D1159614

The Enforceability of Promises in European Contract Law

Civil law and common law systems are held to enforce promises differently: civil law, in principle, will enforce any promise, while common law will enforce only those with 'consideration'. In that respect, modern civil law supposedly differs from the Roman law from which it is descended, where a promise was enforced depending on the type of contract the parties had made. This volume is concerned with the extent to which these characterizations are true, and how these and other differences affect the enforceability of promises. Beginning with a concise history of these distinctions, the volume then considers how twelve European legal systems would deal with fifteen concrete situations. Finally, a comparative section considers why modern legal systems enforce certain promises and not others, and what promises should be enforced. This is the second completed project of The Common Core of European Private Law launched at the University of Trento.

JAMES GORDLEY is Shannon Cecil Turner Professor of Jurisprudence at the University of California at Berkeley.

The Common Core of European Private Law Project

For the transnational lawyer the present European situation is equivalent to that of a traveller compelled to cross legal Europe using a number of different local maps. To assist lawyers in the journey beyond their own locality 'The Common Core of European Private Law Project' was launched in 1993 at the University of Trento under the auspices of the late Professor Rudolf B. Schlesinger.

The aim of this collective scholarly enterprise is to unearth what is already common to the legal systems of European Union member states. Case studies widely circulated and discussed between lawyers of different traditions are employed to draw at least the main lines of a reliable map of the law of Europe.

Books in The Common Core of European Private Law Project

General editors
Mauro Bussani and Ugo Mattei

Good Faith in European Contract Law
edited by Reinhard Zimmermann and Simon Whittaker

The Enforceability of Promises in European Contract Law
edited by James Gordley

The Enforceability of Promises in European Contract Law

edited by

James Gordley

CAMBRIDGE
UNIVERSITY PRESS

PUBLISHED BY THE PRESS SYNDICATE OF THE UNIVERSITY OF CAMBRIDGE
The Pitt Building, Trumpington Street, Cambridge, United Kingdom

CAMBRIDGE UNIVERSITY PRESS
The Edinburgh Building, Cambridge CB2 2RU, UK
40 West 20th Street, New York, NY 10011–4211, USA
10 Stamford Road, Oakleigh, VIC 3166, Australia
Ruiz de Alarcón 13, 28014, Madrid, Spain
Dock House, The Waterfront, Cape Town 8001, South Africa

http://www.cambridge.org

© Cambridge University Press 2001

First published 2001

Printed in the United Kingdom at the University Press, Cambridge

Typeface Swift (EF) 10/13 pt   *System* QuarkXPress™ [SE]

A catalogue record for this book is available from the British Library

Library of Congress cataloguing in publication data

The enforceability of promises in European contract law / edited by James Gordley.
        p.   cm. – (Cambridge studies in international and comparative law;
17. Common core of European private law project)
ISBN 0 521 79021 2 (HB)
1. Contracts – Europe.   2. Promise (Law) – Europe.   I. Gordley, James.
II. Cambridge studies in international and comparative law (Cambridge,
England: 1996).   Common core of European private law project.
KJC1720.E54   2001
346.02′094 – dc 21   00–045552

ISBN 0 521 79021 2 hardback

Contents

General editors' preface	*page* xi	
List of contributors	xiii	
Table of legislation	xv	
List of abbreviations	xxiii	

1	Some perennial problems	1
2	Contemporary solutions	23

Case 1: promises of gifts

Discussions	24
Summaries	62
Preliminary comparisons	65

Case 2: promises of compensation for services rendered without charge

Discussions	67
Summaries	84
Preliminary comparisons	86

Case 3: promises to pay debts not legally due

Discussions	88
Summaries	101
Preliminary comparisons	103

Case 4: a promise to come to dinner

Discussions	105
Summaries	115
Preliminary comparisons	117

Case 5: promises to store goods without charge
 Discussions   118
 Summaries   144
 Preliminary comparisons   149

Case 6: promises to do a favour
 Discussions   151
 Summaries   166
 Preliminary comparisons   169

Case 7: promises to loan goods without charge
 Discussions   171
 Summaries   189
 Preliminary comparisons   191

Case 8: a requirements contract
 Discussions   193
 Summaries   215
 Preliminary comparisons   217

Case 9: promises to pay more than was agreed I
 Discussions   219
 Summaries   236
 Preliminary comparisons   237

Case 10: promises to pay more than was agreed II
 Discussions   239
 Summaries   251
 Preliminary comparisons   253

Case 11: promises to do more than was agreed; promises
to waive a condition
 Discussions   255
 Summaries   265
 Preliminary comparisons   266

Case 12: promises to take less than was agreed
 Discussions   267
 Summaries   276
 Preliminary comparisons   278

Case 13: options given without charge
 Discussions   279
 Summaries   296
 Preliminary comparisons   298

Case 14: promises of rewards
Discussions   300
Summaries   315
Preliminary comparisons   317

Case 15: promises of commissions
Discussions   318
Summaries   332
Preliminary comparisons   334

3 Comparisons   337

Index by country   393
Index by subject   441

General editors' preface

This is the second book in the series 'The Common Core of European Private Law' which will publish its results within Cambridge Studies in International and Comparative Law. The project was launched in 1993 at the University of Trento under the auspices of the late Professor Rudolf B. Schlesinger. The methodology used in the Trento project is novel. By making use of case studies it goes beyond mere description to detailed inquiry into how most European Union legal systems resolve specific legal questions in practice, and to thorough comparison between those systems. It is our hope that these volumes will provide scholars with a valuable tool for research in comparative law and in their own national legal systems. The collection of materials that the Common Core Project is offering to the scholarly community is already quite extensive and will become even more so when more volumes are published. The availability of materials attempting a genuine analysis of how things are is, in our opinion, a prerequisite for an intelligent and critical discussion on how they should be. Perhaps in the future European private law will be authoritatively restated or even codified. The analytical work carried on today by the almost 200 scholars involved in the Common Core Project is a precious asset of knowledge and legitimization for any such normative enterprise.

We must thank not only the editors and contributors to these first published results but also all the participants who continue to contribute to The Common Core of European Private Law project. With a sense of deep gratitude we also wish to recall our late Honorary Editor, Professor Rudolf B. Schlesinger. We are sad that we have not been able to present him with the results of a project in which he believed so firmly. No scholarly project can survive without committed sponsors. The Dipartimento di Scienze Giuridiche of the University of Trento, its past and present directors and its excellent staff must first be thanked. The European Commission is partially sponsoring our annual General Meetings having included them in their High Level

Conferences Program. The Italian Ministry of Scientific Research is now also funding the project, having recognized it as a 'research of national interest'. The Consiglio Nazionale delle Ricerche, the Istituto Subalpino per l'Analisi e l'Insegnamento del Diritto delle Attivatà Transnazionali, the University of Torino, the Fromm Chair in International and Comparative Law at the University of California and the Hastings College of Law have all contributed to the funding of this project. Last but not least we must encourage all those involved in our ongoing Trento projects in contract law, property, tort and other areas whose results will be the subject of future published volumes. Our home page on the internet is at http://www.jus.unitn.it/dsg/common-core. There you can follow our progress in mapping the common core of European private law.

General Editors:

Mauro Bussani (Università di Trento)
Ugo Mattei (European University Institute (Firenze) and University of California, Hastings College of Law)

Honorary Editor:

Rodolfo Sacco (Università di Torino)

Late Honorary Editor:

Rudolf B. Schlesinger (Cornell University – University of California, Hastings)

Contributors

The case studies have been prepared:

for France by Ruth Sefton-Green with the assistance of Christophe André, Muriel Chagny, Gilles Cuniberti, Philippe Jouary, Clothilde Normand, and Judith Rochfeld, Comparative Law Research Group, Centre de droit des obligations, Université de Paris I (Panthéon-Sorbonne)[1]

for Belgium by Isabelle Corbisier, Membre du laboratoire de droit économique; chargé de cours, Faculté universaires NPD Namur; Professeur, l'Ecole supérieure de sciences fiscales, Ichec, Bruxelles[2]

for the Netherlands by Martijn W. Hesselink, Universiteit van Amsterdam

for Spain by Lourdes E. Villar Garcia, Abogado, member of the Madrid Bar, Attorney at Law, member of the Bar of California

for Portugal by Luís Menezes Leitão, Universidade de Lisboa

for Italy by Alberto Monti, Centro Studi di Diritto Civile, Università degli Studi di Milano

for Austria by Georg Graf, Institut für Österreichisches und Europäisches Privatrecht, Universität Salzburg

for Germany by Dirk Kocher, Rechtsreferendar am Landgericht Tübingen

for Greece by Zoe Spyropoulou, University of Athens

for Scotland by Craig Coyle and Joe Thomson, University of Glasgow

---

[1] Ruth Sefton-Green edited and translated the contributions.
[2] Who gratefully acknowledges the assistance of François van der Mensbrugghe for the English translation of the first version of this text.

for England by Stephen A. Smith, McGill University, Canada, formerly of Queen Anne's College, Oxford

for Ireland by Sheena Hickey and Seamus Woulfe, Barristers-at-Law, Ireland

summaries and preliminary observations by James Gordley, Shannon Cecil Turner Professor of Jurisprudence, University of California at Berkeley. Professor Gordley also prepared the introductory and concluding chapters.

Table of legislation

Austria
Bankruptcy Act, 181 ff. 95
Civil Code (ABGB)
  151 95
  285 41
  860a 308
  865 95-6
  865(2) 95
  870 228-9, 245
  881 42, 42 nn. 72; 75
  915 272
  934 291
  936 131, 181, 290
  938 41, 78
  940 246
  943 42
  957 130
  962 131
  969 130
  971 181
  976 181
  1002 158 n. 26
  1035 ff. 78
  1074 290 n. 34
  1151 158, 307
  1220 43
  1231 43
  1295 110
  1295(2) 42 n. 76
  1444 272
Official Recording of Contract Law
  (NZwG) 42 n. 70

Belgium
Civil Code (CC)
  893 ff. 28-31
  894 31
  931 31 n. 27, 32, 242, 269
  932 31-3, 242
  1103 107
  1111-15 224
  1129 197
  1157 284
  1174 283-4
  1184 321-2
  1235 29-30
  1282-8 269
  1304 90-1
  1339 31 n. 27, 32, 242
  1372-5 303
  1591 197
  1675 ff. 284
  1779 302
  1794 302, 321
  1875 ff. 175-6
  1876 176

1888 176
1889 176
1915 ff. 123
1917 123
1919 123
1984 ff. 152
1991(1) 152
1991(2) 152
Labour Contracts Act 1978
  3 241
  7 241
  17 242
  32 241
  40 241
  65 242
  82 242
  86 242

England
Law of Property (Miscellaneous
  Provisions) Act 1989
  1 55
Limitations Act 1980
  29(7) 100
Unfair Terms in Consumer Contracts
  Regulations 1994 211

France
Civil Code (C. civ.)
  102 27
  203 26–7
  204 26, 266
  931 240
  1108 194
  1110 279
  1111-15 220
  1112 220, 221–2, 223
  1114 221
  1126 119
  1129 194, 195

1131 240, 280
1133 28
1134 172, 196, 220, 255, 269
1135 70–1
1142 119, 175, 280, 283
1144 222
1147 120, 175
1148 121–2
1174 195, 282
1235 67–8, 88
1244 268
1282-8 267–8
1341 68–9
1348 69
1348(1) 71
1375 301
1382 25, 106, 121
1583 194, 195, 197
1589 281
1591 194, 219–20
1675 281
1793 219
1794 300–1
1875 ff. 171
1888 ff. 173
1889 172–4
1915 ff. 118
1917 118–19, 122
1919 118, 121
1927 119–20
1927-8 119
1984 318
1991 152
1992 152
1999 318
2271 88–9
2272 88–9
2273 88–9
Civil Procedure Code, 873 222
Code générale des impôts 280

Competition Law of 1 December 1986
  224
Competition Law of 1 July 1996 224
Law of 28 November 1949 supplement-
  ing the Civil Code 281
Law of 2 January 1970 (Hoguet law)
  319–20
  implementing legislation 319–20
Loi de finances 1963 280

Germany
Bankruptcy Law (InsO)
  287 96
  301 96
Brokers Law (*MaklerGesetz*) 325
Civil Code 1900 (BGB)
  104 97
  105(1) 97
  107 97
  108(2) 97
  108(3) 97
  123(1) 229
  125(1) 43
  138(1) 291–2
  142(1) 229
  143 229
  157 272
  222 97
  242 182, 206, 292
  313 291, 325–6
  495 292
  518 43–5, 79, 132, 246, 260
  598-606 182
  605(1) 182
  611-30 308
  612 273
  621(5) 308–9
  631-51 398
  632 273
  652(1)(1) 325

657 309
658(1) 309
662-74 159
665 159
670 79
671(2) 159
675 308
677 79
683 79
688-700 132
689 132, 273
696 132
762(1) 97
762(2) 97
780 43 n. 81, 96–7
781 43 n. 81, 96–7
812 96
826 111
1624(1) 340

Greece
Civil Code 1940 292–3
  150 230
  154 230
  159 45
  166 134
  173 273
  176 327
  179(2) 230–1
  180 45
  181 231
  197 46
  197-8 48
  198 46
  200 135, 207, 273
  201 261, 309
  228 310
  272 98
  281 207, 327
  288 135, 207, 327

330 47 n. 100, 161 n. 34
343 134, 135, 136
349 136
361 134, 183, 247, 261, 273
369 292
371 207
371-3 207
372 207
374 133
380 209
382 209
388 208–9
496 80
496-512 45
498(1) 45
498(2) 45
499 47
512 80
663 247
681 261
681-702 260
703 326–7
703(2) 326–7
703-8 326
709-12 310
710 310
713-29 160
714 161
810 183
810-21 183
816 183
817 184
822-33 133
827 133
828 135
828(1) 134–5
828(2) 135
873 99
906 79
914 231, 327

919 112, 231
1192 292
Code of Civil Procedure, 335 161
L. 308/76 (Civil Brokers Law) 326

Ireland
Infants Relief Act 1874, 2 100
Statute of Frauds (Ireland) 1695, 2 59
Statute of Limitations 1957
  56 100
  58(1) 100

Italy
Civil Code (*Codice civile*) 1942
  555 41
  559 41
  629 228
  770 76
  770(2) 76, 245
  782 40, 76
  785 41 n. 66
  1175 324
  1230 94
  1234 93 n. 15
  1234(2) 94
  1325 129
  1326 288–9
  1327 306, 307
  1328 307
  1329 288, 289
  1331 288
  1333 36, 259–60, 306
  1337 130, 181
  1345 290
  1346 205
  1362-71 271
  1375 324
  1425 94
  1434 228
  1435 228

1441 ff. 94
1444 94
1467(3) 204
1467-8 205
1467-9 204
1703 157
1710 158
1755 324
1756 324
1767 129
1771 129
1803(2) 180
1809(2) 180
1989(1) 305
1989(2) 305
1989 ff. 305
1990 305, 306
2034 76-7
2043 228
2940 93-4
Law 29/1913 (notarial law) 40

Netherlands
Civil Code (*Burgerlijk Wetboek*) (B.W.)
  1992
  3:32(2) 91
  3:33 107, 124, 125, 126, 153, 155, 177,
    178, 201, 202, 256, 322
  3:35 35, 107, 124, 125, 126, 153, 155,
    177, 178, 201, 202, 256, 257, 322
  3:38(1) 303 n. 8
  3:44 226
  3:44(2) 226
  3:44(4) 225
  3:55(1) 91
  6:2 125
  6:2(2) 257, 285
  6:3(1) 72
  6:3(2)(b) 72
  6:5 72

6:5(3) 91
6:20(2) 73
6:21 303 n. 8
6:22 35
6:74 126 n. 13, 155, 225
6:95 ff. 225
6:98 153-4
6:109 154
6:160 257
6:160(2) 269
6:162 107-8, 154
6:162(1) 107
6:162(2) 108
6:200(1) 72
6:201(2) 73
6:216 286
6:219 284-5, 303
6:220 303-4
6:220(2) 303
6:221(1) 285
6:227 200
6:248 125
6:248(1) 155
6:248(2) 201
6:249 35
6:258 200, 201, 285-6
6:296 225-6
7:400 ff. 153
7:401 153
7:600 ff. 124
7:605(2) 125
7A:1719 34-5, 243
7A:1724 34
7A:1777 176, 178
7A:1788 178

Portugal
Bankruptcy Proceedings Code, 209 92
Civil Code 271
  39 40

125 93
125(2) 93
185 ff. 39
227 39
255 227
271 244
282 227
287(2) 93, 227
288 93
303 92
304(1) 92
304(2) 93
402 75
403 75
405 128
406 271
406(1) 227
410(2) 287
411 203, 204, 287
437 203
457 38
459 305
461 305
464 74–5
468 75
469 75
762(2) 203
778(1) 271
798 108, 157, 323
863(72) 271
875 287
940 38
941 75, 244
947 38–9
969 38
974 39
975(b) 75
1129 179
1140 179
1154 108, 157, 304

1156 304
1167 305
1170 304
1185 127
1194 128
1201 128
1753 ff. 40
1765 39
2024 39
2168 39
2172 75
Decree-Law 77/99 of 18 March 1999
    323

Scotland
Requirements of Writing (Scotland)
    Act 1995 9
    1(2) 99, 162, 185, 247
    1(2)(a)(ii) 80–1, 112, 136, 162, 209,
        232, 261, 274
    1(3) 49–51, 113, 136, 162, 185, 247,
        261, 342
    1(4) 49–51, 113, 136–7, 162, 185, 247,
        261, 342
    1(5) 50
    1(7) 274
    2(1) 49
    2(2) 49
    11 48 n. 107

Spain
Civil Code (Catalan), 18 36 n. 49
Civil Code (*Código civil*) 1889
    294 259
    334 259
    406(1) 258
    619 74
    622 74
    632 37
    633 38 n. 55

1101 243
1107 244, 304
1156 38, 257, 270
1177 270
1187(2) 270
1203 226–7, 257
1203-13 257
1218 258
1248 286
1261 36
1263 92
1267 227
1277 108, 126, 243
1280 270, 286
1311 92
1544 156

1710 156
1711 156
1742 179
1749 179
1750 179
1775 127
1776 127
1920 91
Labour Contract Law, 81 243
Law on Urban Leasing 258
Law on Workers, 49(d) 243
Reglamento Hipotecario, 14 286–7

Switzerland, Code of Obligations (CC),
  242 46

Abbreviations

Austria

ABGB	*Allgemeines bürgerliches Gesetzbuch*
ArbSlg	*Sammlung Arbeitsrechtlicher Entscheidungen*
BGBL	*Bundesgesetzblatt*
Ehrenzweig, *System*	A. Ehrenzweig, *System des österreichischen allgemeinen Privatrechts*, 2nd edn (1928)
EvBl	*Evidenzblatt der Rechtsmittelentscheidungen*
GlU (NF)	*Sammlung von zivilrechtlichen Entscheidungen des Obersten Gerichtshofes*, collection founded by J. A Glaser and J. Unger (new series from 1900)
JBl	*Juristische Blätter*
Klang, *ABGB*	H. Klang, *Kommentar zum ABGB*, 2nd edn (1950)
Koziol and Welser, *Grundriß*	H. Koziol and R. Welser, *Grundriß des bürgerlichen Rechts*, 10th edn (1996)
LGZ	*Landesgericht für Zivilrechtssachen*
MaklerG	*MaklerGesetz*
MietSlg	*Sammlung mietrechtlicher Entscheidungen*
NJW	*Neue Juristische Wochenschrift*
NZwG	*Notariatszwangsgesetz*
OGH	*Oberster Gerichtshof*
Rspr	*Rechtsprechung*
Rummel, *ABGB*	P. Rummel (ed.), *Kommentar zum ABGB*, 2nd edn (vol. I 1990, vol. II 1992)
Schwimann, *ABGB*	M. Schwimann (ed.), *Praxiskommentar zum ABGB*, 2nd edn (1997)
SZ	*Entscheidungen des österreichischen Obersten Gerichtshofes in Zivilsachen*

Belgium

Act. dr.	*Actualité du droit*
Cass.	*Cour de cassation*
De Page, *Traité élémentaire*	H. De Page, *Traité élémentaire de droit civil belge*, vol. I, 3rd edn (1962); vol. II, 3rd edn (1964); vol. IV (1938); vol. V (1941); vol. VIII/1 (1944)
de Wilde d'Estmael, *Répertoire notarial*	E. de Wilde d'Estmael, *Répertoire notarial*, vol. III, *Successions, donations et testaments*, book VII, *Les donations* (1995)
Entr. et dr.	*L'entreprise et le droit*
JCB	*Jurisprudence commerciale de Bruxelles*
JL	*Jurisprudence de Liège*
JLMB	*Jurisprudence de Liège, Mons et Bruxelles*
JP	*Justice de paix*
JT	*Journal des tribunaux*
JTT	*Journal des tribunaux du travail*
Les obligations en droit français et en droit belge	*Les obligations en droit français et en droit belge, convergences et divergences: actes des Journées d'étude organisées les 11 et 12 décembre 1992 / par la Faculté de droit de Paris Saint-Maur et la Faculté de droit de l'Université libre de Bruxelles* (1994)
Meinertzhagen-Limpens, *Traité élémentaire*	A. Meinertzhagen-Limpens, *Traité élémentaire de droit civil belge* (1997)
Pas.	*Pasicrisie belge*
Raucent, *Les libéralités*	L. Raucent, *Les libéralités* (1979)
RCJB	*Revue critique de jurisprudence belge*
Répertoire pratique du droit belge	*Répertoire pratique du droit belge, législation, doctrine et jurisprudence* (updated annually)
Rev. aff. eur.	*Revue des affaires européennes*
Rev. not. b.	*Revue du notariat belge*
Rev. trim. dr. fam.	*Revue trimestrielle de droit familial*
RGDC	*Revue générale de droit civil belge*
RIDC	*Revue internationale de droit comparé*
RPS	*Revue pratique des sociétés*
RW	*Rechtskundig weekblad*
Sais.	*Juge des saisies*
TGR	*Tijdschrift voor Gentse rechtspraak*
T. not.	*Tijdschrift voor notarissen*
Trib. civ.	*Tribunal civil*

Trib. comm.   *Tribunal de commerce*
Van Ommeslaghe, *Droit des obligations*   P. Van Ommeslaghe, *Droit des obligations*, 3rd edn (1993–4)

England

A&E   Adolphus & Ellis' Reports (1834–40)
AC   Law Reports, Appeal Cases (from 1891)
All ER   All England Law Reports (from 1936)
App. Cas.   Law Reports, Appeal Cases (1875–90)
Atiyah, *Law of Contract*   P. S. Atiyah, *An Introduction to the Law of Contract*, 5th edn (1995)
Bing.   Bingham's Reports
Camp.   Campbell's Reports (1808–16)
CB   Common Bench Reports (1845–6)
Ch.   Law Reports, Chancery Division (from 1891)
Ch. D.   Law Reports, Chancery Division (1875–90)
Chitty on Contracts   J. Chitty, *Chitty on Contracts*, 27th edn (1994)
CLR   Commonwealth Law Reports (Australia)
Cro. Eliz.   Crooke (Elizabeth) Reports (1582–1603)
De G.F. & J.   De Gex, Fisher & Jones Reports (1859–62)
E & B   Ellis & Blackburn Reports (1851–8)
EGLR   Estates Gazette Law Reports
ER   English Reports
Esp.   Espinasse Law Reports (1793–1807)
Ex D   Law Reports, Exchequer Division (1875–80)
HL   House of Lords
KB   Law Reports, King's Bench (1901–52)
Ld Raym   Lord Raymond Reports (1694–1732)
Lloyd's Rep.   Lloyd's Law Reports
LQ Rev.   *Law Quarterly Review*
LRCP   Law Reports, Common Pleas Cases (1865–75)
LR EX   Law Reports, Exchequer Cases (1865–75)
M & W   Meeson & Welsby's Reports (1836–47)
Mod. L. Rev.   *Modern Law Review*
NI   Northern Ireland Law Reports
Noy   Noy's Reports (1559–1649)
Palmer, *Bailment*   N. Palmer, *Bailment*, 2nd edn (1991)
P & CR   Property and Compensation Reports (formerly Planning and Compensation Reports)

PD   Law Reports, Probate (1864–75)
Pollock, *Contract*   F. Pollock, *Principles of Contract*, 13th edn (1950)
QB   Law Reports, Queen's Bench (1891–1900, from 1952)
R   The Reports (1893–5)
SASR   South Australian State Reports
SI   Statutory Instrument
So.   Southern Reporter (United States)
Treitel, *Contract*   G. H. Treitel, *The Law of Contract*, 9th edn (1995)
VR   Victorian Reports
WLR   Weekly Law Reports

France

Ass. plén.   *Assemblé plénière*
Bull. civ.   *Bulletin civil de la Cour de cassation*
ch.   *chambre*
Chr.   *Chronique*
Civ.   *Cour de cassation, Chambre civile*
Collart-Dutilleul and Delebecque, *Contrats*   F. Collart-Dutilleul and
                            P. Delebecque, *Les contrats civils et commerciaux*, 3rd edn
                            (1996)
Com.   *Cour de cassation, Chambre commerciale*
D   *Dalloz*
DH   *Dalloz, Recueil hebdomadaire de jurisprudence* (1924–40)
DP   *Dalloz périodique*
Flour and Aubert, *Droit civil*   J. Flour and J. L. Aubert, *Droit civil, Les
                            obligations*, vol. I, *L'acte juridique*, 7th edn (1996)
Gaz. Pal.   *Gazette du Palais*
Ghestin, *Traité de droit civil*   J. Ghestin, *Traité de droit civil, Le contrat, La
                            formation*, 3rd edn (1993)
Ghestin, Goubeaux, and Fabre-Magnan, *Traité de droit civil*   J. Ghestin and
                            G. Goubeaux with M. Fabre-Magnan, *Traité de droit
                            civil, Introduction générale*, 4th edn (1994)
Ghestin, Jamin and Billau, *Traité de droit civil*   J. Ghestin, C. Jamin, and
                            M. Billau, *Traité de droit civil: les effets du contrat*, 2nd
                            edn (1994)
IR   *Informations Rapides*
JCP   *La Semaine juridique*
Juris-classeur   *Juris-classeur civil* (1950, updated annually)

Malaurie and Aynès, *Les contrats spéciaux*   P. Malaurie and L. Aynès, *Les contrats spéciaux*, 11th edn (1998)

Malaurie and Aynès, *Les obligations*   P. Malaurie and L. Aynès, *Les obligations*, 8th edn (1998)

PUF   *Presses Universitaires de France*

Rép. Def.   *Répertoire du Notariat Defrénois*

Req.   *Cour de cassation, Chambre des requêtes*

Rev. dr. immobilier   *Revue du droit immobilier*

RTDCiv.   *Revue trimestrielle de droit civil*

S   *Recueil Sirey*

Soc.   *Cour de Cassation, Chambre sociale*

somm.   *sommaires*

Terré, Simler, and Lequette, *Les obligations*   F. Terré, P. Simler, and Y. Lequette, *Les obligations*, 6th edn (1996)

TGI   *Tribunal de grande instance*

Vie jur.   *La Vie juridique*

Germany

BAG   *Bundesarbeitsgericht*

BGH   *Bundesgerichtshof*

BGHZ   *Entscheidungen des Bundesgerichtshofs für Zivilsachen*

InsO   *Insolvenzordnung*

JZ   *Juristenzeitung*

LM   Lindenmaier, Moehring *et al.*, *Nachschlagewerk des Bundesarbeitsgericht*

Mot.   *Motive zum Entwurf einers Bürgerlichen Gesetzbuches* (1887)

NJW   *Neue Juristische Wochenschrift*

NJW-RR   *Neue Juristische Wochenschrift Rechtsprechungsreport*

RGZ   *Entscheidungen des Reichsgerichts in Zivilsachen*

WM   *Wertpapier Mitteilungen*

Greece

Ach.N   *Archio Nomologias* (Archive of Court Decisions)

AP   *Areios Pagos* (Supreme Court of Civil Law)

Arm.   Armenopoulos (a journal)

CC   Civil Code

Deligiannis and Kornilakis, *Law of Obligations*   I. Deligiannis and P.
    Kornilakis, *Law of Obligations* (1992)
Dni   *Dikaiosiyni* (a journal)
EEN   *Ephimearis Hellinon Nomikon* (a journal)
EfAth   *Efetio Athinon* (Athens Court of Appeal)
Erm   interpretation
ErmAK   *Ermineiatou Astikou Kodika* (a collective work on the
                        interpretation of the Civil Code)
Filios, *Law of Obligations*   P. Filios, *Law of Obligations*, Special Part (1988)
Georgiadis, *General Principles*   A. Georgiadis, *General Principles of Civil Law*
    (1996)
Georgiadis and Stathopoulos, *Civil Code*   A. Georgiadis and M.
    Stathopoulos (eds.), *Civil Code* (1978)
Goutos and Levendis, *Labour Legislation*   X. Goutos and G. Levendis,
    Labour Legislation, 7th edn (1988)
HellD   *Helliniki Dikaiosini* (a journal)
Kafkas, *Law of Obligations*   K. Kafkas, *Law of Obligations*, Special Part, 7th
    edn (1993)
Karakatsanis, *The Declaration of Will*   I. Karakatsanis, *The Legal Nature of the
    Type of the Declaration of Will* (1980)
Karakatsanis, *Individual Labour Law*   A. Karakatsanis, *Individual Labour
    Law*, 2nd edn (1988)
NoB   *Nomiko Bima*
Stathopoulos, *Contract Law*   M. Stathopoulos, *Contract Law in Hellas* (1995)
Stathopoulos, *Law of Obligations*   M. Stathopoulos, *Law of Obligations,
    General Part*, 2nd edn (1993)
Varthakokoilis, *Analytical Interpretation*   V. Varthakokoilis, *Analytical
    Interpretation and Court Rulings on the Civil Code* (1989)

Ireland

A&E   Adolphus & Ellis' Reports (1834–40)
AC   Law Reports, Appeal Cases (from 1891)
All ER   All England Law Reports (from 1936)
App. Cas.   Law Reports, Appeal Cases (1875–90)
B & S   Best & Smith's Reports (1861–70)
Camp.   Campbell's Reports (1808–16)
Ch.   Law Reports, Chancery Division (from 1891)
Ch. App.   Chancery Appeals (from 1891)
Chitty on Contracts   J. Chitty, *Chitty on Contracts*, 27th edn (1994)

Clark, *Contract Law*	R. Clark, *Contract Law in Ireland*, 3rd edn (1992)
CLR	Commonwealth Law Reports (Australia)
Exch.	Court of Exchequer
Friel, *Contract*	R. Friel, *The Law of Contract*, 1st edn (1995)
Hare	Hare's Reports (1841–53)
Hob.	Hobart's Reports (1603–25)
ICLR	Irish Company Law Reports
I.Eq.R.	Irish Equity Reports (1838–50)
ILRM	Irish Law Reports Monthly
ILTR	Irish Law Times Reports
IR	Irish Reports (from 1894)
JISL	Journal of the Irish Society for Labour Law
KB	Law Reports, King's Bench (1901–52)
LRCP	Law Reports, Common Pleas Cases (1865–75)
LR Exch.	Law Reports, Exchequer
LRHL	Law Reports, English and Irish Appeals (1866–75)
LT	Law Times Reports (1859–1947)
NI	Northern Ireland Court of Appeal or Northern Ireland Law Reports
NZLR	New Zealand Law Reports
Palmer, *Bailment*	N. Palmer, *Bailment*, 2nd edn (1991)
QB	Law Reports, Queen's Bench (1891–1900, from 1952)
SASR	South Australian State Reports (from 1921)
Treitel, *Contract*	G. H. Treitel, *The Law of Contract*, 9th edn (1995)
WLR	Weekly Law Reports

Italy

Cass. civ.	*Corte di cassazione sezione civile*
Cass. pen.	*Corte di cassazione sezione penale*
Cicu-Messineo, *Tratt. dir. civ. e comm.*	A. Cicu and F. Messineo, *Trattato di diritto civile e commerciale*
Contr. e impr.	*Contratto e impresa*
Corr. giur.	*Corriere giuridico*
Corte app.	*Corte d'appello*
Digesto	*Digesto delle discipline privatistiche*, 4th edn, *sezione civile*
Enc. dir.	*Enciclopedia del diritto*
Enc. giur. Treccani	*Enciclopedia giuridica Treccani*
Foro it.	*Foro italiano*
Foro it. Rep.	*Repertorio del Foro italiano*

Foro pad.   *Foro padano*
Giur. it.   *Giurisprudenza italiana*
Giur. merito   *Giurisprudenza di merito*
Giur. sist. civ. e comm.   *Giurisprudenza sistematica civile e commerciale,*
                     directed by W. Bigiavi
Giust. civ.   *Giustizia civile*
Gorla, *Il contratto*   G. Gorla, *Il contratto. Problemi fondamentali trattati con il*
                     metodo comparativo e casistico (1955)
Marini, *Promessa ed affidamento*   G. Marini, *Promessa ed affidamento nel*
                     diritto dei contratti (1995)
Mass. Foro it.   *Massimario del Foro italiano*
Mass. Giust. civ.   *Massimario di Giustizia civile*
Nuova giur. civ. comm.   *Nuova giurisprudenza civile commentata*
Rass. dir. civ.   *Rassegna di diritto civile*
Rep.   *Repertorio*
Rescigno, *Tratt. di dir. priv.*   P. Rescigno, *Trattato di diritto privato*
Riv. dir. civ.   *Rivista di diritto civile*
Riv. dir. com.   *Rivista di diritto commerciale*
Riv. trim. dir. proc. civ.   *Rivista trimestrale di diritto e procedura civile*
sez. civ.   *sezione civile*
sez. lav.   *sezione del lavoro*
Vassalli, *Tratt. di dir. civ.*   Vassalli, *Trattato di diritto civile*

The Netherlands

AA   *Ars Aequi*
Asser/Hartkamp   A. S. Hartkamp, *Mr C. Asser's handleiding tot de*
                     beoefening van het Nederlands burgerlijk recht,
                     Verbintenissenrecht, vol. I, *De verbintenis in het algemeen,*
                     10th edn (1996); vol. II, *Algemene leer der overeenkomsten,*
                     10th edn (1997); vol. III, *Bijzondere Overeenkomsten,* 7th
                     edn (1997)
Asser/Kortmann   S. C. J. J. Kortmann, L. J. M. de Leede, and H. O.
                     Thunissen, *Mr C. Asser's handleiding tot de beoefening van*
                     het Nederlands burgerlijk recht, Bijzondere overeenkomsten,
                     vol. III, *Overeenkomst von opdracht, arbeidsovereenkomst,*
                     aanneming van werk, 7th edn (1994)
HR   *Hoge Raad der Nederlanden*
NBW   *Nieuw Burgerlijk Wetboek* (Civil Code)
NJ   *Nederlandse Jurisprudentie*

NJB	*Nederlands Juristenblad*
NTBR	*Nederlands Tijdschrift voor Burgerlijk Recht*
PG	*Parlementaire Geschiedenis NBW*
Pitlo/Du Perron	E. Pitlo in E. Du Perron, *Het Nederlands burgerlijk recht*, vol. VI, *Bijzondere overeenkomsten*, 9th edn (1995)
Pitlo/Salomons	A. Salomons in E. Pitlo, *Het Nederlands burgerlijk recht*, vol. VI, *Bijzondere overeenkomsten*, 9th edn (1995)

Tjittes, *De hoedanigheid van contractspartijen*   R.-J. Tjittes, *De hoedanigheid van contractspartijen*, diss. Groningen (1994)

Van Schaick, 'Vriendendienst'   B. van Schaick, 'Vriendendienst en aansprakelijkheidsleniging', NTBR (10/1997)

W	*Weekblad Van Het Recht*
WPNR	*Weekblad voor Privaatrecht, Notariaat en Registratie*

Portugal

BMJ	*Boletim de Ministério da Justica*
CJ	Colectãnea de Jurisprudenca

Cordeiro, *Da Boa Fé no Direito Civil*   A. M. Cordeiro, *Da Boa Fé no Direito Civil* (1984)

Cordeiro, *Direito das Obrigações*   A. M. Cordeiro, *Direito das Obrigações* (1980)

Costa, *Direito das Obrigações*   M. J. A. Costa, *Direito das Obrigações*, 7th edn (1998)

Lima and Varela, *Código Civil Anotado*   F. A. F. Lima and J. A. Varela, *Código Civil Anotado*, 4th edn (1997)

RC	*Relação de Coimbra*
STJ	*Supremo Tribunal de Justiça*

Scotland

All ER	All England Law Reports (from 1936)
D	Dunlop, Bell & Murray's Reports, Court of Session Cases
Inst.	James, Viscount of Stair, *The Institutions of the Law of Scotland*
Mor	Morison's Dictionary of Decisions, Court of Session
R	Rettie's Court of Session Cases, Fourth Series (1873–98)
S	Shaw's Court of Session Cases, First Series (1821–35)
SC	Session Cases

Spain

Castán Tobeñas, *Derecho civil*   J. Castán Tobeñas, *Derecho civil español
común y foral* (1981, 1983, 1984)
Díez Picazo, *Fundamentos de derecho*   L. Díez Picazo, *Fundamentos del
derecho civil patrimonial* (1996)
Díez Picazo and Gullón, *Sistema de derecho civil*   L. Díez Picazo and A.
Gullón, *Sistema de derecho civil* (1979, 1981)
Pérez and Alguer, *Anotaciones*   B. Pérez and J. Alguer, *Anotaciones al
Derecho de obligaciones de Enneccerus and Lehmann*, 2nd
edn (1954)
Puig Brutau, *Fundamentos de derecho civil*   J. Puig Brutau, *Fundamentos de
derecho civil* (1976)
Rebullida, *Notas sobre la naturaleza jurídica*   S. Rebullida, *Notas sobre la
naturaleza jurídica de la condonación de las obligaciones.
Revista de derecho privado* (February 1955)
TS   *Tribunal Supremo*. All *Tribunal Supremo* decisions prior
to 1930 are cited from *Jurisprudencia Civil. Colección
completa de las resoluciones dictadas por el tribunal
supremo* (ed. Reus); thereafter from *Repertorio de
jurisprudencia* (ed. Aranzadi)

Other sections

A.	Atlantic Reporter
Ala.	Alabama
App. Cas.	Law Reports, Appeal Cases (1875–90)
Ark.	Arkansas
Barn. & Ald.	Barnewell and Alderson's Reports
Cal. L. Rev.	*California Law Review*
Cl. & F.	Clark and Finnelly's Reports
Colo.	Colorado
Comb.	Comberbach's Reports
Cowp.	Cowper's Reports
Cro. Eliz.	Crooke (Elizabeth) Reports (1582–1603)
Harv. L. Rev.	*Harvard Law Review*
Holt	Holt's Reports
Int. Eng. Comp. L.	*International Encyclopedia of Comparative Law*
Jur. Rev.	*Juridical Review*
KB	Law Reports, King's Bench (1901–52)

Latch	Latch's Reports
Ld Raym	Lord Raymond Reports (1694–1732)
Leon.	Leonard's Reports
LQ Rev.	*Law Quarterly Review*
Md	Maryland
Mich.	Michigan
Minn.	Minnesota
N.E.	North Eastern Reporter
Neb.	Nebraska
N.W.	North Western Reporter
N.Y.	New York
Owen	Owen's Reports
P.	Pacific Reporter
Plowden	Plowden's Reports
So.	Southern Reporter
Strange	Strange's Reports
S.W.	South Western Reporter
Term. R.	Term Reports
U.S.C.	United States Code

1   Some perennial problems

A basic difference between modern civil law and Roman law is supposed to be that in modern law, in principle, contracts are enforceable upon consent. In Roman law, when they were enforceable depended on the type of contract in question. A basic difference between the modern common law and civil law is supposed to be that the common law requires a contract to have 'consideration'. The civil law does not. This study is concerned with the extent to which these characterizations are true, and how these and other differences affect the enforceability of promises.

The method is that of the Trento Common Core of European Private Law Project. Experts from different legal systems have been asked how their law would resolve a series of hypothetical cases. Because of the larger purposes of the Project, and because one has to draw the line somewhere, the legal systems are those of member states of the European Community. Sometimes, the expert's opinion about a case is conjectural, and the experts were asked to note when it is. In these instances, admittedly, another expert from the same legal system might decide the case differently. But the value of the expert opinions is not that they tell us how the case will come out. It is that they tell us which cases are clear, which are troublesome, the reasons why they are troublesome, and the doctrines that might be applied to resolve the difficulties. That is all one can hope to know, and enough for us to see how different legal systems approach the same problems.

This method focuses less on rules and doctrines than on the results that are reached by applying them. The reason for doing so is not scepticism about whether rules and doctrines matter. They do. Courts look to them for guidance and use them to explain what they are doing. Nevertheless, when the courts of different legal systems reach similar results, it may be that their underlying concerns are the same even though they are

1

reflected in different rules and doctrines. When they reach different results, it may be that their rules and doctrines are similar but that the courts applying them have conflicting concerns. Thus the method helps to identify the underlying concerns.

The questions were chosen to illustrate problems which have arisen. The first part of this study will describe these problems and their historical significance. In the second part, the experts will describe how these problems would be resolved in their legal systems. The third part will try to identify similarities, differences, and underlying concerns.

I. The architecture of contract law

A. Civil law

In Roman law, when a contract became enforceable depended on which contract it was. Some contracts, the contracts *consensu*, were binding on consent. They included sale, lease, partnership, and *mandatum*, a gratuitous agency. Other contracts, the contracts *re* or 'real contracts', were binding only on delivery of the object with which the contract was concerned. They included contracts to loan goods gratuitously for consumption (*mutuum*) or use (*commodatum*), to pledge them (*pignus*), and to deposit them gratuitously for safekeeping (*depositum*). Other contracts were enforceable only when a formality was completed. Large gifts required a formality called *insinuatio*. A document describing the gift was executed before witnesses and officially registered. *Stipulatio* was an all-purpose formality that could be used to make almost any promise binding. Originally it consisted of an oral question and answer. Eventually, it became written, and in medieval and early modern Europe, the accepted formality was to execute a document before a member of the legal profession called a notary. Promises that fell into none of these categories, such as informal agreements to barter, were called 'innominate' contracts, contracts without a name, as distinguished from 'nominate' or 'named contracts' such as the contracts *consensu* and *re*. Initially they were not enforceable. Later, they became enforceable after one party had performed. That party could either reclaim his performance or insist that the other party perform as well.[1] The Roman jurists did not explain why, in theory, these distinctions among contracts made sense. They were not interested in theorizing but in working out rules pragmatically.

---

[1] See generally R. Zimmermann, *The Law of Obligations: Roman Foundations of the Civilian Tradition* (1990), 508–58; A. Watson, *The Law of the Ancient Romans* (1970), 72–3; M. Kaser, *Roman Private Law*, 3rd edn (1980), 196–258.

In medieval and early modern times, in much of continental Europe and in Scotland, the Roman law became a law *in subsidium*, applicable when there was no local statute or custom in point. The medieval jurists preserved the distinctions just described although some found them puzzling. Iacobus de Ravanis noted:

> If I agree that you give me ten for my horse there is an action on the agreement. But if I agree that you give me your ass for my horse there is no action on the agreement. If a layman were to ask the reason for the difference it could not be given for it is mere positive law. And if you ask why the law was so established the reason can be said to be that the contract of sale is more frequent than that of barter. And more efficacy is given to sale than barter.[2]

The greatest medieval jurists, Bartolus of Saxoferrato and Baldus degli Ubaldis, thought they had found a reason, but it was not a very satisfactory one. Bartolus grasped at the term the Roman jurists had used to describe the contracts: they were 'nominate' or 'named' contracts. He thought that the distinction between them and the 'innominate' contracts was not a mere matter of positive law. The nominate contracts, he claimed, derived their name from the *ius gentium* which, according to the Roman texts, was a law 'established among all men by natural reason'.[3] One Roman text said that 'nearly all contracts' belong to the *ius gentium*. According to Bartolus, the 'name' made these contracts actionable, for 'nominate contracts give rise to an action by this alone, that they exist and have a name'.[4] Contracts *consensu* are binding on consent and contracts *re* upon delivery, he said, because of a difference in their names. Consensual contracts such as sale took their names from an act that a party performs by agreeing: I can sell you my house today by agreeing even if I do not deliver it to you until next month. Contracts *re* take their names for an act a party performs by delivering: I cannot say I deposited my goods with you or loaned them to you today if you are not to receive them until next week.[5] Baldus agreed. He concluded that since these rules were not mere matters of Roman positive law, innominate contracts should not be enforceable even in Canon law.[6]

A modern reader is not likely to find this explanation plausible. It appealed to Bartolus and Baldus because it fitted together the Roman texts

[2] Iacobus de Ravanis, *Lectura Super Codice* (publ. under the name of Petrus de Bellapertica) (Paris, 1519, repr. *Opera iuridica rariora*, vol. I, Bologna, 1637), to C. 4.64.3. On the authorship, see E. M. Meijers, *Etudes d'histoire du droit*, vol. III *Le droit romain au moyen âge* (1959), 72–7.   [3] I. 1.2.1; see Dig. 1.1.9.

[4] Bartolus de Saxoferrato, *Commentaria Corpus iuris civilis*, to Dig. 12.14.7 no. 2, in *Omnia quae extant opera* 10 (Venice, 1615).   [5] *Ibid.*

[6] Baldus de Ubaldis, *Commentaria Corpus iuris civilis* (Venice, 1577), to C. 2.3.27.

that spoke of 'nominate contracts', those that spoke of the *ius gentium*, and the Roman rules. While these jurists occasionally borrowed ideas from the Aristotelian philosophical theory that was then popular, for the most part, like the medieval jurists before them, they were not interested in theorizing but in fitting together their Roman texts.

Consequently, a major change took place in the sixteenth century when a group of philosophers and jurists, centred in Spain and known to historians as the late scholastics or Spanish natural law school, tried to synthesize Roman law with the philosophy of their intellectual heroes, Aristotle and Thomas Aquinas.[7] Leaders of the school were Domingo de Soto, Luis de Molina, and Leonard Lessius. They were the first to look systematically for theoretical justifications of the Roman rules. In the seventeenth century, many of their conclusions were borrowed by the founders of the northern natural law school, Hugo Grotius and Samuel Pufendorf. Paradoxically, these conclusions were disseminated throughout northern Europe while the philosophical ideas that had inspired them fell from favour and their roots in this philosophy were forgotten.

The late scholastics explained contract law in terms of three Aristotelian virtues: fidelity, liberality, and commutative justice. For Aristotle, the virtue of fidelity or truth-telling meant keeping one's word.[8] Thomas Aquinas explained that promises should be kept as a matter of fidelity.[9] Liberality, for Aristotle, meant not merely giving resources away, but giving them away sensibly, 'to the right people, [in] the right amounts, and at the right time'.[10] Commutative justice in voluntary transactions meant exchanging resources of equivalent value, so that neither party was enriched at the expense of the other.[11] Thomas Aquinas explained that a person might part with resources either as an act of liberality or as an act of commutative justice.[12] The late scholastics concluded that liberality

---

[7] See generally I. Birocchi, *Saggi sulla formazione storica della categoria generale del contratto* (1988), 25; P. Cappellini, 'Schemi contrattuale e cultura theologico-giuridica nella seconda scolastica: verso una teoria generale' (thesis, Univ. of Florence, 1978/79); M. Diesselhorst, *Die Lehre des Hugo Grotius vom Versprechen* (1959), 6; H. Thieme, 'Qu'est-ce que nous, les juristes, devons à la seconde scolastique espagnole?' in Paolo Grossi (ed.), *La seconda scolastica nella formazione del diritto privato moderno* (1973), 20; H. Thieme, 'Natürliches Privatrecht und Spätscholastik', *Zeitschrift der Savigny-Stiftung für Rechtsgeschichte Romanistische Abteilung* 70 (1953), 230; J. Gordley, *The Philosophical Origins of Modern Contract Doctrine* (1991), 69–133.   [8] *Nicomachean Ethics*, IV.vii.1127a–1127b.

[9] *Summa theologiae*, II–II, Q. 88, a. 3; a. 3 ad 1; Q. 110, a. 3 and 5.

[10] *Nicomachean Ethics*, IV.i.1119b–1120a. Thomas discussed liberality in a similar way. *Summa theologiae*, II–II, Q. 117, aa. 2–4.

[11] Aristotle, *Nicomachean Ethics*, V.ii.1130b–1131a; Thomas Aquinas, *Summa theologiae*, II–II, Q. 61, a. 2.   [12] *Summa theologiae*, II–II, Q. 61, a. 3.

and commutative justice were the two basic types of arrangements one could enter into by promising.[13]

It was easier for them to read this distinction into Roman law because, in the fourteenth century, Baldus had already described liberality and exchange as the two *causae* or reasons that a contract must have, even in Canon law, to be enforceable.[14] This distinction was not to be found in the Roman texts which referred to the *causa* of a contract.[15] There is strong evidence, which I have presented elsewhere, that he took the distinction from Aristotle and Thomas Aquinas.[16] He often drew upon their philosophy to explain Roman texts even though, unlike the late scholastics, he did not try to rebuild Roman law on a philosophical groundplan.

In any event, this distinction cut across the Roman classification of contracts. *Mandatum*, *commodatum*, *mutuum*, and *depositum* were all gratuitous contracts but the first was a contract *consensu* and the last three were contracts *re*. Sale, lease, and barter were all contracts of exchange but the first two were nominate contracts *consensu* and the last was an innominate contract. The late scholastics reclassified these contracts according to whether they were based on liberality or commutative justice, and the northern natural lawyers and those they influenced continued the enterprise. Grotius and Pufendorf presented elaborate schemes of classification in which they showed how the contracts familiar in Roman law could be fitted into these two grand categories.[17] Domat and Pothier explained that these are the two *causes* or reasons for making a binding promise.[18]

The distinction also inspired fresh thought about when a promise became binding. The late scholastics concluded that all contracts of exchange should be binding upon consent. The Roman rules, they said, were mere matters of positive law, established, no doubt, for some sound pragmatic reason, but not founded in principle.

---

[13] L. Lessius, *De iustitia et iure, ceterisque virtutibus cardinalis libri quatuor* (Paris, 1628), lib. 2, cap. 17, dubs. 1, 3; cap. 18, dub. 2; cap. 21, dubs. 2, 4; L. Molina, *De iustitia et iure tractatus* (Venice, 1614), disps. 252, 259, 348; D. Soto, *De iustitia et iure libri decem* (Salamanca, 1553), lib. 3, Q. 5, a. 3; lib. 4, Q. 1, a. 1; lib. 6, Q. 2, aa. 1, 3.

[14] Baldus de Ubaldis, *In decretalium volumen commentaria* (Venice, 1595), to X. 1.4.11 no. 30; Baldus de Ubaldis, *Commentaria Corpus iuris civilis*, to C. 3.36.15 no. 3.

[15] See Dig. 2.14.7.1; 12.7.1; 44.4.2.3.

[16] J. Gordley, 'Good Faith in Contract Law in the Medieval *Ius Commune*', in R. Zimmermann and S. Whittaker (eds.), *Good Faith in European Contract Law* (2000), 93.

[17] H. Grotius, *De iure belli ac pacis libri tres*, ed. B. J. A. de Kanter-van Tromp (Leiden, 1939), II.xii.1–7; S. Pufendorf, *De iure naturae et gentium libri octo* (Amsterdam, 1688), V.ii.8–10.

[18] J. Domat, *Les loix civiles dans leur ordre naturel*, 2nd edn (Paris, 1713), liv. 1, tit. 1, § 1, nos. 5–6; § 5, no. 13; R. Pothier, *Traité des obligations*, in M. Bugnet (ed.), *Oeuvres de Pothier*, 2nd edn, vol. II (Paris, 1861), § 42.

Whether gratuitous promises should be binding on consent was initially less clear. The sixteenth-century theologian and philosopher Cajetan, in his commentary on Thomas Aquinas, claimed that the promisor who broke such a promise was unfaithful to his word. But the disappointed promisee was no poorer. Consequently, the promisee had no claim against the promisor as a matter of commutative justice except if he had suffered harm by changing his position in reliance that the promise would be kept.[19] The French jurist Connanus took a similar position.[20] Soto, Molina, and Lessius disagreed, followed by Grotius and the northern natural lawyers.[21] They pointed out that executory promises to exchange were binding even though no one had become poorer. Gifts were acts of liberality but could not be revoked after delivery. They concluded that, in principle, promises of gifts should be binding as long as the promisor intended to transfer a right to the object to the promisee. Roman law required a formality only as evidence of this intention and to ensure deliberation.[22]

If, in principle, a promise should be enforced whenever the promisor wished to confer a right on the promisee, then gratuitous agreements to make a loan for consumption or for use, or a deposit, or a pledge should be enforceable even before delivery. The Roman rules were, again, mere features of positive law.

According to the late scholastics, these contracts were also acts of liberality. They differed from contracts to make gifts in that the promisor might be able to benefit the promisee without incurring any cost himself. Indeed, according to Lessius and Molina, the promisor normally made a gratuitous loan for use on the assumption that he would not have a use for the property he loaned. If this assumption proved unfounded, he would have the right to withdraw from the transaction even after delivery. He should not have such a right if he promised a gift of money or property because then he was not acting on the assumption that the gift would be costless.[23] Lessius and Molina reached this conclusion even though it seemed to contradict a Roman text:

---

[19] Cajetan (Tommaso de Vio), *Commentaria* to Thomas Aquinas, *Summa theologiae* (Padua, 1698), to II–II, Q. 88, a. 3; Q. 110, a. 1.

[20] F. Connanus, *Commentariorum iuris civilis libri X* (Naples, 1724), I.6.v.1.

[21] Soto, *De iustitia et iure*, lib. 8, q. 2, a. 1; Molina, *De iustitia et iure*, disp. 262; Lessius, *De iustitia et iure*, lib. 2, cap. 18, dub. 2; Grotius, *De iure belli ac pacis*, II.xi.1.5; Pufendorf, *De iure naturae et gentium*, II.v.9.

[22] Molina, *De iustitia et iure*, disp. 278, no. 5; Lessius, *De iustitia et iure*, lib. 2, cap. 18, dubs. 2, 8.

[23] Molina, *De iustitia et iure*, disp. 294, nos. 8–10; Lessius, *De iustitia et iure*, lib. 2, cap. 27, dub. 5.

As lending rests on free will and decency, not on compulsion, so it is the right of the person who does the kindness to fix the terms and duration of the loan. However, once he does it, that is to say, after he has made the loan for use, then not only decency but also obligation undertaken between lender and borrower prevent his fixing time limits, claiming the thing back or walking off with it in disregard of agreed times . . . Favours should help, not lead to trouble.[24]

Molina agreed that, as a general principle, one should not be able to change one's mind in a way that injures another. But, he argued, the borrower should have understood that the loan was made on the tacit condition that the lender had no need for the object. If the need arose, it was an accident for which the promisor should not be held responsible.[25]

The late scholastics were discussing when promises were binding in principle, or, as they put it, as a matter of natural law. They acknowledged that Roman law was different. Nevertheless, their work undermined the Roman rules by providing a coherent, philosophically grounded account of which promises should be enforced.

In time, the rules which the late scholastics ascribed to the natural law became accepted as positive law. In some places such as Castile, innominate contracts were made enforceable by statute.[26] Elsewhere, beginning in the sixteenth century, jurists simply declared that the custom of the courts was to enforce them.[27] As Nanz has shown, the first jurist to mention this custom was Wesenbeck.[28] He cited earlier jurists in support who, in fact, had never taken this position.[29] By the eighteenth century, this view had become almost universal.[30] The Roman rules about innominate contracts were gone. Contracts of exchange were enforceable upon consent. According to many jurists, promises to make gratuitous loans for use or consumption, to accept a deposit, or to give a pledge were binding before delivery, although they often added (following a tradition that went back to Bartolus) that the contracts of *mutuum*, *commodatum*, *depositum*, and *pignus* themselves were formed by delivery since that is what their names implied. This change could not have been caused by a mis-citation.

---

[24] Dig. 13.6.17.3.   [25] Molina, *De iustitia et iure*, disp. 279, no. 10.

[26] Molina, *De iustitia et iure*, disp. 257–8.

[27] J. Voet, *Commentarius ad pandectas* (The Hague, 1698), to Dig. 2.14 § 9; W. A. Lauterbach, *Collegii theoretico-pratici* (Tübingen, 1744), to Dig. 2.14 § 68; J. Wissenbach, *Exercitationum ad I. pandectarum libros* (Frankfurt, 1661), lib. 2, disp. 9, no. 35; see B. Struvius, *Syntagma iurisprudentiae secundum ordinem pandectarium concinnatum*, to Dig. 2.14 no. 32 (Jena, 1692) (arguing that some agreements would still not be enforced when the parties did not so intend).

[28] K. Nanz, *Die Entstehung des allgemeinen Vertragsbegriffs im 16. bis 18. Jahrhundert* (1985), 85.

[29] M. Wesenbeck, *In pandectas iuris civilis et codicis iustinianei libros viii commentaria* (Lyons, 1597).   [30] Zimmermann, *Law of Obligations*, 539–40.

Jurists must have thought that they were moving to a sounder position. They thought the position was sounder because it was the one which the leading jurists of their time believed to be theoretically correct.

When older rules did survive, often they were congenial with the principles of the late scholastics and natural lawyers. Contracts to give money or property still required the formality of registration. Certain traditional exceptions to this requirement were also preserved. One was for promises to charitable causes (*ad pias causas*).[31] Another was for promises to those about to marry (*propter nuptias*).[32] Another concerned the so-called *donatio remuneratoria*: the law would enforce an informal promise to reward someone who had conferred a benefit on the promisor in the past.[33] As mentioned earlier, the late scholastics and natural lawyers explained the formality itself as a way of ensuring deliberation. Liberality, to them, meant not merely giving away money but giving it away sensibly. Although they were not explicit, presumably they thought that in these exceptional cases the gift was more likely to be sensible or, in the case of a *donatio remuneratoria*, that it was not truly an act of liberality but compensation for a benefit received.

This change in early modern times gave the civil law of contracts the shape which it still has today. In most continental countries, informal promises of exchange are binding in principle. Promises to give away money or property still require a formality. The most common formality today is to execute a document before a 'notary' who is not the Anglo-American notary public but a member of the legal profession. Nevertheless, as we will see, the traditional exceptions to this requirement have largely disappeared.

In Scotland, matters took a somewhat different course in early modern times, and, as a result, the shape of Scots law today differs from that of other civil law jurisdictions. As on the continent, the older Roman rules were largely discarded.[34] Jurists such as Stair agreed with the late scholastics and natural lawyers that promises were binding in principle.[35] Nevertheless, Scots law did not adopt the continental solution that promises to give money and property required the formality of registration or, later, notarization. Their rule was that such a promise was enforceable only if the promisor acknowledged the promise in a written document or under oath.[36] By way of exception, it was enforceable if the promisor had

---

[31] Lessius, *De iustitia et iure*, lib. 2, cap. 18, dub. 6, no. 9; Molina, *De iustitia et iure*, disp. 279, no. 2.   [32] Molina, *De iustitia et iure*, disp. 279, no. 7.   [33] *Ibid.*, disp. 279, no. 6.

[34] James, Viscount of Stair, *Institutions of the Law of Scotland*, vol I. ed. D. M. Walker (1981), I.x.4, 12.   [35] *Ibid.*, I.x.10.

[36] D. M. Walker, *The Law of Contracts and Related Obligations in Scotland*, 2nd edn (1985), § 10.2.

acted in a way that acknowledged the existence of the promise (homologation) or allowed the promisee to change his position in reliance upon it (*rei interventus*).[37] These traditional rules have now been replaced by the Requirements of Writing (Scotland) Act 1995, which nevertheless reflects their influence. Under the Act, a gratuitous promise[38] must be made in writing unless undertaken in the ordinary course of business.[39] Absent a writing, the doctrine of *rei interventus* applies in an altered form:[40] the promisee may still have an action if he changes his position in reliance on the promise with the promisor's knowledge and acquiescence.[41]

The civil law retained this shape even after the Aristotelian ideas that had inspired the late scholastics fell from favour. By the nineteenth century, these ideas seemed strange and unacceptable. The contract theories of the late scholastics and the natural lawyers were replaced by the so-called 'will theories'. In these theories, contract was defined in terms of the will of the parties. The innovation was not the concept of will. Jurists had always known that parties enter into contracts by expressing the will to be bound. The innovation was to define contract simply in terms of the will without reference to the types of arrangements that the parties might legitimately will to enter into or the reasons why the law should enforce them.[42]

Consequently, the principle that contracts are binding on consent was now understood differently. It now meant that, in principle, whatever the parties willed should be enforced. The consequence was not so much a change in the rules of contract law. It was that the point of some of these rules now became hard to understand. If whatever the parties willed should be enforced, it was hard to see why the law should only enforce certain promises. The doctrine that there were two kinds of *causa* seemed puzzling. French jurists pointed out that it seemed merely to mean that the promisor must have some reason for promising which might or might not be to receive something in return.[43] Jurists still said that promises of gifts required a formality to ensure deliberation, but the reason why

---

[37] Walker, *Law of Contracts*, §§ 13.35–13.36.

[38] More technically, gratuitous unilateral obligations.

[39] Requirements of Writing (Scotland) Act 1995, s. 2(a)(ii).

[40] W. M. Gloag and R. C. Henderson, *The Law of Scotland*, 10th edn, ed. W. A. Wilson and A. Forte (1995), § 8.3.   [41] Requirements of Writing (Scotland) Act 1995, s. 1(3) and 1(4).

[42] See Gordley, *Philosophical Origins*, 161–213.

[43] C. B. M. Toullier, *Le droit français suivant l'ordre du Code*, 4th edn, vol. VI (Paris, 1869–78) § 166; A. M. Demante and E. Colmet de Santerre, *Cours analytique du Code Civil*, 2nd edn, vol. V (Paris, 1883), § 47; C. Aubry and C. Rau, *Cours de droit civil français d'après la méthode de Zachariae*, 4th edn, vol. IV (Paris, 1869–71), § 345 n. 7; F. Laurent, *Principes de droit civil français*, 3rd edn, vol. XVI (Paris, 1869–78), §§ 110–11.

deliberation was particularly necessary was left obscure. The rules that governed gratuitous loans, deposits, and pledges were often different from those governing either gift or exchange, but the reason why was no longer clear.

On the eve of the twentieth century, then, the civil law was the product of three quite distinct historical influences: the Roman system of particular contracts; the late scholastic and natural law theories of fidelity, liberality, and commutative justice; and the nineteenth-century will theories.

B. Common law

The common law was not taught in universities until the eighteenth century. The common lawyers were either practitioners or judges, and, until the nineteenth century, there was little literature on what we call contract law aside from the reports of decided cases.[44] Blackstone devoted only a few pages to contract. The first treatise on the common law of contract was written by Powell in 1790.[45] Until the nineteenth century, the law was organized, not according to doctrines or principles, but by writs. A writ was needed to bring a case before the royal courts, and eventually the number of writs was limited. To succeed, a plaintiff had to bring his case within one of these writs.

What we call the common law of contract grew out of two writs. One was covenant which could be used to enforce a promise given under seal, a formality originally performed by making an impression in wax on a document containing the promise. The other was assumpsit. To recover in assumpsit, the promise had to have 'consideration'.

There is a famous and inconclusive debate over whether the common law courts borrowed the idea that a promise needs consideration from the civil idea of *causa*. However that may have been, the doctrines had quite different functions. The doctrine of *causa*, as we have seen, identified the reasons why, in principle or in theory, a party might make a promise or the law might enforce one. The doctrine of consideration was a pragmatic tool for limiting actions on a promise to those cases in which courts thought an action was appropriate. These cases were so heterogeneous that the term 'consideration' had no single meaning.

In some of these cases, the promise was made to obtain something in return. But in some it was not. The promise of a father to give money or

---

[44] A. W. B. Simpson, 'Innovation in Nineteenth Century Contract Law', LQ Rev. 91 (1975), 247 at 250–1.   [45] J. Powell, *Essay upon the Law of Contracts and Agreements* (London, 1790).

land to a man who was to marry his daughter had consideration. The consideration was sometimes said to be a gain or benefit the father derived from seeing his daughter married.[46] It was sometimes said to be parental love and affection.[47] Gratuitous loans and bailments had consideration. Sometimes the consideration was said to be the benefit to the party who received the goods.[48] Lord Coke said that 'every consideration . . . must be to the benefit of the defendant or charge to the plaintiff',[49] and this formula – benefit to the promisor or detriment to the promisee – was often repeated. Yet as A. W. B. Simpson has noted, it can only be applied to the marriage cases by very artificial reasoning.[50] Moreover, in one famous case in which the promisor had agreed to transport the promisee's cask of brandy free of charge, the consideration was said to be the delivery of the cask, even though delivering it was neither a benefit to the promisor nor a detriment to the promisee.[51] Sometimes, as Simpson points out, the consideration was that the promisor agreed to do something he already ought to do: for example, return a lost dog, or pay a debt.[52] Promises to pay debts barred by the statute of limitations[53] or discharged in bankruptcy[54] or incurred as a minor[55] were held to be actionable. Sometimes the consideration in such cases was said to be the fulfilment of a moral obligation.

Conversely, sometimes there was held to be no consideration for a promise even though the promise was not made to confer a gratuitous benefit on the promisee. There was no consideration for a creditor's promise to take less than the amount due if he were paid immediately.[56] There was no consideration to pay more for a performance that the promisee had already agreed to do for less.[57]

The common law judges had never felt a need to explain the doctrine of consideration with much precision. Beginning with Blackstone, however, treatise writers tried to describe English law more systematically. One innovation was to say that the rules that governed actions of covenant and assumpsit constituted an English law of contract. Another was to look for a conceptual structure underlying these rules. Part of that task was to try to define consideration. A first step was taken when Blackstone and Powell,

---

[46] *Sharrington v. Strotton* (1556) Plowden 298 at 301.   [47] Plowden 298 at 303.
[48] *Byne v. Playne* (1589) 1 Leon. 220, Cro. Eliz. 218.
[49] *Stone v. Wythipol* (1588) Cro. Eliz. 126, 1 Leon. 113, Owen 94, Latch 21.
[50] A. W. B. Simpson, *A History of the Common Law of Contract: the Rise of the Action of Assumpsit* (1987), 487.   [51] *Coggs v. Bernard* (1703) Holt 13, 131, 528, 2 Ld Raym 909.
[52] Simpson, *History*, 485–6.   [53] *Hylings v. Hastings* (1699) 1 Ld Raym 389, 421.
[54] *Trueman v. Fenton* (1777) 2 Cowp. 544.   [55] *Ball v. Hesketh* (1697) Comb. 381.
[56] *Cumber v. Wane* (1721) 1 Strange 426, followed in the famous case of *Foakes v. Beer* (1884) 9 App. Cas. 605.   [57] *Stilck v. Myrick* (1809) 2 Camp. 317, 6 Esp. 129.

drawing on continental learning, identified consideration with the *causa* of an onerous contract.[58] As Simpson has observed, early nineteenth-century treatise writers regarded consideration as a local version of the doctrine of *causa*.[59] They did not explain why, if that was so, consideration was sometimes present when there was no exchange. Nevertheless, once this step had been taken, the common law of contract began to look on paper as though it had the structure of continental law. Contracts were either bargains, in which case they were enforceable without a formality in assumpsit, or they were liberalities, in which case they were enforceable with the formality of a seal in covenant.

The first truly systematic treatise on the law of contract was written by Sir Frederick Pollock late in the century. Like the earlier treatise writers, he identified consideration with the presence of an exchange or bargain. He thought, however, that he could bring all or most of the decided cases within a single definition of bargain. While consideration had frequently been said to be either a benefit to the promisor or a burden to the promisee, the important element, he said, was that the promisee have incurred some detriment by doing or promising to do something which he was not already obligated to do. If the promisor had 'bargained' for him to incur this detriment, there was consideration. '[W]hatever a man chooses to bargain for must be conclusively taken to be of some value to him.'[60] That was so even if the man himself had received nothing, consideration having moved to a third party. Therefore, consideration meant simply that one party 'abandons some legal right in the present, or limits his legal freedom of action in the future, as an inducement for the promise' of the other party.[61] This formulation became widely accepted not only in England but also in the United States. It was borrowed by Oliver Wendell Holmes[62] and Samuel Williston[63] and has appeared in both the first and second *Restatement of Contracts*.[64]

The formulation could be made to fit the cases in which the promise was to reduce a debt in return for immediate payment or to pay more for a performance than originally agreed. In these cases, supposedly, the promise

---

[58] W. Blackstone, *Commentaries on the Laws of England*, vol. II (London, 1766, repr. Chicago, 1979), *444–6; J. Powell, *Contracts and Agreements*, vol. I (London, 1790), 331.

[59] Simpson, 'Innovation', 262.

[60] F. Pollock, *Principles of Contract*, 9th edn (London, 1921), 186.   [61] *Ibid.*, 177.

[62] O. W. Holmes, Jr, *The Common Law* (1881), 293–4. On the debt to Pollock, see Letter from Holmes to Pollock, 17 June 1880, in M. Howe (ed.), *Holmes–Pollock Letters*, 2nd edn, vol. I (1961), 276.

[63] S. Williston, 'Consideration in Bilateral Contracts', *Harv. L. Rev.* 27 (1914), 503 at 527–8.

[64] *Restatement of Contracts* (1932), § 75; *Restatement (Second) of Contracts* (1979), § 71.

could not have been made to induce the promisee to incur a detriment because, legally, it was not a detriment for him to pay or do what he was already under a legal duty to pay or do. It could fit some of the cases of gratuitous loans or bailments: the borrower's promise to take care of the property loaned was made, at least in part, to induce the lender to make the loan. Pollock even thought that the formula explained why there was consideration for a promise of a gift to those about to marry: it was made, at least in part, so that they would marry.[65] He rejected the explanation an English court had given in *Hammersley* v. *De Beil*[66] that the promisor was bound because he had made 'representations' on which the promisee had 'acted'. Had he not done so, the English might have developed a doctrine of promissory estoppel considerably earlier.[67] Williston, in his edition of Pollock's treatise, noted that the rationale of *Hammersley* explained certain American decisions better than the bargained-for-detriment formula for consideration.[68] Williston included the principle of promissory estoppel along with the bargained-for-detriment formula in the first *Restatement*,[69] and the success of this principle in the United States may have influenced Lord Denning when he adopted a more moderate version of it in *Central London Property Trust* v. *High Trees House Ltd* in 1947.[70]

Nevertheless, there were some cases that the formula did not fit, strain as one might. It did not fit the case in which a person promised gratuitously to take care of property he could not use himself, as in the case of the promise to transport another's cask of brandy. It did not fit any of the cases in which the promise was to perform a pre-existing legal or purely moral obligation.

Paradoxically, these efforts to explain consideration were made at the same time that the common lawyers were also turning to 'will theories'. As Simpson has said, they regarded the will as a sort of *Grundnorm* from which as many rules as possible were to be derived.[71] But if contracts were enforceable simply because of the will of the parties, then it was hard to see why whatever the parties willed should not be enforceable. In the nineteenth century, the common lawyers did not think they had to justify the doctrine of consideration. It was simply part of English positive law, and their job was simply to explain what it meant.

---

[65] See Pollock, *Principles of Contract* 186, 757–8.   [66] (1845) 12 Cl. & F. 45, 62, 88.

[67] Pollock, *Principles of Contract*, 757–65.

[68] F. Pollock in G. H. Wald and S. Williston (eds.), *Principles of Contract*, 3rd American edn (1906), 650 n. 1.

[69] *Restatement of Contracts* § 90 (1932), even though, in his treatise, he had said that the doctrine 'at present . . . is opposed to the great weight of authority'. S. Williston, *The Law of Contracts*, vol. I (1920), § 139.   [70] [1947] KB 130.   [71] Simpson, 'Innovation', 266.

In the nineteenth century, moreover, common lawyers found two additional ways to limit the enforceability of promises that seemed more compatible with will theories. One was to insist that the parties must have intended their promise to be legally binding. As we have seen, civil lawyers had said that they must since at least the time of Molina. In the nineteenth century, English treatise writers such as Pollock began to mention such a requirement,[72] and in the famous case of *Balfour* v. *Balfour*, English courts accepted it.[73]

The second way was the doctrine of offer and acceptance. In civil law, the question of whether an offer was binding without an acceptance had been addressed only obliquely by the Romans. Some late scholastics such as Soto, Molina, and Covarruvias thought that since an offer was a promise and a promise should be binding, in principle, an acceptance was not needed.[74] Lessius disagreed on the grounds that the promisee's acceptance was usually a *sine qua non* condition of the promise.[75] The Scots jurist Stair concluded that a promise was binding as long as it was not conditional on acceptance.[76] His view passed into modern Scots law: a promise not conditional on acceptance constitutes a 'unilateral obligation', in contrast to 'mutual contract', which requires an offer and an acceptance.[77] Grotius simply said that a promise requires an acceptance.[78] His opinion was followed by Pufendorf, Barbeyrac, and Pothier,[79] and passed into continental civil law. The English finally adopted it in the late eighteenth and early nineteenth centuries.[80] Common law treatise writers, like some of the civil lawyers, explained it as a consequence of the will theory: contract was the will of the parties, and therefore each had to express his will to be bound. When they did so seriatim, an offer was followed by an acceptance, and the contract was not formed until the acceptance because, until then, both parties had not expressed their will.[81]

In this study, we will be concerned with only one of the uses to which

---

[72] Pollock, *Principles of Contract*, 3.   [73] (1919) 2 KB 571, 578.

[74] Soto, *De iustitia et iure*, lib. 3, q. 5, art. 3; Molina, *De iustitia et iure*, disp. 263; D. Covarruvias, *Variarum ex iure pontificio, regio et caesareo resolutionum* (Lyons, 1568), p. 2, § 2, no. ult., § 4, no. 6.   [75] Lessius, *De iustitia et iure*, lib. 2, cap. 18, dub. 8.

[76] Stair, *Institutions of the Law of Scotland*, I.x.4. On the influence of Molina on Stair, see A. Rodger, 'Molina, Stair, and the *Ius Quaesitum Tertio*', *Jur. Rev.* 14 (1969), 34.

[77] Gloag and Henderson, *Law of Scotland*, § 5.1.   [78] Grotius, *De iure belli ac pacis*, II.xi.14.

[79] Pufendorf, *De iure naturae et gentium*, III.vi.15; J. Barbeyrac, *La droit de la nature et des gens . . . par le baron de Pufendorf* (Amsterdam, 1734), II.xi.15; Pothier, *Traité des obligations*, § 4.

[80] See *Payne* v. *Cave* (1789) 3 Term. R. 148; *Cooke* v. *Oxley* (1790) 3 Term. R. 653; *Adams* v. *Lindsell* (1818) 1 Barn. & Ald. 681.

[81] Pollock warned against this tendency to regard the need for an offer and acceptance as arising from the very definition of contract. Pollock, *Principles of Contract*, 10–11.

the common lawyers put this doctrine. They used it to explain some further peculiarities of the case law concerning consideration. Traditionally, it had been said that the consideration for a promise might be something done at the time the promise was made. It might instead be something done before the promise was made provided it was done at the promisor's request. Or it might be something the promisee was to do in the future. In that case, the promisee had to plead that he had actually performed this act. Suppose, however, the consideration was a promise made in the present to perform an act in the future. Would the promisee need to plead that he had performed? English courts had traditionally held that he need not because the promise counted as consideration given at the time it was made even though its performance lay in the future. They drew this distinction long before English lawyers considered when the promisee's refusal to perform a promise could be used as a defence by the promisor.[82]

In the nineteenth century, the doctrine of offer and acceptance was pressed into service to explain this difference in pleading. Some offers, it was said, could not be accepted by promising in return but only by doing the act which the promisor requested.[83] If he offered a reward for the return of property, the offeree could only accept by returning the property. Such an offer was sometimes called one of 'unilateral contract', as distinguished from an offer of 'bilateral contract' which could be accepted in the ordinary way by making a promise. It seemed to follow that until the offeree had actually done the act requested, an offer of unilateral contract was an unaccepted offer and therefore revocable. That consequence troubled Pollock since the promisor could then revoke after the promisee had done a substantial part of the work requested. He suggested that the offeree could accept by making 'an unequivocal beginning of the performance requested'.[84] Before that time, however, the promisor could revoke. Thus another reason had been found why a promise might not be enforceable.

II. The questions

Historically, then, both the civil law and the common law were built a layer at a time. Roman law was reshaped through the influence of the late scholastics and natural lawyers to reflect philosophical ideas originally taken from Aristotle. Heterogeneous common law cases which had been decided

---

[82] Simpson, *History*, 452–65.   [83] Pollock, *Principles of Contract*, 23–8.   [84] *Ibid.*, 26.

pragmatically were later explained by the bargained-for-detriment formula for consideration and the doctrine of unilateral contract. In the nineteenth century, both civil and common lawyers were attracted to will theories which made it hard to find any principled explanation of what promises should be enforced. If contract was the will of the parties, it would seem that whatever they willed should be enforceable. Civil and common law systems entered the twentieth century with rules that were the product of very different historical influences and without a principled explanation of them. In the twentieth century, will theories have fallen from favour, but there is no generally accepted explanation of what promises, in principle, the law should enforce.

We will examine what promises the law of European countries does enforce by framing a series of hypothetical questions which are suggested by the historical account just given. In civil law, as we have seen, traditionally, promises of gifts of money and property were treated differently. They required a formality. In common law, such promises were a paradigm case of a promise that lacked consideration and therefore was enforceable only in covenant which also required a formality. We have also seen that at one time, both civil and common law recognized certain exceptions. In civil law, the formality was not required for promises to charities and people about to marry. It was not required for promises to pay compensation for a benefit received in the past such as a rescue. In common law, consideration was found for promises to those about to marry. It was found for promises to pay time-barred debts, debts discharged in bankruptcy, and debts incurred as a minor.

Our first questions test whether a formality is still required, and whether exceptions like these are still recognized.

Case 1: Gaston promised to give a large sum of money (a) to his niece Catherine on her twenty-fifth birthday, (b) to his daughter Clara because she was about to marry, (c) to the United Nations Children's Emergency Fund for famine relief, or (d) to a waitress with a nice smile. Is he bound by the promise? Could he bind himself by making the promise formally or by using a different legal form such as a trust? Is his estate liable if he dies before changing his mind? Does it matter if the promisee incurred expenses in the expectation that the promise would be kept?

Case 2: Kurt promised a large sum of money to Tony who had suffered a permanent back injury saving (a) Kurt or (b) Kurt's adult child from drowning after a boating accident. Can Tony enforce the promise if Kurt changes his mind? Does it matter if Tony was a professional lifeguard or if he had performed the rescue as part of his normal duties?

Case 3: Ian, now solvent and an adult, had once owed money to Anna that she could not claim legally because (a) Ian's debt had been discharged in bankruptcy, (b) the debt was barred by the passage of time (by prescription or by a statute of limitations), or (c) the debt was incurred when Ian was too young to be bound by his contracts. Ian now promises to pay the debt. Can Anna enforce the promise if he changes his mind?

As mentioned earlier, still another ground for refusing to enforce a promise, in civil law as early as Molina, and in common law since the nineteenth century, is the absence of an intention to bind oneself legally. The fourth question tests the limits of this principle.

Case 4: Carlo, a famous musician, agreed to come to a dinner to be held in his honour by a private music conservatory. Two days before the dinner, he was offered a large sum of money if he would give a performance in another city the night of the dinner, taking the place of another musician who had become ill. He notified the conservatory that he could not come because he had accepted a conflicting invitation. The conservatory cancelled the dinner after it had already spent a large amount of money on publicity and food. Can the conservatory recover against Carlo?

Moreover, as we have seen, in civil law gratuitous promises to loan or to store property or to do services were not treated in the same way as gifts. They did not require a formality. In Roman law, contracts to loan and to store property were contracts *re*, binding only on delivery. The late scholastics and natural lawyers thought they should be binding on consent. But they thought that the lender should be able to recover his property if he needed it so that a promise intended to be costless would remain so. They also accepted a special Roman rule applicable to gratuitous contracts: the party who was doing the favour was held to a lower standard of care. As we have seen, English law also treated gratuitous bailments differently. They sometimes had consideration although it was hard to explain why they should, at least if one identifies consideration with bargain. The next three questions examine the extent to which these contracts are still treated differently.

Case 5: Otto sold his house and all his furniture except for a valuable antique table and chairs. Charles promised to store them for three months without charge while Otto found a new house to buy. Is the promise binding? Does it matter (a) if Charles refused to store the table and chairs before they are delivered or a month afterwards? (b) if Charles was a friend of Otto, or the antiques dealer from whom he recently purchased the table and chairs, or a professional storer of furniture? (c) if Charles refused to store them merely because he had changed his mind or because he had unexpectedly inherited furniture which he had no place else to store? (d) if Otto could instead have stored his furniture with Jean, who had also offered to store it without charge, and has now withdrawn that offer? or (e) if Otto had previously contracted with a warehouse to store his furniture, had cancelled the contract because of Charles' offer, and now can only store his furniture at a higher price?

Case 6: Richard promised to mail some documents to Maria's insurance company so that the company would (a) insure, or (b) cancel an insurance policy on Maria's small private plane. He failed to do so. Is he liable (a) if Maria's plane crashes and she cannot recover its value because it was not insured, or (b) if Maria has to pay an extra monthly premium because her insurance was not cancelled? Does it matter if Richard promised to help because he was a friend whose profession was completely unrelated to aircraft, insurance, or the mailing of documents? Does it matter if he promised to help because he had just sold and delivered the plane to Maria?

Case 7: Barbara promised Albert that he could use her car without charge for three months while she was on vacation. She now needs the car because she cancelled her vacation plans after injuring her left foot. Can she have it back? Does it matter if she told Albert he could not have the car a week before she was supposed to deliver it or a week after she actually did? Does it matter if Albert has taken a job that requires him to have a car but does not pay enough for him to rent one?

As we have seen, in common law, just as sometimes consideration was found for some promises that were not bargains, sometimes it was not found for promises which were not favours or gifts. Since these promises are often made in a commercial context, one wonders what reason there might be for refusing to enforce them. Certainly, the reason is not to protect the promisor against his own generous impulses, as it might be in other contexts. One possibility is that covertly, the doctrine was being used to strike down contracts that were unfair because one party was not getting anything in return for his own commitment. If so, perhaps it is still used for that purpose. Or perhaps common law systems have found some more sensitive way to deal with it. The doctrine of consideration is a rather blunt instrument since a commitment is not necessarily unfair because nothing is received in return, and it may be unfair even if something is.

The civil law, by contrast, has traditionally had ways of considering directly whether a transaction was unfair. In some situations, Roman law required the parties to act in good faith.[85] Medieval lawyers developed a

---

[85] See Gordley, 'Good Faith'.

remedy for *laesio enormis* – deviations by more than one-half from the contract price – by generalizing a Roman text concerned with the sale of land.[86] Canon lawyers developed the doctrine that promises are no longer binding when circumstances change sufficiently, and Baldus imported it into civil law.[87] The late scholastics explained the need for good faith and relief for *laesio enormis* by the Aristotelian principle that an act of commutative justice required equality so that each party gave a performance equal in value to what he received. They explained the doctrine of changed circumstances by the Aristotelian idea of equity. Because promise-makers, like law-givers, cannot imagine all the circumstances that might arise, their promises or laws should not extend to all circumstances. These doctrines again became standard among the natural lawyers. The next six questions deal with situations in which a contract may be unfair because a party has committed himself without receiving anything in return. They test whether common law systems still deal with them with the doctrine of consideration and whether civil law systems have used the doctrines just described or other doctrines to give relief.

In some of the situations in Case 8, the promise may be unfair because the other party can order whatever quantity he wishes.

Case 8: Alloy, a steel manufacturer, promised to sell Motor Works, a car manufacturer, as much steel as it ordered during the coming year for a set price per ton. Is the promise binding (a) if the market price rises to 20 per cent more than the contract price, and Motor Works orders the amount of steel it usually needs? (b) if the market price rises to 20 per cent more than the contract price, and Motor Works orders twice the steel it usually needs? (c) if the market price falls to 20 per cent below the contract price, and Motor Works buys no steel from Alloy, buying its requirements of steel on the market instead?

In some of the situations in Cases 9 to 12, a promise may be unfair because the promisor is agreeing to take more (or less) in return for a performance to which he is already entitled.

Case 9: Robert promised (a) to restructure a building for Paul who plans to use it as a restaurant, or (b) to sell Paul restaurant equipment including stoves, tables, chairs, cooking equipment, plates, and glasses. Paul promised him a fixed amount in payment. After performing part of the contract, Robert refused to continue unless he received one and a half times

---

[86] See J. Gordley, 'Just Price', in Peter Newman (ed.), *The New Palgrave Dictionary of Economics and the Law*, vol. II (1998), 410.

[87] See J. Gordley, 'Contract in Pre-Commercial Societies and in Western History', *Int. Enc. Comp. L.* 7 (1997), 2–58–2–59.

the amount originally promised. There had been no change in the circumstances of the parties since the contract was made except that Paul will now experience considerable delay opening his restaurant if he has to turn to someone else to complete the performance promised by Robert. Fearing this delay, Paul promised Robert the amount he demanded. After Robert completed performance, Paul refused to pay more than the amount originally agreed. Must he do so?

Case 10: Vito was an executive working for Company, a business firm, on a contract obligating him to continue working, and Company to continue employing him, for a period of ten years. Company promised to pay him a large sum of money, equal to a year's pay, (a) in the midst of his term of employment because he received an offer of immediate employment at higher pay from a competing firm, or (b) at the end of his term of employment, after he had announced his intention to retire, to thank him for his services. Is Company obliged to keep this promise? Does it matter if Vito has already bought a vacation house he could otherwise not afford?

Case 11: Contractor, a construction company, agreed to build an office building for Realty, a real estate company. According to their agreement, Contractor was to receive a fixed amount 'which shall be due after an architect appointed by Realty certifies that the building is finished according to the specifications' contained in the contract. While the building was under construction, Contractor promised, without demanding or being offered additional payment, to install more expensive glareproof windows than the specifications called for. Some time later, Realty promised that Contractor would be paid without seeking an architect's certificate. Are either of these promises binding? Would it matter if Realty had already advertised the glareproof windows, or Contractor had already covered over portions of the building the architect would have needed to inspect, before the other party threatened not to keep its promise?

Case 12: Realty, a company dealing in land, leased space to Travel, a travel agency, for ten years at a fixed monthly rent. One year later, Travel's business fell off because of an economic recession. Realty agreed that Travel could pay half the agreed rent for the duration of the recession. Two years later, when the recession ended, Realty demanded that Travel pay the remainder of the originally agreed rent for the previous two years. Can it recover that amount from Travel?

In some of the situations in Case 13, the promise may be unfair because one party can choose whether the contract is to be binding.

Case 13: Realty, a company dealing in land, was looking for a site for a new building. It told Simon it might be interested in purchasing a lot that he owned, but that it would need time to conduct a study. Without charging anything, Simon promised that he would sell his land to Realty for a fixed price (a) if Realty chose to buy it at any time within the next month, (b) if Realty chose to buy it at any time within the next two years, or (c) when Realty completed its study of the land, unless, in its sole and absolute judgment, Realty thought the economic prospects were unsatisfactory, in which case Realty had the option to withdraw. Realty accepted. Is the promise binding? Does it matter if there was an abrupt rise in the market price, and Realty wants to buy the land, not for a building, but for immediate resale?

As we have seen, in common law, other promises were said not to be binding because they were 'offers of unilateral contract' which could be revoked before the offeree performed or began to perform. This doctrine may also have covertly played a useful role. It may have allowed the promisor to change his mind when he can do so without harming the promisee. If he should be able to, then perhaps civil law systems have found some way to allow him to do so. Perhaps common law systems have found other ways as well. The last two questions examine these possibilities.

Case 14: A burglar stole Simone's valuable diamond necklace. She offered a large sum of money payable if it was discovered and returned (a) to Raymond, a private detective, or (b) in a newspaper advertisement, to whomever succeeded in finding the necklace. Three months later, after (a) Raymond or (b) others incurred expenses looking for the necklace, she wishes to withdraw her promise because she has changed her mind about how much she is willing to pay for the return of the necklace. Can she do so?

Case 15: Claude, wishing to sell his house, listed it with Homes, an agency that assists sellers in finding buyers. Homes was to receive 5 per cent of the sales price of the house if it found a buyer. Three months later, after Homes had taken various steps to do so and incurred expenses, Claude decided not to sell his house. Is he liable to the agency for 5 per cent of the sales price or for its expenses? Does it matter if the agency has found a buyer who has expressed his willingness to buy the house although no contract has been signed? Does it matter if Claude had promised that he would list the house only with Homes or whether he remained free to list it with other agencies?

2 Contemporary solutions

Case 1: promises of gifts

Case

Gaston promised to give a large sum of money (a) to his niece Catherine on her twenty-fifth birthday, (b) to his daughter Clara because she was about to marry, (c) to the United Nations Children's Emergency Fund for famine relief, or (d) to a waitress with a nice smile. Is he bound by the promise? Could he bind himself by making the promise formally or by using a different legal form such as a trust? Is his estate liable if he dies before changing his mind? Does it matter if the promisee incurred expenses in the expectation that the promise would be kept?

Discussions

FRANCE

In Case 1(a), Gaston's promise to his niece appears to be a gift. One way to make a gift irrevocable in French law is by actual delivery to the donee, but Gaston did not deliver, and, in any case, only gifts of small amounts can be made binding in this way. Consequently, the transaction is governed by art. 931 of the French Civil Code: 'all transactions which constitute gifts *inter vivos* must be executed before a notary', that is, by a notarially authenticated document. Therefore, if the promise is made informally, Gaston will not be bound by it. He would be bound if the gift was made in the legal form by a notarially authenticated document. It would also be necessary for his niece to accept (art. 932 of the Civil Code). If those requirements were met, and then he died before paying the promised sum, his estate will be liable since his heirs inherit the whole of his assets (*patrimoine*), including contractual debts, pursuant to art. 1122 of the Civil Code which provides: 'one is deemed to have stipulated for oneself, one's heirs and assigns . . .'.

It does not matter if Gaston's niece incurred expenses in the expectation that she would receive the money. Under French law there is no legal ground that enables the promisee to recover for reliance on a future benefit to be received under a contract, unless his reliance gives rise to liability in tort under art. 1382 of the Civil Code which allows recovery for harm (*dommage*) that is caused by the fault (*faute*) of another.[1] It is not clear whether Gaston would be liable under art. 1382 for the 'fault' of not fulfilling a promise to make a gift, when the due formalities have not been respected. One can sometimes recover under this article for breaking off commercial negotiations.[2] Nevertheless, that analogy does not seem to be a good one since the parties do not have the same interest in the gift becoming final. It could therefore be difficult for the beneficiary of the promise to claim that the promisor is at fault since only the beneficiary stands to gain and it may be wrong to force the promisor to be generous.

Nevertheless, it is just possible that an analogy could be drawn to the cases where the courts have awarded damages for the fault of creating a certain illusion in the mind of the promisee. An example is a unilateral contract where advertising has created an illusion in the mind of an offeree–consumer that the offeror will give him prize money and the offeror fails to do so. 'Victims' of the false illusion who have spent money in the belief that prize money will be paid have managed to recover on the basis of contract as well as tort.[3] The critical question is whether one can truly compare a promise by a commercial party to a consumer with a promise between two individuals. In the former case, the repercussions

---

[1] Art. 1382 of the Civil Code states that 'any human act whatsoever which causes harm to another creates an obligation in the person by whose fault it has occurred to make compensation'.

[2] For a recent illustration of liability for breaking off commercial negotiations prior to the conclusion of a contract, see Com., 7 Jan. 1997; Com., 22 April 1997, D 1998, 45, note Chauvel. According to this author, since the breaking-off of contractual negotiations is somewhat inevitable in commercial contexts, the victim should only be indemnified when breaking them off can be characterized as a fault. No fault has been committed when the termination of negotiations was justifiable. Nor should the victim be indemnified when his own behaviour was unjustifiable because his reliance on the conclusion of the contract and his hasty expenditure in anticipation were not really reasonable. In this case, French law would explain the denial of recovery in terms of the 'fault of the victim'.

[3] See the observations of J. Mestre, RTDCiv. 1996, 397–8. See also, for example, Civ. 1, 28 March 1995, confirming the analysis of the trial courts on the basis of a unilateral contract (*engagement unilatéral*). Liability has also been imposed in tort, for instance, when a mail-order company gave the beneficiary reason to believe that he had won an important sum of money when in fact he had only gained the right to participate in the lottery. The court awarded the total amount of the prize money offered as a lure on the ground that the victim's 'deception' was equivalent to the hope of the gain on which he could have relied. Cour d'appel, Paris 25 ch., 27 Oct. 1995; Vie jur. 10 March 1996, 9.

are much wider and the potential harm caused to a number of victims is greater. It is clear that the decisions in the cases of prizes or prize money are greatly influenced by the fact that the promisors used misleading advertising. Intuitively, it is not clear that a French court would enforce a promise between two individuals by awarding damages for its breach either in full or in the amount of the promise.

In Case 1(b), where Gaston promised a large sum of money to his daughter Clara because she was about to marry, the answer is the same. If he does not observe the legal formalities he will not be bound. If he does, he and his heirs will be bound provided that there is no confusion between Clara's capacity as heir and as beneficiary.

Nevertheless, it is possible for Gaston to make this type of gift by another means. He may create a dowry: that is, a gift made to a couple by a third party upon their marriage. This type of gift benefits from special rules provided that it is included in the spouses' ante-nuptial settlement. It is not necessary to make the gift in a notarially authenticated document. Mentioning the dowry in the ante-nuptial settlement suffices since this agreement is itself a notarially authenticated document, and the beneficiary's acceptance is not required (art. 1087).

It might be claimed that Gaston's promise is a natural obligation (*obligation naturelle*). A promisor who voluntarily undertakes to perform a natural obligation is bound by his promise and is liable to the promisee if he fails to perform.[4] A unilateral promise to perform converts the natural obligation into a civil one. Nevertheless, that rule does not apply here because the Code contains special provisions that govern parents' gifts of money to their children upon marriage. Under art. 204 of the Civil Code, 'a child does not have an action against his father or mother for a settlement upon marriage or otherwise'.

On the question whether a dowry is a natural obligation or not, case law is in conflict,[5] although the discussion now appears to be obsolete, and the case law emanating from trial courts is of extremely limited value. It should be noted, however, that, in principle, a parent's obligation to maintain his or her children[6] ends when the child reaches the age of majority or marries. That is how the case law has interpreted art. 203 of the Civil

---

[4] Ghestin, Goubeaux, and Fabre-Magnan, *Traité de droit civil* no. 736, pp. 717 f.

[5] For an example in favor, see Cour d'appel, Paris, 26 April 1923: DP 1923, 2, 121, note R. Savatier; for one *contra*, see Cour d'appel, Poitiers, 22 Dec. 1924: Gaz. Pal. 1925, 1, 272. In the latter case it was held that a dowry is a gift and not an onerous act which recognizes a former debt. The gift was thus declared void for failure to comply with formalities.

[6] Maintenance should be distinguished from the concept of settlement under art. 204 of the Civil Code. Civ. 2, 19 Oct. 1977: Gaz. Pal. 1978, 1, somm.

Code, which states that 'spouses contract together, by the very act of marriage, an obligation to feed, maintain and bring up their children'.

The answer might be different if the gift were made subject to the condition subsequent that Clara gets married (*condition subsequent mixte*). In this case Gaston will not be bound until the condition is satisfied on the day of the marriage. That will also be the case if he gives the money in the form of a dowry.

In Case 1(c), in which Gaston promises to give a large sum of money to the United Nations Children's Emergency Fund for famine relief, the same principles apply. Nevertheless, because gifts to legal persons are regarded with suspicion, further restrictions are imposed on such a beneficiary. Their capacity to benefit from a gift is limited depending on the form of the group and, in the case of a charity, whether it is recognized to be of public benefit. It may also be limited by the 'principle of speciality' which means that such groups must stay within the objects set out in the French equivalent of their articles of association.

John Dawson, in his book *Gifts and Promises*,[7] cites some French cases in which courts enforced a promise of gift by applying the concept of a 'moral equivalent'. These courts treated such a promise as an onerous bilateral contract (in the French sense of the word)[8] because the act of the beneficiary compensated the promisor, for example, by giving him the satisfaction of hearing the church bell of his childhood toll again, or having an annual mass said for him. Nevertheless, this case law would not apply to Gaston's promise here. In order to treat a gift as a bargain, the more recent case law requires evidence of a real economic exchange. The existence of any interest whatsoever on the part of the promisor no longer suffices. Whether there is such an exchange is a question of fact for the trial courts to decide and subjective and objective elements will be taken into consideration.[9] In the present case, however, the objective element is absent. There is absolutely no indication that the UN charity has made a concession in return for the promise of the gift. It seems, therefore, that the promise of a gift would be treated as such. Consequently, failure to respect the formalities means that the promise is revocable and cannot be enforced.

---

[7] J. Dawson, *Gifts and Promises, Continental and American Law Compared* (1980), 84–102.

[8] Article 1102 provides: 'A contract is synallagmatic or bilateral whenever the contracting parties contract reciprocal obligations.' According to art. 1106: 'An onerous contract is one that imposes an obligation upon each of the parties to give or to do something.'

[9] F. Terré and Y. Lequette, *Droit civil, Les successions, Les libéralités*, 3rd edn (1997), no. 250, p. 210; G. Marty and P. Raynaud, *Droit civil, Les successions et les libéralitiés*, no. 299, p. 238 f.; see also R. Le Guidec in *Juris-Classeur civil*, arts. 893–5, who suggests that the absence of a *quid pro quo* (*contrepartie*) means that the donor becomes poorer and the donee richer.

In Case 1(d), in which Gaston promises a sum of money to a waitress, once again he will be bound only if he executes a notarially authenticated document. Nevertheless, even if that formality were observed, the gift could be void as against public policy (*cause immorale*) (art. 1133). French judges frequently distinguish according to the different purposes the transaction might serve. If the donor and beneficiary cohabit and the gift is intended to start up or maintain the relationship, then the gift will be annulled. If, on the contrary, the gift is made when the couple are splitting up on account of a duty in conscience (*devoir de conscience*) or a natural obligation (*obligation naturelle*) to compensate for harm that has been done, it will be valid.[10]

Although we have stressed the importance of the legal form to render a promise of a gift enforceable, it may nevertheless be helpful to point out an important difference between French law and English law. Although traditionally, in English law, the formality of a sealed instrument is sufficient to make a gift enforceable, under French law the form does not dispense with the other conditions requisite for the validity of a contract (art. 1108). The judge must satisfy himself that the normal requirements are met as to capacity, freely given consent, subject matter (*objet*), and, above all, the reason for the promise (*cause*). In the gift to Clara, for example, there would be a mistake as to the *cause*, and the gift would be annulled, if Clara turned out not to be his daughter, or, according to a more objective theory of the *cause*, if he did not have the intention required to make a gift, that is, the wish to prefer another to oneself. English law and French law seem to respect legal form for different reasons. In English law, the form is a substitute for consideration and, therefore, a control which cannot be exercised with regard to gifts. Under French law, it is only a formal device, established for the purposes of protection of the donor, his family and third parties since it is considered dangerous to deprive oneself of wealth gratuitously by making a gift.

BELGIUM

This first case involves a gift of a corporeal movable (*bien meuble corporel*): a large sum of money. Belgian law has strict rules as to the enforceability of donations (regulated by arts. 893 f. of the Civil Code).[11] If Gaston's prom-

---

[10] For an example, see Civ. 1, 6 Oct. 1959, D 1960.

[11] These rules reflect the general hostility of the drafters of the Code towards donations, which, unlike onerous transactions (*transactions à titre onéreux*), do nothing to favour commercial transactions and represent a potential danger for the donor and his family

ises are donations within the meaning of these articles, they must meet the conditions necessary for the validity of such a promise: present transfer of the thing given, irrevocability, formality (the requirement of notarial authentication), and express acceptance by the donee. Very likely they do not, as we will see shortly. The first question, however, is whether these promises are donations subject to these articles.

In Case 1(a), Gaston promised to give a large sum of money to his niece Catherine on her twenty-fifth birthday. This promise might be considered to be a 'customary present' (*cadeau d'usage*) because it is quite customary for an uncle to offer a birthday present to his niece. If so, it is not subject to the rules that govern donations and would be enforceable.[12] One possible difficulty, however, is that a customary present must not only be customary; it must also be of relatively moderate importance (*modicité*)[13] considering Gaston's personal means. The question, then, is whether the large sum of money is also large for Gaston considering his means as well as the customs generally followed in Gaston's family for birthday presents. If the sum is immoderate, the gift will be a donation subject to arts. 893 f. of the Civil Code.

In Case 1(b), Gaston promised to give a large sum of money to his daughter Clara who is about to marry. A promise of a gift to those about to marry (*propter nuptias*) is not subject to the formalities that govern donations when it is made by a parent (*ascendant*) in favour of his or her offspring (*descendant*), as is the case here. All that is necessary is the parties' consent.[14] Furthermore, a promise of dowry, even under private signature (*acte sous seing privé*), binds the promisor.[15]

The justification for this result is the theory of the so-called natural obligation (*obligation naturelle*),[16] based on art. 1235, second paragraph, of the

---

especially when the donor finds himself in a delicate situation such as illness. The general tendency of the Code's rules is therefore to protect the donor against himself through rules that ensure he will think the matter over before making a donation. Nevertheless, when the decision to donate has been made in the manner the law prescribes, the Code also contains rules intended to protect the donee by ensuring that the donor will follow through (according to the saying 'donner et reprendre ne vaut'). See generally Raucent, *Les libéralités* nos. 4 f. and 120 f.

[12] See *ibid*. 17–18. This general solution is doctrinal and imposed by case law, proceeding from two specific provisions of the Civil Code (arts. 852 and 1419 (2)) that exclude the application of *some* rules concerning donations for the *présents d'usage*.   [13] See *ibid*.

[14] *Ibid*., 143–4.

[15] *Ibid*. See also de Wilde d'Estmael, *Répertoire notarial* no. 8 (discussing the requirement of an express acceptance for the validity of a donation (see below), the author adds: 'This principle admits only one exception: the promise of dowry, when it is made by the mother and father.').   [16] Raucent, *Les libéralités*, 143–4.

Civil Code[17] (Cass., 12 May 1890[18]). A 'natural obligation' is one that is originally regarded as a moral duty by the obligor and recognized as such by the general *opinio iuris* subject to the final judgment of the courts.[19] This natural obligation becomes a civil obligation, that is, one that is legally enforceable,[20] when it has been expressly or tacitly recognized or accepted voluntarily by the obligor.[21] Moreover, if a natural obligation is voluntarily performed, the obligor cannot recover the performance or its value.[22] Consequently, Gaston's promise is enforceable.

In Case 1(c), Gaston promised to give a large sum of money to the United Nations Children's Emergency Fund. This is a promise of donation governed by arts. 893 f. of the Civil Code. In contrast to the *ius commune* before the nineteenth century,[23] a gift to a charity (*ad pias causas*) does not receive any special treatment in present-day law aside from some tax law advantages that are beyond the scope of our discussion.

In Case 1(d), Gaston promised to give a large sum of money to a waitress with a nice smile. This is a promise of donation governed by arts. 893 f. of the Civil Code. It is not enforceable unless, possibly, there is a 'natural

---

[17] Article 1235 of the Civil Code provides: 'Each payment presupposes a debt: whatever was paid without being due is subject to recovery. Recovery will not be admitted regarding natural obligations that have been voluntarily fulfilled.'

[18] Pas., 1890, I, 197. In this case a father promised a pension as a dowry to his daughter to assist his son-in-law in supporting his wife. The court affirmed the decision of the trial court: 'Considering that the decision of the court of appeal establishes that the parents' duty to dower their children constitutes a natural obligation, and that the obligation undertaken by plaintiff in the disputed agreement had the effect of transforming the said obligation into a contract presenting all the required characteristics to make it legally binding. It appears from these observations that there is no donation submitted to the formalities prescribed by article 931 of the Civil Code in this case.'

[19] Raucent, *Les libéralités* no. 28.   [20] Van Ommeslaghe, *Droit des obligations*, 367.

[21] See *ibid.*, 357 f. Here are some recent illustrations from the case law of valid natural obligations: heirs' conduct in complying with a will they knew to be invalid – their behaviour constitutes the recognition of a natural obligation (Trib. civ. Liège, 7 March 1994, Rev. not. b., 1995, 306); so does supporting an economically weak concubine (Trib. civ. Bruges, 16 Jan. 1996, T. not., 1996, 221); so does the conduct of a man who behaved for years as though he were the father of the children of his concubine so that the man now has a civil obligation to support them (JP, Schaerbeek, 1 April 1992, Rev. trim. dr. fam., 1992, 426; Trib. civ. Bruxelles, 14 Jan. 1992, RGDC, 1993, 387); so does payment of alimony by a father who was no longer under an obligation to do so and who, as a result, cannot recover what he paid after his legal obligation ended (Sais. Gand, 31 July 1991, TGR, 1991, 125). For other illustrations, see Cases 2, 3, and 10, and see S. Stijns, D. Van Gerven, and P. Wéry, 'Chronique de jurisprudence. Les obligations: les sources (1985–1995)', JT, 1996, nos. 5–6.

[22] See art. 1235 of the Civil Code which legally recognizes the concept of natural obligation (cited above).   [23] See Dawson, *Gifts and Promises*, 84–102.

obligation' because the waitress provided Gaston with gratuitous services, for example, by assisting him in his old age by doing his shopping, laundry, cleaning, and the like so that he would have a legitimate reason for gratitude (see Case 10(b)).[24]

We have seen that Cases 1(a) and 1(d) could be donations governed by arts. 893 f. and that Case 1(c) almost certainly is. Very likely, they would be unenforceable under these articles. These cases concern promises to make gifts. According to art. 894 of the Civil Code, however, a donation is an act by which the donor, at the present time, irrevocably divests himself of the thing given.[25] More precisely, art. 894 contains two rules governing the validity of a donation: the donor's dispossession of the thing given must be immediate,[26] and it must be irrevocable.[27] Accordingly, a mere promise to make a donation, even made before a notary,[28] has no legal effect.[29]

Furthermore, under art. 932, no donation is valid until it has been expressly[30] accepted by the donee.[31] This rule treats the offer or the promise of donation differently from how promises or offers are usually treated. The law normally recognizes the binding force of an offer on the theory that a unilateral declaration of will has binding force.[32] It also

---

[24] On gifts made in consideration of services rendered (*donations rémunératoires*) see generally de Wilde d'Estmael, *Répertoire notarial* no. 27.

[25] Article 894 of the Civil Code: 'La donation . . . est un acte par lequel le donateur se dépouille actuellement et irrévocablement de la chose donnée . . .'

[26] Immediate dispossession does not mean immediate delivery. Delivery can take place later (except in the case of a *don manuel*, described below) but the transfer of the right to the thing must be immediate. Therefore the mere promise to donate does not comply with the requirement of immediate dispossession. De Wilde d'Estmael, *Répertoire notarial* nos. 19–20.

[27] The requirement of irrevocability means that the donor cannot make the donation dependent upon a provision the direct or indirect effect of which would be to render the donation ineffective or to permit the donor to reconsider. *Ibid.* no. 11.

[28] That is the formality described by arts. 931, 932, and 1339 of the Civil Code.

[29] Raucent, *Les libéralités* no. 177; de Wilde d'Estmael, *Répertoire notarial* nos. 8, 20.

[30] The requirement of an express acceptance means that a tacit acceptance will not be deemed sufficient. There must be a formal acceptance by the donee which means that his mere signature is not sufficient. De Wilde d'Estmael, *Répertoire notarial* no. 152.

[31] Article 932 of the Civil Code: 'A donation between living persons will not bind the donor and will not produce any effect until the day of its acceptance in express terms.'

[32] Several decisions of the *Cour de cassation* have recognized the binding force of an obligation undertaken by unilateral declaration of will. On the basis of this theory, the *Cour de cassation* has said that an offer may have binding force. Cass., 9 May 1980 (two decisions), Pas., 1980, I, 1127. For a recent overview of the extent to which this theory is accepted, see L. Simont, *Les obligations en droit français et en droit belge* (1994). See also Case 14.

recognizes that sometimes promises to make a contract may be binding.[33] In contrast, under art. 932 of the Civil Code, neither the offer nor the promise of donation has any binding force during the promisor's life or after his death.[34]

In addition, a donation must be evidenced by a solemn notarial act (arts. 931, 932, and 1339 of the Civil Code).[35] A donation made without this formality is absolutely void (*nullité absolue*).[36] Nevertheless, the courts recognize three exceptions from the requirement of notarization. The rule

---

[33] As pointed out by H. De Page, one can distinguish three types of promises. The first is a promise that merely amounts to an offer: for instance, a would-be seller offers to sell something if the buyer-to-be accepts. In this case, although the offer binds the offeror, there is no acceptance by the offeree. This promise is thus a simple unilateral declaration of will: there is no contract. The second kind is a contractual unilateral promise (*promesse unilatérale*) or option contract. In this case, there is a contract where one party undertakes an obligation and the other accepts this undertaking although he/she has not yet decided whether he/she is going to exercise his/her option to enter into the main contract. The third type is a bilateral promise (*promesse bilatérale*). In this case, a contract has actually been entered into whatever the expressions used by the parties (i.e., for instance, one 'promises' to sell and one 'promises' to buy). In some cases, such as sale of real estate, where the effects of the contract as to third parties depend on its notarization, it makes some sense to speak about a 'promise' before the parties proceed with the required formality in order to emphasize that the parties must still go before the notary. The word 'promise' is misleading, however, because the contract already exists and is enforceable between the parties themselves. If one party later refuses to formalize the contract so as to make it effective against third parties, the court will hold that its own decision has the effect of formalization before a notary and its decision will amount to the conclusion of the notarial act (the so-called *jugement tenant lieu d'acte authentique*). This discussion of the distinctions drawn by H. De Page is taken from Meinertzhagen-Limpens, *Traité élémentaire*, no. 103, pp. 278–82.

[34] De Page, *Traité élémentaire* vol. VIII/1, no. 369; de Wilde d'Estmael, *Répertoire notarial* no. 8; P. Delnoy, *Précis de droit civil. Les libéralités et les successions* (1991), no. 25: 'In contrast to [the treatment accorded] a promise and offer when they concern onerous transactions, the promise and offer are deprived of any binding force, even if they were made in the form [notarial document] required for donations. This is a consequence of art. 932, par. 1 of the Civil Code which provides that the donor is not bound in any manner until the donation has been accepted. Moreover, it must be accepted in "express terms".' See the following cases: Bruxelles, 12 March 1975, Pas., II, 141 (a widow signed a document under private signature where she expressed the view that one of her children had to receive an apartment in order for this child to be given the equivalent to what was given to his sister. After the mother's death, the child sought to enforce the promise but to no avail. The court held that a promise of donation, even if it were made in the form of a notarial document, is void when it has been accepted by the donee as required by art. 932 of the Civil Code); Trib. civ. Dinant, 10 April 1991, JLMB, 1993, 392; Gand, 23 Nov. 1993, TGR, 1994, 109.   [35] See Raucent, *Les libéralités* nos. 179–85.

[36] See *ibid.*, no. 123. Note, however, that this absolute invalidity becomes a relative invalidity after the promisor's decease, which means that the promisor's heirs may renounce the right to invoke it.

does not apply (1) when a movable is immediately delivered (*don manuel*, literally, by hand); (2) when a transaction is intended as a gift but is disguised as an onerous transaction (*donation déguisée*, for example, a sale in which it is not intended that the price will be paid); and (3) when the benefit is conferred gratuitously but indirectly through a type of transaction that is neutral or abstract (*donation indirecte*), such as a waiver of a debt (*remise de dette*), a renunciation of a right (*renonciation à un droit*), an assignment of a debt (*cession de créance*), or a stipulation for the benefit of a third party (*stipulation pour autrui*, by which the benefit of a contract between the donor and another person is transferred to the donee).[37] However, one must keep in mind that all the requirements for a donation other than that of a notarial formality apply to *don manuel*, *donation déguisée*, and *donation indirecte*, as well,[38] so that these transactions are not valid unless the donor immediately and irrevocably parts with the object he is giving.

One might ask whether the promise of a *don manuel* could be legally enforceable, and if so, whether the promises in this case would be enforceable on this ground. The answer is clearly in the negative. The *don manuel* belongs indeed to the category of 'real contracts' (contracts *re*) which means that such a contract is formed only on delivery of the object it concerns. Therefore, a promise of a *don manuel*, even when it has been accepted by the donee, has no legal effect.[39]

Applying these principles to this case, we can see that the promises to the United Nations Children's Emergency Fund and to the waitress are not immediate transfers because they are mere promises, not immediate and irrevocable dispositions of property. Additionally, these promises have not been expressly accepted. Finally, the requirement of notarial authentication is not met. The promise to the niece might possibly be regarded as a present transfer subject to a condition (*condition suspensive*). Donations can be made subject to conditions provided that the other requirements for

[37] *Ibid.*, no. 125.
[38] See de Wilde d'Estmael, *Répertoire notarial* no. 11; Raucent, *Les libéralités* nos. 126, 133–4, 136.
[39] De Wilde d'Estmael, *Répertoire notarial* no. 160; Trib. civ. Nivelles, 4 March 1993, Rev. not. b., 1994, 32 (by a written promise under private signature the promisor offered two specified paintings that the promisee could come and get at the address indicated on the document; the court held that the document could not contain a valid donation because it lacked acceptance and the required formality, and that it could not be a valid promise of a *don manuel* because one could not conceive of such a promise in the case of a 'real' contract).

their validity, such as express acceptance, are met.[40] But it is doubtful that the promise should be interpreted in this way. Again, the requirement of notarial authentication has not been met.

Moreover, there is little chance that the promisor will be held liable for violating a pre-contractual duty to act in good faith even if the promisee incurs expenses in the expectation that the promise will be kept. This possibility would certainly be a serious one if the promise had concerned an onerous transaction. In this case, however, the possibility appears very thin considering the very specific regulation of donations and the general distrust of donations expressed by the legislature. We must remember that, in contrast to the general law of obligations, a promise of a donation has no legal effect, the object being to protect the would-be donor and his family.

THE NETHERLANDS

In all four cases, Gaston's promise is a gift. Therefore, he is not bound by his promise unless he actually handed over the money (art. 7A:1724 of the Civil Code[41]), which is not the case here, or executed a notarial document

---

[40] But they may not defeat the requirement of irrevocability described above (de Wilde d'Estmael, *Répertoire notarial* no. 121) and they are impossible in the case of a *don manuel* (*ibid.*). In the case of the promise to the niece, Belgian law prefers to speak of a 'term precedent' (literal translation of *terme suspensif*) rather than a condition precedent. A 'term' is defined as a future and *certain* event, and here the future event – reaching her twenty-fifth birthday – is certain. A donation can be subject to such a 'term' (*ibid.*, nos. 117–18). It is also impossible to conceive of such a 'term' in the case of a *don manuel.*

[41] Article 7A:1724 of the Civil Code: 'Gifts from hand to hand of movable objects, sums of money, or bearer notes do not demand a deed and are valid by the simple delivery to the donee or to a third party who accepts the gift for him' (trans. J. H. M. van Erp).

The Dutch Civil Code has a so-called stratified structure (*gelaagde structuur*) which goes from more general to more specific rules. As a result, rules governing contracts will be found in different places according to the level of abstraction. To give an example: the rules applicable to a sale of goods to a consumer are found in Title 2 (Juridical Acts) of Book 3 (Patrimonial Law in General); in Book 6 (General Part of the Law of Obligations), especially in Title 5 (Contracts in General); and in Title 1 (Sale and Exchange) of Book 7 (Specific (Nominate) Contracts), especially articles such as 5, 11, 13, 18, and 24. In principle (that is, except in case of a specific provision), the rules on formation and validity – the themes that recur in the cases discussed here – are to be found in Title 6.5 and (more importantly) in Title 3.2.

The new Dutch Civil Code is not yet complete. Books 3, 5, and 6, which contain the general part of patrimonial law (contracts, property, and torts), and a part of Book 7 (on specific, nominate contracts) entered into force in 1992. Books 1 (Family Law), 2 (Legal Persons), and 8 (Transport) had entered into force previously. Some of the drafts on specific contracts have not yet taken effect. For those contracts which were dealt with (art. 7A:1719[42]). The promise in Case 1(a) is a promise with a condition precedent (art. 6:22[43]), but that makes no difference.

If he had made the promises through a notarial document, all four of them would be binding. That result is based on the rules on gift (see art. 7A:1719 of the Civil Code). A gift is a contract, and therefore the notarial document must be executed together with the promise.

If a valid contract is concluded by using a notarial document, the estate is liable if Gaston dies. See art. 6:249 of the Civil Code.[44]

If Gaston did not use a notarial document, the promises are not enforceable even if the promisees incurred expenses in the expectation that they would be kept. The reliance principle (art. 3:35 of the Civil Code; see below) will not make the promise binding since that would undermine the purpose of the form requirement, which is to protect people against their own light-hearted generosity. Neither will the duty to act in good faith be of any help. In the *Plas/Valburg* case, the *Hoge Raad* held that a party may recover his expectation interest if the other party breaks off negotiations in a manner contrary to good faith.[45] However, the test the Court adopted was aimed at a situation where protracted negotiations are brutally broken off.[46] Here negotiations were not broken off since a contract is concluded. The question presumes that all promises have been accepted. Therefore agreement has been reached. Nevertheless, it is invalid for lack of form.

In the *Plas/Valburg* case, the *Hoge Raad* also held that a party who breaks off negotiations may be liable to make compensation for expenses that the

---

under the old code (which was very similar to the French Civil Code) these old rules still apply. They are to be found in temporary Book 7A.

  Most of the translations of the Civil Code provisions are taken from: P. P. C. Haanappel and Ejan Mackaay, *New Netherlands Civil Code / Nouveau Code Civil Néerlandais* (1990).

[42] Article 7A:1719 of the Civil Code: 'No gift except the gift which is dealt with in art. 1724 can be done in a different way than by notarial deed of which the original remains with the notary under a sanction of nullity' (trans. J. H. M. Erp).

[43] Article 6:22 of the Civil Code: 'A suspensive condition causes the obligation to take effect upon the occurrence of the event; a resolutory condition extinguishes the obligation upon the occurrence of the event.'

[44] Article 6:249 of the Civil Code: 'Unless the contract produces a different result, its juridical effects also bind successors by general title.'

[45] HR 18 June 1982 (*Plas/Valburg*), NJ 1983, 723, note Brunner, AA 1983, 758, note Van Schilfgaarde.

[46] It does not seem likely that the *Hoge Raad* will broaden the field of application of the *Plas/Valburg* doctrine. Recent case law rather suggests that the *Hoge Raad* intends to limit its application by restricting the test. See M. Hesselink, 'De schadevergoedingsplicht bij afgebroken onderhandelingen in het licht van he Europese privaatrecht', WPNR, 1996, 6248 (pp. 879–83), 6249 (pp. 906–10), at 881.

other party incurred even if negotiations were broken off before the stage at which that party was justified in believing that a contract would certainly be concluded. Allowing expenses, which are part of reliance damages, to be recovered would not, strictly speaking, undermine the protection of a party against his own generosity. It would not be the same as enforcing the promise. Therefore, the rules on gifts should not preclude the courts from awarding reliance damages on the basis of the good faith principle. Nevertheless, there are no Dutch cases that do so when a party has relied on a gift. The reason is that, as noted, the doctrine of precontractual liability has been applied almost exclusively in cases where negotiations were broken off.

SPAIN

Spanish legal scholars maintain that unilateral promises, once accepted, form contracts that are unilateral in the civil law sense of the term: they impose an obligation on only one of the parties.[47] Article 1261 of the Spanish Civil Code provides:

There is no contract unless the following requirements are met:
(1) Consent of the contracting parties,
(2) A certain object that is the subject matter of the contract,
(3) A cause of the obligation that is established.[48]

The Spanish Civil Code does not define unilateral contracts, although those of other civil law systems do (for example, art. 1333 of the Italian Code). The prevalent view, however, is that in contrast to the English common law, there is a unilateral contract when there is a promise, an acceptance, and only one of the parties assumes obligations.

Unilateral promises are not enforced unless they are accepted.[49] Acceptance transforms them into contracts. Some scholars[50] emphasize

---

[47] E.g., Díez Picazo and Gullón, *Sistema de derecho civil*, vol. II, 144.

[48] Unless otherwise noted, all quotations from the Spanish Civil Code are from Julio Romanach's translation, *Civil Code of Spain* (1994).

[49] TS, 17 Oct. 1932, 5 May 1958 (see Case 2), and 13 Nov. 1962. Prior to 1981, however, promises like the one in Case 1(b) to people about to marry were enforceable in Spain even without acceptance: Castán Tobeñas, *Derecho civil*, vol. IV, 234. The former art. 1330 of the Civil Code provided that acceptance is not needed for this kind of donation. This principle has survived in art. 18 of the Catalan Civil Code ('acceptance is not necessary for [donations by reason of marriage] to be valid' (translation by the author from the original code in Catalan)).

[50] E.g., L. Díez Picazo, 'Las declaraciones unilaterales de voluntad como fuentes de obligaciones y la jurisprudencia del tribunal supremo', *Anuario de derecho civil* 27 (1974), 456.

that this is the essential and historic meaning of the characteristic way in which promises are treated in Spanish law. These scholars contend that, with the exception of the *politicatio* and the *votum*, Roman law did not enforce any unaccepted promise. The motto is: 'word given carries duties if it has been taken'. These scholars point out that, conversely, no other European legal system enforces unilateral promises.

Nevertheless, for a promise to make a gift to be enforceable, there must be an intention to give, a *causa donandi*. The determination of whether there is one is purely subjective[51] and psychological.[52]

Moreover, even if these conditions are met, no obligation arises unless the thing promised is actually delivered (*datio rei*) or the promise is made in writing. Article 632 of the Civil Code provides: 'A donation of a movable thing may be made orally or in writing. An oral one requires a simultaneous delivery of the thing donated. In the absence of this requirement, it shall not be effective unless made in writing and the acceptance appears in the same form.' Despite the language of this provision, if the promise is in writing and has not been revoked, then even though there has been no written acceptance, the *Tribunal Supremo* has considered the initiation of legal proceedings in writing by the promisee to enforce the promise to be a de facto acceptance in writing. On these grounds, even though there was no prior written acceptance, it enforced the promise of the owner of a disco club to his out-of-wedlock children that they would have the profits made by the club.[53] It enforced the written promise of an heir to follow the unwritten intentions of her testator.[54]

Therefore, Cases 1(a), 1(b), 1(c), and 1(d) would all be resolved in the same way under Spanish law. In each case, even if there is a *causa donandi*, no obligation arises unless the promise was made in writing or the thing promised is actually delivered.[55]

---

[51] Puig Brutau, *Fundamentos de derecho civil*, vol. II-1, 132.
[52] Díez Picazo, *Fundamentos de derecho*, vol. I, 226.   [53] TS, 6 March 1976.
[54] TS, 13 Nov. 1976.
[55] Since the promise could be made binding by putting it in writing, there is no need to consider whether some other formality might work instead. In any event, a trust would not. In Spain, the institution most similar to a trust would be a 'foundation' (*fundación*). The foundation is a legal person. Goods are given to it to further a certain purpose: for example, education or the fight against hunger in the world. Spanish law allows foundations to be created only when there is a charitable purpose and it has indefinite beneficiaries, like charitable trusts in the United States. There is no such thing as a *fundación* with private goals. All the founding person can do is establish priorities within the foundation such as to assist first his or her relatives in case of need, without excluding strangers.

Foundations are created by unilateral declarations that do not need acceptance. They

Assuming that there was an obligation (for example, because the promise was in writing), if Gaston died before changing his mind, the obligation would not be extinguished by his death.[56]

PORTUGAL

Gaston would not be bound by these promises. He would be bound only if he made them in a written document, and even then, only if they were accepted by the promisee in a written document. Nevertheless, the promisees may be compensated if they incurred expenses in the expectation that the promise would be kept.

Portuguese law distinguishes between unilateral promises, which are not accepted by the beneficiary, and unilateral contracts, which are made by two parties but impose an obligation only on one of them. The general rule is that promises must be accepted. Unilateral promises are valid only in a few cases mentioned in the Portuguese Civil Code (art. 457). Therefore, if the beneficiaries of Gaston's promises have not accepted, Gaston can revoke his promise at any time.

Even if they have accepted, Gaston can still withdraw his proposal unless it was made in a written document (art. 969 of the Civil Code). If he did, and the beneficiaries accepted in a written document, they will have entered into a contract of donation (*contrato de doação*), and Gaston would be legally bound. A donation contract is one in which a person who intends a liberality gratuitously and at his own expense gives another a thing or a right or assumes an obligation for his benefit (art. 940).[57] Such a contract is termed an obligatory donation, meaning that the donor assumes an obligation to give.[58] It is void if it is not made in a written

Footnote 55 (*cont.*)

are irrevocable. Some authors maintain that a foundation must be created in writing even if only personal property is to be given to it. See Castán Tobeñas, *Derecho civil*, vol. I-2, 450. Others disagree. See Díez Picazo and Gullón, *Sistema de derecho civil*. If they are endowed with real property, then, according to the Civil Code, they must be created by a notarial document (art. 633). So although Gaston could create a trust to give the money to the United Nations Children's Emergency Fund, it is not clear whether he would have to do so in writing. In the other cases, his purpose is not charitable, and he would have to satisfy the requirements for a donation.

[56] Article 1156 of the Spanish Civil Code applies. It identifies six instances in which 'obligations are extinguished' and death is not among them: '(1) by payment or performance, (2) by loss of the thing owned, (3) by remission of the debt, (4) by confusion of the rights of the obligor and obligee, (5) by compensation, (6) by novation'.

[57] See Lima and Varela, *Código Civil Anotado*, vol. II, 236 ff.

[58] See J. A. Varela, 'Anotação', *Revista de Legislação e Jurisprudência*, 116 (1984), 30 and 57, at 60–2. The case law agrees that a promise to donate is binding. See A. Relação de Lisboa, 14 Oct. 1993, in CJ 189 (1993), IV, 151.

document (art. 947), even an informal one such as a personal letter, or a public deed if the gift is of immovable property. A public deed is a document subscribed to by the promisor in the presence of a notary. Otherwise, a donation of movable property would be valid only if the property was delivered immediately, which was not the case here.

If a promise of a donation is made and accepted by a written document, the donor can revoke it only if the donee shows ingratitude. Ingratitude means a criminal offence against the donor or his family, a refusal to give them 'due alimony', or coercion of the donor to make a different testamentary disposition of his property (art. 974 of the Civil Code). 'Due alimony' (the phrase used in the statute) has been interpreted to mean an obligation to pay alimony established by a court or in a contract.[59] Only a donation between spouses can be freely revoked (art. 1765).

As obligations are transmitted by death (art. 2024), Gaston's estate would be liable if he dies without performing a valid promise of a donation. However, according to Portuguese law, if the donor dies leaving wife or children as heirs, they are entitled to a mandatory share of his estate (two-thirds), and they are not obligated to perform promises of donations made by the deceased which exceed one-third of the assets he leaves. They can therefore demand that donations in excess of this amount be reduced (art. 2168).[60]

Nevertheless, even if such a promise is void, it could matter whether the promisee has incurred expenses in the expectation that the promise would be kept. In this case, although the promise is not binding, breach of the promise is deemed to violate the rules of good faith. The violation may give rise to pre-contractual liability. If so, the promisor must compensate the promisee for the expenses he has incurred.[61] Pre-contractual liability is governed by art. 227 of the Civil Code which provides: 'A party who enters negotiations to conclude a contract with another one, has a duty, either in its preliminaries or in its formation, to act in accordance with good faith, or he would be liable for losses and damages.' There are no reported cases applying this provision to a gratuitous promise.

We have no trusts in Portuguese law. The institution most similar is the 'foundation' (fundação), governed by arts. 185 ff. of the Civil Code. The foundation is a legal person to whom goods are given in order to further a certain altruistic aim. As foundations are legally obliged to pursue social interests, there are no foundations to pursue private interests. The

[59] RC, 1 June 1993, in BMJ no. 428, 690.
[60] See M. B. Lopes, *Das doações* (1970), 231 ff.; C. P. Corte-Real, *A imputação de liberalidades na sucessão legitimária* (1989), 1041 ff.
[61] On pre-contractual liability, see Cordeiro, *Da Boa Fé no Direito Civil*, 527 ff.

foundation has to be authorized by a public authority, which would not give permission if no public interest is seen to be involved. Therefore, only in Case 1(c) would it be possible to establish a foundation, but there is absolutely no need for it, because, as stated, if the contract of donation is made in a written document, the promisor is bound.

Perhaps it should be mentioned that there is a special rule governing situations like Case 1(b). The donation could be considered a pre-nuptial gift (*donatio propter nuptias*). Such donations are subject to a special rule (arts. 1753 ff. of the Civil Code): if they are included in the pre-nuptial agreement (which is a public deed) they are automatically rescinded if the marriage is not performed or if it is dissolved due to the recipient's fault. However, if they are not included in the pre-nuptial agreement, they are subject to the general rules that have already been described.

ITALY

Gaston is not bound by the informal promise to give a large sum of money in any of these cases. However, he could bind himself by making the promise formally by subscribing to a notarial document in the presence of two witnesses (art. 782 of the Civil Code[62] and the notarial law, art. 48 l. 29/1913). Scholars maintain that the formality of notarization is required by the Civil Code in order to protect the promisor and his family from acting without due deliberation (cautionary function) as well as to save transaction costs when proving the obligation in court (evidentiary function) and to distinguish enforceable from non-enforceable promises so as to encourage reasonable reliance (channelling function).[63]

In Cases 1(a), 1(c), and 1(d), in order to be binding, the formal promise

---

[62] Article 782 of the Civil Code: 'Form of gift: A gift shall be made by public act, under penalty of nullity. If it has movable things as its object, it is only valid for those specified with an indication of their value in the same instrument as the gift, or in a separate note subscribed by the donor, the donee and the notary. The acceptance can be made in the same instrument or by a later public act. In the latter case the gift is not perfected until the donor is notified of the act of acceptance. Until the gift is perfected, both the donor and the donee can revoke their declarations. If the gift is made to a legal person the donor cannot revoke his declaration after he has been notified of the submission of the request to obtain governmental authority to accept. On the passage of a year from the notification without the authority having been granted, the declaration can be revoked.'

For an English version of the Italian Civil Code, see *The Italian Civil Code and Complementary Legislation*, translated by M. Beltramo, G. E. Longo and J. H. Merryman (1991).

[63] See Marini, *Promessa ed affidamento*, 257 ff.; L. Fuller, 'Consideration and form', *Columbia Law Review* 41 (1941), 799; M. Eisenberg, 'Donative Promises', *University of Chicago Law Review* 47 (1979), 1.

requires an equally formal acceptance[64] by the promisee. Hence, Gaston could withdraw his formal promise until it has been formally accepted by the promisee.[65] In contrast, in Case 1(b), the formal promise itself is enforceable without such an acceptance pursuant to art. 785 of the Civil Code.[66]

If Gaston dies before changing his mind, his estate is liable for the amount of money formally promised subject to recall and reduction – as in the case of any gift – in accordance with the rules of succession contained in arts. 555 and 559 of the Civil Code.[67]

The fact that the promisee incurred expenses in the reasonable expectation that the promise would be kept might possibly be considered to support a claim for damages in tort. The outcome of such a claim, however, is presently quite doubtful.

AUSTRIA

In Cases 1(a), 1(c), and 1(d), Gaston is not bound by his promise. All three promises constitute gifts (*Schenkung, Schenkungsvertrag*).[68] Such contracts are valid only if the gift is actually delivered to the donee[69] or if the

---

[64] On the admissibility of peculiar forms of implicit acceptance, see Cass. civ., sez. II, 16 Nov. 1992, no. 12280 (*Calì v. Tomasi*); Cass. civ., sez. II, 16 Nov. 1981, no. 6057 (*Giannò v. Larussa*).

[65] If the acceptance is expressed in a separate deed, the promise can be withdrawn until notice of the acceptance is given.

[66] Article 785 of the Civil Code: 'Gift in contemplation of marriage: A gift made in contemplation of a future marriage whether made between the spouses or by others in favour of one or both spouses or of children to be born of them, is perfected without need of acceptance, but produces no effect until the marriage. Annulment of the marriage imports annulment of the gift. However, the rights acquired by third persons in good faith between the date of the marriage and the date the judgment declaring the marriage annulled becomes final are preserved. The spouse in good faith is not bound to restore the fruits received prior to the application for annulment of the marriage. Gifts in favour of unborn children of a putative marriage remain effective.'

[67] Gifts whose value exceeds the share of which the deceased could dispose are subject to reduction to that share (art. 555 of the Civil Code). Gifts are reduced beginning with the last and proceeding with the next earlier in order (art. 559).

[68] According to § 938 of the Civil Code (ABGB) a contract of donation is a contract whereby the donor promises to transfer ownership in an object gratuitously to the donee. A gift is a contract as the donee has to accept the gift. Section 938 of the ABGB uses the expression *Sache*. This concept is defined in § 285: everything that is not a person and which can be used by human beings is a *Sache*. According to § 285a, animals are not *Sachen* unless otherwise provided. Those rules dealing with objects have to be applied to them.

[69] If the gift is delivered after the making of the promise, the contract becomes effective upon its delivery. The donor therefore cannot demand that the object be returned. The delivery of the object makes the contract effective.

contract is recorded in a notarial document.[70] As Gaston did not deliver the money to the donee, the promises would be binding only if they were recorded in a notarial deed. As Gaston is not bound by the promise, Gaston's estate will not be liable either.

Gaston could bind himself by using a different legal form, namely the contract of *mandatum*. He could instruct a third person, the mandatary, to deliver the money to the donee.[71] Here two questions arise. The first is whether it is necessary that the donee accept the promise. Most jurists say that this is not necessary.[72] The second question is whether the donor must deliver the sum of money in question to the mandatary for the contract of donation to be effective.[73] According to one opinion this is not necessary,[74] but this view has been criticized by other writers.[75]

In general it does not matter if the promisee incurred expenses in the expectation that the promise would be kept. As he should know that a promise of a gift which does not meet the legal requirements is not binding, he incurs such expenses at his own risk. Under exceptional circumstances[76] Gaston could, however, become liable because of *culpa in contrahendo*. It is an accepted doctrine of Austrian law that under special circumstances a person who has signalled a willingness to enter into a contract can be liable even if the contract was never concluded.[77] Liability can arise only if the parties have reached agreement on the content of the future contract and only if the party who refuses to conclude the contract has no reason for doing so. In such a situation that party can be liable for the expenses that the other party incurred in the expectation that the contract will be made. Whether this doctrine will apply to gifts under Austrian law has not yet been determined. If it applies, Gaston could be

---

[70] See § 943 ABGB and § 1 NZwG. Until 1871, it was sufficient that the contract was made in writing.

[71] Such an instruction would constitute a contract in favour of a third party (*Vertrag zugunsten Dritter*).

[72] P. Rummel in Rummel, *ABGB* § 881 no. 8; F. Gschnitzer in Klang, *ABGB* vol. IV/1, 228; K. Spielbüchler, *Der Dritte im Schuldverhältnis* (1973), 20.

[73] There is, of course, the possibility that the mandatary is a debtor of the donator who instructs him to pay the money owed to the donee. In this case the requirement of § 943 of the Civil Code would not apply.

[74] SZ 51/25 & 82; Gschnitzer in Klang, *ABGB* vol. IV/1, 228.   [75] Rummel, *ABGB* § 881 no. 8.

[76] Gaston will be liable, of course, if he acts in bad faith. This would be the case if he makes the promise in order to harm the donee; then § 1295(2) of the Civil Code would apply. According to this provision a person who intentionally inflicts harm on another person becomes liable if he acts *contra bonos mores* (*sittenwidrige Schädigung*).

[77] See P. Apathy in Schwimann, *ABGB* § 861 no. 13.

liable if he has signalled his intention to deliver the money provided he has no reason for refusing to deliver it.[78]

Case 1(b) is more complex. If a child marries, his or her parents are under an obligation to give the child a dowry (*Ausstattung*).[79] The size of the dowry depends on the financial situation of the parents. In Case 1(b), Clara has a claim for a dowry against her father. Gaston's promise therefore could be interpreted as a settlement or an acknowledgment[80] of Clara's claim. As neither a settlement nor an acknowledgment is a contract of donation, the form requirement would not apply. Gaston's promise could constitute a settlement or acknowledgment, however, only if it was preceded by a dispute between Clara and Gaston about the proper amount of the dowry. If there was no such dispute, the promise constitutes a gift to the extent that the amount of money promised exceeds the dowry owed to Clara.

GERMANY

In Case 1(a), Gaston is not bound because a promise to make a gift in the future is valid only if it is recorded in a notarial document (§ 518 of the Civil Code[81]). Otherwise the promise is void (§ 125(1)[82]). This is the only way to make the promise binding. Therefore, Gaston's estate is not liable either.

Even if the promisee incurred expenses, the promise is not binding. The promisee cannot recover these expenses because the purpose of the form is to protect the promisor from making over-hasty promises. And if he would be liable for damages, his decision would no longer really be free. The result would be different only if Gaston had deceived Catherine by telling her that no form was required. Then Catherine would have a

---

[78] For a liability to arise, the signals must have been taken seriously by the other party, and that party must have acted on the basis of these signals and thereby incurred the expenses.

[79] See § 1220 of the Civil Code with respect to a daughter and § 1231 with respect to a son. In general, see Koziol and Welser, *Grundriß* 257.

[80] A party who makes a settlement (*Vergleich*) accepts a compromise between his claims and those of the other party; in contrast, a party who makes an acknowledgment (*Anerkenntnis*) accepts the other party's claims completely.

[81] '(1) A contract which includes the promise to make a gift requires that this promise is recorded by a notary. This rule is also applicable if the gift is an acknowledgment of indebtedness (§§ 780, 781). (2) The lack of this form is immaterial if the promise is fulfilled.'

[82] 'A promise (*Rechtsgeschäft*) which does not meet the formal requirement imposed by the law is void.'

defence which would prevent Gaston from asserting the formal requirement. If this were the case, the promise would be enforceable. Gaston could also be liable for damages (*culpa in contrahendo*[83]) if the promise was void because of Gaston's negligence and if his responsibility for meeting the formal requirements were greater than Catherine's because of his superior knowledge.

In Case 1(b), what somebody gives to his child because the child is about to marry is not a gift in a legal sense as long as the sum is appropriate to the financial circumstances of the parents (§ 1624(1) of the Civil Code[84]). Therefore § 518 is not applicable and the promise is binding without respect to any form.

Gaston's estate is also liable for his promise.

In Case 1(c), the question is whether the promise concerns a gift and therefore whether § 518 of the Civil Code applies. There is no general exception for charitable gifts.

Nevertheless, for there to be a gift, it is necessary that the donee be enriched even after performing a duty connected to the gift.[85] In our case, the United Nations Children's Emergency Fund has to give all the money to famine victims and therefore this requirement is not met. But if a sum of money is given to a legal entity (as distinguished from a natural person), it does not matter if all the money has to be spent for one of the original purposes of the entity. Otherwise it would be virtually impossible to make a gift to a juristic person.[86] Because the Children's Fund (or at least the

---

[83] If a promise is not legally binding, it is still possible that the promisor is liable for the damages the promisee has incurred because he has put his trust in the validity of the promise (*culpa in contrahendo*). But there is no claim for damages if this would be contrary to the purpose of a requirement that there be a formality or if the promisee has to bear the risk of the validity. Also, the promisor is liable only if he did not meet the relevant standard of care.

Culpa in contrahendo can also result in a claim for damages if one party terminates the negotiations for a contract without any reason and the first party has had expenses because it relied on the other party and expected the contract to be concluded. BGHZ 76 (1980), 343 (349). Nevertheless, this doctrine has to be applied very carefully because before a contract is really concluded, the parties are not bound, and they are naturally free to decide whether or not to agree. Therefore, damages can only be awarded if the trust was exceptionally great or if the conduct of the party terminating negotiations was particularly egregious.

[84] Summary of the provision: What parents give to their child because of a marriage or because the child wants to start an independent life is only a gift in respect of the sum which is not appropriate to the financial situation of the parents.

[85] RGZ 62 (1906), 386; RGZ 105 (1923), 305.

[86] RGZ 70 (1909), 15 (17); RGZ 71 (1909), 140 (142, 143); RGZ 105 (1923), 305 (308). See also Dawson, *Gifts and Promises*, 170–3.

United Nations) has its own legal personality and has famine relief as a purpose, § 518 of the Civil Code is applicable in our case and the promise is therefore void.

In Case 1(d), a normal tip is not a gift because it is very similar to remuneration. This doctrine is not undisputed but it is sound because of the close connection between the tip and the service performed by the waitress.[87] Were this a normal tip, the promise would be binding because § 518 of the Civil Code is not applicable. But a large sum of money cannot be regarded as a real tip. It has to be regarded as a gift and consequently § 518 is applicable, and the promise cannot be enforced.

GREECE

Gaston has promised a donation. Donation is a unilateral contract in the civil law sense: only one party assumes an obligation.[88] It is regulated by arts. 496 to 512 of the Greek Civil Code. The donor's promise, the donee's acceptance, and the delivery of the object promised may be simultaneous (an immediately executed donation) or the promise may be made and accepted prior to the delivery (promissory donation).[89]

According to art. 498(1) of the Civil Code, a donation or a promise of donation is valid if, and only if, a notarial document has been drawn up. This form is necessary for such an obligation to exist regardless of the kind and value of the donation, and if it is absent, the donation[90] is void. According to art. 180 of the Civil Code, an 'act which is void is deemed not to have been done'. Therefore, a promise of donation is deemed to have been made, and the donee can ask for the thing promised to be delivered to him, only if a notarial document has been drawn up.[91] The requirement of art. 498(1) is deemed to be a matter of public order and the court can examine it *ex officio*.[92] The invalidity of the donation is complete and the donor, his heirs, his creditors, and anyone who has a legal interest in it can invoke it.[93]

An exception to this rule is created by art. 498(2) of the Civil Code which concerns movables. In the case of movables, when no notarial document

---

[87] H. Kollhosser in K. Rebmann and F. J. Saecker, *Münchener Kommentar zum Bürgerlichen Gesetzbuch*, 3rd edn (1995) § 516 no. 19; O. Mühl in W. Siebert, *Soergel Kommentar zum Bürgerlichen Gesetzbuch*, 12th edn (1997) § 516 no. 18.

[88] Acceptance by the donee is also required by art. 496 of the Civil Code.

[89] Deligiannis and Kornilakis, *Law of Obligations*, Special Part, vol. I, 32.

[90] Art. 159 CC; AP 784/58 NoB 7, 254.   [91] C. Fragistas in ErmAK art. 498 no. 9.

[92] Kafkas, *Law of Obligations*, vol. I, art. 498 CC, pp. 17–21.

[93] I. Karakostas in Georgiadis and Stathopoulos, *Civil Code*, vol. III, art. 498, no. 8.

exists, fulfilment of the donation (namely delivery of the thing to the donee) validates the donation. After delivery, the donor cannot recover what he has given. This is the *donation manuelle* of art. 242 of the Swiss Code of Obligations.[94] The legislator's intention in requiring a formality is to protect the donor from hasty decisions because he may not be aware of the consequences when a simple promise is made. This rationale explains why an exception is made when movables are delivered. The donor is more aware because he experiences the alienation of the gift in a perceptible manner.[95] Therefore, in our case, Gaston is not obliged to keep his promise (namely to deliver the money to the donees), and in case he dies his estate will not be liable, unless a notarial document has been drawn up.

The use of a different legal form such as a trust in order for a promise to be binding is not possible under Greek law, because this legal morpheme (at least as it is defined in common law countries) is not recognized.[96]

Nevertheless, if certain requirements are met, Gaston may be liable because of his pre-contractual conduct for the expenses that the promisees incurred in the expectation that the promise would be kept. Article 197 of the Civil Code provides that 'in the course of negotiations for the conclusion of a contract the parties shall be reciprocally bound to adopt the conduct which is dictated by good faith and business usages'. Article 198 of the Civil Code continues that the person who violates this obligation and causes harm to the other party through his fault is obliged to compensate that party.

The first requirement for these articles to apply is that the violation must occur 'in the course of negotiations'. Negotiations begin from the moment when the parties interested in the conclusion of a contract begin to bargain for this purpose. They end with the conclusion of the contract or the suspension or the final failure of negotiations.[97] The conclusion of an invalid contract – for example, one that does not have the form required by law – does not end the course of negotiations.[98] Thus, in our case, this first requirement is met.

The second requirement is conduct contrary to the principles of good

---

[94] Kafkas, *Law of Obligations*, vol. I, art. 498 CC, pp. 17–21; EfAth 1650/1959 EEN 28, 70.

[95] Karakostas in Georgiadis and Stathopoulos, *Civil Code*, vol. III, art. 498 and Stathopoulos, *Contract Law* 77.

[96] Georgiadis, *General Principles*, 217–18; Stathopoulos, *Contract Law*, 52–5.

[97] Stathopoulos, *Contract Law*, 81–6.

[98] G. Koumantos in ErmAK arts. 197–8 no. 44; Thessaloniki Court of Appeal 348/1980, Arm. 34 (1980) 456; AP 669/1982 NoB 31 (1983) 654; AP 1303/1984 NoB 33 (1985) 993; AP 1505/1988 EEN (1989) 740.

faith and business usage. Whether conduct is contrary to the principles is judged *ad hoc* taking into consideration the facts of the particular case. Normally, good faith does not demand the conclusion of the contract, since contractual freedom includes the freedom to withdraw at least before a party makes a binding offer. A party may terminate negotiations even without a reason without having acted contrary to good faith unless he is at fault for doing so, and the other party strongly believed that the contract would be concluded.[99] Accordingly, Gaston is acting in bad faith if he has decided not to keep his promise (by refusing to draw up a notarial document) and does nothing to prevent the promisees, who strongly believed that the contract would eventually be concluded, from incurring expenses.

The third requirement is fault (*culpa in contrahendo*). The degree of fault required during negotiations is the same as that required for liability to be imposed for breaching the contract itself. So, during negotiations, the promisor could be held liable only for wilful conduct and gross negligence[100] (art. 499 of the Civil Code), for that is the degree of fault required for a person to be held liable for breaching a contract to make a donation.

The fourth requirement is that the other party suffer harm because the trust shown by him has been betrayed through the other party's fault and conduct in bad faith.

The fifth requirement is that the harm that a party suffers be causally related to the fault of the person who acted in bad faith.

All of these requirements must be proven by the party claiming damages.

A party who is held liable must compensate the other party for harm suffered because of his own conduct. The compensation covers only the negative interest or damages[101] suffered through reliance on the conduct of the other party[102] and not the positive or expectation interest owed in the case of contractual liability. The negative interest covers not only the positive damage (expenses that a party incurs in the expectation that the contract would be concluded), but also the lost profit (e.g. rejection of another opportunity).[103]

---

[99] EfAth 1819/75 rm. 29, 131; EfAth 150/75 rm. 29, 677; Karasis in Georgiadis and Stathopoulos, *Civil Code*, vol. I, arts. 197–8.

[100] This is the leading opinion: Stathopoulos, *Contract Law*, 81–6; EfAth 2232/55 rm. 22, 1250, EfAth 1203/69 rm. 23, 937. However, a contrary opinion exists, which claims that the party is liable for all degrees of fault, and it is based on art. 330 CC: Koumantos in ErmAK arta. 197–8 no. 51; Deligiannis and Kornilakis, *Law of Obligations*, Special Part, vol. I, 47, n. 1.

[101] This is the compensation that restores the *status quo* without the contract and negotiations: Stathopoulos, *Contract Law*, 81.   [102] AP 969/1977 NoB 26 (1978) 895.

[103] Georgiadis, *General Principles*, 260–3.

Therefore, Gaston will be liable to compensate the promisees for the expenses that they incurred in the expectation that the contract would be concluded.

There used to be a dispute whether pre-contractual liability of this type was based on contract or tort. Since the enactment of arts. 197–8, it has been accepted that liability is of a special type imposed *ex lege*.[104] In Germany this dispute still goes on because they do not have such provisions governing pre-contractual liability.

Before the regulation of the matter in the Civil Code, pre-contractual liability was imposed by following Jhering's theory of *culpa in contrahendo*. According to this theory, the party who caused the invalidity of the contract or its cancellation would be liable to compensate the other party. Jhering based pre-contractual liability in contract in cases of negligence because, in Roman tort law, an *actio doli* lay only for intentional wrong or *dolus*. Under the Civil Code, however, negotiations and the trust they engender are a source of liability. Greek law has indisputably gone further than it once did or than the law of other countries does.[105]

SCOTLAND

Scots law has long recognized that a voluntary obligation can arise from a promise. Stair describes a promise as 'that which is simple and pure, and hath not implied in it as a condition, the acceptance of another'.[106] Before *contractual* obligations arise, there must be an agreement between the parties, that is, an offer must be met by an acceptance. In the case of promise, in theory, a unilateral obligation arises as soon as the promisor declares his will. The promisor must have the intention to undertake legal obligations. While the test for intention is objective, presumptions apply. For example, there is a presumption of intention to create legal obligations in the context of business and commerce: there is a presumption *against* intention to create legal obligations in family arrangements. These presumptions are, of course, rebuttable.

Since the Requirements of Writing (Scotland) Act 1995,[107] *prima facie* writing is not required to constitute a unilateral obligation: 'subject to

---

[104] Koumantos in ErmAK arts. 197–8 no. 8.
[105] *Ibid.*, art. 197.   [106] Inst. 10, 3.
[107] Before the 1995 Act, *proof* of any unilateral obligation was restricted to the writ or oath of the promisor. This greatly reduced the utility of the *pollicitatio* in Scots law. See generally T. B. Smith, *A Short Commentary on the Law of Scotland* (1962), ch. 32. Proof by writ or oath has been abolished by s. 11 of the 1995 Act.

subsection (2) below and any other enactment, writing shall not be required for the constitution of a contract, unilateral obligation or trust'.

However, the promisor's writing[108] is required to constitute a *gratuitous* unilateral obligation:

(2) Subject to subsection (3) below, a written document complying with section 2 of this Act shall be required for -
(a) the constitution of -
(ii) a gratuitous unilateral obligation except an obligation undertaken in the course of business . . .

Accordingly, non-gratuitous unilateral obligations, for example, a promise to sell property or a promise of a reward for finding lost property, do not require writing. Although a promise is gratuitous, writing is *not* required if it is made in the course of business. Even where the promise is gratuitous and writing is required, a unilateral obligation may nevertheless be constituted without writing if the provisions of s. 1(3) and (4) of the Requirements of Writing (Scotland) Act 1995 are satisfied: *viz*:

(3) Where a contract, obligation or trust mentioned in subsection (2)(a) above is not constituted in a written document complying with section 2 of this Act, but one of the parties to the contract, a creditor in the obligation or a beneficiary under the trust ('the first person') has acted or refrained from acting in reliance on the contract, obligation or trust with the knowledge and acquiescence of the other party to the contract, the debtor in the obligation or the truster ('the second person') -
(a) the second person shall not be entitled to withdraw from the contract, obligation or trust; and
(b) the contract, obligation or trust shall not be regarded as invalid, on the ground that it is not so constituted, if the condition set out in subsection (4) is satisfied.
(4) The condition referred to in subsection (3) above is that the position of the first person -
(a) as a result of acting or refraining from acting as mentioned in the subsection has been affected to a material extent; and
(b) as a result of such a withdrawal as is mentioned in that subsection would be adversely affected to a material extent.

Applying these rules:

Gaston's promise to Catherine is a gratuitous obligation. *Prima facie* it is not binding unless constituted in writing. If constituted in writing, it is submitted that this will rebut the presumption *against* intention to create legal obligations between members of a family. Gaston's promise to Clara

---

[108] I.e., a document subscribed by the promisor: s. 2(1) of the 1995 Act.

raises the same issues. A promise to donate to a charity is gratuitous and again must be constituted in writing: if so, this would suggest sufficient proof of intention to create legal obligations. Gaston's promise to the waitress must also be in writing: if so, this would probably be sufficient to suggest an intention to create legal obligations.

Because the promise is gratuitous, no unilateral obligation is constituted in Scots law unless and until the promise is put in writing. The fact that the promisee incurred expenditure in the expectation that the promise would be kept, could be significant if the promise has not been put in writing. As outlined above, a gratuitous promise will not be invalid owing to the absence of writing and the promisor will be unable to withdraw from the promise if s. 1(3) and (4) of the 1995 Act is satisfied. This is a new provision and there is no relevant authority. In the present writers' view, the decisions on the common law doctrines of *rei interventus* and homologation are of little value: these doctrines were abolished by s. 1(5) of the 1995 Act. The statutory provisions should be interpreted literally.

Accordingly, where the promisee (the first person) has incurred expenditure in the expectation that the promise would be kept, the promisor (the second person) will be bound when the promise is not constituted in writing if:

(a) the first person's expenditure was in reliance on the promise;

(b) the first person's expenditure was done with the knowledge *and* acquiescence of the second person. It would appear that the second person must have knowledge of and acquiesce in the actual expenditure. However, where the purpose of the promise is to enable the promisee to incur expenditure, e.g. A promises to pay to B the cost of B's heating bills, it is thought that it would be sufficient that A could reasonably expect B to rely on the promise by paying the bills;

(c) the expenditure must affect the first person to a material extent. It is thought that in this context, materiality will be construed widely, i.e. provided the effect is greater than *de minimis*, it will be treated as material. (This was the position at common law: 'not unimportant'.) The issue has not yet been the subject of litigation;

(d) the withdrawal of the promise must adversely affect the promisee to a material extent. Again it is thought that material extent should be construed widely, i.e. provided the adverse affect is greater than *de minimis*, then the condition is satisfied. Often the adverse affect will arise from (c), i.e. the promisee's expenditure: but the structure of s. 1(4)(b) does not demand a causative link between s. 1(3) and (4)(a).

In the circumstances of the problem, s. 1(3) and (4) will be triggered if Gaston knows and does not object to the promisee's incurring expenditure in reliance on the promise. Of course, resort to s. 1(3) and (4) only arises if the gratuitous promise is *prima facie* invalid because it is not constituted in writing. If a unilateral obligation is valid, the promisor's estate is liable.

ENGLAND

According to orthodox English law, the promises described in Cases 1(a), 1(b), and 1(c) are each unenforceable. The result is the same if Gaston dies, or the promisees rely on any of the promises, although it is possible through using a formality, or, less simply, the device of a trust, to make the promises enforceable.

The primary reason that the promises are unenforceable is that no 'consideration' was provided in exchange for them, that is, they were 'gratuitous' promises.[109] Although the rule is often criticized, in English law only 'bargains', that is, promises given in exchange for consideration, are enforceable.[110]

As the application of the consideration rule is an issue that arises in nearly all the cases to be discussed, it may be helpful to note in advance that one recurrent problem will be the tension between the rule as stated 'in the books' and the rule as applied in practice. As described in the orthodox formulations found in the leading cases and textbooks, its application to many of the cases discussed below is reasonably clear. The issue that arises in answering the posed questions is whether the consideration rule as it appears 'in the books' accurately reflects how courts apply the rule 'in practice'. It is frequently argued that courts find or 'invent' consideration in a range of cases where, according to the orthodox rules, none should exist. The courts do this, it is alleged, primarily through novel interpretations of the facts (or through creating explicit exceptions to the consideration rule, which does not raise the same issues). The factors which, it is further alleged, courts take into account in deciding whether to enforce so-called gratuitous promises are many, but the most important is undoubtedly detrimental reliance on the promise by the promisee.[111]

---

[109] E.g., *Roscorla* v. *Thomas* [1842] 3 QB 234, where a warranty as to the soundness of a horse already sold was held to be unenforceable.

[110] For a summary of criticisms, see Treitel, *Contract*, 147–9. In 1934, the English body responsible for considering legislative law reform, the Law Revision Committee (now the Law Commission), was charged with examining the desirability of reforming consideration. Their 1937 Report, which recommended certain changes though not wholesale reform, was not acted upon by Parliament.

[111] Atiyah, *Law of Contract*, 118–19, 137–41; P. S. Atiyah, 'Consideration: a Restatement', in P. S. Atiyah, *Essays on Contract* (1986).

Other factors include whether the promisor benefited from the promisee's reliance, the seriousness with which the promise was made, the onerousness of performance, the existence of a moral obligation to benefit the promisee, and the value of the activity supported by the promise.[112] The best-known proponent of the view that 'consideration for a promise' merely means a 'good reason' to enforce the promise, Professor Atiyah, accordingly describes the consideration rule in the following terms:

> The truth is that the courts have never set out to create a doctrine of consideration. They have been concerned with the much more practical problem of deciding in the course of litigation whether a particular promise in a particular case should be enforced . . . When the courts found a sufficient reason for enforcing a promise they enforced it; and when they found that for one reason or another it was undesirable to enforce a promise, they did not enforce it.[113]

Scepticism about the relevance of 'law in the books' is of course found in every area of law, and in all legal systems, but within the common law scepticism about the consideration rule is a particularly strong example of this attitude. It seems clear that at least some scepticism about the strictness with which the consideration rule is applied by the courts is warranted. But it is difficult to say how much scepticism is warranted, that is, exactly how significant is the difference between the consideration rule in the books and the consideration rule in practice. Reasonable lawyers will give different answers to this question. That said, what would appear to be the most common view, and the view that is adopted in the answers below, is that a limited, but not extreme, degree of scepticism about the formal rules is warranted.

Accordingly, what I have tried to do in my answers is, first, to explain the result that would be reached by applying the orthodox rules and, second, to suggest what factors might influence a judge who was willing to go beyond those rules, if this is thought likely or possible on the facts. In some cases, it is reasonably clear that an English judge would not go beyond the orthodox rules (the opposite conclusion – that a judge clearly would go beyond the orthodox rules – is less common). In many cases, however, it is difficult to say definitively whether or not a judge would be likely to go beyond the orthodox rules. This should be borne in mind in the discussion that follows.

I will begin, then, by examining the orthodox formulation of the doctrine. The exact definition of 'consideration' is a matter of some debate

---

[112] Atiyah, 'Consideration'.   [113] *Ibid.*, 181.

amongst English lawyers.[114] The most commonly quoted judicial formulation is from the nineteenth-century case of *Currie* v. *Misa*:[115] 'A valuable consideration, in the sense of the law, may consist either in some right, interest, profit, or benefit accruing to one party or some forbearance, detriment, loss or responsibility, given, suffered or undertaken by the other.' This definition, however, is generally thought to be somewhat narrow. A wider, and more accurate formulation, which was approved of by Lord Dunedin in *Dunlop* v. *Selfridge*,[116] is provided by Pollock in his *Principles of Contract*:[117]

(1) To constitute performance, a performance or a return promise must be bargained for.
(2) A performance or return promise is bargained for if it is sought by the promisor in exchange for his promise and is given by the promisee in exchange for that promise.
(3) The performance may consist of
(a) an act other than a promise, or
(b) a forbearance, or
(c) the creation, modification or destruction of a legal relation.

Different aspects of this definition are relevant to different aspects of the cases discussed below, but it may be useful to highlight in advance three of its important features. First, consideration may consist of doing or not doing something or of *promising* to do or not to do something: an actual transfer is not required. Second, the performance or promise must be done or made *in exchange for* the other promise: simultaneous promises of mutual gifts are not consideration for each other. Third, while mere gratitude or 'natural affection'[118] is not consideration, the performance or promised performance may be of *nominal value* and, indeed, need not be of any economic value in the normal sense of that term. Thus, it is often said that 'a peppercorn' is adequate consideration,[119] and in one case the return to a manufacturer of wrappers from chocolate bars constituted consideration for the manufacturer's promise to make available for sale at a special price certain musical recordings.[120]

It follows that Case 1(a), Gaston's promise to give his niece money on her twenty-fifth birthday, is a straightforward gift, and thus unenforceable in the form it is made. Indeed, a gift of this sort is the classic, and uncontroversial, example of the type of promise that the consideration rule renders unenforceable.

---

[114] Treitel, *Contract*, 64–6.   [115] [1875] LR 10 EX 153, at 162.   [116] [1915] AC 847.
[117] Pollock, *Contract*, 133.   [118] *Bret* v. *JS* [1600] Cro. Eliz. 756.   [119] Treitel, *Contract*, 71.
[120] *Chappell & Co. Ltd.* v. *Nestle Co. Ltd.* [1960] AC 87. See generally S. Smith, 'The Law of Contract – Alive or Dead?' *The Law Teacher* 13 (1979), 73.

Case 1(b), the promise to give money to his daughter 'because she was about to marry', is not so straightforward. Interpreted literally, the promise is unenforceable for lack of consideration because, while agreeing to marry has been held good consideration for a promise,[121] the money in Case 1(b) was not promised *in exchange* for the daughter getting married. Rather, the daughter's marriage was merely the motive for the promise: the money was to be given *because* she was marrying. That said, in a case with similar facts, *Shadwell* v. *Shadwell*,[122] an English court held that the promise was made in exchange for an agreement to marry. There was a strong dissenting judgment, approved of in a later decision,[123] but the case remains a clear example of a court being willing to interpret facts imaginatively in order to find consideration. Whether a court is likely to do this on the facts of Case 1(b) is difficult to predict. The most relevant factor would be whether the daughter relied in some way on the promise; a second factor would be how seriously the promise was made (on which see below).

The promises in Cases 1(c) and 1(d) are, like the promise in Case 1(a), straightforward gifts, and thus are also unenforceable for lack of consideration (but see below).

A further reason for refusing to enforce the promises in Cases 1(a), 1(b), and 1(d) is that the promisor did not intend to create legal relations (there is insufficient information to discuss the status of the third promise in this regard). In English law, a second major limitation, in addition to the requirement of consideration, on the sorts of promises the law will enforce is that the parties must have an 'intention to create legal relations'.[124] This requirement is rarely relevant in litigated cases. There is no requirement of proof of a conscious intent to create legal relations in the ordinary commercial case, it being assumed, lacking clear evidence to the contrary, that such intent exists.[125] One area where the requirement does play a role is in respect of social and family arrangements. There is a presumption that agreements between family members are not intended to create legal relations. For example, in *Balfour* v. *Balfour*[126] a husband's promise to pay his wife a monthly sum while they lived apart was unenforceable. This presumption can be rebutted by evidence of a contrary intent, for example where spouses lived apart and were not on good terms: *Merritt* v. *Merritt*.[127] That the relevant agreement is in writing might provide further evidence of the necessary intent. On this basis, there is a

---

[121] *Shadwell* v. *Shadwell* [1860] 9 CB 159.   [122] [1860] 9 CB (NS) 159.
[123] *Jones* v. *Padavatton* [1969] 1 WLR 328.   [124] Treitel, *Contract,* 150–61.   [125] *Ibid.,* 151.
[126] [1919] 2 KB 571.   [127] [1970] 1 WLR 112.

good chance that the promises in Cases 1(a) and 1(b) would fail for lack of an intent to create legal relations.

Another situation where courts have refused to find an intent to create legal relations is where the promise was a 'mere puff', that is, not seriously meant: for example a father's promise to give £100 to whomsoever married his daughter.[128] It is almost certain that the promise in Case 1(d), the promise to the waitress, would be considered a mere puff, and it is possible, depending on the context in which they were made, that the promises in Cases 1(a) and 1(b) would also fail for this reason.

In respect of each of the four cases, it is possible to make the promise binding, assuming it is not otherwise binding, through the use of a 'formality', in particular through the use of a 'deed' (sometimes known as a 'promise under seal'), which is a special form of a written promise.[129] Where a promise is made by deed, the normal requirement of consideration is waived. Traditionally a deed had to be sealed by a wax seal, but it is now sufficient that the document be in writing, that it make clear on its face that it is intended to be a deed (or 'under seal'), and that it be signed, witnessed, and delivered.[130] At one time, all executory contracts had to be made under seal. This is no longer true, but deeds continue to be used and required for certain purposes,[131] the most significant of which, for our purposes, is as a way – the most important way – of making enforceable a promise that would otherwise be unenforceable for lack of consideration. In English law, a deed can effect the present transfer of an interest, right, or property, but it can also create an obligation to do something in the future, as would be the case if Gaston put his promises into deeds.[132] Furthermore, if a promise is made by a deed the question whether the promisor intended to create legal relations (see above) will not be raised, the deed being evidence of the required intent. Finally, assuming that Gaston has no special knowledge of the law, it is worth noting that he is unlikely to be aware of the need for, or the requirements of, a deed (the same applies to the making of a trust, discussed below, though in the case of a trust, unlike a deed, it is possible to create the legal instrument without knowing that you are doing so).

---

[128] *Weeks* v. *Tybald* [1605] Noy 11.

[129] All contracts under seal are deeds, but not all deeds are contracts under seal, and, furthermore, certain documents other than contracts, for example a share certificate, can be made under seal: see *Chitty on Contracts*, 1–126.

[130] Law of Property (Miscellaneous Provisions) Act 1989, s. 1. See also Treitel, *Contract*, 146.

[131] Deeds are used or required for purposes other than making a gratuitous promise enforceable; for example, the limitation period for suing on breach of a contract under deed is longer than that of ordinary contracts.   [132] See *Chitty on Contracts*, 1–126.

Nominal consideration, for example the payment of £1 in exchange for a promise, is sometimes also described as a formality. Whether this classification is correct or not, it is clear that promises made in exchange for nominal consideration are enforceable under English law because, as noted above, consideration need not be 'adequate'; anything of value, however trivial, is sufficient. Thus, Gaston's various promises would be enforceable if recast as (sham) bargains, that is, as given in exchange for a nominal sum or for something of nominal value.

A trust in English law is an equitable obligation to hold property on behalf of another. In the typical case, a trust is created by one person, the 'settlor', transferring property to another person, the 'trustee', with the stipulation that the trustee should not treat the property as his own, but rather as for the benefit of a third person, the 'beneficiary'.[133] A trust is often used as a way of attaching safeguards to what is essentially a gift, and thus Gaston could create a trust in order to realize an intention to benefit his niece, his daughter, the United Nations Children's Emergency Fund, or even the waitress. No particular formalities are required to make an ordinary trust. Furthermore, it is not necessary for Gaston to introduce a third party into the arrangements, since it is possible, by creating a 'declaratory trust', for the settlor also to be the trustee of the trust. Whether or not the trustee is Gaston or a third person, however, there must be clear evidence of a *present* intention on the part of the settlor, here Gaston, to divest himself of the ownership in the relevant property (though it is not necessary that Gaston actually be aware that he is creating a trust). On the facts as described, such an intention does not exist, since in each case the only intention apparent is an intention to make, in the future, a simple gift. And, despite English courts' occasional willingness to interpret facts liberally so as to avoid the rigours of the consideration rule (see Introduction), courts have hesitated to convert what is essentially a promise of a gift into a trust.[134] A second requirement for the creation of a trust – and a second reason that on the facts no trust would be found in any of the cases, as described – is that the subject of a trust must be specific property, such as shares in a company, a plot of land, or the money in a particular bank account.[135] This requirement of 'certainty of subject matter' would not be satisfied by the promise of a sum of money, although it could be satisfied if, for example, Gaston had put the money

---

[133] S. Gardner, *An Introduction to the Law of Trusts* (1990), 1.

[134] *Milroy v. Lord* [1862] 4 De G.F. & J. 264; but for an exception, see *Re Rose* [1952] Ch. 499, a case dealing with an unperfected transfer of shares and not applied more widely. See generally Gardner, *Introduction*, 51.

[135] See D. J. Heydon, *The Law of Trusts*, 2nd edn (1993), 75–6.

in a special account, which account then became the subject of the trust.

If Gaston dies before changing his mind, his estate is in the same position as Gaston was when he was alive as regards the enforceability of the promises as contracts. That is, if the promises are not contractually binding on Gaston, they are not binding on his estate (and vice versa). An intention that benefits be transferred to another on one's death can of course be enforced against the estate if the intention is expressed in a valid will. On the facts, Gaston has not made a will: aside from not complying with the formal requirements for a will (which are similar to those required for making a deed: see above), his intention is to make a gift while he is still alive, not to transfer property on his death.

The possibility of the promisees in any of the four situations incurring expenses in reliance on the relevant promises is irrelevant, strictly speaking. An act done in reliance on a promise satisfies the consideration requirement only if it is done in exchange for the promise, and, as we have seen, Gaston requested nothing in exchange for any of his promises. There is one important category of promises where the fact of reliance on the promise does, exceptionally, affect the legal significance of the promise, although it is not relevant to Case 1. This category is where the promise purports to release the promisee in whole or in part from a pre-existing legal obligation owed to the promisor: for example, where a landlord informs his tenant that the tenant need pay only half the owed rent.[136] According to the doctrine known as promissory estoppel, a promisor may be barred from enforcing a pre-existing legal relation where he has promised not to enforce the obligation, in full or in part, and the promisee has reasonably relied on that promise. The exact status of the promisee's interest, in particular whether it is an interest to enforce the new promise *qua* promise or an interest merely to recover any detrimental reliance incurred, is not entirely clear.[137] It is clear, however, at least in English law,[138] that, aside from promises to convey an interest in land,[139] estoppel may be raised only as a defence against a claim for the enforcement of pre-existing legal rights. It cannot be used to found a

---

[136] See, e.g., *Central London Property Trust Ltd* v. *High Trees House Ltd* [1947] KB 130, where a landlord's promise to reduce his tenant's rent for the duration of the war was upheld.

[137] In this respect, it is important to note that an 'estoppel' may be raised other than through a promise, for example by a representation, although all of the possible examples considered here (and in other cases discussed below) deal with promises.

[138] Australia has recently allowed promissory estoppel to be used as a cause of action (*Walton Stores (Interstate) Ltd* v. *Maher* [1988] 164 CLR 387), and such actions have long been allowed in the United States: § 90 *Restatement (Second) of Contracts* (1979). The *Walton* decision has attracted much attention in England.

[139] *Crabb* v. *Arun DC* [1976] Ch. 179.

cause of action.[140] Thus, if B incurs expenses in reasonable reliance on A's seriously made promise to make B the gift of a car, B cannot plead estoppel if A fails to deliver the car. The promise is not enforceable, nor can B recover his reliance losses. B's reliance would, however, be relevant, if A had promised B that B need not fulfil his contractual obligation to cut A's lawn that weekend (further examples are provided in Cases 11 and 12 and are discussed in the answers to those questions). The distinction between using estoppel as a defence and using it to found a cause of action is commonly expressed by saying that 'estoppel is a shield not a sword'. This distinction is crucial for the resolution of Case 1 (and for the resolution of many of the questions discussed below), because there are no pre-existing legal relations between any of the parties. This is why reliance on Gaston's promises is legally irrelevant.

Nevertheless, whilst reliance on the promises in Case 1 is irrelevant to their enforceability as a matter of strict or orthodox law, it is undoubtedly relevant to whether the courts in fact apply the law strictly. It is often alleged that English courts invent consideration or find some other way of upholding promises which, according to orthodox law, should not be enforceable, and, furthermore, that the fact of reliance on a promise is the most common reason courts take such an approach. Thus, everything else being equal, courts are more likely to find consideration (or perhaps to hold that a trust was created) where the promisee has detrimentally relied. Whether they in fact do so will depend primarily on the extent of the reliance and the ease with which consideration, or a trust, could be found. As discussed above, it is highly improbable that a trust would be found in any of the cases and a finding of consideration is a strong possibility only in Case 1(b), the promise of a gift on marriage, since Gaston's language here is arguably open to more than one interpretation. It is possible that if the charity in promise 1(c) relied on Gaston's promise, a court might hold that this reliance was requested by Gaston, and thus was consideration in exchange for his promise, but this seems unlikely on the facts. To conclude, reliance is likely to be relevant only to the enforceability of the promise in Case 1(b).

IRELAND

In Irish law a promise is not as a general rule binding as a contract unless it is made in a deed or is supported by some consideration.

---

[140] See, e.g., *Combe* v. *Combe* [1951] 2 KB 215, where the court refused to enforce a husband's relied-upon promise to pay his wife maintenance after a divorce.

Irish law recognizes a promise to be enforceable if the promisee provides consideration in exchange for the promise. A basic feature of that doctrine is the idea of reciprocity: 'something of value in the eye of the law' must be given for a promise in order to make it enforceable as a contract.[141]

In accordance with the above, in Case 1(a), Gaston is not bound by his promise to his niece Catherine because this is simply a promise to make a gift and Catherine has not provided consideration.

In Case 1(b), Gaston is not bound to his daughter Clara because she was about to marry as again there is no consideration. Moreover, the contract has not been evidenced in accordance with the requirements of section 2 of the Statute of Frauds (Ir.) 1695, which provides in part:

No action shall be brought . . . whereby to charge the defendant upon any special promise to answer the debt, default or miscarriage of another person, or to charge a person upon any agreement made upon consideration of marriage . . . unless the agreement upon which such actions shall be brought, or some memorandum or note thereof, shall be in writing, and signed by the party to be charged therewith, and some other party thereunto by him lawfully.[142]

This part of the statute is of little importance today and the English counterpart has been repealed.

In Case 1(c), Gaston is not bound to the United Nations Children's Emergency Fund for famine relief as again there has been no consideration.

Similarly, Gaston is not bound by his promise to a waitress with a nice smile.

Gaston could bind himself by making the promise formally. If the promise is contained in a deed under seal, then it would be binding for the purposes of making a contract at common law. In the days before handwriting became common, the impression upon hot wax of a crest or coat of arms (e.g. by using a signet ring) was of paramount importance. However, this is not so today as only companies have official seals.[143] It

---

[141] *Thomas* v. *Thomas* [1842] 2 QB 851; see also *O'Neil* v. *Murphy* [1936] NI 16.

It is necessary briefly to explain the reasoning behind any references to English case law during the course of this discussion. Contract law litigation and reported cases arising therefrom are more prevalent in England than in Ireland. Having regard to this fact and the similarity between the countries' contract law positions, Irish courts have tended over the years, as a matter of practice, to have regard to English precedents.

However, it is crucial to understand that regard is had to English precedents or case law only in circumstances where there are no earlier Irish precedents or case law on the issue and in such situations the English precedent or case is only considered as persuasive authority and an Irish court is clearly not bound to follow them.

[142] See the judgment of Sugden L. C. in *Saunders* v. *Cramer* [1842] 5 I.Eq.R. 12.

[143] See Friel, *Contract*, ch. 7.

seems clear that some mark or impression must be put on the deed, despite some dicta suggesting the contrary, even if the impression is only caused by the end of a ruler to act as the seal.[144] Once the deed has been sealed, it then takes effect on delivery.[145] Delivery does not mean transfer of possession but merely conduct indicating that the person who has executed the deed intends to be bound by it.[146]

To take effect as a deed an instrument must make it clear on its face that it is intended to be a deed and must be validly executed as such.[147] It appears that the promisor does not even have to sign the document.[148] There is, however, no Irish equivalent to the English Law of Property (Miscellaneous Provisions) Act 1989.

Requirements for a valid deed under seal are not generally known to lay people. While a deed may, in general terms, contain a future covenant, it may not contain a clause by which it is to take effect at a future date. If it does so, much of it as purports to do so is void and the deed will pass an immediate interest.[149]

Gaston could also bind himself by making the promise by way of a trust. A trust is a relationship which arises whenever a party (called the trustee) is compelled in equity to hold property, whether real or personal, and whether by legal or equitable title, for the benefit of some persons (who are termed beneficiaries and of whom he may be one) or for some object permitted by law, in such a way that the real benefit accrues, not to the trustee, but to the beneficiaries or other objects of the trust.[150] Requirements for a valid trust are not generally known to lay people.

However, although a trust is a type of equitable obligation which can be perfectly valid without the element of consideration being present, this undoubtedly is a cumbersome way to bind oneself. The most significant difference between a contract and a trust is that beneficiaries can enforce a trust even though not party to its creation whereas only the actual parties to a contract can enforce it.[151]

In order to bind himself by way of a trust, Gaston must ensure that the following three elements are present: (1) certainty of intention or words;

---

[144] See *Re Smith* [1892] 67 LT 64. See also J. C. W. Wylie, *Irish Conveyancing Law*, 2nd edn (1996), ch. 16.   [145] See *Evans* v. *Gray* [1882] 9 IR 539.

[146] See Treitel, *Contract*, ch. 10. See also *Xenos* v. *Wickhem* [1866] LR 2 HL 296.

[147] See *Evans* v. *Gray* [1882] 9 IR 539.   [148] *Drimmie* v. *Davies* [1889] 1 IR 176.

[149] See *Goodtitle on the Demise of Dodwell against Gibbs*, 1 KB [1827] 716; see also, R. F. Norton, *Norton on Deeds* (1885), ch. 14.

[150] See generally H. Delaney, *Equity and the Law of Trusts in Ireland* (1996).

[151] See *Twiddle* v. *Atkinson* [1861] 1 B & S 393. See also *Dunlop Pneumatic Tyre* v. *Selfridge & Company Limited* [1915] AC 847.

(2) certainty of subject matter; and (3) certainty of objects. Although no formalities are required for the creation of an *inter vivos* express trust for personalty (i.e. personal property), and provided the settlor manifests the intention of creating such a trust,[152] it may be established orally.[153] However, strong evidence is required in such a case.

In light of the above, in Cases 1(a), 1(b), 1(c), and 1(d), Gaston could bind himself either by way of a deed under seal or by using a trust. In the case of the promise to the United Nations Children's Emergency Fund (Case 1(c)), he would use a specific form of trust called a charitable trust.

Gaston's estate is not liable where he was not originally bound by the promises. In the case of a deed under seal, Gaston's estate will be liable where the deed is found to be valid. If the original trust was valid and Gaston was bound by it during the course of his lifetime, then on his death his estate will also be liable.[154]

As established above, there has been no legally binding contract as there has been no consideration by the promisee, nor has a formally sealed legal document been executed to this effect. Where the promisee cannot show consideration he/she may be able to rely on the equitable doctrine of promissory estoppel. Thus, although the needs of the conventional doctrine of consideration cannot be satisfied, some limited compensation may be received through the doctrine of promissory estoppel.

The enforceability of a non-bargain promise was the central issue in the case of *Central London Property Trust* v. *High Trees*.[155] In this case Lord Justice Denning applied the principle that 'a promise intended to be binding, intended to be acted on and in fact acted on, is binding so far as the terms properly apply'. This case was cited with approval in the Irish courts by Mr Justice Barron in *Kenny* v. *Kelly*[156] who decided that the facts of that case came within the principles established in the *High Trees* case.

However, both the English courts and the Irish courts have attempted to limit the principle as enunciated in the *High Trees* case as follows:

First, the right to resile from a statement should be available where reasonable notice is given.[157]

Second, the promisee may have to show an element of detriment, although whether he must is not clear. In *McCambridge* v. *Winters*,[158] Mr Justice Murphy referred to the judgment in *Lowe* v. *Lombank Limited*[159] whereby it was held that where a representation is made and 'believed' to

---

[152] See *Paul* v. *Constance* [1977] 1 WLR 521.   [153] See *Patterson* v. *Murphy* [1853] 11 Hare 88.
[154] See *Jones* v. *Locke* [1865] 1 Ch. App. 25.   [155] [1947] KB 130.   [156] [1988] IR 457.
[157] See *Ajayi* v. *R. G. Briscoe (R.T.) (Nigeria) Ltd* [1964] 1 WLR 1326.
[158] Unreported, 28 May 1984.   [159] [1960] 1 WLR 196.

be true by such person and acted upon by such person to his detriment, it can give rise to an estoppel. However, the passage cited appears to relate to the older doctrine of estoppel by representation rather than promissory estoppel, and it is unclear whether the factor of 'detriment' is necessary for the latter doctrine.

Third, promissory estoppel cannot confer a cause of action where none existed before. Where the original contract is unenforceable, promissory estoppel may only operate to defeat a claim. The principle that promissory estoppel operates as a shield and not a sword is laid down in the cases of *McCambridge* v. *Winters* and *Chartered Trust Limited* v. *Healy*.[160] Mr Justice Murphy, in *McCambridge* v. *Winters*, stated that 'the very essence of the principle of estoppel is that the party making the statement is to be precluded from making a case in conflict with the facts on which the representee has relied as a result of the statements or conduct of the Plaintiff'.

Therefore, the fact that the promisee incurred expenses will only matter where it can be shown that Gaston intended the promise to be binding, that Gaston intended that the promise be acted upon by the promisee, and that the promisee in fact acted upon this. In such an instance the promisee might be able to rely on the doctrine of promissory estoppel. Although it is still unclear under Irish law whether the promisee must show detriment such as incurring expenses, this will undoubtedly be relevant in assessing the level, if any, of compensation. However, the promisee is precluded from instituting proceedings in this regard and may only rely on this principle to defeat a claim. Therefore, none of the promisees in Case 1 can enforce the promise.

Summaries

France: All four promises are gifts and are therefore unenforceable because of the absence of the required formality (notarial authentication, or alternatively in Case 1(b), an ante-nuptial settlement).

Possibly, the promisor is liable in tort for giving the promisee a false impression but none of the decided cases concerns a gratuitous promise.

Case 1(b) does not concern a natural obligation because of the express text of the Civil Code.

Case 1(c) (the gift to the United Nations Children's Emergency Fund) is a gift even though, at least sometimes in the past, gifts to churches and the like were held to be exchanges, and therefore enforceable without a

---

[160] Unreported, 10 Dec. 1985.

formality, if the donor received some benefit such as masses for his soul or hearing a church bell ring that he remembered from childhood.

Belgium: If the promises are gifts, they would be unenforceable, not only because they lack notarial authentication, but also because gifts must be immediate and irrevocable transfers of property and they must be expressly accepted by the promisee.

There is little possibility a court would find a violation of a pre-contractual duty to act in good faith because it would contravene the policy behind the special requirements for gifts.

Nevertheless, the birthday present in Case 1(a) would be enforceable if it is a 'customary present' (*cadeau d'usage*) since then the rules for gifts do not apply. For the present to qualify, it must be customary to give such a present and the amount must be moderate given Gaston's resources.

The gift in Case 1(b) is enforceable because it is *propter nuptias* and so the rules on gifts do not apply because making such a gift is considered to be the fulfilment of a natural obligation.

The presents in Cases 1(c) and 1(d) are gifts (absent any natural obligation in Case 1(d)), and are therefore unenforceable.

The Netherlands: None of the promises are enforceable because they lack notarial authentication. While pre-contractual liability is a possibility, in all the Dutch cases imposing such liability negotiations were broken off.

Spain: None of the promises are enforceable because they were not made in writing. If they had been, they would be enforceable even absent an express acceptance and notarial authentication.

Portugal: None of the promises are enforceable because they were not made in writing. If they had been, and they had been accepted, they would be enforceable even absent notarial authentication.

Nevertheless, if the promisee has relied, the breach of promise would violate good faith and would therefore give rise to pre-contractual liability (in the reporter's view, though there are no decided cases).

Italy: None of the promises are enforceable because they lack notarial authentication. All of them except 1(b) would not be binding, in addition, because they were not formally accepted by the promisee.

If the promisee relied, a claim in tort is possible but doubtful.

Austria: None of the promises are enforceable because they lack notarial authentication.

Possibly one could make such a promise binding by using a contract of *mandatum*: by instructing a third party to deliver money to the donee.

Liability in tort or for breach of good faith is possible, but there are no cases in point.

There might be liability for *culpa in contrahendo* if Gaston indicated his willingness to pay the money promised, if the promisee relied, and if Gaston has no legitimate reason for refusing to pay, but it has not yet been determined whether this doctrine applies to gifts.

Germany: Except as noted below, the promises are not enforceable because they lack notarial authentication.

In Case 1(a), Gaston may be liable for *culpa in contrahendo* if he deceived Catherine about the need for a formality or if he was negligent in not formalizing the promise and he had a greater responsibility than she to do so because, for example, of his superior knowledge.

In Case 1(b), the promise is enforceable because the Civil Code has a special exception for gifts to people about to marry.

In Case 1(c), the promise would have been enforceable if it had been made to a natural person who served as a mere conduit to the ultimate beneficiary. It is not enforceable because the UN is not a natural person.

Greece: None of the promises are enforceable because they lack a notarial formality and acceptance.

There may be an action for bad faith in conducting negotiations if the promisee relied and the promisor was at fault. There is such an action if Gaston knew the promisee expected the promise to be kept but he has already decided not to draw up a notarial document so as to be free to breach it, and Gaston acted wilfully or with gross negligence, and the promisee suffered harm through reliance.

Scotland: None of the promises are enforceable because they are not in writing, as required by statute.

According to the same statute, however, there would be an action if the promisee has incurred expenditure in reliance on them if he did so with the knowledge and acquiescence of the promisor, if his reliance was considerable, and the detriment to him if the promise is not kept is also considerable.

England: The promises in Cases 1(a), 1(c), and 1(d) are unenforceable because they lack consideration. In Cases 1(a), 1(b), and 1(d) the promises might also be unenforceable if the promisor lacked the intention to create legal relations. To be enforceable, the promises must be made by deed (that is, 'under seal'). A wax impression is no longer necessary: just a written document that makes it clear on its face that it is intended to be 'under seal'. They would also be enforceable if cast as sham bargains by giving nominal consideration. They could also be made enforceable by establishing a trust, provided Gaston had in mind, not just money, but a specific sum of money. In that case, no formality would be required, nor even a third party, since Gaston could declare himself to be the trustee.

The promises are not enforceable under the doctrine of promissory estoppel because that doctrine is a shield, not a sword.

In a case similar to 1(b), however, an English court found that there was consideration even though marriage was really the motive for the promise, not something given in exchange for the promise. The judge was 'willing to interpret facts imaginatively in order to find consideration'. Whether other courts would do so is hard to predict, but they might, especially if the couple relied on the promise or it seems to be seriously meant. *Ireland*: None of the promises are enforceable because they lack consideration. Moreover, the promise in Case 1(b) is not enforceable because it fails to comply with a statute requiring that 'an agreement made upon consideration of marriage' be in writing. The promises would be enforceable if made by deed ('under seal') which still requires that some impression be made on the paper, if only with the end of a ruler. They would be enforceable if made by a trust, which requires no formalities. The requirements for a valid deed or trust are not generally known to lay people.

The promises are not enforceable under the doctrine of promissory estoppel because that doctrine is a shield, not a sword.

Preliminary comparisons

General principles:

The significance of form: In none of the systems is an informal executory promise to make a gift enforceable in principle. In one system (Belgium), there is no way to make such a promise binding: to have legal effect, a gratuitous transfer of property must not only be made by a notarial document and expressly accepted but it must be immediate and irrevocable. In the other systems, the promise can be made binding by a formality or by using a different form such as a trust. In Scotland, Spain, and Portugal, a promise in writing is sufficient. In France, the Netherlands, Italy, Austria, Germany, and Greece, the formality is subscription to a document containing the promise before a notary. In Italy and Greece, the promise must also be formally accepted. In England and Ireland, the promise can be made by deed ('under seal') or the property can be placed in trust for the donee. In Austria, it may also be possible to make such a promise binding by using a contract of agency (*mandatum*): that is, by instructing an agent to deliver money to the donee.

The significance of reliance: Even if the proper formality was not used, in Scotland, by a special statute, the promisee will still have an action if he relied on the promise provided he did so with the knowledge and acquiescence of the promisor, and both his reliance and the detriment to him if the promise is not kept are considerable. Although England and Ireland recognize a doctrine of promissory reliance, the promisee could not use it in these cases since it can only serve as a defence, not as the basis of a claim. The English reporter noted, however, that when the promisee has relied, courts are more inclined to be inventive in finding consideration. Other systems impose liability, even though a valid contract has not been concluded, for conduct that misleads the other party and induces him to change his position (France, Belgium, Portugal, Italy, the Netherlands, Austria, Germany, and Greece). Nevertheless, in these systems, courts have not yet applied this doctrine to a promise to make a gift. The Portuguese and Greek reporters thought the courts would; the French, Belgian, and Italian reporters thought they would not; and the others thought they might or might not.

Exceptions

Case 1(a): In Belgium, the informal promise of a birthday present would be enforceable if it is a 'customary present' (*cadeau d'usage*). To qualify, it must be customary to give such a present and the amount must be moderate given Gaston's resources.

b. *Case 1(b):* The promise to the person about to marry is enforceable in Belgium because it is deemed to be a promise to fulfil a natural obligation. In Germany, it is enforceable under a special provision of the German Civil Code. In one English case, such a promise was enforced even though, as the English reporter noted, to find consideration the court had to 'interpret the facts imaginatively' since marrying was the motive for the promise but not something done in return for it. In Ireland, the Statute of Frauds requires such a promise to be in writing to be enforceable.

c. *Case 1(c):* Absent a formality or reliance, in principle, the promise is not enforceable in any system. In France, at least at one time, some such promises were enforced if the promisor himself obtained some particular benefit such as hearing the church bell he remembered from his childhood ring again, or having mass said for him. In Germany, such a promise would be enforceable if made through a natural person who only acts as a conduit rather than, as here, through a legal person. But the promise in this case would not be enforceable in France or Germany.

Case 2: promises of compensation for services rendered without charge

Case

Kurt promised a large sum of money to Tony who had suffered a permanent back injury saving (a) Kurt or (b) Kurt's adult child from drowning after a boating accident. Can Tony enforce the promise if Kurt changes his mind? Does it matter if Tony was a professional lifeguard or if he had performed the rescue as part of his normal duties?

Discussions

FRANCE

Kurt promised Tony a large sum of money for saving him or his adult child because he felt under a moral duty to do so. Under French law, this duty could be considered to be a natural obligation (*obligation naturelle*). As already noted in discussing Case 1, a promisor who voluntarily undertakes to perform a natural obligation is bound by this promise and liable to the promisee if he fails to perform. The natural obligation has been converted into a civil one by a unilateral promise to perform. Nevertheless, his recognition of the natural obligation must be sufficiently unequivocal. Evidence concerning the promise is appreciated by the trial courts and is considered to be a matter of pure fact.[1]

The rule that a promise to perform a natural obligation is binding is a result of judicial interpretation of art. 1235 of the Civil Code.[2] Such a

---

[1] On the question of admissibility of evidence, see below.

[2] Article 1235: 'Every payment presupposes a debt; that which is paid without being due must be repaid. Repayment is not admitted in respect of natural obligations which have been voluntarily satisfied.' For a recent illustration see Civ. 1, 10 Oct. 1995, Bull. civ. I, no. 352, p. 246, note Frata; D 1996, somm. 120, note R. Libchaber; D 1997, 157, note Pignarre,

promise is not specifically enforceable.[3] Yet its breach gives rise to contractual liability.[4] Through Kurt's voluntary undertaking, the natural obligation has been novated (in a non-technical sense) and can thus be considered to be a civil obligation. A promise to perform a natural obligation does not, in principle, constitute a gift, and therefore Kurt does not need to comply with the legal formalities required for making a gift (see Case 1).

The fact that Tony saved Kurt's adult child does not make any difference, nor does the fact that Tony was a professional lifeguard. The promise is enforceable once it is considered to be a promise to perform a natural obligation.

When someone should be compensated for a loss but the conditions for liability in tort are not fulfilled, it may be useful to impose liability on the ground that a promise to perform a natural obligation has been breached. This is the classical instance in which a natural obligation is enforced in the absence of a pre-existing civil obligation. The nature of the unwritten promise which transforms the natural obligation into an enforceable perfect civil obligation is the subject of ongoing scholarly debate.[5] It is agreed, however, that such an act is subject to the usual conditions of validity, interpretation, and rules of evidence.

Tony may nevertheless encounter a problem as to the admissibility of evidence because of the way art. 1341 of the Civil Code has been interpreted in relation to art. 1235. Proof of the transformation of a natural obligation into a civil one is subject to the ordinary rules that govern admissibility of evidence. Normally, an agreement to pay a sum of money greater than 5,000 francs must be made in writing in a notarized document or in a contract signed by the contracting parties in counterpart. These formalities do not seem to have been respected. Nevertheless, there might have been a written document of some sort containing the promise: for example, a letter by Kurt to Tony. If so, it might come within an exception to the rule

---

Footnote 2 (*cont.*)

D 1997, Chr. 85, note Molfessis, which concerned the promise by the winner of the lottery to share the proceeds of the winnings with his friend who had actually filled in the form with the winning numbers on his behalf. After the winner had retracted his promise, the *Cour de cassation* upheld the friend's entitlement to the share on the basis of a natural obligation that constituted a unilateral undertaking by the winner.

[3] Civ. 1, 14 Feb. 1978, Bull. civ. I, no. 59, p. 50, which held: 'a natural obligation not changed into a civil obligation is not specifically enforceable'.

[4] For an analysis of prize money in terms of a unilateral contract, see J. Mestre, RTDCiv. 1996, 398 in a note on Cour d'appel, Toulouse, 14 Feb. 1996. For a criticism of the generalized use of the unilateral contract analysis, see Terré, Simler, and Lequette, *Les obligations* no. 50, p. 46.

[5] Ghestin, Goubeaux, and Fabre-Magnan, *Traité de droit civil* no. 754, pp. 737 f.

just described. The letter might constitute what is called the 'commence-ment of evidence in writing' pursuant to art. 1347 of the Civil Code.[6] If such a letter did exist, proof could be completed by the evidence of witnesses.[7]

The exceptions to the rule of art. 1341 are fairly narrow. In the absence of any writing whatsoever, Tony could perhaps try to claim that he fell within another exception which is set out in art. 1348 of the Civil Code: that it was morally impossible for him to obtain evidence in writing of the contract. Such an argument has succeeded before the courts when proof must be made of the transformation of a natural obligation.[8] Nevertheless, the trial courts have absolute power to determine the issue.[9] Although the case law is contradictory, it seems as though this exception applies primarily to family relationships, or relationships of affection or subordination. It is therefore uncertain whether Tony could benefit from it. If the court decides that Tony has not proven that he falls within one of the exceptions just described, his claim will be inadmissible and therefore no effect can be given to the promise.

As the expression of a duty of conscience, the natural obligation has sometimes been considered to be a legal doctrine which reflects the morality of an elite.[10] To see why such an obligation is rarely enforced by the courts, consider the following alternatives. Either Kurt has such a high idea of his moral duties that it is likely that he will formalize or perform his promise, or Kurt made his promise only lightly in a moment of fear – he will never formalize or perform it and Tony will have difficulty in proving that it was made. In the first case, it is doubtful whether an action would be brought before the courts. In the second, an action may arise, and Tony has standing to bring one since he suffered a definite direct and personal loss. But evidence of the promise that transforms the natural obligation may well be a procedural obstacle.

Nevertheless, even if Tony cannot prove that the promise was made, he may still have a remedy. In analogous cases, the court has sometimes said that a so-called 'rescue agreement' (*convention d'assistance*) has been

---

[6] Evidence in writing is commenced when something is submitted that is written by the defendant or his representative which renders the facts that are alleged probable. The judge may consider that a party's declarations given before him, or his silence or refusal to appear, are equivalent to evidence commenced in writing.

[7] Civ. 1, 28 June 1954, Bull. civ. I, no. 214.

[8] See, for example, Cour d'appel, Paris, 9 April 1957, D 1957, 455.

[9] See Civ. 1, 21 Feb. 1956, D 1956, 287, where it was held that the concept of moral impossibility could not be invoked between people who were cohabiting since the underlying idea is that it is not practical to imagine people in a certain relationship carrying out the necessary formalities. The court also refused to define the concept of moral impossibility.

[10] Ghestin, Goubeaux, and Fabre-Magnan, *Traité de droit civil* no. 743, p. 725.

formed.[11] According to this analysis, by coming to help, that is, by jumping from the boat or diving in from the side, Tony made a clear, firm, and unequivocal offer to help. Even if Kurt or his adult child kept silent during the rescue operation – indeed, even if they were unconscious – their silence would, by way of exception, constitute an acceptance since the offer is deemed to be made in their sole interest.[12] Such a 'rescue agreement' is simply a device by the courts that enables the rescuer and subsequent victim of the rescue operation to be indemnified. In one case, for example, a garage owner was hurt while rescuing a motorcyclist whose vehicle was damaged. It was held that the rescue operation gave rise to an obligation on the part of the person rescued to compensate the rescuer for the physical damage suffered by the latter who had voluntarily offered assistance.[13] Clearly, such a device is highly artificial, not to say fictional. It has been severely criticized by scholars who find it difficult to square the existence of the *convention d'assistance* with the rules on contract formation. How can one imagine that the parties reached an agreement when one of them was under water, or, more generally, in any kind of emergency situation that prevented him from making an acceptance?[14] According to some scholars, it is not only impossible to imagine that consent has been given but also unnecessary. Some consider it more appropriate to allow a claim based on a type of quasi-contract, *gestion d'affaires*. Others have argued that such a claim cannot be brought because the rescuer is under a legal obligation to assist a person in danger. Under French law such an obligation is imposed by legislation and carries criminal sanctions. One could say, in such a case, that the legal obligation carries with it an equitable consequence which the courts can imply under art. 1135 of the Civil Code:[15] namely, that the rescuer should be compensated for any harm he suffers. Nevertheless, art. 1135 says that the

---

[11] In the examples in the case law, the court's conclusion that a contract was formed is open to criticism. The courts have been inventing agreements of this sort since Civ. 1, 27 May 1959, RTDCiv. 1959, 735, note H. Mazeaud. See, for example, Civ. 1, 1 Dec. 1969, Bull. civ. I, no. 375, p. 299, D 1970, p. 422, note Puech, JCP, II, 16445, note Aubert (assistance given by garage owner to motorcyclist); Soc., Bull. civ. V, no. 421, p. 320; RTDCiv. 1987, p. 533, note J. Mestre (assistance given by employee of garage to push a lorry out of a ditch); Civ. 1, 27 Jan. 1993, RTDCiv. 1993, 584; G. Viney, JCP, 1993, I, 3727, no. 4 (help given by a brother to another, the owner, to cut down a tree).

[12] Ghestin, *Traité de droit civil* no. 406, p. 363.

[13] Civ., 1 1 Dec. 1969, Bull. civ. I, no. 375, p. 299, D 1970, p. 422, note Puech, JCP, II, 16445, note Aubert.   [14] See the remarks made by Puech and Aubert, *ibid.*

[15] Article 1135: 'Agreements obligate a party not only as to what is expressly undertaken but also as to all the consequences that equity, custom or law give to the obligation according to its nature.'

parties to an agreement are obligated, not only by its express terms, but by all the consequences which equity, custom, and law attach to it. If there is no agreement, how can the courts have power to recognize such consequences under art. 1135?

With regard to this equitable solution, it may matter whether Tony was a professional lifeguard. The courts may be more anxious to help a benevolent amateur life-saver. Still, the matter is not clear since each case is judged casuistically on the individual merits. In addition, the rescuer's status as a professional or amateur may influence the courts' approach in relation not only to the result but also to its legal foundation. For example, P. Jourdain[16] has suggested that, except in situations where a professional has voluntarily carried out a rescue operation, it is highly artificial to infer that the rescuer had the intention to contract; rather, the act is done out of courtesy. He believes that liability in tort would be more appropriate, particularly in cases where one can apply art. 1384(1)[17] which imposes liability for harm done by a thing in the defendant's custody. That basis for liability is more advantageous for the plaintiff since the defendant is strictly liable.

Nevertheless, this possibility would not be available here. On the facts before us, it is difficult to predict whether the courts would imply retrospectively a duty on Kurt's part to compensate Tony for his back injuries. On balance, it seems more likely that they would do so on the basis of a rescue agreement if Tony were a professional lifeguard. Although this case is exactly the sort which is put by scholars who argue that an agreement could not truly have been concluded, nevertheless, a court might still find that it was a rescue contract in order to reach an equitable solution.

BELGIUM

Kurt's promise would be deemed to have been made out of a sense of moral duty or moral responsibility, that is, to fulfil a 'natural obligation' (*obligation naturelle*) (see Case 1). Debts of gratitude (*dettes de reconnaissance*) are typical illustrations of natural obligations.[18] Tony could therefore enforce Kurt's promise even if Kurt has changed his mind, since the

---

[16] RTDCiv. 1994, 864–6.

[17] Article 1384(1) imposes liability for damage caused 'not only by one's own act but also by persons under one's responsibility, or by things in one's custody'.

[18] This is one of the categories of natural obligations described by Van Ommeslaghe, *Droit des obligations*, 362.

promise converts the natural obligation into a civil obligation.[19] A court would probably conclude that there was a natural obligation, not only in Case 2(a), in which Tony saved Kurt, but in Case 2(b) as well, in which Tony saved Kurt's adult child. It does not matter if Tony was a professional lifeguard performing the rescue as part of his normal duties unless Kurt did not know this, in which case the promise is deemed not to be voluntary.

THE NETHERLANDS

If Kurt changes his mind, the doctrine that a person may recover for the management of the affairs of others (*negotiorum gestio*) is not relevant. In such cases, the manager is entitled to compensation only for damage suffered whereas Kurt's promise was to 'give a large sum of money'. In any event, the compensation due as a result of *negotiorum gestio* is due whether it is promised or not (see art. 6:200(1) of the Civil Code).[20]

In both Cases 2(a) and 2(b), there may be a natural obligation (art. 6:3(2)(b) of the Civil Code[21]) which is unenforceable (art. 6:3(1)[22]), but may be turned into a binding obligation by a contract (art. 6:5[23]). Therefore, the promises may be binding. Generally, however, rewards for services rendered are not considered to be natural obligations but gifts.[24] Consequently, the formal requirements described earlier (Case 1) have to be met. I have not come across any authority which accepts a natural obligation in such a case.

It does not matter if Tony was a professional lifeguard or if he had performed the rescue as part of his normal duties. The rules on management of the affairs of others distinguish between ordinary managers and

---

[19] See *ibid.* 365, referring to a situation whereby an automobile driver pays compensation for humanitarian reasons only: that is, he was under no legal obligation to do so.

[20] Article 6:200(1) of the Civil Code: 'The interested party must compensate the manager for damage which he has suffered as a result of the management, to the extent that his interest has been properly looked after.'

[21] Article 6:3(2) of the Civil Code: 'A natural obligation exists . . . (b) where a person has towards another person an imperative moral duty of such a nature that its performance, although unenforceable at law, must according to societal views be considered as the performance of a prestation to which that other person is entitled.'

[22] Article 6:3(1) of the Civil Code: 'A natural obligation is one which cannot be enforced at law.'

[23] Article 6:5 of the Civil Code: '(1) A natural obligation is transformed into an obligation enforceable at law by contract between debtor and creditor . . . (3) The provisions respecting gifts and other liberalities do not apply to such a contract.'
The rule of art. 6:5(1) of the Civil Code is a codification of what was established by case law under the old code (see Asser/Hartkamp vol. II, no. 81).

[24] See Asser/Hartkamp, vol. I, no. 74; Asser/Hartkamp vol. II, no. 68.

professional managers (art. 6:20 (2) of the Civil Code[25]), but, as already noted, this is not relevant because compensation due as the result of the management of one's affairs by others does not depend on the validity of a promise. As to the natural obligation, there is no reason why Kurt should feel a less 'imperative moral duty' towards a professional rescuer.

SPAIN

One possible ground for enforcing Kurt's promises is that Kurt had a moral obligation to compensate Tony. If so, a promise will be binding even if it is not made in writing.

There is a moral duty to repair the damage one causes.[26] Nevertheless, although the *Tribunal Supremo* has recognized the moral obligation as a valid *causa* for unilateral promises,[27] the duty to repair damage is not the standard type of moral duty that it recognizes. The *Tribunal Supremo* has almost always dealt with moral obligations arising mainly from family relationships. When an older man promised to give a monthly sum to a sixteen-year-old girl with whom he had had an affair and whom he had left, the *Tribunal Supremo* said that the relationship gave rise to

moral obligations, [which] because of their fulfilment during their intimate relationship, became natural obligations, and once the relationship was ended, those same obligations became civil obligations through the formal promise of the alimony, which the debtor must pay, not *donandi* but *solvendi animo*, because the promiser wants to fulfil an obligation of conscience, and does not act simply to reward her or out of liberality.[28]

Similarly, in another decision, a testator changed a will to leave property to the defendant rather than her two nieces, instructing the defendant to give them a sum of money instead. The defendant promised the nieces she would do so. The court enforced the promise on the ground that there was a prior moral obligation to give the money.[29]

It is not clear that the court would find that Kurt was under a moral obligation since no personal relationship was involved between promisor and promisee. Furthermore, it will be even more difficult to prove the existence of a moral obligation if Kurt promised Tony money for saving

---

[25] Article 6:201(2): 'Where the manager has acted in the course of a business or profession, he has, to the extent that this is reasonable, the further right to be paid for his activities in accordance with the prices usually charged for such activities at the time of the management.'   [26] Díez Picazo, *Fundamentos de derecho*, vol. II, 77.
[27] E. Lalaguna, 'La voluntad unilateral como fuente de obligaciones', *Revista de derecho privado* 59 (1975), 801 at 826.   [28] TS, 17 Oct. 1932.   [29] TS, 5 May 1958.

Kurt's adult child because Kurt himself would not be the beneficiary of Tony's act.

Another possibility is that the promise could be considered to be a *donación remuneratoria* (art. 619 of Civil Code). A *donación remuneratoria* is a donation to compensate the recipient for services provided to the donor for which the donor was not legally obligated to pay. Article 622 of the Civil Code provides that *donaciónes remuneratorias* will be governed by the articles on donations only to the extent that they exceed fair compensation for the services. The interpretation of this article is very controversial among Spanish scholars. Some consider the mention of *donaciónes remuneratorias* in art. 622 to be a mistake, and conclude that arts. 632 and 633 should apply to the donation as a whole.[30] If we follow this theory, the promise will not be enforceable at all because the requirements of the donation are not met. Others consider that art. 622 should apply[31] and consequently only the amount in excess of compensation should be treated as a donation.[32] The rest should be treated as an onerous contract.[33] Since onerous contracts do not have to be in writing to be enforceable, Tony could enforce the promise for an amount that is considered a fair compensation for the services he provided.

It does not matter whether Tony was working as a lifeguard. If the promise is enforceable, Tony can enforce it even if his salary was paid by a third party. In a similar case, a sum of money had been offered to whomever discovered the perpetrator of a crime. A policeman did and sued for the reward. According to the *Tribunal Supremo*, he lost, not because there was a prior contractual obligation, but because the police regulations prohibited receiving money as a reward.[34]

PORTUGAL

It is possible that Tony may be able to enforce Kurt's promise in Case 2(a) on the grounds that, even absent a promise, he is entitled to compensation as a *negotiorum gestor*,[35] and the promise is an acknowledgment of the extent of this liability. The *negotiorum gestor* is one who altruistically con-

---

[30] Puig Brutau, *Fundamentos de derecho civil*, vol. II-2, 111; Pérez and Alguer, *Anotaciones*, vol. I, 224.   [31] J. M. Manresa, *Comentarios de derecho civil*, 5th edn, vol. V (1951), 89.

[32] Castán Tobeñas, *Derecho civil*, vol. IV, 256.   [33] *Ibid.*   [34] TS, 6 June 1916.

[35] See Costa, *Direito das Obrigações*, 407 ff.; F. L. P. Jorge, *Direito das Obrigações* (1976), 215 ff.; A. M. Cordeiro, *Direito das Obrigações* (1980), 11 ff.; L. M. Leitão, *A Responsabilidade do Gestor perante o Dono de Negócio no Direito Civil Português* (1991), 159 ff. A comparative reference to this institution can be found in J. P. Dawson, 'Negotiorum Gestio: the Altruistic Intermeddler', Harv. L. R. 74 (1961), 817–65, 1073–129.

ducts another person's business without any obligation or authorization by that person to do so (art. 464 of the Civil Code). The law grants him the right to reimbursement of his expenses and of compensation for damages he suffered (art. 468). If so, Kurt would be legally obligated to compensate Tony for the back injury. The promise could be viewed as an acknowledgment of the obligation pursuant to art. 469 of the Civil Code, which states: 'The approval of the "negotiorum gestio" involves a waiver of compensation for damages caused by the "gestor" and an acknowledgment of the rights granted to him in the previous article [reimbursement of expenses and compensation for damages he suffered].'

On this theory, if Tony was a professional lifeguard, he would also be entitled to compensation unless he had performed the rescue as part of his normal duties, in which case he would not be entitled to anything.

Moreover, on this theory, Tony could not enforce the promise in Case 2(b) unless he could show that Kurt himself was under a duty to rescue, and that Tony therefore performed Kurt's duty. If he can, the solution would be identical to that of Case 2(a).

Most likely, however, the promise would not be considered to be enforceable. If we merely consider the enforceability of the promise itself, Case 2(a) is not much different from Case 1. The only difference is that Kurt's promise would be considered a donation in reward (*doação remuneratória*) which is defined by art. 941 of the Civil Code as a donation to compensate the recipient for services provided to the donor for which the donor was not legally obliged to pay. These donations, however, are subject to almost all the same rules as ordinary donations. The only differences are that they cannot be revoked if the donee shows ingratitude (art. 975(b)), and that they are the last to be reduced if the deceased does not have sufficient assets to leave his heirs their mandatory share (art. 2172 no. 3).

Because a *doação remuneratória* is subject to the same rules as other contracts of donation, to be enforceable, this promise must be made and accepted in a written document during the life of the promisor. It would then be legally enforceable whether or not Tony was a professional lifeguard.

In Case 2(a), Kurt may also have a moral obligation to compensate Tony. Under Portuguese law, moral obligations are moral or social duties that are not legally enforceable but are nevertheless regarded as duties owed as a matter of justice (art. 402 of the Civil Code). If these obligations are performed voluntarily, it is not possible to ask for the restitution of the performance (art. 403). Even if Kurt had a moral obligation, then his promise would still not be enforceable.

Jurists discuss whether a promise to fulfil a moral obligation can be enforceable. The common position is that the law recognizes only its actual fulfilment, and not a mere promise to perform or recognition of the duty.[36]

ITALY

Tony cannot enforce the promise if Kurt changes his mind unless Kurt has promised the amount of money formally through a notarial document and Tony has accepted (art. 782 of the Civil Code), as explained in discussing Case 1. It does not matter if Tony was a professional lifeguard or if he performed the rescue as part of his normal duties.

Kurt promised the money in gratitude for a service rendered by Tony. A promise such as this one which is motivated by gratitude or the desire to make compensation for a past service is termed a 'remunerative gift'. According to art. 770 of the Civil Code,[37] it is subject to the requirements of a contract of donation.

Article 770(2) recognizes certain other types of liberalities for which formalities are not required. This category of gifts is called 'liberality according to usage' (*liberalità d'uso*) and includes all the gratuitous acts which are mandated by social convention. Nevertheless, delivery (*traditio*) seems necessary in these cases. The motivation seems insufficient to make the informal promise enforceable.[38] Courts often distinguish between a 'remunerative gift' and 'liberality according to usage' by an objective test: they ask if the amount given is in proportion to the service received.[39]

Article 2034 of the Civil Code provides that what has been paid in

---

[36] See Costa, *Direito das Obrigações*, 160.

[37] Article 770 of the Civil Code: 'Remunerative gift: A liberality exercised in gratitude or in consideration of the merits of the donee or for special remuneration is also a gift. A liberality that is usual to make for services performed or in any way according to usage does not constitute a gift.' See also Cass. civ., sez. II, 22 Feb. 1995, no. 1989.

[38] See R. Sacco, 'Il Contratto', in Vassalli, *Tratt. di dir. civ.* 6:2 (1975), 607; A. Torrente, 'La Donazione', in Cicu-Messineo, *Tratt. dir. civ. e comm.* 22 (1956), 94; Marini, *Promessa ed affidamento*, 397; *contra* G. Castiglia, 'Promesse unilaterali atipiche', Riv. dir. com. I (1983), 327–41.

[39] See Cass. civ., 28 June 1976, no. 2452, in Foro it. I (1977), 456; Cass. civ., 5 April 1975, no. 1218, in Giust. civ. I (1975), 1310; but see Cass. civ., 10 Dec. 1988, no. 6720, in Nuova giur. civ. comm. I (1989), 614, which considers only the usage. On this controversial distinction see also, most recently: Cass. civ., sez. I, 14 Jan. 1992, no. 324, in Nuova giur. civ. comm. (1992), 654; Cass. civ., sez. II, 2 Feb. 1992, no. 1077, *ibid.*; F. Regine, 'Donazione rimuneratoria e liberalità d'uso: una difficile distinzione', Nuova giur. civ. comm. (1992), 654. See also Marini, *Promessa ed affidamento*, 396; C. Manzini, 'Sugli spostamenti patrimoniali effettuati in esecuzione di obbligazioni naturali', Contr. e impr. (1987), 882 at 911.

fulfilment of a 'natural obligation' cannot be recovered in an action for restitution.[40] A 'natural obligation' arises from a moral or social duty and not from the law. But the Code contains no other special rules governing natural obligations.

Gino Gorla believes that, nevertheless, special rules should govern the enforceability of an informal promise to give a sum of money in remuneration for services one has received gratuitously in the past (*causa praeterita*). The promisor's intention is not to enrich the promisee by making a gift (*animus donandi*) but rather to make compensation (*animus solvendi*). Such promises, in Gorla's view, should be enforced provided two conditions are met. First, the service rendered must have a monetary value (*appréciable à prix d'argent*). Second, the amount promised must be proportionate to the value of the service or the performance received. If these conditions are fulfilled, there is a sufficient basis for enforcing the promise (*cause suffisante*).[41]

In Gorla's view, in order to prevent injustice, whether there is a sufficient basis for enforcing the promise and a sufficiently important natural obligation should be determined case by case. It would be a question of fact, and therefore not reviewable by the highest court, the *Corte di Cassazione*, which decides only questions of law.

Although Gorla's view is very interesting, it has not been accepted by Italian case law and scholars. The fact that a promise was made to compensate for a performance received in the past is not sufficient to make it binding.[42]

AUSTRIA

The promise will be enforceable in both Cases 2(a) and 2(b). According to the prevailing view in the literature and the practice of the courts, a promise of a donation that honours a moral obligation[43] does not constitute a gift.[44] As a result, the form requirement does not apply. According

---

[40] Article 2034 of the Civil Code: 'Natural obligations: Recovery of that which was spontaneously given in performance of moral or social duties is not permissible, unless the performance was made by a person lacking capacity. The duties indicated in the preceding paragraph, and any other duty for which the law accords no action but bars recovery of what was spontaneously paid, shall have no other effect.'

[41] See Gorla, *Il contratto*, 126; but see also Marini, *Promessa ed affidamento*, 389; A. D'Angelo, *Contratto e operazione economica* (1992).

[42] See e.g. Sacco, 'Il Contratto', 582; G. Castiglia, 'Promesse unilaterali atipiche', Riv. dir. com. I (1983), 364 ff.   [43] *Moralische, sittliche oder Anstandspflicht.*

[44] OGH SZ 38/227; EvBl 1964/102; JBl 1967, 257; JBl 1971, 197; JBl 1978, 645.

to a second view such a promise does constitute a gift, but one to which the form requirement is not applicable.[45]

Whether a moral obligation exists depends on the circumstances of the particular case. In Cases 2(a) and 2(b), Austrian courts would come to the conclusion that Kurt has a moral obligation to Tony. Two points seem to be decisive: that Tony's action was of great importance to Kurt and that Tony suffered harm because of this action. Kurt therefore cannot change his mind.

If Tony were a professional lifeguard or if he performed the rescue as part of his normal duties, it could be debated whether Kurt is under a moral obligation to compensate him. As in Case 1(b), the promise can be taken in different ways. If somebody acts as a *negotiorum gestor*, under certain circumstances Austrian law gives him the right to claim compensation from the principal.[46] One type of case where compensation is granted is the so-called necessary *negotiorum gestio* where the *gestor* acts in order to avert an impending harm to the principal and it is not possible to ask the principal's approval first.[47] In such a case the *gestor* is entitled to claim compensation for the costs he incurs and for any harm he suffers because of his action. In Case 2(a), Tony would be acting as a *negotiorum gestor*. The same would be true in Case 2(b) if Tony had rescued a child who was a minor since, by averting the child from harm, he would also avert harm to the parents. In Case 2(b), however, Tony rescued Kurt's adult child. If the child is already grown up and living on his own so that the parents do not have a duty of protection towards the child, Tony may not be able to recover.

If Tony does have the right to claim compensation, then even though he has not incurred any costs, he may claim compensation for the harm he suffered. If he has already made this claim, Kurt's promise may constitute either a settlement or an acknowledgment, in which case the form requirement would not apply.[48]

If Tony were a professional lifeguard or if he performed the rescue as part of his normal duties, it is doubtful whether his action would be qualified as a *negotiorum gestio*. It could be argued that only an action for which there is no antecedent legal duty constitutes a *negotiorum gestio*. The prevailing view in Austria, however, is that even in such situations the *gestor* can have the right to claim compensation, provided the legal rule which makes the action mandatory does not rule out compensation.[49]

---

[45] G. Schubert in Rummel, *ABGB* § 938 no. 4; M. Binder in Schwimann, *ABGB* § 943 no. 29; F. Bydlinski, JBl 1978, 648.   [46] See §§ 1035 ff. of the Civil Code.

[47] *Notwendige Geschäftsführung ohne Auftrag.*   [48] See Case 1.

[49] P. Rummel in Rummel, *ABGB* § 1035 no. 6; Ehrenzweig, *System* vol. II/1, 717. In the case LGZ Wien MietSlg 37.096, a firefighter was allowed to claim compensation although he

GERMANY

In Case 2(a), the promise is not binding because Kurt promised to make a gift without complying with the formalities required by § 518 of the Civil Code (see Case 1). As far as a claim in contract is concerned, it does not matter that Kurt was under a moral obligation to give some money to Tony, nor whether Tony was a lifeguard.

Nevertheless, Kurt could be liable for Tony's damages under §§ 677, 683, and 670 of the Civil Code. If Tony did Kurt a special kind of favour (*Geschäftsführung ohne Auftrag*), Kurt is also liable for the damages which can typically occur in connection with Tony's activity.[50] Kurt's promise could serve as evidence in support of Tony's claim for damages. But this would only be possible if it could be interpreted as an acknowledgment. If Kurt merely wanted to express his gratitude, it would have no effect whatsoever. If, however, Tony acted as a professional lifeguard, it is less clear that he would have such a claim. It would depend on the nature of his duty (public or private law), his relationship with his employer, and Kurt's relationship with Tony's employer.

In Case 2(b), which person Tony rescued does not affect the question whether we have a promise to make a gift. It only makes a difference for Tony's claim for damages. If the child is an adult, Tony could only sue the child for damages because he did not do the favour for Kurt. Kurt had no special responsibility for his child any more.

GREECE

Kurt's promise was made because he feels a special moral duty to Tony.[51] Obligations arising from reasons of a special moral duty or on grounds of decency are termed 'natural obligations', which means that the promisee cannot compel the promisor to perform but if the promisor does so of his own free will then he cannot recover his performance.[52] Article 906 of the Civil Code provides: 'A claim for the return of what was not due cannot be brought when a payment was made by reason of a special moral duty or of reasons of propriety.'

Such an obligation becomes an enforceable contractual obligation if

---

had performed his action as part of his normal duties as a firefighter. If Tony is an employee of Kurt, either Tony's damage will be covered by social security or Kurt will be liable because of § 1014 of the Civil Code.   [50] BGHZ 89 (1984), 153 (157).

[51] Karakostas in Georgiadis and Stathopoulos, *Civil Code*, art. 512; EfAth 1839/55 EEN 23, 45.

[52] A. Ligeropoulos, 'Natural Obligations and Relative Legal Forms', in C. Fragistas, *Miscellany in honor of Ch. Fragistas*, vol. XII, part VI (1970–1), 227. Stathopoulos, *Law of Obligations* 37.

the parties conclude a contract of donation[53] dictated by a special moral duty. According to art. 512 of the Civil Code, 'a donation made by reason of a particular moral duty or on grounds of decency shall not be subject to revocation'. Consequently, in this kind of donation the normal rules that concern the revocation of the donation do not apply. As pointed out in our discussion of Case 1, however, a contract of donation is also subject to the special rule of art. 496 of the Civil Code which requires a notarial document to be drawn up if the promise is to be valid. Nevertheless, it has been suggested in theory that this rule does not apply in cases of donation dictated by a special moral duty because of the special nature of this kind of donation.[54] Furthermore, art. 512 of the Civil Code may be applied here by analogy. According to this article, if a donation exceeds the amount that is reasonable, the surplus is subject to the regulations concerning revocation of donation.[55] So it may be argued here that if the donor promised an unreasonably high amount on account of a moral duty owed to the donee, then the surplus will be considered as a usual donation which would not be valid unless a notarial document is drawn up.

Thus, in the present case, Kurt will be obliged to keep his promise but only for an amount that is reasonable.

If Tony is a professional lifeguard, it matters whether the promise was made before or after the rescue. In the first case a contract to do a job would have been concluded between Kurt and Tony and so Kurt would be obliged to keep his contractual obligation.[56] In the second case, even if Tony performs the rescue as part of his normal duties, Kurt's promise will be considered as a donation dictated by a special moral duty and it will be judged in the way described earlier.

SCOTLAND

Although Kurt *has* received a benefit from Tony, at the time the promise is made there is no potential future benefit for Kurt inherent in the promise. It is submitted, therefore, that this is a gratuitous unilateral obligation. The promise is valid and enforceable only if constituted in writing: s.1(2)(a)(ii) of Requirements of Writing (Scotland) Act 1995.[57] It must be clear that the alleged promise was intended to create a legal obligation: because it must be constituted in writing, this would suggest such an

---

[53] Ligeropoulos, 'Natural Obligations'.
[54] The protection that the notarial deed offers to the donor is not being justified here.
Ibid.; Stathopoulos, *Law of Obligations*, 37.   [55] Ligeropoulos, 'Natural Obligations'.
[56] EfAth 1839/55 EEN 23, 45.   [57] See Case 1.

intention. Once constituted in writing, this is a unilateral obligation. Accordingly, there is no need for any 'acceptance' by the promisee. The promisee can, of course, reject performance, should he so desire. Technically, the promisor is under an obligation as soon as the gratuitous promise is constituted in writing, that is, the promisee does not have to know about the promise. In practice, it cannot be enforced unless the promisee learns of the promise.

It is irrelevant in Scots law whether it was Kurt or his child who was rescued, and also whether or not Tony was a professional rescuer, as there is no requirement of consideration in Scots law.

ENGLAND

According to orthodox English law, none of the promises described in this case are enforceable. The reason is the same as the reason why the promises discussed in the previous answer were unenforceable: nothing was done or promised in return for them, hence they lacked consideration. In each of these cases, Tony suffered a detriment and Kurt obtained a benefit as a result of the rescue. But Kurt's promise is unenforceable because it was not given *in exchange for* the rescue: the promise was made after the rescue.

Exceptionally, English law sometimes allows, under the doctrine of 'implied assumpsit', that something done in the past by the promisee for the promisor can be valid consideration for a subsequent promise. But in none of the promises described in this case are the requirements for implied assumpsit met. In order for the past act to count as good consideration it must have been done at the request of the promisor and with the understanding that the promisee would be rewarded for the act, neither of which appears to have happened here (though we cannot be entirely sure, given the brief facts).[58] There are cases where the courts appear to have interpreted these requirements loosely,[59] but the facts of Case 2, being relatively straightforward, do not easily allow for such an approach. It is worth adding here that the implied assumpsit exception to the consideration rule is arguably not an exception at all, but simply a case of enforcing an agreement in which the price has not been fixed, something which does not ordinarily preclude a contract being concluded.[60]

In certain eighteenth- and early nineteenth-century cases it was held

[58] *Pao On* v. *Lau Yiu Long* [1980] AC 614.
[59] E.g., *Pao On* v. *Lau Yiu Long* [1980] AC 614, which involved a famously complex commercial shipping arrangement.   [60] Atiyah, *Law of Contract*, 124.

that the existence of a pre-existing moral obligation to the promisee could suffice as good consideration.[61] The term 'moral obligation' was given a narrow construction, however, applying essentially to cases where the promisor's prior obligation was not binding because of a specific legal defect. Thus, a promise to pay a statute-barred debt was binding.[62] Many of these exceptions have been overruled (see Case 3 for a current exception), but in any event none cover the situation under consideration, where the promisor's 'moral' obligation is 'moral' in the ordinary, rather than technical sense. Indeed, the facts are similar to the well-known nineteenth-century case, *Eastwood* v. *Kenyon*,[63] where a husband's promise to reimburse expenses incurred by the guardian of his wife when she was a young girl was unenforceable for lack of consideration.

The resolution of Case 2 according to orthodox law, then, is clear: the promises are not enforceable. The facts of Case 2, however, describe the sort of situation in which, according to some commentators – notably Professor Atiyah – English courts will strain hard to find or invent consideration. Kurt's moral obligation to Tony is the sort of 'good reason' that Atiyah has suggested sways courts to find that consideration in the technical sense is satisfied.[64] Indeed, in his text on contract law, Atiyah refers to an American case with facts very similar to Case 2,[65] and suggests that 'the moral appeal of the plaintiff's case would be so great that any court would surely strive to uphold his claim'.[66] It is difficult to deny that an English court would indeed 'strive' to uphold either of Kurt's promises, but, at the same time, an English court, particularly a contemporary English court, would need some factual basis, however slim, on which to support a conclusion that consideration was provided for Kurt's promise. They would refuse, it is suggested, to invent the consideration entirely out of thin air. In the case where Tony is not a professional lifeguard, no such factual basis can easily be found. It appears a clear and unambiguous case of past consideration (and, as such, stands in contrast to the recent examples of allegedly invented consideration cited by Atiyah, where the facts are highly complex[67]). Where Tony is a lifeguard, the court might – though I think this unlikely – imply some sort of prior agreement that Tony be

---

[61] Treitel, *Contract*, 75.   [62] *Hyeling* v. *Hastings* [1699] 1 Ld Raym 389.

[63] [1840] 11 A & E 438.

[64] See P. S. Atiyah, 'Consideration: a Restatement', in P. S. Atiyah, *Essays on Contract* (1986), 179.   [65] *Webb* v. *McGowin* [1935] 168 So. 196.

[66] Atiyah, *Law of Contract*, 125. There does not appear to be a comparable English case.

[67] E.g., *Pao On* v. *Lau Yiu Long* [1980] AC 614.

reimbursed for the cost of his rescue. This is unlikely to happen if Tony did the rescue as part of his normal duties (moreover, in this case Kurt's 'moral obligation' is weaker, since Tony is paid as a lifeguard and presumably will be compensated for his losses by his employer or employer's insurance), but it is a possibility if, say, Tony is off-duty, Kurt is aware that Tony is a professional, and Kurt in some way encourages Tony in the rescue. The request or encouragement would be crucial, since only then could Tony argue implied assumpsit (as described above).

IRELAND

In order to enforce the promise, Tony must show that the promise was made by way of a deed under seal or that there was some consideration made in exchange for the promise (see Case 1). In this instance the promise made by Kurt was made after Tony had performed the act of saving (a) Kurt or (b) Kurt's adult child from drowning after a boating accident.

If a promise is made after some gratuitous act has been performed by the promisee then the subsequent promise is not supported by consideration. The benefit conferred before the promise was made cannot be said to have been made by reference to an antecedent promise.[68]

However, if it can be shown that Kurt expressly asked Tony to save either Kurt himself or Kurt's adult child from drowning after a boating accident and that when this requested act was provided the parties did not intend the act to be gratuitous, the case might fall within the exception in *Lampleigh* v. *Braithwaite*[69] as applied in *Bradford* v. *Roulston*.[70] In *Bradford* v. *Roulston*, it was found that 'where there is a past consideration, consisting of a previous act done at the request of the Defendant, it will support a subsequent promise; the promise being treated as coupled with the previous request'.

If the promise was enforceable, having fallen within the exception above, then Kurt would be liable to Tony irrespective of whether Tony had saved either Kurt himself or Kurt's adult child. Although the principles of contract law provide that consideration must 'move from the promisee',[71] consideration need not move to the promisor. Treitel states that consideration may 'move from the promisee without moving to the promisor

---

[68] See *Provincial Bank of Ireland* v. *Donnell* [1932] 67 ILTR 142.   [69] [1615] Hob. 105.
[70] [1858] 8 ICLR 468.   [71] See *Thomas* v. *Thomas* [1842] 2 QB 851.

where the promisee at the promisor's request confers a benefit on a third party'.[72]

The principle of consideration is essential, therefore, and the promise will only be binding if some consideration other than the past service has been provided by the promisee. The question as to whether consideration is past or otherwise is one of fact and the wording of the agreement is not decisive.[73]

On the facts as presented, it is clear that Tony has provided no consideration in exchange for Kurt's promise and that Kurt's promise was made after the 'gratuitous act' of Tony. Equally, it is unlikely that in an emergency situation such as the above example it could be shown that Kurt had the requisite intention to be contractually bound or otherwise within the meaning of *Bradford v. Roulston*.

It does not matter if Tony was a professional lifeguard or if he had performed the rescue as part of his normal duties. The same principles apply.

Summaries

France: Both promises probably are enforceable because they are promises to perform a natural obligation. Nevertheless, the promisee has an evidentiary problem. He must produce a writing or show that it was morally impossible to obtain one.

Another possibility is that the act of rescuing will be considered an 'offer' which was tacitly accepted, thereby forming a 'contract of rescue' (*convention d'assistance*).

Some might call it a *gestion d'affaires*, but the difficulty in doing so is that French law imposes a duty to rescue.

Belgium: The promise of compensation for saving the promisor's life is enforceable because it is a promise to perform a natural obligation. The promise of compensation for saving the life of his adult child is probably enforceable for the same reason.

The Netherlands: The promises might be enforceable as promises to perform a natural obligation, but it is doubtful because there is no authority squarely in point and promises to make compensation for services received have been held to be promises to make gifts.

The doctrine of *negotiorum gestio* would not apply.

Spain: The promises might be enforceable as promises to perform a natural obligation, but it is doubtful because these are not the typical

---

[72] See Treitel, *Contract*, ch. 3.   [73] See *Re McArdle* [1951] Ch. 669.

instances in which courts have recognized natural obligations. Typical instances involve family relations. A court would be less likely to enforce the promise of compensation for saving the adult child since the promisor himself did not obtain a benefit.

The promises might be enforceable as a *donación remuneratoria*, that is, a gift to compensate the donee for services rendered for which the donor is not legally required to pay. If so, at least according to many scholars, the formality is not required (see Case 1) except to the extent the amount promised exceeds fair compensation.

Portugal: Most likely, the promises are unenforceable because they were not made in writing. But the promise in Case 2(a) (where Kurt himself was rescued) may be enforceable as an acknowledgment of a duty to make compensation to Tony as a *negotiorum gestor*, a duty that would exist even absent a promise. On that theory, the promise would be enforceable even if Tony were a professional lifeguard but not if performing the rescue were part of his normal duties.

Italy: The promises are not enforceable. While Italian law recognizes that one who performs a natural obligation cannot reclaim his performance, it does not accept the doctrine that a promise to pay a natural obligation is enforceable absent compliance with the formalities applicable to gifts. Moreover, although the Civil Code accords special treatment to 'remunerative gifts' (which are motivated by gratitude or a desire to compensate for past services) and 'liberalities according to usage' (which are out of proportion to the value of such services), it does not dispense with the formalities in these cases either. Gino Gorla believes that promises to pay for services received are enforceable if the services have a monetary value and the amount promised is proportionate to their value, but this doctrine has not yet been accepted by the courts or by other scholars.

Austria: Both promises would be enforceable as promises to perform a natural obligation. Alternatively, in Case 2(a) in which the promisor is rescued, the rescuer may be a *negotiorum gestor* since he acted in a situation of urgency for the other party's benefit without time to consult him. If so, the promise could be enforceable as the settlement of the claim which a *negotiorum gestor* has even absent a promise. In Case 2(b), in which the promisor's adult child is rescued, it is harder to apply this theory since the promisor himself has received no benefit. It is hard to apply it even in Case 2(a) if the promisee is a professional rescuer since then he is performing a prior legal duty.

Germany: The formalities required for gifts are also required when promises are made in fulfilment of a moral obligation.

In Case 2(a), in which the promisor is rescued, the rescuer may have a claim for *Geschäftsführung ohne Auftrag* (the German *negotiorum gestio*) and, if so, the promise would be enforceable if it were interpreted, not as a mere expression of gratitude, but as an acknowledgment of this claim. In Case 2(b), in which the promisor's adult child is rescued, there would be no such claim since the promisor himself did not benefit, and so the promise would not be enforceable. In Case 2(a), there would be no such claim if the rescuer were a professional performing a prior legal duty, and so, again, the promise would not be enforceable.

Greece: It has been argued that the normal formalities for gifts do not apply to promises to fulfil a moral obligation. If so, the promises are enforceable, but the question has not yet been resolved.

Scotland: The promises are not enforceable unless made with the normal formality.

England: Unless the rescue was performed at the promisor's request, the promises are not enforceable because they neither have consideration nor are made by deed ('under seal').

Ireland: Unless the rescue was performed at the promisor's request, the promises are not enforceable because they neither have consideration nor are made by deed ('under seal').

Preliminary comparisons

Promise to perform a natural obligation: Some systems enforce informal promises to perform a so-called 'natural obligation'. The French, Belgian, and Austrian reporters believe that their courts would enforce the promises in Case 2 on that ground, although in France the promisor has the evidentiary problem that he must produce a writing or show that it was morally impossible to obtain one. The Greek reporter believes her courts might enforce the promises on these grounds. Although there is no clear authority in the Netherlands and Spain, the reporters from these countries are more doubtful, the Dutch reporter because his courts have held that promises to pay for past services are gifts, the Spanish reporter because her courts have recognized natural obligations primarily in the context of family relationships. In Italy, courts and scholars have not accepted the doctrine that informal promises to perform natural obligations are enforceable although one scholar, Gino Gorla, believes that they should be. This doctrine is not recognized in Germany, Scotland, England or Ireland.

The Belgian and Spanish reporters thought that their courts would be less likely to enforce the promise in Case 2(b) on this ground since the rescue benefited, not the promisor, but his adult child.

Donación remuneratoria: In Spain, many scholars believe that an informal promise to make a *donación remuneratoria* is enforceable, that is, a gift to compensate the donee for services rendered for which the donor is not legally required to pay. If the courts recognize that doctrine, these promises might be enforced. In Portugal, however, a promise to make such a gift (*doaçao remuneratória*) is subject to the same formal requirement as other promises of gifts: it must be made in writing.

Convention d'assistance: In France, possibly, the promises may be enforceable because the act of rescuing will be considered an 'offer' which was tacitly accepted, thereby forming a 'contract of rescue' (*convention d'assistance*).

Negotiorum gestio (gestion d'affaires, Geschäftsführung ohne Auftrag): The Portuguese, Austrian, and German reporters thought it possible (though not likely, in the Portuguese reporter's opinion) that the rescuer might have a claim even absent a promise because he performed a service that was urgently needed when there was no time to ask if it was wanted. If so, then the promise could be enforced if it were interpreted as an acknowledgment or settlement of this claim. This theory could not be applied, or only with difficulty, in Case 2(b) where it was not the promisor who was rescued but his adult child. It could not be applied where the rescuer was performing a prior legal duty, for example, because he was a professional doing his job. The French reporter noted that the theory would not work in France because French law imposes a duty to rescue on everyone, and therefore every rescuer is performing a legal duty.

Prior request: In England and Ireland, the rescuer might recover if the rescue were performed at the promisor's request even though the promise was made afterwards, but, as both reporters noted, on the facts of the case, it is not likely that a prior request was made.

Case 3: promises to pay debts not legally due

Case

Ian, now solvent and an adult, had once owed money to Anna that she could not claim legally because (a) Ian's debt had been discharged in bankruptcy, (b) the debt was barred by the passage of time (by prescription or by a statute of limitations), or (c) the debt was incurred when Ian was too young to be bound by his contracts. Ian now promises to pay the debt. Can Anna enforce the promise if he changes his mind?

Discussions

FRANCE

In Case 3(a), Ian's debt to Anna was discharged in bankruptcy. Under French law, although he is no longer legally bound and cannot be successfully sued, he remains 'naturally' bound. His obligation is not purely moral. If he promises to pay, the debt will become legally due again.[1]

As noted in discussing Case 2, this theory of natural obligations has been developed by case law, and is considered to be an implication of art. 1235 of the French Civil Code. As a consequence, there is no closed list of natural obligations, but French academics agree that a debt discharged in bankruptcy is among them.

In Case 3(b), in which the debt was barred by the passage of time, it is not possible to give a quick answer. French case law has distinguished two types of prescriptions that take place under the French Civil Code: presumed and normal prescriptions.

The so-called presumed (*assumptive*) prescriptions are found in arts.

[1] Civ. 1, 14 Jan. 1952, D 1952, 177.

88

2271, 2272, and 2273. In these situations, a presumption arises that a debt was paid. It is then possible to prove that no payment was ever made. Among the admissible pieces of evidence is any type of acknowledgment from the debtor that he did not pay his debt. Ian's promise to pay would definitely be regarded as such an acknowledgment. Anna could, consequently, claim the original debt, and Ian's new promise would only be taken into account as a piece of evidence.

The so-called normal prescriptions prevent the creditor from suing his debtor when he is not legally bound any more. However, case law has always considered him to be a 'natural debtor' of his former creditor.[2] Consequently, the same rules apply as in Case 3(a). His new promise makes his debt become legally binding again.

In Case 3(c), Ian was too young to be bound by contract. The promise he made was voidable.[3] Nevertheless, because he promised again when he was an adult, Anna may be able to enforce the contract. It depends on whether or not Ian brought an action to have the contract rescinded.

Even if he brought such an action before making a fresh promise to pay, the rescission of the contract does not have a final effect under French law because debts declared void by a court have been recognized as another instance of 'natural' debts.[4] In order to fit into this category, the minor had to be aware of what he was doing when he entered the first contract. Otherwise, not even a natural debt will remain. If he was aware, the rules on natural obligations already discussed will apply, and the new promise will make the natural debt become a legal one and therefore enforceable.

On the other hand, if Ian has not brought an action to rescind the contract before making a fresh promise to pay, then the original promise will remain valid as long as he does not do so. In contrast, debts discharged in bankruptcy (see Case 3(a)) or barred by the passage of time (see Case 3(b)) are no longer valid even when a court has not intervened, unless, as we have seen, a new promise has been made. Nevertheless, Ian could still challenge the contract and ask for its rescission at the time that Anna sues him to enforce it unless he has already made a new promise to pay the debt.

If he has made such a new promise, it will be deemed to confirm the original voidable contract. Under French law, art. 1338 of the Civil Code has been broadly construed to allow some voidable contracts to be

---

[2] Req., 7 Jan. 1938, DP 1940, 1, 5.

[3] A voidable contract has the characteristic that French law calls 'nullité relative'. It is not merely void for all purposes *ab initio*. See Terré, Simler, and Lequette, *Les obligations* no. 92, p. 84.   [4] Civ. 9 March 1896, S. 1897, 1, 225, note Esmein.

confirmed and thereby become unchallengeable.[5] They include contracts voidable because of a vitiating factor or because a party was too young to enter a contract, as is the case here.

BELGIUM

In Case 3(a), Ian is freed from all debts at the conclusion of bankruptcy proceedings. By making the promise, however, Ian is fulfilling a natural obligation which the promise converts into a civil obligation (see Cases 1 and 2). Anna can therefore enforce it.[6]

In Case 3(b), the debt is barred by the passage of time. Passage of time does not affect the existence of the debt itself but only whether its payment can be required (*exigibilité*). Accordingly, one who pays such a debt does not have the right to be reimbursed.[7] Recently, the *Cour de cassation* applied the same line of reasoning to a promise to pay such a debt. It repeated that the passage of time does not affect the existence of a debt but only whether the debtor can be required to pay, and added that the obligation to pay does survive as a natural obligation.[8]

In Case 3(c), Ian's debt is invalid since it was incurred when he lacked legal capacity because of his age. Nevertheless, the invalidity is 'relative'. 'Relative' invalidity means that a debt is voidable and that its invalidity may be asserted by the person for whose protection the law regards it as invalid: in the present case, the minor or his legal representative. In contrast, the invalidity of a debt would be 'absolute' if it is void for everyone and the judge must regard it as invalid even though nobody claims that it is. In the present case, an action to avoid the debt is time-barred unless it

---

[5] Flour and Aubert, *Droit civil* no. 349, p. 250; Terré, Simler, and Lequette, *Les obligations* no. 373, p. 313.

[6] See Van Ommeslaghe, *Droit des obligations*, 361, discussing a situation in which a debtor obtains a release of 50 per cent of his debt, as a result of a legal settlement with his creditors (*concordat*), but the debtor nevertheless pays everything back. The debtor cannot recover the 50 per cent from which he had been freed.

[7] Cass., 22 Sept. 1986, JTT, 1987, 42.

[8] Cass., 14 May 1992, Pas., I, 798. In this case, a lessee owed rent, some of which had not been paid since 1979. (The period for prescription in the case of a lease is one year.) The lessor demanded payment in 1985. The lessee responded by a letter in which he acknowledged all his debts and made a partial payment. The trial court required the lessee to pay the total amount of rent due since 1979. The *Cour de cassation* affirmed, holding that the letter of the lessee acknowledged all the rents, even those which had become time-barred, and that it transformed a natural obligation into a civil obligation to pay the rent that was time-barred. See the comments of S. Stijns, D. Van Gerven, and P. Wéry, 'Chronique de jurisprudence. Les obligations: les sources (1985–1995)', JT, 1996, no. 6.

is brought within ten years of the day on which the incapacity ceased (see art. 1304 of the Civil Code). The action is time-barred after that period because it is presumed that the debtor has confirmed the debt. If the debtor confirms his intention to pay the debt after he is old enough to have legal capacity but before it is time-barred, then the debt ceases to be invalid and no action to avoid it can be brought.[9] Consequently, Ian's promise to pay his debt can be enforced.

THE NETHERLANDS

In Cases 3(a) and 3(b), there is a natural obligation.[10] A natural obligation can be transformed by making a promise into an enforceable obligation (art. 6:5(3) of the Civil Code). The transformation of a natural obligation into an enforceable obligation is not a gift (art. 6:5(3)). Therefore, the formal requirements described earlier need not be met (see Case 1).

In Case 3(c), Ian had a contractual debt to Anna which was unenforceable because Ian was too young to be bound by contract. This is a *casus non dabilis* under Dutch law. Incapacity makes the contract voidable (art. 3:32(2) of the Civil Code[11]). After avoidance there remains no obligation, either civil or natural. Therefore, if there is no counter-promise from Anna, Ian's new promise is a gift which is unenforceable, because the formal requirements are not met (see Case 1). If Ian has not had the contract avoided, he may confirm it now (art. 3:55(1)[12]). But this confirmation is a gift if Anna promised nothing in return.

SPAIN

Case 3(a) could not arise under Spanish law because debts are not discharged by bankruptcy proceedings. Article 1920 of the Civil Code provides: 'In the absence of express stipulation to the contrary between the debtor and his creditors, the latter shall retain their right, following the insolvency proceedings, to collect the uncollected portion of their debts from the assets that the debtor might thereafter acquire.'

---

[9] See C.-L. Closset and F. Lainé, *Répertoire notarial, les personnes*, vol. I, *A capacité juridique en général* (1986), no. 105.

[10] See Asser/Hartkamp, vol. I, no. 70.

[11] Article 3:32(2) of the Civil Code: 'A juridical act of an incapable person may be annulled . . .'

[12] Article 3:55(1) of the Civil Code: 'The power to invoke a ground for annulment in order to annul a juridical act lapses when the person in possession of this right confirms the juridical act after the prescription period for the action to annul upon that ground has started to run.'

In Case 3(b), Anna's claim is barred by prescription. Although Spanish law provides regulation for the prescription of duties and actions, it is generally understood that the Spanish Civil Code refers not to prescription of duties but to prescription of the enforceability (Statute of Limitations in English common law), even though the Code speaks of both things. Some authors contend that only a moral duty remains after prescription.[13] If we assume that a moral obligation exists in Case 3(b), then, after the new promise is made, the moral obligation becomes a legal obligation and is enforceable.

If the debt was incurred by Ian when he was a minor, then Ian is not bound before the unilateral promise is made because the contract lacked mutual assent. According to art. 1263 of the Civil Code, an 'unemancipated minor' 'may not give consent'. But Ian's new promise will be a ratification of his will which makes the prior contract enforceable. Article 1311 of the Civil Code provides: 'Ratification may be made either expressly or tacitly. Tacit ratification shall be considered to exist in instances where having knowledge of the cause of nullity, and such cause having ceased, the person with the right to invoke the nullity executes an act that necessarily implies the intention to renounce it.'

PORTUGAL

Case 3(a) could not occur under Portuguese law. The debts of the bankrupt are not discharged by the bankruptcy proceedings. These proceedings establish only which creditors will be paid from the bankrupt's current assets and to what extent (art. 209 of the Bankruptcy Proceedings Code) but they do not extinguish the creditor's rights. Therefore these rights can always be enforced as to assets the debtor acquires later if his economic situation changes.

In Case 3(b), Anna can enforce the promise to pay the time-barred debt. The effect of the passage of time in Portuguese law is not to extinguish the debt automatically but to allow the debtor legally to refuse to pay it. The debtor has to raise the defence of prescription, and can be forced to pay the debt if he does not (arts. 304(1) and 303 of the Civil Code). If the claim is barred by prescription, the debtor is considered to be under a moral obligation. In one respect, the result is the same as that discussed in Case 2(a): if the debtor voluntarily fulfils the obligation, he cannot ask for restitution

---

[13] Díez Picazo and Gullón, *Sistema de derecho civil*, vol. I, 474; Castán Tobeñas, *Derecho civil*, vol. II–1, 968.

of the payment. In this case, however, the recognition of a duty to pay has the same effect as a voluntary payment. Therefore, if Ian promises to pay Anna a claim barred by prescription, he would not be entitled to raise the defence of prescription afterwards. He can be forced to pay the debt, even if he changes his mind (art. 304(2)).

In Case 3(c), the debt incurred by Ian as a minor is considered to be voidable but not void. Even if it has been paid, it can be annulled at Ian's parents' request within a period of a year after it was incurred or at Ian's request within the same period after he becomes eighteen. If the debt has not yet been paid, annulment can be requested at any time (arts. 125 and 287(2) of the Civil Code). Nevertheless, the debt is no longer voidable if Ian's parents confirm it or if he does so himself after he becomes an adult (arts. 125(2) and 288). Therefore, Ian's promise is regarded as such a confirmation, and it is legally enforceable.

ITALY

Anna would not be able to enforce Ian's informal promise in Case 3(a). She would be able to enforce it in Cases 3(b) and 3(c) only if Ian intentionally renewed his obligation while aware that the debt was barred by the passage of time (Case 3(b)) or that the original contract was voidable (Case 3(c)).

In Case 3(a), Ian promised to fulfil a moral obligation.[14] According to the Civil Code, case law, and a vast majority of scholars, such a promise is not enforceable at all[15] (see Case 2).

In Case 3(b), if Ian promised to pay the debt without knowing that it was already barred by the passage of time, Anna cannot sue him successfully for the payment. The position of Italian law is that Anna's claim is still alive, but nevertheless, when she brings this claim, Ian has the procedural defence of prescription. If he were to pay the debt, he would not be able to reclaim his payment (art. 2940 of the Civil Code). Most Italian scholars do not consider payment of a debt barred by prescription to be fulfilment of a moral obligation because, as just noted, the creditor's claim is deemed to be still alive but subject to a procedural defence. Recent case law takes the position that partial payment of a barred debt does not itself constitute

---

[14] See the discussion of Case 2. See also Gorla, *Il contratto*, 142–3; Marini, *Promessa ed affidamento*, 400 ff.

[15] See L. Nivarra, 'Obbligazione Naturale', *Digesto* (1995), 366; A. Zaccaria, 'Novazione', *Digesto* (1995), 280 at 288, with accompanying references. See also art. 1234 of the Civil Code.

a presumption of the implicit intention to give up the procedural excep-tion of prescription, which, therefore, is still available to the debtor for the unsatisfied portion of debt.[16]

If Ian deliberately promised to pay Anna a barred debt while aware of the fact that it was barred by the passage of time, then the promise would be enforceable because it constituted a renewal, or, in technical terms, a novation of the original debt (art. 1230 of the Civil Code).[17] According to some scholars, however, art. 1234(2) of the Civil Code[18] is applicable by analogy, and, therefore, for the novation to be valid, the intention to waive the right to raise the defence of prescription must appear unequivocally.

In Case 3(c), the obligation originally undertaken may be annulled because Ian lacked legal capacity on account of his age (arts. 1425 and 1441 ff. of the Civil Code). Nevertheless, Ian's promise is enforceable if, as an adult with full capacity, he explicitly ratified the obligation incurred while aware that the original contract can be avoided because he was too young (arts. 1234(2) (novation) and 1444 (validation) of the Civil Code).[19]

By Gorla's view (see Case 2), the promises in Cases 3(a), 3(b) and 3(c) would probably all have a sufficient basis for enforcement (*cause suffisante*), and so be legally binding. As mentioned earlier, his view is not held by the majority of Italian legal scholars.

AUSTRIA

There are two main types of bankruptcy proceedings in Austrian law. The first is called *Ausgleichsverfahren*. Here the insolvent debtor offers to pay his creditors a certain percentage of his debt. The rest of his debt is then dis-charged. There remains, however, a 'natural obligation' (*Naturalobligation*

---

[16] See Cass. civ., sez. lav., 7 Jan. 1994 n. 94, in Giust. civ. I (1995), 567.

[17] Article 1230 of the Civil Code: 'Objective novation: The obligation is extinguished when the parties substitute a new obligation having a different object or a different title for the old obligation. The intention to extinguish the preceding obligation must appear in an unequivocal manner.'

[18] Article 1234 of the Civil Code: 'Lack of effect of novation: The novation is without effect if the original debt did not exist. When the original obligation arose from a voidable transaction, the novation is valid if the debtor validly assumed the new debt knowing the defect in the original transaction.'

[19] Article 1444 of the Civil Code: 'Validation: The contracting party entitled to sue for annulment can validate the voidable contract by a declaration containing a reference to the contract and to the cause for voidability thereof, and a declaration of intention to validate it. A contract is likewise validated if the contracting party entitled to sue for annulment, knowing of the voidability, has voluntarily performed it. The validation has no effect if the person who does it is not in a condition to validly conclude the contract.'

or *obligatio naturalis*). It has the consequence that if the debtor decides to pay a debt that was discharged, he cannot claim the payment back. The second type of bankruptcy proceeding is the so-called *Konkursverfahren*. Its principal purpose is to sell off the assets of the bankrupt in order to pay his creditors. His debts are not discharged.[20]

Consequently, Case 3(a) can arise only with respect to an *Ausgleichsverfahren* if Ian promises to pay Anna a debt which has been discharged. Here the promise is binding.[21] It would be construed as a waiver of the defence to Ian's claim that the debt was discharged through the insolvency proceedings. Such a waiver is possible because the court will take the discharge into account only if the debtor raises it as a defence.

In Case 3(b), Anna can enforce the promise. It would be construed as a waiver of the defence to Ian's claim that it is barred by the passage of time. Such a waiver is possible because the court will take this bar to a claim into account only if the debtor raises it as a defence.

In Case 3(c), two different situations must be distinguished since Austrian law has two different rules governing contracts made by minors or other persons who lack legal capacity. The first rule applies to persons under seven years of age.[22] In general, they are unable to enter into a contract.[23] Any promise they make is invalid.[24] Such a contract cannot be acknowledged after the minor has come of age.[25] If Ian made the contract when he was below seven, he therefore would not be bound by his second promise.[26] He would be bound by it only if it could be interpreted as a new contract for which the form requirement does not apply.

The second rule applies to persons who are at least seven years old.[27] They can make a promise which becomes valid when their legal guardian gives his approval to the contract. The validity of the contract therefore

---

[20] If the bankrupt is not a company, it is possible under certain conditions that a discharge can be granted even within a *Konkursverfahren*. See §§ 181 ff. Konkursordnung (Bankruptcy Act).

[21] See G. Stanzl in Klang, *ABGB* vol. IV/1, 602. OGH Rspr 1932/47; GlU 6902. The other authors (W. Wilburg in Klang, *ABGB* vol. VI, 462 and Ehrenzweig, *System* vol. II/1, 7) to whom Stanzl refers, however, discuss a different topic, namely the question whether a person can reclaim what he has paid in fulfilment of a natural obligation.

[22] § 865 of the Civil Code.   [23] There are some exceptions. See § 151 of the Civil Code.

[24] The court must take this basis for invalidity into consideration even if it is not raised as a defence. OGH EvBl 1973/86.   [25] P. Rummel in Rummel, *ABGB*, § 865 no. 2; SZ 38/217.

[26] It is possible that the first contract was executed and Anna has a claim in unjust enrichment against Ian. The validity of such a claim does not depend on the other party's age. Such a claim could be acknowledged by a second promise after Ian has come of age.

[27] § 865(2) of the Civil Code. Persons aged over seven are also able to accept gifts.

depends on the condition that it is approved by the guardian.[28] After the minor has come of age, he can approve of the contract himself, provided the guardian has not yet refused to approve it.[29] If Ian's guardian has not yet given his approval, Ian's promise would be interpreted as a confirmation of the original promise. If Ian's guardian had refused to approve the contract, there would remain no obligation that could be confirmed. It would therefore be necessary to conclude a second contract.

GERMANY

Case 3(a) could not arise under previous German bankruptcy law because debts are not discharged. Therefore Ian would already be obligated to pay without the additional promise.

German bankruptcy law changed on 1 January 1999. Under the new law a debtor is free after paying his creditors as much as possible for seven years (§§ 287 and 301 InsO). After the seven years, though the creditor no longer has a claim, if the debtor pays, the debtor cannot demand the money back. The payment is not regarded as an unjust enrichment.

Ian's promise is an acknowledgment of indebtedness which is an abstract obligation – abstract from the reason or *causa*[30] for which it is made. If, in fact, there is no *causa*, the acknowledgment can be claimed back as an unjust enrichment (§ 812 of the Civil Code[31]). This enables a court to ensure that a person was really indebted originally.

An acknowledgment of indebtedness is valid only if it is made in writing (§§ 780 and 781 of the Civil Code[32]). The reason is to protect people from making such a promise without enough thought. This protection is

---

[28] The other party can ask the guardian to declare whether he accepts the contract or not. If he declines to make such a declaration within an appropriate period of time, the contract is invalid. See § 865 last sentence of the Civil Code.

[29] In this case the conclusion of a second contract is necessary.

[30] The transfer of property or another right is strictly distinguished from the obligation to transfer the right. The transfer needs an obligation as a *causa*. Otherwise it will be deemed to be an unjust enrichment which can be reclaimed (§§ 812–22 of the Civil Code). The same is true of abstract obligations such as an acknowledgment of indebtedness (§§ 780 and 781). Therefore, the performance of a promise cannot be reclaimed if the promise itself is a valid *causa* for the performance or if there is some other *causa*.

[31] The provision prescribes that every enrichment for which there is no *causa* must be repaid.

[32] Both provisions only impose the formality for the abstract obligation of an acknowledgment of indebtedness.

necessary because the acknowledgment changes the burden of proof when a claim of unjust enrichment is made.

Under the new bankruptcy law, this situation is comparable to a game or a bet because in both cases there is no legal obligation to pay. Nevertheless, a person who pays cannot demand the money back (§ 762(1) of the Civil Code). Therefore, it would be appropriate to apply § 762(2) in this situation as well. Section 762(2) provides that acknowledgments of indebtedness are not enforceable if the original 'obligation' arose from a game or a bet. Therefore, Anna cannot enforce the promise but if Ian pays he cannot claim the money back. This result is not absolutely certain because how the new law will apply has yet to be discussed by scholars.

In Case 3(b), the claim is time-barred. Such a claim does not cease to exist. Rather, the debtor has a defence that entitles him to refuse payment (§ 222 of the Civil Code[33]). In such a situation, even though the obligation is not enforceable, a promise to pay will be interpreted as a renunciation of the defence. Such a renunciation can be declared only after the claim was already time-barred.[34] That is precisely what has happened in our case. Therefore, Anna can enforce the promise because Ian has lost his defence.

The result in Case 3(c) depends on the age of Ian at the time of the original contract and on whether his legal guardian had already refused to approve the contract.

If Ian made the original promise when he was between ages seven and eighteen and his guardian did not refuse to approve it, Ian can approve it himself because he is an adult now (§§ 107[35] and 108(2) and (3) of the Civil Code). The promise he made as an adult can only be interpreted as such an approval, and Ian cannot withdraw it. Therefore, Anna has an enforceable claim.

If Ian concluded the original contract when he was younger than seven years or if his guardian refused to approve it, the contract is void (§ 104, § 105(1), § 108(2) of the Civil Code.) Therefore, he could no longer approve the original contract. His promise and Anna's acceptance have to be interpreted as a new contract with exactly the same content. This new contract is valid unless one of the usual legal requirements is missing. This

---

[33] Section 222: '(1) The debtor is entitled to refuse payment of a claim which is time barred. (2) If he pays, he cannot demand the money back even if he did not know that the claim was time barred. This holds true for acknowledgments and collateral as well.'

[34] RGZ 78 (1912), 130; BGHZ 57 (1972), 204 (209).

[35] The promise of a minor is valid only with the approval of his legal guardian.

question has to be answered from the perspective of the time when the new contract was agreed upon. If all these requirements were met, Anna would have an enforceable claim as well.

GREECE

In Case 3(a), Ian promises to pay a debt discharged in bankruptcy. According to the Greek law of bankruptcy, immediately after the adjudication of bankruptcy the creditors cannot claim their debts individually. Instead, they have to bring their claims in the bankruptcy proceedings.[36] If they do not do that they still cannot proceed against the bankrupt individually, and their claims may eventually be barred by the passage of time. As soon as the bankruptcy proceedings end, the immunity of the bankrupt is over and the creditors can proceed individually to enforce their claims.[37]

In Case 3(b), Ian promises to pay a debt that is barred by the passage of time. In Greek law, with the passage of time, if the holder of a right takes no action, rights lose their force. This means that the right continues to exist but that the claim that stems from it is subject to prescription and can no longer be brought.[38]

Article 272 of the Civil Code[39] provides: 'Upon the term of prescription being completed the obligor has the right to refuse the performance of the undertaking. What has been paid in ignorance of the effect of prescription cannot be claimed back. A written acknowledgment made by contract in ignorance of the prescription of a claim that is extinguished thereby as well as the furnishing of security shall be valid.' Under this provision, Ian's promise would revive Anna's claim only if he did not know that her claim was barred by the passage of time and only if he agreed to pay in a written contract.

Nevertheless, if the parties know that the debt has already been prescribed and Ian now promises to pay it, he has made what is termed a renunciation of the right of prescription. Such a renunciation can be made orally.[40] Therefore, Ian is obliged to keep his promise to Anna.

In Case 3(c), the debt is void initially because a minor has incurred it.

---

[36] K. Rokas, *Bankruptcy*, 13th edn (1978), 136.
[37] In our law bankruptcy does not discharge claims unless there is a bankruptcy composition and the creditors have agreed to that. *Ibid.*
[38] Stathopoulos, *Contract Law*, 207.
[39] Georgiadis in Georgiadis and Stathopoulos, *Civil Code*, art. 272.
[40] Georgiadis, *General Principles*, 173–86; Thessaloniki Court of Appeal 1861/1993 HellD 37 (1996), 1436.

Therefore, Ian's promise is deemed to be one made without a 'cause'. For it to be the basis of a new claim, it would have to comply with art. 873 of the Civil Code,[41] which provides:

A contract whereby a promise is given or a debt is acknowledged in such a manner as to give rise to an obligation irrespective of any consideration for the debt shall be valid if the promise or the declaration of acknowledgment were made in writing. A written promise or declaration of acknowledgment with no reference to consideration for the debt shall in case of doubt be deemed made for the same purpose.

The meaning of this article is that the written acknowledgment of the debt is valid even if the cause of the debt does not exist or is null. Thus, Ian will not be obliged to keep his promise if it was not made in writing.

SCOTLAND

Again, the important provision of the law of Scotland is s. 1(2) of the Requirements of Writing (Scotland) Act 1995, in terms of which the promise will only be enforceable if constituted in writing, as it is a gratuitous unilateral obligation.[42] Therefore Anna can enforce the promise if it is in writing even if Ian changes his mind at a subsequent point. The circumstances in which the debt arose and could not legally be claimed are again an irrelevance in Scots law.

ENGLAND

It is clear in English law that only the last of the three promises is enforceable. The reason the first and second promises are unenforceable is that no consideration was given in exchange for them (see Case 1). What Anna did for Ian, she did in the past; that is, her consideration was 'past consideration' (see Case 2). As noted in the discussion to Case 2, prior obligations that are not binding because of a specific legal defect have been held in certain cases to constitute valid consideration for a subsequent promise (under the misleading heading of 'moral consideration'). The obligations described in Cases 3(a) and 3(b) were indeed considered at one time to fall into this category, and hence to be exceptions to the need for 'fresh' consideration,[43] but these exceptions have since been overruled, and it is clear now that each promise is unenforceable: see, for example, *Jakeman* v.

---

[41] N. Livanis, *Causal Acknowledgement of Debt* (1984).   [42] See Case 1.

[43] See Treitel, *Contract,* 75–6.

Cook[44] (claims discharged in bankruptcy), Limitations Act 1980, s. 29(7) (statute of limitation – barred claims). Case 3(c), the promise to make good a debt unenforceable by reason of minority, is however still a valid exception to the consideration rule: see, for example, *Williams* v. *Moor*.[45] There is no well-accepted explanation for why obligations incurred by minors are treated in this special way, nor for why English law once allowed a relatively large number of exceptions to the rules regarding past consideration.[46]

IRELAND

The principle of past consideration again applies here (see Case 1). Although Ian now promises to pay the debt once owed by him to Anna, she must show that some form of consideration was provided by her or that a deed under seal was executed to this effect.

In Case 3(a), where Ian's debt had been discharged in bankruptcy and Ian is now no longer legally bound to Anna, his subsequent promise to pay the debt is not legally binding as this subsequent promise is not supported by consideration (see Case 2).

The same principles apply in Case 3(b) where the debt is barred by the passage of time. In addition, s. 56 of the Statute of Limitations 1957 provides that where any right of action has accrued to recover any debt and the person liable therefor acknowledges the debt, the right of action shall be deemed to have accrued on and not before the date of the acknowledgment. However, s. 58(1) of the Statute provides that every such acknowledgment shall be in writing and shall be signed by the person making the acknowledgment. Accordingly, an acknowledgment for the purposes of satisfying s. 56 of the Statute of Limitations 1957 has not been made and so no right of action has accrued to Anna under the statute to recover the debt.

Again, in Case 3(c), Ian is not contractually bound by his later promise to pay the debt where the debt was incurred when Ian was too young to be bound by his contract. Section 2 of the Infants Relief Act 1874 provides: 'No action shall be brought whereby to charge any person upon any promise made after full age to pay any debt contracted during infancy or upon any ratification made after full age of any promise or contract made in infancy, whether there shall or shall not be any new consideration for such promise or ratification after full age.'

[44] [1878] 4 Ex D 26.   [45] [1843] 11 M & W 256.   [46] Treitel, *Contract*, 504.

Thus, if a discharged bankrupt, a person whose debt was barred by the passage of time, or an infant promised to pay a debt incurred during bankruptcy, a previous period, or infancy respectively, this promise would not be enforceable.

Around the eighteenth century an attempt was made by the English courts to define consideration so as to include certain pre-existing 'moral' obligations. In certain cases it was found that the consideration for a promise to pay a statute-barred debt or a promise by a discharged bankrupt to pay a debt contracted before the discharge was binding was said to be a 'moral' obligation of the defendant to pay the debt. However, in *Eastwood* v. *Kenyon*,[47] the English court rejected the plaintiff's argument that a promise by the defendant was binding because he was under a moral obligation to perform it. It was clearly stated by Lord Denham CJ that such an argument 'annihilates the necessity for any consideration at all in as much as the mere fact of giving a promise creates a moral obligation to perform it'. This moral consideration theory, which was dismissed as alien to English law in, *inter alia*, *Eastwood* v. *Kenyon*, at no time formed part of the jurisprudence developed by the Irish courts.

Summaries

France: The promises to pay the debts discharged in bankruptcy (Case 3(a)) or incurred as a minor (Case 3(c)) are enforceable because they are promises to fulfil natural obligations. The promise to pay the time-barred debt (Case 3(b)) is enforceable either on this ground, or because the effect of prescription is that the debt is presumed not to have been incurred, and the promise is an acknowledgment proving that it was.

Belgium: The promises to pay the debts discharged in bankruptcy (Case 3(a)) or barred by time (Case 3(b)) are enforceable because they are promises to fulfil natural obligations. The promise to pay the debt incurred as a minor (Case 3(c)) is enforceable because it is invalid 'relatively' rather than 'absolutely', and so becomes enforceable once it is confirmed.

The Netherlands: The promises to pay the debts discharged in bankruptcy (Case 3(a)) or barred by time (Case 3(b)) are enforceable because they are promises to fulfil natural obligations. The promise to pay a debt incurred as a minor (Case 3(c)) counts as a gift, and therefore is unenforceable absent the required formalities.

Spain: Case 3(a) cannot arise since debts are not discharged in bankruptcy.

[47] [1840] A & E 438.

According to some scholars, the promise to pay the debt barred by time (Case 3(b)) is enforceable because it is a promise to pay a natural obligation. The promise to pay a debt incurred as a minor (Case 3(c)) is enforceable because it is a ratification of the debt.

Portugal: Case 3(a) cannot arise since debts are not discharged in bankruptcy. The promise to pay the time-barred debt (Case 3(b)) is enforceable because there is a moral obligation, and, in contrast to other moral obligations, the mere promise to pay this one is binding. The promise to pay the debt incurred as a minor (Case 3(c)) is enforceable because it was confirmed after reaching majority.

Italy: The promise to pay the debt discharged in bankruptcy (Case 3(a)) is not enforceable because courts and most scholars agree that the usual formalities are required even when a promise is made to perform a moral obligation. The other promises are enforceable if the promisor was aware that the debt was barred by the passage of time (Case 3(b)) or voidable due to lack of legal capacity (Case 3(c)) because the promise ratifies these debts.

Austria: The promise to pay a debt discharged in bankruptcy (Case 3(a)) is enforceable because a natural obligation remains, and the promise waives the defence that the debt was discharged. The promise to pay the time-barred debt (Case 3(b)) is enforceable because it also waives the defence. The promise to pay a debt incurred as a minor (Case 3(c)) is enforceable because it ratifies the debt.

Germany: Case 3(a) could not have arisen before 1999 because debts were not discharged in bankruptcy. It can arise under the new bankruptcy statute that took effect on 1 January 1999. The promise will probably not be enforceable but there has been too little discussion to be sure. The promise to pay a time-barred debt (Case 3(b)) is enforceable because the promisor is deemed to have renounced his defence. The promise to pay a debt incurred as a minor (Case 3(c)) is enforceable as an approval of the original contract provided the debt was incurred when the promisor was at least seven years old.

Greece: Case 3(a) could not arise under Greek bankruptcy law. Under special provisions of the Greek Civil Code, the promises in Cases 3(b) and 3(c) are binding only if made in writing, and the promise in 3(b) only if, in addition, the promisor knows that the debt is time-barred.

Scotland: None of the promises is enforceable without the usual formality: a written document.

England: Under current law, the promises to pay the debts discharged in bankruptcy (Case 3(a)) or barred by time (Case 3(b)) are unenforceable because they lack consideration and are not made by deed ('under seal').

At one time they were enforceable on the grounds that they had so-called 'moral consideration'. The promise to pay a debt incurred as a minor (Case 3(c)) is enforceable because English law recognizes an exception in this case to the normal requirement of consideration, although there is no general agreement as to why this exception is made.

Ireland: The doctrine of 'moral consideration' once applied in English courts (see *England*, above) was never acknowledged by the Irish case law. The promise to pay the debt discharged in bankruptcy (Case 3(a)) is unenforceable because it lacks consideration and was not made by deed ('under seal'). The promise to pay the time-barred debt (Case 3(b)) is unenforceable because a statute provides that such a promise is enforceable even without new consideration but only if it is made in writing. The promise to pay the debt incurred as a minor (Case 3(c)) is unenforceable because a statute declares such a promise unenforceable even if it is made for new consideration.

Preliminary comparisons

Most civil law systems would enforce all of these promises on the grounds that a promise to pay a natural obligation is legally enforceable (at least in the case of a time-barred debt), or that the promise ratifies an obligation or waives a defence to enforcing it. (Exceptions: the promise in Case 3(a) is not enforceable in Italy; the one in Case 3(b) is not enforceable in the Netherlands; none are enforceable in Greece and Scotland; and in Spain, Portugal, Austria, Greece, and, until recently, Germany, Case 3(a) could not arise because debts are not discharged in bankruptcy.)

In Austria, and perhaps elsewhere, there is no sharp distinction drawn between these two rationales for enforcing the promise (the natural obligation becomes a civil obligation; the prior debt is ratified). They are distinguished in Italy: the promise in Case 3(a) is not binding because a promise does not make a natural obligation enforceable, but the promises in Cases 3(b) and 3(c) are because they ratify the debts.

In Greece, according to special provisions of the Civil Code, the promises in Cases 3(b) and 3(c) are enforceable if made in writing. All three would be enforceable in Scotland if made in writing where that is the formality required in gratuitous transactions.

In England, all three promises were once enforceable because they were said to have 'moral consideration'. Today, only the third is enforceable and that is an anomaly since consideration is supposed to require that the promisee gives up a legal right.

In Ireland, all three are unenforceable, the first because it lacks consideration, the second because a statute provides that such a promise is binding even without consideration but only if it is in writing, and the third because a statute provides it is not binding even if it is given for new consideration.

Case 4: a promise to come to dinner

Case

Carlo, a famous musician, agreed to come to a dinner to be held in his honour by a private music conservatory. Two days before the dinner, he was offered a large sum of money if he would give a performance in another city the night of the dinner, taking the place of another musician who had become ill. He notified the conservatory that he could not come because he had accepted a conflicting invitation. The conservatory cancelled the dinner after it had already spent a large amount of money on publicity and food. Can the conservatory recover against Carlo?

Discussions

FRANCE

Under French law, the central issue of this case is whether Carlo's promise was legally or morally binding. French courts enforce only legal promises, and never gentlemen's agreements. In order to succeed with its claim the conservatory has to characterize Carlo's promise as a legal one. However, there are no rules whatsoever in French law to help. It is all a question of fact and is left to the lower courts' assessment. In this respect their power is absolute (*appréciation souveraine*), and not subject to the control of the appellate courts or the highest court, the *Cour de cassation*. This means that case law on the subject may be contradictory. It is therefore open to conjecture how a French court would exercise the wide discretion it has in the matter. The fact that Carlo was not given any money to come to the dinner would probably be a factor in favour of describing the promise as a purely moral one. This sort of arrangement looks much more like a purely social arrangement than a legal one.[1] As such it could be outside the bounds of contract law on the grounds that there is no *animus contrahendi*.

The actual case law reflects a certain amount of hesitation. The fact that the service is provided free does not stop a court from holding that a contract exists.[2] The more recent cases ask whether the parties intended to contract, for example, when one of them gave the other a lift in his car. As a result, where such an intention is absent, courts tend to use liability in tort to provide compensation for a loss.[3]

In this case, liability in tort would be possible only if the conservatory could fulfil the three conditions set out in art. 1382: fault, harm, and a causal connection between the two (see Case 1). In our view, the conservatory will find it difficult to show fault in view of the social context in which the promise was made. Consequently, it may be that Carlo was simply performing what P. Jourdain calls an act of courtesy[4] for which he is not liable. However, the matter is open to debate, and such questions are decided purely on a case-by-case basis.

BELGIUM

There is certainly an agreement here but it is not clear that there is a contract imposing obligations that are legally enforceable. For there to be such a contract, the parties must have intended to be legally bound. Such a contract is to be distinguished from a family or social engagement or courtesy promise which, most likely, was all that Carlo made here.[5]

---

[1] B. Oppetit, 'L'engagement d'honneur', D 1979, Chr. 106; A. Viandier, 'La complaisance', JCP 1980, I, 2987; J. Carbonnier, *Flexible droit, textes pour une sociologie du droit sans rigueur*, 8th edn (1995).

[2] Civ. 1, 23 Nov. 1966, D 1967, 313, note M. Cabrillac (in relation to free shows and amusements).

[3] RTDCiv., 1994, 864, note P. Jourdain, who uses the phrase 'act of courtesy' to refer to a situation in which the promisor does not have the intention to contract. Examples include giving a lift to a friend, using the telephone for free in a café, giving a free driving lesson, allowing school children to visit a factory, and giving a neighbour a hand when furniture is delivered.   [4] *Ibid.*

[5] As had already been noted by R. J. Pothier, *Traité de droit des obligations* (Paris, 1761), reprinted in M. Dupin, *Oeuvres de Pothier* (Paris, 1829), 2–3: 'The sort of convention, the object of which is to form an engagement, is what one calls a *contract*: a convention by which two parties reciprocally promise and commit themselves toward the other to give him something or to do or not to do something. I said *promise and commit oneself toward the other*: there are other promises, that we make in good faith, and with the actual intention of complying with them, but without intent to give the promisee the right to request enforcement. This happens when the promisor declares at the time of his promise that he nevertheless does not want to commit himself; or when it so appears

Assuming that the parties intended to be bound (though, at first glance, it seems they did not), this case involves a unilateral contract in the civil law sense of the term: a contract in which only one party – here Carlo – incurred obligations, rather than both parties (see art. 1103 of the Civil Code). It is also a contract *intuitu personae*, meaning that performance by Carlo personally is an essential element which induced the other party to consent. Such a contract is perfectly valid, and Carlo would be liable for non-performance.

THE NETHERLANDS

Carlo is not liable to the conservatory either in contract or in tort.

There was no contract. The parties did not intend their agreement to have any legal effect (art. 3:33 of the Civil Code[6]), nor was the conservatory justified in relying on Carlo (art. 3:35[7]). The agreement was a mere social agreement.[8] Therefore, Carlo will not be liable in contract.

Carlo's conduct does not amount to an unlawful act (art. 6:162 of the Civil Code[9]). Though perhaps morally reprehensible, it is not forbidden by

from the circumstances or from the qualities of the promisor, and from the promisee. For instance, when a father promises to his son, who studies law, to give him what is necessary, at vacation time, to undertake some recreation travelling so that he would make the best use of his time, it is obvious that the father, in making such promise, did not intend to commit himself toward his son in a contractual engagement.' For Belgium, see Cass., 2 Dec. 1875, Pas., 1876, I, 37 (holding that no legal obligation arose among the members of a de facto non-profit musical association absent an intention to do so, the association having been created merely for the musical entertainment of its members); Cass., 9 May 1980, Pas., 1980, I, 1127; De Page, *Traité élémentaire*, vol. II, no. 447: 'Finally, a contract, like any act of will aimed at producing a legal effect, requires an *animus contrahendae obligationis*, an intention to produce *legal effects*. When such an intention does not exist . . . there is no contract . . .' W. Van Gerven, *Algemeen deel. Beginselen van Belgisch Privaatrecht* (1969), no. 102 (translation): 'Furthermore, the will must be directed toward producing legal effects. There is an understanding that mundane and social commitments and agreements (such as, for instance, an agreement to appear as a speaker before one or another circle) will not . . . provide a sufficient basis to constitute a legally binding commitment.' J.V., note under Cass., 11 Jan. 1978, Pas., 1978, I, 530–1.

[6] Article 3:33 of the Civil Code: 'A juridical act requires an intention to produce juridical effects, which intention has manifested itself by a declaration.'

[7] Article 3:35 of the Civil Code: 'The absence of intention in a declaration cannot be invoked against a person who has interpreted another's declaration or conduct, in conformity with the sense which he could reasonably attribute to it in the circumstances, as a declaration of a particular tenor made to him by that other person.'

[8] See Asser/Hartkamp, vol. II, no. 13.

[9] Article 6:162(1): 'A person who commits an unlawful act towards another which can be imputed to him, must repair the damage which the other person suffers as a consequence thereof.'

law. In particular, it does not seem to be a violation of 'a rule of unwritten law pertaining to proper social conduct' (art. 6:162(2) of the Civil Code[10]) (see Case 6). Therefore, although the matter is less clear on the facts given here, since much depends on the circumstances of the case, Carlo will probably not be liable in tort.

SPAIN

In this case the promise is made *causa donandi*, if it has any *causa* at all. There is a presumption of law that a *causa* exists (art. 1277 of the Civil Code). Therefore, Carlo is not under any obligation because the promise has not been given in writing (see Case 1). Since there is no prior duty, the conservatory is not entitled to compensation.

PORTUGAL

Probably, the conservatory cannot recover against Carlo.

In Portuguese law, the acceptance of an invitation to dinner generally does not constitute a contract, because the matter merely concerns social rules, not legal rules. These agreements are considered to be mere gentlemen's agreements which do not constitute legal obligations because the promisor has no intention of assuming a legal obligation.[11]

Nevertheless, if Carlo had assumed a legal obligation to attend the dinner, then he would have entered into a contract to perform a service (art. 1154 of the Civil Code). It would not be a contract of donation because it does not entail any sacrifice of his assets. According to the law, a contract to perform a service is binding even if it was gratuitous and made orally. The conservatory would have therefore had a claim against Carlo, and it would be theoretically possible to demand compensation for non-performance of Carlo's obligation (art. 798 of the Civil Code). In my view, however, it would be very difficult to convince a judge that the mere acceptance of an invitation in a situation like this involved an intention to assume a legal obligation to perform the service of attending the dinner.

ITALY

The conservatory would not be able to recover anything under Italian case law. This case illustrates the uncertain border between 'courtesy promises'

---

[10] Article 6:162(2): 'Except where there is ground of justification, the following acts are deemed to be unlawful: the violation of a right, an act or omission violating a statutory duty or a rule of unwritten law pertaining to proper social conduct.'

[11] See M. de Andrade, *Teoria Geral da Relação Jurídica*, vol. II (1992), 31.

and gratuitous legal obligations. Courtesy promises are made without the intention to be legally bound. They lack a *causa* and, therefore, are not enforceable.[12]

In this case, a court would find the arrangement to be a courtesy promise because the promisor has no clear and immediate economic interest in promising, and the intention of the parties to be legally bound is not apparent. It would have been quite different if the parties, for example, had agreed upon a penalty clause.[13]

In situations of this type, the courts usually say that courtesy promises have no economic value or that they are too indeterminate to be enforceable.[14] The best reason for refusing to enforce them, however, is that the parties to them do not want to be legally bound. Enforcement of their promises is left to informal – but often very effective – mechanisms of social sanction.

The distinction between gratuitous promises and courtesy promises originated in the work of legal scholars. Today, Italian case law distinguishes sharply between courtesy transportation and the contract of gratuitous transportation. The former is governed by general rules of tort liability. As in all other courtesy relationships, the courtesy carrier has the duty not to suspend performance abruptly so as to cause the other party damage. The latter, however, is a contract and is governed by the general rules of contract law.

AUSTRIA

Not every promise results in a legal obligation. For a promise to be binding, the promisor must have the intention to be legally bound.[15] In general, the acceptance of an invitation for a social event such as a dinner with friends does not constitute a legally binding promise. Such

---

[12] See F. Gazzoni, 'Atipicità del contratto, giuridicità del vincolo e funzionalizzazione degli interessi', Riv. dir. civ. I (1978), 52; F. Gazzoni, *Manuale di diritto privato* (1993); G. Ghezzi, 'Cortesia (prestazioni di)', Enc. dir. 10 (1962), 1048; V. Panuccio, 'Cortesia (prestazioni di)', Enc. giur. Treccani 6 (1988), 1–8; N. Lipari, 'Rapporti di cortesia, rapporti di fatto, rapporti di fiducia', Riv. trim. dir. proc. civ. (1968), 415.

[13] In this case it could be reasonable to assume that Carlo reserved his 'right' to change his mind according to the modifications in his schedule. See Marini, *Promessa ed affidamento*, 356.

[14] See Ghezzi, 'Cortesia (prestazioni di)'. For the view that even a promise of a performance with no determined economic value could be legally binding, see F. Carresi, 'Il contratto', in Cicu-Messineo, *Tratt. dir. civ. e comm.* (1987), 18 ff.

[15] Even if he does not have such an intention, he can be bound if the promisee was entitled to understand the promise as a legally binding one because he could assume that there was such an intention.

invitations are purely social matters, where the parties do not intend to create a legal obligation.

Here, the situation is a bit different. The conservatory incurs costs not only for food but also for publicity. It therefore could be argued that the conservatory has an interest that Carlo's promise is binding – an interest that Carlo must have recognized. I do not think, however, that this will be sufficient to credit him with an intention to be legally bound. One must take into consideration that it will not be in Carlo's interest to make such a promise as he then could become liable for the damages caused by his failure to show up. As Carlo was not to receive any payment for the dinner, it cannot be assumed that he accepted such a liability without any payment. The conservatory therefore cannot understand his promise to be a legally binding promise. In other words, if it had wished to receive a binding promise, it should have explicitly asked for one.[16]

Carlo will not be liable in tort, either. As the conservatory suffers only a pure economic loss, Carlo could be liable only if he intentionally caused this loss by acting in a way which is against the *bonos mores* (*Gute Sitten*), as provided by § 1295 II of the Civil Code (ABGB). Section 1295 II could apply if Carlo made the promise with the intention of causing harm to the conservatory by not keeping the promise. This, however, does not seem to be the case.

GERMANY

There would be a contractual claim for damages only if there was a duty to appear at the dinner. Only then could an obligation have been infringed. A binding obligation, however, must be distinguished from the mere promise of a favour which is not binding. For the contract to be binding, Carlo must have intended to be legally bound. German courts will assume he had this intention if the performance promised is of obvious importance to the promisee especially in view of the damage that non-performance might cause.

---

[16] Even if Carlo's promise would constitute a legally binding promise, it is doubtful whether the conservatory could recover the costs incurred. If somebody fails to fulfil a contractual obligation, the other party has the right to demand the expectation interest. The costs the conservatory incurs, however, obviously are part of the reliance interest. Such costs can be recovered if they can be regarded as an indication of the expectation interest, as it can be assumed that a party incurs expenses only if they are covered by his contractual gain. This principle, however, works only in cases where it is clear that the creditor will make a *financial* gain from the contract. With respect to the conservatory, however, it is very doubtful whether there is – or could have been – a direct financial gain. See H. Koziol, *Österreichisches Haftpflichtrecht*, 3rd edn (1997), vol. I, no. 2/86.

This question is often hard to answer. In one case,[17] the highest German court (*Bundesgerichtshof*) held that a promise to make a lorry driver available to another company was binding. The reason was the high value of the lorry. Therefore, the promisor had a contractual duty to select the driver carefully, and was held liable for damages when he failed to do so. In another case,[18] however, the *Bundesgerichtshof* found that a promise to take care of a neighbour's children was not binding. It was regarded as typical social behaviour.

The same difficulty appears in our case. On the one hand, it looks more like a favour. On the other hand, it was clear that the conservatory would incur expenses for the dinner. Nevertheless, in the case of a private dinner, one would not assume that a binding contract was made just because the host has bought food. Therefore, it seems most likely that there is no contractual claim here.

Another possibility is that the claim of the conservatory could be based on tort law. Section 826 of the Civil Code obligates a person to pay damages if he 'has caused the damage intentionally and in a way which offends common decency'. Common decency is defined as the beliefs of those whose thinking is proper and just.[19]

Section 826 requires that the conduct in question be morally reproachable when all aspects of the case are considered.[20] In our case, however, Carlo's behaviour in refusing to turn down the opportunity to earn a large sum does not appear to be immoral, as we can see if we again imagine he did so when invited to a private dinner. The result would be different if Carlo never planned to fulfil his promise or if, for example, the conservatory sold entrance tickets for the dinner and now has to refund the money. Then Carlo's behaviour would be immoral and against common decency. It would also be possible to find that he made a binding contract.

Carlo is under a legal obligation to notify the conservatory as soon as possible that he is not going to appear. But he has not infringed this obligation.

GREECE

We need to ask whether the parties are acting out of courtesy and do not wish to be legally bound or whether they wished to make a contract.

Probably Carlo and the private music conservatory are acting out of courtesy. Their promises do not have legal effects, as the parties do not

---

[17] BGHZ 21 (1956), 102.   [18] BGH JZ (1969), 232.   [19] Mot., vol. II, p. 727.
[20] BGHZ 70 (1978), 277.

want to be bound legally. Someone who cancels a dinner held in his honour does not violate a legal, but rather a social obligation, and, therefore, he is not obliged to pay compensation for the financial damage which the host suffers because of the expenses he made.[21]

In an extreme case, non-performance of a social obligation could result in tort liability. The defendant would have to violate his obligation with the intention to cause harm in a way that is contrary to morality (art. 919 of the Civil Code).[22]

SCOTLAND

As Carlo has *agreed* to come to dinner, it is likely that the courts would adopt a contractual analysis, that is, he had accepted an offer from the conservatory. This would be consistent with the line of reasoning from cases such as *Malcolm* v. *Campbell*.[23] The conservatory would then be able to establish the existence of the contract by parole evidence and sue Carlo for breach of it.

If, however, the problem was analysed in terms of a gratuitous unilateral obligation, once again the conservatory would *prima facie* require the promise to be constituted in writing: s. 1(2)(a)(ii) of the Requirements of Writing (Scotland) Act 1955.[24] Carlo may attempt to argue that there is not a promise but an expression of future intention as in *Gray* v. *Johnston*,[25] where the defender had merely indicated that he would render the pursuer his heir. However, the music conservatory may not require a written promise if the court took the view that Carlo made the promise in the course of his business, in terms of s. 1(2)(a)(ii) of the 1995 Act. This exception is new to the law of Scotland and there is no case law on the point as most business arrangements are bi- or multilateral contracts.

The conservatory could also argue that writing is not required in terms of s. 1(2)(a)(ii) of the Act as the promise is non-gratuitous in that Carlo receives the benefit of a dinner in his honour. As noted in discussing Case 1, it is only gratuitous unilateral obligations which are required to be constituted in writing in terms of the 1995 Act.

It could also be argued by Carlo that going to dinner is merely a social agreement and that therefore an agreement or promise to dine is presumed in Scots law not to create legal obligations. However, in light of his repute, it is likely that it will be seen as a business arrangement and therefore one where intention to enter legal obligations is presumed.

---

[21] Karasis, 'Social Engagement Acts', in *Miscellany in Honour of Andreas Gazis* (1994), 207–25.
[22] *Ibid.*   [23] [1891] 19 R 278.   [24] See Case 1.   [25] [1928] SC 659.

Even if the promise has to be constituted in writing, the conservatory could perhaps rely on s. 1(3) and (4) of the 1995 Act. In order to establish the statutory conditions successfully the conservatory must show that Carlo made the promise. They must then show that their expenditure was in reliance on the promise, and that it was known to and acquiesced in by Carlo. Moreover, the conservatory's expenditure must be material and Carlo's withdrawal must have adverse material consequences for the conservatory.

ENGLAND

The answer to this question is not obvious under English law – no analogous case appears to have been decided – but it is suggested that the conservatory would be unable to recover against Carlo.

The first difficulty for the conservatory is that it is unlikely they will be able to establish that their agreement with Carlo satisfied the requirement of an intent to create legal relations. As discussed in regard to Case 1, there is a rebuttable presumption against finding such an intent in family and social arrangements and a presumption in favour of finding the intent in commercial arrangements. In neither case will a court ordinarily attempt to assess whether the parties were conscious that they were or were not attempting to create legal relations; rather it is assumed that, barring evidence to the contrary, such intent exists in 'commercial' arrangements but not in 'social' or 'domestic' arrangements.[26] Carlo's promise is difficult to categorize, but on balance it would appear to lie in the social rather than the commercial category, because it is not a bargain in an ordinary sense. Neither party, it appears, entered the agreement in order to make a profit. (This factual assumption may be incorrect, since the conservatory is a private body; and if it is incorrect then it is more likely that the requisite intent will be found.) Indeed, a common example of an agreement that lacks the requisite intent to create legal relations is an agreement to have dinner with a friend[27] (though of course Carlo's agreement differs from this example, as the proposed dinner was not merely between friends).

The second barrier to enforcing Carlo's promise is that it does not appear that the conservatory provided or promised anything in

---

[26] For this reason, it has sometimes been suggested that the requirement of intent to create legal relations is not really concerned with finding such an intent, but is instead a means of keeping out of the courts relationships which would be detrimentally affected by actual or threatened legal enforcement.

[27] E.g., *Balfour* v. *Balfour* [1919] 2 KB 571, 578.

exchange, that is, there was no consideration (see Case 1). On the facts as described, the dinner is not to be held in return for Carlo's promise to attend, but is rather the reason for the invitation. And, as explained in the discussion of Case 1, unrequested reliance on a promise – here the conservatory's expenditures on food and publicity – is not valid consideration. The consideration point is not, however, entirely clear cut. If the court has already found an intent to create legal relations, then this intent, together with the conservatory's reliance on Carlo's agreement, might lead the court to interpret the conservatory's invitation as an offer to put on a dinner for Carlo in exchange for Carlo agreeing to attend. As noted in the discussion of Case 1, the fact of detrimental reliance upon a promise is one factor that, it is often alleged, sways a court towards finding consideration. It is suggested, however, that a court would still hesitate to find the necessary consideration in this case. One reason is that in many situations it would be inappropriate to consider Carlo bound to such a promise. Suppose that Carlo became sick – or suppose that Carlo was on bad terms with one of the announced speakers at the dinner. On the other hand, the fact that Carlo's reason for cancelling was financial, though irrelevant in strictly legal terms, would no doubt also sway a court towards viewing the arrangement as binding. Finally, as with the issue of intent to create legal relations, if the conservatory was hoping to make a financial profit on the dinner, and if Carlo was aware of this, a court would be more likely to find that consideration had been given for Carlo's promise.

IRELAND

First, the conservatory must establish that there was consideration and that this consideration was sufficient in law (see Case 1). Second, the conservatory must show that the parties intended the agreement in question to be legally binding, that is, that there was requisite legal intent to create a binding contract.[28]

The conservatory would no doubt argue that the fact that the dinner was to be held in his honour and the fact that they had spent a large amount of money on publicity and food created a legally binding contract. However, it is doubtful whether this consideration is sufficient in law to create a legally binding agreement.[29] Andrews LJ said that while 'it is clear

---

[28] See *Lens* v. *Devonshire Club* [1914] *The Times*. See also Case 6.
[29] See Case 9; *O'Neill* v. *Murphy* [1936] NI 160 Northern Ireland Court of Appeal.

that the Courts will not interfere with the exercise of free will and judgement of the parties by enquiry into the adequacy of consideration it is necessary that it should be sufficient in law. Thus, neither a mere voluntary courtesy nor some act already executed will suffice.'[30]

Even if a court were to hold that the consideration by the music conservatory was sufficient for the purposes of creating a legally binding contract, it is unlikely that they would hold that there was requisite legal intent. This agreement could not be held to come within the scope of a commercial agreement and indeed would most likely fall under a description of a social arrangement.[31]

If the music conservatory were able to establish that the promise by Carlo to come to the dinner was intended by him to be binding, intended to be acted upon, and in fact acted on by them by spending a large amount of money on publicity and food, the principle of promissory estoppel might arise.[32] Although it is unclear whether it is necessary in Ireland to show detriment on the part of the promisee, it is clear that the music conservatory have suffered detriment by spending a large amount of money on publicity and food. However, promissory estoppel operates only as a shield and not as a sword and does not give rise to a cause of action.

For these reasons it is highly unlikely that the conservatory would be able to recover against Carlo.

Summaries

France: Whether there is liability in contract depends on whether the parties intended to be bound legally. The fact that the promisor was not to be paid is one factor to take into account but it is not decisive. It is impossible to tell how the case would be resolved because the trial courts' decisions on the matter are unreviewable, and so the cases are conflicting.

Liability in tort depends on whether Carlo was at fault. Probably he was not.

Belgium: Whether there is liability in contract depends on whether the parties intended to be bound legally, which, most likely, they did not.

The Netherlands: Whether there is liability in contract depends on whether the parties intended to be bound legally, which they did not.

Whether there is liability in tort depends on whether Carlo violated 'a rule of unwritten law pertaining to proper social conduct', which, it seems, he did not.

---

[30] *Ibid.*   [31] See Treitel, *Contract*, ch. 3.   [32] See Case 1.

Spain: The promise will be treated as a gift and is therefore unenforceable without the necessary formality.

Portugal: Probably, the promise would be treated as a gentlemen's agreement or a mere social obligation, and therefore would be unenforceable.

Italy: Whether there is liability in contract depends on whether the parties intended to be bound legally, which they did not.

Austria: Whether there is liability in contract depends on whether the parties intended to be bound legally, which, most likely, they did not.

There would be liability in tort only if Carlo intended to cause harm in a way which is against the *bonos mores* (*Gute Sitten*), and here he did not cause harm intentionally.

Germany: Whether there is liability in contract depends on whether the parties intended to be bound legally. Most likely, they did not, although the question is hard to answer.

For there to be liability in tort, either Carlo's refusal to attend the dinner must have been morally reproachable, which it was not, or he must have intended to cause harm, which he did not.

Greece: Whether there is liability in contract depends on whether the parties intended to be bound legally, which probably they did not.

For there to be liability in tort, Carlo would have had to cause harm intentionally in a way that was contrary to morality. Non-performance of a social obligation could give rise to such liability only in an extreme case.

Scotland: The promise may be a non-gratuitous one, in which case it is enforceable even if it is made informally. Or it may be a gratuitous one, in which case it is enforceable only if it is made in writing or given in the course of business. Here it may have been given in the course of business. In either case, it is enforceable only if it is intended to be legally binding. Although usually a dinner engagement is not so intended, here it may have been since it may have been regarded as a business arrangement.

Even if the promise was one that normally has to be in writing, it may still be enforceable because the conservatory relied on it. To be enforceable, the expenditure must have been known to and acquiesced in by Carlo, it must have been material, and the adverse consequences when Carlo did not come must have been material.

England: There is no liability in contract unless the parties intended to be bound legally, which, most likely, they did not, although the matter is not clear.

Even if they did, the promise is unenforceable because it lacks consideration although, in a sufficiently sympathetic case, a court might manipulate the doctrine of consideration to hold a party liable on similar facts.

The doctrine of promissory estoppel does not make the promise enforceable because that doctrine is a shield, not a sword.

Ireland: There is no liability in contract unless the parties intended to be bound legally, which, most likely, they did not.

Even if they did, the promise is unenforceable because it lacks consideration. Organizing the dinner was more like a voluntary courtesy than something given in return.

The doctrine of promissory estoppel does not make the promise enforceable because that doctrine is a shield, not a sword.

Preliminary comparisons

The intention to be legally bound: In all of the legal systems, the promise is unenforceable unless the parties intended to be legally bound. Most reporters thought it unlikely that they did; some thought it possible; one thought it likely.

Tort: No legal system would impose liability in tort. Some reporters did not think this possibility worth discussing, and those that did said that Carlo was not at fault, or that his conduct was not contrary to morality, or that he did not intentionally cause harm.

Gift: In Spain and Scotland, the promise may be treated like a gift so that it would be binding only if it were made in writing, or, in Scotland, if it were given in the course of business.

Consideration: In addition, in England and Ireland, the promise would be unenforceable because it lacks consideration.

Reliance: Although England and Ireland recognize a doctrine of promissory reliance, the doctrine does not apply here because it is a shield, not a sword.

Case 5: promises to store goods without charge

Case

Otto sold his house and all his furniture except for a valuable antique table and chairs. Charles promised to store them for three months without charge while Otto found a new house to buy. Is the promise binding? Does it matter (a) if Charles refused to store the table and chairs before they are delivered or a month afterwards? (b) if Charles was a friend of Otto, or the antiques dealer from whom he recently purchased the table and chairs, or a professional storer of furniture? (c) if Charles refused to store them merely because he had changed his mind or because he had unexpectedly inherited furniture which he had no place else to store? (d) if Otto could instead have stored his furniture with Jean, who had also offered to store it without charge, and has now withdrawn that offer? or (e) if Otto had previously contracted with a warehouse to store his furniture, had cancelled the contract because of Charles' offer, and now can only store his furniture at a higher price?

Discussions

FRANCE

The agreement between Otto and Charles would constitute a deposit (*contrat de dépôt*) under French law. A deposit is governed by arts. 1915 and following of the French Civil Code. The three main obligations of the depositee are to receive the object, to look after it, and to restore it to its rightful owner. Under French law, a deposit is regarded as an *in rem* unilateral contract, that is to say, as a contract which exists only when the thing is delivered by one party to the other (art. 1919 of the Civil Code). Originally, an essential feature of a deposit, as of a contract of loan, was that it is not made in return for compensation (art. 1917 of the Civil Code). This rule must be understood in conjunction with arts. 1927–8 of the Civil Code which reduce or increase a depositee's liability depending on whether or not the deposit is for compensation. Article 1927 sets out the general rule that a depositee must look after the object with the same degree of care as he takes with his own things. Exceptions are created by art. 1928: a depositee is held to a higher standard of care if (1) the depositee offered to take the object, (2) the depositee is being compensated, or (3) the deposit is for the sole benefit of the depositee.

We will consider, first, Charles' liability if the furniture has been delivered, and then his liability if it has not. In each case, we will consider the significance of his position as a friend, a professional storer of furniture, and so forth.

If the furniture has been delivered, then a contract of deposit has been formed. If Charles now refuses to store the furniture, he is clearly in breach of contract.

If Charles is a friend of Otto, Otto could, in theory, sue Charles successfully to enforce his promise. It is unclear, however, if he could obtain specific performance: that is, compel him to keep the furniture until the end of the term. A depositee's obligations constitute an 'obligation to do' something under art. 1126 of the Civil Code. Originally, art. 1142 was supposed to permit only a damage remedy for breach of such an obligation. The case law has interpreted this article narrowly, and a court will now order specific performance unless it constitutes an infringement of the personal liberty of the promisor. The exception has thus reversed the rule. Nevertheless, because the obligation to look after an object requires active cooperation by the depositee, it may be considered dangerous to order an uncooperative depositee to perform. In addition – and this argument is, in our view, more convincing – a court is not likely specifically to enforce a promise between friends, particularly since that result seems unwarranted or excessive in view of the gratuitous nature of the contract.

Moreover, Otto may not be able to claim damages from Charles on the grounds that the promise is like a gentlemen's agreement and not intended to have legal effect. Indeed, not all deposits are contracts. Sometimes they are characterized as a mere arrangement.[1] In addition, as mentioned already, according to art. 1927 of the Civil Code, the obligations of the depositee vary depending on the type of deposit in question.

---

[1] For example, a barman who agrees to look after a client's bag, Com., 25 Sept. 1984, Bull. civ. IV, no. 242; a vendor who allows its suppliers to stock goods in its premises in order to carry out deliveries, Civ. 2, 25 April 1968, Bull. civ. II, no. 115; Collart-Dutilleul and Delebecque, *Contrats* no. 795, pp. 662 ff.

Traditionally, the case law has interpreted the obligations of a depositee who acts as a friend less rigorously than those of one who acts for compensation. It is thus questionable whether Otto could obtain damages from Charles although he might under art. 1147. In any event, Charles would only have an obligation to use his best efforts (*obligation de moyens*), and would not be liable if he has done so.

Suppose, next, that Charles is not a friend but an antiques dealer from whom Otto bought the furniture. The result depends on a number of considerations, both factual and legal. If Otto removed the furniture after purchasing it and Charles now offers to store it as a favour, it can be assumed that the parties have entered into a deposit without reward, and the answer is the same as in the case just considered in which Charles is a friend. If the gratuitous nature of the contract is the main reason for refusing to award damages in that case, then the same arguments would seem to apply here.

Another possibility is that Otto never removed the furniture, and so the deposit was made immediately after the sale. The obligation to store it would then be an ancillary obligation to the contract of sale. If the deposit is a kind of collateral contract, Otto may be able to obtain specific performance, and his claim for damages looks much more likely to succeed.

Suppose, next, that Charles is a professional storer of furniture. We have already noted that, under French law, the standard of care required of the depositee varies according to whether the deposit is for compensation or not. This means that the fact that Charles is a professional storer is irrelevant provided that the deposit is still gratuitous.

We can now consider how French law would apply if the furniture has not been delivered. If Charles refused to store it before delivery, he would only have made an offer to take a deposit (*promesse de dépôt*).

One possibility is that this offer might give rise to a contract, the content of which is a promise to be depositee (see Case 7 for an analogy). On purely consensualist principles, such a contract could be formed by the exchange of promises and would be a unilateral contract. However, an offer to be a depositee is not an *in rem* contract. Consequently, the rules that were described earlier do not apply. The deposit cannot be specifically enforced because the contract of deposit has not come into existence. Therefore, even if a promise of deposit were held to be enforceable, on analogy with a promise of a loan, the most, if anything, that the disappointed depositor could obtain would be damages.[2]

Moreover, there are two reasons why breach of such an agreement

---

[2] Civ. 1, 20 July 1981, Bull. civ. I, no. 267. See Ghestin, *Traité de droit civil* no. 451, pp. 418 f.

would not give rise to damages. First, where, as here, the contract of deposit is without compensation, it is unclear whether damages can be obtained for its breach although they probably could otherwise.[3] Second, as discussed earlier, if Charles is a friend, it is quite possible that the promise would not be characterized as a contract but as a social agreement. Again, Otto could not obtain damages. As before, even if Charles is a professional storer, as long as he agreed to act gratuitously, his promise would probably be characterized in the same way. Again, Otto could not obtain damages.

It is also possible that purely consensualist principles would not be applied, and Charles' offer would not give rise to a contract. Those who stress the *in rem* nature of a contract of deposit might conclude that no contract can be formed because an essential element is missing. Their conclusion would follow from a narrow interpretation of art. 1919 of the Civil Code, and would represent the more traditional view of deposit contracts. By this analysis, because the formal requirements to make a contract of deposit have not been complied with, there is merely an exchange of promises which fails to constitute an enforceable contract.

Even if, by this approach, there is no contract, Charles could, nevertheless, be liable for breach of his promise if the conditions are met that are required for liability in tort. Liability in tort would be possible only if breach of the promise were considered to be a fault under art. 1382 of the Civil Code.[4] Intuitively, we think it extremely unlikely that failure to fulfil such a promise would constitute a fault. The transaction is not an exchange. The only benefit from the deposit is a unilateral gain by Otto. Common sense suggests that since Charles gets nothing from the arrangement, his liability should be diminished. Thus the considerations of fairness that have led courts to impose liability in tort in other cases are not present here.

In any event, if Charles' promise was legally binding for any of the reasons just discussed, his reasons for breaking the promise, however good they might be, would not discharge his liability under French law. In particular, the mere fact that the performance of the contract will cost him money would not be a sufficient reason. It would do so only if this extra cost constituted *force majeure* under the rules of art. 1148 of the Civil Code.[5]

---

[3] Terré, Simler, and Lequette, *Les obligations* no. 141, p. 123; M. N. Jobard-Bachelier, RTDCiv. 1958, 1 f.; M. Storck, *Juris Classeur, Promesse synallagmatique de contrat*, Fasc. 30, nos. 35 f.

[4] See Cases 1 and 4 for an explanation of these conditions.

[5] Article 1148: 'There are no damages when, as a result of force majeure or an accident, the debtor under an undertaking is prevented from transferring (*donner*) or doing that which he was obliged to do, or had done that which he was forbidden to do.'

The classic interpretation of this article requires three conditions to be met for an event to constitute *force majeure*: it must be unforeseeable, impossible to resist, and external to the will of the parties. The mere fact that it is more costly to store the furniture does not amount to *force majeure* according to the case law.[6] *Force majeure* will only be a defence if there is a complete obstacle to performance, for then the adage applies that 'no one is obliged to do the impossible'. In addition, the fact that performance is more costly does not meet the second condition that the *force majeure* is impossible to resist.

In any event, the possibility that Otto chose one friend, Charles, instead of another, Jean, has no bearing on the enforceability of his promise. Neither does the possibility that he had previously contracted with a warehouse to store his furniture, had cancelled the contract because of Charles' offer, and now can only store his furniture at a higher price. At most, this possibility raises questions about the quantum of damages, or perhaps mitigation, both of which are beyond the scope of our topic.

The interesting and tricky problem raised by this case shows the importance of whether a contract is characterized as *in rem*. Paradoxically, in French law, the prevalence of consensualist principles tends to undercut the traditional requirement for the delivery of the thing. This case therefore underlines a particularity of French law: the possibility, admitted by some academics and courts, of an enforceable contract that consists of mere promises to contract (see also Cases 7 and 13). Notwithstanding debates over formal requirements, this case also illustrates the borderline between contracts with or without compensation. In our view, this characteristic feature – whether the contract is gratuitous or not – matters the most, whichever of the various ways just described one attempts to resolve the problem. Article 1917 characterizes a deposit as 'a contract [that is] essentially gratuitous'. The influence of this characterization still permeates French law's view of this contract.

The case also illustrates another characteristic of French law. The border between contract and tort seems rigid: for example, it is impossible to cumulate the causes of action. Nevertheless, the failure to characterize a situation as contractual does not preclude a party who has suffered a loss (the promisee) from obtaining a remedy. It may still be possible to obtain damages in tort for breach of the promise. Indeed, because the grounds for imposing liability in tort are so extensive in French law, many academics

---

[6] Civ., 4 Aug. 1915, DP 1916, 1, 22; Soc., 8 March 1972; D 1972, 340; nor *force majeure* if the person obliged to perform can do so by substitution, even if it is more costly, Com., 12 Nov. 1969, JCP 1971, II, 16791, note M. Juglart and E. du Pontavice, first case.

are in favour of abolishing the distinction as theoretical and impractical. Since the conditions for recovery in tort are relatively easy to satisfy, despite problems of evidence, to argue over the exact way to analyse a transaction as a contract may be a purely academic exercise.

BELGIUM

This case involves a contract of deposit (*contrat de dépôt*) (arts. 1915 f. of the Civil Code). A contract of deposit is essentially a *gratuitous* agreement (art. 1917). In this case, it is also unilateral in the civil law sense of the term: it imposes obligations on only one of the parties. In addition, it is a 'real contract' (*contrat réel* or *re*) as opposed to a consensual contract (*contrat consensuel*) which means that it is formed and imposes obligations on the depositary only when the thing to be deposited is delivered to him (art. 1919).

In Case 5(a), if Charles refuses the furniture before delivery, no contract of deposit can be said to exist. Nevertheless, there is still a promise of deposit. The promise is perfectly valid, and the depositor can request either performance or damages.[7] If Charles refuses to store the furniture one month after delivery, he will then breach his obligations under a contract of deposit that was formed by delivery and which obligates him to store the furniture for three months. It is quite true that, in the present state of Belgian law, the practical consequences attached to the breaking of a deposit contract and to the breaking of a promise of deposit may appear to be much the same. This seems to be an incidental effect of the modern recognition in Belgian law that the promise has binding force in advance of delivery and even if it has not been accepted by the promisee.

In Case 5(b), if Charles is Otto's friend, the court will have to decide whether there is a contract imposing obligations that are legally enforceable. For there to be such a contract, the parties must have intended to be legally bound. Such a contract is to be distinguished from a family or social engagement or courtesy promise which may have been all the parties intended if they were friends (see Case 4).

In Case 5(c), Charles may refuse to store the furniture as long as no delivery has taken place. If Charles receives the inherited furniture unexpectedly subsequent to the delivery of Otto's furniture, he may be able to escape his obligation to store it by claiming *force majeure*. Admittedly, the two elements necessary to establish *force majeure* are an insurmountable

---

[7] M.-F. De Pover, *Répertoire notarial, principaux contrats usuels*, vol. IX, De Pover, *Le dépôt*, no. 9. See also De Page, *Traité élémentaire*, vol. V, no. 183.

obstacle and the absence of fault. Here, it is still possible for Charles to store the furniture. Nevertheless, in one Belgian case, the defendants, as owners of a coffee shop, had entered into a supply contract with a brewery. When the building where the coffee shop was located was sold in execution upon demand of creditors, they claimed that they were free of their obligation because of *force majeure*. The brewery argued that there could not be *force majeure* since the execution sale did not constitute an insurmountable obstacle to performance by the defendants. The *Cour de cassation* affirmed the decision of the trial court holding that there was *force majeure*, observing, nevertheless, that under the circumstances, the trial court's finding on this issue was unreviewable.[8]

Charles cannot obtain relief on the grounds that unforeseen circumstances have arisen (*imprévision*) for reasons that will be explained in discussing Case 8.

Whether Otto could have stored his furniture with Jean or with a warehouse (Cases 5(d) and 5(e)) matters only as to the amount of damages he can recover.

THE NETHERLANDS

The promise would be binding only if both parties intended their agreement to have legal effect (art. 3:33 of the Civil Code) or if one of the parties so intended and could reasonably think that the other party did as well (art. 3:35). This does not seem to be the case here. Although the outcome is not totally clear since everything depends on the circumstances of the case, the agreement seems to be a mere social agreement.

If there was a contract, it would be a contract of deposit (arts. 7:600 ff. of the Civil Code). This contract was a 'real contract' under the old civil code which means that it was formed only by delivery of the object to be deposited. Under the new code, however, it is a consensual contract, that is, it can be formed even before the object is delivered. This is expressed in the words the Code uses to describe a contract of deposit: 'entrusts or will entrust' (*toevertrouwt of zal toevertrouwen*) (art. 7:600).

It does not matter (Case 5(a)) if Charles refused to store the table and chairs before they were delivered or a month afterwards. The agreement would still be a mere social agreement. The fact that Charles had already started to perform his promise does not in itself make it more likely that the promise was meant to be legally binding. In society, not only contracts

---

[8] See Cass., 9 Dec. 1976, Pas., 1977, I, 408.

but also mere social agreements tend to be performed. The outcome is not totally certain, though. If Otto intended their promise to be legally binding, then, to establish whether he can rely on art. 3:35 of the Civil Code, it is relevant whether he relied on the promise.

Since a deposit is a consensual contract under the new code (see above), delivery of the object is not a prerequisite for its conclusion.

It does matter (Case 5(b)) if Charles was a friend of Otto's, or the antiques dealer from whom he recently purchased the table and chairs, or a professional storer of furniture. If Charles was a friend of Otto's, it is likely that the promise was not meant to be a legally binding promise (art. 3:33 of the Civil Code), and it is less likely that Otto could reasonably think it was (art. 3:35 of the Civil Code). If Charles was the seller, the promise may be a promise collateral to the contract of sale. It would therefore be binding. If Charles was a professional storer, and the promise was gratuitous, it is more likely that the promise was not intended to be a contractual promise (art. 3:33 of the Civil Code), and Otto could not rely on it being so unless he undertook to enquire whether it was (art. 3:35 of the Civil Code).[9] Thus, these facts do make a difference although they may not be decisive. Other facts may lead to a different conclusion.

In deciding whether the arrangement was merely social or had legal effects, it does not matter (Case 5(c)) if Charles refused to store the furniture merely because he had changed his mind or because he had unexpectedly inherited furniture which he had no place else to store. If, however, the agreement is (part of) a legally binding contract, then these facts may constitute an 'important reason' (*gewichtige reden*) which allows the court to change the moment the objects may be given back (art. 7:605(2) of the Civil Code).[10]

One author has argued that when a promise is gratuitous, liability and enforcement should be relaxed.[11] Such a general principle does not follow from the provisions or the *travaux préparatoires* of the new code – on the contrary.[12] Nevertheless, it is not unlikely that in applying provisions like art. 7:605(2) of the Civil Code, possibly, though not necessarily, in connection with good faith (arts. 6:2, 6:248), the courts will take the gratuitousness of the promise into account.

---

[9] See also art. 7:601(1) of the Civil Code which says that in case the depositary is a professional he is entitled to remuneration.

[10] See art. 7:605(2) of the Civil Code: 'The judge of the subdistrict court in whose jurisdiction the thing is located may, for serious reasons and upon the request of one of the parties, determine a date for returning or taking back which differs from the preceding paragraph or from the contract.'   [11] Van Schaick, 'Vriendendienst', 320.

[12] This is recognized by Van Schaick.

It may matter (Case 5(d)) if Otto could instead have stored his furniture with Jean, who had also offered to store it without charge, and has now withdrawn that offer. If Charles knew of Jean's offer, it is somewhat more likely that his own offer was intended to be legally binding. If Charles did not intend it to be but Otto thought that he did, Otto may have been somewhat more justified in relying on it. However, it does not seem to be sufficient to turn the agreement into a contract. The fact that Otto refused Jean's offer is evidence that he actually did rely, but, as just noted, in itself it does not make his reliance any more justified.

If the agreement was intended to have legal effects, and therefore is enforceable, Jean's offer is relevant as evidence of Otto's damages.[13]

It does matter (Case 5(e)) if Otto had previously contracted with a warehouse to store his furniture, had cancelled the contract because of Charles' offer, and now can only store his furniture at a higher price. If he did, it is a strong indication that the promise was regarded by the parties (art. 3:33 of the Civil Code) and could be regarded by Otto (art. 3:35 of the Civil Code) as a legally binding promise rather than a mere social arrangement. Even then, however, the circumstances of the case may still lead to the conclusion that the promise was not a legally binding one.

SPAIN

Here again, the promise is not enforceable unless it has a *causa*, and there is a presumption of law that it does (art. 1277 of the Civil Code). Presumably, the *causa* is mere liberality.

The problem then is that, in Spanish law, a contract of this type is a deposit (*depósito*). A deposit is a contract *re* which means that it does not create an obligation until after the object to be deposited is actually delivered (*datio rei*). After delivery, it is clear that a contract has been formed.

According to the Civil Code, if there is no delivery, there is no contract. Nevertheless, many scholars maintain that duties may arise before the delivery of the object.[14] If so, then the existence of an offer and its acceptance would create an obligation to do what one has promised, although, according to the Civil Code, this obligation is not a contract.

The position of the *Tribunal Supremo* is not clear. There are cases in which physical delivery was not required. In one decision,[15] a party had deposited 175,000 pesetas with a bank as part payment of 350,000 pesetas for the rental of a ship. He later argued that since the deposit with the bank

---

[13] On contractual damages, see arts. 6:74 ff. of the Civil Code.
[14] E.g., Puig Brutau, *Fundamentos de derecho civil*, vol. II-2, 523.   [15] TS, 29 Dec. 1927.

was not paid to the party who was to rent the ship, he had not entered into a contract of deposit with that party. After rejecting this claim as a mere technicality, the court observed: 'a deposit may exist without the physical delivery of the thing in which it consists, as it may as well take place with the non-material or symbolic delivery'. As examples, the court cited the case of agricultural loans, in which the lender can keep as a deposit not only machinery and cattle, but also trees and future crops and harvests. Of course, one can say that delivery may be 'non-material or symbolic' without going as far as do scholars who believe that a promise to deposit can create an obligation even before delivery.

Once Otto and Charles have entered into a contract of deposit, Otto can ask Charles to return his furniture at any time (art. 1775 of the Civil Code), but Charles can only ask Otto to take the furniture back if there is a fair motive (art. 1776). According to legal scholars, examples of fair motives are a lack of space, a change in personal circumstances, the long term of a deposit, and the risk of loss of the goods deposited due to their nature.[16] The motive must be genuine and asserted in a timely fashion. Motives which existed when the deposit was created and not alleged then are insufficient.[17]

If Otto does not accept the goods back, Charles can ask the court to accept the deposit (art. 1776 of the Civil Code).

PORTUGAL

In Case 5(a), Charles is certainly bound by the promise after the delivery of the furniture. It is possible that a court would consider him bound before he does so if both parties have agreed on establishing a legal obligation before delivery. If he is bound, the fact that he had an unexpected inheritance (Case 5(c)) would allow him to discharge the promise. The other circumstances mentioned in Cases 5(b), 5(d), and 5(e) are not relevant.

In Portuguese law, a contract of this type is a deposit (*depósito*), which is defined by art. 1185 of the Civil Code as a contract in which one of the parties gives the other one an object to be taken into custody and later returned. A deposit is a real contract *quoad constitutionem*. That means this contract is formed only with the delivery of the object to the person taking custody. This is an old form of constituting obligations, inherited from the

---

[16] J. L. Albacar López, *Código civil: doctrina y jurisprudencia*, 4th edn (1995), VI-1, 825.

[17] TS, 3 Oct. 1902 (the poor condition of horses and the cost of maintaining them was not a fair reason because nothing had changed since the deposit was accepted).

Roman law, which is called a contract *re* (*obligationes re contracta*). Therefore, the classical idea, expressed in the legal definition of this contract itself, is that it does not create any obligation until after the thing to be deposited is actually delivered (*datio rei*).[18]

Nevertheless, this classical Roman solution has been questioned by some jurists who believe that it is contrary to the principle of freedom of contract. According to these writers, art. 405 of the Civil Code permits the parties to enter into any contract they wish. So there is no reason why the parties could not form a contract that is binding before the delivery of the thing to be deposited, even if the legal definition of deposit requires delivery. Presently, the majority of Portuguese legal writers support this new solution.[19]

Therefore, it is not clear how the courts would solve this case if the object is not delivered. After delivery, however, it is clear that a contract has been formed which is binding on Charles. Therefore, it does not matter at all if Charles was a friend of Otto, the antiques dealer from whom he had purchased the table and chairs, or a professional storer. He would have to fulfil the obligation.

Nevertheless, there are cases in which the deposit contract can be terminated earlier than the time agreed. Otto can ask Charles to return the deposit at any time (art. 1194 of the Civil Code) but Charles can only ask Otto to take the furniture back if there is a fair reason (*justa causa*) (art. 1201). A fair reason is an imprecise concept which can be interpreted in different ways.

According to legal scholars, a fair reason can be found in many different situations which can concern either party or even the thing deposited. Examples include the bad health of the storer, a sudden trip he has to make, and a call for service in the military.[20] In my view, the unexpected inheritance would be considered a fair reason to terminate the deposit earlier than agreed.

The circumstances mentioned in Cases 5(d) and 5(e) have no direct relevance because if a term was agreed upon, Charles cannot terminate the deposit without a fair reason, and if he has a fair reason, the position of Otto is in principle not relevant. However, as the fair reason is evaluated by taking into account the concrete case, these circumstances might make it more difficult for Charles to terminate the deposit.

---

[18] See Lima and Varela, *Código Civil Anotado*, vol. II, 834.

[19] See C. M. Pinto, *Cessão da Posição Contratual* (1982), 14; Costa, *Direito das Obrigações*, 240–2; L. C. Fernandes, *Teoria Geral do Direito Civil*, 2nd edn, vol. II (1996), 58–9; A. M. Cordeiro, *Tratado de Direito Civil Português*, vol. I (1999), *Parte Geral*, I, 260.

[20] See Lima and Varela, *Código Civil Anotado*, vol. II, 856.

ITALY

It makes a fundamental difference whether Charles refused to store the table and chairs before they were delivered or a month afterwards.

Delivery is fundamental because, according to the Italian Civil Code, a contract of deposit[21] is not complete without delivery, and the obligations of the depositary arise from that moment.[22] The depositary has a duty to keep custody of the goods delivered and to return them in their original condition.

The contract of deposit can be gratuitous. Indeed, according to art. 1767 of the Civil Code, it is presumed to be so. According to art. 1771, the depositary must return the goods as soon as the depositor asks for them, and the depositary can ask the depositor to take his goods back at any time unless a time limit in favour of the depositor has been agreed upon.[23]

If the goods have not been delivered, the problem is quite different. According to the case law, such a promise would not be enforceable if the promisor has no economic interest in its fulfilment because then it would lack a *causa*[24] which is essential according to art. 1325 of the Civil Code. Often it would be considered to be a mere 'courtesy promise' that was not intended to have legal effects.[25] The result would be different if the promisor did have an economic interest at stake: for example, if he was an antiques dealer or the promise was made by a professional storer of furniture for publicity.[26]

Legal scholars have discussed the problem of opportunities that are lost and harm that is caused to a promisee who relies on a promise that is not legally binding. Some have said that under circumstances like these, the promisor could be held liable for lost alternatives and for the expenses incurred in the expectation that the promise would be kept, although it is

---

[21] See, e.g., F. Mastropaolo, 'Il deposito', in Rescigno, *Tratt. di dir. priv.* (1985), 441.

[22] Article 1766 of the Civil Code: 'Concept: Deposit is a contract by which one of the parties receives a movable thing from the other under a duty to keep custody of it and return it unchanged.' A. Galasso and G. Galasso, 'Deposito', Digesto (1989), 253, at 255.

[23] Article 1771 of the Civil Code: 'Request for restitution and duty to take back thing: The depositary shall return the thing as soon as the depositor requests it, unless a time limit in favour of the depositary was agreed upon. The depositary can at any time request the depositor to take back the thing, unless a time limit in favour of the depositor was agreed upon. Even if no time limit was agreed upon, unless a time limit in favour of the depositary was agreed upon, the court can grant the depositor an adequate time limit within which to accept the thing.'

[24] In the sense pointed out by R. Sacco, 'Il Contratto', in Vassalli, *Tratt. di dir. civ.* 6:2 (1975), 621.   [25] See *ibid.*, 491 ff.

[26] See A. Gianola, 'Verso il riconoscimento della promessa atipica, informale, gratuita ma interessata', Giur. it. I (1995), 1921.

not clear whether this liability would be contractual or extra-contractual.[27] Whether it can be imposed is quite controversial.

In such cases, some scholars have tried to apply the concept of 'just' or 'reasonable' *causa* introduced by Gino Gorla. He recognizes that to enforce a gratuitous promise of a kind which is not governed by the Code has its costs. There is a social cost to triggering formal machinery for adjudication and a chilling effect on the willingness of people to make such promises. In his view, whether such a promise is enforceable should depend on balancing the harm the promisee would suffer from non-performance and his reliance on it against the cost of keeping the promise for the promisor and his own good or bad faith and reasons for refusing to perform.[28]

Some think that in such a case the promisor could be held liable under the rules of the Civil Code that govern pre-contractual liability imposed for lack of good faith (art. 1337 of the Civil Code).[29] A court might impose such liability by interpreting the promise to receive and store the furniture as part of the negotiations for a contract of deposit which would be formed upon delivery.[30] The liability is deemed to arise in tort, and so is limited to the amount by which a party has been harmed: the so-called 'negative interest' (*interesse negativo*) which would include expenses incurred during negotiations and the loss of other opportunities.[31]

AUSTRIA

The contract of deposit is a 'real' contract in Austrian law, that is to say, a contract that is formed by delivery of the object in question (Civil Code § 957). The promise to store another person's goods constitutes a *pactum de contrahendo*. It creates the obligation to conclude a contract of deposit. There is no special formal requirement for such a contract or agreement. The contract of *depositum* is gratuitous unless a remuneration has been agreed upon (Civil Code § 969). Not every promise to store goods, however,

---

[27] See Marini, *Promessa ed affidamento*, 295–7, 307, 313; Gorla, *Il contratto*, 180 n. 26; A. Checchini, *Rapporti non vincolanti e regola di correttezza* (1977).

[28] See Gorla, *Il contratto*, 180 ff.; Marini, *Promessa ed affidamento*, 297; but see also G. Venezian, 'La causa dei contratti', in *Opere giuridiche*, vol. I (1919), who affirms that those promises are not enforceable to any extent, and A. Ascoli, *Trattato delle donazioni* (1935), for whom this type of promise is a form of donation.

[29] On the rules governing pre-contractual liability affirmed by case law, see, most recently, Cass. civ., sez. III, 13 March 1996, no. 2057, in Foro it. I (1996), 2065; Cass. civ., sez. II, 1 Feb. 1995, no. 1163; Cass. civ., sez. II, 25 Feb. 1992, no. 2335.

[30] See Marini, *Promessa ed affidamento*, 295; Checchini, *Rapporti non vincolanti*.

[31] See Cass. civ., sez. II, 13 Dec. 1994, no. 10649; Cass. civ., sez. I, 30 Aug. 1995, no. 9157; see also Cass. civ., sez. III, 12 March 1993, no. 2973.

creates a legal obligation. If somebody only wishes to do another person a favour (*Gefälligkeitsverhältnis*), and does not intend to bind himself legally, no legal obligation is created.[32]

The promise will be binding if Charles intended to bind himself legally. This undoubtedly will be the case if Charles is the antiques dealer from whom Otto purchased the furniture or if he is a professional storer of furniture. In these two cases Charles' promise belonged to his professional and not his private sphere. If, however, Charles is just a friend of Otto, such an intention probably will be absent (Case 5(b)).

In Case 5(a), if the furniture has been delivered, the 'real' contract of deposit is concluded. As mentioned, before delivery, there is only a *pactum de contrahendo*. In the latter case, according to § 936 of the Civil Code, the agreement is subject to a *clausula rebus sic stantibus*: if there is a significant change in the circumstances, the *pactum de contrahendo* can be cancelled. Section 936 applies only to such an agreement, and therefore not to the contract of deposit. Nevertheless, in Austrian law, any contract can become invalid because of changed and unforeseen circumstances (*Wegfall der Geschäftsgrundlage*, literally, the falling away of the basis of the contract).[33] Consequently, it is really not clear what the difference is between § 936 and this general doctrine. With respect to the contract of deposit, one must also take into consideration that, according to § 962 of the Civil Code, the depositee has the right to return the stored goods to the depositor before the agreed time if, due to unforeseen circumstances, he is unable to store the goods safely or without harming his own interests. The consequence of § 962 is that it really does not matter whether Charles refuses to store the furniture before delivery or afterwards. He will have the right to do so either under § 936 or under § 962.

In Case 5(c), assuming that Charles' promise is binding, § 936 of the Civil Code gives Charles the right to refuse to store the furniture because of changed circumstances. Consequently, he could refuse if he unexpectedly inherited furniture.[34] If he merely changed his mind, neither § 936 nor § 962 of the Civil Code would apply.

In Cases 5(d) and 5(e), the question, of course, is whether these circumstances can be taken to indicate that Charles intended to bind himself legally. I think, however, one cannot conclude that he had such an

---

[32] G. Schubert in Rummel, *ABGB* § 957 no. 1.

[33] See P. Rummel in Rummel, *ABGB* § 90 nos. 1 ff.; G. Graf, *Vertrag und Vernunft* (1997), 131 ff., 276 ff.; A. Fenyves, *Der Einfluß geänderter Verhältnisse auf Langzeitverträge* (1997).

[34] If the furniture were already delivered to Charles, § 962 of the Civil Code would lead to the same result as the inheritance was unexpected.

intention. If Charles is just a friend of Otto, the fact that Otto could have stored the furniture at a warehouse is not sufficient to make Charles' commitment a legal one.[35]

GERMANY

Deposit (*Verwahrung*, §§ 688–700 of the Civil Code) is a type of contract which obligates the promisor to provide a room for storage and to take care of the goods (§ 688). It is up to the parties to agree whether compensation will be paid or not (see § 689) but there is no requirement that it be. Even if the deposit is free of charge, such a contract is not deemed to be a gift. Consequently, no formality is required to enter into a deposit contract. It is not as dangerous for the promisor as the promise to make a gift. Therefore, § 518 of the Civil Code is not applicable (see Case 1), and the promise is binding without any formality.

Nevertheless, § 696 of the Civil Code[36] gives Charles the right to give the things deposited back to Otto before the time agreed if he has an important reason. An important reason means that it is unreasonable for the promisor to have to continue to store them. Thus far, the courts have said little about the meaning of § 696. But one could think of clear cases in which the promisor would have an important reason: for example, if he loses the room (for example, due to a fire in Charles' house), or becomes seriously ill, or if the goods in storage endanger the promisor or his goods, although even then he could not terminate the contract at a moment that would be inopportune given the consequences to the other party. Whether Charles has an important reason depends on weighing his interests against Otto's. The unexpected inheritance could be an important reason depending on how serious the problems caused by the new situation are for Charles. This is especially true because Charles acted altruistically which means that his interests are even more important. If Charles merely changed his mind, he cannot refuse to store the furniture any more.

It does not matter if the furniture has already been delivered when Charles changes his mind except as it bears on the question of whether the moment is inappropriate. If Otto does not have any opportunity to store his furniture elsewhere, the moment is inappropriate. If he still has time enough to find another place, it is not.

As long as the service was meant to be free of charge, Charles' profes-

---

[35] The same argument applies with respect to Case 5(d).
[36] The keeper can give the goods back at any time if no end to the period for keeping them is agreed upon. If such a time is agreed upon, he can only give the goods back before then if he has an important reason.

sion or his relationship with Otto does not matter. It is possible, however, that because of the previous contract, Charles has to take Otto's interests more seriously into consideration.

Whether Otto has lost the opportunity to store the furniture with Jean or to store it with the warehouse at a lower price than he can now obtain matters only to the extent that it shows Otto's own interests are important or that the moment Charles chose to terminate the deposit was inopportune.

GREECE

In Greek law, Charles and Otto wish to make a contract of deposit. This kind of contract is regulated by arts. 822–33 of the Civil Code. According to art. 822 of the Civil Code: 'By a contract of deposit the depositary takes delivery from another person of a movable thing with a view of keeping it (safely) subject to the obligation to return it upon demand. A remuneration may only be claimed if this has been agreed or results from the circumstances.'[37]

In the present case, the contract is a unilateral one (see Case 1) because it is without remuneration and so it creates obligations only on the part of the depositary, namely, the obligations to keep the thing and return it upon demand (art. 827 of the Civil Code).[38] Had remuneration been promised, the contract would be a reciprocal one which would be governed by arts. 374 and following of the Civil Code.[39] Moreover, under the Greek Civil Code, the contract for deposit is based on a fiduciary relationship between the depositor and the depositary.[40]

In Case 5(a), Charles either refuses to store the furniture before it is delivered or refuses to do so a month afterwards. A contract for deposit belongs to the so-called delivery contracts which are concluded *re*. This means that, in addition to the consent of the parties, delivery of the thing is also required for the contract to be formed.[41] Before delivery, the parties

---

[37] Article 822 corresponds to previous law which did not, however, recognize any remuneration for the depositary. A similar provision is contained in §§ 688 and 689 of the German Civil Code, 1915 and 1928(2) of the French Code, and 427 of the Swiss Code of Obligations; Kafkas, *Law of Obligations*, art. 822 CC.

[38] Kafkas, *Law of Obligations*, art. 822 CC; Kritikos in Georgiadis and Stathopoulos, *Civil Code*, art. 822, no. 4.   [39] EfAth 12462/87 HellD 32, 1068 (1991); AP 858/1974 NoB 23, 483.

[40] Kritikos in Georgiadis and Stathopoulos, *Civil Code*, art. 882, no. 8; EfAth 1264/55 EEN 22, 933 (1955); Kafkas, *Law of Obligations*, art. 822 CC; Rammos in ErmAK art. 822 no. 6.

[41] The characteristic of 'delivery' in delivery contracts is that the obligation of the depositary to return the thing (and not the obligation of the depositor to deliver the thing to the depositary) may not be generated prior to the delivery of the thing; Stathopoulos, *Contract Law*, 40–1.

have, not a contract of deposit, but a preliminary agreement to deposit. The leading opinion is that such an agreement obligates them to enter into a contract of deposit.[42] A party who refuses to do so can be forced to enter into the contract.[43] While some deny that an agreement to deposit is enforceable, the leading view seems to be the right one. It is consistent with the principle of freedom of contract (art. 361 of the Civil Code). Such a contract can therefore be formed by mere consent, and delivery of the thing is the fulfilment of a contractual obligation.[44]

Thus, in Case 5(a), if the furniture has not yet been delivered, Charles can be forced to conclude the contract and to take delivery (art. 949 of the Code of Civil Procedure).[45] If he refuses he will be liable for Otto's positive or expectation interest (art. 343 of the Civil Code). The preliminary agreement is a full contract according to art. 166 of the Civil Code and liability is for breach of such a contract, not for pre-contractual conduct.[46]

If the furniture has already been delivered, then the parties have made a contract of deposit. If Charles refuses to store the furniture, he will also be liable for Otto's positive interest according to arts. 343 and following of the Civil Code. The amount of compensation will be the same in both cases.

According to art. 828(1) of the Civil Code, Charles cannot insist that Otto take back the furniture before the end of the term on which they agreed unless some unforeseeable event has occurred.[47] Section 1 provides: 'A

---

[42] Kritikos in Georgiadis and Stathopoulos, *Civil Code*, arts. 822 ff.; Varthakokoilis, *Analytical Interpretation*, art. 822; AP 747/1979 NoB 28, 53.

[43] Kafkas, *Law of Obligations*, art. 822; D. Bosdas, 'The Contract for Deposit', HellD 20 (1979), 1.

[44] Filios, *Law of Obligations*, pars. 27–8; Karakatsanis, *The Declaration of Will*, 212 ff. The Swiss Code of Obligations characterizes the contract for deposit as a *solo consensu* contract.

[45] Some writers doubt whether resort to means of coercion are permitted because they destroy the fiduciary relationship between the depositor and the depositary; Bosdas, 'The Contract for Deposit'.

[46] AP 261/1996 HellD 37, 1560 (1996); Varthakokoilis, *Analytical Interpretation*, art. 166.

[47] Moreover, the depositary cannot get rid of the thing by depositing it with a public body if the thing can be subject to a deposit with a public body (art. 427 of the Civil Code). The deposit with a public body is equivalent to the payment of a debt (art. 431). The debtor has the right to make a deposit with a public body only if certain requirements are met. These are that the creditor must be in default and the debtor insecure, and the object must be one that can be deposited. Furniture, according to art. 2 of the Presidential Degree 30.12.1926/3.1.1927, is not subject to deposit with a public body. Therefore, in this case, art. 428 of the Civil Code applies. It provides: 'If the thing due is a movable, which does not admit of depositing, the debtor, after placing the creditor upon notice and advising him, may sell the thing by public auction and deposit the proceeds of sale with a public body. The advice to the creditor may be omitted if the thing is perishable and a delay would entail risks or if advising the creditor is particularly difficult.' Sxinas in Georgiadis and Stathopoulos, *Civil Code*, art. 428.

depositary shall not be entitled to return the thing deposited before the lapse of the period fixed except if unforeseeable events make it impossible for him to keep further the thing safely and without prejudice to himself.' Section 2 adds: 'If no term has been fixed for safekeeping, a depositary may return the thing at any time.' However, if the depositor recovers the thing, the contract is cancelled.[48]

In Case 5(b), it might matter if Charles is a friend of Otto. If so, one must ask whether there is a contract between them or a mere act of courtesy.[49] If the parties do not intend to bind themselves legally but Charles is acting out of courtesy, he will not be held liable for refusing to store Otto's furniture. Difficulties arise when no remuneration for the deposit has been agreed. The decisive issue will be the real intention of the parties. This issue will be decided *ad hoc*, taking into consideration all the circumstances such as the value of the thing deposited.[50] Here, because of the value of the furniture, it seems probable that the parties intended a contract of deposit even if Charles is a friend of Otto. If so, he is liable.

If Charles is the antiques dealer from whom Otto recently purchased the furniture, their agreement might be an independent contract for deposit or an obligation secondary to the original contract of sale. In either case, the antiques dealer is bound by the contract and will be liable if he breaches for Otto's positive or expectation interest under arts. 343 and following of the Civil Code.

Finally, if Charles is a professional storer of furniture, then the agreement is a contract for deposit, and Charles will be liable if he breaches for the reasons already given.

In Case 5(c), it does matter whether Charles refuses to store the furniture merely because he has changed his mind or because he has inherited furniture which he has no other place to store. If he merely changed his mind, as we have seen, he will be liable. If he inherited furniture he cannot store elsewhere, he is not. He falls within the provision of art. 828 already quoted which entitles the depositary to return the object even before the expiration of the time fixed if unforeseeeable events make it impossible for him to keep further the object safely and without prejudice to himself.

In such a case, however, Charles should, according to the principle of good faith (arts. 200 and 288 of the Civil Code), notify Otto in time for him to take back the furniture.[51] If Otto refuses to do so, he will be in default

---

[48] Kritikos in Georgiadis and Stathopoulos, *Civil Code*, art. 828; Kafkas, *Law of Obligations*, art. 828.

[49] Karasis, 'Gentlemen's Agreement', in *Miscellany in Honor of Andreas Gazis* (1994), 207–25.

[50] Kritikos in Georgiadis and Stathopoulos, *Civil Code*, arts. 822 ff.

[51] *Ibid.*, art. 828, no. 6.

of a creditor (art. 349 of the Civil Code) and the depositary's liability for the furniture will be limited (art. 343 of the Civil Code).

The depositary will also be entitled to deposit the object with a public body if the object can be deposited according to art. 427 of the Civil Code.[52] Furthermore, if the provisions regulating the default of the debtor are being applied, then the depositor will have to compensate the depositary on the basis of art. 343 of the Civil Code.[53]

In Case 5(d), it does not matter if Charles could have stored the furniture with Jean. In Greek law contractual liability requires one to pay the positive or expectation interest and not the negative or reliance interest.[54]

In Case 5(e), for the same reason, if Otto has had to pay any more than originally agreed to have his furniture stored, Charles will be liable for the extra amount.

SCOTLAND

The basis of the law applicable to this problem is once again contained in s. 1(2) of the Requirements of Writing (Scotland) Act 1995, which provides that a gratuitous unilateral obligation will only be enforceable if constituted in writing.[55] The promise is binding in the terms in which it is expressed, and so the point at which Charles breaks it is likely to be relevant only to the quantification of damages.

If Charles is a friend of Otto, it is likely to lead to a presumption that there was no intention to create legal obligations, but merely a social arrangement. This can be shown by the case of *Heslop* v. *Burns*,[56] in which an agreement between friends on contributions to car maintenance was held not to amount to a contract but to be binding in honour only. Obviously, if Otto has the written promise of Charles, that is likely to rebut the presumption. On the other hand, if Charles is a professional storer of furniture, the exemption from the requirements of writing for gratuitous unilateral obligations incurred in the course of business may apply, and Otto may only require to prove the promise by parole evidence: s. 1(2)(a)(ii).

Charles' reasons for breaking his promise are irrelevant. Scots law has a strict doctrine of frustration which requires that the event be unforeseen and the fault of neither party. Therefore, Charles is in breach of his promise.

The circumstances presented in Cases 5(d) and 5(e) are again likely to give rise to reliance upon s. 1(3) and (4) of the 1995 Act, so that the gratuitous unilateral promise can be enforced even if it is not in writing. The

---

[52] See note 47, above.   [53] Kritikos in Georgiadis and Stathopoulos, *Civil Code*, no. 8.
[54] Stathopoulos, *Contract Law*, 84–5.   [55] See Case 1.   [56] [1974] 3 All ER 406.

relevant law can be found in Cases 1 and 4. In all the situations, Otto's acts must be known to and acquiesced in by Charles. They must occur *after* Charles' promise. In both Cases 5(d) and 5(e), it is submitted that s. 1(4) will be satisfied given the wide meaning it has been suggested should be given to 'material' in s. 1(4).

ENGLAND

The resolution of Case 5 involves, in the first instance, consideration of what is known in English law as 'bailment', and in particular 'gratuitous bailment'.[57] A bailment is 'a delivery of goods on condition that the recipient shall ultimately restore the goods to the bailor; they may thus be hired or lent or pledged or deposited for safe custody'.[58] Where, as here, the benefit is entirely to the bailor, the bailment is called *depositum* or *mandatum*. There is little agreement regarding the proper juridical classification of the rules regulating gratuitous bailment. They have been viewed, variously, as part of contract or (less commonly) tort law, as composed of bits of tort, contract, restitution, property, and trusts, or as *sui generis*. Most authors accept that at least some of the rules regulating gratuitous bailment derive from general contractual principles.[59]

It is clear under English law that if the goods have not been delivered, Charles (the potential 'bailee') is not bound by his promise; and this is true regardless of whether Charles is a professional or Otto (the potential 'bailor') has relied in some way on his promise, and also regardless of Charles' reason for changing his mind.[60] In this respect, the law on promises to enter into a gratuitous bailment follows the standard rules on consideration, that is, the promise is not binding unless something has been given in return (see Case 1). Any special rules that apply to bailment come into force only after the bailment relationship has commenced, which requires actual delivery of the goods. Thus, while Otto may, and probably did, promise to deliver his furniture to Charles, Otto's promise is not good consideration for Charles' promise to store the furniture because it was not given in exchange for Charles' promise (see Case 1). In other words, there was no bargain.

As discussed in previous answers, an English court might try to 'invent' consideration if it thought Charles' promise was seriously made and if, as in Cases 5(d) and 5(e), Otto had detrimentally relied on Charles' promise.

---

[57] See generally, Palmer, *Bailment*.

[58] G. C. Cheshire, C. H. S. Fifoot, and M. P. Furmston, *Law of Contract*, 12th edn (1991), 84.

[59] See generally Palmer, *Bailment*, especially 19–31, 566–77.   [60] Treitel, *Contract*, 144.

A court might suggest, for example, that Charles received some benefit in exchange for storing the goods (perhaps he could use them?). If so, then an ordinary contract (albeit a contract to establish a bailment relationship) would exist, and Charles would be bound to store the goods. Judicial manoeuvres of this sort were more common in the past than they are in contemporary decisions, where the clear orthodox law – that gratuitous promises are unenforceable – has been upheld.[61]

Once a bailment relationship has been established by the delivery and taking possession of goods, it is less certain whether and to what extent ordinary contractual rules apply. Clearly, the bailee has certain duties *vis-à-vis* the care of the goods, and the bailor similarly has certain duties, none of which appear founded in contract.[62] It is clear, however, that a bailment relationship is in principle terminable at will, that is, that a bailee can demand that the bailor take back the goods. So as not to be in breach of his duty as a bailee to take care of the goods, Charles would need to give Otto reasonable notice of a decision to hand back Otto's goods, but if this is done then Charles is under no general obligation to continue storing the goods. This rule, however, may not apply where, as here, the bailee has promised to store the goods for a certain period – although predictions here are difficult as the law is unsettled and there do not appear to be any cases directly in point. An initial observation is that delivery does not alter the fact that there was no consideration for Charles' promise, so, as explained above, the promise is not enforceable on ordinary contractual principles. There is, nevertheless, some judicial authority for enforcing promises ancillary to a bailment relationship, that is, promises made in connection with the goods which impose duties greater than those imposed by the bailment relationship itself. In the case of *Mitchell* v. *Ealing London Borough Council*,[63] a local council was held strictly liable for the breach of its gratuitous promise to redeliver goods, that it was holding as a bailee, to a tenant bailor at a particular time and place. If this case were extended, it might cover Charles' promise. It must be stressed, however, that the law in this area is not clear: there is, for example, no consensus amongst commentators as to the basis of liability in *Mitchell*, that is, whether the Council's liability was in contract, tort, or *sui generis*. More importantly, the absence of other cases means it is unclear how far this novel decision would be followed.[64]

---

[61] See Palmer, *Bailment*, 26–7.   [62] *Ibid.*, 505–6.   [63] [1979] QB 1.

[64] Some support can be derived from older cases, such as *Trefitz & Sons Ltd* v. *Canelli* [1872] LRCP 4, where the Privy Council upheld a bailee's promise to release goods only to certain persons without examining the question of consideration for the promise.

The possibility that Charles might be liable on the basis of estoppel or tort must also be considered. Liability here would not be liability to keep the promise to store the goods, but rather liability to make good any loss arising from the breach of that promise. As explained in Case 1, in certain circumstances a promisor may be 'estopped' from going back on his or her word where the promisee has detrimentally relied on the promise. Estoppel cannot, however, be raised by Otto in this case because the parties did not have pre-existing legal relations. As explained in the discussion of Case 1, estoppel may be used in English law only as a defence to a cause of action. It may not be used, as it would be used here, to create legal rights where none existed before.[65]

The possibility of liability in tort is more promising, but also more complex. The relevant area of tort law is in a state of flux, and has not yet been applied to bailment situations (though as noted earlier, some commentators suggest that bailment law itself is at least partly derived from tort principles); thus, it is difficult in the extreme to say confidently how such a case would be decided. Any loss that Otto suffers will presumably be economic loss rather than physical harm to the property itself. Recovery for economic loss in tort is allowed only in a limited range of situations in English law,[66] but one situation where it is allowed is in respect of the negligent provision of services.[67] If the plaintiff suffers harm as a result of relying on the defendant providing the service, the plaintiff can recover for that loss in certain circumstances. In particular, for a claim to succeed on this basis the plaintiff must establish that he or she had a 'special relationship' with the defendant.[68] Exactly what constitutes a 'special relationship' is a notoriously complex and unsettled area of contemporary English tort law, and any brief account of the law here will necessarily be incomplete.[69] That proviso in mind, the most commonly cited tests for establishing a special relationship ask whether the relationship was 'close to contract' or whether the defendant 'assumed responsibility' for the plaintiff's economic welfare.[70] Making a promise does of course

---

Against this can be raised more recent cases, such as the Australian case (Australian law is thought to be consistent with English law in this area) of *Parastatidis* v. *Kotaridis* [1978] VR 449, where it was stated at 454–5 that promissory terms in bailments are unenforceable unless supported by consideration. See generally Palmer, *Bailment*, 572–7.

[65] See Palmer, *Bailment*, 574.

[66] See generally P. Cane, *Economic Interests and the Law of Tort*, 2nd edn (1997).

[67] See *Henderson* v. *Merrett Syndicates Ltd* [1995] 2 AC 145, which involved the provision of services by insurance agents.   [68] *Hedley Byrne* v. *Heller* [1964] AC 465, 486.

[69] See generally D. Howarth, *Textbook on Tort* (1995), 267–99.

[70] See, e.g., Lord Devlin's judgment in *Hedley Byrne* v. *Heller* [1964] AC 465 and Lord Goff's judgment in *Henderson* v. *Merrett Syndicates Ltd* [1995] 2 AC 145.

bring a relationship 'close to contract' (there is a contract save for the needed consideration); equally it is strong evidence of an assumption of responsibility.[71] It is clear, however, that the fact of a mere promise is not enough to satisfy the requirement of a special relationship. In particular, nearly every case in this area has emphasized the importance of the defendant fulfilling a professional role, such as that of a solicitor or a banker.[72] In the recent decision in *Henderson* v. *Merrett Syndicates Ltd*,[73] it was stated explicitly that there is no liability in respect of services rendered on 'an informal occasion'. For this reason, it is suggested that in the scenario where Charles is merely a friend, he is unlikely to be liable in tort. But where Charles is a professional storer of furniture, or an antiques dealer from whom the furniture was recently purchased, the 'close relationship' requirement would likely be satisfied (assuming that the promise was made seriously, and it was understood that it would be acted upon).

A further hurdle to establishing tort liability is that Charles' refusal to store the furniture, while it may have been 'unreasonable', was not negligent. It was nonfeasance, rather than misfeasance, and, in the traditional view, there is no liability for the former in tort law.[74] That a promise has been made is traditionally thought not to change this rule. As one court noted, if a promisor were liable outside of contract for completely failing to perform a promise, this would amount to holding 'that the law of England recognizes the enforceability of a gratuitous promise'.[75] This is not quite correct, since damages in tort would compensate only for detrimental reliance rather than for the value of the promise. But allowing an action for non-performance of a gratuitous promise would, at a minimum, amount to allowing estoppel to be used to support a cause of action, which, as we have seen, is not permitted under the orthodox understanding of estoppel (see Case 1). Consistent with this distinction, Treitel states that there is no liability in contract or tort for 'a complete failure to pursue a *promised course of action*',[76] and two cases support this view.[77] On the other hand, it seems counter-intuitive that Charles could be liable for negligently failing to keep his promise to store the goods, but not liable for completely refusing to store them, given that in the former

---

[71] *Henderson* v. *Merrett Syndicates Ltd* [1995] 2 AC 145.

[72] See, e.g., *Hedley Byrne* v. *Heller* [1964] AC 465; *Smith* v. *Eric S. Bush* [1990] 1 AC 831; *White* v. *Jones* [1993] 3 WLR 730.   [73] [1995] 2 AC 145, 160.

[74] *Argy Trading and Development Co. Ltd* v. *Lapid Developments Ltd* [1977] 1 WLR 444; *The Zephyr* [1985] 2 Lloyd's Rep. 529, 538–9; and see generally, Palmer, *Bailment*, 575–6.

[75] *The Zephyr* [1985] 2 Lloyd's Rep. 529, 328.   [76] Treitel, *Contract*, 145.

[77] *The Zephyr* [1985] 2 Lloyd's Rep. 529; *Argy Trading Co.* v. *Lapid Developments* [1977] 1 WLR 444.

case Charles' liability would rest largely on the fact that he had assumed responsibility for the service. Thus, it is not surprising that other commentators have supported liability for nonfeasance in certain contexts,[78] even if not calling for a general elimination of the sword/shield distinction in estoppel. Consistent with this view, a solicitor was held liable in tort for failing in his promise to register an option, with no distinction being drawn between liability for misfeasance and nonfeasance.[79] It is difficult to predict, therefore, whether a court would find Charles liable in tort. The law is unsettled, and those cases in which liability has been found are not closely related to the case in question. It is suggested that were a court to find Charles liable, it would only be in the case where the goods had already been delivered. Though delivery does not, in itself, make a difference to a tort claim, it would probably influence a court's view of how close the relationship was between the parties and how strong was the assumption of responsibility by Charles – factors which are relevant. Moreover, once delivery has occurred, it is easier for a court to present the question as one of liability for not providing a service, rather than as one of liability for not performing a promise. In short, delivery is a factor that a court wanting to limit the scope of potential liability in tort for failing to perform a promise is likely to fasten upon. That said, the paucity of authority in this area means that any predictions must be treated carefully.

As should be clear from the above, allowing Otto to recover not just for a negligent failure to keep his promise but also for deliberately refusing to keep his promise considerably weakens the force of the consideration requirement in contract. This is one reason why English law in this area is unsettled: tort appears to be intruding into contract. Tort liability for non-performance of promised services is limited (at present anyway) to professional defendants, but in principle promisees are being allowed to recover for losses incurred in reasonable reliance on a broken promise. And if recovery is allowed in respect of the failed provision of services, why not failed sales, and so on? It will be necessary for English law to decide in the near future whether it wishes wholeheartedly to allow recovery in tort for induced-by-promising detrimental reliance or whether it wishes to return to the orthodox position that promises are relevant only to liability in contract. At the moment, the law is unclear, though it appears to be moving in the direction of expanding liability. It is reasonably certain

---

[78] See, e.g., J. Fleming, *The Law of Torts*, 7th edn (1987), 138. See also Case 6.
[79] *Midland Bank* v. *Hett* [1979] Ch. 384. See also *White* v. *Jones* [1993] 3 WLR 730.

that, whichever direction the law moves in, English courts will introduce change relatively gradually in this area. For example, it is unlikely that an English court would extend now the reasoning of the cases dealing with the negligent provision of promised services to cases of non-delivery of promised goods or money.

There is no discussion in the reported cases as to whether the bailee's reason for changing his mind should matter in respect of any of the possible bases for Charles' liability. It might be presumed, therefore, that such factors are irrelevant, but the lack of recent cases in point, and the general confusion in the law in this area, makes it difficult to be certain. Finally, in respect of potential tort liability no distinction appears to have been drawn in the law between different classes of bailees, although if Charles is merely a friend of Otto it might be found that his promise lacked the required intent to create legal relations (see Case 1).

IRELAND

This is not a binding promise, as there has been no formal contract by way of a deed under seal, and Otto has given no consideration in exchange for Charles' promise to store the valuable antique table and chairs. Charles' offer to store Otto's furniture without reward could, however, come within the meaning of a gratuitous bailment where Charles actually acquires the furniture. A gratuitous bailment is one from which only one party benefits. In this example, Otto, as bailor, would clearly benefit from the transaction while Charles, as bailee, would not. Recent case law repudiates the notion of a gratuitous bailment as a contractual relation, and Palmer defines bailment as a legal relationship which, while frequently arising from contract, can exist independently thereof.[80] Recent authorities suggest that a gratuitous bailment may disclose no possible action in contract but gives rise to purely tortious remedies.[81]

Treitel provides that in the case of a bailment for the benefit of the bailor such as in the instant case, Charles' only duty to Otto is that imposed by law. Where Charles promises to do anything which goes beyond the duty imposed by the law (for example, to keep the chattel in repair), Charles would be bound by this promise only if Otto had provided some consideration for it apart from the delivery of the chattel.[82] It is clear that the mere promise by Charles to store the valuable antique table and

[80] See Palmer, *Bailment,* ch. 1.
[81] See *ibid.*, ch. 11. See also *Walker* v. *Watson* [1974] 2 NZLR 175.
[82] See *Charnock* v. *Liverpool Corporation* [1968] 1 WLR 1498.

chairs would be unenforceable in contract under Irish law. However, once the chattels are actually acquired by the bailee he may then become liable with respect to his promise in tort.

As gratuitous bailee, Charles' liability to Otto arises only where Charles actually acquires the furniture.[83] Where Charles refuses to store the furniture before it is delivered, his promise to store the goods would be unenforceable. Otto has provided no consideration for Charles' promise to store the furniture, and he would not be liable in contract to Otto. However, it would appear to matter considerably if Charles refuses to store the furniture after it is delivered. Charles might then be liable to Otto in tort for the storage of the chattels in accordance with his promise.[84] The Irish courts have affirmed that liability may arise between parties where there is no contract between them and further, that the existence of a contract between the parties does not mean that there can be no liability in tort.[85]

In ascertaining whether a promise is binding, if Charles was a friend of Otto, that fact would present difficulties in establishing contractual intention on the part of Charles. Where Otto has provided no consideration, the promise is unenforceable. The enforceability of a contract will depend in part upon proof that a legally enforceable agreement was intended.[86] The fact that Charles was a friend would indicate that the promise was merely a social arrangement and that there was an absence of contractual intention on the part of Charles.[87]

If Charles was the antiques dealer from whom Otto recently purchased the table and chairs, then there is still no consideration, and such a promise amounts to past consideration and is unenforceable.[88] If, however, Charles promised to store the furniture for three months without charge as consideration or as part consideration for Otto's purchase of the table and chairs, then such a promise could amount to sufficient consideration for the purposes of making a binding contract because it was not intended to be gratuitous.[89]

In ascertaining whether Charles' promise is enforceable, his reasons in refusing to store the furniture are irrelevant. Charles' promise is unenforceable because there has been no consideration provided by Otto and the promise was not made by way of a deed under seal. As stated earlier, where Charles actually receives the furniture he may then become liable

---

[83] See Palmer, *Bailment*, ch. 9; *Roufos* v. *Brewster and Brewster* [1971] 2 SASR 218.

[84] See generally B. M. E. McMahon and W. Binchy, *Irish Law of Torts*, 2nd edn (1990).

[85] See *Donoghue* v. *Stevenson* [1932] AC 562.   [86] See *Heslop* v. *Burns* [1974] 1 WLR 1241.

[87] See Case 4; see also Treitel, *Contract*, ch. 3.   [88] See Case 3.

[89] See *Lampleigh* v. *Braithwaite* [1615] Hob. 105; see also Case 2.

in tort in respect of it. The object of damages in tort is to compensate the plaintiff by restoring him to the position which he would have held if the tort had not been committed.[90] The fact that Charles refused to store the furniture merely because he had changed his mind or because he had unexpectedly inherited furniture which he had no place else to store would appear to be irrelevant.

If Otto lost the opportunity to store the furniture with Jean, that fact will not go to the enforceability of the promise.[91] If Charles was held liable in tort to Otto this would be taken into account in seeking to compensate Otto by restoring him to the position which he would have held if the tort had not been committed.

Any detriment incurred by Otto could also be relevant where Otto seeks to raise the principles of estoppel.[92] However, estoppel operates as a shield and not a sword. Accordingly, it is difficult to see how Otto could raise these principles in this instance.

Similarly, if Otto had lost the opportunity to store the furniture with a warehouse at a lower price than is now possible, that fact does not affect the enforceability of the contract. Where Charles was liable in tort to Otto, this would be taken into account in seeking to compensate Otto by restoring him to the position which he would have held if the tort had not been committed.

Summaries

France: There is no liability if the parties did not intend the arrangement to be legally binding, as they may not have, if Charles was a friend or offered to store the furniture as a favour.

If they did, then, if the furniture has been delivered, a contract of deposit is formed upon delivery, and Charles is liable for its breach.

If the furniture has not been delivered, the arrangement would not be a contract of deposit but a promise to enter into such a contract. It is not clear whether such a promise is enforceable. If it is, it is subject to different rules: because it is gratuitous, Otto might not be able to obtain damages.

If Charles is liable in contract, the fact that he needs the space to store the furniture he has inherited will not excuse him because the doctrine of *force majeure* requires that the obstacle to performance be insurmountable. (He cannot obtain relief under the doctrine of *imprévision* or changed

---

[90] See McMahon and Binchy, *Irish Law of Torts*, ch. 1.   [91] See Case 5.   [92] See Case 1.

and unforeseen circumstances because that doctrine is not recognized in France.)

If he is not liable in contract, it is unlikely that he will be held liable in tort because breaking the promise will not be held to constitute fault.

Belgium: There is no liability if the parties did not intend the arrangement to be legally binding, as they may not have, if Charles was a friend.

If they did, then, if the furniture has been delivered, a contract of deposit is formed upon delivery, and Charles is liable for its breach.

If the furniture has not been delivered, the arrangement would not be a contract of deposit but a promise to enter into such a contract. Nevertheless, it would still be enforceable and subject to the same rules.

If Charles is liable in contract, the fact that he needs the space to store the furniture he has inherited may excuse him. Supposedly, the doctrine of *force majeure* requires that the obstacle to performance be insurmountable. But Belgian courts have applied that doctrine in cases in which a performance was simply more difficult. He cannot obtain relief under the doctrine of *imprévision* or changed and unforeseen circumstances because that doctrine is not recognized in Belgium.

The Netherlands: There is no liability if the parties did not intend the arrangement to be legally binding, as they may not have, especially if Charles was a friend. Whether Charles gave up the opportunity to store his furniture elsewhere is relevant to whether they did.

If they did, under the new Civil Code, there is a contract of deposit whether or not the furniture has been delivered.

If there is a contract of deposit, the fact that Charles needs the space to store the furniture he has inherited may excuse him since the court may change the moment at which the things deposited may be returned if he has an 'important reason'.

Because the contract is gratuitous, the rules that usually govern liability may be relaxed.

Spain: If the furniture has been delivered, a contract of deposit is formed upon delivery, and Charles may be liable for its breach.

If the furniture has not been delivered, the arrangement would not be a contract of deposit but a promise to enter into such a contract. It is not clear whether such a contract is enforceable, though some scholars believe that it is.

If there is a contract of deposit, the fact that Charles needs the space to store the furniture he has inherited may excuse him because he can return the things deposited before the time agreed if he has a 'fair motive'.

Portugal: There is no liability if the parties did not intend the arrangement to be legally binding, as they may not have, especially if Charles was a friend.

Otherwise, if the furniture has been delivered, a contract of deposit is formed upon delivery, and Charles may be liable for its breach.

If the furniture has not been delivered, the arrangement would not be a contract of deposit but a promise to enter into such a contract. It is not clear whether such a contract is enforceable, though most scholars believe that it is.

If there is a contract of deposit, the fact that Charles needs the space to store the furniture he has inherited would probably excuse him because he can return the things deposited before the time agreed if he has a 'fair reason'.

Italy: If the furniture has been delivered, a contract of deposit is formed upon delivery, and Charles may be liable for its breach.

If the furniture has not been delivered, the arrangement would not be a contract of deposit but a promise to enter into such a contract. Such a promise is not enforceable unless it is in the economic interest of the promisor since it lacks a *causa*. Some say it is not enforceable because it was not intended to be legally binding. The promise would be enforceable if the promisor did have an economic interest: for example, if he were an antiques dealer or a professional storer of furniture who made the promise for publicity.

One scholar, Gino Gorla, applying what he calls the doctrine of 'just' or 'reasonable' *causa*, believes that whether such a promise is enforceable should depend on balancing the harm the promisee would suffer from non-performance and his reliance on it against the cost to the promisor of keeping it and his own good or bad faith and reasons for refusing to perform.

Some scholars have said that a promisee can recover for opportunities that are lost and harm that is caused by relying on a promise that is not legally binding, but whether he can is controversial.

Some scholars think that in a case like this, the promisor would be liable if he failed to show good faith in pre-contractual negotiations. They would treat the promise to take a deposit as part of the negotiations towards a contract of deposit. To be liable, Charles would have to have acted in bad faith.

Austria: There is no liability if the parties did not intend the arrangement to be legally binding, which is unlikely if Charles is a friend, and likely if he is an antiques dealer or professional storer of furniture. Whether Otto gave up the opportunity to store his furniture elsewhere is relevant to whether they did.

If they did, and the furniture has been delivered, a contract of deposit is formed upon delivery, and Charles may be liable for its breach.

If the furniture has not been delivered, the arrangement would not be a contract of deposit but a promise to enter into such a contract. It is nevertheless enforceable.

According to a provision of the Civil Code, if the contract is a promise to enter into a contract of deposit, relief can be given if circumstances have changed. Nevertheless, in Austrian contract law, any contract can be invalid for changed and unforeseen circumstances. Moreover, according to another provision of the Civil Code, in a contract of deposit, the things deposited may be returned before the time fixed if, due to unforeseen circumstances, the depositee is unable to store them safely or without harm to his own interests. Consequently, whether or not a contract of deposit has been formed, the fact that Charles needs the space to store the furniture he has inherited will excuse him.

Germany: Whether or not the furniture has been delivered, the parties have entered into a contract of deposit.

The fact that Charles needs the space to store the furniture he has inherited will excuse him if it constitutes an 'important reason' for returning the furniture before the date fixed. A court will weigh the burdens to the parties and take into account the fact that the contract was gratuitous.

Greece: There is no liability if the parties did not intend the arrangement to be legally binding, as they may not have if Charles was a friend.

If they did, and the furniture has been delivered, a contract of deposit is formed upon delivery, and Charles may be liable for its breach.

If the furniture has not been delivered, the arrangement would not be a contract of deposit but a promise to enter into such a contract. The leading opinion is that it is enforceable, though some scholars claim it is not.

The fact that Charles needs the space to store the furniture he has inherited will excuse him. He is entitled to return the things deposited before the time agreed if, due to 'unforeseeable events', he cannot keep them 'safely and without prejudice to himself'.

Scotland: There is no liability if the parties did not intend the arrangement to be legally binding, as is likely if Charles was a friend.

If they did, then, since the promise is a gratuitous undertaking, unless Otto has relied upon it, it is unenforceable because it was not made in writing. It is enforceable if Otto relied upon it with the knowledge and acquiescence of Charles in a way that was material and harms him materially if the promise is not kept. Accordingly, Charles is liable in Cases 5(d) and 5(e) where Otto has foregone the opportunity to store the furniture elsewhere.

If the promise is enforceable, the fact that Charles needs the space to store the furniture he has inherited will not excuse him. The doctrine of frustration in Scots law is too strict.

England: There is no liability if the parties did not intend the arrangement to be legally binding, as they may not have if Charles is a friend.

If they did, then, if the furniture has been delivered, the arrangement is a 'gratuitous bailment' which English law calls a *depositum* or *mandatum*. It is subject to special rules, although there is no agreement whether the rules arise in contract or tort or are *sui generis*. For example, the bailee is subject to certain duties as to the care of the goods. It is not clear whether he is bound by a promise to store them for a fixed period of time. The promise could not be enforced on general contractual principles since it lacks consideration. Sometimes, however, courts have enforced promises ancillary to a bailment that impose duties greater than those imposed by the relation itself.

If the furniture has not been delivered, there is no bailment, and the promise is not enforceable because it lacks consideration. It is possible, however, especially if Otto has been harmed by relying on the promise, that a court would invent consideration by finding some benefit to Charles, but courts were more likely to do so in the past than they are today.

Also, Charles might be liable in tort. Normally, one cannot recover in tort for pure economic harm, but exceptions have been made for negligent provision of services where the plaintiff has a 'special relationship' with the defendant. For there to be one, the situation must be 'close to contract' or the defendant must have 'assumed responsibility' for the plaintiff's economic welfare, and typically the defendant has acted in a professional role, for example, as a solicitor or banker. While a court would not find there to be such a 'special relationship' if Charles were a friend, it might if Charles were an antiques dealer or a professional storer of furniture. Even then, a court might not hold him liable because he did not act negligently but failed to act at all, although this distinction is of dubious value. Otto would be more likely to succeed if the furniture had been delivered, since the relationship then seems closer and the case less like mere enforcement of a promise.

It does not matter why Charles refused to store the furniture.

The doctrine of promissory reliance does not apply because it is a shield, not a sword.

Ireland: There is no liability if the parties did not intend the arrangement to be legally binding, as they may not have if Charles is a friend.

If they did, then, if the furniture has been delivered, the arrangement is a 'gratuitous bailment'. The prevailing view is that such an arrangement does not give rise to liability in contract (there being no consideration), but in tort. It is not clear whether this liability would extend to the promise to store the goods for a fixed time, since it was made without consideration and goes beyond the duties imposed by the relationship itself. If so, the damages awarded would be those sufficient to place Otto where he would have been had the tort not been committed.

It does not matter why Charles refused to store the furniture.

The doctrine of promissory estoppel does not apply because it is a shield, not a sword.

Preliminary comparisons

The intention to be legally bound: Nearly all reporters noted that the promise is not enforceable unless the parties intended to be legally bound, and that it is less likely that they did if Charles is a friend.

The significance of delivery: In two civil law systems, a contract of deposit is formed whether or not the furniture has been delivered (the Netherlands and Germany). In seven civil law systems a contract of deposit is formed only upon delivery; before then, the arrangement is a promise to enter into such a contract. In two of these systems, such a promise is enforceable (Belgium and Austria); in two, it is enforceable according to the leading opinion (Greece) or that of most scholars (Portugal); in two it is uncertain whether it is enforceable (France and Spain); and in one it is not enforceable unless made in the economic interest of the promisor, as, possibly, if he were an antiques dealer or a professional storer (Italy). In the two common law systems (England and Ireland), if and only if the furniture is delivered, the arrangement is a 'gratuitous bailment' to which the normal rules of contract law do not apply. The promise to store the furniture for a fixed period lacks consideration; it is not clear whether a court would enforce it as a promise ancillary to a bailment. Absent delivery, the promise is not enforceable in contract or as ancillary to a bailment. In one system, the promise is not enforceable with or without delivery absent a writing or reliance (Scotland).

The significance of reliance: In Scotland, the promise would be enforceable if the promisee relied upon it materially, and would be materially harmed by its breach, if he relied with the knowledge and acquiescence of the promisor. In Italy, reliance might matter if one adopted either of two controversial theories: that the promisee may recover if he relied on a non-legally binding promise; or that he may do so if the harm to him outweighs that to the promisor. In each case, it would also matter if the promisor acted in good faith.

Tort: In England, it might be possible to recover in tort even though the harm is a pure economic loss if the parties had a 'special relationship'. For there to be one, the situation must be 'close to contract' and, typically, the defendant must act in a professional role. Even then, the court might not impose liability since Charles did not act negligently but failed to act at all, although this distinction is of dubious value.

The significance of gratuitousness: In France, even if the promise is binding, recovery of damages may be difficult because the contract is gratuitous. Because it is, in the Netherlands the rules governing recovery may be relaxed. In Scotland, such a promise is unenforceable unless it is in writing or the promisee relied because it is gratuitous. In England and Ireland, if it were not gratuitous, there would be consideration.

Excuse: In six systems, even if Charles is bound contractually, he will likely be excused because of a specific provision in the civil code that a depositee can return the goods before the time fixed if he has an 'important reason' (the Netherlands and Germany) or 'fair motive' or 'fair reason' (Spain and Portugal) for doing so, or if, due to changed or unforeseen circumstances, he cannot store them without harm to his own interests (Austria and Greece). In Belgium, Charles may be excused on account of *force majeure*, even though performance has become more difficult rather than impossible. The reporters from France, Italy, Scotland, England, and Ireland concluded that the reason Charles changed his mind is irrelevant. (It might be worth noting that in Italy, the promise is not binding without delivery; in France, whether it is binding then is doubtful; in Scotland, it is not binding with or without delivery; and in England and Ireland, it may not be binding with delivery and is probably not without.) In the six systems in which the promise is enforceable with or without delivery, at least according to the prevalent opinion, Charles would have an excuse (the Netherlands, Germany, Belgium, Portugal, Austria, and Greece).

Case 6: promises to do a favour

Case

Richard promised to mail some documents to Maria's insurance company so that the company would (a) insure, or (b) cancel an insurance policy on Maria's small private plane. He failed to do so. Is he liable (a) if Maria's plane crashes and she cannot recover its value because it was not insured, or (b) if Maria has to pay an extra monthly premium because her insurance was not cancelled? Does it matter if Richard promised to help because he was a friend whose profession was completely unrelated to aircraft, insurance, or the mailing of documents? Does it matter if he promised to help because he had just sold and delivered the plane to Maria?

Discussions

FRANCE

Once again (see Case 4), the central problem here is the thorny one of distinguishing between promises which are legally enforceable as contracts, and moral promises or gentlemen's agreements which are not. The line between these two is particularly hard to draw in French law, and is left to the judges of the lower courts as a question of fact (see Case 4).

If Richard is a friend whose profession is totally unrelated to the services he carries out, it is very doubtful that the agreement would be regarded as legal and consequently as binding. It is more likely that a French court would characterize the transaction as a favour (*acte de complaisance*) that friends may do for one another. Maria would not recover.

To the extent that the arrangement was between friends, it seems hard to characterize the relationship between the parties as anything other than non-legal. The only legal description that springs to mind – to be ultimately rejected – is one of a *mandat à titre gratuit* under French law: a contract of agency without compensation. An agent's liability for breach of such a contract is governed by art. 1991 of the Civil Code. He must pay damages for his own failure to perform (*inexécution*). The concept of *inexécution* covers complete failure to perform, poor performance, late performance, and so forth. Under art. 1992 of the Code, an agent is liable for intentional wrongdoing (*dol*) as well as any other fault (*faute*) in carrying out his agency. However, art. 1992 provides by way of exception that the liability for fault of an agent who acts without compensation is to be judged less 'rigorously' than if he receives remuneration. Case law has interpreted this exception to apply to the standard of care rather than to the quantum of liability.[1] In our view, however, an agency contract is principally a power given by one party to make a decision or enter into a transaction (see Case 15). Here, the actions undertaken are purely material, and thus the description seems inappropriate. Perhaps we should not be surprised that the favours or services that friends may do for one another are considered outside the realm of legal enforcement.

BELGIUM

If Richard offered his help as a friend of Maria, the preliminary question might be asked whether there is a *contract* imposing obligations that are legally enforceable. For there to be such a contract, the parties must intend to be legally bound. Such a contract is to be distinguished from a family or social engagement or courtesy promise, which may have been all that the parties intended here (see Case 4).

Assuming that a contract has validly been entered into in this case, it is a contract of agency (*contrat de mandat*) (arts. 1984 f. of the Civil Code): Richard is appointed to act on behalf of Maria and in her name. Richard will be held liable if the contract is not performed (art. 1991(1)). However, his liability for faults will be evaluated less severely if the contract was entered into gratuitously (art. 1992(2)).[2] The fact that Richard may have been ignorant in these matters does not, *per se*, mitigate his liability.

---

[1] Civ 1, 4 Jan. 1980, Bull. civ. I, no. 11, p. 9.
[2] Article 1992(2) provides: 'The agent is liable not only for fraud but also for the faults he commits in his management. Nevertheless, liability for faults will be evaluated less severely for the agent whose agency was entered into gratuitously than for an agent who receives a salary.'

If Richard intervened because he had just sold and delivered the plane to Maria, the contract would be one of commercial agency (*mandat commercial*) which is non-gratuitous (*contrat à titre onéreux*) unless the parties provide otherwise.[3] Rules applicable to commercial agents are those generally applicable in matters relating to the liability of professionals (*responsabilités professionnelles*).[4]

THE NETHERLANDS

Probably, Richard is not liable in contract. Therefore, Maria and Richard did not conclude the contract known in Dutch law as *opdracht* (mandate or *mandatum*) (see arts. 7:400 ff. of the Civil Code). There are no special rules on the formation of such a contract. The ordinary rules on contract formation apply. It does not seem that Richard intended to conclude a binding contract (art. 3:33 of the Civil Code) or that Maria could reasonably rely on him wanting to do so (art. 3:35 of the Civil Code). As in Case 5, the promise seems to be a mere social arrangement, not one intended to have legal effects. Therefore, Richard will not be liable.

Although there is no case law, it is generally accepted that agreements to render a service between friends, neighbours, and relatives are not usually considered to be legally binding contracts.[5] The reason there is no case law may be that people will not readily go to court for the performance of a gratuitous, informal promise by a friend.

If Richard was Maria's insurance agent, the agreement would be a contract known in Dutch law as *lastgeving*. *Lastgeving* is a specific type of *opdracht* where a party agrees 'to perform one or more juridical acts on account of' the other party (art. 7:400). In that event, it may make a difference for Richard's liability that the contract was gratuitous.[6] It may matter in several ways. First, and most appropriately, the duty of care may be less strict. According to art. 7:401 of the Civil Code, the standard is 'the care of a good mandatary'[7] which may be lower if the contract was gratuitous. Second, the damages for which Richard would be liable may be less extensive. According to art. 6:98, the damages must be such 'as can be

---

[3] See P. A. Foriers, 'Le droit commun des intermédiaires commerciaux', in L. Simont, P. Foriers, I. Verougstraete, and B. Glansdorff, *Les intermédiaires commerciaux* (1990), 29 f., no. 15.   [4] See *ibid.*, nos. 27–30.

[5] See Pitlo/Du Perron 225; Asser/Kortmann 5-III, no. 54; Van Schaick, 'Vriendendienst', 316.

[6] See Pitlo/Du Perron 226; Parlementaire Geschiedenis boek 7 (invoeringswet boeken 3, 5, 6), 323; Van Schaick, 'Vriendendienst'. Contrast Asser/Kortmann 5-III, no. 72.

[7] Article 7:401 of the Civil Code: 'In his activities, the mandatary must exercise the care of a good mandatary.'

imputed' to the person responsible 'taking into account its nature and that of the liability'.[8] The fact that liability is gratuitous may be one factor to be taken into account. Finally, liability for failure to perform a gratuitous undertaking might be tempered by applying art. 6:109. It provides: 'The judge may reduce a legal obligation to repair damage if awarding full reparation would lead to clearly unacceptable results in the given circumstances, including the nature of the liability, the juridical relation between the parties, and their financial capacity.'[9]

As mentioned earlier (Case 5), one author has argued for general indulgence for gratuitous promisors.[10]

Nevertheless, Richard may be liable in tort. If he knew how important the mailing of the documents was to Maria, and he failed to mail them for no good reason, his conduct may be 'an . . . omission violating a . . . rule of unwritten law pertaining to proper social conduct' (art. 6:162 of the Civil Code). If so, it could constitute a tort.

Article 6:162 is the general tort clause of the Dutch Civil Code. The standard of care (*zorgvuldigheidsnorm*) ('standard for carefulness') in section 2 holds a person responsible, not only when he violates another person's rights or his own statutory duties, but also when he violates 'a rule of unwritten law pertaining to proper social conduct' (*hetgeen volgens ongeschreven recht in het maatschappelijk verkeer betaamt*).[11] This provision codifies a test which was adopted in 1919 in the leading case of *Lindenbaum/Cohen* in which one competitor had bribed an employee of the other in order to get access to his trade secrets.[12] The test is very broad. It has led to a huge amount of case law and has overshadowed the other headings of tort liability. As with the other headings, plaintiffs can recover for pure economic loss.

---

[8] Article 6:98 of the Civil Code: 'Reparation can only be claimed for damage which is related to the event giving rise to the liability of the debtor in such a fashion that the damage, also taking into account its nature and that of the liability, can be imputed to the debtor as a result of this event.'

[9] Article 6:109 of the Civil Code: '(1) The judge may reduce a legal obligation to repair damage if awarding full reparation would lead to clearly unacceptable results in the given circumstances, including the nature of the liability, the juridical relationship between the parties and their financial capacity. (2) The reduction may not exceed the amount for which the debtor has covered his liability by insurance or was obliged to do so. (3) Any stipulation derogating from paragraph 1 is null.'

[10] Van Schaick, 'Vriendendienst', 316.

[11] '[A]n act or omission violating a . . . rule of unwritten law pertaining to proper social conduct' as a translation of 'een nalaten in strijd met . . . hetgeen volgens ongeschreven recht in het maatschappelijk verkeer betaamt' is not very satisfactory. Neither is the French translation: 'l'omission contraire à . . . une règle non écrite qui énonce ce qui est convenable dans le commerce social.'

[12] HR 31 Jan. 1919, NJ 1919, 161, W 10365, 2, note Molengraaff.

Whether Richard is liable in tort depends on the circumstances of the case. It is unlikely he will be held liable because, if the mailing was that important to Maria, she should have taken care of the matter herself. It is somewhat more likely, however, in Case 6(a), in which an insurance policy is not renewed, than in Case 6(b), in which a policy is cancelled, because in the first case, the obvious danger of serious harm to Maria requires Richard to use greater care.

Some have argued that tort liability should be less strict where the damage is caused while rendering a gratuitous service to the victim.[13] This view is shared by lower courts and by arbitrators.[14]

It is clear, then, that there is no contractual liability. Whether there is liability in tort depends on the circumstances, and especially on what Maria told Richard and on what Richard knew otherwise about the importance of the mailing.

It does matter if Richard promised to help because he was a friend whose profession was completely unrelated to aircraft, insurance, and mailing of documents. If Richard was a friend it is most unlikely that the agreement was a legally binding contract. It is also unlikely that he will be held liable in tort because he probably did not have to realize what damage Maria could suffer, and Maria probably was careless herself in entrusting that task to such a person.

It may also matter if Richard promised to help because he had just sold and delivered the plane to Maria. The promise may be part of the agreement to sell and as a consequence the violation of the promise may lead to contractual liability (art. 6:74 of the Civil Code). Whether his promise is part of the sale is a matter of interpretation (arts. 3:33 and 3:35). Since Richard had already sold and delivered the plane, it may be somewhat problematic to regard the promise as part of the same contract. The promise may also lead to a duty based on good faith (art. 6:248(1)).

SPAIN

Under some legal systems Richard's arrangement with Maria might be considered a contract of mandate or gratuitous agency. But it would not be considered such a contract (*contrato de mandato*) in Spanish law. Richard

---

[13] See Van Schaick, 'Vriendendienst', 320; T. Hartlief, 'Aansprakelijkheid bij vriendendiensten' WPNR 6200 (1995), 733.

[14] See the cases mentioned by the authors referred to in the preceding note. Conflicts concerning damage insurances are dealt with by the *Raad van Toezicht op het Schadeverzekeringsbedrijf*.

did not agree to conduct business in Maria's place before third parties. He just promised to mail documents, which is a service that does not need to be performed by someone legally representing or taking the place of Maria. The *Tribunal Supremo* has held that to act before third parties is a necessary condition of all contracts of mandate.[15] Had it been a contract of mandate, it would have been enforceable (art. 1711 of the Civil Code) whether it was express or implied, oral or written (art. 1710).

Neither is it a contract for services because Richard is not getting paid. Remuneration is a requirement of all contracts for services (art. 1544 of the Civil Code).

The legal category that fits it best is 'friendly service' (*servicio amistoso*).[16] All friendly services fall into the category of unilateral contracts or promises (see Case 1). If there is no *causa*, Richard's promise is not enforceable. But the *causa* seems to be liberality. As mentioned earlier, if the *causa* is liberality, then the requirements of the donation must be met: the promisor is not obligated unless there has been actual delivery of an object promised or a promise in writing. Since Maria did not get Richard to put his promise in writing, unfortunately she will not be able to enforce it now, nor will Richard be liable.

The only way Richard's promise might be enforceable is if his profession were the mailing of documents. If so, the case law would conclude that there is a contract of services because it is reasonable to think that a professional postman would want to be paid. His or her services have a price that can easily be established according to custom or regular business practices.[17] This is not the case here.

If the promise to help was included in the sales contract of the plane as an additional obligation, then the promise would be part of the onerous contract and Richard would be liable when the plane crashes.

PORTUGAL

Richard would be held liable in both Case 6(a) and Case 6(b). Nevertheless, although the reason why Richard promised to help is normally not relevant, if the promise was made out of friendship without any intent to create an obligation, Richard would not be liable.

In Portuguese law, the agreement between Richard and Maria would be

---

[15] TS, 26 Feb. 1956.
[16] J. Puig Brutau, *Compendio de derecho civil*, vol. II (1987), 484; J. L. Lacruz Berdejo, *Elementos de derecho civil*, vol. II (1979), 200.   [17] Castán Tobeñas, *Derecho civil*, vol. IV, 465.

considered a contract for services (*contrato de prestação de serviços*). According to art. 1154 of the Civil Code, this contract can be gratuitous. Indeed, the term is a general one which embraces all agreements to render services, whether gratuitous or not.[18] Therefore, it is binding on Richard who has to fulfil the obligation he has assumed. If he fails to perform, he is liable for all the damage he has caused to Maria (art. 798).

Nevertheless, it might matter if Richard is merely a friend of Maria because in this case it is possible that the agreement between the parties is based on a social obligation arising from their friendship without any intent to establish a legal obligation. If so, we would not have a contract but a mere 'gentlemen's agreement'.[19] Richard would not be liable.

ITALY

Richard is liable if he negligently failed to mail the documents for Maria in both Cases 6(a) and 6(b). It does not matter whether Richard promised to help because he was a friend whose profession was completely unrelated to aircraft, insurance, and the mailing of documents or because he had just sold and delivered the plane to Maria.

In these cases, the parties have entered into a contract of mandate (*mandato*) which is a nominate contract whereby one party binds himself to accomplish one or more legal transactions for the account of another (art. 1703 of the Civil Code).[20] Since Richard promised to mail the documents without charge, the contract is one of gratuitous mandate (*mandato gratuito*).[21] Here, Maria actually gave Richard the documents in accordance with his promise to mail them. The handing over of the documents necessary to perform such a task is termed, in Italian law, the *commendatio*

---

[18] In Portuguese law, *mandato* (*mandatum* or agency) is a contract for services which may be gratuitous but is limited to the performance of legal acts on behalf of another, which is not the situation here.

[19] See C. M. Pinto, *Teoria Geral do Direito Civil*, 3rd edn (1983), 382.

[20] U. Carnevali, 'Mandato (diritto civile)', Enc. Giur. Treccani (1990); G. Bavetta, 'Mandato (dir. priv.)', Enc. dir. 25 (1975), 321 ff.; A. Luminoso, 'Mandato, commissione, spedizione', in Cicu-Messineo, *Tratt. dir. civ. e comm.* (1984); G. Minervini, 'Il mandato, la commissione, la spedizione', in Vassalli, *Tratt. di dir. civ.* (1957); C. Santagata, 'Del mandato – Disposizioni generali', in *Commentario al codice civile Scialoja-Branca* (1985).

[21] Article 1709 of the Civil Code states that this contract is presumed not to be a gratuitous one. It is permissible, however, for it to be gratuitous. A court could infer that it is from unequivocal circumstances such as the relationship between the parties or a particular position of the mandatary (see Cass. civ., 27 Jan. 1980, no. 605; Cass. civ., 27 May 1982, no. 3233).

rei.[22] Since it has occurred, under the rules that govern mandate, Richard is liable to Maria if he acts negligently,[23] although art. 1710 of the Civil Code provides that if the mandate is gratuitous, the negligence of his conduct is to be evaluated less strictly. He would be liable if, as in the present case, he fails to perform the mandate when non-performance may cause damage to Maria.

Scholars are divided as to the measure of damages in such cases.[24] Here, however, by beginning the performance (taking the documents to mail them), Richard made it impossible for Maria to mail the documents herself or to find an alternative solution. A basic rule of mandates that require cooperation – and one on which all the scholars agree – is that if by negligently failing to complete performance, Richard caused Maria's situation to change for the worse (*modificatio in peius*), he has to pay damages even if the promise was gratuitous.[25]

AUSTRIA

Here again, the question is whether Richard had the intention to assume a legal obligation.[26] He would have had such an intention if he were the seller of the plane Maria just bought. In this case his promise belonged to his professional and not his private sphere. If, however, Richard is just a friend of Maria, the situation is problematic. Different aspects of it have to be taken into consideration. On the one hand, it must have been obvious to Richard that Maria had a financial interest in the proper mailing of the documents. On the other hand, Maria must have been aware that Richard did not have an interest in accepting a legal obligation which could result in a very expensive liability. One way a court could deal

[22] For the crucial relevance in these cases of the *commendatio rei*, see G. Gorla, 'Il dogma del "consenso" o "accordo" e la formazione del contratto di mandato gratuito nel diritto continentale', Riv. dir. civ. (1956), 923–32; Gorla, *Il contratto,* 173 ff.

[23] See R. Sacco, 'Il Contratto', in Vassalli, *Tratt. di dir. civ.* 6:2 (1975), 625 ff.; G. Castiglia, 'Promesse unilaterali atipiche', Riv. dir. com. I (1983), 348–9.

[24] See, e.g., Castiglia, 'Promesse unilaterali atipiche', 370; Sacco, 'Il contratto', 625; C. M. Bianca, 'Dell'inadempimento delle obbligazioni', in *Commentario a cura di Scialoja e Branca* (1979), 146 ff.   [25] See Sacco, 'Il contratto', 625

[26] The contract concluded would be a *Werkvertrag*. According to § 1151 of the Civil Code, this is a contract by which a party promises to perform a particular piece of work, to produce a certain specified result (*locatio conductio operis*, see R. Zimmermann, *The Law of Obligations: Roman Foundations of the Civilian Tradition* (1990), 393). The contract would *not* constitute a mandate. According to Austrian law (§ 1002 of the Civil Code), there is a mandate only if the mandatary has the obligation to perform legal acts for the mandator such as concluding a contract. The Austrian law in this respect operates with a different conceptual apparatus from the German Civil Code (BGB)

with this problem is to say that there is a contract, but that it is subject to an implied clause exempting Richard from liability for damage caused by ordinary negligence.[27]

If a court concludes that a contract was concluded but that it is *not* subject to a restriction on liability, Richard will be liable in both cases. In both cases, the damage Maria suffers is caused by his failure to fulfil his contractual obligation. Therefore, he is liable. If the contract contains a restriction on liability, Richard would be liable only if he acted with gross negligence.

GERMANY

A contract in which somebody promises to perform a service free of charge is called a mandate (*Auftrag* §§ 662–74 of the Civil Code). Although the promisee has to pay the promisor's expenses if reasonably incurred (§ 670), the contract is not mutual but obligates only the promisor.[28] Even though no compensation is paid, this type of contract is not deemed to be a gift. Since the formalities for a gift (see Case 1) are not required for a mandate, the contract is valid.

If the promisor fails to do what he promised to do, he is liable for damages (breach of contract in violation of § 665 of the Civil Code[29]). The promisor can terminate the contract at any time but the termination is valid only after notice is given. If the promisor terminates the contract at an inopportune moment, the termination is still valid but he is liable for damages (§ 671(2)).

The problem in our case is to distinguish such a contract from a mere favour. In the case of a mere favour, there would be no liability for breach of contract. The way to make the distinction is controversial. The courts ask whether the promisor had the intention to be legally bound.[30] This intention is indicated by the importance of the service for the promisee and especially by the possibility that he will suffer heavy damages if the

---

[27] The German BGH (NJW 1974, 1705) did something similar in the well-known case of the lottery gamblers. Here four friends had pooled their resources for the weekly lottery. One week the one responsible for bringing the ticket to the lottery agent forgot to fulfil his duty. Unfortunately for him they had the right number that week. The BGH did not hold him liable. It argued that the four, although entering into a contract, had made an agreement according to which liability for slight negligence was excluded.

[28] BGHZ 15 (1955), 102 (105).

[29] The promisor may only change the orders of the promisee if he can assume that the promisee would have agreed to that if he had known the circumstances. Before he does so, he has to notify the promisee and await his approval if it is not a case of emergency.

[30] RGZ 157 (1938), 228 (233).

promisor fails to perform. These factors matter only if the promisor was aware of them. As already mentioned in discussing Case 4, in one case,[31] the highest German court (*Bundesgerichtshof*) held that a promise to make a lorry driver available to another company was binding because of the high value of the lorry. In another case,[32] the court enforced a promise to make certain papers available to a company because the fact that this company depended on them in a lawsuit was obvious to the promisor when he made his promise.[33] In our case, the letters were economically very important to Maria, and Richard knew that. Therefore, there is a binding contract. The result would be different if, for example, the letters had contained Christmas cards.

Richard has breached this contract. As a result he is liable for all damages which have been caused by his failure. There is no difference between Cases 6(a) and 6(b).

The question whether Richard was just a friend or the seller of the aircraft may be of some relevance to his intention to be legally bound. If he was the seller, there is no question that there is a contract and that he is liable. If he was just a friend, the result may be less clear, but if he knew about the extreme importance of the matter to Maria, he would still be liable.

GREECE

By agreeing that Richard would mail the documents for Maria, the two entered into a legal relationship that is termed a 'mandate'. Mandate is a unilateral contract in the sense that only one party assumes an obligation (see Case 1). It is governed by arts. 713–29 of the Civil Code. The mandator is not obligated to pay any remuneration. The one essential obligation in such a contract is that of the mandatary to conduct the affairs of the mandator.[34]

---

[31] BGHZ 21 (1956), 102.   [32] RGZ 151 (1936), 203 (208).

[33] Another indication of an intention to be legally bound is whether the promisor has an economic interest in the situation. RGZ 65 (1907), 17 (19).

[34] The contract to conduct the affairs of another person, whether of a material or a legal nature, binds the parties according to art. 361 of the Civil Code even though the arrangement is gratuitous; AP 1169/75 NoB 24, 432; A. Nikolakopoulos, *The Mandate* (1956); Karasis in Georgiadis and Stathopoulos, *Civil Code*, § 713; Stathopoulos, *Contract Law*, 213; art. 713 of the Civil Code (which is similar to § 662 of the German Civil Code, art. 394 of the Swiss Code of Obligations, and art. 1984(1) of the French Civil Code); art. 714 of the Civil Code (which is similar to art. 398(1) and (2) of the Swiss Code of Obligations and art. 1995(1) of the French Civil Code). In the German Civil Code the liability of the mandatary for any fault arises from the general provision § 276 which corresponds to art. 330 of the Greek Civil Code. Kafkas, *Law of Obligations*, arts. 713–14.

The mandatary is responsible for any fault in the course of the performance of his obligation (art. 714 of the Civil Code).[35] He will therefore be liable if he negligently fails to perform his obligation or is seriously late in doing so.[36] In principle, the mandator must prove that he suffered a loss through the mandatary's negligence in fulfilling the obligation he undertook (art. 335 of the Code of Civil Procedure). Nevertheless, the mandatary's failure to perform raises a presumption of fault which he can only overcome by proving it was due to a chance event or to *force majeure*.[37]

If the mandatary is held liable, he must pay the positive or expectation interest of the mandator that is causally related to the mandatary's negligence.[38] Thus, in our case Richard, who fails to perform his obligation to Maria, namely to mail the documents for her, will have to restore the loss which Maria suffers because of his negligence. If, however, Maria was also at fault (e.g., she did not point out the importance of the letter), the compensation that Richard will have to pay to her will be reduced or even discharged.[39]

In the first case this would be the value of the airplane that would have been insured if Richard had mailed the documents. In the second case, when Maria's insurance policy on her small airplane would have been cancelled, Richard will be released from any obligation to her because Maria does not suffer any serious loss.

If Richard has undertaken the obligation to mail the documents for Maria, acting out of courtesy, then we must distinguish whether Richard wanted to bind himself in legal terms or whether this was an act outside the legal sphere. Mandate is a legal relationship and is distinguished from 'accommodation agreements'. Both have the same gratuitous *causa* but mandate contains the intention of the parties to bind themselves in legal terms. The distinction between the two acts is very difficult to make in practice and all the circumstances have to be taken into consideration.

Thus, the undertaking of an obligation to mail urgent business correspondence documents is a mandate if the circumstances (e.g., pointing

---

[35] The mandatary is liable not only for intentional acts and 'gross' negligence but also for 'slight' negligence; AP 9971/75 NoB 24, 286; EfAth 163/62 Ach.N 13, 497. It should be pointed out that the mandatary is held to the higher standard of liability of the common debtor and not to the lower standard of other gratuitous contracts because of the fiduciary character of the mandate. Karasis in Georgiadis and Stathopoulos, *Civil Code*, art. 714.

[36] AP 159/74 NoB 22, 1047; Thessaloniki Court of Appeal 332/78 Arm. 32, 794.

[37] If the mandatary falls in default of a debtor then he is also liable for chance events and *force majeure* acts; Kafkas, *Law of Obligations*, art. 713.   [38] *Ibid.*

[39] M. Stathopoulos in Georgiadis and Stathopoulos, *Civil Code*, art. 300, no. 11.

out the importance of the letter or awareness of the details of the addressee) suggest the existence of an important economic interest or risk for the mandator.[40] In our case, Richard, despite the fact that he is a friend of Maria, will be liable because under the circumstances a contract of mandate exists between them.[41]

Whether Richard had undertaken the obligation because he had just sold and delivered the airplane to Maria would make no difference, because this is a secondary obligation stemming from his main obligation to sell and deliver the airplane to Maria. In this case he will be liable for non-performance of his secondary obligation and he will have to compensate Maria according to the above.

SCOTLAND

Maria will be able to enforce the promise if it is constituted in writing, in accordance with the provisions of s. 1(2) of the Requirements of Writing (Scotland) Act 1995.[42] It is irrelevant whether Richard promised to mail the documents so that the plane could be insured, or so that a policy could be cancelled. It is also irrelevant under Scots law, which has no doctrine of consideration, whether Maria cannot recover after a crash or has to pay an extra monthly premium.

If Richard is a friend of Maria, this is likely to give rise to a presumption that there was no intention to create legal obligations as in Case 5, although this presumption is likely to be rebutted if the promise is constituted in writing. If Richard's business involves selling planes, then Maria may not require the promise to be constituted in writing as he may be seen to be acting in the course of his business in terms of s. 1(2)(a)(ii) of the 1995 Act, as in Case 4.

If the promise has to be in writing, reliance could also be made on s. 1(3) and (4). Richard would have to know the nature of the documents, that is, to insure the plane or cancel the insurance policy. If so, he will know and acquiesce in Maria's refraining to act because of his promise to mail the documents. The materiality criteria in s. 1(4)(a) and (b) are easily satisfied. As has been argued, the adverse effect suffered for the purposes of s. 1(4)(b) does not have to be related to the material act or refraining to act in s1(3) or (4)(a).

---

[40] Karasis in Georgiadis and Stathopoulos, *Civil Code*, art. 713, no. 1.
[41] But Maria can also be at fault, as has been explained above.   [42] See Case 1.

ENGLAND

It is clear under English law that, with the possible exception of the variation where Richard sold Maria the plane, Richard is not liable in contract for failing to keep his promise to mail the documents. Richard may, however, be liable in tort, particularly if he is a professional.

A contractual claim would fail because Maria did not do or promise to do anything in exchange for Richard's promise to mail the documents; that is, there was no consideration for Richard's promise (see Case 1). Thus, in the similar English case of *Argy Trading & Development* v. *Lapid Developments*,[43] a defendant was held not liable in contract for failing to fulfil his gratuitous promise to insure the plaintiff's property. The only possible exception would be the case where Richard sold Maria the plane. Here it is possible that a court might hold that the promise to mail the documents was in substance all part of one sales transaction. As Treitel observes, 'If the consideration and the promise are substantially one transaction, the exact order in which these events occur is not decisive.'[44] A manufacturer's guarantee, for example, may be binding even though it is often given after the goods are bought.[45] However, as mailing insurance documents is not normally attendant to a sale of a plane in the same way that receiving a guarantee is attendant to purchasing goods, it is suggested that an English court is unlikely to reach this conclusion.

Maria may be able to recover in tort, particularly if Richard is a professional. The relevant law here is that discussed in my answer in the previous case. As we noted, it is both complex and in a state of flux. Any predictions made below must be approached cautiously. The non-receipt of insurance coverage or the payment of extra premiums is an economic loss, rather than a physical loss (such as the destruction of the plane, or physical injury to Maria), and, as noted in discussing Case 5, recovery for economic loss in tort is allowed in respect of the negligent provision of services. However, for a claim to succeed on this basis the plaintiff must establish that he or she had a 'special relationship' with the defendant. As discussed in connection with Case 5, the understanding of 'special relationship' is notoriously uncertain, but the most commonly cited tests ask whether the relationship was 'close to contract' or whether the defendant 'assumed responsibility' for the plaintiff's economic welfare.[46] Making a

---

[43] [1977] 1 WLR 444.   [44] Treitel, *Contract*, 73.   [45] *Ibid.*

[46] See, e.g., Lord Devlin's judgment in Hedley *Byrne* v. *Heller* [1964] AC 465 and Lord Goff's judgment in *Henderson* v. *Merrett Syndicates Ltd* [1995] 2 AC 145.

promise brings a relationship 'close to contract' and is also strong evidence of an assumption of responsibility.[47] A further requirement for establishing the necessary special relationship is that the defendant be a professional (see previous answer). Thus, in the scenario where Richard is merely a friend he is unlikely to be liable in tort. But where Richard is a professional, whether in the insurance business, aircraft business, or in respect of delivering documents, tort liability seems possible (assuming that the promise was made seriously, and it was understood that it would be acted upon). Indeed, a close analogy exists in the late eighteenth-century case of *Wilkinson* v. *Coverdale*,[48] where a defendant was held liable for negligently failing to fulfil a gratuitous promise to insure the plaintiff's property.[49] Of course in no case would Richard be held liable unless he knew of the contents of the documents and of their importance; he cannot assume responsibility for that of which he is unaware.

Assuming, then, that a special relationship has been found, the case where tort liability is most likely is where Richard's failure to mail the documents is due to his negligence, for example if he mailed the documents to the wrong address. More difficult is the case where Richard completely fails to act as opposed to where he acts but acts carelessly. As noted in the discussion of Case 5, in principle defendants are liable in tort law only for misfeasance (acting negligently), rather than nonfeasance (refusing to act). But we also noted that it seemed counter-intuitive that Richard could be liable for negligently failing to mail the documents but not liable for deliberately neglecting to mail them, and that various cases appeared to have ignored, or thought not relevant, the misfeasance/nonfeasance distinction here. In particular, in one case not dissimilar to the facts of Case 6, a solicitor was held liable in tort for failing in his promise to register an option, with no distinction being drawn between liability for misfeasance and nonfeasance.[50] It is suggested that this approach would be followed by an English court on the facts of Case 6, rather than allowing the defendant to plead his own wilful wrongdoing as a defence. A court – or at least a trial court – would probably simply ignore the larger implications of the action. Or it might hold that Richard was negligent in failing to deliver the letter, even if the omission was intentional. The fact that Maria had actually handed over the documents to Richard would also, as explained in the discussion of Case 5, support liability. Note also that for the same

---

[47] *Henderson* v. *Merrett Syndicates Ltd* [1995] 2 AC 145.   [48] [1793] 1 Esp. 75.

[49] The juristic basis of this decision may not be the same as that of more recent cases; see W. H. Rogers, *Winfield & Jolowicz on Tort*, 14th edn (1994), 106.

[50] *Midland Bank* v. *Hett* [1979] Ch. 384. See also *White* v. *Jones* [1993] 3 WLR 730.

reasons Richard would probably be held liable if he informs Maria that he will not deliver the letters, but does so only after Maria has detrimentally relied on his earlier promise. In both cases, however, the extent of liability would be Maria's reliance losses (and thus would be less in the second case), as the source of the liability is the fact that Richard induced Maria to rely upon him.

IRELAND

In both Cases 6(a) and 6(b), it is clear that there has been no consideration provided by Maria nor was the promise made by way of a deed under seal. A promise to render a service without reward is not binding contractually as no consideration for it is provided by the promisee and thus Richard would not be liable in contract to Maria.[51] However, although Richard's promise does not create contractual relations between Maria and Richard, he could be liable to Maria in tort. In contract, liability is common both for misfeasance and nonfeasance. In tort, liability is normally imposed because of misfeasance, as liability for nonfeasance in tort requires a duty (usually based on some existing relationship) between the parties. Nonfeasance in the performance of a promise to render gratuitous services means failure to pursue a promised course of action while misfeasance means carelessness in the pursuit of that course of action leading to failure to achieve a promised result.[52] In order to succeed in tort in an action for damages against Richard, Maria would have to show to an Irish court, *inter alia*, that a sufficient proximity existed between the wrongdoer and the person who had suffered damages, that the damage done was reasonably foreseeable, and that there was no compelling exemption based on public policy.[53] The fact that the damage to Maria is purely economic is not in itself a bar to recovery in Ireland. The damage may be to 'property, to the person, financial or economic'.[54] Where Maria succeeded in an action in tort against Richard, the object of damages in such circumstances would be to compensate Maria by restoring her to the position which she would have held if the tort was not committed.

It might matter if Richard promised to help because he was a friend whose profession was completely unrelated to aircraft, insurance, or the mailing of documents. Again, there has been no consideration provided

---

[51] See *Argy Trading & Development Company Ltd* v. *Lapid Developments* [1977] 1 WLR 444.
[52] See Treitel, *Contract*, ch. 3.   [53] See *Ward and McMaster* [1988] IR 33.
[54] See *McShane Wholesale Fruit and Vegetables Ltd* v. *Johnston Haulage Co. Ltd & Carbrook Chemicals Ltd* [1979] ILRM 86.

and, because Richard was a friend, it will be much more difficult to establish any intention on his part to be bound contractually or legally. Treitel notes that many social arrangements do not amount to contracts because they are not intended to be legally binding.[55] By way of an example, Treitel cites the case of *Lens* v. *Devonshire Club*,[56] whereby it was held that the winner of a competition run by a golf club could not sue for his prize where 'no one concerned with that competition ever intended that there should be any legal results flowing from the conditions posted and the acceptance by the competitor of those conditions'.[57]

If the promise to help was made after the contract to sell and deliver the plane to Maria, then the subsequent promise is not supported by consideration. Applying the principles of past consideration as set down in discussing Case 2 above, it is clear that unless it can be shown to come within the scope of *Lampleigh* v. *Braithwaite* or *Bradford* v. *Roulston* then Richard is not liable to Maria. If this promise by Richard to help was coupled 'with the request' involved in selling and delivering the plane to Maria and Maria and Richard both intended that the promise would not be gratuitous then Richard could be liable in such circumstances to Maria.[58]

Where Maria could show that the promise made by Richard was intended by him to be binding and intended by him to be acted on, then, having regard to the context within which the promise was made, the court might award compensation to Maria for a seemingly gratuitous promise made by Richard.[59] However, promissory estoppel cannot confer a cause of action when none existed before and it operates as a shield and not a sword.[60] In such circumstances it is difficult to see what cause of action Richard would bring in order that Maria might raise the principles of promissory estoppel.

Summaries

France: There is no liability if the parties did not intend the arrangement to be legally binding, as they may not have done if Richard was a friend.

If they did, the arrangement might be a gratuitous agency, although perhaps not because Richard is to carry out a physical act rather than act on Maria's behalf. If it is, Richard is liable for breach but he will be held to a lower standard of care if he acts gratuitously.

---

[55] See Treitel, *Contract*, ch. 3.   [56] *The Times*, Dec. 1914.   [57] See Cases 4 and 5.
[58] See Case 2.
[59] See also *Blanford and Houdret Ltd* v. *Bray Travel Holdings Ltd* (unreported, 11 Nov. 1983, Gannon J).   [60] See Case 1.

Belgium: There is no liability if the parties did not intend the arrangement to be legally binding.

If they did, the arrangement is an agency, and Richard is liable for breach, but he will be held to a lower standard of care if he acts gratuitously. He would be held to a higher standard if he had just sold Maria the plane, since then the contract is a commercial agency which is not gratuitous.

The Netherlands: There is no liability if the parties did not intend the arrangement to be legally binding, as is likely, particularly if Richard was a friend.

If they did, the arrangement is an agency, and Richard is liable for breach. If it is a gratuitous agency, however, Richard will be held to a lower standard of care, the damages recoverable will be less extensive, and the judge may reduce the damages awarded still further if necessary to avoid 'unacceptable results'. If Richard has just sold Maria the plane, the promise might be regarded as part of that contract, although this interpretation is problematic since Richard had already sold the plane.

Although it is not likely, Richard may be liable in tort for violating a 'rule of unwritten law pertaining to proper social conduct'. There is no difficulty about recovering for pure economic loss. Some scholars and the lower courts believe that the standard of care should be lower if Richard was acting gratuitously.

Spain: The contract is not one of agency because Richard did not agree to act legally as Maria's representative. Neither is it a contract for the hiring of services since Richard was not paid. It is a contract for 'friendly service'. If the *causa* is liberality, then it is enforceable only if it meets the requirements for a valid donation: the promise must be in writing.

The promise would be enforceable if it could be interpreted to be part of the sales contract for the plane.

Portugal: The contract is one for performing services. As such, it is binding without a formality whether or not the services are to be rendered gratuitously. Nevertheless, it is not binding if the parties were friends who intended a mere social obligation or gentlemen's agreement.

Italy: The contract is one of agency, and Richard is liable for breach. It is a gratuitous agency since Richard is not paid. For the formation of the contract, Maria must actually hand over the documents, but she has done so here. Since the agency is gratuitous, Richard is held to a lower standard of care.

Austria: There is no liability if the parties did not intend the arrangement to be legally binding, as may well be the case if Richard was a friend. They had that intention if Richard has just sold Maria the plane. If Richard was a friend, a court might conclude that the promise is binding but subject to an implied clause that Richard is not liable for slight negligence.

Germany: There is no liability if the parties did not intend the arrangement to be legally binding. They had that intention if Richard has just sold Maria the plane. If Maria was a friend, they probably did because Richard knew the task was very important to Maria.

If they did, the contract is one of agency, and Richard is liable for its breach.

Greece: There is no liability if the parties did not intend the arrangement to be legally binding. It is likely that they did if Richard knew the task was very important to Maria.

If they did, the contract is one of agency, and Richard will be liable for breach. He will be presumed to be at fault, and he can only overcome this presumption by proving a chance event or *force majeure*.

Scotland: There is no liability if the parties did not intend the arrangement to be legally binding, as is likely if Richard was a friend.

If they did, since the promise is gratuitous it may be enforceable even though it was not made in writing if Richard sold the plane and made the promise in the ordinary course of his business. Or it may be enforceable if he knew and acquiesced in Maria's omission to mail the documents herself, and (as is the case) she relied materially and was materially harmed as a result.

England: The promise is not enforceable in contract because it lacks consideration unless Richard sold Maria the plane and the promise is held to be part of the sales contract. Courts have held a subsequent promise to be part of a prior sale, but they are unlikely to do so here because mailing insurance documents is not normally a part of a sale.

As in Case 5, even though Maria's loss was purely economic, Richard might be liable in tort for negligent provision of services if the parties had a 'special relationship'. As before, for there to be one, the situation must be 'close to contract' or the defendant must have 'assumed responsibility' for the plaintiff's economic welfare, and typically the defendant has acted in a professional role, for example, as a solicitor or banker. While a court would not find there to be such a 'special relationship' if Richard were a friend, it might if he had sold Maria the aircraft. Indeed, in one eighteenth-century case, the defendant was held liable for negligently failing to keep a gratuitous promise to insure the plaintiff's property. As before, a court might not hold Richard liable because he did not act negligently but failed to act at all, although this distinction is of dubious value. As before, Maria would be more likely to succeed if the documents had actually been given to Richard since the relationship then seems closer and the case less like mere enforcement of a promise.

Ireland: There is no liability if the parties did not intend the arrangement to place Richard under a legal duty. It is less likely that they did if Richard was a friend.

Even if they did, Richard is not liable in contract if there was no consideration for his promise. There is consideration only if Richard sold Maria the plane, and his promise is considered to be part of that contract. It will not be so considered if it was given after the sale.

Richard might still be liable in tort. In Irish law, it is possible to recover in tort for pure economic loss, for nonfeasance as well as for misfeasance, and for breach of a duty arising out of a relationship voluntarily entered into.

Preliminary comparisons

Intention to be legally bound: Nearly all the reporters observed that Richard is not liable unless the parties intended to be legally bound, and most added that they probably did not if Richard was a friend.

Contract of 'agency' – descendants of the Roman mandatum: In some jurisdictions it mattered whether the contract belonged to a class of contracts descended from the Roman *mandatum* (translated here as 'agency'). It did not matter in Portugal, Germany, and Austria because no special rules applied to such a contract in a case like this one. (In any event, the Portuguese reporter said that this contract was not an agency, the German reporter said that it was, and the Austrian reporter did not discuss the question.) In France, Belgium, the Netherlands, and Italy, the arrangement would be an agency, and the classification does matter because, if the agency is gratuitous, the agent is held to a lower standard of care (and, in the Netherlands, is liable for less extensive damages). (The Austrian reporter arrived at a similar result by another route, suggesting that the contract might be subject to an implied clause excluding liability for slight negligence.) In Greece, on the contrary, the arrangement would be an agency, and the classification matters because the agent's fault is presumed and he can only escape liability by proving a fortuitous event or *force majeure*. In contrast, in Spain, the arrangement would not be an agency because Richard is not authorized to enter into legal transactions on Maria's behalf. The classification matters because, if the transaction is gratuitous but not an agency, it requires the formality necessary for a donation (a writing), and so Richard's promise would not be enforceable. *The prior sale*: Several reporters noted that the promise would not be gratuitous if it could be considered part of the prior sale (Spain, Belgium, England, and Ireland), but most of them thought this possibility unlikely because the promise was made after the sale (the Netherlands and Ireland) or because such a promise is not normally part of a sale (England). *Promising in the course of business*: In Scotland, a gratuitous promise made in the ordinary course of business is enforceable without a formality. The Belgian reporter believes that such a promise does not count as a gratuitous one even if nothing extra is paid to the promisor.

Reliance: In Scotland, reliance matters because a gratuitous promise is enforceable when the promisee relied with the knowledge and acquiescence of the promisor, and the reliance and harm to the promisee are material.

Tort: Richard may be liable in tort in the Netherlands and Ireland, where pure economic loss is ordinarily recoverable. He may be liable in England where ordinarily it is not, if, as in Case 5, the parties had a 'special relationship'. As before, for there to be one, the situation must be 'close to contract' and, typically, the defendant must act in a professional role: here, as seller of the airplane. Even then, the court might not impose liability since Richard did not act negligently but failed to act at all, although this distinction is of dubious value.

Case 7: promises to loan goods without charge

Case

Barbara promised Albert that he could use her car without charge for three months while she was on vacation. She now needs the car because she cancelled her vacation plans after injuring her left foot. Can she have it back? Does it matter if she told Albert he could not have the car a week before she was supposed to deliver it or a week after she actually did? Does it matter if Albert has taken a job that requires him to have a car but does not pay enough for him to rent one?

Discussions

FRANCE

Under French law the arrangement made between Barbara and Albert would constitute a contract of loan for use (*prêt à l'usage* or *commodat*). In such a contract, the lender gives a thing to the borrower for his use which the borrower must later return. Accordingly, it is governed by arts. 1875 and following of the Civil Code.

Such a contract is defined as a contract *in rem* which means that it is formed upon delivery of the thing. It is therefore an exception to the general principle by which contracts are enforceable upon a mere exchange of promises. It does not follow, however, that no contract has been made if the lender has not made the delivery by which a contract of loan for use is formed. Barbara and Albert's arrangement can be classified instead as an offer to lend (*promesse de prêt*), which is an enforceable contract. Which kind of contract has been formed, however, depends on whether delivery has been made. We will discuss each alternative.

If the car has been delivered, then a contract of loan for use has been formed, and it is enforceable. In that case, in principle, the lender cannot recover the thing before the end of the term, and the borrower must return it then. In this case, then, it would seem that Albert may keep the car, and Barbara cannot recover it before the three months have expired. An exception, however, is created by art. 1889 of the Civil Code. It provides that if the lender has an 'urgent and unforeseeable need for the thing, the judge may, depending on the circumstances, force the borrower to return it'.

This exception can be explained by the fact that the lender is doing a favour for his friend. The loan arises because they are friends rather than because of the borrower's need. The essential characteristic of the contract of loan is that it is without compensation. In the absence of an express term to the contrary, the borrower is not obliged to pay for the use of the thing. Since such a loan is aimed at doing a favour for a friend, it should not be turned upside down to cause a loss to the lender. Nevertheless, the lender's right to recover the thing in advance of the time agreed contravenes the principle of the enforceability of contracts enshrined in art. 1134 of the Civil Code. It would seem to allow the promisor to withdraw his promise at will (*condition potestative*) except that it can only be exercised in circumstances outside his control. Since it contravenes the general principle, even if it is justified in the context of an arrangement between friends, it must be interpreted restrictively. Indeed, interestingly enough, art. 1889 can be seen as a specific application of the principle of *imprévision*: the principle that contracts may not be binding in the event of changed or unforeseen circumstances. This principle has been continually rejected as a matter of general contract theory in French private law.

Under art. 1889, to recover the car by court order before the end of the term, Barbara must prove that she has an urgent and unforeseeable need to have her car back. The question whether she does is left to the trial court judge. Moreover, a literal interpretation of the text suggests that the judges are not obliged to order the return of the object loaned before the end of the term but may exercise their discretion in the matter. In other words, the lender's 'urgent and unforeseeable need' is a necessary but not sufficient condition. The reason may be that art. 1889 is an exception to the general principle of art. 1134 that contracts are to be enforced, and so it is made subject to a further exception by taking the borrower's situation into account.

In a recent case, a person had made a loan for use of an apartment for residential purposes for an indefinite term to his brother. The court held that the heirs of the lender could not recover the apartment since they had not met the test of a need that was urgent and unforeseeable and that outweighed the borrower's need to use the thing loaned.[1] This interpretation of art. 1889 seems to limit its scope considerably, although it should be stressed that this case dealt with a contract of unspecified duration, unlike the arrangement between Barbara and Albert. In his comment to this case, A. Bénabent observed that one could read the case narrowly so that the outcome depends on the fact that an apartment was loaned. The court would then be protecting the borrower's right to be housed. Nevertheless, it is possible, he notes, to read it more broadly so that 'someone lending his car for more than one journey will have to wait to take it back as long as the borrower needs to drive it'. He thinks that in the future, to avoid such results, a requirement that all such loans be in writing should be imposed by analogy. In any event, whether the case should be read broadly enough to include the loan of a car is speculative. It could be argued that different considerations apply once a fixed term has been agreed upon, as here, since the loan is not open-ended from the outset.

There is relatively little case law under arts. 1888 and following of the Civil Code, perhaps because a *commodat* concerns arrangements between friends and family.[2] Other cases which we have already cited[3] concern the loan of apartments by parents to children and their families which the parents want to recover when their children's marriage breaks up. The case law is contradictory. In the first case cited, which is published in the *Bulletin de la Cour de Cassation*, and therefore is more authoritative than the second, the daughter-in-law and her children were allowed to keep the apartment. In the second, on similar facts, the lender could recover it. Commentators have suggested that the apparent contradiction can be explained by the fact that the lender's need was not established in the first case. Moreover, in the first case, the borrowers' divorce was pending whereas in the second case it had been final for a number of years, and it was claimed that the apartment should have been subject to the divorce settlement.

Also, art. 1889 must be seen in context. It is an exception or a limitation

---

[1] Civ. 1, 19 Nov. 1996, D 1997, 145, note A. Bénabent who criticizes the solution.
[2] For scholarly opinion on the *commodat*, see G. Cornu, RTDCiv. 1980, 368, who suggests, 'common sense and equity should govern in the context of loans for the use of a thing'; J. Carbonnier, note TGI Briey, 30 June 1966, JCP 1967 ed. G. II 15310, who calls it 'a malleable contract at the border-line between law and non-law'.
[3] JCP 1994, II, 2239, note V. Morgand-Cantegrit; D 1994, 244, note A. Bénabent.

to the general rules set out in art. 1134 of the Civil Code. According to these general rules, a contract cannot be terminated in advance of the term without mutual consent. Moreover, the term is set by the parties, and it is not a question of *ordre publique*. Consequently, the agreement of the parties should override art. 1889, although, in this case, there was no attempt to do so. The reason for the provisions of art. 1889 can be found in Pothier: no one is presumed to want to do a favour for someone to his detriment.[4] Thus, the provision rests on a presumption about the intentions of the parties.

Nevertheless, it must be stressed that art. 1889, as noted, grants a discretionary power to the judge to decide on an equitable basis whether the object should be returned. Barbara will have to go to court to recover her car, and the trial judge has absolute authority (*pouvoir souverain d'appréciation*) to decide whether the conditions of art. 1889 are met because that question is considered a matter of pure fact.[5] It would seem that these conditions are met if Barbara has hurt her foot and cannot walk but can drive. But it is just conceivable that the court would decide otherwise if, for example, Albert had taken a job on the strength of having the use of the car.

The questions that arise are different if the car has not been delivered. In that event, a contract of loan for use has not been formed. Still, it does not follow that there is no enforceable contract between Barbara and Albert. Curiously, despite the absence of a delivery which is necessary to form a contract *in rem*, it is still possible under French law to reclassify Barbara's promise as an offer to lend (*promesse de prêt*), which is in itself a binding contract.

In our view, art. 1889 cannot be applied to an offer to lend. It does not apply because the car has not been delivered, and therefore a contract of loan for use has not been formed. Consequently, Barbara cannot justify her refusal to deliver the car by proving her 'urgent and unforeseeable need' for it as that article provides. Nor can she do so under the general principles of French contract law because, as mentioned earlier, the principle of relief for changed and unforeseen circumstances (*imprévision*) has been consistently rejected.

Supposing that Barbara's promise is an offer to lend, we must consider whether it can be enforced by specific performance, so that Barbara is required to deliver the car, or by an award of damages. The *Cour de cassa-*

---

[4] For an explanation of *commodat*, see F. Grua, *Juris-classeur*, arts. 1888–9.

[5] Civ. 1, 3 Feb. 1993, Bull. civ. I, no. 62; JCP 1994, II, 2239, note V. Morgand-Cantegrit; D 1994, 249, note A. Bénabent.

tion has held that a promise to loan money cannot be specifically enforced since it is not the same as a contract of loan.[6] A promise to loan, according to the Court, is a contract that contains an obligation 'to do' something (see Case 13 for an explanation). Under art. 1142 of the Civil Code, such an obligation cannot be specifically enforced if so doing would constitute an intolerable infringement of the individual rights of the defendant. It would seem that the same result would be reached with an offer to lend something for use.

If Albert cannot have the obligation specifically enforced, he might claim damages under art. 1147 of the Civil Code which is the general provision that damages will be awarded for breach of a contract. He might claim the cost of renting a new car to get to work. The promisee was awarded damages in the case just described. Nevertheless, in that case, the offer to lend was made in relation to a consumer loan, that is, in relation to a contract that is onerous rather than gratuitous. In our view, it is doubtful that Albert can claim damages because Barbara's gratuitous promise does not seem to be truly analogous. The surrounding context is entirely different, and the arrangement is one between friends. In our view, the fact that the promise was made without compensation will probably have a decisive influence on the court's decision whether or not to award damages. Even if the court decided to do so, in the context of a loan between friends it is a matter of speculation whether a court would award Albert damages as high as the cost of his hiring another car.

It is interesting to note, then, that how the contract is analysed may have little effect on the liability of the parties and their ability to enforce the promise. In practice, Albert may not have a remedy even under a consensualist approach which does not require delivery for a contract to be formed. The reason is the context of the promise – an arrangement between friends – and the fact that such a contract follows the original conception of a loan for use (*commodat*). It is entered into without compensation. Perhaps the dearth of case law is indicative. Enforcement is rarely sought, perhaps in the expectation that it will rarely be granted. *Res ipsa loquitur?*

BELGIUM

In this case, the contract is one of loan for use (*prêt à usage*, *commodatum*) (arts. 1875 f. of the Civil Code). It is a 'real contract' (*contrat réel*, contract

---

[6] Civ. 1, 20 July 1981, Bull. civ. I, no. 267, Rép. Def., art. 32915, no. 45, p. 1085.

re), meaning that the contract is only formed on delivery of the object in question.[7] Such a contract is essentially gratuitous (art. 1876). It is unilateral in the civil law sense of the term: it imposes obligations on only one of the parties. The general principle that is applicable here is found in art. 1888: 'The lender may recover the object loaned only after expiration of the contractual term, or, in the absence of an agreement on this matter, only after the object has served the purpose for which it was borrowed.'

Nevertheless, Barbara can have her car back if she has cancelled her vacation plans because she hurt her foot provided she obtains a court's authorization. Article 1889 of the Civil Code provides: 'Notwithstanding, if, during this period of time [i.e. the period of time agreed upon by the parties] or before the borrower's needs cease, the lender has a compelling and unforeseeable need to recover the object, the judge may request that the borrower return it, regard being had to the circumstances of the case.'[8]

If she tells Albert he cannot have the car a week before she is supposed to deliver it, then there is no contract of loan for use since the car has not been delivered. We have instead a mere promise of loan for use.[9] Such a promise is binding (see Case 5(a)). Non-performance of the promise may still not give rise to liability because Barbara may be able to claim *force majeure*, even though it is still possible for Barbara to allow Albert to have the car, for reasons explained in discussing Case 5(c).

Barbara cannot obtain relief under the doctrine of *imprévision* on the grounds that unforeseen circumstances have arisen for reasons that will be explained in discussing Case 8.

It does not matter if Albert suffers some inconvenience if he gives back the car.

THE NETHERLANDS

Barbara can have her car back. She would only be bound by her promise if the agreement were a contract. In Dutch law, the contract under discussion here is a contract of loan for use (*bruikleen*) (*commodatum*) which is a gratuitous contract (art. 7A:1777 of the Civil Code). It is also a 'real con-

---

[7] Van Ommeslaghe, *Droit des obligations*, 32.

[8] See Trib. civ. Liège, 31 March 1987, JLMB, 1987, 1145 and D. Devos, 'Chronique de jurisprudence. Les contrats (1980–1987)', JT, 1993, 77, see in particular no. 2. See also Trib. civ. Liège, 5 May 1989, JLMB, 1989, 111, and the observations of Y. Merchiers and M.-F. De Pover, 'Chronique de jurisprudence: les contrats spéciaux (1988–1995)', *Les dossiers du JT* 13 (1997), no. 11.   [9] See De Page, *Traité élémentaire*, vol. V, no. 111.

tract',[10] the only one remaining under the new code.[11] To conclude a 'real contract', not only must the parties agree, but in addition the object of the contract – the thing loaned – must be handed over.

Because loan for use is a real contract, it is not clear whether a mere agreement to loan an object is a valid contract. The principle of freedom of contract would seem to allow the parties to make a preliminary contract which has, as its object, the conclusion of a contract of a loan for use.[12] But if so, does it not become pointless to recognize a loan for use as a real contract? Not really. Even if such a preliminary contract is binding, there is still a good reason to distinguish a separate contract of loan for use and to give specific rules for it.[13] Because such a contract is gratuitous, it is usually found in informal relations between relatives, friends, and neighbours who do not usually make arrangements about the loss of the object, the right to have it back, and so forth. Therefore, the decision of the legislator to regard loan for use as a 'real contract', though debatable, is not undercut by recognizing the validity of a preliminary contract to conclude a loan for use. The ordinary rules on formation govern the preliminary contract.

An agreement is not a legally binding contract if it was not meant to have legal effect. This follows from the very notion that the formation of a contract 'requires an intention to produce legal effects' (art. 3:33 of the Civil Code).[14] Here, Barbara does not seem to have intended her promise to have had any legal effect. Therefore the agreement is not legally binding unless Albert justifiably believed that she did (art. 3:35). Whether Albert was justified in understanding that Barbara wanted to bind herself depends on the circumstances of the case. It may be relevant whether he acted in reliance, for example, by refusing an offer made by another friend. Here, however, the statement of the facts does not show that Albert believed that Barbara intended to conclude a binding contract. The result is not clear, however, since it is not clear what the parties intended, what they believed the other party intended, and what they could reasonably rely on.

It does matter if Barbara told Albert he could not have the car a week before she was to deliver it or a week after she actually did. If she actually gave the car to Albert, it is likely that a contract of loan for use was

---

[10] See Pitlo/Salomons 209.   [11] See Asser/Hartkamp vol. II, no. 55.
[12] See PG Boek 7, 883; Pitlo/Salomons 209; O. K. Brahn, 'Het irreële karakter van het reële contract van bruikleen in het Nieuw Burgerlijk Wetboek', NJB 1983, 568.
[13] Though one may doubt whether it should be a 'real contract'. This doubt has been expressed by Brahn, 'het irreële karakter'.   [14] See Asser/Hartkamp vol. II, no. 13.

concluded. The requirement that the object be delivered for such a contract to be formed does not mean in itself, as some authors seem to suggest,[15] that mere delivery is sufficient to form such a contract. As in the case of other contracts, the general requirements must be satisfied that apply to the formation of juristic acts (title 3.2 of the Civil Code). Therefore, the parties must have intended their contract to have legal effects (art. 3:33) or one party must have so intended and he must have been justified in thinking that the other did as well (art. 3:35). Nevertheless, delivery of the object and acceptance of it by the borrower seem to be strong indications that the owner wanted to have it back and that the borrower had agreed to give it back, which is his main obligation under the contract of loan for use (art. 7A:1777).

If a contract of loan for use is concluded, the rules in arts. 7A:1777 ff. of the Civil Code apply unless the parties provide otherwise, which is not the case here. Art. 7A:1788 of the Civil Code says that if the owner needs the object himself for an unexpected compelling reason (*dringende reden*), the judge may decide to order the borrower to return it.[16] Here, we are told only that Barbara 'needs' the car but not why: to go to the doctor? to work? to the shopping centre? to see friends? Nor are we told if she owns another car. If her reason is not compelling, Albert may not have to return it before the time agreed.

In a recent article, one author has argued for general indulgence for those who make gratuitous promises.[17] He claims that the courts or the legislator should make rules which are based on the principle that a person who makes a gratuitous promise should be bound to his promise less stringently than is typical of liability in contract or tort.[18]

The final question is whether it matters if Albert has taken a job that requires him to have a car but does not pay enough for him to rent one. How much damage he would suffer if the promise turns out to be legally binding does not matter much for the question whether Albert thought Barbara intended to be legally bound or could reasonably think so (art. 3:35 of the Civil Code). However, if Barbara knew Albert took this job and that he would not earn enough money to rent a car, that might be some evidence that she intended the promise to be legally binding upon her or that Albert was justified in thinking she did.

---

[15] Van Schaick, 'Vriendendienst', 316.

[16] Article 7A:1788 of the Civil Code: 'However, if the lender during that course of time, or before the need of the user has stopped, needs the object lent himself for urgent and sudden reasons, the judge, according to the circumstances, can force the user to return the object lent to the lender.' Trans. by S. von Erp.

[17] Van Schaick, 'Vriendendienst', 318.   [18] *Ibid.*, 320.

SPAIN

This type of arrangement is a loan for use (*comodato*). According to the Civil Code it is a contract *re* which means that the object to be loaned must actually be delivered (*datio rei*) for a contract to be formed (art. 1742). Nevertheless, most scholars maintain that such a contract is consensual, that it can be created by the mere assent of the parties.[19] Its characteristics are that its *causa* is always liberality (otherwise it would be a lease), and it is always temporary (otherwise it would be a sale). By that view, the promise is enforceable even without delivery.

Barbara may terminate her obligations if she needs the car for herself because of an urgent need (art. 1749 of Civil Code).[20] Had the obligation not had a term, she could have terminated it at will (art. 1750). Otherwise, Barbara cannot terminate the contract.

PORTUGAL

Barbara can have the car back. However, her legal position is stronger if the car had not actually been delivered. The fact that Albert has taken a new job which requires him to have a car is not relevant.

The case is very similar to Case 5. This type of agreement is a loan for use which is called a *contrato de comodato* in Portuguese law. According to the definition in art. 1129 of the Civil Code, a loan for use is a contract in which one of the parties delivers to the other something which the recipient is to use and later return. Like a deposit, it is considered a real contract *quoad constitutionem*. Therefore, the classical view is that this contract does not create any obligation until after the thing to be loaned is actually delivered.[21] Today, however, the majority of scholars believe that such a contract can be formed by the mere assent of the parties provided that they agree to establish an obligation immediately.

While a court might decide that a legal obligation did not arise if the car had not actually been delivered, after delivery, it is clear that a contract has been formed, which is binding on Barbara. Generally, she would be entitled to the restitution of the car only after the end of the loan for use. But in this case, she can ask for its restitution immediately. As in Case 5, even if the parties have agreed on a term in the loan for use, Barbara can ask Albert to return her car if there is a fair reason (*justa causa*) (art. 1140 of the Civil Code). As before, *justa causa* is an imprecise concept which

---

[19] Díez Picazo and Gullón, *Sistema de derecho civil*, 427.
[20] The text of the Code says that the need must be urgent but does not require that it be unforeseeable.   [21] See Lima and Varela, *Código Civil Anotado*, vol. II, 741.

can be interpreted in different ways. According to legal scholars, a fair motive can be, for instance, an unexpected and urgent need for the thing loaned.[22] Therefore, in a case like this one, Barbara could terminate the loan for use.

The fact that Albert has taken a new job which requires him to have a car is not relevant because the termination of the contract is in this case allowed by the statute whatever the situation of the other party might be.

ITALY

Barbara can have her car back. The result is the same whether she told Albert he could not have the car a week before she was supposed to deliver it or a week after she actually did, although the legal explanation is slightly different.

If Barbara actually delivered the car, the relationship is governed by the Civil Code rules that govern the contract of loan for use (*comodato*).[23] It is a nominate contract and a *contratto reale* or contract *re*, which means that it is formed when the object in question is delivered, as in the case of a contract of deposit.[24] Also, such a contract must be gratuitous (art. 1803(2)).

Article 1809(2) provides that the lender (Barbara) can ask for the immediate restitution of the object loaned (the car) even before the expiration of the time limit if she has an urgent and unforeseen need for it. So she would be able to demand its return here. The case law does not require the need to be very compelling.[25] The only limits are probably the mere arbitrary demand of the lender or some need that was clearly foreseen when the contract was made.

Before delivery, Barbara's promise is not legally binding according to the Italian case law because it lacks a *causa*, at least in the sense of an economic interest of the lender in performing. It might well be considered merely a courtesy promise.[26] Therefore, as before, Barbara can get her car back, but this time because no contract was formed.

---

[22] See J. B. Machado, 'Pressupostos da Resolução por Incumprimento', in *Estudos em Homenagem ao Prof. Doutor J. J. Teixeira Ribeiro*, II-Iuridica (1979), 343; Lima and Varela, *Código Civil Anotado*, vol. II, 759.

[23] See O. T. Scozzafava, 'Il Comodato', in Rescigno, *Tratt. di dir. priv.* 12 (1985), 611; Giampiccolo, 'Il comodato e il mutuo', in G. Grosso and F. Santoro Passarelli, *Trattato di diretto civile* (1972), 3; F. Carresi, 'Il comodato. Il mutuo', in Vassalli, *Tratt. di dir. civ.* 8:2 (1954), 5; E. M. Barbieri, 'Il comodato', V. Napoletano, E. M. Barbieri, and M. Novità, 'I contratti reali', in Giur. sist. civ. e comm. (1979), 345; R. Teti, 'Il comodato', in Digesto 3 (1988), 37.   [24] See the discussion of Case 5.

[25] See Cass. civ., 5 Feb. 1987, no. 1132; Cass. civ. 2652/1963.

[26] See R. Sacco, 'Il Contratto', in Vassalli, *Tratt. di dir. civ.* 6:2 (1975), 491.

For some scholars, that promise could be considered as part of the negotiations leading towards a contract of loan for use, so that Barbara's refusal to keep the promise could be analysed under the principles governing pre-contractual liability (see art. 1337 of the Civil Code). Under these principles, sometimes, a party can recover damages incurred in reliance that a contract would be completed. Here, however, the reliance would not have been justified given the peculiar kind of contract that the parties were about to conclude. For reasons already discussed, a person would not be justified in relying even upon a completed contract of loan for use.[27]

AUSTRIA

There are two possible ways of describing Barbara's agreement with Albert. First, it might constitute a contract of loan for use (*Leihvertrag*). According to Austrian law (§ 971 of the Civil Code), this is a gratuitous contract.[28] If the contract is made for a certain time period, the lender does not have the right to ask the borrower to return the object before the agreed time. Even if he needs the object urgently himself, he is not entitled to demand its return (§ 976). Barbara therefore cannot have the car back.

A contract of loan for use is a real contract, meaning that it is formed by the delivery of the object in question (see § 971 of the Civil Code). A promise to loan an object constitutes a *pactum de contrahendo*. According to § 936 of the Civil Code, such a contract is subject to a *clausula rebus sic stantibus*: a party can withdraw if circumstances change sufficiently. Barbara would therefore have the right to cancel the contract if she discovered that she will need the car herself provided that the car has not yet been delivered to Albert.

The second possibility is that the contract constitutes a *Prekarium* (§ 974). In that event, the lender has the right to claim the object back at any time.[29] If it does, Barbara can have the car back.[30]

In neither case does it matter if Albert's job requires him to have a car. The fact that it did, however, could be an indication that a contract of loan

---

[27] See Marini, *Promessa ed affidamento*, 295.
[28] If the borrower has to make a payment for the use, the contract constitutes a rental agreement. Such an agreement is governed by §§ 1090 ff. of the Civil Code.
[29] See Koziol and Welser, *Grundriß*, vol. I, 358.
[30] Therefore it is not necessary to ask whether Barbara had the intention to bind herself legally. It is only necessary to ask whether Barbara reserved the right to claim the car back at any time.

for use was concluded since he would not have wanted Barbara to be able to reclaim the car at any time.

GERMANY

A loan for use (§§ 598–606 of the Civil Code) is not a mutual contract because only the lender is obligated: he must allow the borrower to use something for some period of time without remuneration. Neither is it a gift because in a gift something is given away forever. The parties can enter into a loan for use without the formalities necessary to make a promise of gift binding (see Case 1). As in the case of every contract, however, there has to be the intention to be legally bound. But in case of a gratuitous loan for use, the requirements for proving this intention are not very high. Therefore, we have a binding contract here, especially in view of the comparatively long duration of three months which would be very unusual for a mere favour.

A lender may terminate the contract before the agreed point of time if he needs the thing loaned for a reason of which he was unaware when he promised to loan it (§ 605(1) of the Civil Code[31]). Barbara could not have known that she would have to cancel her vacation and would therefore need her car earlier. But she chose a moment that was inopportune for the borrower, and he could therefore claim a violation of good faith (§ 242 of the Civil Code[32]). In such a case, the interests of both parties have to be weighed against each other by the court.

The interests of the lender are generally regarded as more important than those of the borrower because, in principle, the law gives him the right to terminate, and because he did not charge anything. Albert's interests are less important because he did not pay anything in return.[33] Therefore, a court would only regard a moment as inopportune if there were exceptional circumstances involved in the case.

On these principles, Barbara can have the car back because she could not foresee her injury. She is not liable for damages because the right to terminate the contract is granted to her by the law, and she cannot be liable for acting lawfully.

Whether the car has already been delivered when Barbara told Albert

---

[31] 'The lender may terminate the contract: (1) if he needs the good because of unforeseen circumstances . . .'

[32] The debtor has to perform his duties with regard to good faith and ordinary usage. But the notion of good faith is applied generally in order to limit the exercise of rights.

[33] *Entscheidungen der Bayerischen Obersten Landesgerichtes in Zivilsachen* 32, 466.

about her situation matters only as to the question of whether the moment was inopportune.

Whether Albert has taken a job matters because it makes his interest in keeping the car more important. If he has not taken the job, there is no doubt about Barbara's right to terminate the contract. Even if he has, however, it is still doubtful that his hardship would be exceptional enough to make his interest more important than Barbara's.

GREECE

Barbara and Albert have entered into a contract of 'loan for use' for a fixed period of three months. Such a contract is governed by articles 810–21 of the Civil Code. In such a contract, the lender grants to the borrower, without remuneration, the use of a thing which is to be returned upon the expiration of the contract (art. 810 of the Civil Code).[34]

The wording of art. 810 of the Greek Civil Code suggests that a contract of loan for use is a contract *re*,[35] that is, one constituted by the delivery of the thing.[36] If so, then when the thing has not yet been delivered there is no contract of loan for use, but a preliminary agreement.[37] Nevertheless, a contract of loan for use can be concluded *solo consensu* by virtue of the principle of freedom of contract (art. 361 of the Civil Code).[38] Such a contract differs from a preliminary agreement since it is a contract completed even before the delivery of the thing rather than an agreement to enter into another contract. The consensual contract of loan for use is also governed by arts. 810–21 of the Civil Code.

A contract of loan for use ends when the time agreed upon expires (art. 816 of the Civil Code) or, if no time limit is fixed, as soon as the thing is used, unless there is a contrary agreement.[39] Upon the expiration of the

---

[34] Filios, *Law of Obligations*, 148; AP 13/1971 NoB 19 (1971), 432. Article 810 of the Civil Code corresponds in part to previous law. A difference is that art. 810 provides that the borrower is obliged to return the thing when the contract expires. The law previously was that he must return it after having used it. Kafkas, *Law of Obligations*, art. 810.

[35] See Case 5 above for an analysis of the problem of contracts concluded *re* and *solo consensu*. In contracts concluded *re*, the borrower is not obligated before delivery. Stathopoulos, *Contract Law*, 40–1.

[36] Kafkas, *Law of Obligations*, art. 810, § 2b; I. Rokas in Georgiadis and Stathopoulos, *Civil Code*, art. 810, no. 2. In Germany there is still a dispute whether 'the loan for use' contract is one concluded *re* or *solo consensu*.

[37] For the consequences of the preliminary agreement, see Case 5.

[38] Rokas in Georgiadis and Stathopoulos, *Civil Code*, art. 810, no. 2; Filios, *Law of Obligations* 148, follows the opinion that a contract of loan for use is always concluded *solo consensu*.

[39] I. Spiridakis, 'The Loan for Use', NoB 24 (1976), 814; AP 130/1994.

time, the borrower is obliged to return the thing without any formal demand.[40] However, according to art. 817 of the Civil Code,[41] there are some exceptions to this rule. The lender can claim the thing back even before the term expires if (1) the borrower has made use of the thing in a manner contrary to the conditions of the contract; (2) he has caused the thing to deteriorate; (3) he has handed it over without right to a third party; or (4) the lender himself has an urgent need of the thing which the lender could not have foreseen.

Whether the need is 'urgent' will be judged *ad hoc* taking into consideration all the facts.[42] It is agreed that the need is 'urgent' when the lender cannot postpone its fulfilment until the contract expires without a significant detriment to himself.[43] If the need of the lender conflicts with the need of the borrower and they cannot both be fulfilled, then that of the lender prevails.[44] The lender, however, must use his right to reclaim the thing in conformity with the principle of good faith (art. 288 of the Civil Code).[45] Moreover, he must not have been able to foresee the need regardless of whether his inability to do so was due to his own fault or carelessness. In this case, according to one opinion, the lender can ask for the thing without any formal demand;[46] according to another, he must give a notice of termination and set a reasonable period for its return.[47] In these cases, the lender does not have to prove that he suffered loss, and he does not have to compensate the borrower for use.[48]

Thus, in Case 7, if Barbara has delivered the car to Albert, she can reclaim it if her need was considered to be urgent and unforeseeable: she cancelled her vacation after injuring her foot. If she has not yet delivered the car, then she will be discharged from the performance of her obligations under the contract (or of the preliminary contract agreement).

---

[40] Rokas in Georgiadis and Stathopoulos, *Civil Code*, arts. 816–17, no. 1.

[41] Articles 816 and 817 of the Civil Code are similar to §§ 604 and 605 of the German Civil Code, art. 309 of the Swiss Code of Obligations, and art. 1889 of the French Civil Code. Kafkas, *Law of Obligations*, arts. 816–17.

[42] The Thrace Court of Appeal has decided that if an urgent and unforeseeable need arises, the lender can ask for the thing back. Its reasoning was based on principles of good faith. It also decided that cancellation of the re-allotment of land does not constitute an urgent need. Thrace Court of Appeal 151/1984 HellD 25 (1984), 1210.

[43] Rokas in Georgiadis and Stathopoulos, *Civil Code*, arts. 816–17, no. 3; Corfu Court of First Instance 367/65 EEN 32 (1965), 852.

[44] Corfu Court of First Instance 367/65 EEN 32 (1965), 852.

[45] AP 130/1994 EEN 62 (1995), 64.   [46] Kafkas, *Law of Obligations*, arts. 816–17, no. 3.

[47] P. Passias in ErmAK, Introductory Remarks, arts. 810–21; I. Spiridakis and E. Perakis, *Civil Code B/2 Law of Obligations, Special Part* (1978), art. 817.

[48] Kafkas, *Law of Obligations*, arts. 816–17, no. 3.

It is irrelevant that Albert has taken a job that requires him to have a car but does not pay enough for him to rent one. As already noted, the lender's need prevails. Barbara does not owe him any compensation.

SCOTLAND

Section 1(2) of the Requirements of Writing (Scotland) Act 1995[49] again provides that *prima facie* Albert will only be able to enforce Barbara's promise if it is constituted in writing. The time at which he is informed of her change of heart is of no relevance under the law of Scotland.

If Albert has taken a job which requires a car but does not pay enough for him to rent one, then there is a possibility of a plea in terms of s. 1(3) and (4) of the 1995 Act, which will mean that he will no longer require written evidence of the promise. For the plea to be successful, Barbara must be aware of the situation that Albert is now in due to his reliance on her promise. It is clear that Albert will be affected to a material extent by the withdrawal of the car in breach of the promise.

In conclusion, Albert will be able to enforce the promise if he has it in writing. He may be able to avoid this requirement if Barbara is aware that he will lose his job if she fails to fulfil her promise.

ENGLAND

The facts of Case 7 are similar to the facts of Case 5, except that the positions of the parties are reversed. In Case 5, the transfer or contemplated transfer of property was for the benefit of the transferor (the bailor), who was seeking to enforce a promise made by the transferee (the bailee). Here, the transfer is for the benefit of the transferee (bailee), who is seeking to enforce a promise made by the transferor (bailor). Not surprisingly, then, the status of the promise in each case is broadly similar; that is, before delivery it is unenforceable, whilst after delivery it is arguably, and less clearly, enforceable.

Before delivery of the car, Barbara's promise is unenforceable for the same reason that Charles' promise was unenforceable in Case 5: no consideration was provided (see Case 1). Albert did not do, or promise to do, anything in return for Barbara's promise.[50] If Albert relied on the promise then, as discussed in the answer to Case 1, a sympathetic court might try to invent consideration by finding that, for example, Albert had agreed to

---

[49] See Case 1.   [50] Palmer, *Bailment*, 582.

'look after' or 'store' Barbara's car in exchange for her lending it to him. This finding is unlikely, however, where there has been no delivery (as we shall see, it is more likely in the case where delivery has been made).

A further reason which a court might give for refusing to enforce Barbara's promise prior to delivery is that the parties lacked the necessary intent to create legal relations. As discussed in regard to Case 1, an English court will assume, lacking evidence to the contrary, that such an intent, which is required for a valid contract, is lacking in social and domestic arrangements. Presumably Barbara and Albert are friends, so their arrangement would *prima facie* qualify as social.

Once delivery has been made, the relationship becomes one of bailment, more specifically, the relationship is one of *commodatum* or *gratuitous loan* (because the relationship is for the bailee, Albert's, benefit). Absent Barbara's promise, it is clear that the bailment is terminable at will by either party. The effect of Barbara's promise that Albert may have the car for a specified period of time is, like the parallel promise in Case 5, less clear. The author of the leading treatise on bailment, Palmer, states that 'it is uncertain whether an agreement to lend for a particular term, coupled with delivery of the chattel, can be enforced against the bailor',[51] adding later that 'there is remarkably little authority on this point'.[52] As Palmer explains, there are a number of ways the case might be decided. The first is to hold, following ordinary contractual principles, that Barbara's promise is unenforceable for lack of consideration. As noted a moment ago, a court might try to invent consideration for the promise, and cases where this has happened in post-delivery circumstances certainly can be found.[53] Second, and if Albert has detrimentally relied on Barbara's promise, Albert might argue that, in view of his reliance, Barbara is estopped from going back on her word. The difficulty with this argument is that, as explained in the discussion of estoppel in Case 1, in English law estoppel cannot be used to found a cause of action. It might be argued that Albert is not using estoppel to found a cause of action here, since, assuming he was refusing to return the car, he would be the defendant in Barbara's action for repossession of the car. The 'no cause of action by estoppel' rule, however, is understood as requiring that the parties have *pre-existing legal relations* at the time the promise was made. Estoppel can be used only as a defence to the enforcement of those relations. Here, Barbara and Albert had no legal relations at the time of

---

[51] *Ibid.*, 630.   [52] *Ibid.*, 658.

[53] E.g., *Blakermore v. Bristol & Exeter Rly Co.* [1858] 8 E & B 1035; 120 ER 385; and, see generally, Palmer, *Bailment*, 659.

Barbara's promise (this would not be true if the promise was made after delivery of the car). There remains a slim possibility that the promise might be enforceable by analogy to an exception to the 'no cause of action rule' for representations concerning the ownership of land. An owner of land who allows another to make improvements on his or her land on the impression that the land is, or will become, the other party's can be estopped from going back on his word.[54] Some cases have extended this exception to chattels.[55] Furthermore, a few of the land cases have suggested that the exception may apply also to grants of irrevocable licences to occupy.[56] If these two extensions of the land exception are combined, it might be possible to raise estoppel successfully against an attempt by Barbara to regain her car.

Third, it could be argued, as Palmer himself suggests, that bailment is a *sui generis* relationship, and that, by analogy to those cases where a bailee's gratuitous promise was held enforceable (see Case 5), a bailor's gratuitous promise should similarly be enforceable. In other words, Barbara's promise is enforceable because promises ancillary to a bailment relationship are enforceable. But, as discussed in Case 5, the status of promises by unrewarded bailees is itself unclear, so the success of this argument by analogy must be doubly uncertain. Overall, then, the conclusion must be that the status of Barbara's promise once delivery has been made is not clear in English law. Finally, that Albert has relied on the promise would, in theory, make no difference except in the case where estoppel was argued, although in practice it is safe to assume that an English court would be more willing to enforce the promise if Albert has relied on it to his detriment.

IRELAND

On the facts as presented, Albert has provided no consideration for Barbara's promise nor has the promise been made by way of a deed under seal. In these circumstances there is no enforceable contract between the parties, and Barbara would be entitled to have her car back. This example appears also to fall within the definition of a gratuitous bailment.[57] In this instance, however, it is Albert, as bailee, who benefits solely from this transaction while Barbara, as bailor, does not. Where the car has not been actually acquired by Albert then Barbara is not bound by her promise as there has been no consideration provided and the goods have not been

---

[54] *Ramsden* v. *Dyson* [1866] LR 1 HL 129, 140–1.   [55] *Greenwood* v. *Bennett* [1973] QB 195.
[56] *Plimmer* v. *Mayor of Wellington* [1884] 9 App. Cas. 699, 714.   [57] See Case 5.

bailed. The position may be different, however, where Albert actually acquires the goods.[58]

Where Albert is told that he could not have the car a week before Barbara was supposed to deliver, then the contract is unenforceable as there has been no consideration and the promise was not made by way of a deed under seal.[59] However, where Albert is told that he could not have the car a week after she actually delivered the car, a gratuitous bailment arises.[60] In *Bainbridge* v. *Firmstone*,[61] it was held that a gratuitous bailment for the benefit of the bailee gave rise to a detriment to the bailor from 'parting with the possession for even so short a time'. Treitel provides that a mere promise by the bailee to return the chattel might not suffice as consideration as it would only be a promise to perform a duty imposed by law on all bailees, but a promise to look after the chattels or to improve them in some way would probably be regarded as consideration moving from the bailee. Palmer suggests that a gratuitous bailment provides for purely tortious remedies. Whether an Irish court would find that the mere acceptance by Albert of the car could give rise to an enforceable promise remains uncertain. In this regard it could be argued that Albert's acceptance of the car amounts to an implied promise to look after the car and thus amounts to consideration moving from him to Barbara.[62]

Albert might also be able to rely on the equitable principle of estoppel where he had actually acquired the car. In such instance, where Albert refuses to give her the car back and Barbara institutes proceedings for the return of her car, Albert could raise the principles of promissory estoppel in order to defeat her claim. In this regard the issue of whether Albert was told a week before or a week after she was supposed to deliver it might be relevant with regard also to the issue of detriment. As with all equitable remedies, however, all the facts are taken into account and no doubt the fact that she cancelled vacation plans after injuring her left foot would also be taken into account. Furthermore, estoppel operates as a shield and not a sword, allowing Albert to raise the issue of promissory estoppel only to defeat a claim instituted by Barbara.

If Albert took a job that requires him to have a car but does not pay enough for him to rent one, that fact does not go to the enforceability or otherwise of the contract. If there has been no consideration and the promise was not made by way of a deed under seal then the promise is unenforceable (see Case 1). As stated, it is yet uncertain whether an Irish

---

[58] See Case 7.   [59] See Case 5.   [60] See Case 5.   [61] [1838] 8 A & E 743.
[62] See Treitel, *Contract,* ch. 3.

court would find that mere acceptance by the bailee of the chattel would amount to consideration giving rise to an enforceable promise. Where Barbara's promise to Albert was not enforceable in contract she could still be liable to Albert in tort.[63] In tort, the object of damages is to compensate the plaintiff by restoring him to the position which he would have held if the tort was not committed, whereas in contract, an Irish court takes into account loss of expectations and loss of profit as well. In this regard, the fact that Albert has taken a job that requires him to have a car but does not pay enough for him to rent one would matter in assessing the amount of damages, if any, Albert would receive where it could be established that Barbara was liable to Albert, be it in tort or contract.

That Albert took the job would also be relevant where Albert sought to raise promissory estoppel to defeat a claim instituted by Barbara. This could be a factor which could show the intention or otherwise of Barbara to be contractually bound and furthermore which would show detriment on the part of Albert.[64]

Summaries

France: If the car has been delivered, a contract of loan for use is formed but Barbara can reclaim the car before the date agreed if she has an 'urgent and unforeseeable need' for it, although a court will also take hardship to Albert into account. This right is an exception to the general principle that relief will not be given for changed and unforeseen circumstances. If the car has not been delivered, the arrangement is a promise to enter into a loan for use, which is also binding but not subject to this exception, and so Barbara will not have the right to reclaim the car before the time fixed.

Belgium: If the car has been delivered, a contract of loan for use is formed but Barbara can reclaim the car before the date agreed if she has a 'compelling and unforeseeable need' for it. This right is an exception to the general principle that relief will not be given for changed and unforeseen circumstances. If the car has not been delivered, the arrangement is a promise to enter into a loan for use, which is also binding, but not subject to this exception. Barbara may still be able to reclaim the car under the doctrine of *force majeure* which Belgian courts have applied when performance has become difficult even though it is still possible.

---

[63] See Case 5. See also Palmer, *Bailment*, ch. 8; Treitel, *Contract*, ch. 3.
[64] See Case 1 on the issue of promissory estoppel.

The Netherlands: If the car has been delivered, a contract of loan for use is formed. The parties must also have intended to enter into a legally binding contract, which they probably did, although some authors believe their intention to do so does not matter if delivery has been made. If such a contract has been formed, Barbara may still reclaim the car before the date agreed if she has an 'unexpected compelling reason'. If the car has not been delivered, the arrangement is a promise to enter into a loan for use which should also be binding, although the matter is not clear.

Spain: Although the Civil Code provides that a contract of loan for use is formed on delivery, most scholars believe it can be formed by consent as well, and so the parties have entered into such a contract whether or not the car has been delivered. Barbara can reclaim the car if she has an 'urgent' need for it (the text of the Code does not require it to be unforeseeable).

Portugal: Although the Civil Code provides that a contract of loan for use is formed on delivery, most scholars believe it can be formed by consent as well, and so the parties have entered into such a contract whether or not the car has been delivered. Barbara can reclaim the car because she has a 'fair reason' for doing so.

Italy: If the car has been delivered, a contract of loan for use is formed but Barbara can reclaim the car before the date agreed if she has an 'urgent and unforeseen need' for it. If the car has not been delivered, Barbara can reclaim the car because no contract has been formed. Her promise lacks a *causa* unless it served her economic interests. Moreover, she may not have intended to bind herself legally. Some scholars might draw an analogy to pre-contractual liability, but the analogy is not a good one given the special nature of the contract to be entered into.

Austria: If the car has been delivered, and the parties so intended, the contract is a loan for use, and Barbara cannot reclaim the car, even if she needs it urgently herself. If it has not been delivered, and the parties so intended, the contract is a promise to enter into a loan for use, and Barbara can reclaim it if circumstances have changed sufficiently. She can also do so if the parties intended the transaction to be a loan terminable at will (*Prekarium*).

Germany: Whether or not the car has been delivered, the contract is a loan for use as long as the parties intended to be legally bound, as seems likely. If so, Barbara can reclaim the car if she needs it because of 'unforeseen circumstances'. While a court will take Albert's interests into account, it will consider them to be less important than Barbara's because the contract is gratuitous.

Greece: If the car has been delivered, a contract of loan for use has certainly been formed. If it has not been delivered, such a contract may not have been formed, and if not, the arrangement is a promise to enter into a loan for use, which is binding. Barbara can reclaim the car if she has an 'urgent' and 'unforeseeable' need for it. She must exercise this right in good faith, and while Albert's need will be taken into account, in principle, her need will prevail over his.

Scotland: Since the promise is gratuitous, it is unenforceable (unless in writing) unless Barbara knew and acquiesced in Albert's reliance on it, and Albert relied materially and was materially harmed as a result.

England: If the car has not been delivered, the promise is unenforceable because it lacks consideration. If it has been delivered, the parties may not have intended to be legally bound. If the car has been delivered, the arrangement is one of bailment, and more specifically, of *commodatum* or gratuitous loan. It is not clear whether a promise to lend for a fixed term auxiliary to such a relationship is enforceable.

Ireland: If the car has not been delivered, the promise is unenforceable because it lacks consideration. If it has been delivered, the arrangement is a gratuitous bailment. It is not clear whether a promise to lend for a fixed term auxiliary to such a relationship is enforceable, but a court might find a detriment to the bailee, and hence consideration, in a promise to take care of the car.

Barbara might be liable in tort. As before, in Irish law, it is possible to recover in tort for pure economic loss, for nonfeasance as well as for misfeasance, and for breach of a duty arising out of a relationship voluntarily entered into.

Preliminary comparisons

The significance of delivery: In two civil law countries (Spain and Germany), and possibly in a third (Greece), a contract of loan for use is formed whether or not the car is delivered. In the rest, except for Scotland, such a contract is formed only if the car is delivered; otherwise, the arrangement is a promise to enter into a loan for use (France, Belgium, the Netherlands, Portugal, Italy, Austria, and possibly Greece). In Italy, possibly in the Netherlands, and conceivably in Spain and Portugal (where the majority opinion is to the contrary), the distinction matters because such a promise would not be binding. In France and Belgium, it matters because Barbara can reclaim her car if circumstances have changed only if the contract is a loan for use. In Austria, it matters because Barbara can reclaim her car for this reason only if the contract is not a loan for use (see below). Delivery may matter in England and Ireland because without delivery, such a promise is unenforceable for lack of consideration; after delivery, the arrangement is a gratuitous bailment and the promise may be enforceable although it is not clear. In Scotland, the promise is unenforceable (absent a writing or reliance) whether or not the car is delivered.

The significance of reliance: In Scotland, the promise is enforceable if Barbara knew and acquiesced in Albert's reliance on it, and Albert relied materially and was materially harmed as a result.

Tort: In Ireland, Albert may recover in tort since it is possible to recover for pure economic loss, for nonfeasance as well as for misfeasance, and for breach of a duty arising out of a relationship entered into voluntarily.

Intention to be legally bound: Some reporters mentioned that for the promise to be binding, the parties must have intended to be legally bound, but most of them took it for granted that the parties wanted to create legal relations of some sort.

The effect of changed circumstances: The Civil Codes of France, Belgium, the Netherlands, Italy, Austria, Germany, and Greece all provide that, in a loan for use, the lender who has a grave and unforeseen need for the object loaned can reclaim before the time agreed. The Spanish Code has a similar provision that speaks of the gravity of the need but not its unforeseeability. The Portuguese Code allows the lender to reclaim the object if he has a 'fair reason'. The Austrian Code provides that the lender cannot reclaim it. Nevertheless, Austria recognizes a general principle of relief for changed and unforeseen circumstances while France and Belgium do not. Thus the effect of these provisions is that in Austria, Barbara can reclaim the car if circumstances have changed only if the car has not been delivered and so no contract of loan for use has been formed; in France and Belgium, she can do so only if it has been delivered and such a contract formed. In Belgium, however, Barbara may be able to claim *force majeure* since Belgian courts have given relief when performance has become more difficult even though it is not impossible.

Case 8: a requirements contract

Case

Alloy, a steel manufacturer, promised to sell Motor Works, a car manufacturer, as much steel as it ordered during the coming year for a set price per ton. Is the promise binding (a) if the market price rises to 20 per cent more than the contract price, and Motor Works orders the amount of steel it usually needs? (b) if the market price rises to 20 per cent more than the contract price, and Motor Works orders twice the steel it usually needs? (c) if the market price falls to 20 per cent below the contract price, and Motor Works buys no steel from Alloy, buying its requirements of steel on the market instead?

Discussions

FRANCE

The arrangement between Alloy and Motor Works seems to be aimed at fixing the general conditions of sale, which will be the subject of later orders. Under French law, such a contract would be considered a framework contract (*contrat cadre*) as opposed to the sales contracts (*contrats d'application*) which implement the initial contract. It is probably more accurate to view the *contrat cadre* as a convenient and practical category which scholarly opinion (*doctrine*) has constructed so that it will not be necessary to analyse each sale as a new contract with its own conditions. This construction is more elegant.

The only other possible analysis, in our view, would be to consider the arrangement to be a unilateral promise to sell (*promesse unilatérale de vente*) since Alloy is already bound to sell at a fixed price while Motor Works may or may not decide to purchase. Such a promise to sell may be void here because Alloy's own obligation to deliver is uncertain: the amount to be delivered has not been determined. Such an obligation may be void under art. 1129 of the Civil Code[1] and kindred articles which require a contractual obligation to be definite. In any event, such an analysis would require the promise to be transformed into a contract of sale each time Motor Works exercised its option to purchase. It is impracticable to imagine Motor Works repeating such an operation each time it sends an order.

We therefore prefer to analyse the agreement as a framework contract to supply the amount of steel subsequently ordered. Nevertheless, this analysis does not get rid of the difficulty of how to quantify Alloy's obligation: how many tons of steel is it obliged to deliver to Motor Works? If the answer remains 'as many as Motor Works orders', then the contract may still fall foul of the provisions of art. 1129 and related articles of the Civil Code.

These articles require a contractual obligation to be definite. Under art. 1108,[2] the object of the contract must be certain. Under art. 1129, the subject matter of the obligations must be determined or determinable. Similarly, under arts. 1583[3] and 1591,[4] in a sale, if the price of the goods or the amount to be delivered is undetermined or undeterminable, and the contract includes no mechanism for determination, the contract is void for uncertainty (*l'indétermination de l'objet*). If the contract were for the sale of specific goods, the contract would not have to contain any special provision as to quantity. It would be enough to specify the goods. But where, as here, generic goods are sold by quantity, both the type of goods (steel) and the quantity must be determined or determinable. The type of goods must be determined at formation of the contract; the quantity may be set later or may be determinable at the time of performance.

If determining the quantity required a new agreement by both of the parties, then the initial contract would be void for uncertainty. The judge has no power to set a price in the absence of contractual agreement. These principles have been applied by case law to framework contracts.

If the quantity were to be determined at the sole discretion of the promisor under the obligation, who could therefore decide whether or

---

[1] It is necessary that the subject matter of an obligation is at least determinable as to its kind. The quantity of the thing can be uncertain provided that it can be determined.

[2] Article 1108: 'Four conditions are essential for the validity of an agreement (*convention*): the consent of the person who obligates himself; his capacity to contract; certainty of the object which is the subject matter of the undertaking; a licit *cause* for the obligation.'

[3] Article 1583: 'The sale is perfect as between the parties, and the buyer obtains title as of right from the seller, as soon as they have agreed on the thing and the price sold, even if the thing has not yet been delivered nor the price paid.'

[4] Article 1591: 'The price of the sale must be determined and fixed by the parties.'

not to be contractually obligated, it would constitute a *condition potestative*. The contract would then be void under art. 1174 of the Civil Code.[5] This is not the case, as the quantity ordered does not depend on Alloy (the promisor of the relevant obligation) but on Motor Works.

Here, the quantity depends on the sole discretion of the promisee. The cases most closely in point concern contracts in which the price depends on the discretion of one of the parties. For a long time, the *Cour de cassation* held such a contract void for uncertainty under arts. 1129 or 1583 of the Civil Code. Recently, however, the Court overruled its prior decisions by holding that such indeterminacy no longer voids the contract. Nevertheless, a remedy will be granted if there is an abuse in setting the price. Damages may be awarded. Alternatively, or in addition, the contract may be terminated as to the future, although, despite the general rule of French law,[6] it will be deemed valid as to past transactions.[7] Therefore, a party complaining of indeterminacy will now claim relief on the grounds of an abuse of a right.

This result is an application of the theory of 'abuse of right' developed by the case law and by legal scholars which limits the exercise of a right by its owner. Although an abuse of right is most obviously characterized by an intention to harm another person, the concept extends to any behaviour deemed to be illegitimate.[8] Assessing such behaviour is left to the lower court judges but they are subject to review by the *Cour de cassation* as the question raised is one of law: whether a right has been abused by infringing the liberty of another person.

In contracts in which the price is set by one of the parties, the traditional approach which voided the contract for uncertainty was an attempt to deal with the same basic problem as the new one which looks for an abuse of right. It is the problem of fairness. It is self-evident that some degree of certainty is necessary if an agreement is to be enforced. But the requirement of certainty also constitutes a guarantee for the parties, and particularly the promisee, that the other party cannot impose an excessive or unsatisfactory obligation on him.[9] This need for protection has led

---

[5] Article 1174: 'Every obligation is void when it is made under the *condition potestative* of the promisor.'

[6] A. Colin and H. Capitant, *Cours élémentaires de droit civil français*, 3rd edn, vol. II (1920–1), no. 2, p. 350; Ghestin, Jamin, and Billau, *Traité de droit civil* nos. 482 ff.

[7] Ass. plén., 1 Dec. 1995, JCP 1996, II, 22565, concl. Jeol, note J. Ghestin; D 1996, 13, concl. Jeol, note L. Aynès.

[8] Ghestin, Gorbeaux, and Fabre-Magnan, *Traité de droit civil* no. 761, pp. 747 f.; C. Jamin, 'Réseaux intégrés de distribution', JCP, 1996, I, 3959.

[9] See Flour and Aubert, *Droit civil* 1; A. Colin, *L'acte juridique*, 7th edn (1996), no. 244, p. 165.

the courts to refuse to enforce contracts in which a price depends on the sole discretion of one of the parties, for example, in franchising and in contracts for exclusive distribution. Imposing such a requirement in a framework contract might seem artificial since these contracts do not actually include prices, but merely an agreement for future sales contracts. However, the imposition of a limit on the discretion of a party over the content of the contract, and especially the price, was a recognition that in such a situation, the position of the promisee is weak. The policing of the manner in which the parties set the contract price was an indirect way of avoiding economic imbalance. It prevents the weaker party from being subject to the arbitrary economic power of the other.

The new approach to policing unfairness in such contracts by asking if a right has been abused has received both criticism and approval from scholars.[10] It is clear, however, that the remedies it makes available – damages and non-retrospective termination – are easier to administer and more satisfactory in practice. The older approach – voiding the contract for indeterminacy – led to serious practical difficulties concerning restitution, and was not necessarily the appropriate corrective remedy that the promisee was really looking for.

If the cases on an indeterminate price are applied here by analogy,[11] then the contractual obligation to deliver an undetermined quantity of steel will be valid but subject to a claim of abuse of right.

The consequence, in Case 8(a), is that Motor Works may validly order the amount of steel which it usually orders even if the market price has risen 20 per cent above the contract price. It will not have abused its right to determine the quantity it buys. The theory of *imprévision* or relief for changed and unforeseen circumstances is not accepted in French private law and therefore would not be applicable even if a rise in the market price constituted such a change. The French rejection of this theory is based on a strict interpretation by the courts of art. 1134 of the Civil Code. French law does grant relief for *force majeure*, but that is a quite different doctrine which applies only when performance has become impossible.[12]

In Case 8(b), in contrast, Alloy could receive a remedy for abuse of right if it succeeds in proving that Motor Works ordered twice as much steel

[10] For the diversity of opinions, see 'Le contrat-cadre de distribution', JCP 1997, ed. E., and particularly, J. Ghestin, 'La notion de contrat-cadre et les enjeux théoriques et pratiques qui s'y attachent' 7 f.; L. Aynès, 'La question de la détermination du prix', 16 f.

[11] Terré, Simler, and Lequette, *Les obligations* no. 262, p. 219.

[12] For an explanation and criticism of the refusal of French law to accept the theory of *imprévision*, see Ghestin, Jamin, and Billau, *Traité de droit civil* no. 260, pp. 288 ff.

with an intention to do harm (for example, to get rid of a competitor) or for an illegitimate reason. It would then be able to obtain termination of the contract and/or damages for the breach. Characterizing such behaviour as illegitimate is tricky. It would be up to the judges of the lower courts to decide. Although trying to make a profit is not in itself illegitimate, it could be argued that if Motor Works ordered twice as much in order to resell the steel and thus be in competition with Alloy, it would be changing the purpose of their framework contract, which was intended as a supply contract and not a distribution contract.

In Case 8(c), however, where the market price has fallen, Motor Works would be under no obligation to buy any steel. The contract does not contain an exclusive dealing clause, and it imposes an obligation only on Alloy. Under French law, it would be a unilateral contract as opposed to one that is bilateral or synallagmatic (*synallagmatique*) where both parties are under an obligation. It follows that Motor Works need not buy any steel, and obviously will not if the market price is lower than the contract price.

We have already explained why the contract is less likely to be analysed as a unilateral offer to sell, on the part of Alloy, with an option for Motor Works to order as much steel as it wants. Even if this analysis were preferred, it is interesting that a court might then take the traditional approach and void the contract because its content is uncertain. It would probably be held to be uncertain, and therefore void under arts. 1129 and 1583 of the Civil Code, because the quantity to be delivered depends upon the sole discretion of Motor Works.[13]

BELGIUM

The agreement in this case is a supply contract (*contrat d'approvisionnement*). This contract is perfectly valid. The fact that the quantity term is left open does not raise any difficulty under art. 1129 of the Belgian Civil Code (identical to art. 1129 of the French Civil Code) which requires that the object of the contract be certain. The controversy never arose in Belgium, as it did in France, as to the need for complete certainty in quantity (under art. 1129) and price (under art. 1591, also identical in the French and Belgian Civil Codes). Belgian law has always clearly distinguished between a contract that provides a framework for future transactions and the contracts

---

[13] Terré, Simler, and Lequette, *Les obligations* no. 279–3, p. 235; Collart-Dutilleul and Delebecque, *Contrats* no. 148, p. 131.

entered into under this framework.[14] There is very little chance that a Belgian court would think that the situation referred to here would have to be divided into a myriad of unilateral promises of sale that would be void for uncertainty as to quantity.[15]

Although this contract seems undoubtedly valid under Belgian law, it nonetheless appears that Alloy was somewhat negligent as to the protection of its interests. Indeed, the supply contract contains neither (1) an escalation clause (*clause d'adaptation du prix*), which would have addressed the problems of Cases 8(a) and 8(b), nor (2) an exclusivity clause (*clause d'exclusivité*), which would have addressed that of Case 8(c). Alloy could appeal to the principle of good faith performance of agreements. This principle has been developed considerably over the past few years. It is founded on the theory of 'abuse of right in contractual matters' (*abus de droit en matière contractuelle*).[16] The general standard is that 'an abuse of right may result from the exercise of a right which goes grossly beyond the limits of the normal exercise of that right by a careful and diligent person'.[17] Specific criteria enabling a determination of an abuse of right in a given case include (1) whether the person exercising the right intends to do harm (*intention de nuire*), (2) whether he exercises his right without a legitimate, reasonable, and sufficient interest, (3) whether the value of the interest served by the exercise of the right is disproportionate to that of the interest harmed, and (4) whether he has refused to take the other person's legitimate expectations (*confiance légitime*) into consideration.[18] The remedy for abuse of right consists in 'limiting' the right to a normal use of it or in compensating for the damage that was caused by abusing it.[19]

In Case 8(a), the market price rises to 20 per cent more than the contract

---

[14] H. De Page in Meinertzhagen-Limpens, *Traité élémentaire*, vol. IV, no. 42.

[15] As to the commercial pragmatism of Belgian courts in applying the requirement that the object of the contract be certain, see I. Corbisier, 'La détermination du prix dans les contrats commerciaux portant vente de marchandises – Réflexions comparatives', RIDC, 1988, 767 f. For instance, long before the recent French case law recognized that a party to a contract might influence how the price is determined if she does so in good faith, the solution was currently (at least implicitly) accepted in Belgium. See I. Corbisier, 'La validité de la clause de révision unilatérale des taux d'intérêt en Europe (droits belge, luxembourgeois, néerlandais et allemand)', Rev. aff. eur., 1993, no. 3, 27 f.

[16] Cass., 19 Sept. 1983, Pas., 1984, I, 55; Cass., 17 May 1990, Pas., 1990, I, 1061. For a detailed overview, see S. Stijns, D. Van Gerven, and P. Wéry, 'Chronique de jurisprudence. Les obligations: les sources (1985–1995)', JT, 1996, 689 f., in particular no. 33.

[17] Cass., 10 Sept. 1971, Pas., 1972, I, 28 ('l'abus de droit peut résulter de l'exercice d'un droit d'une manière qui dépasse manifestment les limites de l'exercice normal de celui-ci par une personne prudente et diligente').

[18] For an inventory of these criteria, see Stijns, Van Gerven, and Wéry, 'Chronique de jurisprudence', p. 707.   [19] For further details, see JT, 1996, no. 46, pp. 707–8.

price, and Motor Works orders the amount of steel it usually needs. It is highly unlikely that a court would decide that Motor Works is committing an abuse of its contractual right since Motor Works is not taking advantage of the situation to order more steel.

In Case 8(b), the market price rises to 20 per cent more than the contract price, and Motor Works orders twice the steel it usually needs. Here, Alloy could contend that there was an abuse of right. It could argue that the right is exercised absent a legitimate or sufficient interest: Motor Works bought more steel than needed, and did so only to make a profit on its resale. Alloy could argue, moreover, that the value of the interest served is disproportionate to that of the interest harmed if, for example, Motor Works were Alloy's largest client by far, and this operation caused extreme harm to Alloy. Finally, Alloy could argue that Motor Works refused to take its legitimate expectations into account if, for example, Motor Works had bought the same quantity of steel (half the amount) over many years.

In Case 8(c), the market price falls to 20 per cent below the contract price, and Motor Works buys no steel from Alloy, purchasing its requirements of steel on the market instead. *A priori*, Alloy itself would seem at fault since it did not provide for an exclusivity clause in the supply contract. Alloy could again claim that there was an abuse of right if Motor Works were a dominant contractual partner which imposed the contractual provisions on Alloy, and Alloy, a small producer, had to rely entirely on Motor Works. Under these circumstances, Alloy could show that there was a disproportion between the harm it suffered from and the advantage drawn from Motor Works, for whom Alloy would be only one supplier among many others. As a practical matter, Alloy would be unlikely to take this approach since it would prefer to maintain its relationship with a partner it relies upon economically, rather than run the risk that Motor Works will turn towards another, more obliging, producer when the contract is renegotiated.

Alloy will not be able to resort to the theory of *imprévision* which would allow a judge to modify a contract if a change in circumstances upsets the economic balance of the contract (*bouleversement de l'économie contractuelle*).[20] Indeed, this theory has now been clearly rejected by two recent decisions of the *Cour de cassation*.[21] These decisions came after much hesitation in the case law and a long line of articles hostile to this theory.

---

[20] See generally, D. M. Philippe, *Changement de circonstances et bouleversement de l'économie contractuelle* (1986).

[21] Cass., 7 Feb. 1994, Pas., I, 150; Cass., 14 April 1994, JLMB, 1995, 1591.

THE NETHERLANDS

The first question is whether a valid contract has been concluded. A contract is invalid if the obligations that the parties are assuming cannot be determined (art. 6:227 of the Civil Code[22]). Generally, this requirement is easily met. It is not necessary that the precise content of their obligations be determinable at the moment the contract is concluded. It is sufficient if their content can be established afterwards.[23] Therefore, the contract here is probably valid. Thus, if Motor Works orders the amount of steel it usually needs, Alloy is bound to deliver this amount for the set price.[24]

In Case 8(a), however, the market price rises to 20 per cent more than the contract price. The rise in the market price may constitute an 'unforeseen circumstance which [is] of such a nature that the co-contracting party, according to criteria of reasonableness and equity, may not expect that the contract be maintained in an unmodified form' (art. 6:258 of the Civil Code).[25] In that event, Alloy may ask the court to modify the contract or set it aside. Whether the rise in price to 20 per cent more than the contract price constitutes such 'unforeseen circumstances' depends on the circumstances of the case. However, if no additional circumstances can be proven, a mere rise of 20 per cent will probably be insufficient for interference by the court.

In Case 8(b), the market price not only rises by 20 per cent, but Motor Works orders twice the steel it usually needs. The promise is not binding. Several different lines of analysis lead to that result.

First, it can be said that a reasonable interpretation of the contract limits the amount that Motor Works can order to the quantity it really

---

[22] Article 6:227 of the Civil Code: 'The obligations which parties assume must be determinable.'   [23] See Asser/Hartkamp vol. II, no. 227.

[24] The possibility that the courts will interfere on the grounds of good faith if the buyer orders an excessive amount is discussed below.

[25] Article 6:258 of the Civil Code: '(1) Upon the demand of one of the parties, the judge may modify the effects of a contract, or he may set it aside in whole or in part on the basis of unforeseen circumstances which are of such a nature that the contracting party, according to criteria of reasonableness and equity, may not expect that the contract be maintained in an unmodified form. The modification or the setting aside of the contract may be given retroactive force. (2) The modification or the setting aside of the contract is not pronounced to the extent that the person invoking the circumstances should be accountable for them according to the nature of the contract or common opinion. (3) For purposes of this article, a person to whom a contractual right or obligation has been transferred, is assimilated to a contracting party.'

needs (arts. 3:33 and 3:35 of the Civil Code).[26] In a leading case, *Haviltex*,[27] the *Hoge Raad* overturned a decision by a court of appeal which had held that no interpretation of the contract was needed because the meaning of a clause in it was clear. The *Hoge Raad* held that words are never clear. It established a test for interpretation which it has repeated ever since, and which is based on the same principles as those which govern the formation of contracts and other juristic acts, the 'will-reliance doctrine' (*wilsvertrouwensleer*). The *Hoge Raad* recognizes that whether the contract contains a gap cannot be established on the basis of a merely linguistic interpretation of the clauses of the contract. Therefore, in order to establish how the parties have organized their relationship through a written contract, by this test, the court must determine the meaning that each of the parties could reasonably give to those clauses in the given circumstances, and the meaning each could reasonably expect the other party to attribute to them.

Following a different line of reasoning, it would be contrary to good faith for Motor Works to ask for twice the steel now that the market price has risen so much (6:248(2) of the Civil Code[28]). The doctrine of good faith in its so-called limitative function (*beperkende werking*) has been applied very frequently by the courts.[29]

Finally, one can say that even if the contract were interpreted to allow Motor Works to order more steel when the price rises, and even if it were not contrary to good faith to do so, nevertheless Motor Works may still not be able to on the grounds that the contract was not meant to deal with such a large increase in price (art. 6:258 of the Civil Code).[30] Article 6:258 allows the judge to modify the terms of a contract on the basis of 'unforeseen circumstances'. Here, the term 'unforeseen' means 'not provided for'. This article is generally regarded as a particular application of the general rule on good faith in contract law of art. 6:248.

Motor Works probably does not need to buy its steel from Alloy in Case

---

[26] I presume 'Motor Works orders twice the steel it usually needs' implies that Motor Works orders more steel than it needs this year. If, however, this year it needs twice as much as usual the promise may be binding.

[27] HR 13 March 1981, NJ 1981, note Brunner, 635, AA 1981, 355, note Van Schilfgaarde.

[28] Article 6:248(2) of the Civil Code: 'A rule binding upon the parties as a result of the contract does not apply to the extent that, in the given circumstances, this would be unacceptable according to criteria of reasonableness and equity.'

[29] On the functions of good faith, see M. Hesselink, 'Good Faith', in A. Hartkamp *et al.* (eds.), *Towards a European Civil Code*, 2nd edn (1998), 285 at 291.

[30] It is not likely that a Dutch court would invalidate such an arrangement on the grounds of indeterminacy.

8(c) in which the market price falls to 20 per cent below the contract price. Whether Motor Works is under a duty to do so must be established by interpreting the contract (arts. 3:33 and 3:35 of the Civil Code) (see the *Haviltex* case, cited earlier). As the facts are presented here, Motor Works does not seem to be under such a contractual duty. If it were, the rules described earlier would govern whether it could obtain relief on the grounds of a change of circumstances. Therefore, this change in the market price does not in principle have any effect on the binding force of the contract.

SPAIN

Changes in price do not affect such promises in Spanish legal doctrine. The principle *pacta sunt servanda* is generally applied by Spanish courts. The parties should have thought about the conditions in the contract, and, if not, they must bear the burden of it.[31] Provided that the car man-ufacturer gives the money, Alloy has to honour its promise and deliver the steel.

In some instances, the *Tribunal Supremo* has used the principle of *rebus sic stantibus* as a ground for refusing to enforce a contract. According to the Court, this principle applies where (1) there was an extraordinary change in the circumstances between the time of performance and the time of the promise, (2) there is a total lack of proportion between the duties of both parties, (3) the change in circumstances was unpredictable, and (4) no other remedy exists. When this principle is applied, the consequence is not the extinction of the existing obligations but their modification to adapt to the new circumstances. The use of this principle by the *Tribunal Supremo* has been very restrictive.[32] It does not seem that this principle could be applied here but it depends on the effect upon earnings and the reason for the change of price. The *Tribunal Supremo* has applied it when there was a severe decrease in the value of the peseta.[33]

Another possible ground for relief is on the theory that the purpose of the transaction is no longer served (*teoria de la base del negocio*). This theory will be discussed in more detail in dealing with Case 13, along with the leading case decided by the *Tribunal Supremo*.[34] According to the theory, a

---

[31] Díez Picazo, *Fundamentos de derecho*, vol. II, 886.
[32] *Ibid.*, 893. See TS, 23 April 1991 (refusing relief because 'there is no alteration in the circumstances borne in mind by the contracting parties when setting up the binding contracts so extraordinary that it would cause a sharp imbalance between their obligations').   [33] TS, 23 Nov. 1962.   [34] TS, 30 June 1948.

party cannot enforce a contract that no longer serves the purpose for which he entered into it. Applying the theory to this case, a court would probably enforce the contract but just to cover the manufacturing needs of Motor Works, not a quantity in excess of these needs that Motor Works is going to resell.

PORTUGAL

In Case 8(a), the promise is binding. In Case 8(b), although the promise is binding, probably Alloy can refuse to sell the amount of steel that Motor Works does not need. In Case 8(c), the promise is binding but Alloy can ask the court to set a term during which Motor Works can exercise its right to buy if it chooses, but after which its right is cancelled.

If one party promises to sell but the other does not promise to buy, the contract is considered to be one made by a unilateral promise since only one party has made a promise (art. 411 of the Civil Code). The principle *pacta sunt servanda* applies to such a contract, so it must be performed (art. 406(1)). A change in the price does not affect such a promise as it is considered a normal risk of making one. The parties should have considered such a possibility when they decided to enter into the contract.

Alloy can refuse to sell at the price fixed in advance and ask for the rescission of the contract only if there has been a change of circumstances. According to art. 437 of the Civil Code, a change of circumstances occurs when the circumstances in which the parties based their decision to contract have undergone an extraordinary change which is not part of the normal risks of the contract so that a demand for performance violates the principles of good faith.[35] According to the legal scholars, such a change could occur in the event of very high and unexpected inflation, but surely a change of 20 per cent in the price is not enough to justify a refusal to perform. So, in Case 8(a), Alloy must sell.

Case 8(b) seems different. Generally, the mere expectations of the parties to a contract are not relevant, so Alloy could not rely on the amount of steel it had expected that Motor Works would order. However, it is clear that the aim of the contract was to fulfil Motor Works' needs for steel. Therefore if Motor Works is trying to resell the steel in order to obtain an extra profit, it is exploiting Alloy for its own benefit in contravention of the aims of the contract. According to art. 762(2) of the Civil Code, both parties must act in good faith even in the exercise of a claim.

---

[35] See Cordeiro, *Da Boa Fé no Direito Civil*, 903 ff.

Therefore, to demand an amount of steel not needed could be considered illegitimate, in which case Alloy need not fulfil the obligation.[36]

In Case 8(c), although Alloy promised to sell, Motor Works did not promise to buy. Therefore Motor Works is not obliged to buy any steel. However, if it had assumed the obligation to buy steel only from Alloy, it would be held liable if it bought steel from anybody else.

Nevertheless, in a contract made by a unilateral promise in which a term is not fixed, art. 411 of the Civil Code allows the promisor to ask the court to fix a term within which the promisee can exercise its rights if it chooses, but after which its rights are cancelled. If Motor Works does not buy any steel from Alloy it would have that option.

ITALY

In Case 8(a), Alloy's contractual promise would probably be enforceable, while in Case 8(b), it probably would not. In Case 8(c), Motor Works would simply not be obligated to buy any steel, and the case raises no problems worth analysing.

In Case 8(a), Alloy could try to have the contract discharged on the grounds of supervening excessive hardship. According to arts. 1467–9 of the Civil Code, contractual promises can be discharged whenever a supervening event takes place of an extraordinary and unforeseeable nature after the formation of the contract and before performance, and this event makes the performance of one party excessively burdensome in proportion to that of the other. This is a question of fact. The highest court, the *Corte di cassazione*, will not reverse an appellate court's decision on this issue.[37] The only restriction is that the event which took place must lie outside the normal risks assumed under the contract (art. 1467(2)). The promisee can avoid discharge of the contract by offering to modify it equitably (art. 1467(3)).[38]

In Case 8(a), however, Alloy would probably not be able to obtain a discharge of the contract because the courts would probably consider the fluctuation of the market price to be an event which is part of the normal risk of the contract. For example, in a recent decision, the *Tribunale di Monza*[39]

---

[36] See Cordeiro, *Da Boa Fé no Direito Civil*, 853 ff.

[37] Cass. civ., sez. II, 20 June 1996, no. 5690 (*Roccheri c. Mazzara*); Cass. civ., 9 April 1994, no. 3342 (*Soc. Arbos c. Com. Piacenza*).

[38] See G. Criscuoli and D. Pugsley, *The Italian Law of Contract* (1991), 211.

[39] *Tribunale di Monza*, 29 March 1993, *Soc. Nuova Fucinati c. Fondamentall International A. B.*, in Foro it. I (1994), 916, with a case-note by S. Di Paola and in Giur. it. I (1994), 2, 146 with a case-note by J. Bonell. See also Cass. civ., 13 Jan. 1995, no. 369, in Foro it. Rep. (1995), entry 'Contratto in genere', no. 523; Cass. civ., sez. II, 28 Jan. 1995, no. 1027, in Foro it. I

held that a sales contract is not dischargeable under arts. 1467–8 of the Civil Code because of a variation of 30 per cent in the market price of the raw materials sold.

In Case 8(b), Motor Works took advantage of the increase in market price by ordering twice the steel it usually needs, presumably intending to resell the excess. In doing so, it probably violated the general principle that a contract must be performed in good faith, which was recently reaffirmed by the *Corte di cassazione*.[40] The legal analysis would therefore be much the same in Italy as it would be in the United States.[41] Moreover, for Alloy to be bound, the quantity of steel it is obligated to sell must be determinable (art. 1346 of the Civil Code).[42] A court would probably decide that, as a matter of contract interpretation, the quantity was to have been determined by looking at Motor Works' normal requirements.

AUSTRIA

In all three variants, the promise is in principle binding. There could be a different result only if the contract could be interpreted in such a way that the change in market price would give Alloy the right to modify the contract or demand its modification.

In Case 8(a), there are no indications that such an interpretation could be justified. A rise in the market price of 20 per cent is a risk the seller has to bear unless the parties make a different agreement.

In Case 8(b), the question arises whether the contract really gave Motor Works the right to order twice the steel it usually needs. As long as Motor Works uses the steel for its own production, this question will have to be answered in the affirmative. If Motor Works uses the additional steel to make a profit by reselling it on the market, it probably could be argued that such a course of action is not covered by the contract. For such an

---

(1995), 2898; Cass. civ., sez. II, 13 Feb. 1995, no. 1559, in Foro it. I (1995), 2897; F. Macario, 'Inflazione, fluttuazioni del mercato ed eccessiva onerosità', Corr. giur. (1995), 585.

[40] Cass. civ., sez. I, 20 April 1994, no. 3775 (*Comune di Fiuggi c. Ente Fiuggi s.p.a.*), Giur. it. I (1995), 1, 852 and in Foro it. I (1995), 1296. For scholarly writings on this topic, see, e.g., L. Bigliazzi Geri, 'Buona fede nel diritto civile', Digesto 2 (1988), 154; L. Bigliazzi Geri, 'La buona fede nel diritto privato (spunti ricostruttivi)', in *Il principio di buona fede – Quaderni della Scuola Superiore di studi universitari e di perfezionamento*, vol. III (1987), 51 ff.; S. Rodotà, 'Appunti sul principio di buona fede', in Foro pad. I (1964), 1284; C. M. Bianca, 'La nozione di buona fede quale regola di comportamento contrattuale', Riv. dir. civ. I (1983), 205 ff.; U. Natoli, *L'attuazione del rapporto obbligatorio*, vol. I (1974); L. Nanni, *La buona fede contrattuale* (1988).

[41] See, e.g., S. J. Burton and E. G. Andersen, *Contractual Good Faith* (1995), 25–6.

[42] Article 1346 of the Civil Code: 'Requisites: The object of the contract must be possible, lawful, determined, or determinable.'

interpretation to be justified, however, there would have to be indications that the contract was based on the assumption that Motor Works buys steel *only* for its own production. Absent such indications, the contract would be interpreted according to its wording which does not limit the amount of steel Motor Works may order.

Case 8(c) can be analysed in the same way. According to its wording, the contract does not provide for a minimum amount of steel Motor Works has to order. It therefore would be necessary to find circumstances outside the contract which could indicate an intention of the parties that Motor Works should buy a certain minimum of steel. Absent such indications, the contract again would be interpreted according to its terms which do not provide for such a minimum.

GERMANY

If the parties agree upon a fixed price, the debtor bears the risk that prices will rise.[43] In our case the very purpose of the contract was probably that Motor Works did not want to bear that risk itself. Therefore, in Case 8(a), the promise is binding.

In Case 8(b), if Motor Works wants to use the steel for its own production, the promise is binding unless the contract is interpreted to mean that the usual amount should be the limit. But very specific circumstances would be necessary to support such an interpretation. If Motor Works wants to resell the additional steel, their right to do so again depends on how the contract is interpreted: should the promise be binding only for Motor Works' own needs or also for additional amounts which can be used for resale? All the circumstances, including the price and the previous negotiations, would be relevant to this question. Previous contracts between the parties could also give hints.

Questions of interpretation aside, however, there are limits to what terms the contract can contain and how Motor Works can exercise its rights under the contract. It would be a violation of good faith (§ 242 of the Civil Code) for the contract to place Alloy at Motor Works' mercy or for Motor Works to abuse its position excessively. For there to be a violation of good faith in our case, however, the circumstances would have to be exceptional. Alloy consented to the contract, and it is even possible that Alloy demanded a higher price for its consent to the provisions in question. Nevertheless, the limits of good faith may have been reached here.

[43] BGH WM 1979, 582.

The price is 20 per cent higher, the quantity ordered is double the usual one, and the excess amount is ordered for resale. A court would be especially likely to find a violation of good faith if the result of the deal would cause serious problems for Alloy. Again, however, the outcome here depends upon all the circumstances.

In Case 8(c), Motor Works is entitled to buy its steel wherever it wants as long as the contract is not interpreted to require it to deal with Alloy exclusively. If it were, then Motor Works would have to buy Alloy's steel but even then Alloy could not claim it had to buy a certain amount. In the absence of any indications otherwise, the contract would be interpreted as not exclusive simply because that is more usual. Motor Works would not have to buy Alloy's steel.

GREECE

In this case the parties concluded a sales agreement without specifying the amount of steel that Motor Works will order. The problem that arises here is that the performance is undetermined, and its determination is left to the sole judgment of Motor Works. The performance must be determined or at least determinable by the time of performance.[44] If the performance cannot be determined by interpreting the declaration of will of the parties (art. 200 of the Civil Code), then arts. 371–3 of the Civil Code apply. Article 371 of the Civil Code provides that: 'If the determination of a performance has been entrusted to one of the contracting parties or to a third party it is in case of doubt considered that the determination must be made by reference to equitable criteria. If the determination was not based on equitable criteria or has been delayed it shall be made by the Court.' And art. 372 of the Civil Code provides that: 'A contract whereby the determination of a performance has been left to the absolute discretion of one of the contracting parties shall be void.'

In principle, a contract is void if the failure to determine the performance interferes excessively with the liberty of one of the parties or exceeds the limits set by good faith (art. 288 of the Civil Code). Otherwise, art. 371 of the Civil Code applies, which means that the performance should be determined by 'fair' judgment. The criteria for a 'fair' judgment will be based on arts. 200, 288 (good faith), and 281 (morality) of the Civil Code.[45]

A further question is whether the parties will still be bound by their

---

[44] Stathopoulos, *Contract Law*, 109–10.   [45] *Ibid.*, arts. 371–3, no. 28.

agreement despite a change in the circumstances on which their initial agreement was based. This question is governed by art. 388 of the Civil Code.[46] It sets forth five requirements that must be met: (1) there must be a reciprocal contract, (2) a change must have occurred in the circumstances on which the parties based their original agreement taking into consideration the principles of good faith and business usages, (3) the change must take place after the conclusion of the contract, (4) it must have been due to extraordinary and unforeseen circumstances, and (5) as a result of the change, the performance of the contract must have become excessively onerous for the obligor. The balance between the performance and the counter-performance must have been disturbed in a way that does not correspond to the original will of the parties. If these requirements are met, then the court[47] may, at the request of the debtor, reduce his obligation to perform to the appropriate extent or rescind the contract in whole or with regard to the part not yet performed. The judge who determines that the debtor will suffer excessive harm as a result of the change in circumstances is not obliged to adjust the performances in such a way that the harm is fully covered.

Thus, what is crucial is the restoration of the balance that has been disturbed between performance and counter-performance.[48] In Case 8(a), art. 388 of the Civil Code will not warrant relief because the courts have determined that a 20 per cent increase in the value of the performance does not constitute a material disturbance of the original contract.[49] At least a 30 per cent increase is thought to be necessary.[50] Thus, the parties will be

---

[46] Article 338 of the Civil Code is a concretization of the principle of good faith (art. 288) and one of the most basic and forward-looking provisions of the Code. M. Stathopoulos in Georgiadis and Stathopoulos, *Civil Code*, no. 2; AP 133/198 NoB 28, 1452, AP 922/82 NoB 31, 214; AP 16/1983 NoB 31, 1368. This article combines criteria which are drawn from the classic theory that there must be an equilibrium between performance and counter-performance, from the doctrine of *clausula rebus sic stantibus* (which corresponds to the German doctrine of collapse of the underlying basis of the transaction or *Wegfall der Geschäftsgrundlage*), and from the French theory of relief for the unforeseen (*imprévision*). The solution that art. 388 provides would be achieved by art. 288 of the Civil Code as well. The Germans use the corresponding general section of their Civil Code: § 242. Stathopoulos in Georgiadis and Stathopoulos, *Civil Code*, 477 at 485.

[47] Article 388 takes effect through judicial intervention and not *ipso iure*. Stathopoulos in Georgiadis and Stathopoulos, *Civil Code*, art. 388, no. 20.

[48] Stathopoulos, *Contract Law*, 193–4; P. Papanikolaou, 'The Measure of the Harshness of the Performance and the Extent of the Judicial Intervention in the Contract according to art. 388 Civil Code', in *Miscellany in Honour of Andreas Gazis* (1994), 485

[49] AP 1876/85 NoB 34, 1416; EfAth 9781/82 NoB 31, 375.

[50] The courts have not applied this provision in the case of a 35 per cent increase in the value of the performance. EfAth 984/57 EEN 25, 658; EfAth 1407/56 NoB 5, 132; AP 399/61 NoB 10, 83.

bound by their original agreement, and Alloy would not be able to demand a higher price.

In Case 8(b), the performance is not determined according to equitable criteria. Twice the amount of steel that Motor Works usually needs is too much. The quantity demanded must therefore be reduced to accord with good faith and morality. Moreover, Case 8(b) meets the requirement of art. 388 of the Civil Code of the material disturbance of performance and counter-performance.[51] Therefore, Alloy can ask the court for an amount of money that is reasonable and corresponds to the increase in the market price.

In Case 8(c), Motor Works does not perform the contract, thus art. 388 of the Civil Code does not apply. This issue will be judged according to the general principles that govern non-performance. Thus, Alloy can invoke its rights under arts. 382 and 380 of the Civil Code.

SCOTLAND

It is submitted that the promise is non-gratuitous and does not therefore require to be constituted in a written document subscribed by Alloy. Even if writing were required, as Alloy clearly made the promise in the course of their business, Motor Works may be able to take advantage of the exception contained in s. 1(2)(a)(ii) of the Requirements of Writing (Scotland) Act 1995.[52] Any fluctuations in the market price and in the amount of steel ordered are *prima facie* irrelevant in Scots law. It could perhaps be argued that the promise is not valid due to lack of certainty. However, such an argument was dismissed in the case of *Dempster (R and J) Ltd* v. *Motherwell Bridge and Engineering Co.*[53] in which the Lord President (Clyde) noted that 'when a court of law is asked to construe a commercial arrangement couched in terms which are prima facie obligatory . . . the courts will prefer a construction which gives the contract binding effect'. This case is directly in point in the present problem.

In Case 8(a), it is thought that as a matter of construction, Alloy is bound to deliver the same amount of steel to Motor Works as it usually needs: Alloy undertook the risk of the rise in the market price.

In Case 8(b), in ordering twice the amount it usually needs, Motor Works is clearly taking advantage of Alloy's 'bad' bargain. As a matter of

---

[51] The basic principle of the Greek Civil Code, namely the binding nature of contracts (*pacta sunt servanda*) justifies the refusal of the courts to apply art. 388 so as to alter the terms originally agreed in a contract unless there is a material disturbance of the balance between performance and counter-performance. Papanikolaou, 'The Measure of the Harshness', 483.   [52] See Case 1.   [53] [1964] SC 308 at 327–8.

construction the courts would probably 'infer' that the maximum amount to be ordered was to be the same as the year before. However, there is also authority that a contract such as this should be interpreted as *bona fide*. In *MacLelland* v. *Adam and Mathie*,[54] for example, the Court of Session allowed a proof of an averment that purchasers had *increased* the quantity of spirits they wished to buy at a fixed price, when a tax had been imposed while their agreement was effective. In *Wilkie* v. *Bethune*,[55] an employer agreed to give his employee potatoes as part of his remuneration. When the crop failed and the price of potatoes trebled, the court refused to compensate the employee on the basis of the new price and instead ordered damages which would enable him to buy an equivalent amount of other food. Accordingly, since Motor Works is 'snatching' at a bargain, the courts might interpret the promise in good faith and argue that they can only order the same amount as the previous year. If the contract expressly entitled Motor Works to purchase as much as they wanted, I do not think the clause would be struck down as illegal or as a leonine bargain in modern Scots law.

In Case 8(c), as it is a unilateral obligation binding only Alloy, Metal Works is not obliged to buy any steel as it has not undertaken any obligation to do so.

ENGLAND

In English law, a bare promise, such as that which appears to have been made by Alloy, to sell to the promisee such and such goods if the promisee makes an order, is called a 'standing offer'. According to orthodox law, it is not binding in itself, because it has not been accepted nor, as importantly, has any consideration been provided or promised in exchange for it (see Case 1).[56] Note that merely 'agreeing' to the offer does not, in orthodox law, make the offer binding because the promisee, not having promised to do anything, has not provided consideration in exchange for the promise.[57] Thus, until the offer is accepted and paid for, the offeror is free to withdraw the offer at any time.[58] That said, it appears that the orthodox law rules on consideration are not always followed in this area, and that many courts have simply assumed, without much discussion, that,

---

[54] [1796] Mor 142-7.   [55] [1848] 11 D 132.
[56] *Routledge* v. *Grant* [1828] 4 Bing. 653; Treitel, *Contract*, 39.
[57] See, e.g., *Firestone Tyre & Rubber Co. Ltd* v. *Vokins* [1951] 1 Lloyd's Rep. 32.
[58] On the requirements for a proper withdrawal, such as notice, etc., see Treitel, *Contract*, 39–44.

where there is some sort of acceptance of the offer, 'requirements' agreements are binding, regardless of the apparent lack of consideration.[59] For the purposes of this answer, I will, in any event, assume that the offer has been accepted and is *prima facie* binding. This could happen by Motor Works doing something or promising to do something in return for the promise, for example, promising to place a minimum order each year. More typically, however, the promise would become binding by Motor Works actually placing an order, assuming that Alloy had not yet withdrawn its offer (which may be unrealistic if the market price has risen). The latter scenario would then resemble the case of *Great Northern Rly Co. v. Witham*,[60] where the defendant's gratuitous promise to 'undertake to supply the Company for twelve months with such quantities of [specified articles] as the Company may order from time to time' was held to be a standing offer, which was later turned into a series of contracts by the plaintiff's orders.

Assuming, then, that Alloy's promise is *prima facie* binding, is Alloy bound to provide the amount of steel ordered by Motor Works in Cases 8(a) and 8(b), where the market price has risen? According to orthodox law, the answer is clear: Alloy must provide the steel. Alloy's offer is on its face an unambiguous promise to supply whatever amount of steel Motor Works orders at a set price; thus it must supply that amount. There is no general principle in English law, such as a principle of good faith, which would allow a court to invalidate a bargain which has become substantively unfair or to invalidate a bargain where one party is, in lay person's terms, attempting to take advantage of the other party's imprecise contractual drafting. There is English legislation, the Unfair Terms in Consumer Contracts Regulations[61] (based on a recent EEC Directive[62]), that allows courts to invalidate substantively unfair contracts, but it does not apply here because Alloy is not a consumer (and for other reasons as well, including that Alloy itself made the offer).

The question is whether an English court would want, and be able, to find some way of getting around the orthodox rules in order to invalidate the bargain. It is unlikely that a court would seek to invalidate the bargain struck in Case 8(a), where the market price rose by 20 per cent and a normal order was placed. A rise of 20 per cent is, I assume, not unusual, and Motor Works has not attempted to take advantage of the open-ended

---

[59] *Re Gloucester Municipal Election Petition* [1901] 1 KB 683. See generally J. N. Adams, 'Consideration for Requirements Contracts', LQ Rev. 94 (1978), 73.   [60] [1873] LR 9 CP 16.

[61] Unfair Terms in Consumer Contracts Regulations 1994 (SI 1994, No. 3159).

[62] EC Directive on Unfair Terms in Consumer Contracts (93/13/EEC).

nature of the agreement. It is also unlikely that on the facts of Cases 8(b) or 8(c), an English court would seek to invalidate the bargain. The advantage-taking is not that extreme, and, as importantly, there is no easy way for an English court to invalidate. The open-ended nature of the promise is not in itself a problem,[63] the words of the contract are reasonably clear, and no court would wish to hold that such promises are generally unenforceable.

If an English court were to invalidate the order in Case 8(b), it would have to be on the basis that, on the proper interpretation of the contract, it was an implied term that Motor Works would not order more than a certain amount of steel, or perhaps not order more than Motor Works could use itself. The general rule regarding the judicial implication of terms into contracts is that the terms must be 'necessary to give the transaction such business efficacy as the parties must have intended'.[64] Significantly, it is not enough to show merely that the term is a reasonable one.[65] That said, 'business efficacy' is sufficiently vague as to allow courts much leeway.

In the case of scenario 8(c), where the market price dropped and no steel was ordered, the contract would need to be interpreted as requiring that Motor Works would order a certain amount of steel, presumably the amount that it 'needs' for its own production that year. An implied term of this sort is more difficult to imply than a maximum order term since, while it might be implicit in the agreement that Motor Works will not order more than it needs, it is more difficult to assume that Motor Works is agreeing to buy only from Alloy (though the history of their relationship might provide evidence to the contrary). If the contract was an oral contract, implying either a maximum or minimum order term is easier. The imprecision of oral language makes such agreements more amenable to creative interpretation. But if the contract were in writing, it will be more difficult for Alloy to claim that on its proper interpretation the promise was subject to certain conditions. The words of the promise, as stated in the hypothetical, are unambiguous.

It may be thought that in certain cases, for example where a buyer orders 100 times its normal requirements and solely for the purposes of resale, a court surely would find some way of implying a limiting term. That said, there are no clear precedents in English law for such an approach – though there are also no clear examples of English courts

---

[63] In *Great Northern Rly Co.* v. *Witham* [1873] LR 9 CP 16, noted above, a similarly open-ended offer was upheld.   [64] *The Moorcock* [1889] 14 PD 64.

[65] *Liverpool CC* v. *Irwin* [1977] AC 239.

refusing to follow such an approach. Perhaps the closest analogy, and a case which gives some support for implying a term into Alloy's promise, is *Staffordshire Area Health Authority* v. *South Staffordshire Waterworks*.[66] The court interpreted an agreement to supply water at a fixed price 'at all times hereafter' as meaning 'at all times hereafter during the subsistence of the agreement', the agreement being terminable by notice. In general, however, all that can be said with confidence in this area is that the more clear the advantage-taking, the harder a court will try to interpret the agreement as containing an implied term precluding such advantage-taking.

IRELAND

Where a promise appears to be made for some consideration but which consideration is really illusory, the promise must be disregarded.[67] In Case 8(a), Motor Works has provided no consideration for Alloy's promise to sell Motor Works as much steel as it ordered during the coming year. If Motor Works merely counterpromises to buy 'as much steel as it ordered', it is likely that an Irish court would follow English precedent and find that Motor Works' counter-promise does not amount to consideration for the purposes of an enforceable contract.[68]

However, the position could be treated differently by an Irish court where Alloy's promise was treated as a tender. In such instance, Alloy's promise to sell to Motor Works 'as much steel as it ordered' could be considered a tender for an indefinite amount. At this stage neither party is bound by Alloy's tender. English case law provides that Alloy could avoid contractual liability if it withdrew its promise or tender before an order had actually been placed by Motor Works for a specific amount of steel.[69] It is possible that an Irish court would follow this decision in the absence of other factors, such as the provision of some form of consideration by Motor Works. Accordingly, once an order has been placed by Motor Works Alloy may then be bound to fulfil it.[70]

Promissory estoppel, acting as a shield, could arise in a situation where Alloy revokes its tender but Motor Works goes ahead and orders the amount of steel it usually needs but later only pays to Alloy the original contract price. If Alloy instituted proceedings against Motor Works

---

[66] [1979] 1 WLR 203.   [67] See Treitel, *Contract*, ch. 3.
[68] See *Firestone Tyre & Rubber Co. Ltd* v. *Vokins & Co.* [1951] 1 Lloyd's Rep. 32. See also *MacRobertson Miller Airlines* v. *Commissioners of State Taxation* [1975] CLR 125.
[69] See *Great Northern Rly Co.* v. *Witham* [1873] LR 9 CP 16.   [70] See *ibid.*

seeking the difference in the amount payable, Motor Works could then raise promissory estoppel to seek to defeat their claim. Where the promise was intended to be binding, intended to be acted on, and in fact acted on, an Irish court, relying on the principles of estoppel and having regard to all the circumstances of the case, might find it inequitable for Alloy to rely on their revocation of tender.[71]

In Case 8(b), the market price rises to 20 per cent more than the contract price and Motor Works orders twice the steel it usually needs. As stated above, if an Irish court followed the *Firestone Rubber* decision, it would hold that Motor Works' counter-promise to buy 'as much steel as it ordered' did not amount to consideration for Alloy's promise for the purposes of an enforceable contract.

However, once Motor Works places an order with Alloy for a specific amount then the contract may be enforceable in an Irish court. Once the market price in steel rose it was in Alloy's interests to revoke the offer. By failing to revoke the offer, Alloy could become liable to Motor Works to comply with the terms of their tender once their tender was accepted by Motor Works.

If Alloy could establish that Motor Works' acceptance of its tender was made after a reasonable time for acceptance of the tender, the tender might be found to have lapsed. What is reasonable depends entirely upon the circumstances of the offer and the effect of a late acceptance. Clearly, Alloy would be greatly affected by Motor Works' acceptance of Alloy's tender.[72]

Where Motor Works placed an order for twice the steel it usually needs and an Irish court found such acceptance to be sufficient consideration, Alloy could argue that it was an implied term of the contract that Motor Works would only order the amount of steel it usually needed. Traditionally, the courts were reluctant to imply terms in a bargain because this resulted in a modification of the contract as struck between the parties. Indeed, in *Tradox (Ireland) Ltd* v. *Irish Grain Board Ltd*, McCarthy J said, '[it] is not the function of the Court to rewrite a contract for parties met upon commercially equal terms; if such parties want to enter into unreasonable, unfair or even disastrous contracts that is their business not the business of the Court'.[73] In this case, it is possible that an Irish court, having regard to Alloy's promise and the subsequent course of dealings between the parties prior to Motor Works' order, might imply such a

---

[71] See Case 1. See *also Central London Property Trust* v. *High Trees House* [1947] KB 130.
[72] See *Ramsgate Victoria Hotel* v. *Montefiore* [1866] LR 1 Exch. 109. See also Friel, *Contract*, ch. 3.
[73] [1984] IR 1.

term into the contract. However, on the facts as presented, an Irish court would be more likely to rely upon the maxim that 'it is for the parties to strike a bargain; the judiciary serve merely to enforce it'.[74]

In Case 8(c), where Alloy promises to sell to Motor Works 'as much steel as it ordered' during the coming year for a set price per ton and Motor Works buys its requirements elsewhere, it is likely that an Irish court would find no consideration on the part of Motor Works for the purposes of an enforceable promise. Motor Works has provided no consideration at this stage and may accept or reject this tender. On the facts as presented it is clear that Motor Works has rejected Alloy's tender. If, after a reasonable amount of time, the offer has not been accepted or rejected, it will lapse unless Alloy has already revoked the offer.

Summaries

France: French courts are likely to treat such a contract as they do one in which the price is at the discretion of one of the parties. Such contracts were once held to be void for uncertainty. Now they are upheld but a remedy is given if there is an 'abuse of right' in setting the price. They might well give a remedy on that ground in Case 8(b), though not in Cases 8(a) or 8(c).

Belgium: Such a contract is valid but a remedy will be given if there is an abuse of right, as is likely in Case 8(b), though not in Case 8(a), nor in Case 8(c) unless Motor Works were a dominant party who forced the contract on Alloy.

The Netherlands: Such a contract is valid, but in Case 8(b) a remedy will be given either as a matter of interpretation, or because a contract must be conformed to in good faith, or, possibly, on the grounds of changed circumstances. The contract will be enforced in Case 8(a) (unless there are other facts, not described in the case, that would support a claim of changed circumstances) and in Case 8(c).

Spain: In Case 8(b), a court would probably allow Motor Works to purchase only its normal requirements on the grounds that if it buys more, the transaction no longer serves the purpose for which it was entered into (*teoria de la base del negocio*). A court would enforce the contracts in Cases 8(a) and 8(c).

Portugal: In Case 8(b), the court would probably allow Motor Works to purchase the normal amount of steel because the aim of the contract was for

---

[74] See Clark, *Contract Law*, ch. 6.

Motor Works to obtain steel for its own needs, and to demand more would be a violation of good faith. A court would enforce the contract in Cases 8(a) and 8(c).

Italy: In Case 8(b), a court would probably give relief on the grounds that a contract must be performed in good faith, or on the grounds that the quantity is indeterminable unless it is to be determined by Motor Works' normal requirements. A court would enforce the contract in Cases 8(a) and 8(c).

Austria: In Case 8(b), the contract would be interpreted to require that Motor Works buy steel only for its own production provided there were indications that the contract was based on this assumption. A court would enforce the contract as written in Case 8(a), and in Case 8(c) unless there were indications outside the contract that Motor Works was obligated to order a certain amount of steel.

Germany: In Case 8(b), a court might interpret the contract to require Motor Works to buy only for its own needs, or it might well hold that its failure to do so is a violation of good faith. The court would enforce the contract as written in Case 8(a), and in Case 8(c) unless there were indications outside the contract that Motor Works was obligated to order a certain amount of steel.

Greece: In Case 8(b), a court would give relief under a specific provision of the Civil Code that says that if the determination of the performance has been entrusted to one of the parties, that determination must be made under 'equitable criteria'. Relief could also be given on the grounds that circumstances have changed in a way that creates a disproportion between performance and counter-performance. The contract would be enforced in Cases 8(a) and 8(c).

Scotland: None of the promises are gratuitous, and therefore they are binding even absent the formality of a writing. Even if they were gratuitous, a writing would still not be necessary because the promises were made in the course of business. Nevertheless, the contract in Case 8(b) would probably be interpreted to allow Motor Works to buy no more steel than it usually does. Alternatively, a court would likely construe the contract as good faith requires even if it would otherwise be interpreted differently. The contract would be enforced as written in Cases 8(a) and 8(c).

England: Alloy's promise lacks consideration, and so it is not binding until Motor Works commits itself to purchasing a certain amount of steel. Consequently, Cases 8(a) and 8(b) would be unlikely to arise in practice since Alloy would simply withdraw its promise if the market rose. If it did not, then it would be bound in Case 8(a). It might not be bound in Case 8(b) if the promise were interpreted to limit Motor Works' purchases to its own needs, as the court might apply the principle that a contract must be interpreted 'to give the transaction such business efficacy as the parties must have intended'. But it is hard to tell how the contract would be interpreted. A court would enforce the contract in Case 8(c) unless, which is much less likely, it interpreted the contract to require Motor Works to buy some steel.

Ireland: Alloy's promise lacks consideration and so it is not binding. If it is viewed as an offer, it will be binding when Motor Works accepts by ordering steel. It would then be enforced in Case 8(a). In Case 8(b), if Alloy did not revoke its offer when the market price rose, which would be in its interests, then a court might interpret the promise to limit Motor Works' purchases to its own needs, but it would be more likely to enforce the contract as written. In Case 8(c), the court would find that Motor Works has rejected Alloy's offer.

Preliminary comparisons

The reporters from civil law countries thought that the promises in Cases 8(a) and 8(c) would be enforced, but the one in Case 8(b) would not be, or might well not be. The reasons for not enforcing that promise were extraordinarily diverse: abuse of right (France and Belgium), interpretation (the Netherlands, Austria, Germany, and Scotland), the rule of interpretation in accordance with good faith (Scotland), the requirement of negotiation or performance in accordance with good faith (the Netherlands, Portugal, Italy, and Germany), uncertainty (Italy and France at one time), changed circumstances (the Netherlands and Greece), and a specific code provision requiring a party who has discretion over the content of a contract to use it in accordance with 'equitable criteria' (Greece).

The reporters from common law countries (England and Ireland) said that in all three cases, the initial promise was not binding because it lacked consideration. It could constitute, at most, a revocable offer. Cases 8(a) and 8(b) could not arise unless Alloy did not revoke its offer when the market rose, which the English reporter noted was unlikely in practice, and the Irish reporters noted would be against its interest. If Alloy did not revoke its offer in these cases, it would be bound if Motor Works accepted, although, in Case 8(b), a court might interpret the contract to limit Motor

Works to buying for its own needs. Whether it would do so is uncertain (England) or even unlikely (Ireland). In Case 8(c), Motor Works would not be bound because Alloy's offer was never accepted unless, as the English reporter noted, a court interpreted the initial promise to require it to buy a minimum amount, which, he said, is quite unlikely.

Case 9: promises to pay more than was agreed I

Case

Robert promised (a) to restructure a building for Paul who plans to use it as a restaurant, or (b) to sell Paul restaurant equipment including stoves, tables, chairs, cooking equipment, plates, and glasses. Paul promised him a fixed amount in payment. After performing part of the contract, Robert refused to continue unless he received one and a half times the amount originally promised. There had been no change in the circumstances of the parties since the contract was made except that Paul will now experience considerable delay opening his restaurant if he has to turn to someone else to complete the performance promised by Robert. Fearing this delay, Paul promised Robert the amount he demanded. After Robert completed performance, Paul refused to pay more than the amount originally agreed. Must he do so?

Discussions

FRANCE

The promise made by Paul to pay Robert more money than originally promised raises the problem of whether his consent was vitiated by economic duress.

Whether the contract is a construction contract (Case 9(a)) or one for the sale of goods (Case 9(b)), the parties fixed the amount of compensation when they made the contract. Since they have done so, neither party can change that amount without the other's consent. In a construction contract, the builder cannot ask for an increase even if the cost of the work exceeds his estimate (art. 1793 of the Civil Code). Similarly, once the sales price is set in conformity with art. 1591 of the Civil Code, it cannot be unilaterally revised.

Nevertheless, the parties may modify their contract by mutual consent. The modified contract is then binding (art. 1134 of the Civil Code). It does not matter whether the modification is so important that the contract as modified is considered a novation, that is, a new contract substituted for the old one, or so unimportant that the old contract is deemed to continue in existence with the modification.

Paul cannot refuse to pay the increased price on the grounds that Robert failed to perform since he performed fully. He can claim, however, that his consent was not validly given on the account of duress (*violence*) as provided by arts. 1111–15 of the Civil Code. If he is successful, the modified contract will be rescinded, and he may possibly be able to obtain damages. He will then be liable only for the original contract price.

Duress is both a tort and a defence to a contract action because it vitiates the contract. To prevail, Paul must prove (a) that an illegitimate threat was made, and (b) that this threat induced him to make the contract. We will consider these elements in turn.

To constitute duress, according to art. 1112 of the Civil Code, it is sufficient that a threat be directed against one's 'person' or 'fortune'.[1] Nevertheless, according to the case law, economic difficulties do not, in themselves, constitute a case of duress (*contrainte morale*).[2] Thus the question arises whether Robert's refusal to perform until the contract price was raised would be deemed to be an illegitimate threat which could be grounds for annulling the contract.

The *Cour de cassation* is fairly cautious when applying the doctrine of duress to situations where one of the parties is unable to protect its own interests because of its precarious economic situation. In this respect, the French courts' attitude to the question of economic duress may differ from that of courts in other countries such as England. The cases in which such a claim has failed concern the renewal of exclusive distribution agreements where the underlying problem is one of unequal bargaining power: sufficient pressure was exercised to force the distributor to agree to disadvantageous contractual conditions.[3] We have not found any cases

---

[1] Nor, according to art. 1111 of the Civil Code, does it matter if the threat was made by a third party or a contracting party.

[2] Paris, 24 May 1983, RTDCiv. 1984, 708, note J. Mestre.

[3] Com., 20 May 1980, Bull. civ. III, no. 212; D 1978, note H. Souleau, RTDCiv. 1984. This kind of situation is now regulated in two ways: either, in the field of competition law, as an abuse of economic dependence under art. 8 of the ordinance of 1 Dec. 1986 or, in the

where the pressure consisted of a threat by the other party not to perform. French law could be hostile to a claim of economic duress because it takes a formalistic attitude to the modification of the agreement: consent has apparently been given by both parties.[4]

The caution of French courts in extending the concept of *violence* is reflected in the control exercised over the lower courts when they give relief for duress that does not consist of threats of physical harm (*contrainte morale*). If the judges fail to explain fully their basis for doing so, they risk seeing their decision quashed by the *Cour de cassation*.[5] This caution is not required by the express language of the Code but rests on an interpretation by the courts of art. 1114 which provides that mere fear and reverence for one's ancestors is insufficient for a contract to be annulled.

The illegitimate character of the threat may be established from the means used or the objective sought. Here, Paul could claim that Robert blackmailed him into raising the contract price in order to obtain performance in violation of the principle that contracts are to be enforced.

Supposing that the threat is illegitimate and sufficient to constitute duress, Paul still will not obtain relief unless it had a determining influence on his conduct, inducing him to contract. The requirement of art. 1112 of the Civil Code of 'a considerable and present evil' means that the evil must be sufficiently serious for the duress to have been determining. Simple fear would not suffice. Paul must prove that he would never have accepted a revision of the price in the absence of the threat.

The language of art. 1112 is not perfectly clear. When it speaks of a 'present evil', it must mean that the fear must be inspired in the present, for the evil is necessarily in the future. It is not clear how its seriousness should be evaluated since the two paragraphs of art. 1112 are contradictory. The first paragraph requires an objective abstract judgment whereas the second suggests a subjective and concrete approach. Case law has

---

field of consumer law (art. L. 132–1 of the *Code de la consommation*), as a question of unfair contract terms (*clauses abusives*) when there is an 'abuse of weakness' under art. L. 122–8 of the *Code de la consommation*.

[4] Ghestin, *Traité de droit civil* no. 579, pp. 561 ff. suggests that *violence* is rarely used; see also Terré, Simler, and Lequette, *Les obligations* no. 240, p. 197, who discuss whether civil law generally should enlarge their view of duress to make it coincide with that of specialized areas such as competition law (*ibid.*, notes 5 and 6). They suggest that the hostility of the *Cour de cassation* is not necessarily shared by the trial and appeal courts. However, these examples concern attempts to extend the concept of duress to situations of economic dependence. Thus the discussion concerns a problem quite different from the one before us.

[5] See, in particular, Com., 20 May 1980, Bull. civ. III, no. 212, p. 170, quashing Cour d'appel, Paris, 27 Sept. 1977, D 1978, 690, note H. Souleau.

definitely decided in favour of a concrete evaluation, conforming to the role of the intentions of the parties as recognized by French law. The courts therefore evaluate the particular situation of the victim to decide whether the threat had a determining influence. The court would also take into account Paul's business experience. If Paul is inexperienced, it is obvious that he has much more chance of succeeding with his claim. On the facts, it is unclear whether opening the restaurant is the beginning of his business activity or not: he may already own other restaurants, or have other business experience.

It also matters whether Paul had a viable alternative. To see if he did, we must consider the options open to him. Under art. 1144 of the Civil Code, Paul could sue Robert for specific performance (*exécution en nature*) or, in the alternative, for judicial authorization to substitute for Robert's performance that of another contracting party who is able to supply him on time (*faculté de remplacement*). We think this option would be available in Case 9(b) in which the parties have made a contract of sale and even in Case 9(a) in which they have made a construction contract.[6] The option is available as long as it is possible to substitute another party for the party in breach.

If Paul wished to find another contracting party, he would have a choice. First, he could put Robert on notice and go to court. The judge can authorize replacing Robert, or he can order him to perform under *astreinte* (a daily fine is payable as long as performance is not carried out), or he can award damages. If Paul were successful, he could also recover the extra costs of buying the supplies for the restaurant elsewhere. It is also possible to combine these remedies. As the parties are merchants (*commerçants*), any proceedings would be before the *Tribunal de commerce* (art. 873 of the New Code of Civil Procedure).

Second, he could bring the matter before the court very quickly (twenty-four or forty-eight hours) by *référé* (interlocutory proceedings), asking the court to issue an *injonction de faire* ordering performance.

Third, if Paul can show that his situation is urgent, he could replace Robert with another supplier without going to court.[7] If he acts on his own initiative, the courts can always ratify his action subsequently. This exception to the general rule that judicial intervention is required is supported by commercial usage and based on a recognition that it can be impractical to go to court first.

---

[6] Civ. 1, 8 Oct. 1962, Bull. civ. I, no. 400. For an explanation of the mechanism of art. 1144, see generally P. Simler, *Juris-classeur*, arts. 1136–45, Fasc. 10.

[7] For example, Civ., 2 July 1945, D 1946, 4; RTDCiv. 1946, p. 39, note J. Carbonnier; 7 Dec. 1951, D 1952, 144; M. Vasseur, 'Urgence et le droit civil', RTDCiv. 1954, no. 11, 403.

On the facts of this case, however, it is not clear whether obtaining performance from another party would have been a valid alternative for Paul. It depends on such factual matters as the time when the threat was made in relation to the due date for performance and the date the restaurant was supposed to open (a question of hours or days?), and the availability elsewhere and on short notice of the supplies Robert had undertaken to deliver.

If Paul does have considerable business experience, it is likely that he will be considered capable of resisting such intimidation[8] because positive law offers him the remedy of specific performance which would enable him to resist. To succeed, Paul would have to prove that suing Robert would have taken too long and would have caused him a considerable loss, thus putting his business at risk. It seems here that he would have difficulty proving it was so.

Consequently, it is difficult to give a definite answer as to whether Paul would succeed in claiming duress. It also should be emphasized that the power to make a decision in such a case is shared by the various courts of which the French court system is composed. The lower courts (including the courts of appeal) have complete control over all findings of fact (*appréciation souveraine*), whereas the *Cour de cassation* has the final power to decide questions of law. As the distinction between points of fact and of law is rather fine, it is important to note once again that the question of whether a threat is illegitimate, which inevitably involves matters both of fact and of law, is nevertheless subject to the control of the *Cour de cassation*. This division of the power to decide may also help to explain why the case law is difficult to systematize, as each case is decided on its merits on a case-by-case basis.

Ultimately, in a case like this, the law reflects two conflicting concerns. On the one hand, it is essential to ensure that consent is freely given in a legal system which puts so much emphasis on the will of the parties when the contract is made. On the other hand, contracts cannot be annulled lightly without compromising legal certainty which is indispensable. The provisions of the Civil Code reflect the drafters' concern that the remedies available for claims of vitiated consent do not become a source of legal uncertainty. The contradiction contained in art. 1112 of the Civil Code is a good example.

The tension between these concerns persists. The fear that the parties will be unable to rely upon their contract is always present in the minds of judges and scholars. Even if the scope of the doctrine of duress has been

---

[8] Com., 30 Jan. 1974, D 1974, 382.

widened, its applications are relatively rare. On the other hand, special legislation of recent origin has been less reluctant than traditional civil law to protect contracting parties who are in a situation of economic dependence. One can see examples in consumer law (see art. L. 122–8 of the *Code de la consommation* relating to the abuse of a weakness), and in competition law (see art. 8 of the ordinance of 1 December 1986 and arts. 36(3), 36(4) and 36(5) of the same text in the law of 1 July 1996).

BELGIUM

It seems that Paul's promise to Robert of one and a half times the amount originally agreed is invalid because of a defect in consent (*vice du consentement*): it was obtained by duress (*violence*) (arts. 1111–15 of the Civil Code). Duress is defined (art. 1111) as a threat 'capable of overwhelming a reasonable person, and which may create in that person a fear of exposing himself or his fortune to considerable and actual harm'.[9] Duress invalidates consent if four conditions are met.[10] First, it must be capable of overwhelming a reasonable man or woman, due regard being had to the circumstances of the case. Here, Robert's threat to discontinue performance of the contract would likely overwhelm any reasonable restaurant owner, due regard being had to the consequences of a delayed opening of the restaurant. Second, the threat must have induced the victim to consent. Here, surely Paul would not have promised Robert the amount he demanded if Robert had not threatened to discontinue performance of the contract. Third, the threat must arouse the fear of considerable and actual harm. Here, the start of Paul's business was seriously jeopardized. Fourth, the threat must be illegitimate or unjust. Quite obviously, the threat to discontinue performance of a contract entered into validly is not legitimate. Abuse of the economic dependence of the other party (see the discussion of abuse of right in Case 8) may lead a court to find there was duress in entering into a contract.[11] If there was duress, then the agree-

---

[9] '[D]e nature à faire impression sur une personne raisonnable, et qu'elle peut lui inspirer la crainte d'exposer sa personne ou sa fortune à un mal considérable et présent'.

[10] See Cass., 12 Feb. 1988, Pas., I, 697; Gand, 15 Jan. 1991, RW, 1992, 467, and see S. Stijns, D. Van Gerven, and P. Wéry, 'Chronique de jurisprudence. Les obligations: les sources (1985–1995)', JT, 1996, no. 61, p. 712.

[11] See De Page, *Traité élémentaire*, vol. I, no. 60 (discussing the case of an employee forced to consent to a loan to his employer under threat of being fired); Mons, 13 June 1994, JLMB, 1995, 484 (holding that a medical doctor's consent to change the status of his contractual relationship with a medical institution from employed worker to independent worker, thereby reducing his social security benefits and the cost of them to his employer, was obtained under duress by the threat that he would lose his job with the institution). However, the mere discrepancy between the respective economic power

ment to modify the contract price is invalid. Robert must then be satisfied with the original contract price.

THE NETHERLANDS

The principle of freedom of contract implies that parties are free to change their contract by their consent. They may agree that one party has to pay a higher price for something he was already entitled to receive on the basis of the first contract. However, such a contract, like any contract, is voidable if it is concluded as a result of an abuse of circumstances or a threat (art. 3:44(1) of the Civil Code).

Abuse of circumstances is governed by art. 3:44(4) of the Civil Code which provides:

A person who knows or should know that another is being induced to execute a juridical act as a result of special circumstances – such as state of necessity, dependency, wantonness, abnormal mental condition or inexperience – and who promotes the creation of that juridical act, although what he knows or ought to know should prevent him therefrom, commits an abuse of circumstances.

Cases of 'economic duress' are not as such excluded from the application of this article. If nothing changed except that Paul became totally dependent on Robert's promise to perform, then it is likely that Paul may avoid the contract. On the facts of this case, Robert would then seem to have committed an abuse of the circumstances.[12]

Thus, much depends here on the extent to which Paul depended on Robert's promise. Objectively, the promise Paul made does not seem to have been the only possible solution to the problem he confronted after Robert's refusal. If Robert had actually stopped performing, he would have been liable for non-performance (art. 6:74 of the Civil Code). Paul would then have been entitled to compensation for all of the resulting damage (arts. 6:74 and 6:95 ff. of the Civil Code[13]). Moreover, he could have asked the court, in a short procedure, to order specific performance (art. 6:296

of the parties does not in itself constitute duress (Cass., 2 May 1969, Pas., I, 781). There must be an *abuse* of this situation.

[12] He might not have, though, if he had demanded the increase in payment only because of a corresponding increase in his costs.

[13] Article 6:74(1) of the Civil Code: 'Every failure in the performance of an obligation obliges the debtor to repair the damage which the creditor suffers therefrom, unless the failure cannot be imputed to the debtor.'

Article 6:95 (1) of the Civil Code: 'The damage which must be repaired pursuant to a legal obligation to make reparation consists of patrimonial damage and other harm . . .'

Article 6:96 (1) of the Civil Code: 'Patrimonial damage comprises both the loss sustained by the creditor and the profit of which he has been deprived.'

of the Civil Code[14]). Subjectively, however, Paul seems to have felt that he had no other choice. The question is whether he was excused in thinking so. In other words, were the circumstances 'special circumstances' in the sense of art. 3:44 of the Civil Code and, if so, was there a causal link between these circumstances and the conclusion of the contract?

I find this difficult to decide. One might argue that a normal entrepreneur should not overreact as Paul did. But that argument cuts two ways. One could say that Paul should have met the standard of firmness which can be required from someone who is in such a business and is a party to such a contract, and that therefore, he should not be protected. But one could also say that unless there was an emergency, no one would ever have concluded such a contract, and, therefore, he should be protected because he acted only because of an emergency. I am inclined to think that he should be protected.

The contract may also be voidable on the grounds that Robert's refusal to perform unless Paul paid more constitutes a threat. In the case of *Ciba-Geigy* the *Hoge Raad* decided that even absent an abuse of circumstances, a party may nevertheless receive relief because he was the victim of a threat, even an economic threat.[15] In his Conclusion, Advocate-General Hartkamp showed that the test that 'a reasonable person would be influenced by [the threat]'[16] should be less strict than the test of 'special circumstances' since in case of threat the other party commits an unlawful act whereas in case of abuse of circumstances it may not be the other party's fault that the first party was vulnerable.[17]

SPAIN

In Spanish law, a novation of a contract extinguishes the parties' prior obligations or replaces them with new obligations. Spanish scholars have a very broad concept of novation based on art. 1203 of the Civil Code. Article 1203 says that obligations may be amended: their object or main conditions may be changed.[18] According to Castán Tobeñas,[19] the modifi-

---

[14] Article 6:296 of the Civil Code: 'Unless the law, the nature of the obligation or a juridical act produce a different result, the person who is obliged to give, to do or not to do something *vis-à-vis* another is ordered to do so by the judge upon the demand of the person to whom the obligation is owed.'   [15] HR, 27 March 1992, NJ 1992, no. 377.

[16] Article 3:44(2) of the Civil Code: 'A person who induces another to execute a certain juridical act by unlawfully threatening him or a third party with harm to this person or property, makes a threat. The threat must be such that a reasonable person would be influenced by it.'

[17] In the same sense, see Tjittes, *De hoedanigheid van contractspartijen*, 83.

[18] Castán Tobeñas, *Derecho civil*, vol. III, 431.   [19] *Ibid.*, 436.

cation of the prior obligation is the *causa* of the new obligations that come with the novation. In his opinion, however, a change in amount owed does not qualify as a modification of the former obligation, that is, as a novation.[20] He cites a decision of the *Tribunal Supremo* in which the Court refused to enforce an agreement which was ambiguous but which the debtors claimed had reduced the amount they owed from 50,000 pesetas to 25,000 pesetas. The Court held that the modification was not valid under art. 1203 when all the new agreement did was reduce the amount owed.[21]

In this case there has not been a change in the original obligation: Robert has to build the same restaurant. Consequently, by the view just discussed, there is no novation, and the promise is not enforceable.

Duress probably would not be a ground for refusing to enforce Paul's promise. Article 1267 of the Civil Code indicates that the threat has to be of imminent and serious harm. Since Paul would suffer only delays, it could not be considered a serious threat. Also, art. 1267 says that in order to determine whether a party was intimidated, the age and condition of the person has to be considered. These criteria are applied on a case-by-case basis. In any event, duress would not void or invalidate the contract automatically; it would only make it voidable (*anulable*).

PORTUGAL

In Cases 9(a) and 9(b), Paul can refuse to pay more than the amount originally agreed.

Under Portuguese law, it is possible for both parties to modify a contract by agreement (art. 406(1) of the Civil Code). However, in this case the modification agreement can be considered a case of usury. Portuguese law defines a usurious contract as one in which one party exploits the other's situation of necessity to obtain excessive or unjustified benefits (art. 282 of the Civil Code).

A usurious contract is voidable. Because it is voidable, the party exploited can refuse to pay (art. 287(2)). Therefore, in both cases, Paul can legally refuse to pay more than the amount initially agreed.

Another possibility, though in my view a doubtful one, is that Paul has a remedy for duress. According to art. 255 of the Civil Code, the act threatened must be illegal for it to constitute duress. So an unjustified threat which is not illegal, like the one here, would not be enough for duress. Nevertheless, Portuguese case law has found there to be duress when an

[20] *Ibid.*, 441.   [21] TS, 17 March 1933.

electric company threatened to cut off power unless the recipient paid the unpaid debt of the previous owner of a building.[22]

ITALY

In Cases 9(a) and 9(b), Paul is not obliged to pay more than the amount originally agreed.

Robert's demand for extra payment under threat of non-performance which will cause a significant harm to Paul would be considered both a crime[23] – extortion – according to art. 629[24] of the Criminal Code, and a tort according to art. 2043 of the Civil Code.[25] In any event, in contract law, the promise would be voidable under arts. 1434 and 1435 of the Civil Code.[26] In real life, Robert would have no incentive even to request it.

AUSTRIA

Paul can refuse to pay more than the amount originally agreed upon. According to § 870 of the Civil Code, a contract is voidable if it is caused by an unlawful threat. There is a debate among Austrian jurists whether the threat not to perform a contractual obligation is unlawful or not; although Gschnitzer[27] claims that such a threat is unlawful, Rummel[28] argues that not every such threat is unlawful in the sense envisioned by § 870. He fails to make clear, however, where he draws the line between lawful and unlawful threats not to perform one's contractual obligation. Moreover, there are no judicial decisions concerning this question.

---

[22] STJ, 11 March 1997, BMJ 465 at 552.

[23] See, most recently, Cass. pen., sez. III, no. 206858 1996; Cass. pen., sez. II, 17 Oct. 1995, in Cass. pen. (1997), 406; Cass. pen., sez. II, 2 June 1994; Cass. pen., 10 March 1989.

[24] Article 629 of the Criminal Code: 'Whoever, by means of violence or threat that forces someone to do or omit something, obtains an unjust profit for himself or for others by causing someone else harm, is subject to imprisonment for five (5) to ten (10) years and to a fine from one (1) million to four (4) million lire. The sanction is imprisonment for six (6) to twenty (20) years and a fine from two (2) to six (6) million lire if any of the circumstances are present that are enumerated in the last paragraph of the preceding article.'

[25] Article 2043 of the Civil Code: 'Any fraudulent, malicious or negligent act that causes an unjustified injury to another obliges the person who has committed the act to pay damages.'

[26] Article 1434 of the Civil Code: 'Duress: Duress is cause for annulment of a contract even if exerted by a third person.' Article 1435 of the Civil Code: 'Characteristics of duress: Duress must be of such a nature as to impress a reasonable person and to cause him to fear that he or his property will be exposed to an unjust and considerable injury. In this respect, the age, sex and condition of the persons shall be considered.'

[27] In Klang, *ABGB* vol. IV/1, 102 f.   [28] In Rummel, *ABGB* § 871 no. 13.

Not every unlawful threat gives the other party the right to avoid the contract. The threat must be a serious one (*gegründete Furcht*). This means that the threatened harm must not be insignificant and that there must be some probability that the harm will be realized if the contract is not concluded.

Given these rules it is clear that § 870 will apply to both Cases 9(a) and 9(b). In both cases, we have not only the threat not to perform a contractual obligation but also the threat of a serious harm to Paul, namely the considerable delay of the opening of the restaurant. Therefore, under § 870 of the Civil Code, Paul would have the right to avoid the contract.

GERMANY

In Cases 9(a) and 9(b), the new contract is valid but voidable. Robert's threat not to do what he has promised in a binding contract was unlawful and an undue influence. This threat was the cause of Paul's promise. Section 123(1) of the Civil Code allows the promise to be invalidated if it was caused by an unlawful threat. Here, the threat is unlawful if the means threatened are unlawful, even if the person making the threat is not aware of their illegality.[29] A threat is also unlawful if the purpose is illegal,[30] or if both means and purpose are legal but connecting the two of them seems to be wrongful.[31]

Our case fits within the first of these three rules because it is illegal not to perform one's contractual duty without any reason. Therefore, Paul was entitled to invalidate the new contract by so notifying Robert (§§ 123(1), and 143[32] of the Civil Code), and he has already done that.

According to § 142(1) of the Civil Code, the result of invalidating the contract is that it will be regarded as void from the beginning. The termination is retroactive and takes effect not only between the persons involved in the contract but *erga omnes*.[33] Therefore Paul can refuse to pay more than the amount originally agreed because the second contract is deemed never to have existed and so it could not change the original contract between Paul and Robert.

GREECE

Paul can ask for the annulment of his agreement to pay one and a half times more than the amount originally agreed because his declaration of

---

[29] RGZ 108 (1924), 102 (104).   [30] BGH LM § 123 no. 32.   [31] BGHZ 2 (1951), 287 (296).
[32] According to the provision, the invalidation does not have any effect unless notice of it is given.   [33] BGH LM § 2080 no. 1.

will was made under duress. Article 150 of the Civil Code provides: 'A person who has been prompted to make a declaration of will in an unlawful manner or in a manner contrary to morality, through a threat directed against him by the other party to the act or by a third party, shall be entitled to apply for the annulment of such act.' Article 151 provides: 'The threat must be one that would, under the particular circumstances, instil fear in a reasonable man and place in grave and imminent danger the life, limb, freedom, honour or property of the person threatened or of persons very closely connected to him.'

Therefore, the requirements that have to be met are: (1) a threat must have been made of some action that depends directly or indirectly on the will of the person who made it, so that the threat can cause fear to a reasonable man entering into the relevant business transactions;[34] (2) the threat must be unlawful or contrary to morality – a threat not to perform a contractual obligation that will expose the property of the person threatened to a great danger can be deemed unlawful;[35] (3) the threat must expose the life, freedom, honour, or property of the person threatened to a great danger; (4) the person who makes the threat must intend to force the other person to make a declaration of will; (5) there must be a causal connection between the intention of the person to force the other contracting party to a declaration of will and the declaration of will itself.[36] If all these requirements are fulfilled the person threatened can ask for his declaration of will to be annulled.[37] Annulment is declared by the court (art. 154 of the Civil Code).[38]

Robert's threat that he will not complete the performance of his contractual obligations is unlawful because it exposes Paul's property to a great danger. Paul will experience a considerable delay in opening his restaurant. This threat caused Paul fear and would do so to a reasonable man of the same occupation. In addition, Robert intended to force Paul to agree to a much higher amount in payment, since he was aware of the fact that Paul would experience a considerable delay if he had to turn to someone else to complete the performance promised by him. Therefore, Paul can refuse to pay more than the amount originally agreed. He can do so only if he applies to the court for this agreement to be declared null.

Alternatively, the agreement may be void according to art. 179(2) of the Civil Code, which provides:

---

[34] Karakatsanis in Georgiadis and Stathopoulos, *Civil Code*, art. 151, no. 5.
[35] AP 635/1968 NoB 17, 404; Karakatsanis in Georgiadis and Stathopoulos, *Civil Code*, art. 150, no. 8.   [36] I. Karakatsanis in Georgiadis and *Civil Code*, art. 151, no. 5.
[37] Otherwise the contract is in force and the party has to perform his obligation. Georgiadis, *General Principles*, 438 ff.   [38] *Ibid.*, 309.

In particular, an act shall be void as contrary to morality whereby the freedom of a person is hampered excessively or whereby through an exploitation of the need, the levity of character or the lack of experience of the other party, pecuniary advantages are promised or received for one's own benefit or that of a third party and in consideration of something furnished which in the circumstances are obviously out of proportion to the consideration furnished.

The requirements that have to be met for this provision to apply are:[39] (1) there must be an obvious disproportion between the performance and counter-performance; (2) this disproportion must have arisen because of the need, the levity of character, or the lack of experience of the party – a person is in need if he is in a situation (permanent or temporary) of direct danger (financial or otherwise), and he has to face it immediately; (3) the other contracting party must have taken advantage of the need of the other person, which means that he must have been aware of that need and that he used it to obtain more from him.

If art. 179(2) applies, then the contract may be void completely or only in part (art. 181 of the Civil Code).[40] Tort liability is also possible according to arts. 914 and 919 of the Civil Code.[41] Article 179 is construed narrowly and applies only when very strict conditions are met.[42] Nevertheless, Paul should not be required to pay the extra money if his need was great and Robert took advantage of it to obtain a disproportionate amount in return for his own performance.

SCOTLAND

As there are obligations on both sides, the Scottish courts are likely to analyse a problem such as this one as a bilateral contract rather than as two sets of unilateral obligations, as they generally prefer to adopt a contractual analysis. When Robert refuses to perform the contract under the terms originally agreed, he is in material breach of contract, and Paul is entitled to rescind the contract and sue Robert for damages. However, Paul agrees to vary the terms of the contract, and he is therefore bound to fulfil the terms as agreed, as Robert has completed his side of the bargain. Robert will be entitled to sue Paul for specific implement if he does not pay the agreed amount. It is unlikely that any plea Paul makes to the effect that the revision of the contract was invalid will be successful, as the

---

[39] For a thorough discussion of profiteering contracts, see P. Papanikolaou, *The Profiteer Contracts* (1983).

[40] Karasis in Georgiadis and Stathopoulos, *Civil Code*, art. 179, no. 4; Georgiadis, *General Principles*, 275–7.   [41] Karasis in Georgiadis and Stathopoulos, *Civil Code*, art. 179, no. 4.

[42] Stathopoulos, *Contract Law*, 113.

courts are unlikely to find it is invalid through force and fear when Paul could have exercised his contractual remedies and recovered damages in full for Robert's breach. It would therefore appear that Paul must pay the increased amount once Robert fulfils his side of the agreement. If Paul could not have established his loss, there is no authority in Scotland that he could then have the variation set aside on the ground of economic duress.

If the variation is analysed as a unilateral obligation to pay more, it is unlikely that it will need to be established in writing as it is made in the course of Paul's business in terms of s. 1(2)(a)(ii) of the 1995 Act. It can also be argued that the terms of the Act are inapplicable as the promise is non-gratuitous as Paul receives the benefit of performance being completed by Robert.

ENGLAND

It is reasonably clear in English law that in either of these cases, Paul is not obliged to pay the extra sum. Until recently, the reason given for this result would have been that no 'fresh' consideration was provided or promised in exchange for Paul's promise to pay more. Robert agreed to finish the work, but on the traditional view of consideration promising to do no more than that which one already has a legal obligation to do, which is what Robert did, is not consideration.

Thus, in the famous case of *Stilck* v. *Myrick*,[43] a captain's promise to pay his sailors higher wages following the desertion of two of the crew was unenforceable because, according to one report of the case,[44] the sailors were doing no more than they were already legally obliged to do. And in various cases with facts roughly analogous to Case 9, the pre-existing legal duty rule has been applied in refusing to enforce a renegotiation.[45]

Following the landmark decision of *Williams* v. *Roffey Bros. & Nichols (Contractors) Ltd*,[46] however, it is likely that the reason given for refusing to enforce the variation now would be that it was made under duress. According to *Williams*, the consideration rule is satisfied if the promisor

---

[43] [1809] 2 Camp. 317 and 6 Esp. 129.

[44] One reason this case is well known is that there are two reports of the case, and the second, by Espinasse, states that the suit by the sailors failed for 'policy' reasons: an explanation more consistent with the contemporary view that such cases are really about duress.

[45] *D & C Builders* v. *Rees*, where the plaintiff builder agreed to accept less than the sum owed to him by the defendant for work done on the defendant's premises because he was short of cash.   [46] [1991] 1 QB 1.

receives a 'practical benefit', even if not a legal benefit. And the performance of a pre-existing legal duty may, the court held, be a practical benefit. It is likely, though not absolutely certain (we do not yet have a case directly in point), that a court would hold that avoiding the extra expense that Paul will incur if Robert does not perform is of practical benefit to Paul. In *Williams* itself, a subcontractor's agreement to complete works that he was already contractually obliged to complete was held to be a practical benefit, since it appeared that the subcontractor would go bankrupt without a renegotiation of the contract, and that, if he did fail, the main contractor would incur considerable expenses, both in finding an alternative and in paying damages for his own consequent late performance. Here, there is no danger of bankruptcy, but performance clearly is of practical benefit, because of the extra expenses that will be incurred in finding a replacement.

After finding the consideration requirement satisfied, the court in *Williams* said the next question was whether the renegotiation had been formed under duress (or fraud, which need not concern us). The court in *Williams* found no duress, although there was little discussion of this point as the main contractor did not argue duress. The next question to be asked in addressing Case 9, therefore, is whether Paul's promise was made under duress, in particular whether it was made under what is known as 'economic duress'.

Economic duress arises where the relevant threat is to harm the promisor financially rather than physically. The concept of economic duress is little developed in English law (partly because the traditional 'pre-existing legal duty' rule made it unnecessary to do so), and, as just noted, there was little discussion of the point in *Williams*.[47] It is suggested that duress would be found in this case because the promise was made in response to an unlawful threat, which, if carried out, would have harmed Paul. In *Williams*, the facts suggest that, although the subcontractor may have been negligent in pricing his bid, he was not attempting to take advantage of the main contractor. He was not making a 'threat' to breach, but merely warning the main contractor that he would breach unless he received more money. Indeed, it was the head contractor who made the offer to pay more in *Williams*. By contrast, in Case 9 Robert is making a threat, since he has the ability to perform under the original terms of the contract and has indicated that he will not do so unless paid more. The

---

[47] Economic duress was first recognized as a distinct and valid basis of duress in *The Siboen and The Sibotre* [1976] 1 Lloyd's Rep. 293, later affirmed in *Universe Tankships of Monrovia v. International Transport Workers Federation (The Universe Sentinel)* [1983] 1 AC 366.

requirement, to establish duress, that the threat in question be illegitimate or wrongful[48] is satisfied here because a threat to breach a contract is, and has been held to be, wrongful.[49] Furthermore, it seems clear that the threat in this case was operative, that is, it induced Paul's promise of more money, given that Paul had no reasonable alternative but to comply. Such evidence would likely also satisfy the requirement, imposed by some courts, that an invalidating threat 'vitiate the consent' of the promisor.[50] Vitiation of consent, in practice, is understood as meaning an absence of reasonable alternatives.[51] In short, the fact that, in lay person's terms, Robert is trying to take advantage of Paul's vulnerability, would, in this case, mean that he could not enforce Paul's promise.

IRELAND

These two cases concern the enforceability of Paul's promise to pay Robert an extra amount to ensure that Robert would complete performance of his contractual obligations. As described under earlier cases, Irish law requires that a promise not given under seal must be supported by consideration. A promisee must provide something, a *quid pro quo*, in exchange for the promise. The consideration need not be adequate, in a commercial sense, but it must be sufficient in law.

The traditional view has always been that discharge of an existing contractual duty owed by the promisee is insufficient consideration. In *Stilck* v. *Myrick*,[52] two seamen deserted on a voyage to the Baltic. The captain agreed with the rest of the crew that if they worked the ship back to London without the two seamen being replaced, he would divide between them the pay which would have been due to the two deserters. On arrival at London this extra pay was refused and the plaintiff's action to recover his extra pay was dismissed. The court held that the captain's promise of extra pay was unenforceable for want of consideration. The promisees had provided no consideration as they were already bound by their contracts to work the ship home. The traditional approach was endorsed, *obiter*, by O'Hanlon J in *Kenny* v. *An Post*.[53]

This area of the law has been thrown into confusion by the decision of the English Court of Appeal in *Williams* v. *Roffey Bros. & Nichols (Contractors)*

---

[48] See, e.g., *Universe Tankships of Monrovia* v. *International Transport Workers Federation (The Universe Sentinel)* [1983] 1 AC 366.   [49] *Pao On* v. *Lau Yiu Long* [1980] AC 614.

[50] See *The Siboen and The Sibotre* [1976] 1 Lloyd's Rep. 293; but compare *The Evia Luck* [1992] 2 AC 152.   [51] *The Siboen and The Sibotre* [1976] 1 Lloyd's Rep. 293.   [52] [1809] 2 Camp. 317.

[53] [1988] JISL 187.

Ltd.[54] The defendants were main building contractors employed to refurbish a block of flats in London. The defendants engaged the plaintiff to carry out the carpentry work in the refurbishment of the flats for a total price of £20,000. Before the carpentry work was completed, however, the plaintiff ran into financial difficulty, partly because the work had been underpriced. The defendants, fearing that the carpentry work would not be completed on time, and facing a penalty clause in the main contract should it overrun, promised to pay the plaintiff an additional sum of £10,300. After the plaintiff proceeded with the carpentry work the defendant refused to pay the extra money, whereupon the plaintiff ceased working and sued for the additional sum promised.

Notwithstanding the decision in *Stilck* v. *Myrick*, the Court of Appeal held that the defendant's promise to pay the additional sum was enforceable. It held that where a party to a contract promised to make an additional payment in return for the other party's promise to perform his existing contractual obligations and as a result secured a benefit or avoided a detriment, the advantage secured by the promise to make the additional payment was capable of constituting consideration therefor, provided that it was not secured by economic duress or fraud.

In the *Williams* case counsel for the defendants accepted that their clients may have derived, or hoped to derive, practical benefits from their promise to pay the additional sum, by way of ensuring that the plaintiff continued working and did not stop in breach of the sub-contract, avoiding the penalty for delay in the main contract, and avoiding the trouble and expense of engaging other people to complete the carpentry work. The Court of Appeal felt that these potential benefits resulted in a commercial advantage to the defendants and that this benefit accruing to the defendants provided sufficient consideration to support the defendants' promise to pay the additional sums. On the facts of the case the question of duress did not arise.

One Irish commentator has described the propositions enunciated in the *Williams* case as 'controversial and difficult'. It is unclear whether the approach in the *Williams* case would be followed in Ireland. If the *Williams* approach is rejected and the traditional approach maintained, then Paul's promise to pay Robert an extra amount will not be enforceable in the circumstances of either contract in Case 9.

If the *Williams* approach were to be followed in Ireland, would Paul's promise to pay Robert the extra amount be enforceable in Cases 9(a) or

[54] [1991] 1 QB 1.

9(b)? Leaving aside the issue of duress for a moment, it seems that the promise would be enforceable if Robert could show that Paul secured a benefit or avoided a detriment in return for Robert's promise to complete his existing contractual obligations. In the case of the contract to restructure the building (Case 9(a)), this appears quite similar to the contract under discussion in the *Williams* case, and it seems quite possible that Robert could show that Paul gained a commercial advantage by Robert's discharge of his existing contractual duties. The circumstances of the contract for the sale of restaurant equipment (Case 9(b)) appear somewhat weaker and it would be more difficult to show the necessary benefit accruing to Paul from the mere discharge of the contractual obligations. The trouble and expense of having to enter a new contract appear far less in this case.

In any event, the overriding proviso in the *Williams* case was that the promise was not the result of economic duress. In the present case, unlike in *Williams*, Robert refused to continue unless he received the extra amount. An Irish court would almost certainly hold that Paul's promise was vitiated by duress and that he was not obliged to pay the extra amount.

The test for duress is whether the threat actually coerced the will of the person to whom it was addressed. Treitel[55] states that the English courts will consider what alternative courses of action, other than submission to the threat, were reasonably available to that person. For example, taking legal proceedings may have been a viable alternative. There is no Irish authority on this proposition of legal proceedings being a viable alternative and it is unlikely that an Irish court would adopt this approach. The Irish courts tend to accept arguments by parties that legal proceedings are costly and time consuming and therefore amount to a last resort.

Summaries

France: Whether relief would be given for duress is not clear since French courts have been hesitant to consider economic pressure to be duress.
Belgium: Relief would be given for duress.
The Netherlands: If nothing changed except that Paul became completely dependent on Robert to keep his promise, relief would be given for 'abuse of circumstances' which means taking advantage of the other party's 'state of necessity, dependency, wantonness, abnormal mental condition

---

[55] See Treitel, *Contract*, ch. 11.

or inexperience'. Most likely, Paul was completely dependent, but the matter is not clear. Relief may also be given for duress.

Spain: Most likely, the promise is unenforceable on the grounds that it is not a valid novation. The *causa* of a valid novation is the modification of the former obligation, and a change in the amount owed does not count as such a modification. Relief would probably not be given for duress since the harm threatened must be imminent and serious, and here, Paul would suffer only some delay.

Portugal: The promises are probably enforceable despite the claim of duress since the threat was not to commit an illegal act. They probably are unenforceable for 'usury', which is the exploitation of another's state of necessity to obtain unjustified or excessive benefits.

Italy: Relief would be given for duress.

Austria: Most likely, relief would be given for duress.

Germany: Relief would be given for duress.

Greece: Relief would be given for duress. It could also be given for the exploitation of another person's need in a manner contrary to morality.

Scotland: Relief would probably not be given for duress since Paul could have sued for damages if Robert breached.

England: Neither promise is binding. Once it would have been said that there is no fresh consideration. Recently, however, it has been held that there is consideration for a promise if the promisor receives a 'practical benefit', even if the benefit is the performance of a pre-existing legal duty. But relief would be given for duress.

Ireland: Neither promise is binding. Once it would have been said that there is no fresh consideration. Recently, however, an English court held that there is consideration for a promise if the promisor receives a 'practical benefit', even if the benefit is the performance of a pre-existing legal duty. It is not clear whether this decision will be followed in Ireland. Even if it were, relief would be given for duress.

Preliminary comparisons

Duress and exploitation: Virtually all reporters discussed the possibility of relief for duress. Seven thought it likely (Belgium, Italy, Austria, Germany, Greece, England, and Ireland); two thought it possible (France and the Netherlands); three thought it unlikely (Spain, Portugal, Scotland). Nevertheless, relief would be given anyway, in the Netherlands, for 'abuse of circumstances', in Spain, because a mere change in the amount owed does not constitute a novation, and in Portugal, because the agreement was made by exploiting another's state of necessity. Thus only the reporters from two countries thought the promises might be enforceable (France and Scotland). The Greek reporter also believed that the promise might be voidable on the grounds that another person's need was exploited in a manner contrary to morality.

Consideration: The two common law reporters noted that once, the promises would have been unenforceable because they lack fresh consideration, although the approach now taken in England, which may be followed in Ireland, is to count the performance of a pre-existing contractual duty as consideration if the promisor receives a 'practical benefit'.

Case 10: promises to pay more than was agreed II

Case

Vito was an executive working for Company, a business firm, on a contract obligating him to continue working, and Company to continue employing him, for a period of ten years. Company promised to pay him a large sum of money, equal to a year's pay, (a) in the midst of his term of employment because he received an offer of immediate employment at higher pay from a competing firm, or (b) at the end of his term of employment, after he had announced his intention to retire, to thank him for his services. Is Company obliged to keep this promise? Does it matter if Vito has already bought a vacation house he could otherwise not afford?

Discussions

FRANCE

In French law, Cases 10(a) and 10(b) raise quite different questions.

The question in Case 10(a) is whether an agreement that restricts an employee's choice of employment is valid. Such a restriction is valid provided that three conditions are fulfilled: the agreement must be limited as to time; it must be limited as to space; and its purpose must be to serve a legitimate interest of the employer.[1] If these conditions are all satisfied,[2] the restriction is valid, but it is still subject to a special rule that is foreign

---

[1] G. Couturier, *Droit du travail, Les relations individuelles de travail*, 2nd edn (1993), Droit de l'emploi, Dalloz action, 1997.

[2] Soc., 14 May 1992, Bull. civ. V, no. 309, p. 193; D 1992, 351, note Y. Serra; JCP 1992, ed. G. II 21889, note J. Amiel-Donat. See generally, G. Lyon-Caen, J. Pellisier, and A. Supiot, *Droit de travail*, 18th edn (1996), no. 255, pp. 219 f.

to the requirement of *cause*[3] in contract law: the employer is not obliged to give something in exchange for the restriction. There are two exceptions to this special rule: it does not apply when a *quid pro quo* is provided for by a collective agreement with a trade union or by a contract between the employer and the employee. In those cases, the employer will have to pay in exchange for the employee agreeing to be bound by the restrictive covenant. The restriction is regarded as separate from the rest of the contract and subject to the usual requirements of art. 1131. It must be acknowledged, however, that some academic writers on labour law contest this analysis. They suggest that agreeing to such a restriction is not a sacrifice and should as a general rule comply with the ordinary requirement of *cause*.

Company could claim that it only agreed to the modification under duress: Vito was already obliged to work for a definite term at a certain salary and might have threatened to quit unless he received more. It is unlikely to succeed because, as explained in discussing Case 9, French courts have taken a restrictive view of claims of economic duress.

Case 10(a) falls under the second of the exceptions to the special rule. The promise made subsequent to the contract to compensate the employee for staying is a modification of the contract. By this analysis, Vito could argue that he was entitled to the *quid pro quo* contractually agreed upon. If Company refused to pay him, he would be entitled to specific enforcement of the promise or damages, which would amount to the same thing. It should be noted that the courts have no power to revise the amount contractually agreed upon as a *quid pro quo* for Vito agreeing to respect the restriction.

In Case 10(b), Company's promise to pay Vito a large sum of money upon his retirement may be subject to art. 931 of the Civil Code which provides that all gifts must be made in a notarially authenticated document or else are void (see Case 1). The case law generally requires that a promise to make a gift must fulfil the same formal requirements as the gift itself.[4]

There is a dispute among scholars over when a promise to make a contract requires a formality that the law prescribes for that contract itself. Some claim that the promise requires the formality whenever the contract requires it (*contrat solennel*). Others want to distinguish according to the main purpose of the requirement. According to them, the formality should be required only when its main purpose is to ensure that a party

---

[3] Article 1131 of the Civil Code states: 'An obligation without a *cause* or with a false or an illicit *cause* may have no effect.'   [4] Cour d'appel, Dijon, 26 April 1932, DH 1932, 339.

genuinely consented. They are correct that even if the formality some-times protects third parties, the essential reason for requiring it is to protect the donor. Therefore, it seems that the promise of a gift should observe the same formalities as the gift itself.

Nor can Vito claim that the promise falls within one of the exceptions which case law has recognized to the requirement of a formality: indirect or disguised gifts, and gifts made by actual delivery.

He may, however, argue that the promise made by Company is gratui-tous because Company meant to thank him for his previous services. In that case, the promise would not be simply one of a gift but one of a gift in compensation for something already received (*donation rémunératoire*). It is quite unclear, however, whether the moral interest in making com-pensation for services received would be deemed a *quid pro quo* so that the promise would no longer be subject to the requirement of a formality. This question is left by the *Cour de cassation* to be decided by the lower courts. One cannot, therefore, expect the decisions to be consistent. Nevertheless, in view of the significant sum of money involved, it is unlikely that the decision will be in Vito's favour.

Conceivably, the promise is one of payment in return for the services already received. If so, the contract is not gratuitous but onerous (*acte à titre onéreux*). Nevertheless, in order to be considered as a payment for the services rather than as a gift, the services previously rendered must be valued in money, and the amount of the gift must not exceed their value. This claim seems rather tenuous since Vito has already been properly remunerated for his services, and the sum is significant (one year's salary).

BELGIUM

The agreement in this case is an employment contract governed by the Law of 3 July 1978 on employment contracts (see arts. 3 and 7).

Normally, this type of contract expires at the end of the term of employ-ment agreed upon between the parties (art. 32). In Case 10(a), the employee may terminate the contract in advance to accept an offer of employment from a competing firm, provided he complies with art. 40 of the Law, which provides:

If the contract was entered into for a set term of employment . . ., the party who terminates the contract before its end, without serious grounds (*sans motif grave*), is required to pay the other an indemnity equal to the remuneration accruing to the end of the term of employment. This sum may not, however, exceed twice the amount of the remuneration corresponding to the length of the period of advance notice which should be respected had the contract been entered into without a set period of employment.

The length of the period of advance notice for a contract with no determined period of employment (*contrat à durée indéterminée*) depends on both the amount of the annual remuneration and the agreement struck between the employer and the employee (see art. 82). The period of advance notice will lie somewhere between four and six months. Thus, the indemnity could correspond to between nine months and one year of Vito's remuneration. It is also worth noting that the employee has an obligation to keep confidential (*obligation de confidentialité*) any secrets he may have been aware of in the course of his employment (art. 17). He also has an obligation not to compete (*obligation de non-concurrence*), the scope of which varies with the employment contract under consideration (arts. 65 and 86).[5] Consequently, Case 10(a) is unlikely to arise in Belgium. In any event, if Vito decided that it is advantageous to breach his contract and to pay the indemnity just described, nothing could prevent his employer from seeking to keep him working for Company. Company could therefore offer Vito extra money, but it would have to be careful that Vito cannot interpret this gesture as a salary increase which could be due to him for the rest of his contract.

In Case 10(b), the promise is to perform a typical natural obligation (*obligation naturelle*), here, to pay a pension not legally due (*pension extra-légale*) (see Cases 1 and 2). The employer's promise converts it into a civil obligation which is legally enforceable. Consequently, it will not be treated as a donation which would not be enforceable unless evidenced by a notarial document (*acte solennel*) (see arts. 931, 932, and 1339 of the Civil Code, and Case 1).[6] The case law has repeatedly held that the promise to pay a pension not legally due is the acknowledgment of a natural obligation and therefore a valid promise that the employer can be required to perform (*exigibilité*).[7]

THE NETHERLANDS

As noted in discussing Case 9, a contract which changes an existing contract is valid. So the promise to Vito is valid unless Vito threatened to quit

---

[5] See V. Vannes, *Le contrat de travail: aspects théoriques et pratiques* (1996), 291–4: for instance, looking for employment from a competing firm does not constitute a violation of this obligation not to compete.   [6] See Raucent, *Les libéralités* nos. 120–3.

[7] Liège, 27 June 1963, JL, 1963–4, 33; Trib. comm. Bruxelles, 14 March 1967, RPS, 1970, 123; Trib. comm. Bruxelles, 6 May 1971, JCB, 1971, I, 661; Bruxelles, 3 Jan. 1974, RW, 1974–5, column 671, and see Van Ommeslaghe, *Droit des obligations*, 362–3.

and work for the competitor unless he received more money. If he did, then the case would, in principle, be analysed in the same way as the previous one. The question is whether there was an abuse of circumstances or a threat. As before, a great deal depends on whether Company had an alternative.[8] However, the question whether the party who threatens not to perform abuses the circumstances may be answered differently because here the issue of personal freedom may play a role.

The promise in Case 10(b) is a 'remuneratory' gift.[9] Therefore, the formal requirements for gifts have to be met: the promise was binding only if it was made in a notarial document (art. 7A:1719 of the Civil Code).

It does not matter in either Case 10(a) or Case 10(b) whether Vito bought a vacation house he could not otherwise afford.

SPAIN

For the agreement to be enforced, there must be a *causa*. According to art. 1277 of the Civil Code, there is presumed to be a *causa*, and the party who wishes to escape from the contract has the burden of proving that one does not exist. If Company cannot prove that there is no *causa*, the court may consider that the promise was made *causa donandi* as a gift. If it does, then the promise is enforceable only if it meets the requirements for a donation (see Case 1).

A court might decide, however, that the promise was made *causa credendi* because Company made it to keep Vito from leaving the firm. There is *causa credendi* when the promisor hopes to get an advantage by making the promise.[10] The difficulty might seem to be that Vito had already agreed to work for Company for ten years. Nevertheless, Spanish law is very flexible, and it allows the employee to terminate such a contract at will (article 49(d) of the Law on Workers (*Estatuto de los Trabajadores*)). The reasons for this are that (1) the relationship is similar to slavery, and (2) unwilling employees are likely to be unproductive.[11] When an employee wants to terminate a ten-year contract before the time period ends, he is obliged to give notice to the employer. Despite the fact that art. 81 of the Law on the Contract for Labour (*Ley del Contrato de Trabajo*) and art. 1101 of the Civil Code allow the employer to sue for damages, in practice this right is seldom exercised and almost never granted by the courts. Since Vito does have a right to terminate the contract unilaterally, Company's promise to give him extra money if he stays does have a *causa*

---

[8] See also Tjittes, *De hoedanigheid van contractspartijen*, 84.
[9] See Asser/Hartkamp vol. II, no. 68.   [10] Díez Picazo, *Fundamentos de Derecho*, vol. II, 146.
[11] J. Lluis and Navas, *Manual de derecho laboral* (1975), 257.

credendi.[12] Consequently, if Vito stays, the promise is enforceable without meeting the requirements for a donation. Vito can claim damages under art. 1107 of the Civil Code.

In Case 10(b), however, where Vito is about to retire, if Company has promised him money merely to thank him for past services, the promise would be made *causa donandi*.

PORTUGAL

Company is not obliged to keep this promise unless it was made in a written document. Nevertheless, it may have incurred pre-contractual liability. If so, the fact that Vito bought a vacation house may be relevant to the losses he suffered for which Company must compensate him.

According to Portuguese law, this kind of promise would be considered a *doação remuneratória* which is defined by art. 941 of the Civil Code as a donation to compensate the recipient for services provided to the donor for which the donor was not legally obligated to pay. Article 88 of the Labour Contract Statute (*Lei do Contrato de Trabalho*) makes it clear that this kind of donation is not deemed to be part of the wages paid for labour unless it is made regularly.

Therefore, such promises are subject to the normal rules of donation: the sum of money must be actually delivered or the promise must be made in a written document (art. 941 of the Civil Code).

However, as in Case 1, if the contract is void, there may be pre-contractual liability (art. 271 of the Civil Code). Pre-contractual liability is based on the indefinite concept of the breach of a duty of good faith which gives the judge a free hand in deciding cases. In my view and that of other scholars,[13] it is sufficient for liability that a party makes a promise knowing that the other party will rely on it. It is sufficient that the party relying on the promise believes that it will be kept even if he knows it is not legally valid.

ITALY

Company is obligated by its promise in Case 10(a) and probably in Case 10(b) as well. It does not matter if Vito, relying on the promise, has already bought a vacation house he could otherwise not afford.

---

[12] G. Igelmo and A. Jose, *Curso de derecho del trabajo* (1991), 501. TS, 30 Sept. 1975 emphasizes that if the promisee wants to enforce a promise on the grounds of the existence of a *causa credendi*, the promisor must have received the expected advantage.

[13] See Cordeiro, *Da Boa Fé no Direito Civil*, 1243 ff.

A contract obligating Vito to continue working for a period of ten years would definitely be void under Italian labour law. That being so, Company's promise in Case 10(a) would be binding because Company clearly has an economic interest in making it: keeping its valuable employee, giving him a new incentive to work better, and not losing him to the competitors.[14]

Employees stand high in the courts' favour, and so Company's promise in Case 10(b) would probably be enforced as well. The case law does not consider such a bonus promised out of good will to be a gift.[15]

It is worth noting, however, that this situation is quite unusual. I cannot exclude the possibility that the courts would consider such an informal promise to give, based on the services rendered by Vito in the past (*causa praeterita*), to be a 'remunerative gift' (see Case 2). If so, the promise would be unenforceable due to the absence of the formalities required to make a donation binding. Even if it was considered a 'liberality according to usage' (*liberalità d'uso*) (art. 770(2)) (see Case 2), delivery would still be required;[16] a mere informal promise would probably not be considered legally binding.

AUSTRIA

The promise will be binding unless Company can avoid the contract under § 870 of the Civil Code on the grounds of threat in the manner described in discussing Case 9.[17] There are, however, no indications that Vito threatened Company in any way.

The promise does not constitute a gift. As the promise is part of an existing contract, its main purpose is to compensate for services rendered and to motivate the promisee to render the services in the future to the full satisfaction of the promisor. In Austrian law, in such cases, the promisor is deemed not to intend to make a gift (he has no *Schenkungsabsicht*).[18] If, for example, the employer voluntarily increases the salary of the employee, he does not make a gift[19] since the increase is made as a compensation for the services rendered. This is the prevailing view even

---

[14] Close to the point are: Cass. civ., 3 Dec. 1988, no. 6567 (*Tozzi c. Ist. federale credito agrario Italia centrale*); Cass. civ., 25 June 1986, no. 4230 (*Soc. Travertino toscano c. Inail*).

[15] See Cass. civ., 23 Nov. 1984, no. 6053 (*Inps c. Fossi*); Cass. civ., 25 June 1986, no. 4230 (*Soc. Travertino toscano c. Inail*); Cass. civ., 19 July 1983, no. 4986 (*Beccari c. Banca Naz. Agr.*); Cass. civ., sez. lav., 26 March 1994, no. 2968 (*Inps c. Soc. Kodak*), in Foro it. I (1995), 819.

[16] See the discussion of Case 2.   [17] See Case 9.

[18] See G. Schubert in Rummel, *ABGB* § 938 no. 4; SZ 56/30; JBl 1984, 495; SZ 58/209; JBl 1986, 323.   [19] GlU (NF) 4753.

though, according to § 940 of the Civil Code, a gift that has the purpose of rewarding another person for his merits is a genuine gift (*belohnende Schenkung*). According to the prevailing view, § 940 of the Civil Code should be interpreted to apply only if the promisor acts purely out of generosity and with the intention to make a gift. This intention, it is said, is missing when, for example, a salary is increased. Therefore, in Case 10(a), the promise is not a gift, and it will be valid regardless of the form in which it was made.

In Case 10(b), the connection with the services provided by Vito is weaker than in Case 10(a) because Vito is going to retire. There is no connection with future but only with past services. Austrian courts nevertheless consider such payments to be part of the salary rather than gifts even though there is no legal or contractual obligation to make them.[20]

GERMANY

In Cases 10(a) and 10(b), whether the promise is enforceable depends on the question whether the contract to pay the money is a gift or not. If it were a gift, the promise would have to be made formally through a notarial document (§ 518 of the Civil Code) (see Case 1).

A promise made by an employer to pay money to his employee is not a gift even if the employer is not under a legal obligation to make the payment and even if the employee is to receive the payment after his retirement. The reason for this rule is that the payment is closely related to the employee's normal compensation and to the employer's loyalty to him.[21] For example, in one case,[22] the court enforced a promise made by an employer to give a certain amount of red wine per month to an employee after his retirement. It denied that the promise was in the nature of a gift. In another case,[23] the highest German court for tax matters, the *Bundesfinanzhof*, regarded an annual payment on an employee's birthday as part of his income for tax purposes and not as a gift. Therefore, Company's promise was not a gift and it is valid even without the formality.

It does not matter if Vito relied on receiving the extra amount promised.

It does matter if the promise was made because Vito threatened to break his employment contract. If so, the promise could be voidable because the threat is unlawful (see Case 9).

---

[20] ArbSlg 5836 and 7285; JBl 1935, 168; JBl 1959, 218 (the promise of payments to the widow of a deceased employee is not a gift!).   [21] BAG NJW 1967, 2425.
[22] BAG JZ 1956, 322.   [23] NJW 1967, 1776.

GREECE

In Case 10(a), Company's promise to Vito of an extra amount of money is considered to be a supplement to his salary (art. 361 of the Civil Code) which will be governed by the provisions that concern the payment of salaries.[24] If Company refuses to keep its promise then Vito can, *inter alia*: (1) use the special procedure of art. 663 of the Code of Civil Procedure to sue the company for his salary with interest; (2) immediately terminate his fixed term labour contract and ask for compensation.[25]

In Case 10(b), Company's promise is considered to be one dictated by a special moral duty[26] since Company has no legal obligation. It does not have to pay any compensation to him because of his retirement since his contract is of a fixed term.[27]

Company is obliged to keep its promise if the parties, knowing that there was no legal obligation, intended to conclude an agreement for a donation dictated by a special moral duty. As has already been explained in discussing Case 2, the promise of a donation dictated by a special moral duty is valid even if no notarial document has been executed.[28]

If, however, the intention of the parties was not directed to the conclusion of a contract then Company's promise is not enforceable. It is considered to give rise only to a natural obligation.[29] Nevertheless, Company may be liable for its pre-contractual conduct if all the requirements for pre-contractual liability are met (see Case 1). If so, it would be liable to the extent of Vito's negative or reliance interest.[30]

SCOTLAND

As Case 10(b) appears to be a gratuitous unilateral obligation, Company will have to perform its promise if it is constituted in writing in terms of s. 1(2) of the Requirements of Writing (Scotland) Act 1995.[31] Vito may not require written proof as Company may be seen to have made the promise in the course of its business in terms of s. 1(2)(a)(ii) of the 1995 Act (see Case 4). Section 1(3) and (4) of the 1995 Act will also be applicable if Vito bought the house in reliance on Company's promise, and they are aware of this

---

[24] For the meaning of the term 'salary' and the different kinds, see A. Karakatsanis, *Individual Labour Law*, 2nd edn (1988), 191–200; Goutos and Levendis, *Labour Legislation*, 130–79.   [25] Goutos and Levendis, *Labour Legislation*, 170.

[26] M. Stathopoulos in Georgiadis and Stathopoulos, *Civil Code*, art. 906, no. 7.

[27] Z. Zerdelis, *The Law of the Renunciation of the Labour Contract* (1995), 602 ff.

[28] See case 2.   [29] A. Ligeropoulos, *The Law of Obligations* (1960–8).   [30] See Case 1.

[31] See Case 1.

(see Case 1). Vito will then be able to establish the promise by any available evidence in the unlikely event that the court took the view that the promise was not made in the course of Company's business. In Case 10(a), if the payment is made in the course of his employment to prevent him from leaving, then the promise is non-gratuitous as Company will receive the benefit of Vito continuing to work for them, and therefore it need not be established in writing. Even if Vito threatened to leave, the variations would not be challenged on the grounds of economic duress.

ENGLAND

The status of the promise in Case 10(a) is not clear in English law, but the promise in Case 10(b), on the facts as stated, is unenforceable.

Under the traditional approach to contractual variations, the first promise to pay Vito a higher wage is unenforceable because, *inter alia*, in so far as Vito is doing anything in return for the promise, it is only that which he is already contractually obliged to do. On the traditional approach to consideration, doing that which you have a legal obligation to do is not consideration.

But as noted in the previous answer, the 'pre-existing legal duty' rule was overturned in *Williams v. Roffey Bros. & Nichols (Contractors) Ltd*,[32] and replaced by a rule holding that the consideration requirement can be satisfied by the performance of a pre-existing legal duty so long as the pro-misee receives a 'practical benefit'. It is not clear, however, whether the *Williams* ruling would be extended to the facts of Case 10(a) (there are no cases directly in point). The first difficulty is that whether or not Vito con-tinuing to work is a practical benefit to Company, it is not clear that Vito had promised to continue to work 'in exchange' for Company's promise of higher pay. On the facts, it appears that Vito did nothing; he was merely informed of the promise to pay more. This difficulty is avoided if it is found that Vito had in fact agreed to work in exchange for the offer of higher pay.

The second problem is how to find a practical benefit accruing to Company without at the same time finding that Vito implicitly or expli-citly threatened to breach his contract. A threat to breach in these circum-stances, given that Vito was capable of performing the contract, would amount to duress, as explained in the previous answer. Yet it seems clear

---

[32] [1991] 1 QB 1.

that Company is getting a benefit only if there is a risk of Vito breaching. The question, then – a difficult one – is whether the mere risk of such breach amounts to an implicit threat of breach. In theory, at least, there is a distinction between the risk of breach and making a threat to breach. Thinking about making a threat to breach, or simply thinking about quitting full stop (either of which Vito might have been doing at the relevant time) is not the same as making a threat to breach. Thus, a court might reason, first, that Company received a practical benefit from its promise because the chance of Vito going elsewhere was reduced (presumably it will be costly if Vito quits) and, second, there was no duress because Vito had not threatened to quit, explicitly or implicitly.

In the end, I think the distinctions being drawn here are sufficiently fine that external considerations are likely to play a role in the court's reasoning. In particular, Vito's reliance, though strictly speaking irrelevant, would, it is suggested, sway a court towards upholding the contract. But the result cannot be predicted with certainty.

The second promise, to pay Vito a thankyou bonus on his retirement, is unenforceable for lack of consideration (see Case 1). Vito did not do or promise to do anything in return for the extra money. Although there are no cases directly analogous, the orthodox rules would appear to apply fairly clearly to these facts.

In respect of either promise, whether or not Vito relies is strictly irrelevant, because, as explained in regard to Case 1, while detrimental reliance can sometimes be used to give force to a promise that is raised in defence against a claim by the promisor, it cannot be used to found a cause of action on a promise. That said, it is possible, as ever, that a sympathetic court might be able to find ordinary consideration for these promises, and such sympathy is more likely in a case where the promisee has relied. In respect of the second promise, the court might try to argue that Vito had, for example, agreed not to compete in the future or had agreed to retire early. The courts' general willingness to enforce such promises is seen in the enforceability of retirement payments that are made conditional on the employee not competing in future against the employer.[33] The non-competition clause is held to be consideration for the promise, although it seems clear that the clause is a condition of the payment, not the reason for it. As Atiyah observes, the 'pension is not offered in exchange for the employee remaining inactive'.[34]

---

[33] E.g., *Wyatt* v. *Kreglinger* [1933] 1 KB 793.   [34] Atiyah, *Law of Contract*, 124.

IRELAND

Taking the circumstances of Case 10(a) first – Company's promise to pay a large sum during Vito's term of employment because he received an offer of alternative employment – the question of whether the company is obliged to keep this promise again depends on whether the Irish courts would follow the traditional approach of *Stilck* v. *Myrick*[35] or the new approach in the *Williams*[36] case, as described in Case 9 above. Following the traditional approach, the discharge of his existing contractual duty by Vito would not constitute sufficient consideration for Company's promise and it would not be obliged to keep the promise. However, applying the *Williams* approach one could say that Company would derive a benefit by securing Vito's continuing performance of his contract as opposed to losing him to a competitor, and that this would suffice to provide consideration for Company's promise. There is no issue of duress here as there is no threat by Vito to break his existing contract. One way around this problem would be for the parties to discharge the present contract by agreement and to make a new contract incorporating the promise by Company to pay the extra large sum. The agreement to discharge raises no difficulty as regards consideration, for in such a case each party agrees to release his rights under the contract in consideration of a similar release by the other. It seems likely that an Irish court would uphold such an approach.

Turning then to Case 10(b) (Company's promise of a 'golden handshake' payment as thanks for services rendered), in general Irish law follows the English approach and holds that a promise is not binding if the sole consideration is past services previously rendered by the promisee. Such a promise will be binding only if some consideration other than the past service has been provided by the promisee, such as his giving up rights which are outstanding under the original contract, or his promising or performing some other act or forbearance not due from him under the original contract. In the present case none of these elements appear to be present and Company would not be obliged to keep the promise of the golden handshake payment. In another case the additional consideration might consist of some small undertaking by the retiring employee, such as to retire early or not to compete with the company after his retirement. There is no Irish authority on the point but this is the accepted view among Irish lawyers.

---

[35] [1809] 2 Camp. 317.   [36] [1991] 1 QB 1.

Whether it matters if Vito has already bought the vacation home depends on the possible application of the doctrine of promissory estoppel. The conditions for this doctrine have been described above in the answers to previous cases. One particular condition is that the promisee cannot use the doctrine as a sword as well as a shield: see *Combe* v. *Combe*[37] in this regard. Therefore, in the present case Vito's purchase of the vacation house would give rise to no cause of action on his behalf.

Summaries

France: In Case 10(a), where Vito was paid more to induce him to stay, relief would be given for duress if the threat is illegitimate and induced Company to consent, but a court is unlikely to do so since French courts have been hesitant to consider economic pressure to be duress. Absent duress, the promise would be enforceable as, under French labour law, agreements by an employee restricting his freedom to change employment are enforceable if they are reasonable in time and space, and serve a legitimate interest of the employer.

In Case 10(b), the promise may be invalid as a gift which lacks the required formalities. It would be enforceable only if it were considered a gift in compensation for past services – *donation rémunératoire* – or an actual payment for past services, which is unlikely.

Belgium: Case 10(a) is not likely to arise in Belgium because the employee is under an obligation not to compete after his employment ends. Under Belgian labour law, however, the employee may terminate his employment before the end of the term agreed upon if he pays a certain indemnity. Since Vito is free to leave if he pays the indemnity, the employer may promise extra compensation if he does not.

In Case 10(b), the promise is enforceable even absent a formality because it is a promise to pay a natural obligation.

The Netherlands: As in Case 9, the promise in Case 10(a) is valid unless procured by an 'abuse of circumstances' or a threat. In either case, the question is whether the employer had a reasonable alternative. In this case, however, the court is less likely to give relief because there is an issue of personal freedom.

In Case 10(b), the promise is unenforceable because it is a 'remuneratory gift' which requires the same formalities as other gifts.

Spain: In Case 10(a), Spanish labour law gives an employee the right to

---

[37] [1951] 2 KB 215.

terminate his employment before the time agreed upon, and while the employer has a right to sue for damages if he does, this right is almost never recognized by the courts. Since Vito therefore has the right to leave, the employer's promise is valid if it is made *causa credendi* to induce him to stay.

In Case 10(b), the promise is made *causa donandi* and therefore it is not valid without the formality required for a gift.

Portugal: The promise is not enforceable because it is a gift and such promises must be made in writing. Nevertheless, if Vito has relied on the promise, there may be pre-contractual liability for violation of good faith since a promise was made and then broken knowing the promisee might rely on it.

Italy: In Case 10(a), the original promise to work for ten years would be void under Italian labour law, and so Company's promise to induce him to stay would be valid.

In Case 10(b), the promise would probably not be considered a gift and so would be enforceable without a formality because Italian courts favour employees. Possibly, a court might consider it a 'remunerative gift' (one for past services) which does require the same formality as other gifts.

Austria: In Case 10(a), the promise will be enforceable unless it can be avoided for duress, which is unlikely since there is no indication that Vito actually threatened Company. The promise is not a gift since the employer will not be deemed to have acted purely out of generosity. Therefore the promise is enforceable without the formality required for a gift.

In Case 10(b), the promise is enforceable without a formality because it will be deemed to be part of Vito's salary rather than a gift even though it is connected only with his past services.

Germany: In Case 10(a), the promise will be voidable for duress if Vito threatened to break his employment contract. Otherwise, it and the promise in Case 10(b) will be enforceable. Such promises are not deemed to be gifts even if made after retirement because they are related to the employee's normal services and the employer's loyalty to him.

Greece: In Case 10(a), the promise is enforceable since it will be considered a supplement to Vito's salary.

In Case 10(b), the promise is enforceable even absent a formality since it is deemed a promise to perform a special moral duty.

Scotland: In Case 10(a), if the payment is made to prevent Vito from leaving, it is not gratuitous. Even if Vito had threatened to leave, the threat does not constitute duress.

In Case 10(b), the promise is gratuitous but enforceable absent a writing because it was made in the course of business. If Vito bought a house, it is also enforceable because he relied on it.

England: In Case 10(a), it would once have been said that there is no fresh consideration. Recently, however, it has been held that there is consideration for a promise if the promisor receives a 'practical benefit' even if the benefit is the performance of a pre-existing legal duty. Here, Company gets a practical benefit if the increase in pay keeps Vito from leaving, and yet, if Vito had threatened to leave, the threat would constitute duress. A court might decide that Company did receive this practical benefit, and that there would be duress only if Vito actually threatened to leave. Vito's reliance on the promise might influence what a court did.

In Case 10(b), the promise is unenforceable since Company did not receive a practical benefit.

Ireland: In Case 10(a), it would once have been said that there is no fresh consideration. Recently, however, an English court held that there is consideration for a promise if the promisor receives a 'practical benefit' even if the benefit is the performance of a pre-existing legal duty. This decision may not be followed in Ireland. If it were, a court might decide that the Company did receive a practical benefit by inducing Vito to stay. A court would not find there to be duress because Vito never threatened to leave. Even if the traditional approach were followed, the parties could make the new promise binding by first agreeing to discharge the existing contract and then agreeing to make a new one.

In Case 10(b), the promise is unenforceable because it lacks consideration. It could be made binding by having Vito promise some small undertaking in return, such as to retire early or not to compete with the company.

Preliminary comparisons

In one jurisdiction, Portugal, the reporter believed that the promise in Case 10(a) is not enforceable though there may be a remedy for violation of good faith. In all other jurisdictions, the reporters thought it would be enforceable. In three cases, the reason was that the initial promise to work for a fixed term was either invalid (Italy) or one which the employee was entitled to break though he would then be liable for an indemnity (Belgium) or for damages which, as a practical matter, the employer could not recover (Spain). The two common law reporters noted that at one time, the promise would have been unenforceable because it lacked consideration, but under the new English approach, which may be followed in

Ireland, it will be enforceable because the employer received a 'practical benefit'. The Irish reporter observed that the parties could get around the traditional approach by first agreeing to cancel their contract and then agreeing to make a new one. In Italy, Belgium, and Spain, duress was not an issue because the employee had the right to leave. In Scotland, it was not because threatening to leave would not constitute duress. Elsewhere, it was not because Vito did not threaten to do so.

The promise in Case 10(b) would be considered a gift and therefore unenforceable without the required formalities in France, the Netherlands, Spain, and Portugal, although in Portugal there may be a remedy for violation of good faith. The promise would be unenforceable for lack of consideration in England and Ireland. It would be considered gratuitous in Scotland but nevertheless enforceable because it was made in the course of business (and even if it were not, if it had been relied upon). It would be enforceable as a promise to fulfil a natural or moral obligation in Belgium and Greece. It would be enforceable in Austria and Germany because it would be considered part of, or linked to, the employee's past services. In Italy, it would be treated as a gift if it were regarded as payment for past services, but the Italian reporter believes a court would enforce it because Italian courts favour employees.

Case 11: promises to do more than was agreed; promises to waive a condition

Case

Contractor, a construction company, agreed to build an office building for Realty, a real estate company. According to their agreement, Contractor was to receive a fixed amount 'which shall be due after an architect appointed by Realty certifies that the building is finished according to the specifications' contained in the contract. While the building was under construction, Contractor promised, without demanding or being offered additional payment, to install more expensive glareproof windows than the specifications called for. Some time later, Realty promised that Contractor would be paid without seeking an architect's certificate. Are either of these promises binding? Would it matter if Realty had already advertised the glareproof windows, or Contractor had already covered over portions of the building the architect would have needed to inspect, before the other party threatened not to keep its promise?

Discussions

FRANCE

Once a contract exists, as a general principle under art. 1134 of the Civil Code, it cannot be modified unilaterally. However, French law recognizes that a party can agree to modify the contract in his sole interest, provided that the conditions for the formation of a contract are satisfied. Whether they are is a question of fact which is within the absolute authority of the trial courts.[1] In our view, the oral promises here would be enforceable.

---

[1] Terré, Simler, and Lequette, *Les obligations* no. 118, p. 103; Ghestin, *Traité de droit civil* no. 406, p. 363 (see Case 2).

They may be considered to be unilateral offers to modify the contract. They must be accepted, and, as a general rule, silence does not amount to acceptance. But the case law recognizes an exception where, as here, the offer is made in the exclusive interest of the party who is silent.[2] Such an offer is deemed to be accepted tacitly.

Moreover, the courts would take into account the way in which Realty reacted after the windows have been installed, and Contractor reacted after the announcement that an architect's certificate would no longer be required. If Realty had included the modifications in its advertisements and if Contractor had covered over portions of the building which should have been inspected, it means that they each accepted the other contracting party's offer upon which they had reasonably relied (*confiance légitime*).

BELGIUM

While this case may raise problems under the Anglo-American doctrine of consideration, it does not in Belgian law. As long as the two promises were made freely and accepted, they are binding. The only possible problem with regard to Realty's promise is that it will have no effect if it is interpreted as a waiver of the warranty of hidden defects in the building (*garantie des vices cachés*).

THE NETHERLANDS

Both promises are binding. As in Case 9, the principle of freedom of contract permits the parties to change their contract. Of course, the promisor must have intended his promise to be legally binding (art. 3:33 of the Civil Code) or the promisee must have justifiably understood it to be so (art. 3:35).[3]

The promise in Case 11(a) may also be regarded as a unilateral promise (*eenzijdige toezegging*). However, that term is usually used for promises, especially by public authorities, in situations in which there is no contract between the parties. In any event, the result would not be much different since it is held that, in so far as possible, the same rules should be applied to unilateral promises as to contracts.[4] Many of the same rules necessarily apply because Title 3.2 (including arts. 3:33 and 3:35 of the Civil Code) governs both unilateral promises and contracts.

---

[2] Req., 29 March 1938, DP 1939, I, 5 (solution applied in relation to a waiver of debt).
[3] See Case 4 for the text of these articles.   [4] Asser/Hartkamp vol. II, no. 84.

The promise in Case 11(b) resembles a renunciation (*kwijtschelding*). In the new code, a renunciation is a contract, albeit with a specific rule which makes the acceptance of a gratuitous renunciation easy (art. 6:160 of the Civil Code).[5] Nevertheless, a renunciation involves the extinction of an obligation, and one cannot really speak of one in this case.

If the promisor did not intend his promise to be legally binding, it might matter if Realty had already advertised the glareproof windows, or Contractor had already covered over portions of the building the architect would have needed to inspect, before the promisor threatened not to keep his promise. These facts may be relevant for establishing whether he is bound on the basis of art. 3:35 of the Civil Code (reliance principle). It provides that a party is bound, not only to what he intended, but to what the other party could reasonably think he meant.

Moreover, because of these facts, the promisor may also be estopped from claiming that he is not bound (*venire contra factum proprium*) under art. 6:2(2).

SPAIN

As in Case 9, since the promises modify a previous contractual obligation, their enforceability depends on whether they qualify as novations. Novations are mentioned in art. 1156 of the Civil Code and governed by arts. 1203–13. A novation requires *animus novandi*.[6] This requirement means that a party must express his will to replace one obligation with another or to modify an existing obligation.

In addition, following art. 1203 of the Civil Code, a novation must modify an obligation, which means that the novation must change its object or conditions, or the debtor or creditor. As we saw in discussing Case 9, a mere change in the amount owed has been thought to be insufficient. Nevertheless, Contractor's modification of its obligation by promising to install glareproof quality in windows is enforceable as a novation that makes an objective modification. It changes the object of the prior obligation: one thing (lower quality windows) is replaced with another (glareproof ones).[7] Realty's modification of its obligation by promising to

---

[5] Article 6:160 of the Civil Code: '(1) An obligation is extinguished by a contract between creditor and debtor whereby the creditor renounces his claim. (2) An offer to renounce gratuitously, addressed by the creditor to the debtor, is deemed accepted when it has come to the attention of the debtor and he has not rejected it without delay.'

[6] Castán Tobeñas, *Derecho civil*, vol. III, 438; Díez Picazo, *Fundamentos de derecho*, vol. II, 796.

[7] See Castán Tobeñas, *Derecho civil*, vol. III, 441.

pay without an architect's certificate is also enforceable as a novation of conditions of the obligation.[8] It replaces one conditional obligation (paying if the architect approves) with an unconditional obligation (paying).

Since the novations establish new contractual obligations, it does not matter whether or not Contractor had covered portions of the building or Realty had advertised the glareproof windows before the other party refused to fulfil its obligations as modified.

It also does not matter that the novations may increase the burden of the contract to one of the parties without any increase in compensation. In one decision of the *Tribunal Supremo*[9] a tenant rented a shop and then received the landlady's permission to modify the lease so as to permit installation of a chimney. When the chimney needed repairs, the landlady refused to pay on the grounds that she should not have to do so for something that was not included in the lease in the first place. The Court held that she must make the repairs because there had been a 'transformation of the space from one for mercantile use into one for mercantile and industrial use; which constitutes an essential modification of the primitive obligation and, hence, a novation'. The landlady was therefore required to make repairs by art. 107 of the Law on Urban Leasing (*Ley de Arrendamientos Urbanos*) and art. 1554(3) of the Civil Code.

PORTUGAL

The promise of Contractor is binding whether or not Realty had already advertised the glareproof windows. The promise of Realty is not binding. However, the fact that Contractor had already covered over portions of the building the architect would have needed to inspect can be a cause for frustration of the right of inspection without liability for Contractor.

The contract here is one to do a job (*contrato de empreitada*). As mentioned in Case 9, it is possible for both parties to modify any contract by agreement (art. 406(1) of the Civil Code). Therefore, if Realty accepts the promise of Contractor, Contractor would be obligated to install more expensive glareproof windows whether or not Realty relies on that promise.

Nevertheless, Realty's promise to pay Contractor without an architect's certificate is not binding because it is illegal. The completion of work done under a contract to do a job must always be verified by an expert (art. 1218 of the Civil Code). The right of inspection can be exercised by the party

---

[8] See Puig Brutau, *Fundamentos de derecho civil*, vol. I-2, 467 and Díez Picazo, *Fundamentos de derecho*, vol. II, 793.   [9] TS, 24 April 1959.

itself or by an expert acting on its account. The waiver of that right is not permitted, so an agreement in which the parties agree that they will not inspect is illegal. A promise such as this one which is against the law is void (art. 294 of the Civil Code).[10]

The fact that Contractor had already covered over portions of the building the architect would have needed to inspect does not make the promise binding. It can, however, be a reason why the right of inspection has been frustrated and is therefore lost. The only way Realty could exercise this right would be to insist that part of the work already done by Contractor be destroyed. That would be regarded as an abuse of right because Realty, by making the promise, caused the work to be completed before it was inspected. Therefore, according to the doctrine of the abuse of right expressed in art. 334 of the Civil Code, the right of inspection would be lost as to the portions of the work already covered over.[11]

ITALY

Both promises are binding. It does not matter if Realty had already advertised the glareproof windows, or Contractor had already covered over portions of the building the architect would have needed to inspect, before the other party threatened not to keep its promise. In such a situation, modifications of the original contract such as Contractor's promise and waivers of right such as Realty's promise are not examined by the courts in isolation. They are evaluated as part of the whole contractual agreement so that the question whether there is a *causa* is asked of the transaction as a whole.[12] In the Italian legal system, viewing the transaction in this way is a matter of established doctrine.[13]

The enforceability of both modifications and waivers is governed by art.

---

[10] See Lima and Varela, *Código Civil Anotado*, vol. II, 759.

[11] According to legal scholars, in a situation like this *venire contra factum proprium*, or going back on your word, can constitute an abuse of right. See Cordeiro, *Da Boa Fé no Direito Civil*, 742 ff.

[12] See L. Moscarini, 'Rinunzia (diritto civile)', Enc. giur. Treccani, 27 (1991), 5; M. Giorgianni, 'Causa (diritto privato)', Enc. dir. (1960), 565

[13] See e.g., L. Vacca, 'Causa e contratto nella prospettiva storico-comparatistica', *Atti del IIIo convegno internazionale ARISTEC* (1997); G. Venezian, 'La causa dei contratti', in *Opere giuridiche*, vol. I (1919); G. Astuti, 'Contratto', Enc. dir. 9 (1961), 780; G. Astuti, *I contratti obbligatori nella storia del diritto italiano*, vol. I (1952); M. Bessone, *Adempimento e rischio contrattuale* (1969); C. Massimo Bianca, *Diritto civile*, vol. III, *Il contratto* (1984), 419; L. Bigliazzi Geri, U. Breccia, F. D. Busnelli, and U. Natoli, *Diritto civile*, vol. III, *Obbligazioni e contratti* (1989); I. Birocchi, *Causa e categoria generale del contratto* (1997); E. Roppo, *Il Contratto* (1977); E. Roppo, 'Contratto', in Digesto (1989), 90; R. Sacco, 'Il Contratto', in Vassalli, *Tratt. di dir. civ.* 6:2 (1975), 595.

1333 of the Civil Code.[14] Provided that they burden only the promisor, both types of promises are irrevocable as soon as they come to the knowledge of the promisee. They are legally binding with no need for an express or implied acceptance by the promisee unless they are rejected within the time limit that is customary or appropriate given the nature of the transaction.

AUSTRIA

Both promises are binding. They will not be considered to be gifts. As they are made within the context of a contractual relationship they are not made with the intention to make a gift. They will rather be considered as modifications to the original contract. As they are not gifts, the form requirement does not apply. It does not matter whether Realty has already advertised the glareproof windows or whether Contractor has covered over portions of the building.

GERMANY

If the promises were accepted by the other party, they are both binding because a contract which modifies an already existing contract is not a gift even if only one party makes a promise in the new contract. Additional compensation is not required. A contract that modifies another contract is regarded as a revaluation of the original contractual duties. Its connection with these duties is deemed to be ongoing. The courts do not look at the promise modifying the contract in isolation.[15] Therefore, the formalities that § 518 of the Civil Code requires for gifts are not necessary (see Case 1).

It does not matter whether the other party has changed his position in reliance on the promise.

GREECE

Contractor and Realty entered into what is termed a contract for work. Such a contract is governed by arts. 681–702 of the Civil Code. It is a

---

[14] Article 1333 of the Civil Code: 'Contract binding on offeror only: An offer for the purpose of forming a contract that creates obligations only for the offeror is irrevocable as soon as it comes to the knowledge of the party to whom it is directed. The offeree can reject the offer within the time requested by the nature of the transaction or by usage. In the absence of such rejection the contract is concluded.'

[15] BGH NJW-RR 1986, 1135.

reciprocal contract by which the contractor undertakes the obligation to complete a work and the other contracting party, the commissioner of the work, is obliged to pay the agreed remuneration (art. 681 of the Civil Code).[16]

The remuneration is payable on completion of the work unless the parties agree otherwise: for example, on pre-payment or payment by instalments. The parties may, however, agree that the fee will be paid under the condition that the commissioner of the work approves it (art. 201 of the Civil Code).[17]

Provided that they have both consented, the parties are bound by the changes in the terms of their original agreement: that Contractor would do some additional work without further remuneration or that the fee is payable regardless of the architect's approval (art. 361 of the Civil Code). Moreover, here it would be contrary to good faith to threaten not to keep such a promise after the advertisement of the windows or the covering of portions of the building so that the architect cannot inspect them.[18]

SCOTLAND

If they are regarded as gratuitous unilateral obligations, s. 1(2) of the Requirements of Writing (Scotland) Act 1995[19] provides that both promises will be binding and enforceable if constituted in writing. However, as has been noted above, s. 1(2)(a)(ii) dispenses with this requirement where the promise is made in the course of the promisor's business, and therefore it is likely that either side will be able to establish the promise in question by any available evidence.

The requirement that the promise be constituted in writing will also be unnecessary if there has been a change of position in reliance on the promise which is known to the other party. This will give rise to a plea in terms of s. 1(3) and (4) of the 1995 Act (see Case 1). The unilateral gratuitous promise is valid even though it is not constituted in writing.

ENGLAND

It is reasonably clear in English law that the promise by Contractor to install more expensive windows is unenforceable regardless of whether Realty relied in some way. The reason is that Realty did not do or promise to do anything in exchange for Contractor's promise, hence the promise

---

[16] A. Kardaras in Georgiadis and Stathopoulos, *Civil Code*, arts. 681–702; Stathopoulos, *Contract Law*, 226.   [17] AP 1274/1993 HellD 37 (1996), 147.   [18] *Ibid.*   [19] See Case 1.

lacks consideration (see Case 1). Realty's possible reliance on Contractor's promise is in principle irrelevant since, while induced detrimental reliance on a promise can give rise to certain obligations under the doctrine of estoppel (see Case 1 and below), this is the case only where the promise is raised in defence to an attempt to enforce a pre-existing legal duty or right. Estoppel cannot be used to create a cause of action where none existed before, as would be required here. As discussed elsewhere, courts sometimes invent consideration where there has been reliance upon an apparently gratuitous promise. Thus, a court might find, for example, that Realty's advertisement of the glareproof windows was of benefit to Contractor and, furthermore, was given in exchange for Contractor's promise to install the windows. Such a conclusion seems unlikely on the facts, but it is possible.

The second promise, that Contractor would be paid without the architect's certificate, is clearly enforceable if Contractor has relied on the promise and probably enforceable even if Contractor has not relied. As with the first promise, there is no consideration for Realty's promise not to require an architect's certificate, and thus, according to the ordinary understanding of the consideration requirement, the promise is unenforceable. And if Contractor has not relied on the promise, estoppel is not a possibility (see Case 1). Nevertheless, even in the no-reliance situation Contractor may be able to enforce the promise by using the concept of waiver. A 'waiver' is said to occur when one party agrees to forgo rights owed to him or her.[20]

There is little consensus on the meaning of waiver, its juristic foundation, or its legal consequences;[21] and many commentators and courts now regard it as virtually indistinguishable from estoppel (see Case 1).[22] Certainly, waiver and estoppel are closely related. Under the doctrine of waiver, a party who has agreed or promised to forgo his rights cannot reassert those rights without giving reasonable notice.[23] Thus, like estoppel, waiver is used as a defence to an attempt to reassert pre-existing legal rights. The usual case of waiver is where a buyer has agreed that delivery may be made later than the date specified in the original contract. The buyer may not change his mind and demand delivery at the original date without giving reasonable notice, and then only if the seller has not relied on the new agreement. In the case now under consideration, the

---

[20] Waiver also has other meanings in other contexts, but we can ignore these for our purposes.   [21] See, e.g., *The Kanchenjunga* [1990] 1 Lloyd's Rep. 391.

[22] See, e.g., *Prosper Homes v. Hambro's Bank Executor & Trustee Co.* [1979] 39 P & CR 395, 401.

[23] See Treitel, *Contract*, 98.

promisee, Contractor, did not rely upon the promisor's promise to forgo his rights. This suggests the promise is not binding. But against this conclusion is the fact that no notice was given prior to Contractor's completion of its part of the contract. Thus, it is arguably too late for Realty to reinvoke the original agreement. As Treitel notes, where 'the varied performance is actually made and accepted, neither party can claim damages on the ground that performance was not in accordance with the contract'.[24] For example, a seller who delivers late at the buyer's request is not liable if the buyer has accepted delivery. It is not entirely clear what is the equivalent to acceptance of goods in the case under consideration (the reported cases nearly all deal with variations regarding delivery of goods), but it is suggested that a court would likely hold that acceptance had occurred if everything under the contract was done save for obtaining the architect's certificate. Thus it seems possible that, even where there is no reliance, Realty may not be able to go back on its promise not to seek this certificate.

Where Contractor has relied on Realty's promise, Realty is liable if it breaks the promise. Realty is liable under the doctrine of either waiver or estoppel. As noted above, where a party agrees to forgo rights, as Realty has done, that party cannot go back on its word without giving reasonable notice and then only if the other party has not yet relied on the forbearance. Similarly, under the doctrine of estoppel (see Case 1), a party who has induced another party to alter its position detrimentally through a representation that she would not enforce her strict legal rights is estopped from going back on her word. The requirements of estoppel would appear to be met in this case, the reliance requirement being satisfied by Contractor covering up some of the work. Estoppel is being used as a shield, not a sword, because it is raised as a defence against Realty's attempt to reassert its original rights – the pre-existing legal relations – in full.

Note that, as discussed in more detail in the next answer, it might be argued that Contractor should not be able to use estoppel to enforce the promise *qua* promise, but should be limited instead to a claim for damages incurred in reliance on the promise (which would be difficult to assess, though it might be less than the value of the promise). An English court, however, is unlikely to pursue this line of argument (see Case 12), and in practice will almost certainly simply bar Realty from demanding the certificate before payment.

[24] *Ibid.*, 99.

IRELAND

It is necessary to look at the two promises separately, as they would be classified in a different manner under Irish law. The promise by Contractor would be classified as a variation of the agreement made wholly for the benefit of one party, Realty. Under Irish law such a variation requires consideration and in the present case Realty has provided no consideration and the promise by Contractor is not binding.[25]

The promise by Realty that Contractor would be paid without seeking an architect's certificate would be classified under Irish law not as a variation, but as a waiver or forbearance. Under this doctrine a promise by a party to relinquish some or all of his rights under a contract may amount to a waiver of those rights. If, by words or conduct, a party has agreed or led the other party to believe that he will accept performance of an agreement in a different manner from that provided in the contract, he will not be able to refuse that performance when tendered. A waiver is distinguishable from a variation of a contract in that there is no consideration for the forbearance moving from the party to whom it is given.[26] The party granting the forbearance may, however, be entitled upon reasonable notice to require the other party to comply with the original mode of performance, unless in the mean time circumstances have so changed as to render it impossible or inequitable so to do. In the present case, therefore, Realty's promise may be binding, but this will depend upon the circumstances which arise following the waiver. This will be dealt with further below.

Whether it matters that Realty has acted to its detriment in advertising the glareproof windows depends on the possible application of the doctrine of promissory estoppel, the conditions for which were set out in discussing Case 1. Once again, a limiting condition is that the promisee cannot use the doctrine as a sword as well as a shield, to confer a cause of action where none existed before. Therefore in the present case Realty's actions in advertising the glareproof windows would give rise to no cause of action on its behalf.

It would matter if Contractor had already covered over portions of the building the architect would have needed to inspect, before Realty threatened not to keep its promise regarding payment without an architect's certificate. As described above, a party may waive a term of the contract regarding the mode of performance and he may be bound by such a waiver. He may be entitled, upon reasonable notice, to require the other

---

[25] See Clark, *Contract Law*, ch. 18.   [26] *Chitty on Contracts*, ch. 22.

party to comply with the original mode of performance, unless in the mean time circumstances so change as to render it impossible or inequitable so to do. In the present case Contractor has acted on the basis of Realty's promise to make payment without seeking an architect's certificate. Circumstances have so changed following the waiver by Realty of the architect's certificate requirement as to render it inequitable to permit Realty now to require Contractor to comply with the original requirement. In the circumstances, Realty would not be permitted to repudiate the waiver and rely on the original term of the agreement.

Summaries

France: Both promises are enforceable. They are unilateral offers to modify the contract in the other party's favour which are enforceable when the other party accepts, which he may do tacitly or by changing his position in reliance.

Belgium: Both promises are enforceable.

The Netherlands: Both promises are enforceable.

Spain: The promises are valid as novations. As already noted (Case 9), the *causa* of a valid novation is the modification of the former obligation. Here, unlike in Case 9, the content of the obligations has changed. It does not matter that the burden to one party has increased without any increase in compensation.

Portugal: The promise to install the glareproof windows is enforceable. The promise to pay without an architect's certificate is not, since it is illegal to dispense with an inspection. Nevertheless, the owner cannot demand an inspection after the area in question has been covered up since that would be an abuse of right.

Italy: Both promises are enforceable because modifications of a contract and waivers of contractual rights which only burden the promisor are binding without acceptance as soon as they come to the notice of the promisee.

Austria: Both promises are binding, and will be considered to be modifications of the original contract rather than gifts.

Germany: Both promises are binding if accepted because they are not considered to be gifts but a revaluation of the original contractual duties.

Greece: Both promises are binding.

Scotland: Both promises are binding because, even if they are gratuitous, they are made in the course of business. They would also be enforceable if the promisee changes his position in reliance on them.

England: The promise to install the windows is not enforceable because it lacks consideration. The promise not to require an architect's certificate is enforceable if Contractor relies on it, and perhaps if it does not, because it is a 'waiver', and therefore does not need consideration.

Ireland: The promise to install the windows is not enforceable because it lacks consideration. The promise not to require the architect's certificate is enforceable if Contractor relies on it. It does not need consideration because it is a 'waiver'. If Contractor has not relied on it, then Realty can revoke it.

Preliminary comparisons

In all civil law jurisdictions except Portugal, both promises are enforceable. In Portugal, the promise to pay without an architect's certificate is not enforceable because it is illegal to dispense with an inspection, although, if the area in question has been covered up, to demand an inspection is an abuse of right. In all civil law jurisdictions except Scotland, the promises are not considered to be gifts. In Scotland they are enforceable anyway because they were made in the course of business (and would be enforceable even if they were not if the promisee relied upon them).

In England and Ireland, the promise to install the windows is unenforceable because it lacks consideration. The promise not to require an architect's certificate is enforceable if the promisee relies upon it because it is a 'waiver' which does not need consideration. If the promisee does not rely, then Realty will be able to revoke it in Ireland and may be able to do so in England.

Case 12: promises to take less than was agreed

Case

Realty, a company dealing in land, leased space to Travel, a travel agency, for ten years at a fixed monthly rent. One year later, Travel's business fell off because of an economic recession. Realty agreed that Travel could pay half the agreed rent for the duration of the recession. Two years later, when the recession ended, Realty demanded that Travel pay the remainder of the originally agreed rent for the previous two years. Can it recover that amount from Travel?

Discussions

FRANCE

Whether Realty will recover half the rent in arrears for two years from Travel depends on how the agreement reached by the parties is construed. The parties have clearly reached an agreement. The question is, what exactly have they agreed? It is assumed that no variation to the lease has been made, since a lease must be modified in writing (law of 6 July 1989). Either they agreed to cancel Travel's obligation to pay the full rent during the recession or they agreed to postpone the date at which it is to be paid. In the first case, the agreement would be characterized under French law as the waiver of a debt (*remise de dette*), and in the second, as an extension of the term.

Waiver of a debt is governed by arts. 1282–8 of the French Civil Code. If the new agreement waives a part of the debt under scrutiny (half of the previously agreed rent, as long as the recession will last), then there is no way that Realty will be allowed to recover the money at some point in the future. That part of the debt is now extinguished. However, it boils down to a question of evidence. Can Travel prove that this is what Realty actually agreed to do? Under French law, there is insufficient evidence to conclude that Realty has expressly agreed to waive the debt. Travel can probably only claim that Realty tacitly agreed to do so. Construing the promise this way will prevent Realty from reneging on it. But trial judges are very wary of finding that there was tacit consent. They are not likely to find that there was an intention to extinguish a debt or waive a right in the absence of clear terms. In such cases, consent must be unambiguous[1] since French law follows an unwritten rule that waiving or renouncing a right cannot be presumed. The case law therefore requires that the creditor express an unequivocal desire to release the debtor.[2] Tacit acceptance by the debtor may indicate his agreement that the debt is waived, but it is unlikely that such an agreement can be inferred from a creditor's silence. Alternatively, the parties may merely have agreed that the term of the debt has been extended, that is, that the time for paying the rent due under the original contract has merely been postponed. In that event, the contested part of the debt is not cancelled but cannot be claimed for the duration of the recession. At the end of the recession, Travel will have to pay both the full amount of the rent and the part of the arrears outstanding from the recession. Such an agreement to postpone payment of a debt is called in French law a clause 'for the return of better fortune' (*clause de retour à meilleure fortune*).

Once again, characterizing the content of the agreement is a question of fact left to the trial judges to decide. In the absence of clear language, the courts must examine the parties' intentions, which is a factual issue. The *Cour de cassation* refuses to intervene in such matters. If, on the contrary, the contract were very clear about what the parties meant, the question of which way to characterize their agreement – as a waiver of the debt or extension of the term – would be regarded as one of law, and, consequently, one which the *Cour de cassation* would review.

One might add that even if the agreement is interpreted as the extension of a term, the promisee could still claim more time to pay if the promisor unexpectedly asked for immediate payment. The idea is not exactly the same as estoppel under English law, but may amount to the same thing. Although the promisee cannot escape the debt, under art. 1244 of the Civil Code he may ask for more time to pay (*délai de grace*), or under art.

---

[1] Req., 12 Dec. 1904, S. 1905, I, 321, DP 1906, I, 163.
[2] See, e.g., Versailles, 20 May 1994, RTDCiv. 1994, 863, note J. Mestre.

1134 he may claim that the promisor acted in bad faith by asking for the entire amount in arrears at once. The promisor may therefore recover the amount in arrears but not if he behaves unreasonably.[3]

BELGIUM

By agreeing that Travel can pay half the agreed rent for the duration of the recession, Realty waived a debt (*remise de dette*) (arts. 1282–8 of the Civil Code). In this type of contract, the debtor's consent will often be tacit. Since the debt is waived gratuitously it could constitute a donation but only if the donor acted *animus donandi*, with the intention of benefiting another (*l'intention libérale*). That intention is absent if, as here, the creditor waives part of the debt in order to preserve the greater part of it. In any event, even if it were a donation, it would not have to be evidenced by a notarial document (*acte solennel*) (see art. 931 of the Civil Code) since it would constitute a *donation indirecte* (see Case 1). The waiver of a debt extinguishes the obligation.[4] Realty could not recover the amount waived unless Travel later promised to pay that amount on its own initiative, thereby acknowledging a natural obligation (see Case 3).

THE NETHERLANDS

Realty cannot recover from Travel. It has renounced its right to the amount of rent originally due. Article 6:160(2) of the Civil Code provides: 'An obligation is extinguished by a contract between creditor and debtor whereby the creditor renounces his claim.'[5] Renunciation in the sense of this article may also consist of renunciation of part of a claim.[6] A gratuitous renunciation is not a gift if, as seems to be the case here, the party who renounces does so because he hopes the other party will recover and be able to pay his remaining debts: in this case, the full rent for the next seven years.[7] If, however, the renunciation here was a 'material gift' it would still not be a 'formal' one, which means that a notarial document would not be required.[8]

---

[3] Com., 7 Jan. 1963, Bull. civ. IV, no. 16, p. 14; Civ. 3, 8 April 1987, Bull. civ. III, no. 88, p. 53.

[4] On waiver of a debt, see Van Ommeslaghe, *Droit des obligations*, 1100–3.

[5] See also section 2: 'An offer to renounce by gratuitous title, addressed by the creditor to the debtor, is deemed accepted when it has come to the attention of the debtor and he has not rejected it without delay.'   [6] See Asser/Hartkamp vol. I, no. 618.

[7] *Ibid.*   [8] *Ibid.*

SPAIN

Realty has granted Travel a tacit remission of the debt. Article 1156 of the Civil Code provides: 'Obligations are extinguished: (1) by payment or performance, (2) by loss of the thing owned, (3) by remission of the debt, (4) by confusion of the rights of the obligor and obligee, (5) by compensation, (6) by novation.'

Scholars distinguish between remission (*condonación*) and *pactum de non petendo*.[9] In the latter case, the creditor agrees not to require the payment of the debt only while certain circumstances are present.

According to the Civil Code, remission may be express or tacit. If express, then it must meet the requirements of a donation (art. 1187(2): see Case 1) and therefore it must be accepted. On one occasion the *Tribunal Supremo* held that both the promise and the acceptance must be in writing[10] in order to meet all the requirements for a donation. On another occasion, it held that a debt was cancelled by a remission made by one party only and not in writing.[11] Most scholars think the *Tribunal Supremo* was mistaken in the former case and right in the latter.[12] The reasoning is that, if tacit remission is allowed (art. 1177), it does not make sense to require written form in case of an express remission. Article 1280, which requires all contracts of more than 1,500 pesetas in value to be in writing for purposes of proof, will apply to this remission (see Case 13).

Although a remission is usually an act of liberality, made *causa donandi*,[13] some scholars say that the remission is of 'abstract nature', that is, it has legal effect even without a *causa*. For example, it would be effective even if the person remitting the debt did not intend to enrich the debtor (as he would in an act of liberality) but did so to avoid the hassle and expenses that would come with a lawsuit,[14] or if he did not claim the debt because he forgot or because it is such a small amount that it is not worth it to him.[15] In one decision, the *Tribunal Supremo* agreed.[16] The buyer of a new house remitted the seller's obligation to deliver the house free of

[9] Puig Brutau, *Fundamentos de derecho civil*, vol. I-2, 434.   [10] TS, 24 Oct. 1955.
[11] *Ibid.* See below.   [12] Puig Brutau, *Fundamentos de derecho civil*, vol. I-2, 438.
[13] *Ibid.*, 368.   [14] Pérez and Alguer, *Anotaciones*, vol. I, 366.
[15] In a case cited in discussing Case 9, the court refused to enforce an agreement that was ambiguous but which the debtors claimed had reduced the amount they owed from 50,000 pesetas to 25,000 pesetas. TS, 17 March 1933. In that case, there was no remission because there was no *causa liberatoria* or intention to relieve the other party of part of his obligation. It is true that the authors just cited contend that a remission need not have a *causa*. But they have in mind cases in which the creditor was oblivious or in which he decided that collecting the debt was not worth it.   [16] TS, 24 Oct. 1955.

tenants. Later he changed his mind and asked the seller to get rid of a tenant. The court held that the remission was valid although it was not in writing and was without apparent *causa donandi* or intention to confer a liberality. The buyer had allowed the tenant to stay and continue to use garage space because the tenant happened to own another house in which the buyer himself was a tenant, and so he was looking after his own interests.

PORTUGAL

Realty can recover the unpaid rent from Travel unless the parties have agreed to extinguish the debt or to a modification of the contract. Whether they have is not clear.

According to art. 863 of the Civil Code, the creditor can always extinguish his claim by a contract with the debtor. Such a contract is called a remission (*remissão*). If the remission were done with the intention of acting out of liberality, the transaction is considered a donation (art. 863(72)), and it would have to be contained in a written document. Here, however, Realty was not acting with such an intention. Therefore, it would not be able to recover that amount.

The situation might also be considered as a conditional modification of the lease by agreement of the parties. According to art. 406 of the Civil Code, the parties can always modify the contract if they both agree. If they have, Realty cannot rely on the initial contract.

It is possible, however, that the agreement between Realty and Travel should be construed, not as one to reduce the amount of rent due, but as one not to claim the amount due until Travel is in a position to pay. In this case the duty to pay the other part of the original rent remains as an obligation *cum potuerit*. According to art. 778(1) of the Civil Code, it can be claimed only if the creditor proves that the debtor is able to pay.

Thus the solution of this case depends on a question of fact as to how the agreement between Realty and Travel is interpreted.

ITALY

If the judge determines that Realty meant to reduce the rent and not merely to accept partial payment, reserving its right to receive full payment at a subsequent time, Realty cannot recover the remainder from Travel. The question is one of interpretation to be resolved by the rules provided by arts. 1362–71 of the Civil Code.

As already explained (Case 11), waivers of a contractual duty are enforceable even if they advantage only the other party. Their enforceability is said to follow from the principle of freedom of contract. As noted (Case 12), Realty's promise will not be considered to lack a *causa* because the judge will examine it not in isolation but as part of the entire rental agreement.

AUSTRIA

Realty cannot recover the amount from Travel. The agreement constitutes a relinquishment (*Verzicht*, see Civil Code § 1444) of the claim for half of the rent. According to § 939 of the Civil Code, such a relinquishment is not a gift. Therefore, the form requirement does not apply.

Nevertheless, the result would be different if the agreement were interpreted merely to defer payment. Then Realty would not have lost its right to be paid. Whether such an interpretation is warranted would depend on the circumstances of the case and the formulation of the promise. In case of doubt, § 915 of the Civil Code would apply. According to this provision, if a unilateral promise is unclear it is to be assumed that the promisor wished to incur a smaller rather than a larger obligation. With respect to the present case, that would mean that the promise would have to be interpreted as deferring payment without relinquishing the right to it.

GERMANY

As in Case 11, the promise to change the amount due per month is not considered to be a gift. Therefore, it is binding without the formalities that gifts require (see Case 1).

Realty's claim, however, depends on how the modification is interpreted. It may be just a deferment of payment. In this case Realty would be able to recover the money. But it may be interpreted as a partial renunciation of the rent.

According to § 157 of the Civil Code, the interpretation of a contract depends on good faith and the *Verkehrssitte*, which is defined by the courts as the actual beliefs and customs of daily life of the group involved in the contractual relation in question.[17] The purpose of the interpretation is to determine what the parties objectively willed, or, if they did not take the

---

[17] RGZ 55 (1904), 375 (377).

point in question into consideration, to find out what kind of agreement reasonable people would have made (*ergänzende Auslegung*).[18] All of the circumstances of the case have to be taken into account, but if there are no contrary indications, it is more likely that the parties intended to defer payment because people are not expected to act altruistically in a business relationship.

Although there is no authority on this point, there are provisions in the Civil Code that reflect the same idea. Sections 612, 632, and 689 provide that certain kinds of contracts are presumed to be made in return for compensation, even if the contract does not mention it, when the service in question is not normally performed free of charge. Here, it is unlikely that Realty wanted to renounce its claim forever even if Travel's economic situation improved.

GREECE

Realty's agreement that Travel could pay half the agreed rent for the duration of the economic recession is valid by virtue of the principle of freedom of contracts (art. 361 of the Civil Code).

If Realty had expressly reserved its right to recover the other half of the rent originally agreed after the end of the economic recession then Realty would be able to do so. If it did not do so expressly, then the agreement must be interpreted in accordance with arts. 173 and 200 of the Civil Code. Article 173 provides: 'When interpreting a declaration of will, the true intention shall be sought without adhering to (the literal meaning of) the words.' Article 200 provides: 'Contracts shall be interpreted according to the requirements of good faith taking into consideration business usage.'

The question, then, is what the parties intended, taking into account good faith and usage. If the parties did not understand the same thing, then the meaning prevails which the declarant expected that the recipient could and should have understood.[19] Accepted views on business transactions would play a role but the specific circumstances and the capabilities of the parties would be crucial.[20]

Consequently, in the present case, Realty would not be entitled to recover the amount from Travel.[21]

---

[18] BGHZ 9 (1953), 273 (278).
[19] Stathopoulos in Georgiadis and Stathopoulos, *Civil Code*, art. 173, no. 8; art. 200, no. 11; AP 269/72, NoB 20, 1025.   [20] Stathopoulos, *Contract Law*, 125–9.
[21] The proper application of the rules of interpretation is subject to judicial control. *Ibid.*

SCOTLAND

By s. 1(2)(a)(i) of the Requirements of Writing (Scotland) Act 1995,[22] 'a contract or unilateral obligation for the creation, transfer, variation or extinction of an interest in land' must be constituted in a written document. This applies to leases of more than a year: s. 1(7). The original lease must be in writing. The variation of the lease must be in writing whether it be regarded as a contractual variation or as a unilateral obligation on the part of Realty to forgo half the rent. It is then a matter of construction to determine the extent and duration of the variation. It would appear that Realty will not be able to recover the amount in question as they contracted to the effect that payment of that amount was no longer due, that is, no longer due for the extent of the recession. After the recession, the original rent is due for the remainder of the lease.

ENGLAND

It is clear in English law that, despite the apparent lack of consideration for its promise to reduce the rent, Realty cannot recover the remainder of the original rent owed. The example is almost identical to the leading case of *Central London Property Ltd* v. *High Trees House Ltd*,[23] where it was held, in similar circumstances, that the landlord could not go back on his representation to reduce the rent. The legal basis of the *High Trees* decision is the doctrine of promissory estoppel, which, as already discussed (see Case 1), holds that if A induces B to alter his position detrimentally by a representation that A will not enforce her strict legal rights, A is then estopped from going back on her word. The primary limitation on the scope of estoppel – that it may be used only as a defence to a cause of action – is not a barrier here because the promise would be raised as a defence against Realty's attempt to enforce in full the original agreement.

It should be noted that while the result here is clear because of the precedent of *High Trees*, in *High Trees* itself the court did not discuss whether the tenant had in fact relied nor whether the tenant should be able to rely on the defence of estoppel only to the extent of his reliance. It may have been assumed that substantial reliance had occurred or it may have been thought that the extent of reliance was irrelevant. The latter point is significant because there is no consensus (but also relatively little discussion)

---

[22] See Case 1.   [23] [1947] KB 130.

in English law as to whether estoppel is an alternative to consideration for the enforcement of promises or whether it is a non-contractual doctrine concerned solely with protecting people who have been induced to rely upon representations, whether promissory or otherwise, and hence closer to tort.[24]

It is generally assumed that if the latter interpretation is correct, then the remedy should be limited to compensating the representee to the extent that he has relied. The English cases are not clear on what remedy – reliance or the value of the promise – is appropriate where estoppel has been raised. Thus, while I think it is clear that, because of the strong similarity between the example and *High Trees*, Realty will be unable to claim back any of the remainder, it is possible that were similar facts put into a different setting Travel might be limited to enforcing Realty's promise only to the extent that it had relied on that promise.

Case 12 would almost certainly be decided using estoppel, but it should be mentioned that in light of the ruling, in *Williams* v. *Roffey Bros. & Nichols (Contractors) Ltd* (discussed in Case 9),[25] that performance of a pre-existing legal duty is good consideration if of practical benefit, Travel could also argue that, by not breaking the lease, it provided consideration for Realty's promise (see Case 9). If this argument were successful, Realty could enforce the variation as a binding contract.

IRELAND

Realty will be unable to recover the extra amount of rent from Travel, despite the absence of consideration for its promise to accept half the agreed rent for the duration of the recession. This result flows from the doctrine of promissory or equitable estoppel which has been endorsed by the Irish courts.

In the case of *Hughes* v. *Metropolitan Railway Company*[26] Lord Cairns stated that where a promise by a contracting party has the effect of leading the other party to suppose that the strict legal rights arising out of the contract will not be enforced and will be kept in suspense, the party making the promise will not be allowed to enforce those rights where it would be inequitable, having regard to the dealings which have thus taken place between the parties. In *Central London Property Ltd* v. *High Trees House Ltd*[27] (hereinafter 'the *High Trees* case'), Denning J stated *obiter* that he would

---

[24] See Atiyah, *Law of Contract*, 137–41.   [25] [1991] 1 QB 1.   [26] [1877] 2 App. Cas. 43.
[27] [1947] KB 130.

apply Lord Cairns' principle to hold the landlord estopped from going back on a promise to reduce the rent for a given period. Denning J indicated that in his view the proper principle is that 'a promise intended to be binding, intended to be acted on, and in fact acted on, is binding so far as its terms properly apply'. He added that the logical consequence was that a promise to accept a smaller sum in discharge of a larger sum, if acted upon, is binding notwithstanding the absence of consideration.

In the Irish case of *Kenny* v. *Kelly*,[28] Barron J approved of the decision in the *High Trees* case and the principle of promissory estoppel laid down by Denning J. In the present case Realty has made a promise intended to be binding, intended to be acted upon by Travel, and Travel has in fact acted upon the promise by making the part payment of the rent. Therefore the facts of this problem come within the principle of promissory estoppel and Realty would be unable to recover the extra amount of rent.

While the outcome of this problem is clear on the facts presented, one might mention that there are some doubts concerning possible limitations on the principle of promissory estoppel which have arisen in later English cases. One such limitation is the principle that promissory estoppel is a shield not a sword: see the earlier discussion of Case 1. In the present case Travel is using the doctrine as a shield to resist a claim rather than as a sword to advance a cause of action.

A further possible limitation concerns whether the promisee must show detrimental reliance, by having acted on the promise to his detriment. Treitel[29] points out a perceived difficulty about the *High Trees* case, in that a tenant who is contractually bound to pay a particular rent for a given period suffers no 'detriment', in the sense in which that word is used in the law of estoppel, by paying half that rent for part of the period. However, there is no requirement of 'detriment' mentioned in the *High Trees* case itself and it does not, at least not yet, form part of the promissory estoppel doctrine in English or Irish law.

Summaries

France: If the agreement is interpreted to cancel the debt rather than postpone the time it is due, Realty cannot recover. In case of doubt, courts will interpret it as a postponement.

Belgium: The agreement is valid without a formality because it is a waiver of a debt.

---

[28] [1988] IR 547.   [29] See Treitel, *Contract*, ch. 3.

The Netherlands: The agreement is valid without a formality because it is the renunciation of a claim.

Spain: The agreement is probably valid without a formality because it is the remission of a debt. Even though express remissions must meet the same requirements as gifts, some courts (though not others) have held that while the remission must be accepted it need not be made with the same formalities as a gift, and that is the view of most scholars. In any event, here the remission was tacit, and therefore does not have to meet the same requirements as a gift. Moreover, some scholars believe that if the remission of a debt that is not made *causa donandi*, to benefit the other party, but in the creditor's own interest, it is no longer a gift but a promise with an 'abstract nature' that is enforceable without a *causa*.

Portugal: The agreement is valid as a modification of the original contract, and so Realty can recover if the promise is interpreted as a relinquishment of its claim but not if it is interpreted as a postponement.

Italy: As noted (Case 11), waivers of contractual rights that burden only one party are binding as soon as they come to the notice of the promisee, and so Realty cannot recover the rent provided its promise is interpreted as a waiver rather than a postponement.

Austria: The promise to relinquish a claim is not considered to be a gift, and therefore is binding without a formality. Consequently, Realty cannot recover unless its promise is interpreted as a postponement rather than a relinquishment of its claim. It would be interpreted as a postponement in case of doubt.

Germany: Realty cannot recover if its promise is interpreted as a reduction of rent rather than a postponement because, as noted earlier (Case 11), such promises are considered to be revaluations of the contractual obligations rather than gifts. In case of doubt, the promise would be interpreted as a postponement.

Greece: Realty is bound by its promise to reduce the rent unless that promise is interpreted as a postponement, which is unlikely.

Scotland: The promise should be interpreted as a reduction of the rent, not a postponement. Nevertheless, it is not enforceable because contracts to transfer interests in land must be in writing, including the modification of a lease.

England: The doctrine of promissory estoppel will prevent Realty from recovering the rent despite the lack of consideration for its promise.

Ireland: The doctrine of promissory estoppel will prevent Realty from recovering the rent despite the lack of consideration for its promise.

Preliminary comparisons

Assuming it is interpreted as a reduction in rent and not a postponement of the time it is due, the promise is valid in every jurisdiction except Scotland, where it would not be because it is a contract affecting an interest in land which, for that reason, must be in writing. In all the other civil law jurisdictions, the promise is enforceable because the reduction of a contractual claim is not considered to be a gift and therefore does not require a formality. In the two common law jurisdictions, it is enforceable under the doctrine of promissory estoppel even though the promisee seems to have done nothing in reliance except comply with his pre-existing contractual obligations.

Case 13: options given without charge

Case

Realty, a company dealing in land, was looking for a site for a new build-ing. It told Simon it might be interested in purchasing a lot that he owned, but that it would need time to conduct a study. Without charging any-thing, Simon promised that he would sell his land to Realty for a fixed price (a) if Realty chose to buy it at any time within the next month, (b) if Realty chose to buy it at any time within the next two years, or (c) when Realty completed its study of the land, unless, in its sole and absolute judgment, Realty thought the economic prospects were unsatisfactory, in which case Realty had the option to withdraw. Realty accepted. Is the promise binding? Does it matter if there was an abrupt rise in the market price, and Realty wants to buy the land, not for a building, but for immediate resale?

Discussions

FRANCE

We note at the outset that it does not matter if, because of an abrupt rise in the market price, Realty wants to buy the land, not for building, but for resale unless the purpose for which the land is bought was an essential element of the contract. We will not examine that possibility in any detail. Suffice it to say that, had the purpose of the sale been one of the determining factors which induced Simon to contract, he would need to prove that such a condition belonged to the parties' agreement (*dans le champ contractuel*). Even if he could do so, he would only be able to have the sale annulled on the ground of either mistake (*erreur*) (art. 1110 of the Civil

Code) or the absence of *cause* (art. 1131) if there was a mistake about the purpose of the sale or its achievement was impossible at the time the contract was made.

In both Cases 13(a) and 13(b), Simon has made a unilateral promise to sell (*promesse unilatérale de vente*) in favour of Realty. Although the promisee, Realty, has not undertaken to buy the land, Simon's unilateral promise gives it an option to do so within the time specified. The length of this period (one month or two years) makes no difference.

Simon could argue that the promise is not binding if Realty failed to comply with the registration requirements of art. 1840A of the *Code général des Impôts*, enacted as art. 7 of the *Loi de finances* of 1963. These provisions require that a unilateral promise of sale which is not made in a notarially authenticated document must be registered within ten days of its acceptance by the beneficiary. Simon could claim that the promise is void for want of registration. This argument may not succeed since registration formalities are primarily a protection against tax evasion, and this much-criticized provision has been interpreted restrictively. The case law has thus tried to ensure that this provision is not exploited by contracting parties who are acting in bad faith.[1] Moreover, in the case of an option, it has been held that the promise has not been accepted, in so far as these provisions are concerned, until the option is exercised.[2]

In principle, therefore, Simon's promise is binding. He cannot revoke it during the period of the option, and it is valid until the option period has expired. Nevertheless, the promisee cannot have it specifically enforced. Specific enforcement of a contract of sale is possible, but, if the promise is revoked before the option is exercised, a contract of sale has not yet been made. Moreover, the case law has held that a promise such as this one creates an obligation 'to do' something (*obligation de faire*) (see art. 1126 of the Civil Code). Promises 'to do' cannot be specifically enforced. Therefore, the promisee's only remedy would be to claim damages. This is a strict application of art. 1142 of the Civil Code which provides that 'every obligation to do or not to do (something) gives rise to a claim in damages in the event of breach by the promisor'. Thus, in a recent decision, the *Cour de cassation*[3] held that 'as long as the promisees of a promise to sell have not announced their decision to buy, the promisor's undertaking only constitutes an obligation to do, and the exercise of the option subsequent

---

[1] See, e.g., Civ. 3, 10 Oct. 1968, D 1969, 271.   [2] Civ. 3, 19 Oct. 1971, Bull. civ., no. 500.

[3] Civ. 3, 15 Dec. 1993, JCP 1995, II, 22366, note D. Mazeaud; Rép. Def. 1994, art. 35845, note P. Delebecque; RTDCiv. 1994, 588, obs. J. Mestre; confirmed afterwards, Civ. 3, 5 April 1995, Bull. civ. III, no. 101.

to the promisor's revocation excludes the possibility that the parties had the common intention of buying and selling'. Although this view has been received with almost unanimous disapproval by scholars, nevertheless Realty would have a great deal of difficulty in enforcing such a promise. If, however, Simon refused to sell after the option was exercised, Realty could claim specific performance.

Article 1589 of the Civil Code clearly states that a promise to sell is equivalent to a sale as long as the parties have agreed on the subject matter and the price. When a binding contract exists, normally the courts cannot interfere with the bargain. By way of exception, however, another remedy may be available to Simon. If he does not refuse to sell but wishes to contest the price for the sale because of the sharp rise in the market price (but regardless of the purpose for which Realty has bought), he may bring an action for rescission for *lésion*. Such an action may be brought if, because of the increase in market value, the contract price is less than seven-twelfths of the market value of the land.

The aim of the remedy of *lésion* is to protect sellers from making foolish sales. The drafters of the Civil Code considered that a person might be coerced into selling (though not into buying) when, for example, the parties are in a situation of inequality.[4] Nevertheless, the view of the case law is that *lésion* is an autonomous remedy which does not depend on proof of circumstances such as coercion or mistake that might vitiate consent (*vices du consentement*).[5] The time limit to bring an action for *lésion* is, as a general rule, two years from the date of the contract of sale. Moreover, the Law of 28 November 1949, which supplements art. 1675 of the Civil Code, provides that the date for evaluating the market price of the land is the date on which the sale is completed, that is, the day upon which the option is exercised.

The 1949 law increases the protection given to the seller. One might argue that it is consistent with the approach of the case law which distinguishes *lésion* from factors that vitiate consent.[6] Nevertheless, the fact that the date that matters is not that of the promise is an exception to the rule set out in art. 1589 of the Code that 'a promise of sale equals a sale'. Moreover, the 1949 law constitutes an exception to the hostility of French law to the theory of *imprévision*, since using the later date allows market fluctuations to be taken into account, and so ensures that the remedy is of genuine, rather than theoretical, value to the seller.

---

[4] Terré, Simler, and Lequette, *Les obligations* no. 295, p. 246; no. 299, p. 250.
[5] Req., 28 Dec. 1932, DP 1933, I. 87; Ghestin, *Traité de droit civil* no. 791, pp. 791 f.
[6] Flour and Aubert, *Droit civil* no. 252, pp. 171–2.

Whether Simon can keep the land thus depends on whether the option has been exercised. If not, the *Cour de cassation*[7] has held that the breach of an option contract (*contrat de promesse*) entitles the disappointed buyer only to damages and not to specific performance. If so, the seller has an action for *lésion*. Even if that action succeeds, Simon would still not be sure he could keep his land since, under art. 1681, the buyer can always take the land and pay its full value. If the buyer is willing to pay this amount, he can have the contract specifically enforced. If he is not, he can allow it to be rescinded.

In Case 13(c), the parties have made a bilateral contract to buy and sell (*promesse synallagmatique*). In exchange for Simon's promise to sell, Realty has promised to buy unless it considers that the economic prospects are unsatisfactory. Realty is the sole and absolute judge of whether they are or not. It may not be possible to make a valid contract subject to such a condition.

Under French law such a condition might be considered to be a condition within the power of a party (*condition potestative*) under art. 1170 of the Civil Code since the fulfilment of the condition (the decision to purchase) lies within the sole discretion of Realty. After carrying out the study, Realty is under no obligation to justify its refusal to purchase. Such a clause gives it a right to be released from the contract at will. Consequently, under art. 1174 of the Civil Code, the contract is void (see Case 8), and therefore Simon can refuse to sell the land.

It is undeniable that pre-sale contracts have their uses in view of the complicated nature of transactions involving the sale of land. Such contracts enable purchasers to ensure that they will be able to buy while they undertake various and necessary time-consuming formalities and enquiries. French law has offered much more protection to potential purchasers than, for example, English law which offers no protection whatsoever before both parties are committed. In France, this protection has been provided by the case law which has recognized the validity of promises to sell and gone well beyond anything originally envisaged by the Civil Code.

The most recent decisions of the *Cour de cassation* must be understood in the light of this effort to protect purchasers. The case law makes it quite clear that the security granted to future purchasers by unilateral promises is only partial. Although such a contract is binding, its breach only gives rise to a claim for damages.

There is a gulf between the approach of the case law and the opinion of

---

[7] Civ. 3, 15 Dec. 1993, JCP 1995, II, 22366.

legal scholars. They have claimed, first, that characterizing the promisor's obligation as an obligation 'to do' something is very dubious. Second, even if this classification were correct, it would not follow that breach of such an obligation only gives rise to a claim for damages. The only reason it does that is that art. 1142 has been interpreted restrictively by case law (see Case 7). Finally, the approach of the case law ignores the fact that the promisor has definitively consented to sell, and thereby confuses a mere offer, which may be revoked, with a promise which is binding as a contract.

BELGIUM

In Cases 13(a), 13(b), and 13(c), the agreements are options to buy (*promesse de vente*, *option d'achat*).[8] In the first two cases, the agreement is unilateral in the civil law sense: it imposes an obligation only upon Simon,[9] an obligation to sell which is held open for a set period of time. The third case is not clear. It could be a unilateral agreement. In that event, the fact that Realty can withdraw depending on its own judgment does not raise any particular difficulty since the unilateral promise to sell, by its very nature, obligates only the prospective seller and not the prospective buyer. Article 1174 of the Civil Code, which deals with purely potestative conditions, is therefore not applicable to it.[10] The clause allowing Realty to withdraw would then merely restate its right not to exercise the option if it does not choose to do so. Alternatively, the agreement could be bilateral: Simon undertakes to sell and Realty undertakes to buy upon completion of the study. In this case, the fact that Realty can withdraw depending on its own judgment might be a purely potestative condition, that is, a condition that allows one party to determine whether a contract is binding. If so, the

[8] See arts. 1589 f. of the Civil Code and see De Page, *Traité élémentaire*, vol. IV, nos. 240 f.; P. Harmel, *Répertoire notarial. La vente*, vol. VII, Part 1, *Théorie générale de la vente* (1985), nos. 70 f.

[9] See Case 1, for the description of the three types of promises to be distinguished in Belgian law: the mere offer, the unilateral promise (where only *one* of the parties obligates him or herself), and the bilateral promise (where the *two* parties undertake an obligation). The court will hold that its own decision shall have the same effect as the notarial formality when the effectiveness of the contract as to third parties depends on its formalization, as, for instance, when real estate is sold.

[10] Let us recall that art. 1174 of the Civil Code, which invalidates obligation subject to a purely potestative condition, clearly states that the rule applies only when the condition is purely potestative for the party who undertakes the obligation. It speaks of a potestative condition by the party committing him or herself. See Cass., 13 Oct. 1984, Pas., 1984, I, 151. *A contrario*, a purely potestative condition in favour of the party who is owed the obligation is valid. Trib. comm. Bruxelles, 8 June 1966, JCB, 1966, 248 and see Van Ommeslaghe, *Droit des obligations*, 762.

contract is void under art. 1174 of the Civil Code. But it is also possible that the court would apply art. 1157 which says that when a clause is susceptible of two possible interpretations (in this case, that the agreement is unilateral or that it is bilateral), one should favour the interpretation that enables the clause to have some effect rather than no effect.[11] In this case, the fact that the parties used the words 'promise' and 'option to withdraw' might lead the court to interpret the parties' language as an expression of their intent to have entered into an option contract, that is, a unilateral agreement to sell.

If the market price had risen sufficiently, there might be a right to relief for *lésion*. Such relief is given when the seller of real estate receives a price less than seven-twelfths of the market price (see arts. 1675 f.). The sale is then rescinded unless the buyer pays the difference between contract and market price. In an option contract, whether there has been a sufficiently great deviation between contract and market price is determined as of the time the option is exercised, not the time when the option contract was entered into.[12]

It does not matter whether Realty decides to buy the land for resale rather than for a building unless Simon manages to prove that the purchase of the site for a new building only was part of the essence of the contract and the reason (applying the doctrine of *cause*) that it was entered into.[13]

THE NETHERLANDS

The promise is binding in all three situations. Simon has made an irrevocable offer, and Realty's acceptance is sufficient to conclude a contract. Art. 6:219 of the Civil Code provides:

[11] See Van Ommeslaghe, *Droit des obligations*, pp. 220–1. According to the case law, the judge should prefer the interpretation that would uphold the validity of a clause. The *Cour de cassation* observed that, nevertheless, a judge is not *obligated* by art. 1157 of the Civil Code to choose an interpretation that will sustain a right or an obligation (Cass., 25 Sept. 1981, Pas., I, 158).

[12] See H. De Page in Meinertzhagen-Limpens, *Traité élémentaire*, vol. IV, nos. 396 f. (on rescission for *lésion* of the seven-twelfths in a contract for the sale of real estate generally), and, in particular, no. 406 (*lésion* of seven-twelfths in option contracts).

[13] See P. Van Ommeslaghe, 'Observations sur la théorie de la cause dans la jurisprudence et dans la doctrine moderne', note under Cass., 13 Nov. 1969, RCJB, 1970, 328 f.; P. A. Foriers, 'Observations sur la caducité des contrats par suite de la disparition de leur objet ou de leur causel', note under Cass., 28 Nov. 1980, RCJB, 1987, 74; X. Dieux, 'Les chaînes et les groupes de contrat en droit belge', in X. Dieux, *Les obligations en droit belge et en droit français: convergences et divergences* (1993), no. 5.

(1) An offer may be revoked, unless it includes a term for acceptance, or irrevocability results otherwise from the offer.

. . .

(3) A stipulation whereby one party binds himself to enter into a certain contract with another party at the latter's option is deemed to be an irrevocable offer.

If there had been no way to determine how long the offer would be irrevocable, things would have been different, but 'one month', 'two years', and 'the end of the study' are sufficiently certain.

Would the result be different if the option were for fifty years, and nothing were paid for it? At some point, would the contract be so unfair that the courts would interfere? That may well be the case. If the result is particularly unfair a court may find several ways out. First of all, it may look for factors which show that the offeror did not intend his promises to have this effect, and that the offeree was not reasonable to think so (arts. 3:33 and 3:35 of the Civil Code). In particular, the court may find that the time limit was not meant to make the offer irrevocable but merely to indicate when the offer would lapse if not accepted (that is, to fix a 'reasonable period': (art. 6:221(1)[14]).[15] Furthermore, the court may regard the attempt to hold the offeror to the offer as a violation of good faith, particularly if the offeree by his conduct has induced the offeror to think he is no longer interested in accepting the offer (*rechtsverwerking/venire contra factum proprium*).

It may matter if there was an abrupt rise in the market price, and Realty wants to buy the land, not for a building, but for immediate resale. In principle, the buyer's motive is not relevant, unless it is in some way incorporated into the offer. This is a matter of interpretation. Here there is no indication that the offer should be interpreted in this way. Nevertheless, because of the abrupt rise in the market price, it may be contrary to good faith to insist that the offer is irrevocable (art. 6:2(2) of the Civil Code). Whether it is depends on such circumstances as the characteristics of the parties, the circumstances in which the offer was made, and, especially, the period for which it was made. In particular, if there is an abrupt and unforeseen rise in the market price after a non-professional makes a gratuitous two-year irrevocable offer, it is likely to be contrary to good faith for the offeree to insist that it is irrevocable. If the option is considered to be a contract,[16] the same result can be reached on the basis of an

---

[14] Article 6:221(1) of the Civil Code: 'A verbal offer lapses when it is not immediately accepted; a written offer lapses when it has not been accepted within a reasonable period.'   [15] See Asser/Hartkamp vol. II, no. 146.   [16] *Ibid.*, no. 74.

unforeseeable change of circumstances (art. 6:258 of the Civil Code in connection with art. 6:216).

The phrase 'sole and absolute' judgment in itself does not exclude the applicability of the principle of good faith. The parties are not allowed to exclude the application of the provisions of art. 6:2 as such. However, such a clause will naturally have an influence on determining what good faith requires in the particular case.

It should be mentioned here that good faith (*redelijkheid en billijkheid*) in Dutch law is an objective standard. Subjective good faith ('I thought my conduct was right') is not an excuse for failing to meet this standard. Moreover, not any subjective bad faith violates this standard. Therefore, Realty would not necessarily violate good faith if it announced it was satisfied with the economic prospects for its new building when, in fact, it was dissatisfied, and merely wanted to take advantage of the increase in the market price to resell the land. Nor would it necessarily violate good faith in the reverse case in which the market value of the land falls if it decided to locate its building elsewhere where land is cheaper, and announced it was dissatisfied with the economic prospects of the location merely to escape its contract. Realty's subjective bad faith would not be decisive. What matters is the objective unfairness of its conduct. Since, as noted earlier, the motive of the buyer is irrelevant in principle, it is not in itself contrary to good faith to declare oneself satisfied when one really is not and vice versa, even assuming such conduct is subjectively dishonest.

SPAIN

This is a case of an enforceable unilateral promise. The parties have entered into an option contract. Spanish courts will enforce such a contract whether it was entered into in exchange for money or not.[17] A person who gives an option on his property and then sells it to another must pay damages.

All contracts of a value above 1,500 pesetas are required to be in writing for purposes of proof (art. 1280 of the Civil Code), but if they are not it does not mean that they do not exist.[18] They can still be proven by means of other types of evidence such as witnesses (art. 1248 of the Civil Code).[19]

An option on real property must be recorded in the Property Registry to affect the rights of third parties (art. 14 of *Reglamento Hipotecario*).[20] After

---

[17] Díez Picazo and Gullón, *Sistema de derecho civil*, 83.   [18] TS, 17 July 1956.
[19] Puig Brutau, *Fundamentos de derecho civil*, vol. II-1, 163.
[20] Castán Tobeñas, *Derecho civil*, vol. III, 543.

the option is registered, a third party will have the same obligations as the person who gave the option on it. One cannot register the option if the period within which it can be exercised is greater than four years (art. 14 of *Reglamento Hipotecario*).

As a general rule, all option contracts need to specify a term explicitly. If they do not, the court will set a term.[21] The party granting the option cannot be obligated indefinitely.

In itself, a change in the market price does not matter. Courts will follow the principle of *pacta sunt servanda* (see Case 8). Nevertheless, if Realty wants to buy the land not to develop it but to resell it, it is likely that the *Tribunal Supremo* would not enforce the contract on the theory that the original purpose of the transaction is no longer being achieved (*teoria de la base del negocio*). The leading case is its decision of 30 June 1948. The defendant had agreed to an option contract which would allow the plaintiffs to buy a piece of land which would provide their property with access to a public street. The plaintiffs sold their property but still wanted the defendant to sell his piece of land to them. The Court held that since the plaintiffs no longer owned their piece of land, the purpose of the contract no longer existed. Therefore the contract was not enforceable by the plaintiffs.[22]

PORTUGAL

In Cases 13(a), 13(b), and 13(c), the promise would be binding only if it were made in a written document signed by the promisor. The abrupt rise in the market price is not relevant.

This is a contract made by a unilateral promise because one of the parties promises to sell but the other does not promise to buy. According to art. 411 of the Civil Code, such a contract may be binding even if the promisor does not receive any money in return for his promise. But here the promise is to sell land, and that requires a public deed (art. 875), which means that the promise has to be made in a document subscribed to by the promisor in the presence of a notary (art. 410(2)). If such a document is issued, the promise is binding. Otherwise it is void.

An abrupt rise in the market price is relevant only if it is considered a change in circumstances. As noted in discussing Case 8, however, the change would have to be so great that the enforcement of the promise

---

[21] TS, 17 Nov. 1966 (term read into option for 300,000 kilos of olive oil which did not expressly set one), cited in Puig Brutau, *Fundamentos de derecho civil*, vol. III-3, 504.
[22] Díez Picazo, *Fundamentos de derecho*, vol. II, 887.

would be against good faith. A normal variation in the price of the land is therefore irrelevant. It does not make any difference what Realty intends to do with the land. The new owner always has the right to decide what to do with his property, and the previous owner is not entitled to say a word about it. The mere expectations of one of the parties are not relevant.

ITALY

Simon's promise would be considered binding in Cases 13(a), 13(b), and 13(c). It does not matter if there was an abrupt rise in the market price, and Realty wants to buy the land, not for a building, but for immediate resale.

In all three situations, the parties have entered into a gratuitous option contract which is governed by art. 1331 of the Civil Code[23] and by the case law which holds that such agreements are enforceable.[24]

Many scholars agree that they are.[25] Others say that an option must be paid for.[26] Otherwise, the option would amount to an offer which is irrevocable for a fixed time and which is governed by art. 1329 of the Civil Code.[27] Such an offer cannot be revoked provided that the intention to make the offer irrevocable is expressly stated. According to the case law,[28] setting a time limit for the validity of an offer (art. 1326 of the Civil

---

[23] Article 1331 of the Civil Code: 'Option: When the parties agree that one of them is to remain bound by his declaration and that the other has the power to accept or not, the declaration of the first is considered an irrevocable offer within the meaning of article 1329. If no time limit has been fixed for the acceptance, it can be established by the court.'

[24] See Cass civ., 6 May 1981, no. 1944, in Giust. civ. I (1981), 2272, with case-note by E. Perego, 'Trattative, proposta irrevocabile e patto d'opzione'.

[25] E. Gabrielli, 'Opzione', Enc. giur. Treccani (1990), 1–9; E. Gabrielli, Il rapporto giuridico preparatorio (1974); E. Perego, I vincoli preliminari e il contratto (1974); Ravazzoni, La formazione del contratto, I (1966).

[26] R. Sacco, 'Il Contratto', in Vassalli, Tratt. di dir. civ. 6:2 (1975), 221, 710 ff.; A. Chianale, 'Opzione', Digesto 13 (1995), 140.

[27] Article 1329 of the Civil Code: 'Irrevocable offer: If the offeror has bound himself to keep the offer open for a certain time, the revocation is without effect. In the case contemplated in the preceding paragraph, the death or supervening incapacity of the offeror does not deprive the offer of effect, unless the nature of the transaction or other circumstances preclude such effect.'

On the relationship between irrevocable offer and option see, e.g., G. Gorla, 'Note sulla distinzione fra opzione e proposta irrevocabile', Riv. dir. civ. (1962), 213; P. Menti, 'Il dualismo tra proposta ferma per patto e contratto di opzione', Riv. trim. dir. proc. civ. (1984), 681; A. Jannuzzi, 'Proposta irrevocabile e patti d'opzione', Foro it. I (1949), 179; E. Cesarò, Il contratto e l'opzione (1969); S. Gulotta, 'Proposta irrevocabile e opzione gratuita', Riv. dir. com. II (1988), 154.

[28] See Cass. civ., 11 Jan. 1990, no. 41, in Corr. giur. (1990), 842.

Code)[29] is not considered to be the same as setting a period during which the offer will be irrevocable (art. 1329 of the Civil Code).

According to the case law, however, the effects of options and irrevocable offers are much the same.[30] For example, both must specify all the elements of the final contract.[31] Otherwise, we have a mere negotiation.

In the present case, if Simon stated that his offer was to be irrevocable and not only valid for the time period indicated, the promise is binding whether it was regarded as a gratuitous option or an irrevocable offer. If Simon did not state that it was irrevocable, then, if we take the view of those scholars who consider gratuitous options to be void, Simon could revoke his offer as long as Realty has not yet accepted it.

Case 13(b) raises the problem of how long a revocable offer or gratuitous option can be valid before it is accepted or exercised. In the present case, two years are a long time but the justification may be that Realty had to perform a complex geological survey on the land, and Simon wanted to give Realty an incentive to do so. If the time limit is manifestly excessive given the nature of the transaction – for example, if it were fifty years in a case like this one – the judge would probably consider the offer to be revocable or would reduce the time limit to one that would normally be appropriate.

Case 13(c) is peculiar because, in contrast to Cases 13(a) and 13(b), a court would probably conclude that Realty did not have an absolute right to refuse to conclude the final contract. Realty might be required to act in good faith in exercising its right to declare itself dissatisfied. The general principle of good faith obliges the party who has discretion to take the other party's interest into account. Realty would probably have to explain its grounds for dissatisfaction even if the express terms of the contract leave the matter to its sole and absolute judgment.[32] This kind of judicial control over the behaviour of the party with discretion would probably be

---

[29] Article 1326 of the Civil Code: 'Formation of contract: A contract is formed at the moment when he who made the offer has knowledge of the acceptance of the other party. The acceptance must reach the offeror within the time set by him or within that ordinarily necessary according to the nature of the transaction or usage. The offeror can treat late acceptance as effective, provided that he immediately so informs the other party. When the offeror requires a specific form of acceptance, the acceptance is ineffective if given in a different form. An acceptance that does not conform to the offer is equivalent to another offer.'

[30] On this point, see F. Messineo, 'Contratto', Enc. dir. IX (1961), 902.

[31] See Cass. civ., 29 Oct. 1993, no. 10777, in Corr. giur. (1993), 1401. See also G. Tamburrino, *I vincoli unilaterali nella formazione progressiva del contratto*, 2nd edn. (1991); P. Meoli, 'Termine di irrevocabilità ed efficacia della proposta irrevocabile', Rass. dir. civ. (1994), 129.

[32] Cass. civ., sez. I, 20 April 1994, no. 3775 (*Comune di Fiuggi c. Ente Fiuggi s.p.a.*), in Giur. it. I (1995), 852.

exercised only if Realty did not want to buy the land. Nevertheless, how the standard of good faith would apply to the case is far from clear. The case law on this issue is still confused.

The reasons why Realty wants to buy the land are irrelevant to the case. Motives are subjective and they are generally irrelevant in contract law. An exception to this rule is provided by art. 1345 of the Civil Code, which states that a contract is unlawful when the parties are led to conclude it solely by an unlawful motive common to both.

AUSTRIA

Simon's promise in Cases 13(a) and 13(b) constitutes an option. An option is an agreement which gives the other party the right to conclude a contract with predetermined content with the promisor.[33] An option is not considered to be a gift because the promisor does not have the intention to make one. His interest lies in the conclusion of the second contract which is the object of the option. Therefore, an option is not subject to the form required of gifts. Indeed, it is not subject to any form requirement because, under Austrian law, a contract to sell real property does not have to be made in a special form. Simon's promise will therefore be binding in these two cases. There are no restrictions on the length of the time during which the other side can bring the contract into existence. An option for two years is therefore unproblematic.[34]

The analysis is different in Case 13(c), but the result is the same. Here it could be argued that we already have a sales contract, but that Realty has the right to cancel it without giving any reason for doing so. Such an agreement is valid in Austrian law.

Although an option is not described as a *pactum de contrahendo*, § 936 of the Civil Code is applied to such a contract.[35] If there is an abrupt rise in the market price, it is possible that the *clausula rebus sic stantibus* allows Simon to withdraw his promise.

Whether Realty has the right to buy the land for immediate resale would depend on the interpretation of the contract. An interpretation according to which Realty does not have this right, however, would be

---

[33] Courts and commentators accept the possibility of making such a contract although it is not mentioned in the Civil Code. The option is defined as a contract made under the condition that the other side wishes to bring the contract into existence (see M. Binder in Schwimann, *ABGB* § 936 no. 12).

[34] According to § 1074 of the Civil Code, the right of pre-emption is not transferable by succession. F. Bydlinski (in Klang, *ABGB* vol. IV/2, 798) argues that § 1074 should be applied to options as well.   [35] See M. Binder, in Schwimann, *ABGB* § 936 no. 13.

warranted only if the circumstances indicate that such was the intention of the parties.

Another legal provision that could apply if the market price rises is § 934 of the Civil Code. This provision gives a party the right to avoid a contract if the price paid (or received) is more (or less) than half the value of the goods bought, provided the party did not know their real value. The application of § 934 of the Civil Code, however, would be problematic as the disparity between the price and the value of the goods must exist at the moment that the contract granting the option is concluded.[36]

GERMANY

In all three cases, the promise is not binding without compliance with the formalities for assuming an obligation to transfer real estate of § 313 of the Civil Code.[37] The formalities are required to provide proof of the obligation and to caution the parties themselves because real property is regarded as an extremely important asset.

Because Realty can choose freely whether to buy or not, the contract in Case 13(a) is an option. An option is not deemed to be a gift. It is valid even if nothing is paid for it. Therefore the promise is binding. It does not matter if the market price has risen (Case 8(a)).

The question of what Realty wants to do with the land merely concerns Realty's motives. They are not part of the contract as long as it does not prohibit an immediate resale.

The only difference between Cases 13(a) and 13(b) is the duration of the option. In general, contracts that are binding for a very long time can offend common decency and therefore be void according to § 138(1) of the Civil Code.[38] Here again, common decency is defined as the beliefs of those whose thinking is proper and just.[39] For common decency to be violated, there must be an extreme limitation of a person's economic liberty.

Section 138(1) of the Civil Code would only apply to an option if no reasonable remuneration were paid in return for it. Because remuneration was inadequate, the highest German court (*Bundesgerichtshof*) held an option to be void that gave an editor the right to publish all further works

---

[36] *Ibid.*, § 934 no. 13; OGH JBl 1987, 718.
[37] A contract which obliges one party to transfer or acquire real property has to be recorded by a notary. The absence of this formality is immaterial if the real property has actually been transferred.
[38] A promise (*Rechtsgeschäft*) which offends common decency is void.
[39] Mot. vol. II, 727; BGHZ 52 (1970), 20.

of a certain author without any time limit.[40] Therefore, the permissible duration of an option always depends on what was paid for it. It is not possible to say exactly how long the time limit can be. In our case, however, the option for two years should be valid even with little compensation or even without any if Simon had some interest of his own in the deal, and this interest was the reason he granted the option.

In Case 13(c), Realty can refuse to buy if, in its 'sole and absolute judgment', it thinks the economic prospects of the property are unsatisfactory. If a contract provides that the buyer has the right to examine goods or real estate, the contract is deemed to be concluded already but subject to the condition that the buyer approves the goods. In the absence of an explicit contractual provision to the contrary, the buyer is absolutely free in his decision to approve the goods according to § 495 of the Civil Code. Again, the motives of Realty and the rise in the market price are immaterial as long as they are not explicitly included in the contract. It would not be a violation of good faith even if Realty did not tell the truth about its motives since under § 495 of the Civil Code the buyer is not even obliged to disclose his motives.

Because the law provides that the buyer has this right, his exercise of it would be held to violate good faith (§ 242 of the Civil Code) only under very exceptional circumstances. They would have to be much more compelling than they are here.

GREECE

An agreement to transfer the ownership of immovable property must take the form of a notarial document (art. 369 of the Civil Code) and it must also be entered in the public land register (art. 1192 of the Civil Code).[41]

The agreement undertaking to transfer the ownership of immovable property must take the form of a notarial document because it leads to a transfer of such property (art. 369 of the Civil Code). If this form is not used, then the agreement is invalid.[42]

Moreover, the terms and conditions that the parties agree upon must also appear in a notarial document in order to be valid, and they must be entered in the public land register so that the buyer can be protected as long as a condition of the transfer is not yet fulfilled.[43] If there is a change

---

[40] BGHZ 22 (1957), 34.   [41] Georgiadis, *General Principles*, 226–33.
[42] G. Tambakis in Georgiadis and Stathopoulos, *Civil Code*, art. 369.   [43] *Ibid.*, art. 201, no. 2.

in the circumstances before the fulfilment of the condition, art. 388 of the Civil Code does not apply.[44]

The present case concerns an option contract, by which one of the two parties is given the right to bring about the conclusion of a contract by his unilateral declaration to the other party. Because it concerns immovable property, it is not valid unless it takes the form of a notarial document.[45]

SCOTLAND

As outlined in Case 12, because this is a unilateral obligation in relation to an interest in land, it must be constituted in writing even though it is non-gratuitous or made in the course of business. Once constituted in writing, any change in the market price, or in Realty's reasons for purchasing the land, are irrelevant in the law of Scotland which has no doctrine of consideration. Realty can hence enforce the promise if it has written proof of it. It may be possible that the promise is binding only if the land is used for building on and not for resale but this, of course, would depend on the construction of the promise.

ENGLAND

It is clear in English law that promises 13(a) and 13(b) are not binding. They have the status of mere offers, and as such can be withdrawn any time before Realty agrees to buy the land on the offered terms.[46] Merely agreeing to the promise to keep open the offer is not enough, because, like any other promise, a 'firm offer' (i.e., a promise to keep open an offer for a certain time period) is not binding unless consideration was provided in exchange for it (see Case 1). Here, nothing was given or promised in return for either promise, so the offeror is free to withdraw the offer at any time before it was accepted, so long as that withdrawal is communicated to the offeree. Thus, it was held in *Dickinson* v. *Dodds*[47] that the defendant's offer of land for sale, 'to be left over until Friday', could be withdrawn on Thursday and, moreover, that the withdrawal was effective where the offeree had heard from a third party that the land had been sold on Thursday.

As I have noted elsewhere, where a promisee has relied on a gratuitous offer a court may be tempted to invent consideration for the promise. In

---

[44] *Ibid.*; AP 223/74 NoB 21, 1070.   [45] Stathopoulos, *Contract Law*, 74.
[46] See Treitel, *Contract*, 141.   [47] [1876] 2 Ch. D. 463.

this case, a court might be tempted to hold, for example, that Realty had promised to conduct a survey (which, though arguably of no benefit to Simon, is a detriment to Realty and hence meets the classical test for consideration) or to apply for a mortgage, in exchange for Simon's promise to keep the offer open. In general, it can be predicted that English courts will try fairly hard to find ways of enforcing such a promise, especially if it is made in a commercial context.[48] The rule that firm offers are unenforceable is often criticized by English lawyers,[49] and the English Law Commission has recommended that firm offers made in the course of business and for a definite period should be binding.[50]

The status of Simon's third promise ('sole and absolute judgment') is less clear. On the one hand, Realty appears to have agreed to buy the land if certain conditions prevail, thereby fulfilling the requirement of consideration. On the other hand, because the determination of whether the 'economic prospects were unsatisfactory' is left entirely to Realty's discretion it is arguable that Realty has not bound itself to do anything. If performance is entirely at the discretion of Realty, the promise is unenforceable for lack of consideration.[51] It would also be unenforceable on the grounds that the contractual terms are too uncertain to be enforced.[52]

There is no doctrine of 'good faith' in English law such that Realty is bound to exercise its discretion only on certain grounds. In English law, the question is one of interpretation: Does the contract, on its proper construction, bind Realty in any way, however slight? There do not appear to be any cases directly in point, but it is suggested that a court would hold that Realty was at least weakly bound in that it could exercise its discretion only on the basis of its view of the 'economic prospects' of building on the land and not, for example, on the basis of external economic considerations (e.g., it found cheaper land elsewhere). Earlier cases have held that sales which were subject to a 'satisfactory mortgage' or to a 'satisfactory survey' were unenforceable,[53] but more recent cases have tended to construe such discretion as subject to an implied condition that it be exercised *bona fide*, and hence that the contract is valid.[54]

A further point in regard to the third promise is that because the

---

[48] See, e.g., *Pitt v. P.H.H. Asset Management Ltd* [1994] 1 WLR 327, where it was held that a prospective purchaser's promise to get on by limiting himself to just two weeks was consideration for the vendor's promise not to consider other offers during that period.

[49] See, e.g., Treitel, *Contract*, 142.   [50] Law Commission, Working Paper No. 60 (1975).

[51] Treitel, *Contract*, 80.   [52] *G. Scammell & Nephew Ltd v. Ouston* [1941] AC 251.

[53] *Montreal Gas Co. v. Vasey* [1900] AC 595; *Astra Trust v. Adams & Williams* [1969] 1 Lloyd's Rep. 81.

[54] *Albion Sugar Co. Ltd v. Williams Tankers Ltd (The John S Darbyshire)* [1977] 2 Lloyd's Rep. 457.

promise specifically envisages Realty conducting a survey, a court would be more willing, in this case, to find that Realty had undertaken to do a survey in return for Simon's promise. As noted above, a court will be anxious to uphold such a promise if possible. As ever, if Realty relies on Simon's promise – which may be the case if they do a survey – then the court will normally try harder to find a binding contract. In the end, it is not certain that this third promise would be enforced in English law, though it probably would be, especially if Realty has relied.

The change in market price is strictly speaking irrelevant in all of the above, though it is possible that if the result was not clear cut, as in Case 13(c), a court might be influenced by the prospect of Simon getting a bad deal. On the other hand, price rises in land are so common that it is unlikely that a court would be greatly influenced by such an event.

IRELAND

There can be a problem in seeing the consideration for a promise when the promisee is not yet bound. The promise by Simon in each of the three cases cited would be classified in Irish law as a 'firm' offer, meaning one containing a promise not to revoke it for a period of time. Chitty[55] points out that the mere fact that such a promise has been made does not prevent the offeror from revoking the offer within that period where the promise is unsupported by consideration.

In some cases consideration will be provided, for example, where the offeree pays or promises to pay a sum of money for the promise and so buys an option. Chitty suggests that it is also possible for a person, to whom a promise not to revoke an offer for the sale of property has been made, to provide consideration for that promise by incurring the expense of a survey.[56]

In the present case, Simon has made his promise in each case 'without charging anything'. Therefore on the face of it the promise is unsupported by consideration and is consequently not binding and can be revoked before performance by Realty. However, the situation would probably be different if Realty does some act before revocation such as incurring the expense of conducting a study. In such circumstances an Irish court would probably follow the suggestion by Chitty[57] and hold that Realty had provided consideration for Simon's promise and thus rendered the promise binding.

[55] *Chitty on Contracts*, par. 128.   [56] See *ibid*.   [57] *Ibid*.

It is possible that a binding contract could arise in Case 13(c) if the clause relating to the 'sole and absolute judgment' of Realty were removed. In that event the Irish courts could treat the contract as a conditional contract, conditional upon Realty obtaining a satisfactory economic study. The Irish case of *Draisey v Fitzpatrick*[58] concerned a contract for sale which was subject to the purchaser obtaining loan approval. Ellis J held that the contract was subject to the implied terms that the loan approval conditions should be reasonable, should reasonably have been in the contemplation of the parties when the contract was made, and should be to the satisfaction of the purchaser acting reasonably. It would be possible to apply this approach to Case 13(c) on the altered facts as set out above. It might be necessary for the contract to specify more closely the scope and purpose of the economic study, and therefore the parameters of what Realty might be dissatisfied about.

In any event, the change in market conditions, and in Realty's motives for buying the land, would appear to be irrelevant in Irish law.

Summaries

France: The promises do not comply with a formality required for options to sell land, but those in Cases 13(a) and 13(b) are probably enforceable anyway since the purpose of the formality is to prevent tax evasion. The promise in Case 13(c) may be invalid as subject to a *condition potestative*: a condition allowing one of the parties to determine if there is a valid contract. In all of these cases, if the contract price when the option is exercised is less than seven-twelfths of the market value of the land, the seller has a remedy for *lésion*: the contract is void unless the buyer chooses to make up the difference. Moreover, the remedy for breach of an option contract is damages, not specific performance.

Belgium: The promises in Cases 13(a) and 13(b) are valid as option contracts. The promise in Case 13(c) is valid if it is interpreted as an option contract; if it is interpreted as a bilateral contract it is void since it is subject to a *condition potestative*: a condition allowing one of the parties to determine if there is a valid contract. In all of these cases, if the contract price when the option is exercised is less than seven-twelfths of the market value of the land, the seller has a remedy for *lésion*: the contract is void unless the buyer chooses to make up the difference.

---

[58] [1981] ILRM 219.

The Netherlands: The promise is enforceable in all three cases. Nevertheless, if the option were so long term as to be unfair, a court would likely give relief by interpreting it as revocable or by finding that its exercise is a violation of good faith. Also, if there were an abrupt rise in the market price and Realty wants the land for resale, exercise of the option might be a violation of good faith.

Spain: The promise is enforceable in all three cases. Nevertheless, if Realty wants to buy the land not to develop it but to resell it, it is likely the contract is not enforceable on the ground that the original purpose of the transaction is no longer being achieved (*teoria de la base del negocio*).

Portugal: The promise is unenforceable in all three cases but only because they concern sale of land which requires a notarial formality.

Italy: According to the case law and many scholars, these promises are enforceable. According to some scholars, however, if an option is not paid for, it is an offer irrevocable for a fixed term. According to the case, such an option is irrevocable only if the promisor expressly says that it is; it is not enough if he says it is valid for a fixed term. By this view, these promises would be irrevocable only if the promisor said so expressly.

In Case 13(b), the option is probably valid because the length of time was probably justified by Realty's business needs – for example, conducting a complex study – but if an option is for an excessive period, a court will hold it to be revocable or reduce the period to what is appropriate.

In Case 13(c), a court would hold that Realty does not have an absolute right to decline the contract but a right that must be exercised in good faith.

Austria: In Cases 13(a) and 13(b), the promises are options and enforceable without a formality. They are not deemed to be gifts because they are not so intended. The promise in Case 13(c) is enforceable as well although it is considered, not an option, but a sales contract that Realty has the right to cancel. If there is an abrupt rise in the market price, however, Simon may be able to cancel on account of changed circumstances. A party does have the right to void a contract if the price is more or less than half the value of the object sold, but the disparity between value and price must exist at the time the contract is concluded.

Germany: Options are enforceable even if nothing is paid for them, but these options must comply with the formalities required to transfer real estate. The option in Case 13(b) would be void if it is for such a long time as to offend common decency. In evaluating whether it does, a court will take into account the amount that was paid for it. Here, the option might be valid if Simon had an interest of his own in the deal. The promise in Case 13(c) is valid. Realty would have to exercise its right in good faith, but a court would find that it did not do so only under very exceptional circumstances.

Greece: Options are enforceable even if nothing is paid for them, but these options must comply with the formalities required to transfer real estate.

Scotland: This promise concerns an interest in land and so is unenforceable unless it is in writing. If it were in writing, it would be enforceable.

England: In Cases 13(a) and 13(b), the promises are not binding because they lack consideration. It is not clear whether the promise in Case 13(c) is binding, but a court might well decide that it is because Realty had agreed to do a survey and it can refuse to go forward only on the basis of its view of the economic prospects.

Ireland: It would seem that the promises are not binding because they lack consideration, but consideration might be found if the promisee was to do something such as make a survey. The promise in Case 13(c) might be held to be binding because Realty can refuse to go forward only on the basis of its view of the economic prospects, but the matter is not clear.

Preliminary comparisons

No civil law jurisdiction considered these promises to be gifts but in several jurisdictions they would be unenforceable for failure to comply with the formalities required in transfers of land (Portugal, Germany, Greece, and Scotland). In Italy, the promisor might have to state expressly that the promise is irrevocable rather than to say it is valid for a fixed term. In England and Ireland, the promises in Cases 13(a) and 13(b) are unenforceable because they lack consideration, although, as the Irish reporter noted, they would be enforceable if Realty promised to do something such as make a survey. The promise in Case 13(c) might be enforceable because Realty's right to withdraw depended on its view of the economic prospects.

Some reporters thought that if the term of the option was too long, a court would require it to be exercised in good faith (the Netherlands) or would hold it to be revocable or reduce the term (Italy, and Germany if the length of the term offends 'common decency').

If exercise of the option were seriously unfair, for example if there were an abrupt price rise and Realty decided to buy the land for resale, relief might be given on a variety of grounds: because of a severe disparity in value and contract price at the time the option is exercised (*lésion*) (France and Belgium); for failure to act in good faith (the Netherlands, Italy, and Germany); because the purpose of the original transaction is no longer achieved (*teoria de la base del negocio*) (Spain); or for changed circumstances (Austria).

Case 14: promises of rewards

Case

A burglar stole Simone's valuable diamond necklace. She offered a large sum of money payable if it was discovered and returned (a) to Raymond, a private detective, or (b) in a newspaper advertisement, to whomever succeeded in finding the necklace. Three months later, after (a) Raymond or (b) others incurred expenses looking for the necklace, she wishes to withdraw her promise because she has changed her mind about how much she is willing to pay for the return of the necklace. Can she do so?

Discussions

FRANCE

When Simone promises Raymond a sum of money to find her necklace, she makes an offer to a specified person which is clear, precise, and unequivocal. By undertaking the investigation, Raymond has tacitly accepted this offer and a contract to find the jewellery has accordingly been made. It can be analysed either as a contract to undertake an investigation (*contrat d'entreprise*) or as a promise of reward.

If it is a contract to undertake an investigation (*contrat d'entreprise*), it may be that no payment is due until Raymond achieves the desired result, and Raymond is under an obligation to use his best endeavours to achieve it. Such an obligation is termed an *obligation de moyens*. Under this analysis, because the contract resembles one for a lump sum, it might seem that Raymond cannot be reimbursed for his costs if Simone revokes her offer as no express provisions have been made to that effect. However, art. 1794 of the Civil Code contains a provision which enables the employer to terminate in mid-performance and compensate the other contracting party for his expenses. If the contract was analysed as a *contrat d'entreprise*, Raymond might be able to invoke this provision and claim his expenses.

Alternatively, Simone's offer could be interpreted as a promise of a reward, that is, as a unilateral contract. If Raymond expressly accepts, the contract then becomes a *contrat d'entreprise* – a bilateral contract – as before. If Raymond tacitly accepts, by way of exception, his silence will suffice as an acceptance because the offer is made in his sole interest (see Case 11). Once again, a bilateral contract will be formed on the basis that the offer is made in his sole interest (see Case 11 above).

In Case 14(b), when Simone advertises in the newspaper, she makes an offer to the public at large. Under French law, such an offer binds the promisor and the promisee under the same conditions as an offer to a specified person.[1] Thus an offer to the public at large is not freely revocable. It must be kept open until the fixed term has expired or until the end of a reasonable time. After this period, the offer will be deemed to have lapsed. On these facts, the courts will probably consider that the offer to the public at large has lapsed after three months.

French law has always been very attached to an analysis of a promise of a reward as a bilateral contract. The theory that it is a unilateral undertaking has not really been accepted. Recently, however, a judgment of the Court of Appeal of Toulouse adopted the unilateral contract analysis[2] (see Case 1). Here, however, the facts can be distinguished. That case was one in which a prize could be won with no effort on the part of the winner. In this case, to obtain the reward, one must search for the necklace. Also, in this case, analysing the transaction as a unilateral undertaking does not seem very realistic: the performance of the contract (finding the jewellery) would then be simultaneous with the acceptance of the offer.

In equity, following principles of unjust enrichment, the judges may be tempted to consider the conscientious but unsuccessful searcher as a person who has undertaken the management of another's affairs (*gestion d'affaires*). Such a person is reimbursed for all 'useful and necessary costs' (art. 1375 of the Civil Code).

In practice, however, the circumstances where damages can be obtained for the withdrawal of an offer are rare, except if the withdrawal is characterized as intemperate and indicates a manifest change of mind or a breach of an express undertaking. The reasonable period implied by the courts is generally very short.

---

[1] Ghestin, *Traité de droit civil* no. 297, pp. 365 ff.
[2] Cour d'appel, Toulouse, 14 Feb. 1996, Bull. Civ., 1 July 1996, IR no. 433.

BELGIUM

The contract between Simone and the private detective in Case 14(a) is a *contrat d'entreprise*, literally, an 'enterprise contract' or contract to achieve a particular result. It belongs to the category of *louage d'ouvrage*, literally, hiring of labour. In contrast to an employment contract, it does not create a relationship of subordination between the parties (see arts. 1710 and 1779 of the Civil Code). Having entered into such an agreement, it is hard to see how Simone could unilaterally change her mind about how much she is willing to pay unless this possibility were specifically provided for in the contract.[3] If Simone wishes to terminate the contract with the detective, she may do so provided she complies with art. 1794 of the Civil Code which provides: 'The master may terminate the *marché à forfait* [the specific work to be performed] on his own initiative, even though the work has commenced, if he compensates the contractor for all expenses incurred, for all the work, and for everything he could have gained in this undertaking'.[4] The extent of the compensation depends on whether the termination of the contract is attributable to the contractor's negligence. If so, compensation covers only costs incurred; if not, it includes gains which would have resulted from the undertaking. Here, awarding compensation for these gains raises the difficulty that we do not know whether the detective would have found the necklace or not. The judge will have to make a decision *ex aequo et bono* based on the case law that deals with the so-called 'loss of a chance' (*perte d'une chance*).[5]

The advertisement in Case 14(b) is a promise of a reward (*promesse de récompense*) which constitutes a commitment through a unilateral declaration of will.[6] According to some, it is enforceable because a unilateral act

---

[3] See P. A. Foriers, 'L'objet et la cause du contrat', in Dieux, *Les obligations*, 131.

[4] 'Le maître peut résilier, par sa seule volonté, le marché à forfait, quoique l'ouvrage soit déjà commencé, en dédommageant l'entrepreneur de toutes ses dépenses, de tous ses travaux, et de tout ce qu'il aurait pu gagner dans cette entreprise.' See A. Fettweis and A. Delvaux, 'La fin du contrat d'entreprise, du contrat d'architecte et du contrat de marché public de travaux ou de services (résiliation, résolution, décès et faillite)', Act. dr., 1992, 387; C. Levintoff and P. A. Foriers, 'De la réalisation unilatérale du contrat d'entreprise par le maître de l'ouvrage', Entr. et dr., 1977, 21.

[5] See S. Stijns, D. Van Gerven, and P. Wéry, 'Chronique de jurisprudence. Les obligations: les sources (1985–1995)', JT, 1996, nos. 115 f.

[6] See Van Ommeslaghe, *Droit des obligations*, 72. A unilateral act is in principle irrevocable. On these questions, see *ibid.* 379. See also Stijns, Van Gerven, and Wéry, 'Chronique de jurisprudence', 689–90, 692–3, nos. 7–9; L. Simont, 'L'engagement unilatéral', in *Les obligations en droit français et en droit belge* (1990). For recent case law, see two decisions of the Belgian *Cour de cassation*: Cass., 9 May 1980, JT, 1981, 206 and Cass., 16 March 1989, Pas., I, 737.

may be binding.[7] Others might find it to be enforceable on a different ground. For example, Simone might be liable because a person who suddenly withdraws an offer commits an abuse of right (see Case 8). Or she might be liable because there was a *gestion d'affaires*, literally, the management of another's business: whoever searched for the necklace could claim compensation on the grounds that their intervention was necessary and urgent to protect Simone's interests (arts. 1372–5 of the Civil Code).

THE NETHERLANDS

In Case 14(a), Simone's promise is binding. She concluded a conditional contract with Raymond, which created a conditional obligation for her.[8] A contract cannot be revoked unilaterally.

In Case 14(b) she is not bound. An offer is revocable unless it is made irrevocable (art. 6:219 of the Civil Code[9]). The public offer Simone made was revocable. It did not contain a time period within which it could be accepted nor did anything about the offer imply it was irrevocable.

Nevertheless, art. 6:220(2) provides that '[i]n the event of revocation or modification of an offer of reward, the judge may grant equitable compensation to a person who, on the basis of the offer, has begun to prepare the requested prestation [performance]'. Therefore, if the fact that 'others' have incurred expenses looking for the necklace counts as beginning to prepare the performance, they may be entitled to equitable compensation. However, it does not seem likely that any member of the public who has looked for the necklace should be entitled to do so even if they incurred expenses. Therefore, it seems that beginning 'to prepare the requested prestation [performance]' should be interpreted quite strictly in case of an offer of reward made to the public. In any event, it is clear that she can withdraw, but not clear whether she has to pay compensation.

Even if the offer of reward had been made irrevocable by including a clause to that effect, it could nevertheless have been revoked 'for serious

---

[7] The promisor can of course specify the scope of his or her commitment, for instance through the setting of a date at which it would lapse.

[8] On conditional juristic acts, see art. 3:38(1) of the Civil Code: 'Unless the law or the nature of a juridical act produces a different result, a juridical act can be performed subject to . . . a condition.' (In French: 'Un acte juridique peut être assorti . . . d'une condition . . .') On conditional obligations, see art. 6:21 of the Civil Code: 'An obligation is conditional where, in virtue of a juridical act, its effect has been made dependent upon a future and uncertain event.'   [9] For the text of art. 6:219 of the Civil Code, see Case 13.

reasons' (art. 6:220 of the Civil Code[10]). Whether Simone's reasons here can be said to be serious is doubtful. If, indeed, such an offer could not have been revoked, a member of the public could have accepted it and so made it binding. For some time it was thought that an offer of reward is accepted by performing the required act such as finding the object.[11] Today, however, it is thought that in addition to performance, one must declare one's will (wilsverklaring) to accept.[12]

SPAIN

The promise in Case 14(a) is binding. When Simone makes her promise to Raymond, there is a *causa credendi* (see Case 10). Therefore, the promise is enforceable provided that it is accepted. If Raymond finds the necklace, Simone has to pay (art. 1107 of the Civil Code).[13]

In Case 14(b), Simone makes her offer to the public rather than to a particular person. Spanish law has followed § 657 of the German Civil Code. If someone offers a reward to the general public for either doing an act or getting a result, he or she is obligated without the need for an acceptance.[14] Moreover, in contrast to English common law, the promisor is obligated even if the one who returned the necklace was unaware of the promise. The promise may be revoked if the revocation is made public to the same extent as the promise was.

PORTUGAL

Simone can withdraw the promise in both cases but in Case 14(a) she can be forced to compensate Raymond for the expenses he has incurred.

The promise made to the private detective in Case 14(a) is binding provided that it was accepted. After acceptance, a contract for services has been formed (art. 1154) to which the Portuguese Civil Code applies the rules that govern an agency contract (*contrato de mandato*) pursuant to art. 1156. According to these rules, the contract can be unilaterally revoked by either of the parties at will (art. 1170). Therefore Simone can withdraw the promise, but in this case she would have to compensate Raymond for any

---

[10] Article 6:220(1) of the Civil Code: 'An offer of reward made for a specific period can be revoked or modified for serious reasons.'

[11] See Bei Weissmann, *Verbintennissenrecht*, art. 220, no. 23.

[12] Asser-Hartkamp vol. II, no. 142.

[13] L. Díez Picazo, 'Las declaraciones unilaterales de voluntad como fuentes de obligaciones y la jurisprudencia del tribunal supremo', *Anuario de derecho civil* 27 (1974), 456 at 465.

[14] Díez Picazo and Gullón, *Sistema de derecho civil*, vol. II, 145.

loss he incurred. In an agency contract, any necessary expenses the agent incurs must always be reimbursed by the principal (art. 1167).

Case 14(b) concerns a promise made to the public which in Portuguese law is one of the exceptional cases in which a unilateral promise will constitute an obligation. According to art. 459 of the Civil Code, if someone, by a public announcement, offers a reward to any member of the public either for being in a certain situation or for taking some action or omission, the promise is immediately binding without the need for an acceptance. The promisor is even obligated to those who are in the situation or perform the act without attempting to earn the reward or even in ignorance of it.

However, if no term was fixed for the duration of the promise, it can be revoked up until the time that the action is performed if the revocation is made in the same way as the promise (art. 461). Therefore, if the necklace has not yet been found, Simone can revoke her promise by another announcement made public to the same extent. In this case, the expenses incurred by people who tried to find the necklace need not be reimbursed.

ITALY

In both Cases 14(a) and 14(b), Simone cannot withdraw her promise because she has changed her mind. In Case 14(b), she can revoke her promise only for just cause.

Case 14(b) is a promise to the public which is governed by arts. 1989 ff. of the Civil Code.[15] The promise is binding as soon as it is made public (art. 1989(1)). If no time limit is set for the performance, and one cannot be inferred from the nature or the purpose of the promise, the limit will be deemed to be one year (art. 1989(2)). The promise may be revoked before the end of this period only if the revocation is made public in the same way as the promise or in an equivalent way. But it can only be revoked for a just cause (art. 1990).

---

[15] Article 1989 of the Civil Code: 'Promise to the public: A person who, addressing himself to the public, promises a given performance in favour of a person who is found in a specific situation or who performs a specific action, is bound by such promise as soon as it is made public. If no time limit is set in the promise or is implicit in its nature or purpose, the promisor is freed from his obligation if he is not notified within one year from the time of the promise that the specified situation or performance called for in the promise has occurred.' Article 1990 of the Civil Code: 'Revocation of promise: Before the end of the period indicated in the preceding article, a promise can be revoked only for just cause, provided that the revocation be made public in the same manner as the promise or in an equivalent form. In no case shall the revocation be effective if the situation called for in the promise has already materialized or if the act called for has already been performed.'

There is a just cause for revocation when, due to supervening events that are not due to the negligence of the promisor, the goal he is pursuing becomes impossible, or the act in return for which he has made the promise becomes completely useless even if it is still possible.[16] 'Just cause' means that the promisor's interest in revoking is allowed to prevail over the other party's interest in holding him to his promise.[17] A mere change of mind, of course, is not considered by case law a just cause for revocation.[18]

In Case 14(a), Simone has promised Raymond money if he finds her necklace. Raymond undertook no obligation to do so explicitly or implicitly but if he finds the necklace he is to receive the money. Scholars differ as to how conditional promises of this sort should be analysed.[19] Some[20] claim that they are governed by art. 1333 of the Civil Code.[21] It provides that an offer that creates obligations only for the offeror is irrevocable as soon as it comes to the notice of the person to whom it is directed. According to others,[22] such a promise is governed by art. 1327.[23] It provides that when a performance is to take place without a prior acceptance of an offer, the offer is binding when the performance begins. By the one opinion, then, such a promise is irrevocable as soon as it comes to the promisee's notice. Scholars who take this approach say that nevertheless, by analogy to art. 1990, the promise could still be revoked for just cause.

---

[16] See G. Sbisà, *La promessa al pubblico* (1974), 272.

[17] F. Carnelutti, 'Del recesso unilaterale nel mandato di commercio', in F. Larnelutti, *Studi di diritto commerciale* (1917), 26, n. 11.

[18] See, e.g., Sbisà, *La promessa al pubblico*; C.A. Graziani, 'Le promesse unilaterali', in Rescigno, *Tratt. di dir. priv.* 9 (1982), 661.

[19] G. Gorla, 'Promesse "condizionate" ad una prestazione', *Riv. dir. com.* I (1968), 431.

[20] See, e.g., R. Sacco, 'Il Contratto', in Vassalli, *Tratt. di dir. civ.* 6:2 (1975), 32 ff.; C. A. Graziani, 'Le promesse unilaterali'; P. Spada, 'Cautio quae indiscrete loquitur: lineamenti funzionali e strutturali della promessa di pagamento', *Riv. dir. civ.* (1978), 742 n. 173.

[21] Article 1333 of the Civil Code: 'Contract binding on offeror only: An offer for the purpose of forming a contract that creates obligations only for the offeror is irrevocable as soon as it comes to the knowledge of the party to whom it is directed. The offeree can reject the offer within the time requested by the nature of the transaction or by usage. In the absence of such rejection the contract is concluded.'

[22] See, e.g., G. Gorla, 'Promesse "condizionate" ad una prestazione'; Sbisà, *La promessa al pubblico*; G. Castiglia, 'Promesse unilaterali atipiche', *Riv. dir. com.* I (1983), 378.

[23] Article 1327 of the Civil Code: 'Performance before reply by acceptor: When, at the request of the offeror or by the nature of the transaction or according to usage, the performance should take place without a prior reply, the contract is concluded at the time and place in which performance begins. The acceptor must promptly give notice of the beginning of performance to the other party and, if he does not, is liable for damages.'

Consequently, according to their view, such a promise does not differ at all from a promise made to the public under art. 1989.[24] By the other opinion, such a promise becomes irrevocable as soon as the promisee begins to perform.[25] Scholars who take this approach do not believe that thereafter such a promise can be revoked for just cause. They believe that such a promise is governed by the general principles of contract formation and, in particular, by arts. 1327 and 1328.[26]

Here, however, Raymond began performance by starting to search for the necklace: inspecting the site, collecting information, and so forth. Simone merely changed her mind about how much she is willing to pay for its return. Thus, regardless of which approach one takes, the offer is now irrevocable.

In real life, Simone would probably manage to settle the claim against Raymond by paying him the expenses he incurred. If, however, he refuses the offer of settlement and wants to try to find the necklace and obtain the reward, he would have the right to do so.

AUSTRIA

In Case 14(a), the contract is a *Werkvertrag*[27] which, according to § 1151 of the Civil Code, is a contract to perform a particular piece of work, to produce a certain specified result (*locatio conductio operis*). Raymond will get the money if he produces the necklace. The person for whom the work is to be done has the right to cancel such a contract at any time. If he does, however, he must compensate the other party for the work already done and for the profit that would have been made had the contract been completed.[28] Simone therefore has to pay Raymond his expenses and his profit. Raymond will not get the whole sum since he

---

[24] See Sacco, 'Il Contratto', 39. This author, moreover, considers that most of the legal consequences of a promise to the public according to art. 1989 of the Civil Code could be reached equally well through the joint application of arts. 1333 (contract binding on offeror only) and 1336 (offer to the public).   [25] *Ibid.*, 42–3.

[26] Article 1328 of the Civil Code: 'Revocation of offer and acceptance: An offer can be revoked until the contract is concluded. However, if the acceptor has begun performance in good faith before having notice of revocation, the offeror is bound to indemnify him for the expenses and losses sustained in beginning performance of the contract. The acceptance can be revoked, provided that the revocation comes to the knowledge of the offeror before the acceptance.'

[27] The contract is not a *Dienstvertrag* (contract for services) because Raymond can claim the money only if he produces the necklace. By contrast, the person employed pursuant to a contract for services can claim his compensation even if the desired result has not been realized.   [28] See H. Krejci in Rummel, *ABGB* § 1168 nos. 11 and 13.

cannot claim compensation for work that he does not have to do because the contract was cancelled.

In Case 14(b), the promise is a public offer of a reward (*Auslobung*, see § 860 of the Civil Code). According to § 860a of the Civil Code, the promisor has the right to withdraw the promise. Withdrawal does not affect the rights of a person who has achieved the result for which the reward was offered, provided this person did not know and did not have reason to know of the withdrawal. Since nobody had produced the necklace by the time the offer was withdrawn, Simone does not have to make any payments.

GERMANY

In Case 14(a), Simone and Raymond have entered into a contract with a contingent fee. It is binding because, since Raymond is to receive remuneration, he is deemed to be under an obligation to act unless the contract expressly provides otherwise. If Simone does not terminate the contract at all, she has to pay the agreed sum if Raymond finds the necklace.

Whether she may terminate the contract does not depend on the question whether Raymond incurred expenses before she changed her mind. It depends on whether the contract is a *Dienstvertrag* (§§ 611–630 of the Civil Code), a *Werkvertrag* (§§ 631–51), or a *Geschäftsbesorgungsvertrag* (§ 675).

If it is a *Werkvertrag*, Simone is entitled to terminate the contract but then she has to pay the agreed fee (§ 649[29]). But it would be difficult to determine the amount of the fee. According to § 649, Raymond would only be able to claim the fee that he would have been paid if Simone had not terminated the contract, and we do not know if Raymond would have been able to find the necklace.

If the contract is a *Dienstvertrag*, Simone has a right to terminate according to § 621(5).[30] But in this case Raymond could not claim the agreed remuneration. The same is true if the contract is a *Geschäftsbesorgungsvertrag*.

The nature of the contract, then, is crucial to whether Raymond can claim his fee. The contract is a *Werkvertrag* if Raymond is obligated to find the necklace. It is a *Dienstvertrag* or a *Geschäftsbesorgungsvertrag* if he is

---

[29] 'The client can terminate the contract at any time as long as the performance is not completed. If the client terminates the contract, the other party (*Unternehmer*) can claim the agreed remuneration minus the expenses he has saved . . .'

[30] According to this provision, if labour law is not applicable and the remuneration does not depend on the length of the service, the contract may be terminated at any time. If, however, the service occupies the principal part of the time of the person performing it, the termination is valid only for two weeks after notification is given.

merely obligated to look for it.[31] Which of these obligations he has assumed depends on how the contract is interpreted. In our case, Raymond could not be sure that he would be able to find the necklace even if he tried his utmost. Therefore it seems very unlikely that he would accept an obligation to do so. It does not seem to be a *Werkvertrag*.

It is not a *Dienstvertrag* either because, typically, in such a contract Raymond would have to follow all orders given by Simone, and private detectives usually work quite independently.

Therefore, the contract must be described as a *Geschäftsbesorgungsvertrag* but one with the basic structure of a *Dienstvertrag*. Consequently, Simone can terminate the contract without having to pay the fee (§ 621(5) of the Civil Code) as long as she does not do so in violation of good faith: for example, just as Raymond was about to find the necklace. Good faith may require Simone to terminate the contract only with due notice.

In Case 14(b), the promise has been made by a public declaration (*Auslobung*). The promisor must pay for the performance requested even if it is made by a person who did not know about the promise (§ 657 of the Civil Code[32]).

Nevertheless, § 658(1) gives Simone the right to withdraw the promise in a way similar to that in which the promise was made provided that nobody has yet found the necklace. It does not matter if anyone has already incurred expenses. If she withdraws the promise, she does not have to pay for any expenses that have been incurred since that would restrict her right to withdraw.[33]

GREECE

In Case 14(a), Simone promised Raymond a sum of money on condition that he finds her necklace. Such a condition is termed suspensive because the effects of the contract are suspended until the occurrence of the future and uncertain event on which the duty to pay the money is conditioned (art. 201 of the Civil Code). As long as the suspensive condition is unfulfilled, Raymond does not have a right to the reward and Simone is not obliged to pay it. Raymond has only a right of expectation to the reward.[34] If the condition is not fulfilled then the contract is cancelled.

---

[31] BGHZ 31 (1960), 224.
[32] If someone offers a reward for performing an action by public announcement, he has to pay the reward to anyone who has performed this action even if this person has not acted with regard to the announcement.   [33] Mot. vol. II, 521.
[34] M. Stathopoulos, *Contract Law in Hellas* (1995), 129.

Therefore, after three months, which is a reasonable period of time, according to art. 288 of the Civil Code, Simone can withdraw her offer, and, as the condition has not been fulfilled, she will not be obliged to pay anything.

In Case 14(b), Simone's announcement in the newspaper advertisement is governed by arts. 709–12 of the Civil Code which govern unilateral acts by which a person publicly declares that he will give a reward for achieving a result. By so doing, the person offering the reward becomes obligated to pay the reward to whoever achieves the result, even if that person had acted without reference to the announcement.[35]

Until the result is achieved, the offeror may revoke his promise according to art. 710 of the Civil Code, which states:

A person who made the announcement may until the achievement of the act revoke the announcement in the same manner in which it was made or nearly so, or by special notification, except if this person had renounced the possibility of revoking in his announcement. In case of doubt the fixing of a term for the accomplishment of the act shall be deemed to be a renunciation. If a revocation has not been made known in such manner it shall be null in regard to a party which in ignorance of the revocation and prompted by the announcement accomplished the act.

Thus, the announcement can be revoked. If the revocation is not made as this provision requires, it will be ineffective but only as to someone who accomplished the act in ignorance of the revocation. These requirements need not be followed if a right to revoke in some other way was reserved in the announcement.[36]

SCOTLAND

A non-gratuitous promise is binding as soon as it is made. There is no need for it to be met by an acceptance. Therefore Simone's promise is binding on her. It is irrevocable when she communicates it to Raymond or when the others read the newspaper advertisement. It is not revocable thereafter, as in *Campbell* v *Glasgow Police Comrs*.[37] (defender promised gratuities to children of injured or deceased policemen). It is questionable whether it may be revoked after a reasonable time has passed, but the three months in this problem are highly unlikely to lead to the courts seeing the

[35] Karasis in Georgiadis and Stathopoulos, *Civil Code*, art. 709, no. 1; Varthakokoilis, *Analytical Interpretation*, art. 709; AP 566/79 NoB 27, 602; EfAth 11713/86 HellD 27, 144; EfAth 2720/88 HellD 31 (1990), 1459.

[36] Karasis in Georgiadis and Stathopoulos, *Civil Code*, art. 709, no. 1.   [37] [1895] 22 R 621.

promise as being revocable. Simone's promise can be seen as being non-gratuitous because when the condition is purified by the discovery and return of the necklace she will clearly receive a benefit, and therefore writing is not required for the constitution of the promise. A potential benefit inherent in the promise is sufficient to render it non-gratuitous. Alternatively, the courts could adopt a contractual analysis such as that used in *Carlill* v. *Carbolic Smoke Ball Co.*[38] in which an advertisement such as the present one was held to be an offer (offer of £100 to purchaser of defender's product who suffered flu after using it).

ENGLAND

The answer in either case is not clear in English law although it is suggested that whilst Raymond could recover against Simone, other persons who had relied on the offer/promise made in the newspaper could not recover.

In English law, an offer of a reward is described as an offer of a unilateral contract. In civil law systems, a 'unilateral contract' is one in which only one party assumes an obligation. In English law, the expression 'unilateral contract' is used in a much different sense. The defining characteristic of such a contract is that acceptance occurs – or is at least said to occur – by the performance of the requested act. Whether the performing party must know about the offer and be performing in order to satisfy the condition is less clear, but need not concern us here. The question of consideration is not generally raised in such cases, it being assumed that performance is consideration. It should be mentioned, however, that, as various commentators have noted,[39] performance in such cases is arguably more properly interpreted as a condition of receiving the benefit, rather than as something done in exchange for the promise.

In practice, the main difficulty raised by unilateral contracts is that raised by this case: what is the effect of a purported withdrawal once a party has commenced performance of the condition? In principle, the offeror should be able to withdraw at any point prior to complete performance, since offers can in general be withdrawn prior to acceptance. Where no reliance has been placed on the offer, this principle is indeed applied, and the offer can be withdrawn. The withdrawal must be communicated, but, while there are no English cases in point, English commentators have assumed that notice of withdrawal need not reach everyone

---

[38] [1893] 1 QB 256.   [39] E.g., Atiyah, *Law of Contract*, 137.

who has heard the offer; it is enough if a reasonable method of communication is used, such as the original medium.[40]

The result is less clear where a party has incurred expenses in reliance on the offer. According to the orthodox rules, the offer should be capable of being withdrawn at any point prior to acceptance, that is, before completion of the performance. But strict application of this rule would appear capable of leading to injustice and thus it is not surprising that in some cases courts have held that the offer cannot be withdrawn once the plaintiff has commenced performance. In *Daulia Ltd v. Four Millbank Nominees Ltd*,[41] a vendor told buyers that if the buyers showed up the next morning with their part of a contract for sale of land engrossed and signed together with a banker's draft deposit, the vendors would enter a written contract. It was held that the vendor could not withdraw the next morning after the buyers showed up and, more generally, that there was an implied obligation on the part of the offeror not to prevent the condition becoming satisfied, which obligation arose as soon as the offeree started to perform.[42] Precisely what constitutes 'starting to perform', and whether and how this is different from 'preparations to perform', has not been discussed in English cases, though presumably the courts would try to draw some sort of distinction between the two.

More significantly, the *Daulia* decision is not followed consistently. In *Luxor (Eastbourne) Ltd v. Cooper*,[43] the appellants promised that if the respondent agent introduced a buyer for their cinemas at the stated price, on completion of the sale the respondent would be paid £5,000. The respondent introduced a buyer, but the appellants refused to proceed with the sale. The court held that the unilateral contract was complete only on actual sale so that the respondent received nothing. The distinction between *Luxor* and *Daulia* would appear to be that, in the court's view, in the former case, but not the latter, it was the normal understanding of parties that the risk of non-completion lay entirely on the agent. This risk was offset by the high rewards earned in cases where completion occurred.

It is difficult to say how a court would apply this distinction to a revocation of reward case (none of the cases in point deal with rewards). Treitel suggests, in the absence of any clear authority, that 'it is probable that an

---

[40] See, e.g., Treitel, *Contract*, 40, which cites an American case as authority.
[41] [1978] Ch. 231.
[42] See also *Errington* v. *Errington* [1952] 1 KB 290, where it was held that a father's promise to turn over a house to his son and daughter-in-law if they paid all the mortgage could not be revoked once they had begun performance.   [43] [1941] AC 108.

offer of a reward for the return of lost property could still be withdrawn after someone had spent time looking for the property without success, but not after he had actually found it and was in the process of returning it to the owner'.[44]

It is suggested that this approach is most likely to be followed in Case 14(b), where the advertisement is made 'to the world' in a newspaper. No court is going to be very keen on a ruling which in theory could allow thousands of disappointed reward-seekers to claim compensation from Simone. Raymond has a stronger claim because in his case (as in *Daulia*) the offer was made to him personally, rather than to the world at large. In tort cases dealing with detrimental reliance (e.g., negligent misrepresentation, negligent provision of services), the closer the relationship of the parties the more likely a finding of liability (see Case 5).[45] The significance of Raymond being a private detective is unclear. On the one hand, it can be assumed that he would not look for the necklace without some hope of collecting the reward, and that Simone would be aware of this. On the other hand, a court might reason that the possibility of a reward being revoked is, as in *Luxor*, one of the risks of the business. On balance, I think it unlikely a court would allow revocation once Raymond had begun to search.

Assuming that it is too late for Simone to withdraw her offer to Raymond, what is the effect of attempting to withdraw? In theory an ineffective withdrawal has no effect, and, in the case of a unilateral contract, the other party should be free to try, if he wishes, to complete performance just as if nothing had happened. Performance would of course need to be complete by the relevant expiry date, here the date indicated on the reward or, lacking such a date, a reasonable period. If Raymond failed to find the necklace, he could not collect anything.

The situation is more complex if Raymond ceases looking for the necklace because he wrongly believes that the purported withdrawal is effective or because he believes, perhaps rightly, that Simone is no longer interested in recovering the necklace. It seems likely that an English court would seek to allow Raymond a measure of recovery here, assuming that Raymond was acting reasonably, but the basis on which an award could be made is not clear. There are no cases in point.

One possibility is that Raymond could claim that the withdrawal was in effect an 'anticipatory breach' of the contract. An anticipatory breach occurs where one party, before the time at which he is to perform, informs

---

[44] Treitel, *Contract*, 37.   [45] *Hedley Byrne* v. *Heller* [1964] AC 465.

the other party that he will not perform.[46] Where such a 'breach' occurs, the innocent party can 'accept the repudiation' and claim damages as of that time. Raymond might be able to argue that Simone's purported withdrawal was in effect an anticipatory breach. If so, then Raymond could claim damages, which would presumably be based on the value to him, at that time, of the possibility of getting the reward. This means that Raymond would almost certainly not receive the entire reward, but only a percentage reflecting his loss of a chance. A second possibility is that an English court would find that Simone had in fact withdrawn the offer, but was in breach of an implied obligation not to do so, and hence that damages could be recovered on that basis.

A final general observation is that, as should be evident by now, withdrawal of offers to make a 'unilateral' contract raises problems that cannot be accommodated easily by orthodox English law.

IRELAND

These cases concern a unilateral contract. Irish law and English law use the expression 'unilateral contract' in a quite different sense from continental legal systems. In Irish law and English law, a unilateral contract is where only one party makes a promise inviting the other, not to promise in return, but to make some performance. In contrast, a bilateral contract is where both parties are bound, and it comprises the exchange of a promise for a promise.

There is no difficulty in seeing the consideration for such a promise when the stipulated act has actually been completed. Thus in this case, Simone clearly obtains a benefit where she promises a reward for the return of the stolen necklace and it is actually returned to her.

Chitty[47] suggests that just as commencement of performance can amount to acceptance of an offer of a unilateral contract, in the same way such commencement can also amount to consideration. It may be a sufficient detriment to the promisee to commence efforts in finding the necklace and incurring expenses thereby. Thus commencement of performance may provide consideration, and may accordingly deprive the promisor of his right to revoke the promise.

There is slight Irish authority on this point but, in my opinion, an Irish court would probably adopt the approach suggested by Chitty. If so, an Irish court will hold that Raymond or others have commenced performance by

---

[46] See Treitel, *Contract*, 769–71.   [47] *Chitty on Contracts*, par. 127.

incurring expenses looking for the necklace and have thus provided consideration. As a result they have deprived Simone of her right to revoke the promise. Of course, full performance of the stipulated act, i.e. finding the stolen necklace, is necessary before Simone's promise to pay the large reward can be enforced.

In Case 14(a) as described Raymond has made no promise to look for the necklace. If an Irish court found on the facts that Simone wanted such a counter-promise in return for her own, and that Raymond had so promised expressly or impliedly, then the court would probably conclude that there was a bilateral contract binding on both parties in which one party's obligations were conditional on the other's success.

Summaries

France: In Case 14(a), Simone may terminate the contract but she must pay Raymond's expenses. In Case 14(b), the promise to the general public can be revoked under the same conditions as a promise to a specific person, but the courts will deem such a promise to be valid for only a short period of time. Possibly, Raymond can claim compensation for the management of another's business (*gestion d'affaires*).

Belgium: In Case 14(a), Simone may terminate the contract but she must compensate Raymond for his expenses and the loss of the chance to earn the sum offered for finding the necklace. In Case 14(b), the promise of reward is enforceable because it is unilaterally binding or because revoking it would be an abuse of right. Possibly, Raymond can claim compensation for the management of another's business (*gestion d'affaires*).

The Netherlands: In Case 14(a), Simone's promise to Raymond is binding. In Case 14(b), the promise is not binding but, when Simone revokes it, the court can require her to pay 'equitable compensation' to anyone who has 'begun to prepare' the performance requested. Here, most likely, a member of the public would not have 'begun to prepare' simply because he has incurred expenses looking for the necklace. If Simone had declared her offer to be irrevocable, then she would not be entitled to revoke it unless she had 'serious reasons', which she did not in this case.

Spain: The promise in Case 14(a) is binding. The promise in Case 14(b) may be revoked if the revocation is made public to the same extent as the promise.

Portugal: The promise in Case 14(a) is binding. Nevertheless, Simone has the right to revoke it, although, if she does, she must compensate Raymond for any loss he incurred. The promise in Case 14(b) is binding, but it can be revoked before the necklace is found by making the revocation in the same way as the original offer. If it is revoked, Simone need not compensate those who have incurred expenses.

Italy: In Case 14(a), if Raymond undertook no obligation to try to find the necklace, express or implied, some believe that Simone's offer is irrevocable as soon as it comes to the promisee's notice (except possibly for a just cause, as described below), and some that it is revocable until Raymond begins to perform (and thereafter, not even for a just cause). Even by the second view, the promise is irrevocable if Raymond has begun to try to find the necklace.

In Case 14(b), the promise to the public can be revoked only if the revocation is made public in the same way as the offer, and only then for a just cause. Just cause means that the performance has become impossible or useless; it is not enough that she changed her mind.

Austria: In Case 14(a), the contract is valid, but Simone has the right to cancel it provided she compensates Raymond for work already done and for the profit he would have made had the contract been completed.

In Case 14(b), the promise is valid, but Simone can revoke it. Revocation does not affect the rights of a person who achieves the result for which a reward is offered provided they did not know or have reason to know of the revocation, but here, no one has yet found the necklace.

Germany: In Case 14(a), if Raymond is actually obligated to find the necklace, Simone may cancel the contract but only if she pays him the fee agreed upon, which would be problematic here because he earns the fee only if he finds the necklace. If, as is more likely, Raymond is only obligated to try to find the necklace, Simone has a right to cancel it without paying Raymond's fee. She must do so in good faith: for example, not when he is about to find the necklace.

In Case 14(b), the promise is valid but Simone can revoke it provided she does so in the same way as she made the promise. She need not pay anyone for expenses they have incurred.

Greece: In Case 14(a), Simone can withdraw her offer if the result has not been achieved in a reasonable period of time, as seems to be the case here where three months have passed.

In Case 14(b), the promise is valid but Simone can revoke it in the same way as it was made.

Scotland: Both promises are non-gratuitous and therefore irrevocable. Possibly, they could be revoked after a reasonable time has passed, but three months is not a reasonable time.

England: The promises are offers of unilateral contract in the common law sense: offers that are said to be accepted by performing the act requested. They can be withdrawn before they have been relied upon, in the case of the advertisement, in the same way that the original offer was made. In principle, it would seem that the offer could be withdrawn even afterwards, but some English cases have held that it could not be after the promisee has begun to perform, as distinguished from making preparations to perform. It is not clear that these cases would be followed here, or how this distinction would be applied. In any event, a court would be unlikely to enforce the promise in the newspaper advertisement.

Ireland: The promises are offers of unilateral contract in the common law sense: offers that are said to be accepted by performing the act requested. They can be withdrawn before they have been relied upon. They probably will be held to be irrevocable when the offeree begins performance, and to incur expenses looking for the necklace is probably to begin performance.

Preliminary comparisons

The promise in Case 14(a) was revocable at will only in Germany, and even then, the revocation must be made in good faith. It is revocable in France and Portugal, but Simone would be liable for Raymond's expenses. It is revocable in Belgium and Austria only if she pays his expenses and lost profit, and so, while the promise is revocable, she must pay the same amount as if it were not. It is irrevocable in the Netherlands, Spain, Greece, and Scotland, and, in Italy, it may be revocable only for just cause. It may be irrevocable after Raymond has 'begun to perform' in Italy, according to one opinion, and in England and Ireland, where the promise is deemed to be an offer of unilateral contract in the common law sense, that is, an offer that can be accepted only by performing.

The promise in Case 14(b) is freely revocable in Austria, and in Spain, Portugal, Germany, and Greece as well provided that the revocation is given the same publicity as the original offer. It is revocable in France if Simone pays for the expenses anyone has incurred; in the Netherlands provided she pays 'equitable compensation' to whoever has begun to perform. It is irrevocable in Belgium either because unilateral obligations (in the civil law sense) are binding or because revocation would be an abuse of right. It is irrevocable in Scotland because it is not a gratuitous obligation. It is irrevocable except for just cause in Italy. It is probably irrevocable only after performance has begun in England and Ireland, where, as before, it is deemed to be an offer of unilateral contract in the common law sense.

Case 15: promises of commissions

Case

Claude, wishing to sell his house, listed it with Homes, an agency that assists sellers in finding buyers. Homes was to receive 5 per cent of the sales price of the house if it found a buyer. Three months later, after Homes had taken various steps to do so and incurred expenses, Claude decided not to sell his house. Is he liable to the agency for 5 per cent of the sales price or for its expenses? Does it matter if the agency has found a buyer who has expressed his willingness to buy the house although no contract has been signed? Does it matter if Claude had promised that he would list the house only with Homes or whether he remained free to list it with other agencies?

Discussions

FRANCE

Under French law, the contract between Claude and Homes would be classified as one of agency (*mandat*). Claude grants Homes the power to do something in his name (art. 1984 of the Civil Code): to find a buyer for his house. More precisely, this contract would probably be considered to be a real estate agency contract, although some would consider it a contract for services on the ground that, traditionally, a contract of agency is deemed to be gratuitous, unlike a contract with a real estate agent, who receives compensation.

The Civil Code provides some general rules to govern an agent's remuneration. According to art. 1999, 'the principal must reimburse the agent for advance payments and costs that the latter has incurred while performing the agency, and pay the salary promised to him'. If the agent has committed some fault, the principal cannot refuse to reimburse him even though the matter has not been successful, nor can he reduce the amount on the basis that his costs could have been less.

However, special legislation has been enacted to protect the clients of estate agents: the 'Hoguet' law of 2 January 1970, with rules for its implementation (decree of 20 July 1972, amended on 29 June 1995 and 31 May 1996). This legislation covers all those persons, physical or legal, whose business it is to assist in real property transactions or real property management, as is the case here.

Nevertheless, this law is even more stringent as to the amount of remuneration that is due. First, it makes payment subject to the contract that sets this remuneration. The contract, however, must be valid and in writing and must name the person to whom payment is to be made (art. 6 of the 'Hoguet' law). These formalities are a necessary condition for payment to be made.[1]

Moreover, this remuneration is not linked to the services rendered (research, advertising, and effecting the transaction) but to the actual result of the steps taken by the agent. Article 139 of the decree of 31 May 1996 also provides that if a professional's activity does not achieve a satisfactory result, he will have no right to a commission, nor to any reimbursement of the costs that he has incurred. Moreover, the 'Hoguet' law has been interpreted to restrict even further the right to claim it. Remuneration is due only when the real estate agent has achieved a 'substantial result', and his intervention has had a determining effect on the completion of the transaction. The commission is due on account of the result achieved and not for the time or effort spent. Applying this rule can sometimes be rather tricky.

If Claude changes his mind three months after making the contract with Homes, Claude might be liable for the 5 per cent commission if Homes had achieved a 'substantial result', and an offer to purchase had been made. This requirement would seem to be satisfied as soon as the agent introduces a serious buyer who satisfies the conditions laid down by the principal. Thus, it would seem to be satisfied if Homes has found a willing buyer although no contract has been signed. All that the real estate agent would then have to prove is that his intervention was essential for realizing the sale. This is a question of fact and, as such, left to the absolute authority of the trial court judges to answer. In any event, according to the 'Hoguet' law, either Homes is entitled to the commission agreed

---

[1] Civ. 1, 26 Nov. 1985, Bull. civ. I, no. 317, p. 280.

upon in writing or it is entitled to nothing. The commission is paid for achieving the desired result and not for the time and expenses incurred by the agent.

Nevertheless, the case law does not seem to accept this conclusion. It has admitted that the seller 'may have perfectly legitimate reasons for not selling despite the agency given',[2] and that 'not completing the principal act may be due to purely personal reasons of convenience'.[3] As a result, the agent would not be able to earn anything. Moreover, the real estate agent only has an obligation to use his best endeavours (*obligation de moyen*) since this type of agency is only one of 'involvement consisting in looking for clients and negotiating just one of these transactions'.[4] Remuneration would be due only if Homes could prove that the sale has been effectively concluded.[5]

Nevertheless, it would still be possible for him to bring an action in tort for the loss caused by withdrawing the agency on the grounds that by doing so, Claude has committed a fault under art. 1382 of the Civil Code. As a general rule, damages are awarded in full to place the plaintiff where he would have been if no harm had been suffered.

Finally, we will consider whether it matters whether the contract was one for an exclusive agency to sell the house. If it is an exclusive agency, then, according to art. 6, final paragraph of the law and art. 78 of the decree, the agent's right to remuneration is considerably reinforced. He has the right to be paid even if he achieves the result in question with the help of a third party, which is not the case here. Moreover, he is allowed to include a penalty clause which provides that the owner is liable to pay a specified amount of damages if a sale has not been concluded although the real estate agent has found a buyer who satisfies his principal's requirements. Thus, if the contract was for an exclusive agency, Homes could have included such a clause, and if it had, Claude could be liable for the amount specified. In a sole agency a penalty clause may even take effect when a contract has been concluded without the real estate agent's involvement, which is not the case here.[6]

Litigation over real estate agents' remuneration is frequent. On average,

[2] Report of the *Cour de cassation* for 1987.
[3] Civ. 1, 15 Dec. 1987, Bull. civ. I, no. 271, p. 203.
[4] Civ. 1, 8 July 1986, Rev. dr. immobilier 1986, 481.
[5] Civ. 1, 7 June 1988, Bull. civ. I, no. 170, p. 119.
[6] If the agency is not exclusive, nevertheless, a provision may be included allowing the agent to earn a commission if the sale is effected without his intervention but with the buyer whom he found. This, again, is not the case here.

seven decisions per year are handed down by the First Civil Chamber of the *Cour de cassation*. Scholarly writing is also voluminous,[7] and the case law is complex.

What is surprising is the rule that the remuneration is not linked to the agent's services but solely to the result achieved. It is sometimes criticized because it derogates from general rules of law (*droit commun*) which require that a service actually rendered should be duly paid for. It is justified, however, by the need to protect clients from abuses that agents might otherwise commit. There is another way as well in which the rules that govern agency contracts seem to derogate from general principles. It is one of the rare instances in which French judges have asserted the power to reduce the remuneration stipulated for if they consider that it is excessive in relation to the services rendered. Traditionally, a contract of agency was deemed by French law to be a gratuitous contract, and so it is subject to strict control whenever it is entered into for compensation.

BELGIUM

The agreement in this case is a brokerage contract (*contrat de courtage*). It is not a contract of agency (*mandat*) because the role of Homes is limited to mediating between the parties. It does not represent the seller. The contract belongs to the category of *louage d'ouvrage*, literally, the hiring of labour.[8] Here, as in Case 14, art. 1794 of the Civil Code allows Claude to terminate the contract unilaterally provided it is a contract with no set term (*contrat à durée indéterminée*).[9] If he does, Homes is entitled to compensation,[10] although, because its mission was unsuccessful, the 5 per cent commission on the price of the house need not be paid. Nevertheless, if the failure of the mission were attributable to Claude, the broker could seek the rescission of the contract (*action en résolution du contrat*) with damages for the failure of the principal to perform his contractual obligations (art.

---

[7] See, e.g., D. Tomasin, 'La rémunération des agents immobiliers', Rev. dr. immobilier, 1989, 125 f.; J.-L. Bergel, 'Observations sur le droit à rémunération de l'agent immobilier', JCP 1989, 73 f.; F. Dagot, 'La commission de l'agent immobilier', JCP 1986, 255 f.; S. Sanz, 'Le droit à commission de l'agent immobilier', RTDCiv. 1981, 507.

[8] See P. A. Foriers, 'Le droit commun des intermédiaires commerciaux', in L. Simont, P. Foriers, I. Verougstraete, and B. Glansdorff, *Les intermédiaires commerciaux* (1990), nos. 95 f.   [9] See, on this point, *ibid.*, no. 117.

[10] See *Répertoire pratique du droit belge*, 'Courtier', no. 124 (expenses incurred must have been necessary or useful).

1184 of the Civil Code). In particular, a broker who finds a buyer who expresses his willingness to buy the house and makes a reasonable offer which is arbitrarily rejected by the principal would be entitled to damages which reflect the gain he would otherwise have made. The amount of damages would coincide with the amount of the commission originally provided for in the contract if that is the gain he would otherwise have made.[11]

THE NETHERLANDS

In this case, everything depends on what the parties agreed. In the Netherlands, most real estate agents are members of an association (NVM) that uses standard contracts. These contracts prescribe that a client who decides that he no longer wants to sell the house has to pay the agent 10 per cent of the fee he would get if the house was sold for the price for which it was listed. They also forbid clients to list their houses with other agencies. Moreover, they require arbitration in case of a dispute, and so there is little case law on such contracts.

If there were no such standard contracts everything would depend on what the parties agreed to. If the parties did not make explicit provisions on these points, the matter would be decided by interpretation (arts. 3:33 and 3:35 of the Civil Code).

SPAIN

This type of contract is termed *corretaje* in Spanish law. The *corretaje* is not one of the types governed by the Spanish codes. Under the rules developed by the courts, Claude is obligated to pay Homes 5 per cent of the sales price if a sale takes place due to Homes' efforts.[12] Generally, for Homes to recover, there must be a causal link between its actions and the sale. In a case where the broker found a buyer and the seller prevented completion of the sale the *Tribunal Supremo* decided to allow the broker to recover its commission.[13] Thus if Homes finds a buyer and Claude does not want to sell, Homes can recover its commission of 5 per cent. If the property were sold but the sale was not attributable to Homes' efforts, Homes could not recover its commission. If Claude changes his mind and

---

[11] See *ibid.*; J. Van Ryn and J. Heenen, *Principes de droit commercial*, 2nd edn (1988), vol. IV, no. 160; Foriers, 'Le droit commun', no. 99; Bruxelles, 5 March 1913, JCB, 1914, 147.
[12] TS, 2 Dec. 1902; TS, 3 June 1950; TS, 23 Oct. 1959; TS, 27 Dec. 1962; TS, 2 May 1963; TS, 21 Oct. 1965.   [13] TS, 17 May 1966.

decides not to sell before Homes finds a buyer, then it cannot recover.[14] Homes runs this risk.

PORTUGAL

Claude is liable to Homes neither for 5 per cent of the price nor for its expenses even if the agency has found a buyer. He would however be obliged to compensate Homes for its expenses if he has promised in a written document to list the house only with Homes and then decides not to sell it before the term expires which is fixed for the duration of the contract. Moreover, Homes would be entitled to its commission if it found a buyer during this period.

This type of contract is called *mediação imobiliária* in Portuguese law, and is governed by Decree-Law 77/99 of 18 March 1999. According to art. 20 of this law, such a contract has to be made in a written document which describes the compensation and sets a term for the duration of the contract. If these conditions are not complied with, the contract is void and not binding on Claude.

The *mediação imobiliária* is considered a contract for services in which the agency, Homes, is obligated to find a buyer for a building, Claude's, by the established deadline. Therefore, Claude would be obliged to pay Homes 5 per cent of the sales price only if a sale takes place due to Homes' efforts. This solution is expressly provided by the law (art. 19(1)). Therefore, if a sale did not take place Homes is not entitled to any compensation.

Nevertheless, if Claude promised to list the house only with Homes, the law provides for a different solution. If the agency has the right to an exclusive listing, it is entitled to its commission if the sale did not take place due to Claude's fault (art. 19(2)(a)). If the term fixed for the duration of the contract has expired, however, Claude would not have any obligation towards Homes if he decided not to sell, even if Homes had incurred expenses. If the term has not expired, Claude would be at fault if he decided not to sell the house and so would be liable to Homes (art. 798 of the Civil Code). In any case, he would have to pay for the expenses Homes has incurred. His obligation to pay the commission, however, would depend on whether Homes could prove that it could have found a buyer before the expiration of the contract. Therefore, if the agency had already found a buyer, it would be easy to convince a court to grant it compensation for the 5 per cent of the price that it lost.

[14] *Ibid.*

ITALY

Claude is liable to the agency for its expenses if it has not found a buyer. Claude is liable instead for 5 per cent of the sales price if Homes has found a buyer although no sales contract has been signed.

If Homes has not yet found a buyer, it nevertheless has the right to recover its expenses[15] according to art. 1756 of the Civil Code.[16]

The contract says that Homes would receive the 5 per cent commission 'if it found a buyer'. Therefore, Claude is bound by his promise to pay the commission even if he decides not to sell the house as long as Homes found a buyer, and so this condition has been met.

Absent such a provision, the case would probably be decided differently. According to art. 1755 of the Civil Code,[17] the agent is entitled to a commission only if the deal is concluded as a result of his intervention. Doctrinally, the right to receive the commission arises as soon as the economic interest of the parties is safeguarded.[18]

As in all contractual relationships, the parties must behave in accordance with the general principle of good faith (arts. 1175 and 1375 of the Civil Code). Claude has no duty to sell his house if he changes his mind, even if he listed it with Homes, but he is certainly obligated to disclose his intentions as soon as possible so as to avoid useless efforts of the real estate agent.[19]

Real estate agencies in Italy generally insist that they have the exclusive right to list a house.

AUSTRIA

Claude can cancel the contract without having to pay any money to Homes. The contract with a real estate agent is regulated by the 'Makler-

---

[15] See G. Giordano, D. Iannelli, and Santoro, 'Il contratto di agenzia. La mediazione', Giur. sist. civ. e comm. I (1974), 133; G. Di Chio, 'La mediazione', in G. Cottino, *Contratti commerciali, Trattato di diritto commerciale e di diritto pubblico dell'economia diretto da Galgano* 16 (1991), 619 ff.

[16] Article 1756 of the Civil Code: 'Expenses: Subject to agreement or usage to the contrary, the broker is entitled to reimbursement of his expenses from the person on whose behalf they were incurred, even if the transaction is not concluded.'

[17] Article 1755 of the Civil Code: 'Commission: The broker is entitled to a commission from each of the parties if the transaction is concluded as a result of his intervention. In the absence of agreement, fee schedule, or usage, the amount of such commission and the proportion in which it is chargeable to each of the parties are determined by the court on an equitable basis.'

[18] See Di Chio, 'La mediazione', 624; C. Varelli, *La mediazione* (1953), 78; U. Azzolina, 'La mediazione', in Vassalli, *Tratt. di dir. civ.* 8:2 (1943), 133; M. Stolfi, 'La mediazione', in *Commentario a cura di Scialoja e Branca* (1976), 27 ff.

[19] See Giordano, Iannelli, and Santoro, 'Il contratto di agenzia', 510.

Gesetz' (Act on Brokers, BGBl 1996/262). According to § 6 of this Act, the real estate agent is entitled to claim his brokerage fee only if a contract for the sale of the land is concluded. The seller, who has the contract with the agent, is under no obligation to conclude the contract with the persons found by the agent who are interested in buying the house.[20] This rule is obligatory and cannot be changed by the parties in their contract.[21] If no contract is concluded, the agent cannot claim compensation for his expenses.[22] If the contract with the agent is not made for a certain period of time, both parties can cancel it at any time.

If Claude promised to list the house only with Homes, the contract would constitute an *Alleinvermittlungsauftrag*. In such a case it is possible[23] for the parties to agree that the customer must pay the agent's fee if he cancels the contract and does not have an important reason for the cancellation, provided the contract with the agent was concluded for a certain period of time.

GERMANY

Section 652(1)(1) of the Civil Code provides that an agency like Homes can claim the agreed percentage of the sales price only if someone really agrees to buy the house, and this agreement was brought about by the actions of the agency. It is not enough if the agency finds somebody who is willing to buy. That is so even if the contract is exclusive or the agency has incurred expenses. There is no obligation on Claude to sell his house. He is absolutely free to make that decision without regard for Homes' interests. The only limitation on Claude's freedom to decide is, as usual, that he must act in good faith.[24]

The result would be different only if the contract included an express provision that money would be due if Homes finds a buyer. But when the sum due is 5 per cent of the sales price, and it is due without the completion of the sale, the promise to sell real estate would require compliance with the formalities of § 313 of the Civil Code. The reason is that it creates an economic pressure to sell real estate. That was the conclusion of the highest German court (*Bundesgerichtshof*) when a client of a real

---

[20] § 4 I MaklerG.   [21] See § 18 MaklerG.

[22] This is justified by the fact that the real estate agent – unless otherwise agreed – is under no obligation to try to find a buyer for the house (see § 4 I MaklerG). It is, however, possible for the parties to make an agreement according to which expenses which exceed the costs for the normal business activity of the broker have to be reimbursed by the customer (see § 9 MaklerG).   [23] See § 15 II N 1 MaklerG.

[24] BGH NJW 1975, 647 (648).

estate agency promised in writing to pay 4 per cent of the proposed price of a house just for the work of the agency and without regard to its success. The court held that the formalities of § 313 had to be complied with because the economic pressure on the client demanded the protection that these formalities were supposed to afford.[25] An agency like Homes can claim its expenses (as distinguished from its fee) only if the contract expressly so provides (§ 652 II of the Civil Code[26]). As a compensation for these disadvantages, agencies like Homes are not under a legal obligation to find a buyer. They are not even obligated to make any efforts to do so.

GREECE

A brokerage contract such as this one is governed by arts. 703–8 of the Civil Code. The provisions of the Civil Code concerning brokerage are basically dispositive law. For certain categories of brokerage contracts there are special laws (for example, L 308/76 on brokers of civil contracts).

A brokerage contract is related to the contract of agency or mandate,[27] but it is entered into for remuneration. In such a contract, which establishes a fiduciary relationship, the broker (who corresponds to the mandatary) promises to the other contracting party (the mandator) to find him an opportunity to conclude a contract that is in his interest in return for a fee promised to the broker (art. 703 of the Civil Code).[28] The fee must be paid only if the contract is actually concluded as a consequence of the actions of the broker (art. 703 of the Civil Code). If a contract is not concluded but a promise to enter into one has been made, half the fee is due. The parties may agree, on the contrary, that the fee is due for the actions of the broker even if a contract is not concluded.[29] The broker can also claim his expenses if the other party has agreed to reimburse him for

---

[25] BGH NJW 1971, 93.

[26] The agency (*Makler*) has a claim for expenses only if this was especially agreed. This is so even if the proposed contract is never agreed upon.

[27] The leading opinion in theory and in the case law considers brokerage as a mandate. P. Zepos, *Law of Obligations* (1965), Special Part, vol. II, 43–8; EfAth 2319/56 NoB 5, 258; AP 474/1979 NoB 27, 1473. However, some commentators believe that brokerage differs from mandate. Karasis in Georgiadis and Stathopoulos, *Civil Code*, art. 703.

[28] Article 703 of the Civil Code comes from art. 413(1) and (3) of the Swiss Code of Obligations and from § 652(1) of the German Civil Code. Kafkas, *Law of Obligations*, vol. A, art. 703. As far as procedural law is concerned, if the broker has been legally appointed then any disputes between him and the mandator are governed by art. 667 of the Code of Civil Procedure. In any other case the regular procedure is followed. Karasis in Georgiadis and Stathopoulos, *Civil Code* art. 703.

[29] AP 687/80 NoB 28, 2014; AP 180/66 NoB 14, 1017.

them. In that event, reimbursement is due even if a contract was not concluded (art. 703(2) of the Civil Code).

The mandator is free to recall his mandate at any time without giving a reason (art. 186 of the Civil Code). In that event, the mandator does not owe the fee unless the parties agreed otherwise. The revocation of the brokerage relationship is valid *ex nunc*. This means that the broker cannot earn his fee after revocation by taking an action that leads to a contract unless the mandator agrees to pay one and so enters into a new brokerage contract. The fee is payable if the actions of the broker before revocation lead to the conclusion of a contract.

Claude, then, had the right to revoke. Nevertheless, if he did so in a way that is contrary to good faith or *bonos mores* or the social and economic purpose of the right (art. 281 of the Civil Code) or if he did so negligently (art. 914 of the Civil Code), he must pay damages to the broker which would include the brokerage fee. For example, he would be liable if he revoked during a crucial period of negotiations with the intention of frustrating the broker's rights when a contract is about to be concluded.[30]

In a brokerage contract, the mandator of a brokerage contract is free to employ other brokers unless the parties agree otherwise. An agreement for exclusive brokerage is valid.[31] If the brokerage is exclusive, all the requirements that we have analysed above must also be fulfilled. Usually in this kind of brokerage it is agreed that the mandator is not free to revoke his mandate for a limited period unless he can prove that the contrary was understood (art. 288 of the Civil Code). He would still have the right to revoke on serious grounds. If the mandator employs other brokers or if he revokes his mandate before the time agreed or he revokes it in a manner contrary to good faith, he must compensate the broker for the damages suffered. These include the loss of the opportunity to earn the fee because the mandator violated his agreement. The broker could receive the same fee if he could prove that his actions would have led to the conclusion of the contract if the agreement had not been violated.[32]

SCOTLAND

The Scottish courts would approach this problem from a contractual standpoint. The solution will therefore depend on whether the terms of

---

[30] Karasis in Georgiadis and Stathopoulos, *Civil Code*, art. 703, no. 16.

[31] *Ibid.*, art. 709, no. 21; Varthakokoilis, *Analytical Interpretation*, art. 703; Athens Court of First Instance 4029/82, Dni 25/849.

[32] Karasis in Georgiadis and Stathopoulos, *Civil Code*, art. 703, no. 21; N. Farmakidis, *The Brokerage Contract* (1989), 64–5, 90–1.

the contract permit Claude to withdraw from it without penalty. If the contract is silent on this matter, it would appear that Claude is in breach and will have to pay damages. If the agreement allowed him to list the house with other agencies, then it would seem clear that he was free to withdraw from his contract with Homes at any time without penalty: to allow him to list with other agencies would suggest that since the original agency was non-exclusive, he was free to withdraw.

The problem could also be analysed from the viewpoint that Claude makes a promise *sub conditione*. If this were the case then Claude would be liable if he changed his mind within a reasonable time as he would then be acting in such a way as to prevent the promisee fulfilling (purifying) the condition, as in *Petrie* v. *Earl of Airlie*[33] (defender held to his promise to provide a reward for the detection *and conviction* of a criminal, even though conviction failed: this was because the *defender* refused to cooperate in the proceedings, leading to the case against the accused being dropped). The promise need not be constituted in writing as it is non-gratuitous since Claude will receive a benefit if the condition is purified.

ENGLAND

It is reasonably clear in English law that if Homes has not found a buyer then, even if Homes has incurred expenses, Claude is free to withdraw his offer and is not liable for either 5 per cent of the sale price or Homes' expenses.

As discussed in the previous answer, in the case of *Luxor (Eastbourne) Ltd.* v. *Cooper*[34] the court held that an agent who had found a requested buyer for the defendant's house was not owed the £5,000 that the vendor promised would be his on completion of the sale when, as happened, the vendor refused to go through with the sale. We noted that this decision appeared to turn largely on the court's understanding of what the normal expectations and understandings of such an arrangement are in the relevant business community. In Lord Russell's words: 'No general rule can be laid down by which the rights of the agents or the liability of the principal under commission contracts are to be determined. In each case these must depend upon the exact terms of the contract in question, and upon the true construction of those terms.' As the arrangement in Case 15, and the context in which that arrangement arose, appear similar to *Luxor*, it can be assumed that the same result would be reached. And of course in

---

[33] [1834] 13 S 6.   [34] 8[1941] AC 108.

Case 15 the vendor's position is stronger because no buyer has yet been found. Finally, courts have generally construed terms strictly against real estate agents in such cases.[35]

Regarding a claim for expenses incurred, a principal, such as Claude, is in general under no obligation to continue in business (which in this case means to continue trying to sell his house) for the sake of his agent (here Homes), but if on the true construction of the contract the principal has given such an undertaking, then he can be held liable in damages for breaching that undertaking.[36] It is not clear from the facts whether Claude gave such an undertaking, but it would not be normal in such a contract (since the agent cannot force the vendor to agree to a sale, there is little point in forcing the vendor to continue offering the property for sale).

Would it matter if Homes had an exclusive listing? In *Luxor*, it appeared that the agent did not have an exclusive listing, but no weight was placed on this point there or in other cases. Arguably, in a non-exclusive listing the possibility that the agent may not earn a commission, even if he finds a willing buyer, is more evident from the start, but I do not think that great weight would be placed on this factor.

Claude's position if Homes has found a buyer depends, again, on the precise terms of Claude's offer. If Claude offered to pay Homes merely for finding a willing buyer, then he must pay if a willing buyer is found, since Homes has fully performed the requested condition. Courts require clear language before finding such an intention.[37] The phrase 'if it found a buyer' is ambiguous (must a 'buyer' actually buy the house?), and the fact that the commission in the example was '5 per cent of the *sales* price' would probably be taken as indicating that payment was, as in the *Luxor* case, conditional on an actual sale being completed. If so, then the *Luxor* ruling would again be applied. Note that it is clear from *Luxor* that it does not matter why Claude did not go through with the deal. There is no doctrine of good faith in English law that could be applied to a case such as this. The situation is unchanged if Homes is appointed a sole agent, except that if Claude sells through a different agent before the expiry of the agreement with Homes, then Homes can recover damages for breach (which damages would be calculated, it appears – though the law here is not much developed – by the amount of commission promised).[38]

---

[35] Treitel, *Contract*, 658 and cases cited therein.   [36] *Turner* v. *Goldsmith* [1891] 1 QB 544.
[37] *Fairvale* v. *Sabharwall* [1992] 2 EGLR 27.
[38] *Hampton & Sons Ltd* v. *George* [1939] 3 All ER 627.

IRELAND

Commission agency contracts turn 'in the main on the particular terms of the contract between the person who employs the agent and the agent'.[39]

In ascertaining whether the estate agent should be entitled to recover his commission and/or expenses the court will look primarily to the agreement made between the parties. In this instance, Homes was to receive '5 per cent of the sales price of the house if it found a buyer.' On the facts as presented it is clear that Homes has not found a buyer.

In *Fowler* v. *Bratt*, Lord Evershed MR relied on the following statement of Lord Russell in *Luxor (Eastbourne) Ltd.* v. *Cooper*:[40] 'where there is a bargain whereby the agent has to find a purchaser, or introduce a purchaser, then the agent in order to earn the commission, must produce the result of a binding contract made between vendor and purchaser'. Applying the dicta of Lord Russell and Lord Romer in *Luxor*, it was held that in order to earn the commission, the plaintiff had to find a purchaser who was bound in law to buy. In that case the real estate agent was also instructed to 'find a purchaser' or buyer.

There was no agreement between the parties in respect of the expenses to be incurred by Homes in finding a buyer. In *Murphy Buckley and Keogh* v. *Pye*,[41] the defendant vendors did not contest their liability to the plaintiff real estate agents for the money expended by them on advertising and so forth. However, it was clear from the facts of that case that the defendant had, prior to the advertising, agreed to specific expenditures being made in advertising the property in question. The plaintiffs were also found to be sole agents for the purposes of obtaining a purchaser of the property. An agreement such as that has clearly not taken place in Case 15.

The position of a real estate agent where no express agreement has been made with regard to the agency's entitlement to expenses is unclear in Ireland. However, there is some authority for the proposition that a real estate agent would be entitled to recover expenses, despite the absence of an express agreement to that effect.[42] In ascertaining whether the agent is entitled to his expenses, an Irish court might well take into account circumstances such as whether the principal was aware that the agent intended to, and actually did, incur outlay.

---

[39] Per *Somervell LJ in Boots* v. *Christopher & Co.* [1952] 1 KB 89.

[40] [1941] AC 105. It is to be noted that this case was cited as a precedent on a related issue in the Irish case of *Murphy Buckley and Keogh* v. *Pye (I) Ltd* [1971] IR 57.   [41] [1971] IR 57.

[42] See *Meacock & Co* v. *Abrahams* [1956] 3 All ER 660.

On the facts as presented it is possible that Homes might be entitled to recoup its expenses despite an absence of express agreement between the parties to that effect. However, if Homes could show that Claude was aware of possible expenditure to be incurred by Homes and any other such circumstances, then Homes would be in a far stronger position in seeking to recoup its expenses.

Whether it matters if the agency has found someone willing to buy depends upon the terms of the agreement between the parties. The agreement was to 'find a buyer'. Lord Evershed MR found that the phrase 'to find a purchaser' meant that the agent had to produce for his principal a purchaser who was bound at law to buy.[43]

There has been no signed contract and the real estate agent is not entitled to insist upon the principal instituting proceedings for specific performance.[44] In this regard, in accordance with the judgment in the *Fowler* case, Homes would not be entitled to the 5 per cent commission unless the behaviour of the parties was such as amounted to the purchaser being 'bound at law to buy'. Accordingly, if proceedings for specific performance are taken and are successful, the real estate agent's commission becomes payable.[45]

Again it is not clear whether Claude would be liable to Homes for its expenses for the reasons already discussed. However, the fact that Homes had found a buyer and that clearly their advertising costs and any other expenses involved had realized a buyer would strongly favour Homes when seeking to recoup any expenses incurred in an Irish court.

Irrespective of whether Homes was the sole agent for Claude or otherwise, unless Homes produces a buyer who was bound at law to buy, then Homes is not entitled to the commission.

In the Irish case of *Murphy Buckley and Keogh* v. *Pye (I) Ltd*[46] the sale of a factory, the subject matter of the proceedings, had been effected privately by the vendors or defendants with a third party during the continuance of the term of sole agency of the real estate agent or plaintiff. The agents sought commission for the sale but were refused by Henchy J who held, *inter alia*, that the plaintiffs' extensive exertions as sole agents had not played any effective part in effecting the sale of the factory to the purchaser.

The question as to whether Homes was the sole agent or not might be relevant in the context of expenses incurred. In *Murphy Buckley and Keogh*

---

[43] *Fowler* v. *Bratt* [1950] 2 KB 96.   [44] See *Boots* v. *Christopher & Co.* [1952] 1 KB 89.
[45] *Ibid.*   [46] [1971] IR 57.

v. *Pye (I) Ltd*, the plaintiffs were found to be sole agents for the purpose of obtaining a purchaser of the property in question. Although it was admitted by the defendant vendors that the plaintiff real estate agents were entitled to their expenses claimed, it is interesting that Henchy J noted the fact that they were sole agents for the defendant vendors and that there was certain correspondence which appeared to affirm the defendant vendors' liability to the plaintiffs in respect of expenses.

Applying the obiter dicta of Lord Justice Denning in the *Meacock* case,[47] Homes could be entitled to its expenses irrespective of whether there was an express agreement between Claude and Homes as to expenses. However, this view relies only on the obiter of Lord Justice Denning and the position is as yet unclear in Ireland.

If Homes was appointed sole agent by Claude then this no doubt would show a greater intention on the part of Claude that Homes should incur expenses on his behalf than if he remained free to list it with other agencies. Thus, if the fact that Homes was sole agent for Claude was combined with other factors, then this would go further to show the intention of Claude to be bound to Homes for its expenses.

Summaries

France: This contract is governed by special legislation that requires it to be in writing. This legislation provides that the agent can claim his commission once he has achieved a 'substantial result', and so it would seem that Homes can do so if it has found a willing buyer even though no contract has been signed. Nevertheless, the case law has recognized that the principal may have perfectly legitimate reasons for changing his mind, and would not allow Homes its commission unless a sale is actually concluded. Still, Homes may be able to recover in tort for harm it suffered if, by changing his mind, Claude committed a 'fault'. Under the legislation just mentioned, if the agency were exclusive, Homes would have the right to include a clause requiring Claude to pay a penalty if it found a satisfactory buyer but Claude refused to sell.

Belgium: If Homes has not yet found a buyer, Claude is entitled to terminate the contract but he must pay Homes' expenses. If Homes has found a willing buyer who makes a reasonable offer which Claude has arbitrarily rejected, Claude is liable for the commission Homes would have earned.

The Netherlands: In principle, whatever the parties agreed to will be

[47] [1956] 3 All ER 660.

enforced, and if their agreement is not explicit, the court will resolve the matter by interpretation. In practice, most real estate agencies use a standard form contract which requires the owner to list with them exclusively and provides that if he decides not to sell the house, he must pay the agent 10 per cent of the fee the agent would have received had the house been sold for the price at which it was listed.

Spain: Under rules developed by the courts, Homes cannot recover if Claude changes his mind before it finds a buyer. If it finds a buyer and then Claude changes his mind, it can recover the commission.

Portugal: Claude is liable to Homes only if the listing is exclusive, in which case he is liable for the expenses that Homes incurred, and he will be liable for the commission as well if Homes proves it would have sold the property.

Italy: Claude is liable to Homes for its expenses if it has not found a buyer, and for its commission if it has. Real estate agencies in Italy generally insist that the listing be exclusive.

Austria: Special legislation provides that Claude is under no obligation to sell to a buyer that Homes finds, and that Homes is not entitled to its commission unless a contract of sale is actually concluded. If the contract is for an exclusive listing, then the parties are allowed to change this rule by express agreement so that Claude is liable for the commission if he cancels the contract without an important reason. Otherwise, the parties cannot change the rule even by express agreement.

Germany: Whether or not the contract is exclusive, Homes can claim its commission only if a sale is actually concluded, not if it merely finds a willing buyer. While Claude must act in good faith, he can change his mind without taking account of Homes' interests. If the contract expressly provided that Homes could have its commission if it found a willing buyer, it would be valid only if it complied with the formalities for transferring real estate because, while it does not constitute a transfer, it creates economic pressure to make such a transfer. Homes cannot even claim its expenses. On the other hand, it is under no obligation even to try to find a buyer.

Greece: Claude does not owe the commission unless a sale is actually concluded. Up to then, he can change his mind for any reason. He must exercise this right in good faith: for example, he could not revoke as a contract is about to be concluded with the intention of harming the broker. These rules can be changed, however, by express agreement. Usually, if the parties agree that the listing is exclusive, they also agree that the owner is not free to change his mind for a limited period of time.

Scotland: Whether Claude is free to withdraw depends on how the contract is interpreted. If the agency is non-exclusive, it would seem clear that he may. If it is not and the agreement is silent on his right to withdraw, he would probably be deemed to be in breach. The promise might also be viewed as one subject to a condition, in which case Claude is in breach if he prevents the fulfilment of a condition in the contract.

England: Claude is free to withdraw and is not liable for Homes' expenses or its commission. The promise is, again, an offer of unilateral contract which is accepted by performance, but a court will refuse to enforce, not merely because it was not accepted, but because the normal expectation of the parties would be that Claude can withdraw. In the case in point, the listing was non-exclusive, but the court attached no weight to that circumstance.

Ireland: The contract will be interpreted to allow Claude to withdraw without paying the commission. There is some authority for interpreting the contract to allow Homes to recover its expenses. Homes would be much more likely to do so if it could show that Claude expected it to incur expenses. If Homes was sole agent, that fact might show that the parties intended Homes' expenses to be recoverable.

Preliminary comparisons

In Scotland, England, and Ireland, the effect of the agreement depends on its interpretation. The Scots reporter believes that if the agency were non-exclusive, Claude could withdraw before sale, but that if it were exclusive, he could not. The English and Irish reporters believe that he could withdraw before sale.

In Portugal, Claude is liable to Homes only if the listing is exclusive, in which case he is liable for the expenses that Homes incurred, and will be liable for the commission as well if Homes proves it would have sold the property.

In Belgium, Italy, and Spain, Homes could claim its commission if it finds a willing buyer, although in Belgium and Italy, if Claude withdraws before that time, he must pay Homes' expenses. In France, if the agency is exclusive, the parties may agree to a penalty if Claude withdraws before Homes finds a willing buyer, although otherwise Homes can claim its commission only if there is a sale.

In other jurisdictions, supposedly, Homes can claim its commission only if a sale is actually concluded, and before then, Claude can withdraw (in the Netherlands, this result may be reached as a matter of interpretation). But the parties are permitted to contract around the principle in certain ways. In Austria, if and only if the agency is exclusive, the parties can agree that the agent earns his commission if the principal changes his mind without an important reason. In Germany, they can change the rule provided they do so in writing. In Greece, if the agency is exclusive, the parties usually agree that the principal cannot revoke for a period of time. In France, the principal who revokes may be liable in tort. In the Netherlands, although in principle the effect of the contract is a matter of interpretation, in practice, agencies use a standard form contract which would require Claude to pay a penalty of 10 per cent of its commission if he withdraws before sale.

3   Comparisons

We can now examine the similarities and differences in the results that European legal systems reach and the doctrines by which they arrive at them. We will first consider promises which are meant to confer a benefit gratis on the promisee, and then those that are not. We will ask to what extent these results can be explained as responses to common underlying problems. In the end, we will discuss how the problems we identify might be solved most straightforwardly.

I. Gifts and favours

We will consider promises to confer a benefit on the promisee that necessarily entail a significant cost to the promisor because he has promised money or property. We will then turn to those that could be performed costlessly.

A. Promises of money or property

1. Obstacles to giving gifts

None of the legal systems under examination will ordinarily enforce an informal promise to give away money or property. One reason is generally acknowledged: to prevent the promisor from making ill-advised gifts. Nevertheless, no legal systems prevent the promisor from making any gifts at all. Nor, with some exceptions to be noted, are any legal systems willing to consider on the merits whether a particular gift is well or ill-advised. Instead, they interpose obstacles to gift-giving so that the would-be donor will deliberate.

As one might expect, the principal differences concern the size of the obstacle since there are advantages and disadvantages to making it larger or smaller. The difficulty of making a gift is the greatest in Belgium. In principle, a promise to do so cannot be made enforceable. To have legal effect, a gratuitous transfer of property must not only be subscribed to formally before a notary but it must transfer the property immediately and irrevocably. The advantage is that the promisor can decide his promise was ill-advised up to the very moment when the intended beneficiary is to receive the property.

In most civil law countries, promises to make a gift can be made enforceable but only by completing a formality that requires the help of a legal professional: the promisor must execute a document containing the promise before a notary (France, the Netherlands, Italy, Austria, Germany, and Greece). This requirement is the descendant of the old Roman formality of *insinuatio* or registration before a court. While these systems will presumably enforce more ill-advised promises than Belgian law, they do recognize that the promisor may have a good reason for deciding to commit himself in advance. He may think his decision to make the gift is better advised than any later decision he may make not to follow through. He may wish to assure the promisee that the promise will be kept.

In three legal systems (Spain, Portugal, and Scotland), the formality is so simple that the promisor can complete it himself: he need only put the promise in writing. The advantage is that the promisor can decide for himself where and when to make a commitment. This decision may actually be better advised than the one he makes if he is forced to visit a legal professional. In any case, it need not be less deliberate since his reason for not visiting a notary might be, not that he is acting on impulse, but that he wants to avoid the trouble and expense. On the other hand, one can imagine many occasions – a birthday party, for example, or a visit to a favourite nephew – when he might act under the influence of a warm but transitory impulse. If he needs to see a legal professional, the impulse may pass, and he may receive some good advice.

In the common law jurisdictions, England and Ireland, an informal promise to make a gift is not enforceable because it lacks consideration. The promisor can commit himself irrevocably either by completing a formality or by establishing a trust.

The formality is to make a 'deed' which is 'under seal'. In England, the promisor needs merely to state in a written document that it is intended to be under seal. In Ireland, he must still make some impression on the paper if only with the end of a ruler.

When a trust is established, ownership of the property in question passes from its owner, the 'settlor', to the trust. It is administered according to the settlor's instructions by the trustee for the benefit of the trust beneficiary. A promisor who, like Gaston in Case 1(a), wants to give his niece a large sum of money on her twenty-fifth birthday, could deposit the money in an account and place the account in trust with instructions to dissolve the trust and pay her the money when she turns twenty-five but until that time to pay the interest to himself. He could even name himself as the trustee who is obligated to act on these instructions. If the trust is made irrevocable, he is committed.

A trust requires no formalities. In principle, a lay person could execute a deed under seal or establish a trust without the help of a lawyer. In practice, very often he will not. To the extent he does not seek help, the advantages and disadvantages are like those of Scots and Spanish law, although with an additional disadvantage: it is easier for the promisor who does without professional help to make a mistake that renders the promise unenforceable. To the extent that he does seek help, the advantages and disadvantages are like those of continental systems that require the help of a notary, although with the additional advantage that one does not need to pay the notary's fee which can be quite high.

All of the legal systems, then, place obstacles in the way of making binding promises to give gifts, and the advantages and disadvantages of each depend on the size of the obstacles. It would be a mistake, however, to assume that all of the rules we have described were the result of a conscious decision about how large the obstacle should be. Sometimes such a decision was made. As we have seen, the drafters of the Belgian and Spanish Civil Codes broke with the pre-existing law governing promises of gifts in opposite ways. In Belgium, such promises became unenforceable. In Spain they became enforceable without notarization. Presumably, in each case, a decision was made about just how difficult gift-giving should be. Sometimes, however, decisions are made incrementally over time by adapting or finding new jobs for inherited rules rather than by tailoring a rule to produce exactly the results that it does. As we have seen, there are advantages and disadvantages to the formality of notarization as compared with that of a deed under seal. But civil law systems do not require the one formality, and common law systems the other, because anyone compared the two. Civil law systems require notarization because they substituted this formality for *insinuatio*. Some did so to make the formality more difficult and some to make it simpler.[1] Notarization seemed appropriate because since the Middle Ages, this formality had replaced

---

[1] R. Zimmermann, *The Law of Obligations: Roman Foundations of the Civilian Tradition* (1996), 500–1 (comparing France and Germany).

the Roman *stipulatio* in other transactions. *Insinuatio* had previously been required because the Emperor Constantine had thought it appropriate. Common law systems require a promise under seal because such promises were once enforceable in an action in covenant. Initially, that action was the only one that could be brought on an executory promise. Centuries later, when an action could also be brought in assumpsit, the seal acquired its modern role of making a promise enforceable when a promise lacked consideration as in the case of a gift. Today, as the Irish reporter mentioned, that formality is no longer easily understood and correctly performed by lay people. It no longer has the same advantages and disadvantages as it did when it was used by nobles with signet rings.

2. Exceptions for meritorious gifts

An alternative approach would be to enforce informal promises of gifts when, on the merits, the promise is unlikely to be ill-advised. The *ius commune* did so, in effect, when it created exceptions for promises to charitable causes (*ad pias causas*) and to those about to marry (*propter nuptias*).

Today, almost nothing is left of the first of these exceptions. In France, sometimes, in the past, promises of gifts to churches were enforced by characterizing them as exchanges because the promisor received some benefit such as hearing a church bell ring as it did in his childhood, or having mass said for his soul. In Germany, sometimes promises of gifts to a natural person who is to use them to benefit another have been upheld on the grounds that they are not really gifts if the recipient is obliged to give in turn to the ultimate beneficiary. But these are very exceptional cases. No system under examination will enforce an informal promise like that in Case 1(c) to the United Nations Children's Emergency Fund.

A few legal systems do make an exception for promises to people about to marry (Case 1(b)). In Belgium, such a promise is considered to be one to fulfil a 'natural obligation', and is therefore enforceable. It should be remembered that in Belgium it is not possible to make a promise of a gift binding. Where the rules are rigid, it is not surprising to find a greater willingness to make an exception. In Germany, such a promise is binding under a specific provision of the Civil Code (§ 1624(1)) which says that what parents give a child because of marriage or to live an independent life is counted as a gift only to the extent that it exceeds what is appropriate to their financial circumstances. In England, such a promise has sometimes been enforced despite the doctrine of consideration. As we saw earlier, such promises were traditionally enforced before the rise of the bargain theory of consideration, and in this case, the tradition has continued despite it. In Ireland, by statute, such a promise is enforceable if the promisor complies with the fairly simple formality of putting it in writing.

One might think that these exceptions are less common today because culture has changed since medieval and early modern times. People then might have had more definite ideas of what should count as 'pious causes' and why they should be supported. Family ties and inherited wealth counted for more, and so promises to those about to marry were more important. But that cannot be the entire explanation, as we can see if we look briefly at the law of the United States. Promises of both sorts are enforced. For a long time, American courts said that the consideration for promises to charitable causes was the commitment of other subscribers to donate money,[2] or the commitment of a charity to name a fund after the donor,[3] to locate a college in a particular town,[4] or even to use the money for charitable purposes.[5] They said that the consideration for a promise to those about to marry was the marriage itself.[6] With the rise of the doctrine of promissory reliance, American courts said that such promises were enforceable because the charitable organization or the couple had changed their position in reliance upon them. Yet the courts asked for proof of reliance so rarely that, according to the authoritative Second Restatement of Contracts, promises of both types are enforceable 'without proof that the promise induced action or forbearance'.[7] If modern conditions explain why the enforcement of such promises is rare in Europe, then it is surprising that they are enforced in the United States, and, indeed, enforced by using one fiction after another.

A better explanation is that the ends served by enforcing these promises are achieved in other ways in the societies that do not enforce them. In most of Europe, contributions to charitable causes play a less critical role than they once did and still do in the United States because European governments take much more extensive measures to safeguard the

---

[2] *Congregation B'nai Sholom v. Martin*, 173 N.W.2d 504, 510 (Mich. 1969); *First Presbyterian Church v. Dennis*, 161 N.W. 183, 187–8 (Iowa 1917).

[3] *Allegheny College v. National Chautauqua County Bank*, 159 N.E. 173, 176 (N.Y. 1927).

[4] *Rogers v. Galloway Female College*, 44 S.W. 454, 455 (Ark. 1898).

[5] *Nebraska Wesleyan University v. Griswold's Estate*, 202 N.W. 609, 616 (Neb. 1925).

[6] Even then, in the famous case of *De Cicco v. Schweitzer*, 117 N.E. 807 (N.Y. 1917), it was hard to arrive at the desired result since the promise was made to a fiancé who, having already engaged himself to marry, was legally obligated to do so. Cardozo ingeniously observed that the affianced couple might still have given up their legal right to dissolve their engagement by mutual consent. 117 N.E. at 809–10. In effect, the parent's promise was treated as though it were made to induce them to marry should they no longer wish to do so. [7] *Restatement (Second) of Contracts* (1979), § 90(2).

welfare of their citizens. As E. Allan Farnsworth, Reporter for the Second Restatement, has stated, enforcing such promises is 'particularly desirable as a means of allowing decisions about the distribution of wealth to be made at an individual level'.[8] To the extent that such decisions are made on the social level, as they commonly are in Europe, enforcing them is less necessary.

Again, in Europe, except in the northern countries, it has been traditional to draw up formal contracts that arrange the property rights of those about to marry, at least among families rich enough to be concerned with the matter. To the extent that there is such a custom, it is not necessary and may be positively undesirable to enforce the informal promises of parents. It is not surprising that such promises are enforced where such a practice is uncommon: in the United States, Germany, and England, and, provided they are made with the simple formality of a writing, in Ireland and Scotland as well.

3. Protecting reliance

One might also have expected to find an exception to the formal requirements when the promisee has been harmed by changing his position in reliance that the promise will be kept. As we have seen, even Cajetan thought the promisee should be protected if he did. In the United States, protecting him is supposed to be one of the advantages of the doctrine of promissory estoppel. Nevertheless, European systems rarely do so.

Scotland is an exception. Section 1(3) and (4) of the Requirements of Writing (Scotland) Act 1995 provides that a gratuitous promise is enforceable without a writing if the promisee has acted or refrained from acting in reliance on it with the knowledge and acquiescence of the promisor provided that he is affected to a material extent by his reliance and the failure of the promisor to keep his promise.

England and Ireland recognize a doctrine of promissory estoppel according to which a promise can be binding without consideration if the promisee changes his position in reliance that it will be kept. In contrast to the United States, however, this doctrine is not supposed to allow the promisee an action on a gratuitous promise. In England and Ireland, it can only be used as a shield, to defend against a claim, and not as a sword, to assert one.

In other jurisdictions, protection is spotty when it even exists. Belgian

---

[8] E. A. Farnsworth and W. F. Young, *Cases and Materials on Contracts*, 4th edn (1988), 98.

law will enforce one kind of promise on which the promisee would be particularly likely to rely: the *cadeau d'usage*, a present that has been made customarily to the promisee. It is enforceable whether the promisee has relied on it or not. According to the Belgian reporter, Gaston's promise to his niece of a birthday present in Case 1(a) might qualify if he had given her such promises regularly.

A number of reporters suggested that where a valid contract was not concluded, a person might be liable in tort or for acting in bad faith for misleading the other party and inducing him to change his position (France, Belgium, Portugal, Italy, the Netherlands, Austria, Germany, and Greece). It is striking, however, that reporters from all these countries noted that the cases in which courts have actually found a person liable all concern misleading conduct preliminary to an exchange. Courts have not yet done so for breach of a promise to make a gift.

Arthur Corbin, who played a critical role in developing the American doctrine of promissory estoppel, once speculated on why it was not found in civil law systems. '[I]t would be unnecessary for the Roman and Continental jurists to develop an action in reliance doctrine', he said, if their law 'make[s] enforceable every promise on which it would be reasonable to rely.'[9] We have seen the contrary. In continental law, with few exceptions, the promisee who relies on a promise of gift is not protected. The parallel with the United States is actually just the reverse of the one Corbin expected. American courts have enforced promises of gifts much less frequently than one would expect, given the broad formulation of the doctrine of promissory estoppel,[10] and when they have, usually some additional element was present: the promisor had died before changing his mind,[11] the gift was of land and the promisee had moved on and made repairs,[12] or, as already noted, the promise was to a charitable organization or to people about to marry.

When one considers the matter, it is really not surprising that a person who relies on a promise of gift is protected so rarely. By hypothesis, the promise itself would not be enforceable absent reliance because the proper formality has not been observed. One reason for requiring the formality is that without it, one cannot be sure that the promise was made

---

[9] A. Corbin, *Corbin on Contracts* (1963), 1A, § 196, at 199–200.

[10] See J. Gordley, 'Enforcing Promises', *Cal. L. Rev.* 83 (1995), 547, 573–9.

[11] E.g., *Ricketts* v. *Scothorn*, 77 N.W. 365 (Neb. 1898); *Devecmon* v. *Shaw*, 14 A. 464 (Md. 1888); *Sandoval* v. *Bucci (In re Estate of Bucci)*, 488 P.2d 216 (Colo. Ct App. 1971).

[12] E.g., *Evenson* v. *Aamodt*, 189 N.W. 584 (Minn. 1922). In that case, the court defended the result by drawing an analogy to the delivery of personal property.

with sufficient deliberation. If the promisee himself suspected that the promisor had acted on impulse and might later regret his promise, then he is not a sympathetic figure. If he is protected if he changes his position in reliance, he may do so just because he is afraid the promisor will change his mind. Of course, the promisee may know the promisor better than the court does, and may have good reason to believe that the promisor will not regret his promise. But how is the promisee to convince a court that he had that belief, especially in a case in which the promisor has actually changed his mind? If it were thought that a court could accurately determine whether an informal promise was sufficiently deliberate by looking at evidence presented by the promisee, then very likely, the law would not have required a formality in the first place.

B. *Favours that need not entail expense*

Promises to benefit the promisee by giving him money or property necessarily entail a corresponding cost to the promisor. Other promises to benefit him gratis need entail no significant cost at all: for example, promises to loan the promisor's property (Case 7), or to store the promisee's property (Case 5), or to do a service (Case 6). One question is whether such promises, if made informally, are binding. Another is what to do if the promise can no longer be, as intended, both costless to the promisor and beneficial rather than harmful to the promisee. That can happen in two ways. First, the performance of a promise might entail an unexpected cost, for example, because the promisor now needs the object he has loaned for his own use (Case 7) or the space for storing his own goods (Case 5). The promisee, however, may have changed his position so that he will now be harmed if the promise is not kept. The other possibility is that, although the promise could have been kept costlessly, it was not kept, and as a result, the promisee has been harmed. To make up for the harm, the promisor would have to compensate the promisee at significant cost to himself. While such a problem could arise when goods are loaned or stored, we will examine it in the context of a broken promise to do a service (Case 6).

1. Favours that can no longer be performed costlessly

As we have seen, in Roman law, gratuitous contracts to loan or store goods (*commodatum* and *depositum*) were contracts *re*. They became binding at the moment when the goods were delivered. As we saw earlier, in Roman law, so far as one can tell, if the parties agreed that goods were to be loaned for a fixed term, the lender could not take them back earlier. As we have seen, the late scholastics and natural lawyers disagreed. Even if a term had been fixed, they thought the lender should be able to reclaim them if he had an unexpected need.

Those were two ways of dealing with the problem that the promise can no longer be, as it was intended, both costless to the promisor and helpful rather than harmful to the promisee. The Roman jurist Paulus said that the promise should be kept because 'favours should help, not lead to trouble'.[13] Nevertheless, the lender received a certain measure of protection because the contract was formed only upon delivery. Here, as with gifts, the delivery would be more likely to be accompanied by reflection and a realization that there could be legal consequences. Moreover, the requirement of delivery limited the length of time during which the lender had to foresee his needs accurately and the buyer's reliance was protected. In contrast, the late scholastic solution protected the lender even though the borrower was harmed. Molina argued that the borrower should have been aware that the lender did not expect to part with the goods to his own cost.[14] The approaches of modern legal systems reflect the same concerns although sometimes they protect the parties differently.

a. Promises to loan goods

In Spain and Germany, probably in Portugal, and possibly in the Netherlands and Greece, the lender is protected in the manner endorsed by the late scholastics and natural lawyers: the promise is binding in advance of delivery but the lender can reclaim his property in case of need. The promise is binding in advance of delivery in Spain and Germany and probably Greece, because a contract of loan for use is formed when the promise is made even before delivery. In any event, in Greece and probably in Portugal, a promise to enter into such an agreement is binding. In the Netherlands, where a loan for use is formed only on delivery, such an agreement may or may not be binding. In all of these countries, a loan for use is subject to a specific provision of the civil code which allows the lender to reclaim his property before the time agreed upon if he has an urgent and unforeseen need for it (Germany, the Netherlands, and Greece) or an urgent need (Spain, where the text of the Code does not mention foreseeability) or a 'fair reason' (Portugal). The Greek and Dutch reporters believe that this provision would apply by analogy to a promise to enter

---

[13] Dig. 13.6.17.3.   [14] L. Molina, *De iustitia et iure tractatus* (Venice, 1614), disp. 279 no. 10.

into a contract of loan for use. The German and Greek reporters note that a court would take some account of the harm the borrower suffers through reliance, although it would attach more importance to the lender's need.

No civil law system protects the parties in precisely the same way as Roman law. Austria comes close. A contract of loan for use is formed by delivery, and after that the lender cannot reclaim the object before the time agreed even in case of urgent need. In contrast to Roman law, however, a promise to enter into a loan for use is binding before delivery although it is subject to the general principle that relief will be given for changed circumstances.

Interestingly enough, English and Irish law may afford the same kind of protection as Roman law though the doctrinal justification is quite different. In Case 7, the promise to lend the car is not binding in advance of delivery because there is no consideration. Upon delivery, the contract formed is called a 'gratuitous bailment'. A party is liable for breaching it, according to some, in contract, according to others, in tort, and according to still others his liability is *sui generis*. At any rate, the normal rules of contract law do not apply. Absent an agreement to the contrary, the lender can take back the object at any time. It is possible, however, that the lender's promise to let the borrower keep an object for a fixed term is enforceable as a promise ancillary to a gratuitous bailment. If so, then the result (though not the doctrinal justification) is the same as in Roman law. The Irish reporter believes that the result might be the same, although the matter is far from clear, but that the lender would be liable in tort.

It is possible, however, that an English or Irish court would not enforce the promise to keep the object for a fixed term. If not, then, in England, and in Ireland as well unless he is liable in tort, the lender will receive the most extreme form of protection possible. His promise to the borrower is never binding. He can go back on it at any time, for any reason, regardless of whether the borrower has relied.

In Italian law, the lender receives protection which is extensive but not so extreme: his promise is not binding before delivery because a loan for use is not yet formed, and he can reclaim the goods after delivery if he has an urgent and unforeseeable need because of a code provision like those described earlier. He has both the protection that Roman law gave the lender and that which the late scholastics and natural lawyers endorsed.

In Scots law, in contrast, as long as the borrower relied, he is protected whatever the lender's need. Delivery does not matter. The promise is gratuitous, and therefore enforceable only if the promisee relies with the knowledge and acquiescence of the promisor provided both his reliance and the harm he suffers are material. It is also enforceable if it is made in the ordinary course of business.

In Ireland, the promisee who relies may receive similar protection although the doctrinal justification is different: he may be able to recover in tort. In Irish law, unlike English law, the plaintiff can do so for pure economic losses, for the defendant's nonfeasance as well as misfeasance, and for breach of a duty that arises out of a relationship the defendant entered into voluntarily.

So far, then, the rules we have examined can be understood as responses to the two concerns one might have when a transaction that was supposed to be costless to the promisor and beneficial to the promisee can no longer be both: that of the late scholastics, that it remain costless, and that of the Romans, that favours not cause troubles. The rules differ in the degree to which they respond to one of these concerns at the expense of the other.

We should note, however, that only some of the rules we have examined were laid down specifically to address this problem. For example, in Scotland the protection given to the borrower is a consequence of a general rule that if a gratuitous promise is not in writing, the promisee must have relied and been harmed to a significant extent, or the promise must have been given in the course of business. Those who adopted this rule may or may not have thought of the case in which the lender or depositee or promisor of a service will incur an unexpected cost. Even if they had, one could not conclude that they adopted the general rule because they wished to protect the borrower this extensively in such a case. They might simply have wanted a general rule rather than a clutter of specific ones.

Similarly, the results in England and Ireland may be shaped by the generality of the rules that come into play. Liability depends on whether a court will enforce a promise ancillary to a gratuitous bailment. If it will, the result is much the same as in Roman law. If it will not, the lender is protected more extensively than in any other legal system since he can break his promise for any reason at any time. If an English court enforces the ancillary promise, it may be because, like Paulus, it believes that favours should not cause trouble. But it may be because the court's only alternative is the extreme one just described. The court does not have the option of allowing the lender or depositee to break his promise only in case of urgent and unexpected need because it has only general rules to work with. To frame a specific one would require a degree of judicial creativity that would be condemned in England and could even raise an eyebrow in California. Conversely, if the court refuses to enforce the promise, the reason for the extreme consequences may not be a desire to protect the promisor, but that there is no middle alternative. Indeed, the court might refuse to enforce the promise, not to protect the promisor, but simply because of the general rule that promises must have consideration.

These considerations suggest why, in this case, the solutions in Scots, English, and Irish law seem more extreme than the others. Their rules are general ones which extend beyond gratuitous loans. They are not decisions about precisely how the parties should be treated in a more specific situation. Perhaps if they had been, the solutions would have been more moderate.

Finally, we must note that the law of France and Belgium cannot be explained as a response to these underlying concerns. The French and Belgian Civil Codes contain a provision like those we have seen elsewhere: in a loan for use, the lender can reclaim his property if he has an urgent and unexpected need. Nevertheless, according to the French and Belgian reporters, a contract of loan for use is formed only upon delivery, and this provision applies only to such a contract. A promise to enter into a loan for use made before delivery is binding, but the provision just described will not apply to it even after delivery has been made. Moreover, in such a case, the promisor cannot seek relief on the grounds of changed circumstances (*imprévision*) because neither French nor Belgian law accepts that doctrine. In Belgium, he might obtain relief for *force majeure* because Belgian courts have sometimes applied that doctrine when performance has become more difficult than expected rather than impossible. Thus the lender who has an unexpected need is protected only if he did not commit himself before delivery. That result cannot be explained by a concern for the position of the borrower. Whether the lender committed himself before delivery has little to do with whether the borrower will be harmed if the promise is broken. Nor can this result be explained by a concern for the position of the lender. If he commits himself in advance, he is less likely to have been able to anticipate his own need.

The French and Belgians seem to have arrived at their rules, not by considering how the parties should be protected, but by applying the maxim of statutory construction that exceptions to a general principle should be construed narrowly. To them, the special provisions in their codes allowing the lender to reclaim his property if he has an urgent and unforeseeable need seem to be deviations from general principle because French and Belgian law does not accept the doctrine of changed circumstances (*imprévision*). Therefore, these provisions are limited to the case to which they expressly apply. The result is the odd one we have seen. It was not reached by asking whether the lender is less worthy of protection when he commits himself before delivery. Thus it does not represent a decision as to how that question should be resolved.

b. Promises to take care of goods

In the Netherlands, Austria, Germany, probably in Portugal and Greece, and possibly in Spain, the parties are protected in the manner endorsed by the late scholastics and natural lawyers in the case of a loan for use. The promise is binding in advance of delivery. The reason, in the Netherlands and Germany, is that a contract of deposit is already formed. In Austria, probably in Portugal and Greece, and possibly in Spain, the reason is that even though such a contract is formed only on delivery, a promise to enter into such a contract is binding. Provisions in the civil codes of these countries allow the depositee to return the goods before the time agreed if he has an 'important reason' (the Netherlands and Germany) or a 'fair reason' (Spain and Portugal) for doing so, or if, due to changed and unforeseen circumstances, he cannot store them without harm to his own interests (Austria and Greece).

In Italy and France, a contract of deposit is formed only on delivery. In Italy, a promise to enter into such a contract is not binding in advance of delivery unless the promisor is acting in his own economic interest. In France, it may or may not be binding. In neither country may the depositee return the goods before the time agreed. Thus, sometimes in Italy and perhaps in France, the parties receive the sort of protection that Roman law gave to the parties to a loan for use. The agreement is not binding until delivery, but the depositee must keep the goods as long as agreed.

As in the case of a loan for use, it is possible that the parties would be protected in the same way in England. A promise to look after another's goods without compensation lacks consideration, and so is not binding before delivery. Upon delivery, the arrangement is a 'gratuitous bailment', which, as before, is regarded as an exceptional case to which the usual rules do not apply. In England (though, according to the Irish reporter, not in Ireland), it is possible that a court would enforce the promise to keep the goods for a fixed term because it is ancillary to a gratuitous bailment. If so, the parties are protected in the same way that Roman law protected the parties to a loan for use; they are, at least if the depositee is not liable in tort, which is a possibility we will consider later on.

If he is not liable in tort, and if the promise is not enforced as one ancillary to a gratuitous bailment, then, in England and Ireland, the depositee receives the most extreme form of protection: he can change his mind at any time for any reason or no reason regardless of the reliance of the depositor. As before, if a court reached that conclusion, the reason might not be a judgment as to how extensively he should be protected but a consequence of having only very general rules to apply.

Possibly, in Spain, Portugal, and Greece, the depositee may receive protection which is extensive but not so extreme. A contract of deposit is not formed until delivery, and possibly a promise to enter into such a contract may not be binding, although in Portugal and Greece, the prevailing view is the opposite. Moreover, as mentioned, in both countries, the depositee can return the goods in advance of the time fixed if he has a good reason. It is possible, then, that he has both the protection that Roman law gave the parties to a loan for use, and that which the late scholastics and natural lawyers endorsed.

In Belgium, possibly in France, and sometimes in Italy, the depositor may receive an extreme form of protection. In all these countries, a contract of deposit is formed only on delivery. Nevertheless, in Belgium, a promise to enter into such a contract is binding, in France it may or may not be binding, and in Italy it is binding if and only if the promise, though gratuitous, was made in the depositee's economic interest. Moreover, in these countries, the debtor cannot return the goods even if he has an important reason, although in Belgium he might have a defence of *force majeure* if storing them is more costly even if it is not impossible. The depositor is protected, then, whether or not he has made delivery, whether or not he has relied, and the depositee is not protected, even if he has unanticipated costs.

In Scots law, the depositor is protected despite the depositee's unanticipated costs if he relied with the depositor's knowledge and acquiescence, provided both his reliance and the harm he suffers are material. He is also protected if the promise was made in the ordinary course of the depositor's business. Delivery does not matter. Like the gratuitous borrower, the depositee therefore receives more extensive protection than many legal systems would give him. As before, however, that result may be due to the fact that the rule was laid down generally to apply to other situations as well.

The depositor who has relied may be protected in Irish and English law by an action in tort. In Ireland, as mentioned earlier, the plaintiff can recover in tort for pure economic losses, for the defendant's nonfeasance as well as misfeasance, and for breach of a duty that arises out of a relationship the defendant entered into voluntarily. In England, these are obstacles but in this case it is possible that they might be overcome. English courts have sometimes allowed recovery in tort for pure economic loss where the parties had a 'special relationship'. For there to be one, the situation must be 'close to contract' and, typically, the defendant must act in a professional role. Supposedly, such an action can be brought only for misfeasance, not nonfeasance, but in this case the English reporter found this distinction of 'dubious value' since a depositor would then be liable if he did his job poorly but not if he did nothing at all. Perhaps a court would agree.

Thus, all of the solutions we have examined range between the two extremes of protecting the depositor against a cost he did not intend to incur and protecting the depositee against a harm he was not supposed to suffer. Again, the more extreme solutions were common in systems in which the rules in play were more general.

2. A broken promise to do a service

In Case 6, unlike Cases 5 and 7, the cost to the promisor of performing his promise has not changed. The promise could have been kept costlessly but, because it was not, the promisee was harmed. Consequently, the same concerns as before arise although in a different way. If the promisor is made to compensate the promisee, a promise that he expected to be costless will entail a significant cost to himself. If he does not, a promise that was intended to benefit the promisee will have harmed him.

Another difference is historical. In Roman law, as we have seen in Part I, *commodatum* and *depositum* were contracts *re*, formed only by delivery. As we have seen, that distinction has consequences in some modern legal systems. In contrast, a promise to do a service gratuitously was a contract of *mandatum* which was formed by consent. Consequently, in modern civil law systems, it rarely matters if anything has been delivered. The one exception is Italy, where, for a contract of gratuitous agency to be formed, documents must actually be handed over.

Moreover, in common law, as we have seen, delivery of goods as a loan or for safekeeping formed an arrangement called a 'gratuitous bailment' which was subject to special rules. There were no special rules for a promise to do a service gratuitously. Such a promise lacked consideration and so, as we will see, the promisor was not liable except possibly in tort.

A first question is whether one who promises to do a service gratuitously may be liable for failing to perform. In nearly all civil law jurisdictions he may be. In the others, he is liable only if some simple act or formality is added to the informal promise. In Spain, the agreement to mail a letter does not count as a *mandato*, which is the Spanish descendant of *mandatum*, unless the promisor is to enter into legal transactions on the promisee's behalf. Other gratuitous promises to do service must comply with the formality for gifts, which is the simple one of a writing. In Italy, as mentioned, documents must be handed over, as they were in Case 6. In Scotland, because the promise is gratuitous, it is not binding unless it is in writing, or it was given in the ordinary course of business (as in Case 6 if Richard sold Maria the plane). In Scotland, as before, the promise would also be binding if the promisee relied with the knowledge and acquiescence of the promisor provided both his reliance and the harm he suffers are material. Again, the degree of protection is extensive and the product of a general rule rather than one framed for this specific situation.

In England and Ireland, while the promise is not binding because it lacks consideration, the promisee who relies on it might recover in tort. The considerations are the same as in Case 5.

A further question is whether the promisor is held to the same standard of care and liable to the same extent as in the case of an ordinary non-gratuitous contract. In Scotland, England, and Ireland, if relief is given at all, the standard of care would be the same as for a non-gratuitous promise. It is the same in Greece, and the standard is a high one, since fault is presumed, and to escape liability the defendant must prove accident or *force majeure*. The standard of care is also the same as in a non-gratuitous transaction in Germany and Austria where no special rules are applicable to an *Auftrag*, the descendant of *mandatum*. Nevertheless, the Austrian reporter thought that a court might escape that result by finding that the contract was subject to an implied clause excluding liability for ordinary negligence.

In contrast, the promisor is held to a lower standard of care in France, Belgium, the Netherlands, and Italy because of a special rule that applies to contracts of *mandat*, *opdracht*, or *mandato*, the descendants of the Roman *mandatum*. In Belgium, however, if Richard had sold Maria the plane, so that the promise was given in the course of his business, a Belgian court would consider it to be non-gratuitous. Richard would be held to the ordinary standard of care even if he did not charge anything for the service. In the Netherlands, he would not only be held to a lower standard of care but would be liable for less extensive damages.

There are, then, three solutions: the promisor is held to the same standard of care as in other transactions; the promisor is not liable at all; and the promisor is held to a lower standard of care. These are three obvious ways to treat a transaction that can no longer – as the parties intended – be both costless to one party and helpful rather than harmful to the other. One can hold the promisor liable because favours should not lead to trouble. One can exonerate him so that the transaction will be costless. Or, following a middle course, one can exonerate him as long as he was not too negligent.

3. A note on the 'intention to be legally bound'

In Cases 5 and 6, nearly all the reporters noted that the promise is not enforceable unless the parties intended to be legally bound, and that it is less likely that they did if they were friends. This issue is obviously quite important but also very difficult to understand. Clearly, the word 'intention' is used here in a strange sense. None of the reporters meant that the promisor must have had the conscious intention of incurring legal liability if he broke his promise. It is extremely unlikely that the promisor would have consciously considered that possibility. Therefore, what must be involved is some constellation of facts which do not concern the parties' conscious intentions but which influence a court's decision that a promise ought to be enforced.

It is hard to see what facts these might be. In Cases 5 and 6, the ones most frequently mentioned by the reporters were that nothing was given in return for the promise, and that, in some of the situations, the parties were friends. In Case 6, the German and Greek reporters said that a court would be more likely to conclude that the promisor intended to be legally bound if he knew the promise was important to the promisee. But how tricky it is to see what facts matter is illustrated by Cases 7 and 4. In Case 7, while some reporters mentioned that the parties must have intended to be legally bound, most of them took it for granted that they did, even though the car was lent gratuitously, and even when the lender was a friend. In Case 4, the parties were not friends. Moreover, while the transaction was not an exchange, each stood to gain from it. Carlo was to have the prestige of a dinner in his honour, and the music conservatory was to have the prestige of hosting a famous musician. Moreover, it was important to the conservatory that the promise be kept because of the expense that it incurred. Yet every reporter noted that the promise might be unenforceable since the parties might not have intended to be legally bound.

Most reporters thought it unlikely that they did; some thought it possible; one thought it likely.[15] That is more of a consensus of opinion than in Cases 5 and 6. And yet, none of the facts that were said to matter in those cases seem to have mattered in this one.

When the parties are deemed 'to intend to be legally bound' is therefore an issue on which this study cannot shed much light. There is more agreement among the reporters in Case 4 than in any other about the result courts will reach and the doctrine by which they will do so. And yet the meaning of the doctrine and the facts that call for its application will have to remain a mystery.

C. What is left of Roman contract law?

It is common to say that Roman law was a law of particular contracts without any general principles governing what to enforce, in contrast to modern civil law, in which, as a general principle, agreements freely entered into are binding. We can now ask to what extent this view is correct.

One resemblance between Roman law and modern civil law is the survival in most of the systems we have examined of a special formality for promises of gifts of money. In Belgium, such promises cannot be made binding. In Scotland and Spain, they can be made binding by the simple formality of a writing, which is required in the case of other gratuitous promises as well. But in the other civil law systems we have looked at, modern law is like Roman law except that notarization has replaced registration.

In contrast, in most of them, the Roman distinction between contracts *re* and *consensu* has either disappeared or lost its original significance. Originally, the contracts of loan for use and deposit became binding on delivery. Today, in some legal systems, they are formed by consent; and in others, an agreement to enter into such a contract is binding. In a few systems, it is not clear whether such an agreement is binding in advance of delivery (loan for use in the Netherlands, deposit in Spain and possibly Portugal and Greece). Only in Italy has something like the Roman rule survived: loan for use and deposit are binding only upon delivery except in the case of a promise to accept a deposit made in one's own economic interest.

---

[15] In some systems, it might be unenforceable on other grounds as well. In Spain and Scotland, it might be treated as a gift so that it would require a formality which, in these countries, is a writing. In England and Ireland, it would be unenforceable because it lacks consideration.

It would seem, then, that except in the case of gifts, the voluntaristic principle has prevailed: contracts freely entered into are binding. If we look at some special rules that are applicable to these contracts, however, we may want to qualify that opinion. Nearly all civil law systems have a rule that the lender can reclaim his property if he now needs it (France, Belgium, the Netherlands, Spain, Portugal, Italy, Germany, and Greece). Only Austria and Scotland do not. Many have a rule allowing a depositee to return a deposit if he finds he needs the space for himself (the Netherlands, Spain, Portugal, Austria, Germany, and Greece). Many have a rule that a party who gratuitously promises to perform services is held to a lower standard of care (France, Belgium, the Netherlands, and Italy, and in Austria, this rule might be applied as a matter of interpretation).

If we ask why these rules have survived, the reason is not the triumph of the voluntaristic principle. These are rules which, in whole or in part, exempt a party from the consequences of a promise that he made voluntarily. The reason he is exempted seems to be that the promise was gratuitous and did not necessarily entail a significant cost to the promisor. The underlying concern, then, is that the promisor's attempt to do a favour for the promisee should not have the unintended effect of making him poorer. That concern made sense to the late scholastics and the natural lawyers. They believed that one party should not grow poorer for another party's benefit except as an act of liberality. Liberality meant not merely giving money away but giving it away sensibly. They approved of the Roman formality for making gifts because it encouraged people to be sensible. That rule and the one that holds the promisor to a lower standard of care are the two Roman rules that many legal systems still preserve. They invented the rule that a lender can reclaim his goods in case of unexpected need. Many modern systems not only have preserved that rule but apply it to deposits as well. These legal systems look neither voluntaristic nor Roman. They look much as they did before the rise of the will theories when jurists thought that, except for liberalities, a transaction should not reduce a party's wealth.

II. Promises to pay for benefits received or owed

We will now turn to cases that are not gifts or favours, at least not in the same sense. The promise is made, not out of generosity, but to pay for a benefit received or to be received from the promisee. Of course, if the promise is made in return for a benefit that the promisee has not yet conferred and is under no obligation to confer, the transaction is an ordinary exchange. The enforceability of such a promise raises no special problems. This study will be concerned with cases in which the benefit has already been conferred, or in which the promisee is contractually obligated to confer it.

A. Promises to pay for benefits already conferred

In the case of a gift of money or property, one party intends to enrich the other at his own expense. A party who has already received a benefit, however, may promise compensation because he wants to even the scales. Unless the promise is enforced, he will have been enriched at the promisee's expense. Many legal systems treat such promises differently.

In one type of case, the promisor received the benefit pursuant to a contract, and he would be obligated to pay for the benefit he received except that the contract is legally unenforceable. In another type of case, the promisor did not receive the benefit pursuant to a contract.

1. Promises to perform contractual obligations that are legally unenforceable

A contractual obligation might be unenforceable because it has been discharged in bankruptcy (Case 3(a)), or barred by the passage of time (Case 3(b)), or because it was incurred by a minor (Case 3(c)).

Once, common law courts enforced promises to pay debts that were unenforceable in all three situations. Such promises were said to have 'moral consideration'. As we have seen, however, they could not be explained by the formulation of the doctrine of consideration that became generally accepted in the nineteenth century. The promisor did not promise to induce the promisee to do anything in return but rather on account of something the promisee had done in the past. Today, the promises to pay a debt discharged in bankruptcy or barred by the passage of time are not enforceable in England or Ireland. They still are in the United States where these exceptions to the normal requirements of consideration have been preserved.[16] The change in England and Ireland may be due to a desire for doctrinal consistency rather than a decision about how these specific situations should be treated. The promise to pay the debt incurred as a minor would still be enforceable in England but it is

---

[16] *Restatement (Second) of Contracts* (1979), §§ 82, 83, 85. Nevertheless, the Bankruptcy Reform Act, 11 U.S.C. § 524 severely limits the enforceability of a promise to pay a debt discharged in bankruptcy.

regarded as an anomaly. It would not be enforceable in Ireland. A statute provides that such a promise will not be enforced even if it is given for fresh consideration.

Many of the civil law systems under examination would enforce these promises. Sometimes it is said that the promisor had a 'natural obligation' to the promisee which, after the promise is made, becomes a legally enforceable civil obligation; sometimes that the promise ratifies the obligation or waives a defence to it.

In France and Belgium, all of these promises would be enforceable. Case 3(a) could not arise in Spain, Portugal, Austria, or, until recently, in Germany because debts are not discharged in bankruptcy. But the other promises would be enforced in these countries. In Italy, the promise to pay such a debt discharged in bankruptcy would not be enforced because Italian law does not recognize the doctrine that promises to pay natural obligations are enforceable. Nevertheless, the other two promises would be enforced on the grounds that a debt has been ratified. In the Netherlands, although the other promises would be enforced, the one in Case 3(c) to pay a debt incurred as a minor is considered to be a promise of gift, and therefore unenforceable without a formality.

The only civil law systems that would refuse to enforce all of them are Scotland and Greece. In Scotland, however, as in the case of gifts, promises can be made binding by complying with the fairly simple formality of reducing the promise to writing. As before, however, this result is the consequence of a general rule applicable to all gratuitous promises. It may not represent a decision about how these specific situations should be treated. In Greece, special provisions of the Civil Code reduce the difficulty of complying with the formality. Promises to pay obligations barred by the passage of time or incurred as a minor need only be in writing even though promises to make gifts must be made before a notary. Since, in Greece, debts are not dischargeable in bankruptcy, Case 3(a) could not arise.

The formality of appearing before a notary is almost never required. The only exceptions are Case 3(a) (discharge in bankruptcy) in Italy and Case 3(c) (debt incurred as a minor) in the Netherlands.

If the reason for refusing to enforce an informal promise of gift is to protect the promisor from himself, then it is not surprising that the formality is not generally required in cases like these. In the case of a gift, the promisee is enriched at the expense of the promisor. In these cases, the promisor has been enriched at the expense of the promisee even though no gift was intended. It is the promisee who has been hurt. In each case, moreover, the law has erected a barrier to the enforcement of the original obligation on account of certain fears which, to a large extent, the new promise eliminates. Where debts are dischargeable in bankruptcy, the fear is that if they are not, the bankrupt's entire future will have been sacrificed by his improvidence or bad luck in the past. The new promise, at least if it is made advisedly, removes the fear that he will be unable to pay without such a sacrifice. Debts become time-barred, in part, because of a fear of trumped-up claims, and in part, because the debtor may have changed his position in the belief that the creditor will never insist on payment. When the debtor acknowledges the claim, those concerns are removed. The promises of minors are not enforced for fear that their judgment may not be as good as that of an adult. That fear is removed when the promisor confirms it after becoming an adult.

2. Promises to pay for benefits received absent a contract

The matter is more difficult when a promise is to pay for benefits that were not conferred pursuant to contract. An example is Case 2 in which Kurt promises a large sum of money to Tony who suffered a permanent back injury saving either Kurt or Kurt's adult child. Here, Kurt was never under a legal obligation to pay for Tony's services except possibly, in Portugal, Austria, and Germany, where he might be held liable on the grounds of unjust enrichment because the services were rendered under circumstances of urgent need (*negotiorum gestio*, *Geschäftsführung ohne Auftrag*). Where Kurt is not liable, his promise must not merely remove a legal barrier to what would otherwise be an enforceable obligation but create a legal obligation where previously there was none.

In some of the legal systems, the promise might have this effect. In others it would not. One approach, as before, would be to enforce it on the grounds that it is a promise to fulfil a natural obligation. The French, Belgian, and Austrian reporters believe that their courts would do so, although in France, Tony would have the evidentiary problem that he must either produce a writing or show that it was morally impossible to obtain one. The Greek reporter believes that her courts might enforce the promise on these grounds. Although there is no clear authority in the Netherlands or Spain, the reporters from these countries are doubtful, the Dutch reporter because his courts have held that promises to pay for past services are gifts, and the Spanish reporter because her courts have recognized natural obligations primarily in the context of family relationships. The Belgian and Spanish reporters thought that a court would be less likely to enforce the promise if Kurt's adult child were rescued rather than Kurt. In Italy, Germany, Scotland, England, and Ireland, the promise could not be enforced on these grounds because these legal systems have not accepted the doctrine that informal promises to pay natural obligations are binding, although one influential Italian scholar, Gino Gorla, believes that they should be.

In Spain, even if the rescue did not create a natural obligation, many scholars believe that a promise like Kurt's would be enforceable without a formality because it is a *donación remuneratoria*: a promise to compensate the donee for services rendered in the past for which the donor is not legally required to pay (although the doctrine has not yet been recognized by the courts). In Portugal, a promise of such a gift (*doaçao remuneratória*) is subject to the same formal requirement as other promises to give: it must be made in writing.

As mentioned earlier, the German and Austrian reporters thought that if Kurt himself were rescued, Tony might have an action against him even absent a promise on the grounds of unjust enrichment by services received under circumstances of urgent need (*negotiorum gestio*, *Geschäftsführung ohne Auftrag*). If so, the consequences of refusing to enforce Kurt's promise are considerably less severe for Tony since at least he will be compensated for his back injury. In any event, according to the Austrian and German reporters, because Tony might have such an action, the promise would be enforceable if it could be interpreted as an acknowledgment or settlement of Tony's claim rather than as a mere expression of gratitude. The Portuguese reporter agreed but thought this interpretation unlikely.

In England and Ireland, the promises would be unenforceable because they lack consideration since Tony's services had already been rendered before they were made. In contrast, some American courts have enforced promises like Kurt's to pay when he himself was rescued,[17] and the authoritative second *Restatement of Contracts* believes that they should in order to avoid unjust enrichment.[18] Nevertheless, if Kurt had asked Tony to rescue him or his adult child, then Tony would have an action in contract in England and Ireland. All that is necessary is that the services be performed at his request, not that they agreed in advance upon a price. A great deal would depend on what, if anything, Kurt said to Tony before the rescue and how it should be interpreted.

The possibility that Kurt and Tony entered into a contract at the time

---

[17] *Webb* v. *McGowin*, 168 So. 199 (Ala. 1936).   [18] *Restatement (Second) of Contracts* (1979) § 86.

the rescue was performed and before Kurt's promise was made was also suggested by the French reporters. Although it involves twisting the usual doctrines that govern contract formation, the act of rescuing might be considered an 'offer' which Kurt tacitly accepted, thereby forming a 'contract of rescue' (*convention d'assistance*).

In Scotland, neither promise would be enforceable unless it were made with the formality required for promises of gifts, which is a writing.

To sum up, in two legal systems (Italy and Scotland), Tony would have no claim of any kind (although in Scotland, the formality required is the simple one of a writing). In two others (England and Ireland), Tony would have an action only if Kurt said something before the rescue that could be interpreted as a request to render services. In Portugal and Germany, Tony could have a claim in unjust enrichment only for rescuing Kurt himself, and to be enforceable, the promise must be interpreted as an acknowledgment or settlement of such a claim. In Spain, he might have a claim because the promise is a *donación remuneratoria*. In the remaining legal systems, the promise might be enforceable as one to fulfil a natural obligation, a result that seemed likely to the reporters from three countries (France, Belgium and Austria), possible to one reporter (Greece), and doubtful to another (the Netherlands).

In contrast to Case 3, then, there is fairly widespread agreement that this case presents a problem, and much less agreement about what to do about it. In part, the reason is that promises are made in cases like this far less often than promises to pay debts that are discharged in bankruptcy, time-barred, or incurred as a minor. Most legal systems have had less experience with such promises, and consequently less opportunity to decide what to do.

In part, however, the reason may be that in this case, it is less clear what should be done. As in Case 3, the promisor has benefited at a cost to the promisee even though no gift was intended. Moreover, as in Case 3, one might regard the promise as removing an obstacle that would otherwise exist to an enforceable legal claim, here, a claim in unjust enrichment. As we have seen, only the Portuguese, German, and Austrian reporters regarded such a claim as possible. There is a good reason why most jurisdictions would not recognize such a claim and why the German and Austrian reporters were uncertain and the Portuguese reporter was sceptical that it would succeed even in their own countries. Even in a case as extreme as a rescue, it is hard to be certain that the promisor wanted the services and how much he would have been willing to pay for them had he been asked in advance. Presumably, if Kurt thought he would die without the rescue, he would have been willing to pay almost any amount, and one hopes he would feel that way about his adult child. But Kurt might not have thought the danger was so great that he would be willing to pay for whatever harm Tony suffered in rescuing him. To some extent, the promise removes these doubts. Kurt evidently did want to be rescued, and, at least when he made the promise, he was willing to pay the promised amount.

But the promise removes these doubts only to a certain extent. Kurt might have made the promise even if he thought he was in little or no danger because he felt grateful that Tony wanted to rescue him or sorry that Tony had suffered in doing so. If so, although these are noble motives, one can no longer say that Kurt was trying to compensate Tony for a benefit Kurt received. If Kurt thought he was in danger, he might still promise Tony more than the amount needed to compensate for the back injury, and, at the time Kurt promised, he may not have been aware of the extent of the danger. Thus the promise does not remove the obstacle to a legally enforceable claim – here a claim for unjust enrichment – as clearly as the promise of a former bankrupt, who presumably does think he now has sufficient funds, or the person owing a time-barred debt, who would presumably not promise if the creditor's claim were groundless, or the person who incurred a debt as a minor, who presumably now does have the judgment of an adult. There are good reasons why legal systems are less certain and unanimous.

3. Promises to pay an additional amount when a benefit has already been received and paid for under a contract

In Case 10(b), Company agrees to pay an additional amount to an employee who is about to retire. We will defer consideration of this case until we see how the different legal systems treat promises to pay more than originally agreed for benefits one is yet to receive under a contract.

B. Promises to pay for benefits to which one has a contractual right

We will now turn to promises that modify the terms of a contract to make them more favourable to the promisee. In Case 9, the promise is to pay more than agreed originally for remodelling or for equipment; in Case 10(a), to pay a larger salary; in Case 11, to install more expensive windows or to waive the requirement of an architect's certificate; in Case 12, to lower the rent (assuming the promise is interpreted as a reduction in rent and not a postponement of the time it is due).

Most legal systems do not treat these promises like promises to pay for benefits one has already received. There is far less difficulty about enforcing them absent some distinct ground for relief such as duress.

Absent such a ground for relief, all of the civil law systems we are examining would enforce all of these promises with four exceptions. In Scotland, the promise to lower the rent in Case 12 would have to be in writing because it concerns an interest in land. In Spain, the promise in Case 9 to pay more for remodelling or equipment would not be enforced, even absent duress, because a mere change in the amount owed does not constitute a novation. In contrast, the promise to reduce the rent in Case 12 would be valid because it is the remission of a debt. In Portugal, the promise in Case 10(a) is unenforceable because it is considered a gift and lacks the requisite formality. Nevertheless, the promisor may be liable for violating a pre-contractual duty to act in good faith. Also in Portugal, the promise to do without an architect's certificate in Case 11 is illegal, and therefore unenforceable.

In civil law systems other than Scotland, these promises are enforceable because they are not considered to be gifts. In Scotland, the promises in Case 11 might be regarded as gratuitous, but they would be enforceable anyway absent the usual formality because they are made in the course of business. In addition, in some civil law jurisdictions the promise of a higher salary in Case 10(a) does not raise a problem because the employee has a right to leave despite the terms of his contract. The employee's initial promise to work for a fixed term for a certain salary was either invalid (Italy) or one which the employee is entitled to break although if he does he will be liable for an indemnity (Belgium) or for damages which, as a practical matter, the employer cannot recover (Spain).

In the common law jurisdictions, at one time, all but one of these promises would have been unenforceable on the grounds that they lack consideration. The exception is the promise in Case 11 to dispense with the requirement that an architect certify that the building has been properly completed before the builder is paid. It does not need consideration because it is a waiver of a condition. It would be enforceable at least if the builder changed his position in reliance upon it.

Today, only the builder's promise to install more expensive windows would be unenforceable for lack of consideration. Absent duress, the promises to pay more money in Cases 9 and 10(a) would be enforceable as long as the promisor receives a 'practical benefit' even if the benefit is the performance of a pre-existing legal duty.

The promise to reduce the rent in Case 12 is enforceable under the doctrine of promissory estoppel. Under this doctrine, the promisor may be bound by a promise that does not have consideration. In England and Ireland (unlike the United States), the promisee can invoke this doctrine even if he has not changed his position in reliance on the promise. The limitation (again, unlike the United States) is that the doctrine can be used only as a shield, to defend against a claim, and not as a sword, to raise one. In Case 12, the doctrine is used as a shield because the lessor is suing for the back rent. Thus, not only will the common law systems enforce these promises, but they have carved out exceptions to the general requirement of consideration in order to do so.

Nevertheless, if the promisee threatened not to perform unless he was promised more (as in Case 9), the promise may be unenforceable on the grounds of duress. The only exception was in Portugal where the threat must be to perform an 'illegal act'. All of the other reporters agreed that it would be unenforceable if the promisor would suffer imminent and serious harm if he refused to comply, although they disagreed on whether this requirement was met in Case 9. Seven reporters thought it probably was (Belgium, Italy, Austria, Germany, Greece, England, and Ireland); two thought it might be (France and the Netherlands); and two thought that it was not met (Spain and Scotland). Three reporters thought that relief might be given even absent duress for 'abuse of circumstances' (the Netherlands), or for exploitation of another's need (Portugal and Greece).

Absent duress, then, the legal systems we are examining are far less reluctant to enforce the promises in these cases than to enforce promises of gifts. With gifts, where the promisee is to be enriched at the promisor's expense, there is a concern that the promisor act with deliberation which we do not find here. The reason may be that, absent duress or some other ground for relief, such a promise is regarded as a revaluation of the promisee's performance rather than an enrichment of the promisee. It is made in a business context. The promisor has no reason to be altruistically interested in the promisee's welfare as he did when he promised a gift in Case 1. He has no reason to feel grateful as he did when he made a promise to his rescuer in Case 2. If he is promising more, very likely he feels that the performance he receives in return is worth it.

Originally, of course, a different value was placed upon the same performance. By doing so, one might think, the parties have allocated the risk that the promise will prove more or less valuable. It is no different, one might think, than when the value of a share of stock or painting rises after it has been sold. The profit belongs to the buyer. If he shares it with the seller, he will be enriching him just as if he makes a gift. But that argument presupposes that the parties meant to allocate this risk between them when they originally fixed the price. In cases like 10(a), 11, and 12 they may not have. When a person is hired (Case 10(a)) or property is leased for a long period of time (Case 12), it is usually hard to know what the value will be in the future. The reason the parties did not expressly agree to determine this matter in the future may be that they would have had to agree upon how it is to be determined. That is tricky if they want to make a firm commitment to each other now and do not want the matter determined by third parties. Consequently, they might fix a salary or rent with the expectation that it will be adjusted if the employee proves to be more valuable or economic conditions alter the value of the lease. When the contract is not long term, as in Case 11, the parties still might expect each other to be flexible about such matters as deadlines or the quality of the windows without each change calling for a renegotiation of the price. The fact that one party agreed, absent a threat, to modify the contract in the other's favour suggests that they did have such expectations. In contrast, in the situation described in Case 9, Paul would not have expected that he might have to pay 50 per cent more than he had agreed a short time ago when Robert's circumstances have not changed. Consequently, he would not have made such a promise if he had not been threatened. His promise is not a revaluation of the value of Robert's performance but a response to the harm that Robert can cause him.

We can now turn to Case 10(b) and see why it is less clear. To thank Vito for his services, Company promised him a large sum of money at the end of his term of employment after he had already announced his intention to retire. In France, the Netherlands, Spain, and Portugal, the promise would be considered a gift, and therefore unenforceable without the usual formalities, although in Portugal, the promisor may be liable for violating a pre-contractual duty to act in good faith. In England and Ireland, it would be unenforceable for lack of consideration, although the Irish reporter noted that it could be made enforceable by having Vito promise some small undertaking in return such as to retire early or not to compete with Company. In Belgium and Greece, it would be enforceable as a promise to fulfil a natural or moral obligation. In Austria and Germany, it would be enforceable because it would be deemed part of or linked to the employee's past services. In Italy, it is supposed to be unenforceable because it is a gift even if it is given in return for the employee's past service. Nevertheless, the Italian reporter believes it would be enforced anyway because Italian courts favour employees.

There are, then, greater differences than before in the results reached and in the grounds for reaching them. That is as one might expect since it is far less clear in Case 10(b) that the money promised Vito on retirement represents a judgment by Company as to what his services were worth. In Case 10(a), Company is paying to induce him to render his services. Presumably, the services are worth it unless Company is really paying because, as in Case 9, it has changed its position and will suffer some harm if he leaves other than the loss of his services. In Case 10(b), however, the officers of the company may have been using its money to express their own gratitude or friendship to a retiring colleague, or to set a precedent that they hope will be followed in their own case, or to improve company morale generally. Or they may indeed have believed that his salary did not reflect the value of his past services, and they think it fair to make up the difference. Since it is less clear that they are revaluing his services as in Cases 10(a), 11, and 12, rather than making a gift intended to enrich him beyond what he has earned, as in Case 1, it is not surprising that different legal systems reach different results.

III. The absence of commitment

In the cases examined thus far, the question was whether a party who had decided to commit himself was legally committed. We will now turn to the question of whether a party can remain uncommitted. We will first examine cases in which the parties have agreed that one of them will not be committed. The question is whether that agreement will be honoured. We will then turn to cases in which the parties have not so agreed, and the question is whether, nevertheless, one party should have the option to withdraw.

A. Open terms and options

In Case 8, one party to a contract to buy steel is not committed to buy any particular quantity. In Case 13, one party has the option to buy land which the other party must sell to him if he chooses.

In both cases, the one-sided commitment could benefit both parties. In Case 8, it allows the promisee to adjust the quantity he orders to his own requirements. In Case 13, it allows the party who wants to buy land to conduct a study before committing himself. In either case, because the promisee benefits, he may be more willing to buy or to buy at a favourable price, and, if so, the promisor will benefit as well, which is most likely why he was willing to make the promise. On the other hand, in both cases, the promise may be unfair to the committed party since the party who is free may be able to speculate at his expense. He can buy steel or buy the land if the market price goes up and refuse to do so if the price falls.

Most of the legal systems under examination protect the committed party, at least in the cases in which he needs the protection most. In the common law jurisdictions, until the promisee commits himself, none of the promises in Cases 8, 13(a), and 13(b) are enforceable because they all lack consideration: the promisee was not committed and therefore gave up nothing in return for the promise. Possibly, however, the promise in Case 13(c) would be enforced. In that case, Realty was obligated to buy the land at a certain price at the conclusion of its study 'unless, in its sole and absolute judgment, [it] thought the economic prospects were unsatisfactory'. The English and Irish reporters thought that a court might decide that this provision is not the same as one that allows Realty to withdraw from the contract if it chooses to do so since Realty is allowed to withdraw only on the basis of its view of the economic prospects.

If the underlying concern is that the promisee will speculate at the promisor's expense, then this approach is in one way too broad and in another too narrow. It is too broad in that it will knock down promises even when there is little chance the promisee will be unfairly advantaged and in which the promise serves one of the useful purposes just described. Examples are Case 8(a) where Motor Works buys the amount of steel it ordinarily orders and Case 13(a) where Realty's option is short term. It is too narrow in that even if the promisor could be exploited, the promise would be enforceable if the promisee made some commitment in return. For example, he could agree to buy a minimum amount of steel in Case 8 or to withdraw only if dissatisfied with the economic prospects, as in Case 13, which could be hard to verify.

The civil law approach is to take the parties' need for protection into account more directly. Reporters from civil law systems had no difficulties with the enforceability of the promises in Cases 8(a), 8(c), 13(a), and 13(c) where the danger of unfairness is small (except that in Germany, Greece, and Scotland, the promises in Case 13 could not be made informally because they concerned interests in land). The reporters thought that there might be difficulties in Case 8(b) in which the market price of steel rises, and Motor Works buys twice its normal requirements of steel, and in Case 13, in which the market price of land rises and Realty buys, not to develop the land as originally planned, but to resell the property.

The doctrines applicable in these cases were quite diverse. The promise in Case 8(b) might not be enforceable because Motor Works committed an 'abuse of right' (France and Belgium), because the contract should be interpreted so that it cannot buy more than its normal requirements (the Netherlands, Austria, and Germany), because the contract should be interpreted to accord with good faith (Scotland), because parties to a contract must perform in good faith (the Netherlands, Portugal, Italy, and Germany), because the terms of a contract must be certain (Italy, and France at one time), because relief is given for changed and unforeseen circumstances (the Netherlands and Greece), and because a specific code provision requires a party with discretion over the content of a contract to act by 'equitable criteria' (Greece).

In Case 13(b), some reporters thought that if the term of the option were too long, a court would require that it be exercised in good faith (the Netherlands) or would reduce the term (Italy, and Germany if the term offends 'common decency'). If the exercise of the option were seriously unfair, for example if there were an abrupt price rise and Realty bought the land for resale, relief might be given because Realty did not act in good faith (the Netherlands, Italy, and Germany), because the purpose of the original transaction is not achieved (Spain, the *teoria de la base del negocio*), or because circumstances have changed (Austria). In France and Belgium, relief might be given for *lésion*. Relief for *lésion* is given when the contract price is less than seven-twelfths of the market price of the land. A court will evaluate whether the discrepancy is sufficiently large, in a sale, at the time the land is sold, and in an option, at the time the option is exercised.

Thus the one precise rule encountered in civil law jurisdictions is this last one in France and Belgium: that relief will be given if the contract price of the land is less than seven-twelfths of the market price of the land at the time an option to buy land is exercised. Like the common law rule, however, it seems both too broad and too narrow. It takes no account of how much was paid for the option, of the length of its term, or of the volatility expected in market prices at the time the option was given. A party who paid a fair amount for the option might make a profit of more than five-twelfths. A party who paid less than this amount or nothing at all, as in Case 13(b), might make a profit of less than five-twelfths.

With this exception, however, the remedies in civil law systems in Case

8(b) and in Case 13 if Realty buys in order to resell and make a profit have the opposite disadvantage. They are not under- or over-inclusive. They are imprecise.

B. Locus poenitentiae

In the cases just examined, the parties agreed that one of them would not be committed, and the question was whether he should have that option. We will now turn to cases in which the promisor seems to have committed himself and the question is whether he should nevertheless have the option to withdraw. This question, of course, opens up a large subject. We will merely examine two cases in which many legal systems allow him to withdraw.

In Case 14, the promisor offered a reward for finding her necklace. In Case 15, the promisor listed his house with a real estate agent. In each case, both parties might benefit if the promise is enforceable. The promisees can try to find the necklace and sell the house knowing that they will be paid if they succeed. Without that assurance, they may be unwilling to make these efforts, and so the promisor may benefit as well. Moreover, there is no danger, as in the previous cases, that they will speculate at the promisor's expense. But there is a problem. If the promisor cannot change his mind, he may be forced to pay for a service that he does not want and which has not yet been rendered.

Again, these concerns are reflected in the results that different legal systems reach in these cases although the doctrinal justifications for them are different. In Case 14(a), Simone promised a particular detective, Raymond, a reward for finding her necklace. In Case 14(b), she made this promise to the public in a newspaper advertisement. English and Irish law treat both promises as offers of unilateral contract in the common law sense of the term. They are offers which the offeree cannot accept by making a promise in return but only by performing the action requested. Neither the detective nor the members of the public can accept by promising to find the necklace; they must actually find it. Since, until they do, the offer is not yet accepted, in principle, it can be revoked on the grounds that an offer is not binding until its acceptance. According to the English and Irish reporters, the harshness of this principle will probably be mitigated by holding that the offerer cannot revoke after the offeree has begun to perform. It would not be enough for him to make preparations to perform. It is not at all clear what the offerees would have to do in this case to be held to have begun performance. The Irish reporter thinks it would be enough to incur expenses looking for the necklace. The English reporter thinks that would not be enough, at least in the case of the newspaper advertisement.

Many civil law jurisdictions would treat Case 14(a) differently from Case 14(b). The promise to the detective is revocable at will only in Germany, and even then, the revocation must be made in good faith. It is revocable in France and Portugal, but Simone would be liable for Raymond's expenses. It is revocable in Belgium and Austria only if she pays his expenses and lost profit, and so, while the promise is revocable, she must pay the same amount as if it were not. It is irrevocable in the Netherlands, Spain, Greece, and Scotland, and in Italy it may be revoked only for just cause. In Italy, it may also be irrevocable after Raymond has 'begun to perform' as in the common law jurisdictions.

The promise in Case 14(b) is freely revocable in Austria, and in Spain, Portugal, Germany, and Greece as well provided that the revocation is given the same publicity as the original offer. It is revocable in France if Simone pays for the expenses anyone has incurred, and in the Netherlands provided she pays 'equitable compensation' to whoever has begun to perform. It is irrevocable in Belgium either because unilateral obligations (in the civil law sense) are binding, or because revocation would be an abuse of right. It is irrevocable in Scotland because it is not a gratuitous obligation. It is irrevocable except for just cause in Italy.

In short, we have a range of solutions stretching from the one extreme of protecting only the offeror to the other of protecting only the offeree. Either or both of the promises are freely revocable; revocable except in bad faith; revocable if the promisee's expenses are paid; revocable if an equitable amount is paid; revocable if his expenses and lost profit are paid; irrevocable if the promisee has begun to perform; irrevocable except for just cause; or simply irrevocable. That is as we would expect if the underlying concerns are in tension. As noted, on the one hand, enforcing the promise serves the useful purpose of encouraging effort by the promisee. On the other, the promisor may be forced to pay for work he does not want and that has not yet been done.

Moreover, in civil law systems, when the promise is to a particular person (Case 14(a)), the promisee is protected more often: the promise is freely revocable only in Germany, and then only in good faith; irrevocable in at least four systems; and revocable only on payment of full damages including lost profit in one system. In contrast, the promise to the public (Case 14(b)) is freely revocable in four systems, and irrevocable (or revocable for just cause) in three. That is as one would expect since the detective is more likely to make extensive efforts than a member of the public who reads an advertisement. Indeed, the purpose of the promise to the detective is to induce him to make such efforts. That of the advertisement may not be to encourage people to look for the necklace but to come forward if they happen to know where it is.

In Case 15, Claude promised to list a house with a broker. Again, there are different approaches but they can be understood in terms of these same concerns. In Scotland, England, and Ireland, the effect of the agreement depends on its interpretation. The Scots reporter believes that if the agency were non-exclusive, he could withdraw before sale, but that if it were exclusive, he could not. The English and Irish reporters believe that he could withdraw before sale.

In Portugal, Claude is liable to Homes only if the listing is exclusive, in which case he is liable for the expenses that Homes incurred, and will be liable for the commission if Homes proves it would have sold the property.

In Belgium, Italy, and Spain, Claude could claim his commission if he finds a willing buyer, although in Belgium and Italy, if he withdraws before that time, he must pay the broker's expenses. In France, if the agency is exclusive, the parties may agree to a penalty if Claude withdraws before the broker finds a willing buyer, although otherwise the broker can claim its commission only if there is a sale.

In the remaining jurisdictions, supposedly, the broker can claim his commission only if a sale is actually concluded, and before then, Claude can withdraw. In the Netherlands, this result may be reached as a matter of interpretation. But Claude's ability to do so may be more restricted than this principle suggests. In Austria, if and only if the agency is exclusive, the parties can agree that the agent earns his commission if the principal changes his mind without an important reason. In Germany, they can change the rule provided they do so in writing. In Greece, if the agency is exclusive, the parties usually agree that the principal cannot revoke for a period of time. In France, the principal who revokes may be liable in tort. In the Netherlands, in practice, agencies use a standard form contract that would require Claude to pay a penalty of 10 per cent of their commission if he withdraws before sale.

In this case, then, Claude is more likely to be able to revoke his promise than Simone in Case 14. That is as one would expect. The importance of allowing the promisor to change his mind is greater here. Simone may have changed her mind about how much she values her necklace but presumably she would still like it back. Claude no longer wants to sell his house. Moreover, if the agency is exclusive, as a matter of practice if not of principle, a person who lists a house with a broker is unlikely to be able to withdraw without either giving him a chance to sell it or paying his expenses or a penalty. That is as one would expect if it is also important for the broker to incur expenses in reliance on the promise. When the listing is exclusive, a broker is particularly likely to do so since he is not afraid that the sale will be made by another broker.

IV. Epilogue

We found more order in the results that different legal systems reach than in the doctrines by which they do so. We will examine the results and then the doctrines.

A. The results

We did not find that the same results are always reached everywhere. We did find that, generally, these results reflect similar underlying concerns.

When we examined gifts and favours, we saw that promises that are intended to enrich the promisee at the promisor's expense invariably required a formality. The acknowledged reason was to encourage deliberation. Favours that could be performed without expense generally did not. The problem instead was what to do when, because of the promise, either the promisor will incur an unexpected cost or the promisee will suffer an unexpected harm. A promise to loan or store property can no longer be performed costlessly. A promise to do a service was broken and the promisee will be worse off than before unless the promisor compensates him. Solutions ranged, as one might expect, between protecting the promisor and protecting the promisee.

When we examined promises to pay for benefits received pursuant to a now unenforceable contract, we saw that usually they were not treated like promises of gifts. Promises to pay debts that had become unenforceable because they were time-barred, discharged in bankruptcy, or incurred as a minor rarely required a formality, and when they did, the formality was rarely the one required for gifts. These are cases in which the promisor will be enriched at the promisee's expense if the promise is not enforced. Moreover, the promise alleviates some of the concerns that led the law to bar enforcement of the original debt: concern that evidence has been lost or the debtor has changed his position with the passage of time; concern that the bankrupt should have a fresh start; concern that minors have bad judgment. The legal systems we examined were much less consistent in enforcing promises to pay for benefits that had been conferred absent a contract, such as a promise to pay a rescuer. In such a case, it is less clear that the promise should be interpreted as one of compensation for the service that has been rendered rather than as an act of generosity.

Again, most often, promises to pay more (or take less) for benefits already due under contract were not treated like gifts. Almost everywhere, they were enforceable absent duress. Most of them have become enforceable even in English and Irish law by making special exceptions to the doctrine of consideration (waiver, receipt of a 'practical benefit', promissory estoppel). These promises are made in a business context where the promisor is not motivated by a concern for the promisee's welfare. They are treated, not as attempts to enrich the promisee at the promisor's expense, but as revaluations of the performance due from the promisee. In one situation it was plausible to regard the promise as motivated by gratitude or generosity: the promise of money to an employee about to retire. Roughly half the legal systems examined would enforce that promise and half would not, which is as one might expect when the promise could either be a reappraisal of the value of his services or an act of generosity. In one situation it was not plausible to regard the promise in either way: the promise was made because the promisee threatened not to perform otherwise. In that case, all legal systems would refuse to enforce the promise on the grounds of duress if the party threatened would suffer immanent and serious harm. Reporters disagreed, however, whether the harm was immanent and serious in the hypothetical cases.

When the parties expressly agreed that one of them would not be bound, most of the legal systems would give relief in the two situations in which the uncommitted party could most easily enrich himself at the other party's expense: the promise to sell whatever quantity is ordered at a fixed price, and the long-term option in an unstable market. Admittedly, English and Irish law go considerably further and strike down all agreements in which one side is not committed. Conversely, in the cases in which the one could change his mind without either harming the other or enriching himself at the other party's expense, many legal systems found ways of allowing him to do so.

Not only are the underlying concerns similar, but one of them continually reappears: that one party be enriched at the other's expense only when the promisor intended to do so with sufficient deliberation. That is a conclusion that would have appealed to the late scholastics and natural lawyers.

B. *The doctrines*

While these results seem to reflect similar underlying concerns, the doctrinal structures were different. There was one structure in most civil law systems, another in Scotland, and still another in the common law systems.

To begin with, most civil law systems had preserved, with or without modifications, some old doctrines that were in place at the time of the late scholastics and natural lawyers: gifts of money and property require a special formality that cannot be performed without a legal professional; promises to loan or care for property or to do a service gratuitously are subject to special rules, often, to ensure that they remain costless; promises to pay compensation for benefits received are often enforceable without a formality. It is not surprising that these rules reflect a concern that neither party be enriched at the other's expense except by a deliberate decision to do so. That was a concern of the late scholastics and the natural lawyers who either invented these rules or preserved them when so many other rules of Roman contract law were weeded out.

When these doctrines were not available, most civil law systems turned to one or more less concrete and rather general doctrines which, for the most part, were directly concerned with the fairness of a transaction. Which of these doctrines would be applied to a given problem often varied considerably from one system to the next. For example, to explain why promises to sell whatever quantity the other party ordered or to give him a long-term option might not be enforced, different civil law systems would apply doctrines of 'abuse of right', changed circumstances, good faith, 'equitable criteria', offence to 'common decency', *lésion*, frustration of the purpose of the original transaction (*teoria de la base del negocio*), or canons of interpretation. Only the doctrine of *lésion* is fairly specific.

Sometimes, moreover, general rules of this sort were not used to resolve a problem because a much more specific rule was available which had been framed for a particular situation. The content of this rule differed from one system to another. An example is the wide variety of detailed rules used to decide when promises to detectives or brokers could be revoked. These rules were intended to strike a fair balance between the interests of the promisor and promisee but, unlike the more general ones, they specify how this balance is to be struck.

In light of the account given earlier in this study, this structure should not be surprising. Historically, the civil law is the product, not only of Roman law, but of two systematic efforts to find principled justifications for its rules, one made in the sixteenth and seventeenth centuries, and one made in the nineteenth century. One idea that played a key role in the earlier of these attempts was the Aristotelian principle that it would violate commutative justice for one person to be enriched at another's expense. As we have seen, the older doctrines reflect this principle. In the nineteenth century, an effort was made to explain as much of contract law as possible by the idea of will. As noted earlier, it was difficult for the will theories to explain what promises the law should and should not enforce. It would seem, according to the theory, that anything the parties willed should be enforceable. It was also hard for these theories to explain relief from an unfair contract. Supposedly, contract law should not concern itself with whether a transaction is fair or not but merely enforce the terms the parties have chosen. Even in the nineteenth century, however, the civil law did not enforce whatever promises the parties had made without regard to their fairness. The old doctrines were preserved even though their rationale became obscure. In the twentieth century, will theories fell from favour and courts were more explicitly concerned with fairness. Nevertheless, we have not seen another great rethinking of the principles behind the civil law, as happened in the sixteenth/seventeenth and nineteenth centuries. It is not surprising, then, that when problems of fairness arise that the old doctrines do not address, there are two alternatives: to have recourse to blurry doctrines that say little more than that a contract should be fair, or to turn the problem over to draftsmen who can frame particular rules to deal with a specific situation. So it will remain, perhaps, until the next time a systematic effort is made to bring theoretical coherence to private law.

Although we have spoken of Scotland as a civil law jurisdiction, in fact its doctrinal structure is much different, one might almost say *sui generis*. Scottish law resolves many of the problems we have discussed by reference to the rather simple rules of a statute, the Requirements of Writing (Scotland) Act 1995. As we have seen, the statute provides that a gratuitous promise must be in writing unless the promisee has relied upon it in a significant way or the promise was made in the ordinary course of business. This statute classifies together as 'gratuitous' types of transactions which other civil law systems treat differently. Yet, the statute is remarkably successful at reaching results that are sensible given the underlying concerns we have identified. Gifts of money and property are 'gratuitous' and so require a formality in Scotland as they do elsewhere. Favours that can be performed without cost are also 'gratuitous' and so Scots law requires a formality when most other civil law systems do not. But it may not matter much in practical terms because as long as the promise remains costless, the promisor is likely to perform. If it ceases to be costless, he is not bound (absent a formality, absent reliance), but some civil law systems would reach the same result by a special rule excusing him from performance. The promisee who relies is completely protected, but, as we have seen, some civil law systems give the promisee some protection although none of them to this extent. Finally, in Scots law, some promises that entail a cost to the promisor for which he receives nothing in return can also be 'gratuitous': for example, the promises in Case 11 to install better windows or waive the need for an architect's certificate. Other civil law systems do not treat them as gifts which require a formality. Scots law achieves similar results by dispensing with the formality when a promise is made in the ordinary course of business. That is precisely the context in which a promise is unlikely to be made out of a concern for the promisee's welfare and is more likely to represent a reassessment of the terms of exchange. The remaining problem is how to avoid enforcing an unfair promise in a business context, and that is met by the doctrine of duress (Case 9 if the harm were imminent), and by interpreting the contract to accord with good faith (Cases 8(b), 13(a), and possibly 15). In short, Scots law arrives with a few simple rules at a large number of results within the range that would be sensible in other civil law systems, but which they would produce with a large number of rules.

The advantages are a high degree of economy and simplicity and, perhaps, certainty in how the law will be applied. The disadvantage may be the loss of a certain amount of fine tuning. As we have seen, when Scots law protects either the promisor or promisee of a gratuitous favour, the protection is often more extreme than in other civil law systems; it will not enforce promises to pay for benefits conferred under contracts that have become unenforceable; it has fewer tools for scrutinizing the fairness of a promise that has been given in the course of business. We have had to wonder continually to what extent these results are reached because they are thought proper and to what extent the reason is merely that the rules are so general. One reason it is difficult to tell is that because the rules are so general, the underlying concerns to which they respond are less visible than in other civil law systems. Indeed, a Scots lawyer might claim that the concerns this study has identified are not those his law is addressing. And it must be conceded that the only reason for thinking they are is that otherwise Scots law would be reaching results that reflect these concerns surprisingly often.

The doctrinal structure of the common law systems is different again.

It does not have the simplicity of Scots law. Unlike the civil law systems, it was not systematized in the sixteenth and seventeenth centuries, and so does not have doctrines based on ideas in favour at that time. Unlike them, it does not have a vague and general doctrine such as good faith which allows courts to consider directly whether a promise is fair. Nor are the problems we have examined resolved by special rules enacted for particular situations.

Instead, there is a doctrine of consideration which is stated generally and then made subject to a number of exceptions. A promise has consideration when it is made to induce the promisee to give up something in return. A promise to make a gift of money or property therefore lacks consideration, and consequently, as in other legal systems, it can be made binding only by using a special formality. Gifts to those about to be married, gratuitous bailments, promises to do services gratuitously, and promises to pay for benefits received in the past or already due under contract should all lack consideration. Yet, gifts to those about to marry have been enforced by way of exception. Gratuitous bailment is admitted to be an exceptional case although the rules applicable to it are unclear. The promise of a gratuitous service might support an action in tort even though tort actions are not usually based on promises. Promises to pay time-barred debts, debts discharged in bankruptcy, and debts incurred as a minor were all once enforceable by way of exception and the last of them still is. Promises to pay for a rescue are unenforceable unless the person in danger managed, before the rescue, to say or do something that would count as a 'request' and therefore constitute an 'implied assumpsit'. But the leading scholar Atiyah thinks the English courts should make an exception in this case as American courts have done. Promises to pay more (or take less) for benefits already due under contract were enforced by recognizing three further exceptions: waiver, receipt of a 'practical benefit', and promissory estoppel.

There is a parallel to the state of the common law for much of its history. As we saw earlier, the formula for consideration which is now generally accepted was a nineteenth-century innovation. Before then, the requirement of consideration had been described in different ways. Judges did not decide whether there was consideration by applying a formula but by seeing if the facts of the case before them were similar to those in which consideration had been found to be present or absent in the past. The result was a law that was structured, not so much by rules or doctrines or principles, but by lines of cases kept distinct by close attention to their facts. Looking at the list of exceptions we have encountered in this study, one wonders if those days have not returned. If so, the difference today is that, in these exceptional cases, judges say that the doctrine of consideration does not apply, whereas once, when they wished to enforce a promise, they would find consideration for it without worrying too much about what consideration meant.

This way of proceeding has certain advantages. Judges, whether in civil law or common law systems, often find it much easier to see that certain cases are similar and should be decided in a certain way than they do to frame an abstract rule that expresses what the cases have in common, let alone to identify a still more abstract principle that explains why this rule is appropriate. Indeed, unless such a rule or principle can be stated with reasonable coherence, the attempt to formulate it may simply lead to uncertainty and muddy thought because the formulation lacks any real content. It may be better to pay close attention to the facts of cases, and to state rules, not abstractly, but in terms of facts that seem to distinguish one line of cases from another.

The disadvantage is that when rules are stated by identifying such facts, it is perfectly possible that, in some cases, the presence of these facts does not call for a particular result even though it may in others. Courts will either create more exceptions, or their decisions will turn on the presence or absence of a fact that they know should not matter. Thus, according to the English reporter, many circumstances can influence an English court to enforce a promise that are not part of the doctrine of consideration or any recognized exception to it. An example is the promise to compensate someone who has been injured in rescuing the promisor (Case 2). According to Atiyah, 'any court would surely strive to uphold' the rescuer's claim,[19] and the English reporter agrees. But, as the English reporter put it, the court cannot 'invent the consideration entirely out of thin air'. It 'would need some factual basis, however slim, on which to support a conclusion' that there was consideration. That comes close to saying that sometimes, when a court believes a party should win his case, whether he will win depends on the presence or absence of some fact which has little or nothing to do with the court's conviction that he should. Words that would not be construed as a request for aid in other circumstances, would be so construed to enforce the promise to the rescuer, but absent any such words, the rescuer will lose.

---

[19] P. S. Atiyah, *An Introduction to the Law of Contract*, 5th edn (1995), 125.

Conversely, the presence of a certain fact may compel a court to reach a result which seems ill-advised. For a long time, English courts said there was no consideration for one party's promise to modify his contractual duties when the other party did not modify his own. As we have seen, they finally recognized exceptions when the promisor received a 'practical benefit' or the promisee relied. Surely, before these exceptions were created, English courts must have refused many times to enforce promises which they thought should be enforced. Today, promises are unenforceable when only the promisor has committed himself. Such promises can sometimes be unfair, as we saw in Cases 8(b) and 13(c) when the promisee could buy as much steel as he wished at a fixed price or held a long-term option on the promisor's property. If they are sufficiently unfair, other legal systems will not enforce them either. The consequence of the doctrine of consideration, however, is that other promises are not enforced, such as those in Cases 8(a), 8(c), and 13(a), because only the promisor is committed even though they do not seem unfair, and other legal systems enforce them routinely. It may be that English courts see no reason for refusing to enforce them except that the absence of mutual commitment is a fact that requires them to apply the doctrine of consideration.

In any event, as we have seen, common law courts reach many of the same results as those in civil law systems, in part, because of the exceptions that they have recognized. If one wishes, one can speak of the carving out of these exceptions as 'convergence'. But, in this area of law, the doctrinal structure has not converged.

C. The search for solutions

We have examined the results that different legal systems reach and seen that they can most often be explained as responses to common underlying problems. That does not mean that the rules were adopted with these problems distinctly in mind. It is often easier to see that a result makes sense than to explain why it does, or even what problem it addresses. Indeed, one of the advantages of the comparative study of law is that by examining the approaches of different legal systems, we may gain a better understanding of the underlying problems.

Having gained a better understanding, we should be in a better position to see how a problem can be solved. We should at least be able to frame a solution that addresses the problem straightforwardly. Many of the solutions we have examined, in contrast, address problems obliquely, so much so that one cannot see right away what problem is being addressed. Often, we could identify a common underlying problem only after examining several different solutions.

Our last task, then, will be to ask what is the most straightforward way to address the problems we have identified. By the most straightforward solution, I mean the one that comes the closest to giving the right result – the one that resolves the problem – in the largest number of cases. It is the rule that directs the judges' attention to what is ultimately at stake. Paradoxically, such a rule may not be the best one in practice. What ultimately matters may require factual determinations that are too difficult to make directly. One might be better off with a rule that gives the wrong answer more of the time but is clearer and simpler. As we have seen, nearly all the rules we have examined have their advantages and disadvantages, many of a practical nature. Nevertheless, it will still be useful to formulate a rule that states so far as possible what really does matter. It at least provides a bench-mark for gauging how often the clearer simpler rule gives the wrong result.

1. Gifts and favours

a. Promises of money or property

As we have seen, in all the legal systems we have examined, the promisor must surmount some obstacle in order to obligate himself to give away money or property. The difference is in the height of the obstacle. In one system (Belgium), he cannot give it away in advance of making the actual transfer; in most, he cannot do so without completing a formality that typically requires the help of a legal professional; in two systems (Spain and Scotland), he must promise to do so in writing.

It is generally acknowledged that one of the underlying problems is to prevent the donor from rashly making himself poorer. If that were the only problem, surely the most straightforward solution is not simply to refuse to enforce a promise unless a formality is completed. With some informal promises of gifts, that problem might not arise, or it might not be serious. Suppose, for example, that the promise was small compared with the promisor's resources and commitments, and made to an apparently deserving person or cause. It is hard to see why a court should treat the promise as without legal significance if the only problem were a fear of rashness.

Admittedly, there may be other problems as well. The American jurist Melvin Eisenberg has described two of them. First, for the promisee to demand performance as a matter of right might be inconsistent with the relationship of trust and affection that led the promisor to make the promise.[20] If Gaston promises his niece Catherine a large sum of money for her birthday, part of what is important to their relationship may be that she must trust him to perform – that she cannot legally compel him to do so. Second, both parties may be aware that the promise is subject to implicit conditions which are inchoate in the sense that a court would find it hard to identify them.[21] Both Gaston and Catherine may understand that he need not perform if his business fails or his house burns down or he needs an operation for which his medical insurance will not pay.

Again, however, the most straightforward solution to those problems is not to require a formality. With some informal promises of gifts, such problems may not arise. In principle, such promises should be enforced even if the formality was not completed. That does not mean that the formality should be abolished. It serves the useful function of creating what American jurists sometimes call a 'safe harbour': it permits a promisor who does wish to bind himself to ensure he is bound by completing the relevant formality. But the more straightforward rule would consider directly whether these reasons for caution about enforcing informal promises apply.

For example, suppose that the promisor clearly indicated that he wished to be legally bound. One might still be afraid he was acting rashly. But the two reasons for caution just mentioned would not be present or would be far less significant. It would be presumptuous to assume his relationship with the promisee would be impaired if he succeeded in binding himself, or that his obligation is subject to implicit conditions that a court cannot determine. Indeed, under some circumstances, these reasons would be unlikely to matter even if the promisor did not indicate that he meant to be legally bound. Perhaps there is no relationship of trust or affection to be impaired, as, for example, in a promise to a charity. Perhaps the promise is unlikely to be subject to implicit conditions, as, for example, if it is made so that the promisee can change his position in reliance upon it.

Thus, the problems which dictate a need for caution in the enforcement of donative promises themselves suggest that one need not always be cautious. The straightforward approach would be to enforce any such promise when the court is convinced (1) that it was not rashly made, taking into

---

[20] Melvin Aron Eisenberg, 'The Theory of Contracts', forthcoming in *The Theory of Contract Law: New Essays* (ed. P. Benson, Cambridge Univ. Press).

[21] Melvin Aron Eisenberg, 'The World of Contract and the World of Gift', *Cal. L. Rev.* 85 (1997), 821, 850.

account the promisor's motive and the amount of the gift in proportion to his resources, and (2) that to treat it as a legal obligation is consistent with the parties' intentions, given their relationship and the likelihood that it was subject to inchoate tacit conditions.

How this approach might work can be illustrated by traditional exceptions to the requirement of a formality which disappeared with the rise of modern codes even though this approach would not be to list exceptions but to ask, in each case, whether the usual reasons for caution in enforcing donative promises are present. Two of these traditional exceptions concern situations in which the usual reasons would not normally be present.

One exception was for informal promises made *ad pias causas*, to a charitable cause. Such a promise is unlikely to be rash as long as it is small in proportion to the promisor's resources. It is not inspired by a relationship of trust or affection. It is unlikely to be subject to implicit and inchoate provisions: indeed, the reason for making it in advance of performance is often so that the charitable organization will be able to rely (whether it does so or not).

Another traditional exception was for informal promises made *propter nuptias*, on account of the marriage of a child. Today, such a rule is found only in Germany. Here again, the promise is unlikely to be rash as long as it is in proportion to one's resources. Thus, in Germany, it is enforceable only when it is not immoderate in light of the parents' wealth.[22] Moreover, such a promise is often made to confer independence on the new couple so that they can regard what they receive as their own. They can use it without their needs being weighed against those of other family members as when they were part of their parents' household. If so, while the promise is inspired by affection, allowing them to claim what they were promised as of right is consonant with the donor's intention. It need not undermine the relationship any more than recognizing their right to refuse to return any property which their parents have given them. Moreover, such a promise is unlikely to be subject to implicit and inchoate conditions.

If such an approach were adopted, it could matter whether the promisee was likely to change his position in reliance on the promise, but not for the reason one might expect. One might think that the reason would be to protect the promisee who does rely. Actually, to determine whether he should be protected one would have to answer the same questions as to

---

[22] German Civil Code (*Bürgerlichesgesetzbuch*) § 1624(1).

determine whether the promise should be enforced whether or not he relied upon it. The promisee who relied upon a rash promise is not a sympathetic figure, particularly if there is any possibility that he relied on the promise in order to be legally protected. The promisee who relied upon a promise subject to a tacit condition cannot complain that the promise is broken unless the condition is fulfilled. And if enforcing the promise would undermine a relationship of affection and trust, so, presumably, would holding the promisor liable because the promisee relied.

Nevertheless, it might matter if the promise was made so that the promisee could act in reliance on it. In that case, it is unlikely that the promise was subject to the sort of inchoate conditions we have described. It is unlikely, in other words, that the parties imagined that there were all sorts of unspoken reasons why the promisor might not have to perform. In that event, the promise should be enforced if it is not rash and if enforcing it would not undermine a relationship of trust and affection.

b. Favours that need not entail expense

As we have seen, most legal systems will enforce a promise to do a favour which can be performed without significant cost provided, as most of the reporters mentioned, that the arrangement was meant to have legal consequences. That is as it should be since, in such cases, the reasons for caution that we have seen in the enforcement of promises of gifts are not present. If there is no significant cost, there is no danger that the promisor rashly decided to enrich the promisee at his own expense. It might be, as in the case of gifts, that enforcing the promise would be inconsistent with a relationship of trust and affection between the parties. But if so, the promise would not be enforceable because the arrangement was not meant to have legal consequences – ambiguous as that requirement may be in other contexts.

The problem, as we have seen, is what to do when the promise unexpectedly entails a significant cost. We have examined two such situations. In one, exemplified by our cases of the loan of a car and the deposit of furniture, the promisor unexpectedly developed a need of his own: for the car (Case 7) or for the storage space (Case 5). In the other situation, exemplified by the promise to insure the plane (Case 6), the promise is broken, and the cost to the promisor will be significant if he is held liable.

We can come closer to a solution if we bear in mind the principle that explains why legal systems are cautious about enforcing donative promises: the promisee should not be enriched at the promisor's expense unless the promisor has deliberately decided that he should be.

In the first situation, a benefit that was meant to be conferred costlessly is no longer costless since the promisor needs the car or the storage space himself. Let us first suppose that if the promise is enforced, the promisor will have to purchase a replacement – he will have to rent another car or other storage space – but that if it is not enforced, the promisee will have to do so. Suppose also that the promisee would have to rent the car or storage space and could have done so as cheaply if the promise had never been made. Enforcing the promise under these circumstances violates the principle just mentioned. It confers a benefit on the promisee at the promisor's expense. Moreover, the promisor has not decided to do so at his own expense. He thought the arrangement would be costless.

On the assumptions we have just made, the promisee is no worse off than if the promise had never been given. He would have had to rent a car or storage space anyway. Of course, he could be made worse off. Perhaps he cannot rent the car or the space now, or cannot do so as cheaply, or perhaps he could have borrowed a car or stored his goods gratuitously with someone else and has now lost the chance to do so. The problem in such cases is like the one raised by the next situation we have to consider: the promise to insure the plane. In that case, the promisee is also worse off than if the promise had never been made. Indeed, she is worse off due to the promisor's negligence. If the promisor should not be liable in that situation, *a fortiori*, he should not be liable simply because the promisee is worse off.

In the case of the plane, the promisee is worse off because the promisor negligently failed to perform a service which he could have performed costlessly. To see how to deal with this case, we should recognize that the promisor incurs a cost if he has to run the risk of being held liable for negligence just as he would if he promised to indemnify the promisee for the consequences of a chance event. It would be like a promise to insure someone against a risk. As economists and people in business look at the matter, a risk of loss is itself a cost. Here, admittedly, the promisor can reduce the size of this risk by trying not to act negligently. But people sometimes act negligently even when they have resolved to act with care. The risk could only be reduced to zero for conduct that is so careless that it can be avoided by anyone who makes the effort. Otherwise, there will be a risk of liability, and therefore the promise will not be costless.

Of course, if the promisor is not held liable for his own negligence, the risk of suffering the consequences will fall on the promisee. That, too, is a cost. It may be, however, that the net benefit to the promisee is positive even taking the risk of these consequences into account. The value of the benefit that promisee is to receive may be sufficiently great as to outweigh the risk. In that case, at the time the promise was made, the promisee would consider himself to be better off even after taking into account the possibility that the promisor will be negligent. Consequently, it would seem that the promisor should not be liable for negligence. To hold him liable is to make the promisee better off at his expense.

It might be, however, that the promisee is worse off, even if the matter is viewed *ex ante* at the time the promise is made. The consequences of the promisor's negligence may be sufficiently severe, and the chance that he will be negligent sufficiently great, to outweigh the benefit the promisee is to receive. In that case, the promisee would not have wanted the promise to be made. He would not have relied upon it if he had understood the risks. Since he did rely on the promise, it is likely that he did not understand the risks because he did not understand how likely it was that the promisor would be negligent. In that event, it would seem that the promisor should be held liable. He has not benefited the promisee even when the matter is viewed *ex ante*. He has harmed him by leading him to rely on a promise while failing to inform him of the risk of doing so.

We can see, then, that the legal systems that hold the promisor liable only for gross negligence are not far off the mark. Gross negligence can be defined in two ways. It can be defined as conduct so careless that it can be avoided by anyone who tries to do so. In this sense, gross negligence is like an intentional wrong: *culpa lata dolo aequiparatur.* Liability for gross negligence is more like liability for a choice one makes than for a chance event. A person who does not make this choice runs no risk of liability. Thus, a promise is still costless if the promisor is held liable for gross negligence in this sense. It is not if he is held liable for ordinary negligence.

Gross negligence can also be defined in terms of the risks and consequences to others. In this sense, it is conduct which is exceptionally likely to harm them or to do them serious harm. If the promisor is grossly negligent in this sense, the risk of harm to the promisee is likely to outweigh whatever benefit he was promised. If so, as we have seen, the promisor should be held liable. We can conclude then, that the promisor should be liable for gross negligence in either of these two senses but not for ordinary negligence.

2. Promises to pay for benefits received or owed

a. Promises to pay for benefits already conferred

As we have already seen, many legal systems will enforce a promise to pay a debt discharged in bankruptcy, a time-barred debt, or a debt contracted before reaching one's majority. Some will enforce a promise to compensate a person who was injured rescuing the promisor. The doctrines used to reach these results are quite varied. Yet the cases are similar. In each case, unless the promise is enforced, the promisor will have benefited at the promisee's expense even though the promisee did not intend to make him a gift. In each case, there is a reason why, even absent a promise, the promisor should have to pay for the benefit. In three of the cases, he had obtained the benefit by agreeing to pay for it. In the other, because he was benefited at the rescuer's expense, one would expect the rescuer to have a claim for unjust enrichment. Yet in each case, absent a promise, the party who conferred the benefit faces some obstacle to recovery: the discharge in bankruptcy (in some jurisdictions); the passage of time; the rules protecting minors; and reluctance (in some jurisdictions) to allow an action in unjust enrichment for the performance of an unrequested service.

As suggested earlier, enforcing these promises makes sense if, because the promise was made, the law no longer has a reason to interpose an obstacle to recovery. When debts are discharged in bankruptcy, the reason is to allow the debtor to make a new start. The fact that he made the promise is evidence that he can now repay the debt without compromising his new start. The reason debts become time-barred is the fear that evidence has been lost or that the debtor has changed his position in the belief that he will not be called upon to pay. The promise is evidence that the debt was truly owed and that the debtor expects to pay. The contracts of a minor are unenforceable for fear that minors have bad judgment. The promise is evidence that payment is consistent with the debtor's now mature judgment. In some jurisdictions, it is difficult to recover in unjust enrichment for unrequested services because of doubts as to whether the service was desired and what it was worth to the recipient. The promise may remove these doubts.

If so, however, the promise is not important, as promises usually are, because it is a commitment. It is important because it is evidence. The straightforward approach would not be to lay down a general rule such as 'promises to perform a natural obligation will be enforced'. It would be to treat the promise as evidence and give it whatever weight seems appropriate. It may be that the bankrupt can now afford to repay the debt, or it may be that he blurted out the promise rashly. It may be that the promise proves the time-barred debt was genuine, but if the promise is vague, it may not be clear evidence. The promise made upon majority may reflect a judgment that the prior contract was a fair one or it may reflect an exaggerated view of the obligations one should be bound to honour. In such cases, one cannot say what weight to give the promise until one has looked at the other relevant evidence: the financial circumstances of the bankrupt, the other indications that the debt was genuine, the terms of the contract with the minor, and the circumstances in which it was entered into.

The same is true of the rescue. The promise may resolve doubts as to whether the rescue was needed and what it was worth to the promisor. But the extent to which it will do so depends on the seriousness of these doubts. It may be obvious that the rescue was needed and was worth a great deal. Or it may be unlikely. Similarly, how far the promise will resolve these doubts depends upon the circumstances. The promisor might or might not have been in a position to decide whether he needed to be rescued. The promise may have expressed a sense of obligation to pay for what he has received, or it may merely have expressed generosity or admiration. Again, the most straightforward approach would be to treat the promise merely as evidence bearing on the ultimate question of whether the person rescued was benefited and by what amount.

b. Promises to pay for benefits to which one has a contractual right

As we have seen, when someone agrees to pay more or take less than originally agreed for a benefit to which he is contractually entitled, there are two possibilities. It may be that the parties envisioned from the beginning that the contract price would be adjusted from time to time to reflect changed economic conditions or new information about the value of the performance received in return. The adjustment in question was made in an effort to be fair and to honour this original understanding. Or it may be that the contract price was not intended to be flexible. It was an allocation of risks between the parties. The promisee who demands an adjustment is reneging on a bet which he has lost. Since he cannot appeal to the promisor's sense of fairness, he will normally have to appeal instead to his own power to harm the promisor by breaching the contract and withholding performance.

In the first of these situations, the price set originally does not reflect the risks of new information and changed conditions since the parties meant to adjust the price in response to this risk. In the second situation, the price will be set to reflect these risks. Thus, in the first situation, if the party who was trusted to act fairly refused to adjust the contract price, he would in effect be enriching himself at the other party's expense since the contract price was set in the expectation that he would agree to adjust it. In the second situation, the party who demands that the price be changed is trying to enrich himself at the other party's expense since the original price was set in the expectation that he would bear the risks in question. Consequently, if neither party should be enriched at the expense of the other, the promise should be enforced in the first situation but not in the second.

The straightforward approach, then, would be to ask which of these two situations we are dealing with. A number of indicia could help a court to decide. One important consideration is the likelihood that the parties would have intended the terms of the contract to be flexible, at least with respect to the sort of event that allegedly led to the later adjustment. One reason they may have done so is that allowing for that event in the original contract would have been difficult. The difficulty is greater when the contract is long term, and when current information is known to be much less accurate than later information. It is not surprising, then, that courts often uphold later adjustments in long-term leases and employment contracts. Again, the difficulty is greater when it is hard to state in the contract in advance how its terms are to be modified in response to future events. It may be hard to specify in advance exactly the sort of event that warrants an adjustment and how much the contract price should be adjusted. For example, in long-term leases and employment contracts it is hard to specify when economic conditions are so much worse than expected, or when an employee's services are so much more valuable, that the rent or salary should be adjusted. It is hard to state in advance how large the adjustment should be since that may depend on how economic conditions have affected the lessor or employer. Again, the contract may include certain terms in order to ensure that a party gets the performance he wants when he needs it. Examples are dates of delivery or the requirement of an architect's certificate. These terms may prove to be unnecessary. The party they protect may discover that he does not need the performance to be made at the time called for, or that he can tell if the work is satisfactory without the architect's inspection. For that very reason, it is more likely that the parties inserted these terms with the expectation that the beneficiary will be flexible if he discovers he does not need their protection.

Another important consideration is the promisor's reason for agreeing to take less or pay more than the contract provided. We have been assuming it was either a sense of fairness (the first situation) or fear (the second). Yet it may have been generosity as when Company promises Vito money on his retirement. If so, the promise is not meant as fair compensation but to enrich Vito at Company's expense, and it should receive the same scrutiny as other donative promises. Indeed, the executives voting to enrich

Vito may have done so in hopes of some day seeing themselves enriched, in which case their decision may amount to a raid on company funds.

Assuming that the motive was either a sense of fairness or a fear of insisting on one's rights, then the question is which is more likely. The promisor is more likely to have been acting out of a sense of fairness if an event occurred that makes the adjustment seem fair. The event might be new information, a change in economic conditions, or a reason not to insist on timely performance or an architect's inspection. Again, the action is more likely to have been motivated by a sense of fairness when the promisor was not threatened, and still more likely when he proposed the change himself or accepted it readily when the promisee proposed it. Similarly, he is less likely to have made the promise through fear when he can protect himself in other ways against the threat (for example, by suing for damages) or when the consequences he would suffer if the threat were carried out are less severe, or when the consequences he would suffer by performing his promise are less serious, as they may be, for example, when he waives the architect's certificate.

The ultimate question is which situation we are confronting: one in which the promisor made a concession to adjust fairly a matter that the parties had not finally settled; or one in which the issue in question had already been settled in his favour, and in which he made the concession only because the promisee could do him harm. If that is what ultimately matters, it would seem that a court should examine all the considerations just described because they all bear on how it should be answered.

3. The absence of commitment

We examined two types of cases: those in which one of the parties was given the option of deciding whether to contract, or for what quantity; and those in which one of the parties committed himself to pay only if the other succeeded in producing a certain result.

a. Open terms and options

In one of our cases (Case 13), a party had the option to buy or not; in another (Case 8), he had the option of how much to buy. As we saw, although their doctrines are quite varied, most of the legal systems we examined protect the committed party against the danger that the other party will speculate at his expense, at least when he most needs that protection.

If, as before, a party should not be able to enrich himself at the expense of someone who does not wish to make him a gift, then we can see why most legal systems afford this protection. The principle is violated when one can speculate at another's expense. To do so is like playing cards and deciding on the stakes at the end of the evening. On the other hand, options and open terms sometimes benefit even the party who is committed. They may increase the value of the contract to the uncommitted party and thereby increase the amount that the committed party can charge. They may benefit the non-committed party by allowing him to obtain information about the value of the performance to him which he does not currently have. In Case 13, the option enables him to conduct a study of the value of the land. In Case 8, it allows him to order steel only after he knows how much he will need. Without the opportunity to gain this information, he might not have been willing to contract, or to contract on terms as favourable to the committed party.

The straightforward approach would be to ask directly whether the arrangement actually did serve as a means of providing these legitimate benefits without allowing one party to enrich himself at the other's expense. To make this determination, a court would ask first about the benefits: did the arrangement allow one party to remain uncommitted so that he could learn more about the value to him of the performance he was to receive? How important was this information? Second, a court would ask about the cost to the committed party of allowing the other party to remain uncommitted. It is small if there is little opportunity to speculate at his expense, as, for example if the option is short term or the quantity purchased corresponds to the buyer's normal requirements or the market prices are generally stable. Third, a court would ask whether, because of an unexpectedly large change in the market price, the uncommitted party actually did use his freedom to speculate at the other party's expense rather than to obtain the information he wanted. He did if he changed his plans because the market price rose and is buying for resale rather than to put the land or goods to his own use.

b. Promises conditional upon success

As we saw, most legal systems will enforce a promise to pay money conditional upon finding a necklace (Case 14) or finding a buyer for the promisor's house (Case 15). The problem is whether the promisor can change his mind and announce that he will not pay before the necklace or a buyer is found.

In one respect, these promises may resemble those just considered. The point of them may be to allow one of the parties to learn more than he can know at the time he contracts. In the case of the options and open price terms, the uncommitted party learns more about the value of the performance he is to receive. In the case of the promises conditional on success, the promisee learns more about the difficulty of performing. It may be expensive or impossible to find the necklace or the buyer. Consequently, because of his lack of knowledge, the promisee may be unwilling to commit himself to do so. The promisor may be unwilling to pay the promisee merely for trying. Yet the promisee may be unwilling to try unless he has some assurance he will be paid. The solution is for the promisor to be obligated to pay but only if the promisee succeeds.

Here, however, the promisee is usually not able to speculate at the promisor's expense. He is hardly likely to increase or decrease his efforts in response to a change in market prices. It would seem, then, that the one reason for caution in the case of options and open terms has disappeared. Why, then, should we not enforce all promises conditional upon success? And yet, as we have seen, many legal systems allow the promisor to withdraw.

The answer, it would seem, is that not all of the promises that are conditional upon success are a solution to the problem just described. That problem was how to deal with uncertainty about the difficulty and expense of making a performance. Because of that uncertainty, the promisee will not commit himself to succeeding, the promisor will not pay him merely for trying, and yet the promisee will not try (or try as hard) unless he has some assurance of being paid. Sometimes a promise conditional upon success is not made to give the promisee this reassurance. It may be that the promisee can perform without incurring any expense. He may already have information – for example, as to who stole the necklace or where it is now – and need only impart it. Or it may be that the promisee need not incur any extra expense. For example, the real estate agent may have incurred considerable expense establishing and publicizing his listings, but listing one more house does not cost any more. If so, it would be peculiar to hold the promisor to his promise if he changes his mind before anyone has claimed the reward. As in one class of cases considered earlier, a party is in a position to confer a benefit on another at no cost to himself. This time, however, so far as the promisor is aware, the promisee will not do so without a reward. In general, it is sensible to enforce a promise offering him a reward since, if it is unenforceable, the promisee may not confer the benefit. But if the promisee has not yet done so, it is hard to see why the promisor should be bound or why he would want to be. No one is either committing himself in return or incurring a cost in reliance on his promise.

Whether the promisor can change his mind should therefore depend on whether or not he made his promise, conditional on success, to induce the promisee to incur extra expense. The answer will depend upon the circumstances. It is probably in the negative in the case of the reward for the necklace offered in a newspaper advertisement. No one is likely to go to significant trouble and expense on the strength of such an offer. The same is probably true when the house is listed non-exclusively with a broker. Indeed, the broker may incur no extra expense at all. That may be why these promises are freely revocable in many legal systems. Nevertheless, the straightforward approach would be to ask whether, under the circumstances, the promise is made so that the promisee would incur trouble and expense in hope of earning the reward.[23]

---

[23] For an argument that the promisor should then be bound even if the promisee has not yet incurred the trouble and expense, see Gordley, 'Enforcing Promises', 603–7.

Index by country

(See also Table of Legislation)

Austria
Alleinvermittlungsauftrag 325
Ausgleichsverfahren 94
bad faith (*contra bonos mores*), breach of
 promise and 42 n. 76, 63, 110, 116
bankruptcy proceedings
 payment of percentage of debt
  (*Ausgleichsverfahren*) 94
 sale of assets (*Konkursverfahren*) 95
changed circumstances 131
 change in market price 290, 297
 contract, modification 205
 pre-contractual/contractual obligations
  131, 147, 181, 290
contract
 interpretation, determination of
  quantity 216
 modification: changed circumstances
  and 205; gift distinguished 260, 265
 offer: revocability 290, 297, motivation,
  relevance 290–1
 requirements: contract replacing
  earlier contract invalid for defect of
  age 95; guardian's consent in case of
  minor 95–6; intention to create legal
  relationship 116
 voidable: disproportion between price
  and value 291, 297; for defect of age,
  court's duty to consider on own
  initiative 95; for unlawful threat of
  non-performance 228–9; promise to
  comply as confirmation of contract,
  in case of, defect of age 95–6

contract of agency (*mandatum*) 63, 65
 definition 42; *Vertrag zugunsten Dritter*
  42 n. 71
 requirements: acceptance by donee 42;
  delivery 42; obligation to represent
  legally before third parties 158
 work contract (*Werkvertrag*)
  distinguished 158 n. 26
contract of deposit/promise to store
 goods without charge
 as pre-contractual obligation 130, 131
 definition 130; remuneration,
  relevance 130
 liability: after delivery 131; between
  friends 131–2, 136–7; cancellation of
  alternative contract, relevance 132;
  gratuitous contract 130; loss of
  alternative possibility, relevance 132,
  147; professional storer of furniture
  131; seller of goods 131
 release from liability, grounds: delivery
  of goods, relevance 131; harm to own
  interests 131, 349; inability to store
  goods safely 131; *rebus sic stantibus*
  131, 147
 requirements: absence of formality
  132; intention to create legal
  relationship 131–2, 146–7
contract of donation
 definition 41 n. 68
 requirements: acceptance of gift 41 n.
  68; immediate delivery 41–2;
  notarization 41–2

Austria (cont.)

contract of loan for use (*prêt à l'usage/commodatum*)
  as contract *re* 181
  as *Leihvertrag* 181
  delivery and 180, 190
  release from liability, grounds, urgency 181, 190
  requirements: absence of remuneration 181; intention to establish legal obligation 190

contract *re*
  contract of deposit as 130
  contract of loan for use (*prêt à l'usage/commodatum*) as 181
  delivery of goods, need for 131, 181, 190

contract for services, work contract distinguished 307 n. 27

contract for work, modification 258

culpa in contrahendo 42–3
  gifts, applicability to 42–3, 64
  requirements 42–4, 64

damages for breach of
  agreement to keep social engagement 110; reliance damages 110 n. 16
  contract, expectation interest 110 n. 16
  work contract (*contrat d'entreprise/Werkvertrag*), lost profit 307, 316, 317, 369

debt not legally due, enforceability of promise to pay
  natural obligation, debt discharged in bankruptcy 95, 102; new promise, need for 95; recovery of paid debt 95
  prescription, effect, promise to pay subsequent to, as waiver of defence 95, 102
  voidable contract, promise as confirmation of contract, defect of age and 95–6, 102; new contract, need for 95, 96

debt, right to reclaim arrears in case of promise to reduce rent
  promise as: deferral of payment 272, 277; gift/donation 272, 277
  waiver of debt, formalities 272

delivery of goods, relevance
  contract of agency 42
  contract of deposit/promise to store goods without charge 131, 147
  contract of donation 41–2
  contract/promise of loan of goods without charge 180, 190
  gift/donation 41–2

Dienstvertrag 307 n. 27

dowry/gift *propter nuptias*
  obligation to give 43
  promise of as settlement or acknowledgment of claim to 43
  proportionality and 43

economic duress
  remedies, avoidance/rescission of contract 229
  requirements: illegitimate or unjust threat 245, 252; imminent and serious harm 228–9

employment contract, termination, terminal bonus
  gift, whether 246
  obligation, whether 246

Gefälligkeitshältnis 131

gift/donation
  classification as: honouring of moral obligation 77–8; promise of dowry exceeding obligation 43; reward for merits 246
  distinguished from: option contract 290, 297; terminal bonus 246, 364; unilateral modification of contract 260, 265

gift/donation, enforceability of promise of, recovery of expenses incurred in expectation of, good faith, relevance 42

gift/donation, legal formalities/ requirements
  acceptance of promise 42
  delivery to donee 41–2
  intention to give, *Schenkungsabsicht* 245, 246, 252

gift/promise of gift as, contract 41–2

gratuitous contract
  gift distinguished 132

promise to store goods without charge
as 130
Gute Sitten 110
Konkursverfahren 95
Leihvertrag 181
lésion
  critical date 291, 297
  economic duress and 229
liability in tort
  economic loss, sufficiency 110
  failure to keep promise, free
    services/social engagement, bad
    faith, need for 110
  nonfeasance 168
loan of goods without charge, promise
  as: rental agreement 181 n. 28; *pactum
    de contrahendo* 181; *Prekarium* (loan
    terminable at will) 181, 190
  release from liability, grounds: in case
    of *Prekarium* 181, 190; inconvenience
    to borrower, relevance 181–2
mandatum 42, 63, 65
moral obligation, promise of
  remuneration for fulfilling
  enforceability 77–8
  gift, whether 77–8
  legal formalities/requirements 77–8;
    harm to donor 78; importance to
    donee of services rendered 78
  professional status of promisee,
    relevance 78
natural obligation/*obligation naturelle*,
  applicability, debt
  discharged in bankruptcy 94–5, 102
  time-barred 95
negligence in case of
  gross negligence 159
  promise to do favour 159, 168, 352
  work contract (*contrat d'entreprise*/
    Werkvertrag) 159, 168
negotiorum gestio
  remuneration for damage/harm
    suffered: in case of necessary action
    78, 85; legal duty, relevance 78;
    professional status of person
    rendering service, relevance 78;
    promise, as acknowledgment of claim

78, 85; promise of payment, relevance
  85; status of person receiving service,
  relevance 85, duty of that person to
  provide service, need for 78, parent of
  adult/minor child distinguished 78, 85
unjust enrichment and 359
notarization
  contract of donation 41–2
  enforceability of promise, of gift 41–2,
    63
obligation of result (*locatio conductio
  operis*) 307
option contract (*contrat de promesse*)
  gift distinguished 290, 297
  pre-contractual agreement
    distinguished 290
  time limits for exercise of option 290
pactum de contrahendo 130, 131, 181, 290
pre-contractual obligation
  basis of liability, *culpa in contrahendo* 42
  changed circumstances and 131, 147,
    181, 290
  promise to: lend goods without charge
    181; store goods without charge 130,
    131
Prekarium 181, 190
promise, intention to create legal
  relations, need for 109, 131–2
  professional status, relevance 131,
    147–8
  promisee's right to assume 109
promise of reward
  as work contract (*contrat
    d'entreprise*/*Werkvertrag*) 307–8
  recovery of expenses and 307–8, 316,
    367
  revocability of promise to general
    public: *Auslobung* 308, 316; relevance
    of, knowledge of withdrawal of offer
    308, 316
  revocability of promise to individual,
    relevance of, performance in
    response to promise 308
promise to do favour
  as contract to perform a particular
    piece of work (*Werkvertrag*) 158;
    professional status, relevance 158

Austria (cont.)

promise to do favour (*cont.*)

liability, negligence: gross 159; implied clause exempting from 159, 168, 352

requirements, intention to create legal relations 158, 167–8

promise to do more than agreed

as offer to modify/modification of contract 260

formalities 260

promise to sell at fixed price, whether binding in case of change of market price 205–6

in absence of: agreement that sale for own consumption 205–6, 216; minimum/usual purchase requirement 206

proportionality

dowry/gift *propter nuptias* 43

voidable contract and 43

protection of promisor/donor in case of dowry/gift *propter nuptias* 43

real estate agency contract

remuneration of agent: dependence on result 324–5, 333; termination of contract, effect, fixed term, relevance 325

seller, obligation to sell, whether 325, 333

sole agency: remuneration of agent, seller's fault 325, 333, 370; requirement 325

termination, fixed term, relevance 325

real property transactions, requirements 290, 297

rental agreement 181 n. 28

reward for merits, as gift 246

Schenkungsabsicht 245, 246

services rendered [without charge], promise to pay remuneration for

as moral obligation 77–8

as natural obligation 358

as salary, increase in 245

as terminal bonus 246, 364

negotiorum gestio, relevance of doctrine 78

social engagement, agreement to keep

as legally binding promise 109–10; intention/cause, need for 110

specific performance, contract of deposit/promise to store goods without charge in absence of contract 131, 147

sums exceeding usual or obligatory level or financial means, treatment as gift or remunatory donation, dowry/gift *pro nuptias* 43

unilateral contract, promise to sell, revocability, motivation, relevance 290–1

unilateral promise

presumption of intention to incur smaller obligation 272

to sell (*promesse unilatérale de vente*), as contract 290, 297

unjust enrichment, *negotiorum gestio* 359

waiver of right, binding nature 260

Wegfall der Geschäftsgrundlage 131

work contract (*Werkvertrag*) 158

classification as: promise of reward to individual 307–8; promise to do favour 158–9, professional status of promisor, relevance 158

distinguished from, contract for services (*Dienstvertrag*) 307

liability, negligence: gross 159; implied exemption 159, 168

obligation of result 307

unilateral termination 307–8; right to recover: expenses 307–8, 316, 369, lost profit 307, 316, 317, 369

Belgium

abuse of economic dependence 224

abuse of right

abus de droit en matière contractuelle 198

definition/requirements: disproportion between interest benefited and harm caused 198, 199; exercise of right without legitimate, reasonable and sufficient excuse 198, 199; failure to consider legitimate expectations 198, 199; intention to do harm 198; untimely withdrawal of offer 303, 369 inequality of bargaining power 199, 215

remedies: damages 198, 303, 315; limitation of right to normal use 198

acte sous seing privé 29

ad pias causas 30

animus contrahendi 106 n. 3

animus donandi/animus solvendi 269

biens meuble corporel 28

brokerage contract

as hiring of labour (*louage d'ouvrage*) contract 321

breach by person hiring: arbitrary rejection of reasonable offer 322; damages for 321–2; rescission of contract 321

remuneration in case of termination 321, 332; where buyer found 332, 370

unilateral termination: broker's right to, [necessary and useful] expenses 321, 332; right of, in case of contract without fixed term 321, 332

cadeau d'usage 29, 63, 342–3

changed circumstances

change in economic balance of contract 199

loan of goods without charge 176, 189, 348–9

promise to sell and 284

charitable gift

ad pias causas 30

applicable rules 30

clause d'adaptation du prix 198

commercial agency 153

condition potestative 283–4, 296

contract

bilateral promise as 32 n. 33

conditional: *condition suspensive* 33–4; suspensive condition 33–4

interpretation, effectiveness principle 284

offer, binding, whether 31–2

release from obligations, grounds, unforeseen circumstances, change to economic balance of contract 199

requirements, certainty of obligation:

condition potestative 283–4, 296; price at discretion of one of parties 197; quantity at discretion of one of parties 197

requirements, intention to create legal relationship 106–7, 115

voidable, promise to comply as confirmation of contract 90–1; in case of, defect of age 90, 91

contract of agency, hiring of labour (*louage d'ouvrage*) distinguished 321

contract of agency (*mandatum*)

commercial agency (*mandat commerciale*) 153

distinguished from brokerage contract 321

liability: in absence of remuneration 152, 167; failure to perform/ *inexécution* 152; ignorance of obligations, relevance 152; standard of care 152, 167; under commercial agency 153

requirements, intention to contract 152, 167

contract of deposit/promise to store goods without charge

alternatives to contract: *promesse de dépôt* 123; social engagement or courtesy promise 123

as gratuitous unilateral obligation 123

as *in rem* unilateral contract 123

definition 123; remuneration, relevance 123

liability: after delivery 123, 145; before delivery 123; between friends 123; cancellation of alternative contract, relevance 124; loss of alternative possibility, relevance 124; professional storer of furniture 123

release from liability, grounds: delivery of goods, relevance 350; *force majeure* 123–4, 145, 348, 350; unforeseen circumstances 124, 145

requirements, protection of promisor, relevance 348–9

contract *intuiti personae* 107

Belgium (cont.)

contract of loan for use (*prêt à l'usage/commodatum*)
  as contract *re* 175–6
  as gratuitous unilateral obligation 176
  delivery and 176, 189, 348
  distinguished from promise of loan 176, 189
  release from liability, grounds: court's authorization, need for 176; urgency 176, 189, 348–9
  requirements, absence of remuneration 176
  rights, to keep until end of term 176
contract *re*
  contract of deposit as 123
  contract of loan for use (*prêt à l'usage/commodatum*) as 175–6
  delivery of goods, need for 123
  don manuel as 33
  promise of, enforceability 33
courtesy act/promise 106–7, 123, 152
  agreement to keep social engagement 106–7, 123
  contract of deposit/promise to store goods without charge 123
  promise to do favour 152
damages for abuse of right 303, 315
damages for breach of
  brokerage contract, amount of commission contracted for 322
  employment contract (termination before term) 241–2, 251, 253, 362
  lost opportunity (*perte de chance*) 302
  promise to reward 302–3, 315
  work contract (*contrat d'entreprise/Werkvertrag*): *ex aequo et bono* 302; lost profit 302, 315, 317, 369
debt not legally due, enforceability of promise to pay
  natural obligation, debt declared void 90
  prescription, effect: on action to rescind 90–1; obligation to pay 90, 91, 101; presumptive prescription 91, payment of debt 91, rebuttal 91; recovery of paid debt 90

voidable contract: action to rescind, time limits 90–1; promise as confirmation of contract 90–1, 101, defect of age and 90–1, 101, time-barred action 91
debt, right to reclaim arrears in case of promise to reduce rent
  promise as gift/donation 269
  promise by debtor to pay as natural obligation 269
  promise made in order to secure future payment of part or all of rent 269
  waiver of debt: effect 269; implied, tacit acceptance by debtor 269; *remise de dette* 269
delivery of goods, relevance
  contract of deposit/promise to store goods without charge 123, 145
  contract/promise of loan of goods without charge 176, 189
  don manuel/donation manuelle 33
  gift/donation 29, 31, 33, 63
dette de reconnaissance 71
dowry/gift *propter nuptias*
  enforceability, *acte sous seing privé* 29
  legal formalities/requirements, acceptance, relevance 29
  obligation to give, natural obligation (*obligation naturelle*) 29–30, 63, 66
economic duress
  requirements: determining influence 224; fear of considerable and actual harm 224; illegitimate or unjust threat 224; 'threat capable of overwhelming a reasonable person' 224
  specific performance of original contract and 224–5
employment contract
  hiring of labour (*louage d'ouvrage*) distinguished 302
  work contract distinguished 302
employment contract, termination
  contract without fixed term, notice 242
  fixed-term contract before term:

damages/indemnity 241–2, 251, 253, 362; inducement to stay, employer's right to offer 242, 251; obligations of: confidentiality 242, non-competition 242, 251

ex aequo et bono, damages/compensation 302

exclusive dealing clause 198, 199

exigibilité 90

force majeure
  obligations of depositee and 350
  promise to lend goods without charge 176, 189, 192, 348
  requirements: absence of fault 124; impossibility of performance 123–4, 145

gift/donation
  disguised donation (*donation déguisée*) 33
  distinguished from promise of gift 31
  don manuel 33; conditional 33–4; promise, enforceability 33
  indirect donation (*donation indirecte*): assignment of debt (*cession de créance*) 33; reduction of rent 269; renunciation of a right (*renonciation á un droit*) 33; stipulation for benefit of third party (*stipulation pour autrui*) 33; waiver of debt (*remise de dette*) 33

gift/donation, enforceability of promise of
  compliance with legal formalities, need for 29, 32, 34
  conditional promise, *condition suspensive* 33–4; condition precedent distinguished 34 n. 40
  form of promise, relevance 31
  recovery of expenses incurred in expectation of, pre-contractual obligation to act in good faith 34, 35, 63

gift/donation, legal formalities/requirements
  acceptance of gift 29; express 29, 31, 33, 63
  compliance with formal requirements, effect 31

delivery to donee 29, 31, 33, 63
  failure to comply, effect 34; nullity 32; renunciation of right to invoke 32 n. 36
  immediate divestment of right to 31, 33
  intention to give 269
  irrevocability 29, 31, 33–4, 63
  purpose, protection of donor 28, 34

gift/promise of gift as
  'customary present' (*cadeau d'usage*) 29, 63, 342–3
  natural obligation/*obligation naturelle* 29–30

gratuitous unilateral obligation, promise to
  loan goods 175
  store goods without charge 123

hiring of labour (*louage d'ouvrage*) contract
  distinguished from: contract of agency 321; employment contract 302
  unilateral termination, right of 302, 321

inequality of bargaining power 199, 215

legitimate expectations 198, 199

lésion
  critical date 284, 296, 367
  option contract (*contrat de promesse*) and 284
  requirements 367

loan of goods without charge, promise
  binding nature 176, 189
  release from liability, grounds: *force majeure* 176, 189, 192, 348; inconvenience to borrower, relevance 176; unforeseen circumstances 176, 189

modicité 29

natural obligation/*obligation naturelle* 29–30
  applicability 30 n. 21; debt: discharged in bankruptcy 90, 101, of gratitude (*dette de reconnaissance*) 71, recovery of arrears of rent in case of debtor's promise to pay 269, time-barred 90, 101

Belgium (cont.)
natural obligation/*obligation naturelle*
(*cont.*)
conversion to civil obligation 30;
promise to: pay discharged debt 90,
pay pension not due 242, 251,
remunerate 71–2
definition 30
pension 242, 364
promise, enforceability 71–2, 242,
251, 364; professional status of
person rendering service, relevance
72
recovery of performance or value 30
statutory basis 29–30
negotiorum gestio
remuneration for damage/harm
suffered, in case of necessary action
303
search for lost property in response to
offer of reward 303
notarization
enforceability of promise of gift 32,
33–4, 63, 242
exemption: disguised gift (*donation
déguisée*) 33; immediate delivery of
movable (*don manuel/donation
manuelle*) 33; indirect gift (*donation
indirecte*) 33; limitation to small
amounts/*modicité* 29
nullité absolue 32
obligation of result 302
pension, promise to pay as natural
obligation 242, 251, 364
pre-contractual obligation, breach of
promise and 34, 63
prescription, presumptive 91
professional status, relevance, liability
(*responsabilités professionnelles*) 153
commercial agency 153
promesse bilaterale 32 n. 33
promesse unilaterale 32 n. 33
promise
as bilateral promise (*promesse bilaterale*)
32 n. 33
as offer 32 n. 33
as unilateral contract 32 n. 33; *promesse
unilatérale* 32 n. 33

intention to create legal relations, need
for, between friends 123, 145, 152
promise of reward
as *gestion d'affaires* 303
as hiring of labour (*louage d'ouvrage*)
contract 302
as unilateral contract 303, 369
as work contract (*contrat
d'entreprise/Werkvertrag*) 302
recovery of expenses and 302, 315, 367;
gestion d'affaires 303
revocability of promise to general
public, relevance of, undertaking
not to revoke 303–4, 315
promise to do favour
as contract of agency, *contrat de mandat*
152, 352
as courtesy act/promise 152
promise to do more than agreed, binding
nature 256
promise to sell at fixed price, whether
binding in case of change of market
price 197–9, 213–15
in absence of exclusive dealing clause
198, 199
abuse of right and 198, 199
unforeseen circumstances theory and
199
proportionality, abuse of right and 198,
199
protection of promisor/donor in case of
loan without charge 348–9
promise of gift/donation 29, 34
remedies, limitation of right to normal
use 198
remise de dette 269, 276
services rendered [without charge],
promise to pay remuneration for, as
natural obligation 30–1, 63, 71–2,
358–9
social engagement, agreement to keep
as contract 106–7
as courtesy promise 106–7, 123
specific performance
contract of deposit/promise to store
goods without charge 123, 145; in
absence of contract 350
sums exceeding usual or obligatory level

or financial means, treatment as gift
or remunatory donation, customary
gift 29, 63
supply contract
escalation clause 198
exclusive dealing clause 198, 199
requirements, certainty of
price/quantity 197–8
transaction à titre onéreux 28 n. 11
unforeseeable circumstances 124, 145
unilateral contract
definition/requirements 107
promise to reward 303, 369;
revocability 302, 315
unilateral promise, to sell (*promesse
unilatérale de vente*)
as option contract (*contrat de promesse*)
6, 284
changed circumstances 284
obligation limited to promisor 283
offer distinguished 283 n. 9
waiver of warranty of hidden defects
(*garantie des vices cachés*) 256
work contract (*contrat d'entreprise/
Werkvertrag*)
classification as, promise of reward to
individual 302
distinguished from employment
contract 302
obligation of result 302
unilateral termination 302, 315; right
to recover: *ex aequo et bono*
determination 302, expenses 302,
315, 369, lost profit 302, 315, 317,
369

England
abuse of right, inequality of bargaining
power 215
changed circumstances
change in market price 295
good faith and 211
promise to sell and 295
common law of contract, historical
development
consideration: *causa* and 10–12,
exchange, relevance 12; origin in
assumpsit 10, 12, 14–15

intention to be bound 14
moral obligation 82–3
origin in procedure by writ, covenant
10, 12
unilateral contract 15
'will theories' and: consideration 13;
intention to be bound 14
consideration/cause
agreement to marry as 11, 13, 54
circumvention of rule by courts 51–2,
54, 82, 186, 376–7; detrimental
reliance on promise and 11, 12, 51,
58, 114, 137–8, 148, 185–6, 249, 253,
262, 266, 293–4
definition 52–3; actual transfer,
relevance 53; natural affection 53;
real exchange 53, motive
distinguished 54, 65, nominal value
53, 56, 64
estoppel and 13, 274–5, 277, 363
implied assumpsit/act at request of
promisor 14–15, 81, 87, 359, 376–7;
as agreement with unfixed price
81; intention to reward, need for
81, 83
legal formalities as substitute 55–6
liability in tort, effect of changes in
law 141–2
moral consideration 11, 81–2, 99–100,
103; limitation to cases of legally
defective prior obligation 82
need for 51, 53, 81–3, 86; bailment 137,
138, 376; confirmation of voidable
contract 100, 103; option contract
(*contrat de promesse*) 366; promise of
gift 52, 58, 64, 81; promise to: do
favour 163, 168, do more than
agreed 11, 261–2, 266, lend goods
without charge 185, 186, pay
discharged debt 99, 102, 376, pay
more than agreed 232–3, 362, pay
time-barred debt 11, 99, 102, reward
311, 359, sell 293, 298, sell at fixed
price 210–11, 216, 366; social
engagement, agreement to keep
113–14, 116–17, 354 n. 15; unilateral
contract 311, 368–9; waiver of right
362

England (cont.)

consideration/cause (*cont.*)

non-competition clause 249

performance of contract 248–9, 253, 311, 368–9

practical benefit (employee's agreement to stay) 248, 253, 362–3, 378

pre-existing legal duty 11, 232–3, 237, 275, 363

reciprocal promises 53, 137, 185, 210–11, 294–5, 298

services previously rendered 359

'sole discretion' clause and 294, 298

'will theories' and 13

contract

executory 55

implied terms 212–13, 216–17

interpretation, business efficacy and 212, 216

modification, increase in salary as inducement to employee to stay 248–9; reliance on promise and 249

offer: acceptance 210–11, performance as 311, 317, 368–9, 'starting to perform'/'preparations to perform' 312–13, 317; binding, whether 293; 'firm' offer 293; revocability in absence of: acceptance 293, 312, consideration/cause 293, 298; withdrawal, notification to offeree 293

requirements: certainty of obligation 294; intention to create legal relationship 116, 186

sole discretion clause 294

contract of deposit/promise to store goods without charge

as collateral contract 347, 349

liability, special relationship requirement 139–40, 148

requirements, intention to create legal relationship 142, 148

contract of loan for use (*prêt à l'usage/commodatum*)

as arrangement between friends/family 186

as bailment 186–7

as gratuitous unilateral obligation 186

consideration/cause 185, 186, 191

damages for breach of

bailment, as negligent provision of services 139–40

contract: anticipatory breach 313–14; implied condition not to withdraw offer 314

promise: reliance on promise, need for 164–5, 263, 275; to do favour, reliance losses 165; to reward 313–14

real estate agency contract: breach of agent's obligations 329; lost commission 329, 334; sole agency agreement 329

debt not legally due, enforceability of promise to pay in absence of consideration

discharged debt 99, 102

time-barred debt 99, 102

voidable contract, promise as confirmation of contract 100, 103

debt, right to reclaim arrears in case of promise to reduce rent

estoppel and 274–5, 277, 363

promise as, modification of contract 275

deed/promise under seal

applicability 55; promise to, remunerate for services rendered without charge 86

as evidence of intention to create legal obligations 55, 64

procedure 55

requirements 55; intention to create deed on face of instrument 64

delivery of goods, relevance

as evidence of special relationship 141, 148

bailment 137, 141

promise to do favour 164

depositum 137

dowry/gift *propter nuptias*, agreement to marry as consideration 11, 13, 54

reliance on promise, need for 54, 65

economic duress
  as distinct form of duress 233
  requirements: determining influence
    234; illegitimate or unjust threat
    233–4; vitiation of consent 234
  threat to terminate employment
    before term 248–9, 253
estoppel 65
  consideration and 13, 274–5, 277, 363
  damages and 263, 275
  definition 57
  estoppel by representation
    distinguished 13
  failure to keep promise to: lend
    without charge 186–7; pay more
    than agreed 249; reduce rent 274–5;
    store goods without charge 139, 141
  liability in tort and 141, 149, 275
  requirements: detriment 186, 187, 263,
    363; pre-existing legal rights 57–8,
    65, 66, 115, 117, 139, 149, 186–7, 249,
    263, 274, 363; reliance on promise
    66, 187, 262, 263, 274–5, 363
  waiver distinguished 262–3
evidence of
  assumption of responsibility, promise
    163–4
  intention to create legal obligation:
    between family members 54, 55, 113;
    between friends 186; promise to lend
    goods without charge 187
  special relationship: delivery of goods
    141, 148, 168–9; professional status
    of promisor 148, 164, 168
gift/donation, enforceability of promise
  of
  liability of estate 51, 57; intention
    expressed in will 57
  recovery of expenses incurred in
    expectation of 57–8
gift/donation, legal
    formalities/requirements
  intention to create legal obligation 113
  intention to give 54–5; presumption
    of/against 54; seriousness, need for
    55
  promise under seal 55

gift/promise of gift as, gratuitous
    unilateral obligation, between
    family members 54–5
good faith
  change of circumstances and,
    unfairness and 211
  in common law jurisdictions 376
  real estate agency contract 329
  'sole discretion' clause, relevance 294
gratuitous bailment
  definition 137, 148
  estoppel and 139, 141, 186–7
  legal classification: contract 137;
    mixed 137; sui generis 137; tort 137,
    139; uncertainty 137, 138, 148
  liability: after delivery 138, 148, 187;
    before delivery 137, 141,
    consideration, need for 137, 148,
    150, 186–7, 191, 376; between
    friends 142; collateral contract
    138, 148, 187, 346, 347, 349;
    professional status of bailee,
    relevance 137, 139, 142, 148; seller
    of goods 140, 142
  loan of goods without charge as 186–7,
    191, 346
  obligations: care of goods 138;
    restoration of goods, termination at
    will 138, 346; uncertainty 148, 187
  release from liability, grounds 137,
    142, 186, 349–50; in case of fixed
    term 138, 346; timeliness of
    termination of bailment, relevance
    138
gratuitous promise
  enforceability 138, 140
  liability for breach: misfeasance
    139–40, 164; nonfeasance 140–1, 148,
    164
gratuitous unilateral obligation, promise
    to, make gift 54–5
liability in tort
  detrimental reliance and 313
  economic loss, sufficiency 139, 150,
    163, 168, 350–1
  effect of changes on doctrine of
    consideration 141–2

England (cont.)

liability in tort (*cont.*)

failure to keep promise: as breach of duty arising out of voluntary relationship 31; loan without charge 346; storage of goods without charge 139–42, delivery of goods, relevance 141, 148, 150, status of promisee/ bailee, relevance 142; to do favour 163–5, 352, reliance on promise and 164–5

negligent provision of services, special relationship, need for 139–40, 148, 150, 163–4, 350–1; professional status of promisor 148, 164, 168

nonfeasance 140–1, 148, 164, 350–1

loan of goods without charge, promise estoppel 186–7, 191

release from liability, grounds, inconvenience to borrower, relevance 187

requirements: consideration 185; delivery, relevance 185, 186; reliance on promise 186, 187

mandatum 137, 148

moral obligation, promise of remuneration for fulfilling consideration, need for 81–3

professional status of promisee, relevance 82–3

negligence in case of

bailment 139–40

promise to do favour 164, 168

provision of services 139–40, 148, 150, 163–4, 168, 350–1

option contract (*contrat de promesse*), consideration/cause, relevance 366

promise

as offer, standing offer 210, 211

in course of business 294

intention to create legal relations, need for 142; between friends 113; business relations 113

promise of reward

as offer of unilateral contract 311, 317, 368–9

as unilateral contract 311–14, 368

revocability of promise to general public: notice of revocation as for original promise 311–12, 317; relevance of: acceptance of offer 312, expenditure on search 312–13, performance in response to promise 311–13, 317, 368

revocability of promise to individual, relevance of, expenditure on search 312–13

promise to do favour

as part of contract of sale 163, 168

contract, consideration, need for 163, 168

liability for negligence 164, 168

requirements, intention to create legal relations 166

promise to pay more than agreed consideration: need for 232–3, 261–2, 266, 364, 376; performance of contract as 232–3

expenditure in expectation of, relevance 249, 253

promise to sell at fixed price, whether binding in case of change of market price 210–13

in absence of: consideration 210–11, 216, acceptance of offer 210; minimum/usual purchase requirement, interpretation of contract and 212

good faith and 211

interpretation of contract and 212

protection of promisor/donor in case of, storage of goods without charge 349

real estate agency contract

agent's obligations: in case of termination 329; damages for breach 329

agent's right to recover expenses 329

as unilateral contract 334

good faith and 329

remuneration of agent, dependence on, result 329, 334

seller: obligation to sell, whether 312, 328–9, 334; protection of 329 sole agency: damages for breach 329; remuneration of agent 329, termination and 329, 334; seller's right to terminate 370

specific performance 329, 334

reliance on promise, relevance 51, 58

consideration/*causa*, circumvention of rule 51, 58, 114, 137–8, 148, 185– 6, 293–4

dowry/gift *propter nuptias* 54, 65

estoppel 66, 187, 262, 274–5, 363

failure to keep social engagement 113–14

negligent provision of services 139

promise of, reward 313

promise to: do favour 164–5; lend goods without charge 186, 187; sell 295

waiver of right 263

services rendered [without charge], promise to pay remuneration for

as contract, implied assumpsit/act at request of promisor 81, 87, 359

as moral obligation 81–3

enforceability, requirements, consideration 359, 376

social engagement, agreement to keep

as contract 117

as creation of legal relationship 113

sole discretion clause 294, 298

special relationship

evidence of: delivery of goods 141, 148, 168–9; professional status of promisor 148, 164, 168

relevance: contract of deposit/promise to store goods without charge 139–40, 148; negligent provision of services 139–40, 148, 150, 163–4, 350–1

specific performance

contract of deposit/promise to store goods without charge, breach of collateral contract 138, 148, 349

contract/promise of loan for use 187

real estate agency contract 329, 334

trust

definition 56

gift distinguished 56

requirements: certainty of, subject matter 56–7, 64; immediate divestment of ownership 56

third party, as intermediary 56, 64

unilateral contract

definition/requirements, common/civil law distinguished 311, 316–17

offer, acceptance: knowledge of offer, relevance 311; need for 15

offer, withdrawal 311–14, 317; as anticipatory breach of contract 313–14; effect 313–14

performance as: acceptance of offer 15, 311, 317, 334, 368–9, 'starting to perform'/'preparations to perform' 312–13, 317; condition of benefit 311, 317; consideration for promise 311

promise to reward 311–14, 317, 368–9; revocability 15, 311–14, 317

unilateral promise to sell (*promesse unilatérale de vente*)

changed circumstances 295

offer distinguished 293

waiver of right

consideration, relevance 262, 266, 362, 376

definition 262

estoppel compared 262–3

reliance on, relevance 263, 362

right to revoke 262

France

abuse of economic dependence 220 n. 3, 224

abuse of right

advantages/disadvantages of concept 196

definition/requirements 195; intention to do harm 196–7

difficulty of determining 197

fairness and 195, 196

remedies: damages 197; termination of contract 197

in setting price 195, 215

acte de complaisance 151

France (cont.)

animus contrahendi 106

appréciation souveraine 105

astreinte 222

bad faith (*contra bonos mores*), improper exploitation of tax evasion legislation 280, 296

cause immorale 28

changed circumstances
balance of interests and 173, 189
change in market price 196
contract, release from obligations 196
contract of loan for use 172, 189
loan of goods without charge 174, 348–9

charitable gift
eligibility: principle of speciality 27; public benefit and 27
requirements, benefit to donor 27, 62–3, 66

clause de retour à meilleur fortune 268

clauses abusives 220 n. 3

commodat/comodato 171, 173, 175

competition law, abuse of economic dependence and 220 n. 3, 221 n. 4, 224

condition potestative 194–5, 282, 296

condition subsequent mixte 27

confiance légitime 256

consideration/cause
definition, real exchange, economic 27
employment restrictions imposed by employer 239–40
legal formalities as substitute 28
'moral equivalent' 27, 62–3, 66
need for, promise of gift 28
services offered free and 106

construction contract, cost of work exceeding estimate, right to increase price 219

consumer law, unfair contract terms 220 n. 3, 224

contract
act of courtesy distinguished 106 n. 3
breaking-off of negotiations, liability in tort 25, 62; 'fault of the victim' 25

modification: by agreement 220; courts' power 240; novation distinguished 220; post-contractual promise to award retirement bonus 240; unilateral, requirements 255–6, 265

offer: acceptance: parties' conduct as evidence of 256, 265, performance as 301, where offer in favour of accepting party 256, 301; promise of reward as 360; promise to do distinguished 283; revocability, in case of, 'best endeavours' obligation 300, employment contract 300–1

'onerous bilateral contract' 27

pre-sale contract 282

release from obligations, grounds: *force majeure* 196; unforeseen circumstances 196, change in market price as 196

requirements: agreement on subject matter and price 281; certainty of obligation 193–6, 215, 367, *condition potestative* 194–5, 282, 296, *condition subsequent mixte* 194–5, price at discretion of one of parties 195, 196, protection of parties and 195–6, quantity at discretion of one of parties 197, remedy in case of 195, subsequent determination, possibility of 194; consent freely given 223–4; economic exchange 27; intention to be create legal relationship 106, 115; object 28

termination: before term, consent of parties, need for 174; retroactive 195, 196

unfair contract terms (*clauses abusives*) 220 n. 3

voidable: for: absence of cause 279–80, mistake (*erreur*) 279–80; *nullité relative* 89 n. 3; promise to comply as confirmation of contract 89–90, in case of, vitiating factor 90; rescission/avoidance of contract, effect 89; *vices de consentement* 281

contract of agency (*mandatum*)

definition: gratuitous nature 318, 321; *mandat à titre gratuit* 152, 318
distinguished from: contract for services 318; real estate agency 318
liability: in absence of remuneration 152, 166; failure to perform/*inexécution* 152; fault (*faute*) 152, 318–19; intentional wrongdoing (*dol*) 152; standard of care 166, quantum of damages distinguished 152
remuneration of agent 318–19
contract of deposit/promise to store goods without charge
alternatives to contract: gentlemen's agreement 119; non-contractual arrangement 119; *promesse de dépôt* 120
as collateral contract 120
as *in rem* unilateral contract 118, 120, 121, 122; promise to store distinguished 120
contracts of loan/deposit compared 119, 120
definition 118–19; remuneration, relevance 119
liability: after delivery 119–20; before delivery 120–1; between friends 119, 144; cancellation of alternative contract, relevance 122; gratuitous contract 119, 120, 122, 150; loss of alternative possibility, relevance 122; professional storer of furniture 120; remuneration for storage, relevance 118–19, 122; seller of goods: in case of goods remaining *in situ* 120, offering to store after removal 120
obligations of depositee: care of goods 118; cost of meeting, relevance 121; receipt of goods 118; restoration of goods 118
release from liability, grounds: delivery of goods, relevance 349, 350; *force majeure* 121–2, 144; unforeseen circumstances 144–5
requirements, protection of promisor, relevance 348–9

standard of care 119; best efforts 120; depositee as friend 119–20
contract of loan for use (*prêt à l'usage/commodatum*) 119, 171
as arrangement between friends/family 173
as *commodat* 171, 175, 273
as contract *re* 171, 175
delivery and 171–2, 174, 348
obligations, return, at end of term 172
release from liability, grounds: courts' discretion 172, 174; unforeseen circumstances 172, 189, balance of interests 173, 189; urgency 172–3, 189, 348, as breach of contract 12
requirements: absence of remuneration 172, 175; writing 173
rights, to keep until end of term 172, 189
contract *re*
as consensual contract 122, 175
contract of deposit as 118, 121, 122
contract of loan for use (*prêt à l'usage/commodatum*) as 171, 175
delivery of goods, need for 119, 171
relevance of classification as 122
contract of rescue (*convention d'assistance*) 69–71, 84, 87
legal obligation to assist person in danger and: liability in tort as alternative 71; status of rescuer, relevance 71
rescue as offer 360
contract for sale of goods, price, right to increase 219–20
contrat cadre 193, 194, 196
breach 197
courtesy act/promise 106 n. 3
agreement to keep social engagement 106 n. 3
damages for abuse of right 195, 215
damages for breach of
contract of agency, in absence of remuneration 152
contract of deposit/promise to store goods without charge 119–20, 122; in absence of contract 119–20, 144,

France (cont.)

damages for breach of (*cont.*)
 enforceable promise compared 120;
 in case of gratuitous contract 120–1,
 150; collateral contract 120;
 gentlemen's agreement 119, 121; lost
 opportunity and 122
 contract for gratuitous services 175
 gentlemen's agreement 105
 option contract (*contrat de promesse*)
 282, 296
 promise of gift: in amount of promise
 26; in full 26
 promise to lend goods without charge
 175
 promise to reward 300–1
 promise to sell 280, 282–3
 real estate agency contract, *restitutio in
 integrum* 320
debt not legally due, enforceability of
 promise to pay
 natural obligation: debt declared void
 89, in case of minor 89; debt
 discharged in bankruptcy 89, new
 promise, need for 88, 89; time-barred
 debt 89, 90, new promise, need for
 89
 prescription, effect: presumptive
 prescription 88–9, 101, payment of
 debt 88–9, promise to pay as
 evidence of non-payment 89, 101,
 rebuttal 89; promise to pay
 subsequent to 89
 voidable contract: action to rescind: in
 absence of 89–90, as response to
 action to enforce promise 89;
 promise as confirmation of contract
 89–90
debt, right to reclaim arrears in case of
 promise to reduce rent
 extension of term (*clause de retour à
 meilleur fortune*) 268; effect 268;
 further period of grace 268–9
 promise as, deferral of payment 276
 waiver of debt: effect 267–8; implied
 268, tacit acceptance by debtor 268;
 remise de dette 267

délai de grâce 268
delivery of goods, relevance
 contract of deposit/promise to store
 goods without charge 119–21, 144,
 349
 contract/promise of loan of goods
 without charge 171–2, 174
devoir de conscience 28
dowry/gift *propter nuptias*
 definition 26
 enforceability: heir/beneficiary,
 importance of distinction 26; where
 conditional on marriage (*condition
 subsequent mixte*) 27
 legal formalities/requirements:
 acceptance, relevance 26;
 notarization 26
 obligation to give: maintenance
 obligations distinguished 26; natural
 obligation (*obligation naturelle*) 26–7
economic duress
 as defence to action in contract 220
 as tort 220
 distinguished from: abuse of economic
 dependence 220 n. 3; economic
 difficulties 220; unfair contract
 terms (*clauses abusives*) 220 n. 3
 French/English approach distinguished
 220
 jurisdiction in relation to 223
 limited applicability 221, 240, 251
 remedies: avoidance/rescission of
 contract 220, 281; damages 220
 requirements: determining influence
 220, 221–2, 251, imminent and
 serious harm 221, status of parties,
 relevance 221, 223; direct or indirect
 dependence on person making
 threat, third party as originator of
 'threat', relevance 220; illegitimate
 or unjust threat 220, 221, 251;
 relevance of right to, judicial
 authorization to substitute
 performance 222–3, seek specific
 performance 222, 223, take
 emergency action 222
employment contract, termination

promise of reward 300–1
terminal bonus, gift, whether 240
employment restrictions imposed by
    employer, requirements 239, 251
consideration/cause, relevance 239–40
estoppel, grace period compared 268–9
evidence, writing supplemented by
    witnesses 69
evidence of
    acceptance of offer 256
    contractual agreement, acceptance of
        offer 256, 265
    intention to create legal obligation,
        between family members 69
    natural obligation/*obligation naturelle*
        68–9, 84
    non-payment of debt 89
exclusive dealing clause 197
exécution en nature 222
faculté de remplacement 222
fairness
    abuse of right and 195
    voiding of contract and 195
fault/*faute*/*dol* 25, 121, 145, 152
force majeure
    obligations of depositee and 121–2, 144
    requirements: impossibility of
        performance 122, 196; independence
        of parties' will 122; unforeseeability
        122
general rules of law (*droit commun*),
    derogation from, real estate agency
    contract 321
gentlemen's agreement
    damages for breach 105
    promise to do favour 151
    promise to store goods without charge
        119
gift/donation
    disguised donation (*donation déguisée*)
        241
    indirect donation (*donation indirecte*)
        241
gift/donation, enforceability of promise
    of
    compliance with legal formalities,
        need for 24, 25, 26, 27, 28, 240–1, 251

conditional promise, *condition
    subsequent mixte* 27
legal person as beneficiary 27
liability of estate 24
public policy and 28
recovery of expenses incurred in
    expectation of 25; contractual
    liability 25; deception of victim 25,
    62; inequality of bargain 25; tortious
    liability 25, 62
gift/donation, legal
    formalities/requirements
    acceptance of gift 24, 26
    capacity of parties 28
    compliance with formal requirements,
        effect 28
    delivery to donee 241
    irrevocability 27
    purpose, protection of donor, consent
        freely given 28
gift/promise of gift as
    contractual debt 24
    natural obligation/*obligation naturelle*
        26–7
    onerous bilateral contract 27
    unilateral contract 25
gratuitous contract
    promise to store goods without charge
        as 119, 120–1, 122, 144
    relevance of classification as 122
gratuitous promise, *donation
    rémunératoire* 241
imprévision 21
inequality of bargaining power 25
legal persons as beneficiaries of gifts 27
lésion
    attempt to change contract price and
        281
    critical date 281, 296, 367
    economic duress and 220, 281
    invalidity of consent distinguished
        281
    option contract (*contrat de promesse*) and
        282
    protection of promisor and 281
    requirements 96, 281, 367
    time limits 281

France (cont.)
liability in tort
  contract/tort, relevance of distinction
    122–3
  failure to keep promise: free
    services/social engagement 106, 115;
    gift/donation 25, 62; storage of goods
    without charge 121, 122–3, fault,
    need for 121, 145
  fairness as basis 121
  fault (*faute*): breaking-off of
    commercial negotiations 25; failure
    to complete formalities, whether 25;
    need for 25, 121, 145
  harm (*dommage*) 25; liability to rescuer
    acting voluntarily 71
  natural obligation liability as
    alternative 68
  strict 71
  termination of real estate agency 320,
    332, 370
loan of goods without charge, promise
  promesse de prêt 171
  release from liability, grounds,
    unforeseen circumstances 174
maintenance obligations 26–7
moral equivalent 27
moral impossibility 69
natural obligation/*obligation naturelle*
  applicability: debt: declared void 89,
    discharged in bankruptcy 88, 101,
    time-barred 89, 101; remuneration
    in absence of liability in tort 68
  conversion to civil obligation 26, 68–9;
    evidence of 68–9
  dowry 26–7, 62
  promise: as unilateral contract 68;
    enforceability 67–9, difficulty/rarity
    of enforcement by courts 69,
    professional status of person
    rendering service, relevance 68,
    promisor's status, relevance 68; gift
    distinguished 68; novation 68
  recovery of performance or value 67 n.
    2
  requirements: evidence of 68–9, 84;
    interpretation 68; notarization 68–9;

  unequivocal recognition of obligation
    67; validity 68; writing 68–9
  statutory basis 67–8, 89
negotiorum gestio
  quasi-contract 70; equitable
    consequences deriving from
    agreement, applicability 70–1
  remuneration for damage/harm
    suffered: legal duty, relevance 70–1;
    professional status of person
    rendering service, relevance 70–1;
    useful and necessary expenses 301,
    315
  search for lost property in response to
    offer of reward 301
notarization
  agreement to pay sum above a certain
    level 68
  dowry 26
  enforceability of promise, to sell 280
  exemption: disguised gift (*donation
    déguisée*) 241; immediate delivery of
    movable (*don manuel/donation
    manuelle*) 241; indirect gift (*donation
    indirecte*) 241; limitation to small
    amounts/*modicité* 24
novation
  increase in burden on one of parties,
    relevance 265
  modification of contract and 220
  natural obligation/*obligation naturelle*
    and 68
obligation of best endeavours (*obligation
    de moyens*) 120, 300, 301, 320
obligation de faire 280, 282–3
option contract (*contrat de promesse*),
    remedies for breach
  damages 282, 296;
  specific performance 282
prescription
  presumptive 88–9, 101
  reactivation of obligation 89
prêt à l'usage 171
promesse de prêt 171, 174–5
promesse unilatérale de vente 193–4
promise
  as unilateral contract 25

breach, damages for 26
moral/legal promise, distinction 105–6,
    151–2; court's discretion 105, 115,
    151; remedy in tort in absence of
    contract 106, 115
promise of reward
    as contract 301
    as employment contract 300–1
    as *gestion d'affaires* 301, 315
    as unilateral contract 301
    as work contract (*contrat
        d'entreprise/Werkvertrag*) 300–1
    recovery of expenses and 300–1, 315,
        369; *gestion d'affaires* 301
    revocability of promise to general
        public 301, 315; relevance of, passage
        of time 301, 315
    revocability of promise to individual
        300–1, 315
    unjust enrichment and 301
promise to do favour
    as *acte de complaisance* 151
    as contract of agency (*mandat à titre
        gratuit*) 152
    as gentlemen's agreement 151
    as moral obligation 151
promise to do more than agreed, as offer
    to modify/modification of contract
    255–6, 265
promise to sell at fixed price, whether
    binding in case of change of market
    price 193–7
    in absence of, exclusive dealing clause
        197
    abuse of right and 195–7
    unforeseen circumstances theory and
        196
    unilateral offer to sell, uncertainty of
        obligation and 193–4, 197
proportionality, services rendered,
    promise of remuneration 241
protection of promisor/donor in case of
    coercion 281
    loan without charge 348–9
    promise to, contract 240–1
    storage of goods without charge 349
public benefit 27

public policy, promise of gift/donation,
    enforceability 28
quasi-contract, *negotiorum gestio* 70
real estate agency contract
    agent's obligations, obligation of best
        endeavours (*obligation de moyens*) 320
    agent's right to recover expenses
        319–20
    as contract for services 318
    general rules of law (*droit commun*),
        derogation from 321
    legal requirements: name of person to
        whom payment is to be made 319;
        writing 319, 332
    remuneration of agent 319; court's
        power to reduce 321; dependence
        on; effectiveness of agent's role 319,
        result 319–21, 332, 370, terms of
        valid contract 319; termination of
        contract, effect 319–20
    seller, protection of 321
    sole agency, remuneration of agent
        320; contract concluded other than
        by agent 320; penalty clause 320;
        332; termination and 320, 370; third
        party's help, relevance 320
    termination, liability in tort 320, 332,
        370
real property transactions, requirements
    296
    notarization 280
    registration 280
reliance on promise, relevance,
    modification of contract 256, 265
remedies, termination of contract 197
remise de dette 267, 276
restitution, practical difficulties 196
services rendered [without charge],
    promise to pay remuneration for
    as moral obligation,
        consideration/cause, whether 241
    as natural obligation 67–71, 358
    as onerous contract 241
    as remunatory donation 241, 251
    as rescue agreement (*convention
        d'assistance*) 69–71, 359–60; rescue as
        offer 359–60

France (cont.)

services rendered [without charge], promise to pay remuneration for (*cont.*)
  as terminal bonus 241
  enforceability, requirements: monetary value for service 241; proportionality 241
  negotiorum gestio, relevance of doctrine 70–1
social engagement, agreement to keep
  as contract 105–6, 115
  as courtesy promise 106 n. 3
speciality principle 27
specific performance 119
  contract of deposit/promise to store goods without charge: in absence of contract 120, 350; between friends 119, in case of gratuitous contract 119, 120; breach of collateral contract 120
  contract/promise of loan for use 172; distinction 174–5
  infringement of rights of defendant and 175
  option contract (*contrat de promesse*) 282
  promise to do (*obligation de faire*) 280, 282–3
supply contract, exclusive dealing clause 197
unforeseeable circumstances 144–5
unilateral contract 25 n. 3
  conversion to bilateral contract 301
  exchange of contracts giving rise to 120–1
  natural obligation (*obligation naturelle*) and 68
  promise to reward 301
  synallagmatic contract distinguished 27, 197, 282
  unilateral promise, distinguished 68
unilateral promise
  acceptance, in case of options 280–1
  to sell (*promesse unilatérale de vente*) 193–4; as option contract (*contrat de promesse*) 282, 296; as sale 281; offer distinguished 283; requirements: notarization 280, registration 280

validity/enforceability distinguished 280
unjust enrichment, breach of promise to reward and 301
work contract (*contrat d'entreprise*)
  classification as: contract to undertake investigation 300–1; promise of reward to individual 300–1
  obligation of best endeavours (*obligation de moyens*) 300
  unilateral termination, right to recover expenses 300–1

Germany

bad faith (*contra bonos mores*), breach of promise and 111
burden of proof, unjust enrichment 97
changed circumstances
  balance of interests and 182, 183, 190
  change in market price 291, 292
  contract of loan for use 182, 190
  good faith and 206–7
  promise to sell and 291
charitable gift
  applicable rules 44
  eligibility, legal person 44–5, 64, 66
  requirements, enrichment of donee 44–5
common decency 111, 291–2, 297, 367
consideration/cause
  adequacy 292
  implied 273
  need for: modification of contract 260; option contract (*contrat de promesse*) 291–2, 297; transfer of property without *causa*, unjust enrichment 96 n. 30
contract
  conditional, promise of reward to investigator 308
  interpretation: aids 206, usual practice (*Verkehrssitte*) 272–3; good faith 272; parties' intention/*ergänzende Auslegung* 272–3
  modification: by agreement 260; consideration/cause 260; gift

distinguished 260, 265; invalid
subsequent contract, effect 229
offer, revocability, motivation,
relevance 291
requirements: 'common decency'
291–2, 297, 367; contract replacing
earlier contract invalid for defect of
age 97–8, 102; guardian's consent in
case of minor 97; intention to create
legal relationship 116
sole discretion clause 292
termination: *erga omnes* 229;
retroactive 229
voidable: for, unlawful threat of non-
performance 229, 246, 252;
notification of invalidation, need for
229; promise to comply as
confirmation of contract, in case of,
defect of age 97, 102; retroactive
invalidation 229; void/invalid
contract distinguished 229
contract of agency (*mandatum*), liability,
in absence of remuneration 159
contract of deposit/promise to store
goods without charge
definition 132; remuneration,
relevance 133
liability: cancellation of alternative
contract, relevance 133; gratuitous
contract 132–3; loss of alternative
possibility, relevance 133;
professional storer of furniture 132–3;
seller of goods 132–3; timeliness of
termination of deposit, relevance 133
obligations of depositee, restoration of
goods, on request or expiry of time
limit 132
release from liability, grounds: 'an
important reason' 132, 147, 349;
balance of mutual interests, need for
132, 147; delivery of goods, relevance
132
requirements, protection of promisor,
relevance 132
contract for gratuitous services,
intention to create legal
relationship, need for 159–60, 168

contract of loan for use (*prêt à
l'usage/commodatum*)
delivery and 182–3, 190
distinguished from: bilateral contract
182; gift 182
release from liability, grounds:
promisee's situation, relevance 183;
unforeseen circumstances 182, 190,
balance of interests 182, 183, 190
requirements: intention to establish
legal obligation 182, 190; limited
nature 182
rights, termination 182; in good faith
182
contract for services
termination, right to recover agreed
fee 308
work contract distinguished 308
contract for services without charge
(*mandatum*) 159
termination 159; damages in case of
untimely 159, 168
culpa in contrahendo 44
gifts, applicability to 44 n. 83
requirements 44
damages for breach of
contract for loan of goods without
charge 182
contract for services 159, 160, 168;
untimely termination 159
pre-contractual obligation, reliance
damages 43
promise to do favour 159–60
debt not legally due, enforceability of
promise to pay
discharged debt, absence of provision
for discharge 96, 102
expiry of obligations 96; recovery of
paid debt 96, 97; unjust enrichment
and 96
prescription, effect: obligation to pay
97; promise to pay subsequent to, as
waiver of defence 97, 102
promise as acknowledgment of
indebtedness 96; requirements 96–7,
protection of promisor and 96–7,
writing 96

Germany (cont.)

debt not legally due, enforceability of
   promise to pay (cont.)
   voidable contract, promise as
      confirmation of contract, defect of
      age and, new contract, need for
      97–8, 102
debt, right to reclaim arrears in case of
   promise to reduce rent
   promise as: deferral of payment 272,
      277; gift/donation 272, 277;
      modification of contract 273, 277
delivery of goods, relevance,
   contract/promise of loan of goods
   without charge 182–3, 190
dowry/gift propter nuptias
   legal formalities/requirements,
      exceptional rules 44, 64
   liability of estate 44
   proportionality and 44 n. 84, 381
employment contract, termination,
   terminal bonus
   gift, whether 246, 252
   obligation, whether 246
employment contract, work contract
   distinguished 308
evidence of, intention to create legal
   obligation
   professional status of promisor 160
   services rendered gratuitously,
      importance of services 159–60, 168
exclusive dealing clause 207
Geschäftsbesorgungsvertrag
   good faith and 309, 316, 317, 367, 369
   termination, right of 309; good faith
      and 309, 317
   work contract (Werkvertrag)
      distinguished 308–9
gift/donation, distinguished from
   option contract 291
   terminal bonus 246, 252
   tip 45
   unilateral modification of contract
      260, 265
gift/donation, enforceability of promise of
   legal person as beneficiary 44–5
   liability of estate 43, 44

gift/donation, legal formalities/
   requirements
   enrichment 44–5
   failure to comply, effect 79; nullity 43
   purpose, protection of donor 43
gift/promise of gift as, gratuitous
   contract of deposit distinguished
   132
good faith
   as limitation of exercise of rights 182
      n. 32
   change of circumstances and 206–7,
      216
   Geschäftsbesorgungsvertrag and 309, 316,
      317, 367, 369
   interpretation of contract and 272
   real estate agency contract 325, 333
   revocability of, promise of reward 309,
      316, 317, 369
   'sole discretion' clause, relevance 292,
      298
   timeliness of termination of:
      Geschäftsbesorgungsvertrag 309; loan of
      goods 182
gratuitous contract
   gift distinguished 159
   promise to: do favour 159–60; store
      goods without charge as 132–3, 147
gratuitous unilateral obligation, promise
   to do favour 159
liability in tort, failure to keep promise,
   bad faith, need for 111, 116
moral obligation, social engagement,
   failure to keep and 110–11, 116
negotiorum gestio
   remuneration for damage/harm
      suffered: legal duty, relevance 86;
      professional status of person
      rendering service, relevance 79, 86;
      promise as acknowledgment of claim
      79, 86; status of person receiving
      service, relevance, parent of
      adult/minor child distinguished 79
   unjust enrichment and 359
notarization
   enforceability of promise of gift 43, 64,
      246

real property transactions 291, 297
obligation of
  best endeavours (*obligation de moyens*)
    308–9, 316
  result 308, 316
option contract (*contrat de promesse*)
  changed circumstances, relevance 291
  consideration/cause, relevance 291, 297
  gift distinguished 291
  time limits for exercise of option 291–2
promise, moral/legal promise, distinction
  110–11, 116
promise of reward
  as conditional contract 308
  as work contract (*Werkvertrag*) 308–9
  contract for services 308–9
  recovery of expenses and 316
  revocability of promise to general
    public: *Auslobung* 308, 316; notice of
    revocation as for original promise
    309; relevance of: knowledge of offer
    309, performance in response to
    promise 309
  revocability of promise to individual,
    good faith, need for 316, 369
promise to do favour
  as contract of agency 159–60
  as contract for services: professional
    status, relevance 160; remuneration,
    relevance 159
  intention to create legal relations,
    need for 159–60
promise to pay more than agreed,
  expenditure in expectation of,
  relevance 246
promise to sell at fixed price, whether
  binding in case of change of market
  price 206–7
  in absence of: exclusive dealing clause
    207; minimum/usual purchase
    requirement 206
  abuse of right and 206
  good faith and 206–7
  interpretation of contract and 206, 216
proportionality, dowry/gift *propter nuptias*
  44 n. 84, 381
protection of promisor/donor in case of

dowry/gift *propter nuptias* 44 n. 84, 381
  promise of gift/donation 43
  promise to pay debt not legally due
    96–7
  storage of goods without charge 132
real estate agency contract
  agent's obligations, absence 326, 333
  agent's right to recover expenses 325,
    326
  good faith and 325, 333
  remuneration of agent, dependence
    on: effectiveness of agent's role 325;
    result 325, 333; terms of valid
    contract 326
  seller: obligation to sell, whether 325;
    protection of 325–6, 333
  sole agency, remuneration of agent 325
real property transactions, requirements
  notarization 291, 297
  protection of parties and 291
reliance on promise, relevance 43
services rendered [without charge],
    promise to pay remuneration for
  as contract: moral obligation, relevance
    79; professional status of person
    rendering service, relevance 79
  as gift 79
  as salary 246, 364
  as terminal bonus 246
  negotiorum gestio, relevance of doctrine
    86
social engagement, agreement to keep
    as contract 111
  duty to notify of inability to fulfil 111
sole discretion clause 292, 298
sums exceeding usual or obligatory level
    or financial means, treatment as gift
    or remuneratory donation, services
    rendered without charge, dowry/gift
    pro nuptias 44 n. 84
supply contract, exclusive dealing clause
  207
unilateral contract, promise to sell,
    revocability, motivation, relevance
  291
unilateral promise, to sell, changed
    circumstances 291

Germany (cont.)

unjust enrichment
    absence of *causa* and 96
    burden of proof 97
    negotiorum gestio 359
    payment of debt not legally due 96
    transfer of property without *causa* 96
Verwahrung 132
waiver of right, binding nature 260
work contract (*contrat d'entreprise/
    Werkvertrag*), unilateral
    termination, right to recover,
    agreed fee 308, 316
work contract (*Werkvertrag*)
    distinguished from: employment
        contract 308; *Geschäftsbesorgungs-
        vertrag* 308–9
    obligation of: best endeavours
        (*obligation de moyens*) 308–9, 316;
        result 308–9

Greece

bad faith (*contra bonos mores*)
    breach of promise and 47, 64, 112
    termination of brokerage contract 327
bonos mores, termination of brokerage
    contract 327
brokerage contract
    as contract of agency 326
    exclusive brokerage: damages for
        breach 327; requirements 327; right
        to terminate 327, within given
        period 327, 333
    fiduciary relationship 326
    remuneration, causal link with sale,
        need for 326
    remuneration in case of termination
        327; in accordance with terms of
        contract 326; exclusive brokerage
        and 327; where buyer found 326;
        where contract concluded 326, 327,
        333; where contract concluded after
        termination 327
    unilateral termination: broker's right
        to: damages 327, expenses 326–7;
        right of: at will and without reason
        327, *bonos mores* and 327, in case of
        exclusive brokerage agreement 327,

good faith and 327, 333, negligence
    327
burden of proof, breach of pre-
    contractual obligation 47
changed circumstances
    balance of interests and 185, 191
    change in economic balance of
        contract 208, 216
    contract: modification 208; release
        from obligations 208
    contract of loan for use 184
    good faith and 209
    loan of goods without charge 184, 191
    promise to sell and 292–3
    real property transactions 292–3
    requirements: change subsequent to
        contract 208; change in underlying
        circumstances 208; disproportion
        between parties 208; excessive
        onerousness 208; extraordinary
        change 208; reciprocal contract 208;
        unforeseen/unpredictable change
        208
consideration/cause
    definition, real economic exchange
        161–2
    need for: confirmation of voidable
        contract 99; option contract (*contrat
        de promesse*) 298
contract
    act of courtesy distinguished 135
    conditional: *condition suspensive* 309;
        promise of reward to investigator
        309–10
    interpretation: aids, business usage
        273; good faith 273; parties'
        intention 273; status of parties and
        273
    modification: by agreement 261;
        changed circumstances and 208
    performance, failure because of
        changes to market price 209
    release from obligations, grounds,
        unforeseen circumstances, change to
        economic balance of contract 208,
        216
    requirements: certainty of obligation

207, good faith and 207, liberty of party and 207, price at discretion of one of parties 207, 216, quantity at discretion of one of parties 207, 216, subsequent determination, possibility of 207; intention to create legal relationship 112; performance in good faith 207, 209, equitable criteria 216, 367

sole discretion clause 293

voidable, promise to comply as confirmation of contract, writing, need for 99

contract of agency (*mandatum*)
definition: gratuitous nature 326; mandate 160, 326
distinguished from accommodation agreement 161
liability: in absence of remuneration 160; failure to perform/*inexécution* 161; *force majeure* and 161, 168, 352; loss, need for 161; negligence 161, contributory negligence 161
requirements: consideration/*causa* 161; intention to contract 161, 168; obligation to represent legally before third parties 160

contract of deposit/promise to store goods without charge
as collateral contract 135
as fiduciary relationship 133
as gratuitous unilateral obligation 133
as pre-contractual obligation 134, 147
as *solo consensu* contract 134 n. 44
intention to create legal relationship, need for 147
liability: after delivery 134–5; before delivery 350; between friends 135; cancellation of alternative contract, relevance 136; loss of alternative possibility, relevance 136; professional storer of furniture 135; remuneration for storage, relevance 135; seller of goods 135; timeliness of termination of deposit, relevance 135–6
obligations of depositee: custody of

goods 133; dependence on delivery 133 n. 41; restoration of goods, as cancellation of contract 135, on request or expiry of time limit 133, timing in absence of time limit 135
release from liability, grounds: deposit with public authority 134 n. 47, 136, obligation in case of debt 136; harm to own interests 135, 349; inability to store goods safely 135; obligations of depositor and 136; unforeseen circumstances 134–5, 147
social engagement or courtesy promise as alternative 135

contract of donation
requirements: notarization 80; proportionality 80
revocation 80
services rendered, promise of remuneration 79–80; professional status of person rendering service, relevance 80; sum above usual level 80

contract for gratuitous services
intention to create legal relationship, need for 162
liability, for collateral contract 162

contract of loan for use (*prêt à l'usage/commodatum*)
as contract *re* 183; preliminary consensual contract distinguished 183, 191
as *solo consensu* contract 183
delivery and 183, 191
obligations, return: after use 183; at end of term 183; without demand 183–4
release from liability, grounds: allowing goods to deteriorate 184; transfer of goods to third party 184; unforeseen circumstances 184, balance of interests 185, 191; urgency 184, 191; use contrary to conditions of contract 184
requirements, absence of remuneration 183

Greece (cont.)

contract of loan for use (*prêt à l'usage/ commodatum*) (*cont.*)

rights, termination: compensation 184, 185; in good faith 184, 191; method 184

contract *re*

as consensual contract 133–4

contract of loan for use (*prêt à l'usage/commodatum*) as 183

delivery of goods, need for 133, 183, 191; as fulfilment of contractual obligation 134

contract *solo consensu* 134 n. 44, 183

conversion to civil obligation 79–80

courtesy act/promise 111–12

agreement to keep social engagement 111–12

contract of deposit/promise to store goods without charge 135

promise to do favour 161

culpa in contrahendo 48

damages for breach of

agreement to keep social engagement 112

brokerage contract 327; exclusive brokerage agreement 327; lost opportunity 327

contract, expectation interest 136

contract of agency, contributory negligence and 161

contract of deposit/promise to store goods without charge: in absence of contract 134; collateral contract 135, expectation interest 135; contract 134

contract for gratuitous services, collateral contract 162

contract for loan of goods without charge 184, 185

contract to supply at fixed price 29

pre-contractual obligation: negative interest 247; reliance damages 47, 134, 247

promise of gift, negative 47

promise to pay more than agreed 247

debt not legally due, enforceability of promise to pay

discharged debt, absence of provision for discharge 98 n. 37, 102

prescription, effect: obligation to pay 97; promise made in knowledge that debt time-barred, promise in writing in ignorance that debt time-barred 98, 102; promise to pay subsequent to: as waiver of defence 98, oral 98; recovery of paid debt 98

voidable contract, promise as confirmation of contract, writing, need for 99, 102

debt, right to reclaim arrears in case of promise to reduce rent, promise as, modification of contract 273, 277

delivery of goods, relevance

contract of deposit/promise to store goods without charge 133–4

contract/promise of loan of goods without charge 183, 191

don manuel/donation manuelle 45–6

economic duress

remedies, avoidance/rescission of contract, annulment by court 230

requirements: determining influence 230, status of parties, relevance 230; direct or indirect dependence on person making threat 230, 363; illegitimate or unjust threat 230; imminent and serious harm 230

employment contract, termination before term

inducement to stay: enforceability 247, 252; right to terminate for non-payment 247

equitable criteria 216, 367

evidence of

breach of pre-contractual obligation 47

intention to create legal obligation: between friends 135; services rendered gratuitously, importance of services 161–2

fairness, performance of contract and 207

fault/faute/dol 47

fiduciary relationship

brokerage contract 326

contract of deposit/promise to store
goods without charge 133
force majeure, contract of agency and 161,
168, 352
gift/donation
classification as, honouring of moral
obligation 247
distinguished from, terminal bonus
364
gift/donation, enforceability of promise of
liability of estate 46
recovery of expenses incurred in
expectation of, pre-contractual
obligation to act in good faith 46–8,
64
gift/donation, legal formalities/
requirements
acceptance of gift: on delivery 45; prior
to delivery 45
delivery to donee, donor's right to
recover 46
failure to comply, effect, nullity 45;
right to invoke 45
intention to create legal obligation 247
purpose, protection of donor 46; in
case of movable property 46
gift/promise of gift as, unilateral contract
45
good faith
brokerage contract 327, 333
change of circumstances and 209
interpretation of contract and 273
performance of contract and 207, 209
promise to do more than agreed and
261
timeliness of termination of: contract
of deposit 135–6; loan of goods 184,
191
gratuitous unilateral obligation, promise
to, store goods without charge 133
immoral act, liability in tort 231, 237
imprévision 208 n. 46
interest on unpaid salary 247
liability for breach of contract/pre-
contractual obligation
gross negligence 47, 161
wilful conduct 47

liability in tort
act contrary to morality 231, 237
failure to keep promise, free
services/social engagement, bad
faith, need for 112
loan of goods without charge, promise
as preliminary consensual contract
183, 191
release from liability, grounds,
unforeseen circumstances 184, 191
moral obligation, promise of
remuneration for fulfilling
enforceability 79–80, 86, 247, 252, 364
legal formalities/requirements 86
natural obligation/*obligation naturelle*
applicability, promise to pay terminal
bonus 247, 252, 364
conversion to civil obligation: by
contract 79–80; in case of prior
moral obligation 79–80
moral or social duty as basis 79
recovery of performance or value 79
negligence in case of
brokerage contract 327
contract of agency 161
contract/pre-contractual obligation 47,
161
gross negligence 47, 161
promise to do favour 161
notarization
agreement to pay sum above a certain
level 80
contract of donation 80
court's right to examine requirement
on own initiative 45
enforceability of promise, of gift 45–6, 64
exemption, immediate delivery of
movable (*don manuel/donation
manuelle*) 45–6
real property transactions 292, 298
option contract (*contrat de promesse*)
consideration/cause, relevance 298
notarization 293
pacta sunt servanda 209 n. 51
pre-contractual obligation
basis of liability 48, 134; *culpa in
contrahendo* 48; negotiations 48

Greece (cont.)
pre-contractual obligation (*cont.*)
  breach of promise and 46–8, 64
  liability for breach, requirements:
    burden of proof 47; conduct
    contrary to good faith and business
    practices 46–7; harm 47, causally
    related to fault 47; violation in
    course of negotiations 46
  promise to: pay more than agreed 247;
    store goods without charge 134, 147
  remedies, specific performance 134
  withdrawal from negotiations 47; fault
    47
promise, as unilateral contract 45
promise of reward
  as conditional contract 309–10
  revocability of promise to general
    public: notice of revocation as for
    original promise 310, 316; relevance
    of, knowledge of offer 310,
    knowledge of withdrawal of offer
    310, reservation of right to revoke
    310
  revocability of promise to individual
    309–10; relevance of, passage of time
    309–10, 316
promise to do favour
  as courtesy act/promise 161
  liability, negligence 161; gross 161
promise to do more than agreed
  binding nature 261
  parties' conduct, relevance 261
promise to sell at fixed price, whether
    binding in case of change of market
    price 207–8
  good faith and 207, 216
  pacta sunt servanda and 209 n. 51
proportionality
  changed circumstances and 208
  immoral act and 231
  services rendered, promise of
    remuneration 80
  usurious contract 231
protection of promisor/donor in case of,
    promise of, gift/donation 46
real property transactions, requirements

changed circumstances, relevance
    292–3
notarization 291
registration 292
services rendered [without charge],
    promise to pay remuneration for
  as contract, professional status of
    person rendering service, relevance
    80
  as contract of donation 79–80
  as remunatory donation, sum above
    usual level 80
  as salary, increase in 247, 252
  enforceability, requirements,
    proportionality 80
social engagement, agreement to keep
  as contract 111–12, 116
  as courtesy promise 111–12
sole discretion clause 293
specific performance, contract of
    deposit/promise to store goods
    without charge, pre-contractual
    obligation 134, 147
sums exceeding usual or obligatory level
    or financial means, treatment as gift
    or remunatory donation, services
    rendered without charge 80
trust, absence of concept in civil law 46
unforeseeable circumstances 134–5
unilateral contract, definition/
    requirements 133
unilateral promise
  to sell (*promesse unilatérale de vente*): as
    option contract (*contrat de promesse*)
    293; changed circumstances 292–3;
    requirements, notarization 292–3,
    registration 292–3
usurious contract
  definition 231; disproportion 231;
    improper advantage 231; relative
    status of parties and 231
  remedies/effect: tort liability 231;
    voidness 231
waiver of right, binding nature 261–2
Wegfall der Geschäftsgrundlage 208
work contract (*contrat d'entreprise/*
    Werkvertrag) 260–1

modification 261
payment due on completion 261

Ireland

changed circumstances, change in
    market price 296
charitable gift, charitable trust 61
consideration/cause
    circumvention of rule by courts 376–7;
        detrimental reliance on promise and
        266
    definition, real exchange 59, 234
    early retirement 250, 253, 364
    estoppel and 275, 277, 363
    implied assumpsit/act at request of
        promisor 87, 359, 376–7
    moral consideration 101, 103
    need for 58–9, 83–4, 86; bailment
        142–3, 187–9, 376, promise to look
        after goods as consideration 188,
        storage of goods as consideration for
        purchase 143; confirmation of
        voidable contract 103; option
        contract (*contrat de promesse*) 366;
        promise of gift 58; promise to: do
        favour 165, 168, do more than
        agreed 264, 266, lend goods without
        charge 187, pay discharged debt 100,
        104, 376, pay more than agreed 362,
        pay time-barred debt 100, 103,
        reward 314, 359, sell 295, 298, sell at
        fixed price 213, 215, 366; social
        engagement, agreement to keep
        114–15, 117; unilateral contract 314,
        368–9; waiver of right 262
    non-competition clause 250, 253
    past consideration 166
    performance of contract 235–6, 314,
        368–9
    practical benefit (employee's
        agreement to stay) 250, 253, 362–3
    pre-existing legal duty 234–6, 237, 363
    reciprocal promises 213, 295, 298, 315
    reciprocal release from rights 250, 253,
        254
    services previously rendered 250, 359
    third party as beneficiary 83–4

contract
    implied terms 214–15
    modification: consideration/cause 264;
        courts' reluctance 214–15; for sole
        benefit of one party 264
    offer: acceptance 213, performance as
        368–9, 'starting to perform'/
        'preparations to perform' 314–15;
        'firm' offer 295; revocability, in
        absence of, consideration/cause 295,
        298, motivation, relevance 296
    requirements: certainty of obligation,
        conditional contract 296; intention
        to create legal relationship 114–15,
        165–6
    sole discretion clause 296, 298
contract of deposit/promise to store
    goods without charge
    as collateral contract 347, 349
    requirements, intention to create legal
        relationship 143
contract for gratuitous services,
    intention to create legal
    relationship, need for 166
contract of loan for use (*prêt à l'usage*/
    commodatum)
    as bailment 187–9
    consideration/cause 187–8, 191
courtesy act/promise 115
    agreement to keep social engagement
        115, 117
damages for breach of
    bailment, *restitutio in integrum* 144
    contract of deposit/promise to store
        goods without charge, lost
        opportunity and 144, 347
    promise, reliance on promise, need for
        275–6
    promise to do favour 166; *restitutio in
        integrum* 165
    promise to lend goods without charge,
        liability in tort/contract
        distinguished 189
debt not legally due, enforceability of
    promise to pay
    discharged debt, in absence of
        consideration 100, 104

Ireland (*cont.*)

debt not legally due, enforceability of
promise to pay (*cont.*)
prescription, effect, right of action
accruing on date of written
promise/acknowledgment 100
promise as acknowledgment of
indebtedness, requirements:
signature of person making
acknowledgment 100; writing 100,
104
time-barred debt in absence of
consideration 100
voidable contract, promise as
confirmation of contract: in absence
of consideration/cause 103; defect of
age and 100–1, 103, 104
debt, right to reclaim arrears in case of
promise to reduce rent, estoppel and
275–6, 277, 363
deed/promise under seal
applicability, promise to: lend goods
without charge 187, 188; remunerate
for services rendered without charge
83, 86; store goods without charge
142, 143
delivery, relevance 60
procedure 59–60, 65
requirements 65; immediate
effectiveness 60; intention to create
deed on face of instrument 60;
signature, relevance 60; valid
execution 60
delivery of goods, relevance
bailment 142–3
deed/promise under seal 60
dowry/gift *propter nuptias*, writing, need
for 59
economic duress
as distinct form of duress 236
requirements: determining influence
236; illegitimate or unjust threat
250, 253; relevance of right to, take
legal proceedings 236
English law and 59 n. 141
estoppel 65
balance of interests and 188

consideration and 275, 277, 363
estoppel by representation
distinguished 62
failure to keep promise to: attend
social engagement 115; do favour
166; lend without charge 188, 189;
pay more than agreed 251; store
goods without charge 144
requirements: detriment 61–2, 189,
276, 363; intention that promisee
should act on promise 62, 214;
intention to be bound 62, 189, 214,
276; pre-existing legal rights 62, 66,
117, 144, 149, 166, 188, 214, 251, 264,
363; reliance on promise 62, 66, 115,
213, 214, 363
right to withdraw from statement and
61
evidence of intention to create legal
obligation
between friends 143
professional status of promisor 165–6
promise to lend goods without charge
189
gift/donation, enforceability of promise
of, recovery of expenses incurred in
expectation of, consideration
doctrine and 58
gift/donation, legal formalities/
requirements, writing, signature of
donor and witness 59, 65
good faith, in common law jurisdictions
376
gratuitous bailment
definition 142
estoppel and 144, 187, 188, 189
legal classification: contract 142; tort
142, 149
liability: after delivery 188; before
delivery, consideration, need for 130,
142–3, 149, 189, 191, 376; between
friends 143; cancellation of
alternative contract, relevance 144;
collateral contract 346, 347, 349,
storage as consideration for
purchase 143; loss of alternative
possibility, relevance 144

loan of goods without charge as 187–9, 191, 346

obligations: limitation in absence of consideration to those imposed by law 142, 149; restoration of goods 188, termination at will 346

release from liability, grounds 143, 144, 149, 349–50; in case of fixed term 236, 346

gratuitous promise

enforceability 143

liability for breach, nonfeasance 165

liability for breach of contract/pre-contractual obligation, misfeasance/nonfeasance 165, 347

liability in tort

contractual relationship, relevance 143

economic loss, sufficiency 165, 169, 347, 350–1

failure to keep promise: as breach of duty arising out of voluntary relationship 192, 347, 351; loan without charge 189, 191, 192, 346, 347; storage of goods without charge 142, delivery of goods, relevance 143–4

negligent provision of services, special relationship, need for 165, 350–1

nonfeasance 165, 169, 191, 250–1, 347

requirements: absence of public policy objection 165; foreseeability 165; proximity between wrong-doer and person suffering damage 165

loan of goods without charge, promise, estoppel 188, 189, 191

negligence in case of, provision of services 165, 350–1

option contract (*contrat de promesse*), consideration/cause, relevance 366

promise

as offer 213, 217

intention to create legal relations, need for 143; business relations 115

promise of reward

as contract, reciprocal promises 315

as offer of unilateral contract 368–9

as unilateral contract 314–15, 317, 368

revocability of promise to general public, relevance of: expenditure on search 314–15, 317; performance in response to promise 368

revocability of promise to individual, relevance of expenditure on search 314–15, 317

promise to do favour, as part of contract of sale 166, 169

promise to do more than agreed

as offer to modify/modification of contract 264

consideration, need for 264, 266, 376

parties' conduct, relevance 264–5

promise to pay more than agreed

consideration: need for 234–6, 250, 364, 376; non-competition undertaking 250; performance of contract as 234–6, 250

expenditure in expectation of, relevance 251

promise to sell at fixed price, whether binding in case of change of market price 213–15

in absence of consideration 213, 215, 217

real estate agency contract

agent's right to recover expenses 330–2, 334; seller's knowledge of, relevance 330–1, 334

remuneration of agent, dependence on: effectiveness of agent's role 331; result 330; terms of valid contract 330–2

seller, obligation to sell, whether 331

sole agency: remuneration of agent: contract concluded other than by agent 331, termination and 331; seller's right to terminate 370

specific performance 331

reliance on promise, relevance 62

estoppel 62, 66, 115, 213, 214, 363

services rendered [without charge], promise to pay remuneration for

as contract, implied assumpsit/act at request of promisor 87, 359

enforceability, requirements, consideration 359, 376

Ireland (cont.)
social engagement, agreement to keep
as contract 114–15, 117
as courtesy promise 115, 117
sole discretion clause 296, 298
special relationship, negligent provision
of services and 165, 350–1
specific performance
contract of deposit/promise to store
goods without charge: between
friends 143; breach of collateral
contract 349; liability in tort 144
contract/promise of loan for use 188
inconvenience of claimant, relevance
188
real estate agency contract 331
trust
charitable trust 61
definition 60
requirements 65; certainty of:
intention 60, object 61, subject
matter 61; evidentiary 61
third party's right to enforce 60
unilateral contract
definition/requirements: common/civil
law distinguished 34; promise
inviting performance 314
performance as: acceptance of offer
368–9, 'starting to perform'/
'preparations to perform' 314–15,
317; condition of benefit 317;
consideration for promise 314
promise to reward 368–9
promise to sell, revocability,
motivation, relevance 296
unilateral promise to sell (*promesse
unilatérale de vente*)
binding effect 295
changed circumstances 296
offer distinguished 295
waiver of right
binding nature 264
consideration, relevance 264, 266, 362,
376
implicit 264
modification of contract distinguished
264

reliance on, relevance 362
right to revoke 264, 266
Italy
animus donandi/animus solvendi 77
brokerage contract
remuneration, causal link with sale,
need for 324
remuneration in case of termination
324; exclusive brokerage and 333;
where buyer found 324, 333, 370
unilateral termination: broker's right
to [necessary and useful] expenses
324, 333; right of in good faith 324
causa praeterita 77, 245
cause suffisante 77, 94
changed circumstances
change in market price 204–5
disproportion between parties, need
for 204
release from obligations 204–5
commendatio 157–8
commodat/comodato 181
consideration/cause
'just' or reasonable consideration 130,
146, 150
need for: modification of contract 259,
272; option contract 288, 297
real economic exchange 146, 180, 190
services offered free and 109, 129, 146
contract
act of courtesy distinguished 108–9
interpretation, determination of
quantity 205
modification: changed circumstances
and, agreement by party affected
204; consideration/cause 259, 272;
post-contractual promise to award
retirement bonus 245
nominate 157
offer: acceptance: performance as
306–7, requirements 288–9, where
offer in favour of accepting party
260, 265, 272, 306; revocability: in
absence of, acceptance 289,
consideration/cause 288, 297,
express intention of irrevocability
288, 297, motivation, relevance 290,

time limit on exercise of options,
relevance 288, 289, 297
release from obligations, grounds,
unforeseen circumstances 204
requirements: certainty of obligation
205, 367; economic exchange 109;
intention to create legal relationship
109, 116; performance in good faith
205, 216
sole discretion clause 289–90
supervening excessive hardship 204
voidable: promise to comply as
confirmation of contract, defect of
age and 94, enforceability, *cause
suffisante* 94; validation,
requirements 94 n. 19
contract of agency (*mandatum*)
definition: *mandato* 157; *mandato
gratuito* 157
liability: in absence of remuneration
157–8, 167; incomplete performance
167, *modificatio in peius* 158;
negligence 157–8; standard of care
158, 167
requirements: delivery (*commendatio*)
157–8, 167; obligation to represent
legally before third parties 157
contract of deposit/promise to store
goods without charge
as pre-contractual obligation 130, 146
liability: after delivery 129; before
delivery 129; gratuitous contract
129; professional storer of furniture
129, 146; seller of goods 129, 146
obligations of depositee: custody of
goods 129; restoration of goods, in
original condition 129, on request or
expiry of time limit 129
release from liability, grounds, delivery
of goods, relevance 349, 350
remuneration, relevance 129
social engagement or courtesy promise
as alternative 129
contract of donation, services rendered,
promise of remuneration as 76
contract of loan for use
as *comodato* 180

as contract *re* 180
release from liability, grounds,
urgency 180, 190, 346
requirements, absence of
remuneration 18
contract *re*
contract of loan for use as 180
delivery of goods, need for 129, 180, 190
courtesy act/promise 108–9, 129
agreement to keep social engagement
108–9
contract of deposit/promise to store
goods without charge 129
promise to lend goods without charge
180
courtesy transportation 109
damages for breach of
contract of agency: in absence of
remuneration 158, incomplete
performance, effect 158
contract of deposit/promise to store
goods without charge: lost
opportunity and 129–30, 146, nature
of liability 130
pre-contractual obligation: negative
interest 130; reliance damages 181
debt not legally due, enforceability of
promise to pay
partial payment, effect 93–4
prescription, effect 93–4; promise
made in knowledge that debt time-
barred 93, 102, novation 94; recovery
of paid debt 93
voidable contract, promise as
confirmation of contract, promise
made in knowledge that contract
voidable, need for 93, 94, 102
debt, right to reclaim arrears in case of
promise to reduce rent, promise
made in order to secure future
payment of part or all of rent 271
delivery of goods, relevance
contract of agency 157–8
contract of deposit/promise to store
goods without charge 129, 146, 346,
349
promise to do favour 352

Italy (cont.)

dowry/gift *propter nuptias*
    critical date 41 n. 66
    legal formalities/requirements,
      acceptance, relevance 41
    rescission, on dissolution of marriage
      41 n. 66
    third party rights acquired before
      marriage 41 n. 66
economic duress, requirements
    determining influence, status of
      parties, relevance 228 n. 26
    fear of considerable and actual harm
      228 n. 26
employment contract
    termination before term, inducement
      to stay, employer's right to offer 245,
      252
    validity in case of fixed 10-year term
      245, 252, 253, 362
extortion, unjustified demand for extra
    payment 228
gift/donation
    distinguished from terminal bonus
      245, 252, 364–5
    'liberality of usage': definition 76;
      delivery, need for 76; proportionality
      and 76, 85; terminal bonus 245
gift/donation, enforceability of promise of
    liability of estate, recall and reduction
      41
    recovery of expenses incurred in
      expectation of, tortious liability 41
gift/donation, legal formalities/
    requirements
    acceptance of gift, formal 40–1, 63
    delivery to donee, 'liberality according
      to usage' 76, 245
    purpose: distinction between enforceable
      and non-enforceable promises 40;
      evidentiary function 40; protection of
      donor, 'cautionary function' 40
good faith
    brokerage contract 324
    performance of contract and 205, 216
    requirement to take other party's
      interests into account 289

'sole discretion' clause, relevance
    289–90, 297
gratuitous contract, promise to store
    goods without charge as 129
gratuitous promise
    courtesy promise distinguished,
      transportation promises 109
    'just' or reasonable consideration 130
    liability for breach, tort 130
just cause 305–7, 316, 317, 369
liability in tort
    courtesy transportation, suspension of
      performance 109
    failure to keep promise: gift/donation
      41, 63; storage of goods without
      charge 130
    unjustified demand for extra payment
      228
loan of goods without charge, promise
    as courtesy promise 180
    pre-contractual liability 181, 190
    release from liability, grounds, absence
      of contract 180
    reliance on promise, need for 181
modificatio in peius 158
moral obligation
    payment of debt 93
    promise of remuneration for fulfilling,
      legal formalities/requirements 102
natural obligation/*obligation naturelle*
    moral or social duty as basis 77
    recovery of performance or value 76–7,
      85
negligence in case of
    contract of agency 157–8
    promise to do favour 157–8
notarization, enforceability of promise
    of gift 40, 63
    to pay for services rendered without
      charge 76; status of person providing
      services, relevance 76
novation
    contract voidable for defect of age 94
    time-barred debt 94; unequivocal
      intention to waive right of
      prescription, need for 94
option contract (*contrat de promesse*)

consideration/cause, relevance 288,
   297
enforceability 288
pre-contractual agreement
   distinguished 289
pre-contractual obligation
   bad faith and 130, 146, 150
   breach of promise and, negative
      interest damages 130
   promise to: lend goods without charge
      181, 190; sell goods 289; store goods
      without charge 130
promise of reward
   as contract 307
   recovery of expenses and 307
   revocability of promise to general
      public: in case of just cause 305–7,
      316, 317, 369; notice of revocation as
      for original promise 305, 316;
      relevance of, date of publication 305,
      fixed term 305, performance in
      response to promise 307
   revocability of promise to individual
      306–7; in case of just cause 306, 316,
      317; relevance of, acceptance 306,
      knowledge of offer 306, 316,
      performance in response to promise
      306–7, 316
promise to do favour
   as contract of agency (contrato de
      mandato) 157, 352
   liability, negligence 157–8
promise to do more than agreed
   as offer to modify/modification of
      contract 259–60
   binding nature 260; acceptance,
      relevance 260
promise to sell at fixed price, whether
      binding in case of change of market
      price 204–5
   good faith and 205, 216
   interpretation of contract and 205
   supervening hardship and 204
   unforeseen circumstances theory and
      204–5
proportionality
   changed circumstances and 204

liberality of usage 76, 85
services rendered, promise to pay
   remuneration for 77, 85
protection of promisor/donor in case of
   notarization and 40
   storage of goods without charge 349
real estate agency contract, sole agency,
   requirement 324, 333
recall and reduction 41
reliance on promise, relevance, promise
   to lend goods without charge 181
services rendered [without charge],
   promise to pay remuneration for
   as contract of donation 76
   as gift 76
   as natural obligation 76–7
   as remunatory donation 76; definition
      76 n. 37; 'liberality according to usage'
      distinguished 76; requirements:
      delivery 245, rules applying to
      ordinary gifts/donations 76
   as salary, payment as part 252
   as terminal bonus 245, 252
   enforceability 77, 85, 86; ad hoc nature
      of decision 77; causa praeterita 77,
      245, 364–5; requirements, cause
      suffisante 77, monetary value for
      service 77, 85, proportionality 77, 85
   legal formalities/requirements,
      intention of promisor, animus donandi/
      animus solvendi distinguished 77
social engagement, agreement to keep, as
   courtesy promise 108–9
sole discretion clause 289–90, 297
specific performance, contract of
   deposit/promise to store goods
      without charge 129
   in absence of contract 350
unilateral promise to sell (promesse
   unilatérale de vente)
   as option contract (contrat de promesse)
      288–9
   binding effect 289
   offer distinguished 288–9
   pre-contractual agreement 289
waiver of right, binding nature 259–60,
   272, 277

Netherlands
abuse of circumstances
  definition 225, 236–7
  economic duress as 225, 363
  illegitimate threat as alternative
    source of liability 226
  requirements: availability of
    alternative course of action,
    relevance 225; dependence on
    promise 225, 237
  threat to terminate employment
    contract before term 242–3, 251
  urgency of situation and 226
beperkende werking 201
bruikleen 176
casus non dabilis 91
changed circumstances
  change in market price 200, 285–6
  contract: modification 200, 201, 215;
    release from obligations 200, 202, 215
  contract of loan for use 178
  good faith and 201, 215
  option contract 291, 299
  promise to sell and 285–6
consideration/cause, confirmation of
  voidable contract 91, 101
contract
  conditional, promise of reward to
    investigator 303
  interpretatation, *wilsvertrouwensleer*
    201
  interpretation, will/reliance doctrine
    (*wilsvertrouwensleer*) 201
  modification: by agreement 225, 242,
    256; changed circumstances and
    200, 201, 215; circumstances
    unprovided for 201
  offer: acceptance, performance as 304,
    'starting to perform'/'preparations to
    perform' 303, 315, *wilsverklarung* 304;
    revocability 284–6, good faith and
    285, 297, motivation, relevance 285,
    serious reasons 303–4, 315, time
    limit on exercise of options,
    relevance 285, 297
  release from obligations, grounds,

    unforeseen circumstances 200, 202,
    215, change in market price as 200
  requirements: certainty of obligation
    200, 201 n. 30, subsequent
    determination, possibility of 200;
    consent freely given 256; intention
    to create legal relationship 107, 115,
    256, 304
  sole discretion clause 286
  voidable: promise to comply as
    confirmation of contract 92;
    rescission/avoidance of contract,
    effect 91
contract of agency (*mandatum*)
  definition, *opdracht* 153
  liability: in absence of remuneration
    153–4; standard of care, quantum of
    damages distinguished 153, 167
  obligations, 'care of good mandatary'
    153
  requirements, intention to contract
    153, 167
contract of deposit/promise to store
    goods without charge
  alternatives to contract: *promesse de
    depôt* 125; social engagement or
    courtesy promise 124–5
  as, collateral contract 125
  date of return, factors determining
    125
  liability: after delivery 124; before
    delivery 124; between friends 125;
    cancellation of alternative contract,
    relevance 126; gratuitous promise
    125, 145; loss of alternative
    possibility, relevance 126;
    professional storer of furniture 125;
    seller of goods 125
  release from liability, grounds, 'an
    important reason' (*gewichtige reden*)
    125, 145, 349
  requirements, intention to create legal
    relationship 124
  toevertouwt of zal toevertrouwen 124
contract of loan for use (*prêt à l'usage/
    commodatum*)

as, gratuitous unilateral obligation,
  bruikleen 176
as contract *re* 176–7; preliminary
  consensual contract distinguished 177
obligations, return, at end of term
  178
release from liability, grounds:
  promisee's situation, relevance 178;
  unforeseen circumstances 178;
  urgency 178
contract *re*
  as consensual contract 124
  consensual preliminary contract
    distinguished 177
  contract of deposit as 124
  contract of loan for use (*prêt à
    l'usage/commodatum*) as 176–7
  delivery of goods, need for 124, 125,
    177, 190
courtesy act/promise, contract of
  deposit/promise to store goods
  without charge 124–5
damages for breach of
  contract of agency, in absence of
    remuneration 153–4
  contract of deposit/promise to store
    goods without charge, lost
    opportunity and 126
  pre-contractual obligation, reliance
    damages 35–6
  promise to reward, *ex aequo et bono*
    303–4, 315, 317
debt not legally due, enforceability of
  promise to pay, voidable contract
  promise as confirmation of contract, in
    absence of consideration/cause 91
  promise as gift 91, 101
debt, right to reclaim arrears in case of
  promise to reduce rent
  promise as: contract of 'renunciation'
    269, 277, formalities 269 n. 5, 277,
    renunciation of part of claim 269;
    gratuitous renunciation 269
  promise made in order to secure
    future payment of part or all of rent
    269

delivery of goods, relevance
  contract of deposit/promise to store
    goods without charge 124, 125, 145
  gift/donation 34 n. 41
dringende reden 178
economic duress, requirements
  determining influence 225, 226; status
    of parties, relevance 226
  relevance of right to, damages for non-
    performance 225; seek specific
    performance 225–6
employment contract, termination
  fixed-term contract before term, as
    abuse of circumstances 243
  terminal bonus, gift, whether 243, 364
estoppel, requirements, reliance on
  promise 257
evidence of intention to create legal
  obligation
  promise to lend goods without charge
    178
  services rendered gratuitously 126
ex aequo et bono, damages/compensation
  303–4, 315, 317, 369
exclusive dealing clause 202
gewichtige reden 125
gift/donation, classification as,
  confirmation of voidable contract
  without consideration/cause 91
gift/donation, enforceability of promise of
  conditional promise, condition
    precedent 35
  liability of estate 35
  recovery of expenses incurred in
    expectation of 35; pre-contractual
    obligation to act in good faith 35–6;
    reliance damages 34–5
gift/donation, legal formalities/
  requirements
  delivery to donee 34 n. 41
  purpose, protection of donor 35–6
gift/promise of gift as contract 35
good faith (*redelijkheid en billijkheid*)
  as limitation of exercise of rights 201
  change of circumstances and 201, 215;
    circumstances 'unprovided for' 201

Netherlands (cont.)
good faith (*redelijkheid en billijkheid*) (*cont.*)
objective fairness as test 286
revocability of offer 285
'sole discretion' clause, relevance 286
gratuitous promise, liability for breach
125
gratuitous nature, relevance 125, 154,
155
professional status of promisor,
relevance 125, 155
insurance agency
lastgeving 153
liability, remuneration, relevance 153–4
lastgeving 153
liability in tort
economic loss, sufficiency 154, 167
failure to keep promise: free
services/social engagement 107–8;
gratuitous nature, relevance 125,
154, 155; to do favour 154–5,
standard of care, relevance 155, 167
violation of 'rule of unwritten law
pertaining to proper social conduct'
108, 115, 154, 167
loan of goods without charge, promise
as preliminary consensual contract
177, 190; enforceability 177, 190;
requirements 177
release from liability, grounds,
inconvenience to borrower,
relevance 178
requirements: delivery, relevance 178;
intention to create legal obligation
177, 178, evidence of 178, promisee's
right to assume 178; reliance on
promise 177
natural obligation/*obligation naturelle*
applicability, debt: discharged in
bankruptcy 91, 101; time-barred 91,
101
conversion to civil obligation 91; by
contract 72
promise: enforceability, professional
status of person rendering service,
relevance 73; gift distinguished 358
requirements 91

negotiorum gestio, remuneration for
damage/harm suffered 72
professional status of person rendering
service, relevance 84
notarization, enforceability of promise,
of gift 34–5, 243
opdracht 153, 352
lastgeving 153
pre-contractual obligation, breach of
promise and 35
promise, intention to create legal
relations, need for 124, 145
between friends 153
promisee's right to assume 124, 125,
126, 178
promise of reward
as conditional contract 303
as offer 303–4
recovery of expenses and 303–4, 369
revocability of promise to general
public 303–4, 315; in case of, serious
reasons 304
promise to do favour
as contract of agency, *opdracht* 153, 352
as good faith obligation 155
as part of contract of sale 155, 167
promise to do more than agreed, as offer
to modify/modification of contract
256
promise to pay more than agreed,
expenditure in expectation of,
relevance 243
promise to sell at fixed price, whether
binding in case of change of market
price 200–2
in absence of, exclusive dealing clause
202
good faith and 201
interpretation of contract and 201
unforeseen circumstances theory and
200, 202, 215
protection of promisor/donor in case of,
promise of, gift/donation 35–6
real estate agency contract
remuneration of agent, dependence
on, terms of valid contract 322,
332–3

sole agency: remuneration of agent, termination and 322; requirement 322, 333
standard contract 322, 333, 335, 370
redelijkjeid en billijkheid 286
reliance on promise, relevance 34–6, 257
estoppel 257
promise to, lend goods without charge 177
services rendered [without charge], promise to pay remuneration for
as gift 72, 84, 358
as natural obligation 72–3
as remunatory donation, rules applying to ordinary gifts/donations 243, 251
negotiorum gestio, relevance of doctrine 72–3, 84
social engagement, agreement to keep, as, contract 107
sole discretion clause 286
standard of care (*zorgvuldigheidsnorm*) 154
supply contract, exclusive dealing clause 202
unilateral contract, performance as, acceptance of offer, 'starting to perform'/'preparations to perform' 303, 315
unilateral promise
in absence of contract 256
to sell (*promesse unilatérale de vente*): as contract 284–6; changed circumstances 285–6
venire contra factum proprium 257, 285
waiver of right (*kwijtschelding*), 'renunciation' as contract 257, 269, 277
effect 257, 269
formalities 269 n. 5, 277
gratuitous 257, 269

Portugal
abuse of right, loss of right as remedy 259, 265, 266
changed circumstances
change in market price 203, 287–8
good faith and 203, 215
promise to sell and 287–8
requirements, extraordinary change 203
charitable organization, foundation (*fundação*)
as legal person 39
requirements 39–40; public interest 40
commodat/comodato 179
consideration/cause, services offered free and 108
contract
conditional modification 271, 277
offer/acceptance, reliance on promise, relevance 258, 288
requirements, intention to create legal relationship 108
termination, unilateral promise with unfixed term 204
unforeseen circumstances: change in market price as 203; extraordinary change 203
voidable, promise to comply as confirmation of contract, defect of age and 93, 102
contract of agency (*mandatum*)
definition 157
liability in absence of remuneration 157
obligation to represent legally before third parties, need for 157
termination at will 304, 315
contract of deposit/promise to store goods without charge
as *in rem* contract *quoad constitutionem* 127
liability: after delivery 127, 128, 146; before delivery 127, 128, 350; between friends 128; cancellation of alternative contract, relevance 128; loss of alternative possibility, relevance 128; professional storer of furniture 128; seller of goods 128
release from liability, grounds 127; fair reason/motive 128, 146, 349, 350
requirements, intention to create legal relationship 127, 145–6

Portugal (cont.)

contract of donation 38
  definition 38
  requirements: immediate delivery 39;
    notarization 39; sacrifice of assets
    108; writing 38–9
contract for gratuitous services,
    intention to create legal
    relationship, need for 157, 167
contract of loan for use (*prêt à
    l'usage/commodatum*)
  as *comodato* 179
  as consensual contract 179, 190
  as contract *re quoad constitutionem* 179
  definition 179
  delivery and 179
  intention to establish legal obligation,
    need for 179
  release from liability, grounds:
    delivery, relevance 179; fair reason
    179–80, 190, 192; promisee's
    situation, relevance 180; urgency
    180, 190
contract *re*
  as consensual contract 128
  contract of deposit as 127–8
  delivery of goods, need for 127–8, 146
  quoad constitutionem 127, 179
  Roman law origin 127–8
contract for services (*contrato de prestação
    de serviços*), remuneration, relevance
    157, 167
damages for breach of
  contract of agency, loss or necessary
    expense 304–5, 315
  gentlemen's agreement 108, 116, 157
  promise to do favour 157
  promise to pay more than agreed,
    expenditure in dependence on 244
  real estate agency contract, lost
    commission 323, 333
debt not legally due, enforceability of
    promise to pay
  discharged debt, absence of provision
    for discharge 92, 102
  natural obligation, time-barred debt,
    as moral obligation 92, 102

voidable contract: promise as
    confirmation of contract, defect of
    age and 93, 102; recovery of paid
    debt 93
debt, right to reclaim arrears in case of
    promise to reduce rent
  promise as: deferral of payment 271,
    277; modification of contract 271,
    277
  waiver of debt: contract of *remissão* 271;
    writing, need for 271
delivery of goods, relevance
  contract of deposit/promise to store
    goods without charge 127–8, 146
  contract of donation 39
  contract/promise of loan of goods
    without charge 179
dowry/gift *propter nuptias*
  applicable rules 40
  legal formalities/requirements,
    notarization 40
  rescission: on dissolution of marriage
    40; marriage not performed 40
economic duress, illegitimate or unjust
    threat 227–8, 363
exclusive dealing clause 204
frustration of right of inspection 258,
    259
gentlemen's agreement
  damages for breach 108, 116, 157
  promise to do favour 157, 167
gift/donation, enforceability of promise
    of
  liability of estate: remunatory
    donation 75; rights of wife and
    children 39
  recovery of expenses incurred in
    expectation of 38; pre-contractual
    obligation to act in good faith 39
gift/donation, legal formalities/
    requirements
  acceptance of gift: contract of
    donation (*contrato de remissão*) 271; in
    writing 38, contract of donation
    (*contrato de doaçao*) 38
  intention to give 271
  writing 38–9, 63

gift/donation, revocability of promise on grounds of ingratitude 39, 75

gift/promise of gift as unilateral contract, unilateral promise distinguished 38

good faith, change of circumstances and 203, 215, 288–9

just cause 179–80

legitimate expectations 203

loan of goods without charge, promise, release from liability, grounds, inconvenience to borrower, relevance 180

moral obligation, promise of remuneration for fulfilling enforceability 75–6, 102

legal formalities/requirements 102

moral obligation, recovery of performance or value 75

natural obligation/*obligation naturelle*, applicability, debt, time-barred 92

negotiorum gestio

definition 74–5

remuneration for damage/harm suffered 75; in case of necessary action 87; legal duty, relevance 74–5, 87; professional status of person rendering service, relevance 75, 85; promise as acknowledgment of claim 85; promise of payment, relevance 74–5, 85; status of person receiving service, relevance 85, duty of that person to provide service, need for 75

notarization

contract of donation 39

dowry 40

enforceability of promise to sell 287

real property transactions 39, 287, 297

obligation *cum potuerit* 271

pacta sunt servanda 203

pre-contractual obligation

bad faith and 244, 252, 362, 364

breach of promise and 39

damages 244

liability for breach, dependence on promise and 244, 252

promise to pay more than agreed 244, 252, 253, 362

promise

as unilateral contract 38, 203

intention to create legal relations, need for 127, 145–6; between friends 156

promise of reward

as contract of agency 304

as unilateral promise 305

recovery of expenses and 304–5, 316

revocability of promise to general public: notice of revocation as for original promise 305, 315–16; relevance of, acceptance of offer 305, fixed term 305, knowledge of offer 305, specific action to secure 305

revocability of promise to individual 305; acceptance, relevance 305

promise to do favour

as contract for services, remuneration, relevance 156–7

as gentlemen's agreement 157, 167

requirements, intention to create legal relations 156, 157

promise to do more than agreed

as offer to modify/modification of contract 258

binding nature 258; illegal promise 258

promise to sell at fixed price, whether binding in case of change of market price 203–4

in absence of exclusive dealing clause 204

good faith and 203–4

pacta sunt servanda and 203

unforeseen circumstances theory and 203

proportionality, services rendered, promise of remuneration 85

public benefit 40

real estate agency contract, agent's right to recover expenses 333, 370

real estate agency contract (*mediação imobiliára*)

as contract for services 323

Portugal (cont.)

real estate agency contract (*mediação
imobiliára*) (*cont.*)
legal requirements: fixed term 323;
remuneration 323; writing 323
remuneration of agent: dependence
on, result 323; termination of
contract, effect, fixed term,
relevance 323
sole agency, remuneration of agent:
seller's fault 323; termination after
conclusion of fixed term 323;
termination and 323, 333, 370
real property transactions, requirements
gift 39
notarization 39, 287, 297
reliance on promise, relevance
modification of contract 258
promise to, sell 288
remissão 271
services rendered [without charge],
promise to pay remuneration for
as remunatory donation 75, 85;
definition 75, 87, 244; exceptions 75;
requirements, delivery 244, rules
applying to ordinary gifts/donations
75, 87, 244, 359, 362, writing 87, 244,
252, 359; sum above usual level 85
as salary, payment as part 244
negotiorum gestio, relevance of doctrine
74–5, 85
social engagement, agreement to keep
as contract 108
as contract of donation 108
specific performance, contract of
deposit/promise to store goods
without charge
in absence of contract 128, 146
contractual obligation 128
sums exceeding usual or obligatory level
or financial means, treatment as gift
or remunatory donation 85
supply contract, exclusive dealing clause
204
unilateral contract
offer, acceptance, need for 38
promise to sell at fixed price 203

revocability, motivation, relevance 288
unilateral promise, as 203, 204, 287
unilateral promise distinguished 38
unilateral promise to sell (*promesse
unilatérale de vente*)
as contract 287–8
changed circumstances 287–8
requirements: notarization 287;
writing 287
usurious contract
definition 227, 237
remedies/effect, voidability of contract
227, 363
venire contra factum proprium 259 n. 11
waiver of right, illegality 258–9, 265, 266,
362
parties' conduct, relevance 259
work contract 258

Scotland

business arrangement
factors determining whether 112
implications 112, 136
changed circumstances
good faith and 209–10, 216
promise to sell and 293
real property transactions 293
charitable gift, requirements, writing as
evidence of intention 50
consideration/cause
need for: gratuitous unilateral
obligation 81, 99, 232; promise to,
pay more than agreed 232, 248;
social engagement, agreement to
keep 112
performance of contract 232
practical benefit (employee's
agreement to stay) 248
contract
interpretation: in favour of binding
effect 209, 216; good faith 209–10,
367, 375
modification by agreement 231
offer, promise of reward as 311
parallel unilateral obligations
distinguished 231
requirements: agreement of

contracting parties 48; certainty of
obligation 209, interpretation of
contract favouring 209
contract of deposit/promise to store
goods without charge
as, gratuitous unilateral obligation 136
frustration 136, 148
liability: loss of alternative possibility,
relevance 148; material damage,
need for 136–7, 346–7, 350; reliance
on promise, need for 350
requirements: intention to create legal
relationship 136, 147; protection of
promisor, relevance 347; writing 136
social engagement or courtesy promise
as alternative 136
contract law, historical development,
early modern developments 8–9
damages for breach of
agreement to keep social engagement
113, 116
contract 231
promise, requirements: acquiescence
of promisor 113, 116, 137, 148, 150,
162, 168; material damage 112, 113,
116, 137, 148, 150, 162, 168, 352;
reliance on promise 113, 116, 148,
150, 162, 168, 352
debt not legally due, enforceability of
promise to pay
promise as acknowledgment of
indebtedness, writing, need for 99
promise as gratuitous unilateral
obligation, writing, need for 99, 102
debt, right to reclaim arrears in case of
promise to reduce rent, promise as,
variation of lease 274, 277
economic duress
requirements: fear of considerable and
actual harm 232, 375; relevance of
right to, damages for non-
performance 231–2, 237, 363
threat to terminate employment
before term 248
evidence of
contractual agreement, oral/parole
112, 136

intention to create legal obligation:
between friends 162, 168; services
rendered gratuitously 80–1
promise to do more than agreed 261
promise to pay terminal bonus 248
unilateral obligation 48–9
frustration 136, 148
gift/donation, enforceability of promise
of recovery of expenses incurred in
expectation of,
in case of obligation created despite
failure to comply with formalities,
requirements: causation 50;
knowledge and acquiescence of
donor 9, 50–1, 64, 247; material
effect ('not unimportant') 50–1, 64;
reasonableness 50–1; reliance on
promise 50–1, 64, 247, 253, 254
compliance with legal formalities and
50–1
gift/donation, evidence of 48–9
gift/donation, legal
formalities/requirements
acceptance of promise 81
failure to comply, effect 49–51; on
entitlement to withdraw 49–50;
validity of contract and 49–50
intention to create legal obligation
80–1
intention to give 48; presumption
of/against 48
writing 48–50, 64, 80–1, 86, 360
gift/promise of gift as gratuitous
unilateral obligation 49
between family members 49–50
consideration, relevance 81, 99
critical date 81
services rendered gratuitously 80–1, 86
good faith
change of circumstances and 209–10,
216
interpretation of contract and 209–10,
367, 375
gratuitous promise
enforceability 191
potential benefit to promisor, effect
311

Scotland (*cont.*)
gratuitous unilateral obligation
  historical origin 14
  promise to: do favour 352; do more
    than agreed 261, 265; make gift
    49–50; pay debt not legally due 99,
    102; pay more than agreed 232,
    247–8, 252; pay remuneration for
    services rendered 80–1, 86, 360; store
    goods without charge 136
  writing, need for 112, 136, 147–8, 149,
    162, 232, 247, 252–3, 261, 352, 374
homologation, statutory provisions on
  promises distinguished 8–9, 50
lease, variation, writing, need for 274,
  277, 278, 362
liability in tort, failure to keep promise
  to store goods without charge 351
loan of goods without charge, promise
  release from liability, grounds:
    inconvenience to borrower,
    relevance 185; timeliness, relevance
    185
  requirements: reliance on promise 185,
    191; writing 185, 191
material damage, need for
  contract of deposit/promise to store
    without charge 350
  enforceability of promise to lend goods
    without charge 185, 191, 346–7
  recovery of expenses incurred in
    reliance on promise 50–1, 64, 112,
    113, 116, 136–7, 148
natural law 8–9
promise
  as expression of future intention 112
  conditional, liability for frustration of
    condition 328
  in course of business 9, 112, 116, 117,
    162, 168, 209, 216, 246–7, 248, 253,
    254, 261, 265, 266, 347, 375
  intention to create legal relations,
    need for: business relations 136;
    professional status, relevance 136
  non-gratuitous 209, 216, 310–11, 316,
    317, 328, 369; writing, need for 328
promise of reward

  as non-gratuitous contract, benefit to
    promisor 311
  as non-gratuitous promise 310–11, 316,
    317, 369
  as offer 311
  revocability of promise to general
    public, passage of time, relevance
    310–11, 316
  revocability of promise to individual,
    relevance of, acceptance 310; passage
    of time 310–11, 316
promise to do favour, requirements
  intention to create legal relations
    162
  writing 162, 168
promise to do more than agreed,
  formalities 261
promise to pay more than agreed
  as unilateral obligation, writing, need
    for 232
  consideration, performance of contract
    as 232
promise to sell at fixed price, whether
  binding in case of change of market
  price 209–10
  absence of minimum/usual purchase
    requirement, interpretation of
    contract and 209–10
  as non-gratuitous promise 209, 216
  good faith and 209–10, 216
protection of promisee 375
protection of promisor/donor in case of
  gratuitous transactions 374–5
  loan without charge 347
real estate agency contract
  as contract 327–8
  as non-gratuitous promise 328
  as promise *sub conditione* 328
  remuneration of agent, dependence
    on, terms of valid contract 327–8
  sole agency, seller's right to terminate
    328, 334, 370
real property transactions,
    requirements
  changed circumstances, relevance 293
  motivation of parties, relevance 293
  writing 274, 293, 298, 362

rei interventus 9
  statutory provisions on promises
    distinguished 9, 50
  reliance on promise, relevance
    breach of contract of deposit/promise to
      store without charge 136, 150, 346–7
    failure to keep social engagement 113,
      116
    promise to: do favour 113, 116, 148,
      150, 162, 168, 352; do more than
      agreed 261, 265, 266; lend goods
      without charge 185, 191; store goods
      without charge 350
    recovery of expenses in expectation of
      enforcement of promise 50–1, 64
    rei interventus 9
  services rendered [without charge],
      promise to pay remuneration for
    as gratuitous unilateral obligation
      80–1, 86, 360; professional status of
      person rendering service, relevance
      81; status of person receiving
      service, relevance 81
    as remuniratory donation, writing, need
      for 248
    as salary, increase in 248
  social engagement, agreement to keep
    as contract 112
    as expression of future intention 112
    as gratuitous unilateral promise: given
      in course of business 112, 116, 117;
      writing, need for 112, 116, 354 n. 15
    as intention to keep legal obligations 112
  specific performance
    contract/promise of loan for use 185;
      requirements, detriment 185, 191,
      knowledge and acquiescence of
      donor 185, 191, 350
    promise to do favour 162
  sui generis nature of legal system 374–5
  unilateral promise to sell (*promesse
    unilatérale de vente*), changed
    circumstances 293

Spain
animus novandi 257
breach of promise to marry, acceptance,
    relevance 36 n. 49

brokerage contract
  remuneration, causal link with sale,
    need for 322
  remuneration in case of termination
    322–3, 333; where buyer found 322,
    332, 370
burden of proof, consideration/cause
    243
business arrangement, promise to do
    favour as 156
causa credendi 243–4, 252, 304
causa donandi 37, 108, 243, 252, 270–1,
    277
causa liberatoria 270
changed circumstances 202
  contract, modification 202
  option contract 287
  promise to sell and 287
  requirements: absence of other remedy
    202; disproportion between parties
    202; extraordinary change 202;
    unforeseen/unpredictable change
    202
charitable organization, foundation
    (*fundación/fundação*)
  as legal person 37 n. 55
  requirements 37 n. 55
condonación, pactum de non petendo
    distinguished 270
consideration/cause
  burden of proof 243
  definition, real exchange, 'liberality'
    distinguished 126, 156, 167, 179
  modification of original contract as
    226–7, 237
  need for 36; promise to, lend goods
    without charge 179; social
    engagement, agreement to keep 108,
    116; waiver of right 270–1, 277
  services offered free and 108
contract
  evidence of 286
  modification, changed circumstances
    and 202–3
  release from obligations, grounds,
    unforeseen circumstances, *teoria de
    la base del negocio* 205–6, 215

Spain *(cont.)*
  contract *(cont.)*
    requirements: agreement of
      contracting parties 36; object 36
    voidable *(anulable)*, void/invalid
      contract distinguished 227
  contract of agency *(mandatum)*
    definition, *contrato de mandato* 155–6
    requirements: consideration/*causa* 156,
      167; express/implied undertaking
      156; obligation to represent legally
      before third parties 155–6, 167;
      oral/written undertaking 156
  contract of deposit/promise to store
    goods without charge
    as *in rem* unilateral contract 126–7;
      promise to store distinguished 126
    date of return, factors determining 127
    liability before delivery 126–7, 350
    release from liability, grounds, fair
      reason/motive 3, 127, 145, 350
  contract of donation
    services rendered, promise of
      remuneration, sum above usual level
      74
    writing, need for 156
  contract of loan for use *(prêt à l'usage/*
    commodatum)
    as consensual contract 179, 190
    as contract *re* 179
    consideration/*causa*, liberality 179
    delivery and 190
    distinguished from lease 179
    release from liability, grounds,
      urgency 179, 190
    right of termination 179, 190
    temporary nature 179
  contract *re*
    as consensual contract 179, 190
    contract of deposit as 126–7
    contract of loan for use *(prêt à*
      l'usage/commodatum) as 179
    delivery of goods, need for 126, 179, 190
    promise of, enforceability 126–7
  contract for services
    implied, professional status, relevance
      156

    remuneration, relevance 156, 167
  conversion to civil obligation 73–4, 92
  damages for breach of
    employment contract (termination
      before term) 243, 252, 253, 362
    option contract *(contrat de promesse)* 286
  debt not legally due, enforceability of
    promise to pay
    discharged debt, absence of provision
      for discharge 91, 101
    natural obligation, time-barred debt as
      moral obligation 92, 102
    voidable contract, promise as
      confirmation of contract 92; defect
      of age and 92, 102
  debt, right to reclaim arrears in case of
    promise to reduce rent
    condonación/pactum de non petendo
      distinguished 270
    promise as gift/donation 270, 277
    waiver of debt 362; consideration/
      cause, need for 270–1; formalities,
      writing, need for 270; implied 270,
      277
  delivery of goods, relevance
    contract of deposit/promise to store
      goods without charge 126–7, 145
    contract/promise of loan of goods
      without charge 190
    promise to do favour 156
  economic duress
    remedies, avoidance/rescission of
      contract 227
    requirements: determining influence,
      status of parties, relevance 227; fear
      of considerable and actual harm
      227; illegitimate or unjust threat
      227–8; imminent and serious harm
      227, 237
  employment contract, termination
    at will 243–4, 251–2
    fixed-term contract before term: as
      abuse of circumstances 251;
      damages/indemnity 243, 252, 253,
      362; inducement to stay, as *causa*
      credendi 243–4, 252, enforceability 244
    terminal bonus, gift, whether 244, 364

evidence of
    contractual agreement, witnesses 286
    waiver of debt 270
gift/donation, enforceability of promise
        of
    liability of estate 38
    liability of heir, in case of written
        promise 37
gift/donation, legal formalities/
        requirements
    acceptance of gift in writing 37;
        institution of proceedings as 37
    causa donandi 37, 252, 270–1, 277
    compliance with formal requirements,
        effect 37
    intention to give 37
    writing 37, 63, 156
gift/promise of gift as
    onerous bilateral contract 36–8
    unilateral contract 36
gratuitous unilateral obligation
    promise to do favour 156, 352
    writing, need for 156
lésion, economic duress and 227
moral obligation, promise of
        remuneration for fulfilling,
        enforceability 76
natural obligation/*obligation naturelle*
    applicability, debt, time-barred 92, 102
    conversion to civil obligation, in case
        of prior moral obligation 73–4, 92
    family relationship as basis 73, 358
    promise, enforceability 73; promisor's
        status, relevance 73–4
novation
    effect: creation of new contractual
        obligations 258; extinction of
        previous obligations 226
    increase in burden on one of parties,
        relevance 258
    modification of contract and 227; as
        consideration/*causa* for new contract
        226–7, 237
    parties' conduct, relevance 258
    requirements 226–7, 257–8, 265;
        animus novandi 257; change of price,
        sufficiency 227, 237, 257

option contract (*contrat de promesse*)
    changed circumstances, relevance 287;
        'basis of contract' theory and 287,
        297, 367
    registration 286–7
    remedies for breach: damages 286;
        specific performance 286
    third party rights 286–7
    time limits for exercise of option 287
pacta sunt servanda 202, 287
pactum de non petendo 270
promise
    as unilateral contract 36–7
    in course of business 156
promise of reward
    revocability of promise to general
        public 304; notice of revocation as
        for original promise 304, 315;
        relevance of, acceptance of offer 304,
        knowledge of offer 304
    revocability of promise to individual,
        causa credendi and 304, 315
promise to do favour
    as contract of agency (*contrato de
        mandato*) 155–6, 352
    as contract for services: professional
        status, relevance 156, 352;
        remuneration, relevance 156
    as friendly service (*servicio amistoso*) 156,
        167
    as part of contract of sale 156
    requirements: consideration/*causa*,
        liberality as 156, 167; delivery 156;
        writing 156, 352
promise to do more than agreed
    as novation 257–8
    as offer to modify/modification of
        contract 257
promise to pay more than agreed
    in absence of modification/novation of
        contract 227, 362
    consideration, need for 243
promise to sell at fixed price, whether
        binding in case of change of market
        price 202–3
    pacta sunt servanda and 202
    rebus sic stantibus 202

Spain (cont.)
promise to sell at fixed price, whether
    binding in case of change of market
    price (*cont.*)
    unforeseen circumstances theory and
        202
proportionality, services rendered,
    promise of remuneration 74
real property transaction, registration,
    need for 286
services rendered [without charge],
    promise to pay remuneration for
    as natural obligation 73–4, 84–5, 358–9
    as onerous contract 74
    as remunatory donation 74, 359; *causa
        donandi* 244, 252; definition 87;
        requirements, writing 74; status of
        parties, relevance 74; sum above
        usual level 74
    legal formalities/requirements 74
servicio amistoso 156
social engagement, agreement to keep,
    as, contract, writing, need for 108,
    116
specific performance
    contract of agency 156
    contract of deposit/promise to store
        goods without charge 126, 145; in
        absence of contract 145; contractual
        obligation 127
    contract/promise of loan for use 179
    option contract (*contrat de promesse*) 286
sums exceeding usual or obligatory level
    or financial means, treatment as gift
    or remunatory donation, services
    rendered without charge 74
teoria de la base del negocio 202–3, 215

unilateral contract 36
    definition/requirements 36;
        common/civil law distinguished 36
    offer, acceptance, need for 36–7
    promise to sell, revocability,
        motivation, relevance 29
unilateral promise to sell (*promesse
        unilatérale de vente*)
    as option contract (*contrat de promesse*)
        286–7
    changed circumstances 287
    pacta sunt servanda and 287
    waiver of right, consideration, relevance
        270–1, 277

United States
consideration/cause
    circumvention of rule by courts,
        detrimental reliance on promise
        and, *Restatement of Contracts (First and
        Second)* 12
    estoppel and 13
estoppel
    consideration and 13
    requirements, pre-existing legal rights
        363
moral consideration 82
Restatement of Contracts (First) 12, 13
Restatement of Contracts (Second) 12, 13, 359
services rendered [without charge],
    promise to pay remuneration for,
    enforceability, unjust enrichment
    and, *Second Restatement of Contracts*
    359
unjust enrichment, services previously
    rendered without charge, *Restatement
    of Contracts (Second)* 359

Index by subject

Note 1: To assist the reader to locate references, each reference has a bold number indicating the country or section in question according to the following table. (Numbers not in bold indicate the page.)

Introduction/Roman law **1**	Greece **10**
France **2**	Scotland **11**
Belgium **3**	England **12**
Netherlands **4**	Ireland **13**
Spain **5**	United States **14**
Portugal **6**	Summaries **15**
Italy **7**	Preliminary comparisons **16**
Austria **8**	Comparisons **17**
Germany **9**	

Note 2: Discussion in the various case studies usually takes the shape of a discussion of a more general legal concept. (For example, 'contract of deposit' is sometimes treated simply as a 'contract *re*'.) In this situation, the item is indexed under both the narrow heading and the more general, the more detailed treatment appearing under the general heading.

Note 3: Headings follow closely the headings of the cases themselves, and are not extensively cross-referenced.

Note 4: Except where it would seem to be a matter of a minor difference of translation, apparently identical or near identical concepts having different terminology (e.g., bailment/deposit) have usually been separately indexed.

abuse of circumstances
definition **4**.225, 236–7, **15**.236–7
economic duress as **4**.225, 363, **17**.363
See also economic duress
illegitimate threat as alternative source
of liability **4**.226
requirements
availability of alternative course of
action, relevance **4**.225
dependence on promise **4**.225, 237,
15.237

threat to terminate employment
contract before term **4**.242–3, 251,
15.251
urgency of situation and **4**.226
abuse of economic dependence 2.220 n. 3,
224, **3**.224
abuse of right 16.217, **17**.367, 373
See also good faith
abus de droit en matière contractuelle **3**.198
advantages/disadvantages of concept
2.196

abuse of right (*cont.*)

definition/requirements **2**.195

disproportion between interest benefited and harm caused **3**.198, 199

exercise of right without legitimate, reasonable and sufficient excuse **3**.198, 199

failure to consider legitimate expectations **3**.198, 199

intention to do harm **2**.196–7, **3**.198

untimely withdrawal of offer **3**.303, 369, **16**.317, **17**.369

difficulty of determining **2**.197

fairness and **2**.195, 196

inequality of bargaining power **3**.199, 215, **12**.215, **16**.217

remedies

damages **2**.197, **3**.198, 303, 315, **15**.315

limitation of right to normal use **3**.198

loss of right **6**.259, 265, 266, **15**.265, **16**.266

termination of contract **2**.197

in setting price **2**.195, 215, **15**.215

acte de complaisance **2**.151

acte sous seing privé **3**.29

ad pias causas **1**.8, **3**.30, **17**.340, 341, 381

agency contract. *See* contract of agency

Alleinvermittlungsauftrag **8**.325

animus contrahendi **2**.106, **3**.106 n. 3

animus donandi/animus solvendi **3**.269, **7**.77

animus novandi **5**.257

appréciation souveraine **2**.105

astreinte **2**.222

Ausgleichsverfahren **8**.94

Auslobung **8**.308, 316, **9**.308, 316, **15**.316

bad faith (*contra bonos mores*)

breach of promise and **8**.42 n. 76, 63, 110, 116, **9**.111, **10**.47, 64, 112, **15**.63, 64, 116, **17**.343

improper exploitation of tax evasion legislation **2**.280, 296, **15**.296

termination of brokerage contract **10**.327

bailment

See also gratuitous bailment

definition **12**.137

bankruptcy proceedings

payment of percentage of debt (*Ausgleichsverfahren*) **8**.94

natural obligation to pay remainder of debt. *See also* debt not legally due, enforceability of promise to pay; natural obligation/*obligation naturelle*

sale of assets (*Konkursverfahren*) **8**.95

beperkende werking **4**.201

biens meuble corporel **3**.28

bonos mores. *See* bad faith (*contra bonos mores*)

breach of promise to marry, acceptance, relevance **5**.36 n. 49

brokerage contract

as

contract of agency **10**.326

hiring of labour (*louage d'ouvrage*) contract **3**.321

breach by person hiring

arbitrary rejection of reasonable offer **3**.322

damages for **3**.321–2

rescission of contract **3**.321

exclusive brokerage

damages for breach **10**.327

requirements **10**.327

right to terminate **10**.327; within given period **10**.327, 333, **15**.333, **17**.370

fiduciary relationship **10**.326

remuneration, causal link with sale, need for **5**.322, **7**.324, **10**.326

remuneration in case of termination **3**.321, 332, **5**.322–3, **7**.324, **10**.327, **15**.332, 333

in accordance with terms of contract **10**.326

exclusive brokerage and **7**.333, **10**.327, **15**.333

where buyer found **3**.332, 370, **5**.322, 332, 370, **7**.324, 333, 370, **10**.326, **15**.332, 333, **16**.333, **17**.370

where contract concluded **10**.326, 327, 333, **15**.333

where contract concluded after termination **10**.327

unilateral termination

broker's right to: damages **10**.327; [necessary and useful] expenses **3**.321, 332, **7**.324, 333, **10**.326–7, **15**.332, 333; remuneration. *See* remuneration in case of termination *above*

right of **17**.389–91; at will and without reason **10**.327; *bonos mores* and **10**.327; in case of contract without fixed term **3**.321, 332, **15**.332; in case of exclusive brokerage agreement **10**.327; good faith and **7**.324, **10**.327, 333, **15**.333; negligence **10**.327

bruikleen **4**.176

burden of proof
breach of pre-contractual obligation **10**.47
consideration/cause **5**.243
unjust enrichment **9**.97

business arrangement
factors determining whether **11**.112
implications **11**.112, 136
promise to do favour as **5**.156

cadeau d'usage **3**.29, 63, 342–3, **15**.63, **17**.342–3
casus non dabilis **4**.91
causa credendi **5**.243–4, 252, 304, **15**.252
causa donandi **5**.37, 108, 243, 252, 270–1, 277, **15**.252, 277
causa liberatoria **5**.270
causa praeterita **7**.77, 245
cause. See consideration/cause
cause immorale **2**.28
cause suffisante **7**.77, 94
changed circumstances **5**.202, **8**.131, **17**.373
See also unforeseeable circumstances
balance of interests and **2**.173, 189, **9**.182, 183, 190, **10**.185, 191, **15**.189
change in economic balance of contract **3**.199, **10**.208, 216, **15**.216
change in market price **2**.196, **4**.200, 285–6, **6**.203, 287–8, **7**.204–5, **8**.290, 297, **9**.291, 292, **12**.295, **13**.296, **15**.297, **17**.367
contract
modification **4**.200, 201, 215, **5**.202, **8**.205, **10**.208, **17**.387–8

release from obligations **2**.196, **4**.200, 202, 215, **7**.204–5, **10**.208, **15**.215
contract of loan for use **2**.172, 189, **4**.178, **9**.182, 190, **10**.184, **15**.189, 190, **16**.192
fairness and **1**.19
good faith and **4**.201, 215, **6**.203, 215, **9**.206–7, **10**.209, **11**.209–10, 216, **12**.211, **15**.215, 216, **16**.299, **17**.367
loan of goods without charge **2**.174, 348–9, **3**.176, 189, 348–9, **10**.184, 191, **15**.189, **16**.192, **17**.348–9
option contract **4**.291, 299, **5**.287
pre-contractual/contractual obligations **8**.131, 147, 181, 290, **15**.147
promise to sell and **3**.284, **4**.285–6, **5**.287, **6**.287–8, **9**.291, **10**.292–3, **11**.293, **12**.295
real property transactions **10**.292–3, **11**.293
requirements
absence of other remedy **5**.202
change subsequent to contract **10**.208
change in underlying circumstances **10**.208
disproportion between parties **5**.202, **7**.204, **10**.208
excessive onerousness **10**.208
extraordinary change **5**.202, **6**.203, **10**.208
reciprocal contract **10**.208
unforeseen/unpredictable change **5**.202, **10**.208

charitable gift
ad pias causas **3**.30, **17**.340, 341
historical origin **1**.8
applicable rules **3**.30, **9**.44
charitable trust **13**.61
eligibility
legal person **9**.44–5, 64, 66, **15**.64, **16**.66
principle of speciality **2**.27
public benefit and **2**.27
enforceability **17**.340
reasons for changes to **17**.341–2
reliance on promise, relevance **17**.381
requirements
benefit to donor **2**.27, 62–3, 66, **15**.62–3, **16**.66, **17**.340

charitable gift (cont.)
  requirements (*cont.*)
    enrichment of donee **9**.44–5
    proportionality **17**.381
    protection of donor and **17**.381
    writing, as evidence of intention **11**.50
charitable organization
  foundation (*fundación/fundação*)
    requirements **5**.37 n. 55, **6**.39–40;
      public interest **6**.40
  foundation (*fundación/fundação*), as legal
    person **5**.37 n. 55, **6**.39
civil law of contract, historical development
  See also common law of contract,
    historical development
  ad pias causas **3**.30
  canon law **1**.3
  causae
    canon law **1**.5
    early modern law **1**.9–10
    exchange **1**.5
    liberality **1**.5, 6
    medieval law **1**.5
    Roman law **1**.5
  changed circumstances **1**.19
  early modern developments **1**.8–10
    in Scotland **1**.8–9, **11**.8–9
    'will theories' **1**.9
  gratuitous loan, enforceability **1**.6–7
  gratuitous promise, enforceability,
    detrimental reliance, need for **1**.6
  ius gentium **1**.3–4
  laesio enormis/lésion **1**.18–19
  medieval
    contract *consensu* **1**.3
    contract *re* **1**.3
    nominate/innominate contracts,
      distinction **1**.3–4
    Roman law as law *in subsidium* **1**.3
    Roman law distinguished **1**.7
    Roman law origin. *See* Roman law
    scholastics **1**.4–8
      commutative justice (exchange) **1**.4–5;
        enforcement of promise and **1**.6
      fidelity **1**.4
      gratuitous promise, binding effect **1**.5–7
      liberality **1**.4–5, 8

clause d'adaptation du prix **3**.198
clause de retour à meilleur fortune **2**.268
clauses abusives **2**.220 n. 3
commendatio **7**.157–8
commercial agency **3**.153
commission agency contract. *See* contract
    of agency; real estate agency
    contract
commodat/comodato **2**.171, 173, 175, **6**.179,
    7.181
common decency **9**.111, 291–2, 297, 367,
    15.297, **16**.298, **17**.367, 373
  See also good faith
**common law of contract, historical
    development**
  consideration
    See also consideration/cause
    causa and **1**.10–12, **12**.10–12; exchange,
      relevance **1**.12, **12**.12
    moral obligation **12**.82–3
    origin in assumpsit **1**.10, 12, 14–15,
      12.10, 12, 14–15
    protection of promisor, relevance **1**.18
    intention to be bound **1**.14, **12**.14
    origin in procedure by writ, covenant
      1.10, 12, **12**.10, 12
    unilateral contract **1**.15, **12**.15
    'will theories' and
      consideration **1**.13, **12**.13
      intention to be bound **1**.14, **12**.14
competition law, abuse of economic
    dependence and **2**.220 n. 3, 221 n. 4,
    224
condition potestative **2**.194–5, 282, 296,
    3.283–4, 296, **15**.296
  See also sole discretion clause
condition subsequent mixte **2**.27
condition suspensive **3**.33–4, **10**.309
condonación, *pactum de non petendo*
    distinguished **5**.270
confiance légitime **2**.256
consideration/cause
  See also civil law of contract, historical
    development; common law of
    contract, historical development;
    Roman law
  adequacy **9**.292

agreement to marry as **1**.11, 13, **12**.11, 13, 54, **16**.66, **17**.340-1, 376

burden of proof **5**.243

circumvention of rule by courts **12**.51-2, 54, 82, 186, 376-7, **13**.376-7, **17**.376-7

detrimental reliance on promise and **1**.11, 12, **12**.11, 12, 51, 58, 114, 137-8, 148, 185-6, 249, 253, 262, 266, 293-4, **13**.266, **15**.148, 253, 266, **17**.342; *Restatement of Contracts (First and Second)* **1**.12, **14**.12

common law system and **17**.376-8

definition **12**.52-3, **17**.376

actual transfer, relevance **12**.53

natural affection **12**.53

real exchange **12**.53, **13**.59, 234; economic **2**.27, **7**.146, 180, 190, **10**.161-2, **15**.146, 190; 'liberality' distinguished **5**.126, 156, 167, 179, **15**.167; motive distinguished **12**.54, 65, **15**.65; nominal value **12**.53, 56, 64, **15**.64

early retirement **13**.250, 253, 364, **15**.253, **17**.364

employment restrictions imposed by employer **2**.239-40

estoppel and **1**.13, **12**.13, 274-5, 277, 363, **13**.275, 277, 363, **14**.13, **15**.277, **16**.278, **17**.342, 363

implied **9**.273

implied assumpsit/act at request of promisor **1**.14-15, **12**.14-15, 81, 87, 359, 376-7, **13**.87, 359, 376-7, **15**.87, **17**.340, 359, 376-7

as agreement with unfixed price **12**.81

intention to reward, need for **12**.81, 83

'just' or reasonable consideration **7**.130, 146, 150, **15**.146, **16**.150

legal formalities as substitute **2**.28, **12**.55-6, **17**.376

liability in tort, effect of changes in law **12**.141-2

modification of original contract as **5**.226-7, 237, **15**.237

moral consideration **1**.11, **12**.11, 81-2, 99-100, 103, **13**.101, 103, **14**.82, **15**.103, **16**.103, **17**.356

limitation to cases of legally defective prior obligation **12**.82

'moral equivalent' **2**.27, 62-3, 66, **15**.62-3, **16**.66, **17**.340

need for **5**.36, **12**.51, 53, 81-3, 86, **13**.58-9, 83-4, 86, **15**.86, **17**.338

See also circumvention of rule by courts *above*

bailment **12**.137, 138, 376, **13**.142-3, 187-9, 376, **16**.192, **17**.376; promise to look after goods as consideration **13**.188; storage of goods as consideration for purchase **13**.143

confirmation of voidable contract **4**.91, 101, **10**.99, **12**.100, 103, **13**.103, **15**.101, 103

gratuitous unilateral obligation **11**.81, 99, 232

modification of contract **7**.259, 272, **9**.260

option contract (*contrat de promesse*) **7**.288, 297, **9**.291-2, 297, **10**.298, **12**.366, **13**.366, **15**.297, 298, **17**.366

promise of gift **2**.28, **12**.52, 58, 64, 81, **13**.58, **15**.64

promise to: do favour **12**.163, 168, **13**.165, 168; do more than agreed **1**.11, **12**.11, 261-2, 266, **13**.264, 266, **15**.266; lend goods without charge **5**.179, **12**.185, 186, **13**.187, **16**.192; pay discharged debt **12**.99, 102, 376, **13**.100, 104, 376, **15**.10, **16**.104, **17**.356-7, 376; pay more than agreed **1**.11, 12, **11**.232, 248, **12**.232-3, 362, **13**.362, **16**.253-4, **17**.362; pay time-barred debt **1**.11, **12**.11, 99, 102, **13**.100, 103, 104, **15**.102, 103, **16**.104, **17**.356-7; reward **12**.311, 359, **13**.314, 359, **17**.359, 360; sell **12**.293, 298, **13**.295, 298, **15**.298, **16**.298; sell at fixed price **12**.210-11, 216, 366, **13**.213, 215, 366, **15**.216, **16**.217, **17**.366

social engagement, agreement to keep **5**.108, 116, **11**.112, **12**.113-14, 116-17, 354 n. 15, **13**.114-15, 117, **15**.116, 117, **17**.354 n. 15

consideration/cause (*cont.*)

need for (*cont.*)

transfer of property without *causa*, unjust enrichment **9**.96 n. 30

unilateral contract **12**.311, 368–9, **13**.314, 368–9, **17**.368–9

waiver of right **5**.270–1, 277, **12**.362, **13**.262, **15**.277, **17**.362

non-competition clause **12**.249, **13**.250, 253, **15**.253

past consideration **13**.166

performance of contract **11**.232, **12**.248–9, 253, 311, 368–9, **13**.235–6, 314, 368–9, **15**.253, **17**.368–9

practical benefit (employee's agreement to stay) **11**.248, **12**.248, 253, 362–3, 378, **13**.250, 253, 362–3, **15**.253, **16**.253–4, **17**.362–3, 378

pre-existing legal duty **1**.11, 238, **12**.11, 232–3, 237, 275, 363, **13**.234–6, 237, 363, **15**.237, **17**.363

reciprocal promises **12**.53, 137, 185, 210–11, 294–5, 298, **13**.213, 295, 298, 315, **15**.298

reciprocal release from rights **13**.250, 253, 254, **15**.253, **16**.254

services offered free and **2**.106, **5**.108, **6**.108, **7**.109, 129, 146, **15**.146

services previously rendered **12**.359, **13**.250, 359, **17**.356, 359, 360

'sole discretion' clause and **12**.294, 298, **15**.298

third party as beneficiary **13**.83–4

'will theories' and **1**.13, **12**.13

construction contract, cost of work exceeding estimate, right to increase price **2**.219

consumer law, unfair contract terms **2**.220 n. 3, 224

contract

See also brokerage contract; construction contract; contract of agency (*mandatum*); contract of donation; contract for gratuitous services; contract of rescue (*convention d'assistance*); contract for sale of goods; contract for services; contract for services without charge (*mandatum*); contract *solo consensu*; *contrat cadre*; employment contract; hiring of labour (*louage d'ouvrage*) contract; lease; option contract (*contrat de promesse*); real estate agency contract; unilateral contract; usurious contract; waiver of right; work contract (*contrat d'entreprise/Werkvertrag*)

act of courtesy distinguished **2**.106 n. 3, **7**.108–9, **10**.135

bilateral promise as **3**.32 n. 33

breaking-off of negotiations, liability in tort **2**.25, 62

'fault of the victim' **2**.25

civil law contracts. *See* civil law of contract, historical development

conditional

condition potestative **2**.194–5, 282, 296, **3**.283–4, 296, **15**.296

condition subsequent mixte **2**.27

condition suspensive **3**.33–4, **10**.309

promise of reward to investigator **4**.303, **9**.308, **10**.309–10

evidence of **5**.286

executory **12**.55

gratuitous. *See* gratuitous contract

implied terms **12**.212–13, 216–17, **13**.214–15, **15**.216–17

interpretation

aids **9**.206; business usage **10**.273; usual practice (*Verkehrssitte*) **9**.272–3

business efficacy and **12**.212, 216, **15**.216

determination of quantity **7**.205, **8**.216, **15**.216, **16**.218

effectiveness principle **3**.284

in favour of binding effect **11**.209, 216, **15**.216

good faith **9**.272, **10**.273, **11**.209–10, 367, 375, **17**.367, 375

parties' intention **9**.272–3, **10**.273

status of parties and **10**.273

will/reliance doctrine (*wilsvertrouwensleer*) **4**.201

modification

by agreement **2**.220, **4**.225, 242, 256, **9**.260, **10**.261, **11**.231

changed circumstances and **4**.200, 201, 215, **5**.202–3, **8**.205, **10**.208, **17**.387–8; agreement by party affected and **7**.204

circumstances unprovided for **4**.201

conditional **6**.271, 277, **15**.277

consideration/cause **7**.259, 272, **9**.260, **13**.264

courts' power **2**.240, **17**.387

courts' reluctance **13**.214–15

gift distinguished **8**.260, 265, **9**.260, 265, **15**.265, **16**.266

increase in salary as inducement to employee to stay **12**.248–9; reliance on promise and **12**.249

invalid subsequent contract, effect **9**.229

novation distinguished **2**.220

post-contractual promise to award retirement bonus **2**.240, **7**.245

for sole benefit of one party **13**.264

unilateral, requirements **2**.255–6, 265, **15**.265

nominate **7**.157

offer

See also option contract (*contrat de promesse*)

acceptance **12**.210–11, **13**.213, **16**.217–18; parties' conduct as evidence of **2**.256, 265, **15**.265; performance as **2**.301, **4**.304, **7**.306–7, **12**.311, 317, 368–9, **13**.368–9, **15**.317, **17**.368–9; reliance on promise, relevance **6**.258, 288; requirements **7**.288–9; 'starting to perform'/'preparations to perform' **4**.303, 315, **12**.312–13, 317, **13**.314–15, **15**.315, 317, **16**.317, **17**.369; where offer in favour of accepting party **2**.256, 301, **7**.260, 265, 272, 306, **15**.265

binding, whether **3**.31–2, **12**.293

'firm' offer **12**.293, **13**.295

promise of reward as **2**.360, **11**.311, **17**.360

promise to do distinguished **2**.283

revocability **4**.284–6, **8**.290, 297, **15**.297; in absence of: acceptance **7**.289, **12**.293, 312, consideration/cause **7**.288, 297, **12**.293, 298, **13**.295, 298, **15**.297, 298, **16**.298; in case of: 'best endeavours' obligation **2**.300, employment contract **2**.300–1. *See also* employment contract, termination; changed circumstances. *See* changed circumstances; express intention of irrevocability **7**.288, 297, **15**.297; good faith and **4**.285, 297, **15**.297; motivation, relevance **4**.285, **7**.290, **8**.290–1, **9**.291, **13**.296; serious reasons **4**.303–4, 315, **15**.315; time limit on exercise of options, relevance **4**.285, 297, **7**.288, 289, 297, **15**.297

withdrawal, notification to offeree **12**.293

'onerous bilateral contract' **2**.27

parallel unilateral obligations distinguished **11**.231

performance, failure because of changes to market price **10**.209

pre-sale contract **2**.282

release from obligations, grounds *force majeure* **2**.196

unforeseen circumstances **2**.196, **4**.200, 202, 215, **7**.204, **15**.215; change in market price as **2**.196, **4**.200, **6**.203; change to economic balance of contract **3**.199, **10**.208, 216, **15**.216; extraordinary change **6**.203; *teoria de la base del negocio* **5**.205–6, 215, **15**.215

requirements

agreement of contracting parties **5**.36, **11**.48

agreement on subject matter and price **2**.281

certainty of obligation **2**.193–6, 215, 367, **4**.200, 201 n. 30, **7**.205, 367, **10**.207, **11**.209, **12**.294, **15**.215, 216, **17**.367; *condition potestative* **2**.194–5, 282, 296, **3**.283–4, 296, **15**.296;

contract (*cont.*)
requirements (*cont.*)
certainty of obligation (*cont.*)
condition subsequent mixte **2**.194–5;
conditional contract **13**.296; good
faith and **10**.207; interpretation of
contract favouring **11**.209; liberty of
party and **10**.207; price at discretion of
one of parties **2**.195, 196, **3**.197, **10**.207,
216, **15**.216; protection of parties and
2.195–6; quantity at discretion of one
of parties **2**.197, **3**.197, **10**.207, 216,
15.216; remedy in case of **2**.195;
subsequent determination, possibility
of **2**.194, **4**.200, **10**.207
'common decency' **9**.291–2, 297, 367,
15.297, **16**.298, **17**.367
consent freely given **2**.223–4, **4**.256. *See
also* economic duress
consideration/cause. *See*
consideration/cause
contract replacing earlier contract
invalid for defect of age **8**.95, **9**.97–8,
102, **15**.102
economic exchange **2**.27, **7**.109
guardian's consent in case of minor
8.95–6, **9**.97
intention to create legal relationship
2.106, 115, **3**.106–7, 115, **4**.107, 115,
256, 304, **6**.108, **7**.109, 116, **8**.116,
9.116, **10**.112, **12**.116, 186, **13**.114–15,
165–6, **15**.115, 116
object **2**.28, **5**.36
offer/acceptance *See* offer, acceptance
above
performance in good faith **7**.205, 216,
10.207, 209, **15**.216; equitable criteria
10.216, 367, **15**.216, **17**.367
rescission. *See* lésion
sole discretion clause **4**.286, **7**.289–90,
9.292, **10**.293, **12**.294, **13**.296, 298,
15.298
supervening excessive hardship **7**.204
termination
for abuse of right. *See* abuse of right
before term, consent of parties, need
for **2**.174

erga omnes **9**.229
retroactive **2**.195, 196, **9**.229
unilateral promise with unfixed term
6.204
unfair contract terms (*clauses abusives*)
2.220 n. 3
voidable
See also lésion
disproportion between price and value
8.291, 297, **15**.297
for: absence of cause **2**.279–80; abuse
of circumstances. *See* abuse of
circumstances; defect of age, court's
duty to consider on own initiative
8.95; economic duress. *See* economic
duress; mistake **2**.279–80; unlawful
threat of non-performance **8**.228–9,
9.229, 246, 252, **15**.252
notification of invalidation, need for
9.229
novation. *See* novation
nullité relative **2**.89 n. 3
promise to comply as confirmation of
contract **2**.89–90, **3**.90–1, **4**.92; in
case of: defect of age **3**.90, 91, **6**.93,
102, **7**.94, **8**.95–6, **9**.97, 102, **15**.102,
vitiating factor **2**.90; enforceability,
cause suffisante **7**.94; writing, need for
10.99
rescission/avoidance of contract, effect
2.89, **4**.91
retroactive invalidation **9**.229
validation. *See also* promise to comply
as confirmation of contract *above*;
requirements **7**.94 n. 19
void/invalid contract distinguished
5.227, **9**.229
voidness. *See* requirements *above*
'will theory' **1**.9
contract of agency (*mandatum*) **8**.63, 65,
15.63, **16**.65.
See also contract for services; real estate
agency contract
commercial agency (*mandat commerciale*)
3.153
damages for breach. *See* damages for
breach of

definition **6**.157, **8**.42
  contrato de mandato **5**.155–6, **7**.157
  gratuitous nature **2**.318, 321, **10**.326
  mandat à titre gratuit **2**.152, 318
  mandate **10**.160, 326
  mandato gratuito **7**.157
  opdracht **4**.153
  Vertrag zugunsten Dritter **8**.42 n. 71
distinguished from
  accommodation agreement **10**.161
  brokerage contract **3**.321
  contract for services **2**.318
  real estate agency **2**.318
hiring of labour (*louage d'ouvrage*)
  distinguished **3**.321
insurance agency. *See* insurance agency
liability
  in absence of remuneration **2**.152, 166,
    3.152, 167, **4**.153–4, **6**.157, **7**.157–8,
    167, **9**.159, **10**.160, **15**.166, 167
  failure to perform/*inexécution* **2**.152,
    3.152, **10**.161
  fault (*faute*) **2**.152, 318–19
  force majeure and **10**.161, 168, 352,
    15.168, **16**.169, **17**.352
  ignorance of obligations, relevance
    3.152
  incomplete performance **7**.167, **15**.167;
    modificatio in peius **7**.158
  intentional wrongdoing (*dol*) **2**.152
  loss, need for **10**.161
  negligence **7**.157–8, **10**.161;
    contributory negligence **10**.161
  standard of care **2**.166, **3**.152, 167,
    7.158, 167, **15**.167, **16**.169; quantum
    of damages distinguished **2**.152,
    4.153, 167, **15**.166, 167, **16**.169
  under commercial agency **3**.153
obligations, 'care of good mandatary'
  4.153
remuneration of agent **2**.318–19
requirements
  acceptance by donee **8**.42
  consideration/*causa* **5**.156, 167, **10**.161,
    15.167
  delivery **8**.42; *commendatio* **7**.157–8, 167,
    15.167

express/implied undertaking **5**.156
intention to contract **3**.152, 167, **4**.153,
  167, **10**.161, 168, **15**.167, 168, **16**.169
obligation to represent legally before
  third parties **5**.155–6, 167, **6**.157,
  7.157, **8**.158, **10**.160, **15**.167, **16**.169
oral/written undertaking **5**.156
Roman law basis **16**.169
termination at will **6**.304, 315
work contract (*Werkvertrag*) distinguished
  8.158 n. 26
contract of deposit/promise to store goods
  without charge
See also civil law of contract, historical
  development; gratuitous bailment;
  Roman law
alternatives to contract
  gentlemen's agreement **2**.119
  non-contractual arrangement **2**.119
  promesse de dépôt **2**.120, **3**.123, **4**.125
  social engagement or courtesy promise
    3.123, **4**.124–5, **7**.129, **10**.135, **11**.136
as
  collateral contract **1**.16, **2**.120, **4**.125,
    10.135, **12**.347, 349, **13**.347, 349,
    16.149, **17**.347, 349
  fiduciary relationship **10**.133
  gratuitous unilateral obligation **3**.123,
    10.133, **11**.136
  in rem contract *quoad constitutionem*
    6.127
  in rem unilateral contract **2**.118, 120,
    121, 122, **3**.123, **5**.126–7; promise to
    store distinguished **2**.120, **5**.126
  pre-contractual obligation **7**.130, 146,
    8.130, 131, **10**.134, 147, **15**.146, 147
  solo consensu contract **10**.134 n. 44
contracts of loan/deposit compared **2**.119,
  120
damages. *See* damages for breach of,
  contract of deposit/promise to store
  goods without charge
date of return, factors determining **4**.125,
  5.127
definition **2**.118–19, **3**.123, **8**.130, **9**.132
  remuneration, relevance **2**.119, **3**.123,
    7.129, **8**.130, **9**.133

contract of deposit/promise to store goods without charge (*cont.*)

enforceability of promise. *See* specific performance, contract of deposit/promise to store goods without charge

liability

after delivery **2**.119–20, **3**.123, 145, **4**.124, **6**.127, 128, 146, **7**.129, **8**.131, **10**.134–5, **15**.145, **17**.354

before delivery **2**.120–1, **3**.123, **4**.124, **5**.126–7, 350, **6**.127, 128, 350, **7**.129, **10**.350, **16**.149, **17**.350

between friends **2**.119, 144, **3**.123, **4**.125, **6**.128, **8**.131–2, 136–7, **10**.135, **15**.144, 146–7

cancellation of alternative contract, relevance **2**.122, **3**.124, **4**.126, **6**.128, **8**.132, **9**.133, **10**.136

discharge. *See* release from liability, grounds *below*

gratuitous contract **2**.119, 120, 122, 150, **7**.129, **8**.130, **9**.132–3, **16**.150, **17**.344–5

gratuitous promise **4**.125, 145, **15**.145

loss of alternative possibility, relevance **2**.122, **3**.124, **4**.126, **6**.128, **8**.132, 147, **9**.133, **10**.136, **11**.148, **15**.147, 148

material damage, need for **11**.136–7, 346–7, 350, **17**.346–7, 350

professional storer of furniture **2**.120, **3**.123, **4**.125, **6**.128, **7**.129, 146, **8**.131, **9**.132–3, **10**.135, **15**.146

reliance on promise, need for **11**.350, **17**.350

remuneration for storage, relevance **2**.118–19, 122, **10**.135

seller of goods **4**.125, **6**.128, **7**.129, 146, **8**.131, **9**.132–3, **10**.135, **15**.146; in case of goods remaining *in situ* **2**.120; offering to store after removal **2**.120

special relationship requirement **12**.139–40, 148, **15**.148

timeliness of termination of deposit, relevance **9**.133, **10**.135–6

in tort. *See* liability in tort

obligations of depositee

care of goods **2**.118; standard of care. *See* standard of care *below*

cost of meeting, relevance **2**.121

custody of goods **7**.129, **10**.133

dependence on delivery **10**.133 n. 41

receipt of goods **2**.118

restoration of goods **2**.118; as cancellation of contract **10**.135; in original condition **7**.129; on request or expiry of time limit **7**.129, **9**.132, **10**.133; timing in absence of time limit **10**.135

release from liability, grounds **6**.127

'an important reason' **4**.125, 145, 349, **9**.132, 147, 349, **15**.147, **16**.150, **17**.349, 350

balance of mutual interests, need for **9**.132, 147, **15**.147

delivery of goods, relevance **2**.349, 350, **3**.350, **7**.349, 350, **8**.131, **9**.132, **16**.150, **17**.345, 349, 350

deposit with public authority **10**.134 n. 47, 136; obligation in case of debt **10**.136

fair reason/motive **5**.3, 127, 145, 350, **6**.128, 146, 349, 350, **15**.145, 146, **16**.150, **17**.349, 350

force majeure **2**.121–2, 144, **3**.123–4, 145, 348, 350, **15**.144, 145, **16**.150, **17**.348, 350

frustration **11**.136, 148, **15**.148

harm to own interests **8**.131, 349, **10**.135, 349, **17**.349, 351, 355, 382–4

inability to store goods safely **8**.131, **10**.135

obligations of depositor and **10**.136

rebus sic stantibus **8**.131, 147

unforeseen circumstances **2**.144–5, **3**.124, 145, **10**.134–5, 147, **15**.144–5, 147

remedies. *See* damages; specific performance

requirements

absence of formality **8**.132

consideration. *See* consideration/cause

intention to create legal relationship **4**.124, **6**.127, 145–6, **8**.131–2, 146–7,

10.147, **11**.136, 147, **12**.142, 148,
13.143, **15**.127, 145, 146, 147, 148,
16.149, **17**.353–4
protection of promisor, relevance
2.348–9, **3**.348–9, **9**.132, **11**.347,
17.347, 348–51, 355, 371
reasons for **17**.347–9
writing **11**.136
standard of care **2**.119
best efforts **2**.120
depositee as friend **2**.119–20
contract of donation 6.38
See also services rendered [without
charge], promise to pay
remuneration for, as remunatory
donation
definition **6**.38, **8**.41 n. 68
requirements
acceptance of gift **8**.41 n. 68
immediate delivery **6**.39, **8**.41–2, **17**.338
notarization **6**.39, **8**.41–2, **10**.80
proportionality **10**.80
sacrifice of assets **6**.108
writing **5**.156, **6**.38–9
revocation **10**.80
services rendered, promise of
remuneration **7**.76, **10**.79–80
professional status of person rendering
service, relevance **10**.80
sum above usual level **5**.74, **10**.80
contract for gratuitous services
intention to create legal relationship,
need for **6**.157, 167, **9**.159–60, 168,
10.162, **13**.166, **15**.167, 168, **17**.353–4
liability
for collateral contract **10**.162
in tort **17**.351
contract intuiti personae **3**.107
**contract of loan for use (*prêt à l'usage/
commodatum*) 2**.119, 171, **17**.345–9
See also loan of goods without charge,
promise
as
arrangement between friends/family
2.173, **12**.186
bailment **12**.186–7, **13**.187–9. *See also*
gratuitous bailment

commodat **2**.171, 175, 273
comodato **6**.179, **7**.180
consensual contract **5**.179, 190, **6**.179,
190, **15**.190
contract *re* **2**.171, 175, **3**.175–6, **4**.176–7,
5.179, **7**.180, **8**.181, **10**.183;
preliminary consensual contract
distinguished **4**.177, **10**.183, 191,
15.191
contract *re quoad constitutionem* **6**.179
gratuitous unilateral obligation **3**.176,
12.186; *bruikleen* **4**.176
Leihvertrag **8**.181
solo consensu contract **10**.183
consideration/*causa*, liberality **5**.179
consideration/*cause* **12**.185, 186, 191,
13.187–8, 191, **15**.191
definition **6**.179
delivery and **2**.171–2, 174, 348, **3**.176, 189,
348, **5**.190, **6**.179, **8**.180, 190, **9**.182–3,
190, **10**.183, 191, **15**.189, 190, 191,
16.191–2, **17**.345, 346, 348, 354
distinguished from
bilateral contract **9**.182
gift **9**.182
lease **5**.179
promise of loan **3**.176, 189, **15**.189
obligations
return: after use **10**.183; at end of term
2.172, **4**.178, **10**.183; without demand
10.183–4
release from liability, grounds
allowing goods to deteriorate **10**.184
court's authorization, need for **3**.176
courts' discretion **2**.172, 174
delivery, relevance **6**.179, **17**.345, 346
fair reason **6**.179–80, 190, 192, **15**.190,
16.192, **17**.345–6
promisee's situation, relevance **4**.178,
6.180, **9**.183, **17**.346
transfer of goods to third party
10.184
unforeseen circumstances **2**.172, 189,
4.178, **9**.182, 190, **10**.184, **15**.189, 190,
16.192; balance of interests **2**.173,
189, **9**.182, 183, 190, **10**.185, 191,
15.189

**contract of loan for use (*prêt à l'usage/
commodatum*) (*cont.*)**
release from liability, grounds (*cont.*)
urgency **2**.172-3, 189, 348, **3**.176, 189,
348-9, **4**.178, **5**.179, 190, **6**.180, 190,
7.180, 190, 346, **8**.181, 190, **10**.184,
191, **15**.189, 190, 191, **17**.345, 346,
355; as breach of contract **2**.12
use contrary to conditions of contract
10.184
requirements
absence of remuneration **2**.172, 175,
3.176, **7**.18, **8**.181, **10**.183
intention to establish legal obligation
6.179, **8**.190, **9**.182, 190, **16**.192,
17.353-4
limited nature **9**.182
writing **2**.173
rights
See also release from liability, grounds
above
termination **5**.179, 190, **9**.182, **15**.190;
compensation **10**.184, 185; in good
faith **9**.182, **10**.184, 191; method **10**.184
to keep until end of term **2**.172, 189,
3.176
temporary nature **5**.179
contract re
See also contract *intuiti personae*; contract
of loan for use (*prêt à
l'usage/commodatum*)
as consensual contract **2**.122, 175, **4**.124,
5.179, 190, **6**.128, **10**.133-4, **15**.190
consensual preliminary contract
distinguished **4**.177
contract of deposit as **2**.118, 121, 122,
3.123, **4**.124, **5**.126-7, **6**.127-8, **8**.130
See also contract of deposit/promise to
store goods without charge
contract of loan for use (*prêt à
l'usage/commodatum*) as **1**.344-5, **2**.171,
175, **3**.175-6, **4**.176-7, **5**.179, **7**.180,
8.181, **10**.183, **17**.344-5
delivery of goods, need for **1**.344-5, **2**.119,
171, **3**.123, **4**.124, 125, 177, 190, **5**.126,
179, 190, **6**.127-8, 146, **7**.129, 180,
190, **8**.131, 181, 190, **10**.133, 183, 191,
15.146, **17**.344-5, 354

as fulfilment of contractual obligation
10.134
don manuel as **3**.33
promise of, enforceability **3**.33, **5**.126-7
quoad constitutionem **6**.127, 179
relevance of classification as **2**.122
Roman law origin **1**.127-8, 344-5,
6.127-8, **17**.4-5, 354-5
contract of rescue (*convention d'assistance*)
2.69-71, 84, 87, **15**.84, **16**.87
legal obligation to assist person in
danger and
liability in tort as alternative **2**.71
status of rescuer, relevance **2**.71
rescue as offer **2**.360, **17**.360
contract for sale of goods, price, right to
increase **2**.219-20
contract for services
implied, professional status, relevance
5.156
requirements
remuneration, relevance **5**.156, 167,
6.157, 167, **15**.167. *See also* contract for
services without charge (*mandatum*)
termination, right to recover agreed fee
9.308
work contract distinguished **8**.307 n. 27,
9.308
**contract for services without charge
(*mandatum*) 9**.159
termination **9**.159
damages in case of untimely **9**.159, 168
contract solo consensu 10.134 n. 44, 183
contract for work. *See* work contract (*contrat
d'entreprise/Werkvertrag*)
***contrat cadre* 2**.193, 194, 196
breach **2**.197
contrat d'approvisionnement. *See* supply
contract
contrat de courtage. *See* brokerage contract
contrat de dépôt. *See* contract of deposit
contrat de promesse. *See* option contract
(*contrat de promesse*)
contrat d'entreprise. *See* work contract
(*contrat d'entreprise/Werkvertrag*)
contrato de doação. *See* contract of donation
convention d'assistance. *See* contract of
rescue (*convention d'assistance*)

conversion to civil obligation 5.73–4, 92, **10**.79–80

corretaje. See brokerage contract

courtesy act/promise 2.106 n. 3, **3**.106–7, 123, 152, **7**.108–9, 129, **10**.111–12, **13**.115

See also gentlemen's agreement

agreement to keep social engagement 2.106 n. 3, **3**.106–7, 123, **7**.108–9, **10**.111–12, **13**.115, 117

contract of deposit/promise to store goods without charge 3.123, **4**.124–5, **7**.129, **10**.135

promise to do favour 3.152, **10**.161

promise to lend goods without charge **7**.180

courtesy transportation 7.109

culpa in contrahendo **8**.42–3, **9**.44, **10**.48

gifts, applicability to **8**.42–3, 64, **9**.44 n. 83, **15**.64

requirements **8**.42–4, 64, **9**.44, **15**.64

culpa lata dolo aequiparatur. See negligence in case of, gross negligence

damages for abuse of right 2.195, 215, **3**.303, 315, **15**.215, 315

damages for breach of

agreement to keep social engagement **8**.110, **10**.112, **11**.113, 116, **15**.116

reliance damages **8**.110 n. 16

bailment

as negligent provision of services **12**.139–40

restitutio in integrum **13**.144

brokerage contract **10**.327

amount of commission contracted for **3**.322

exclusive brokerage agreement **10**.327

lost opportunity **10**.327

contract **11**.231

anticipatory breach **12**.313–14

expectation interest **8**.110 n. 16, **10**.136

implied condition not to withdraw offer **12**.314

contract of agency

in absence of remuneration 2.152, **4**.153–4, **7**.158; incomplete performance, effect **7**.158

contributory negligence and **10**.161

loss or necessary expense **6**.304–5, 315

contract of deposit/promise to store goods without charge 2.119–20, 122

See also bailment *above*

in absence of contract 2.119–20, 144, **10**.134, **15**.144; enforceable promise compared **2**.120

in case of gratuitous contract **2**.120–1, 150, **16**.150

collateral contract 2.120, **10**.135; expectation interest **10**.135

contract **10**.134

gentlemen's agreement 2.119, 121

lost opportunity and 2.122, **4**.126, **7**.129–30, 146, **13**.144, 347, **15**.146, **17**.347; nature of liability **7**.130

contract for gratuitous services **2**.175

collateral contract **10**.162

contract for loan of goods without charge **9**.182, **10**.184, 185

contract for services **9**.159, 160, 168, **15**.168

untimely termination **9**.159

contract to supply at fixed price **10**.29

employment contract (termination before term) 3.241–2, 251, 253, 362, **5**.243, 252, 253, 362, **15**.251, 252, 253, **17**.362

gentlemen's agreement 2.105, **6**.108, 116, 157, **15**.116

option contract (*contrat de promesse*) 2.282, 296, **5**.286, **15**.296

pre-contractual obligation

negative interest **7**.130, **10**.247

reliance damages **4**.35–6, **7**.181, **9**.43, **10**.47, 134, 247

promise

requirements: acquiescence of promisor **11**.113, 116, 137, 148, 150, 162, 168, **15**.116, 148, 168, **16**.150, 170; material damage **11**.112, 113, 116, 137, 148, 150, 162, 168, 352, **15**.116, 148, 168, **16**.150, 170, **17**.352; reliance on promise **11**.113, 116, 148, 150, 162, 168, 352, **12**.164–5, 263, 275, **13**.275–6, **15**.116, 148, 168, **16**.150, 170, **17**.352

damages for breach of (*cont.*)

promise of gift

in amount of promise **2**.26

expenses incurred **10**.47

in full **2**.26

lost opportunity **10**.47

negative interest **10**.47

promise to do favour **6**.157, **9**.159–60, **13**.166

reliance losses **12**.165

restitutio in integrum **13**.165

promise to lend goods without charge **2**.175

liability in tort/contract distinguished **13**.189

promise to pay more than agreed **10**.247

expenditure in dependence on **6**.244

promise to reward **2**.300–1, **3**.302–3, 315, **12**.313–14, **15**.315

ex aequo et bono **4**.303–4, 315, 317, **15**.315, **16**.317

promise to sell **2**.280, 282–3

real estate agency contract

breach of agent's obligations **12**.329

lost commission **6**.323, 333, **12**.329, 334, **15**.333, 334, **17**.370

restitutio in integrum **2**.320

sole agency agreement **12**.329

work contract (*contrat d'entreprise/ Werkvertrag*)

ex aequo et bono **3**.302

lost profit **3**.302, 315, 317, 369, **8**.307, 316, 317, 369, **15**.316, **16**.317, **17**.369

debt not legally due, enforceability of promise to pay

discharged debt **17**.384–6

in absence of consideration **12**.99, 102, **13**.100, 104, **15**.102, **16**.104, **17**.356–7

absence of provision for discharge **5**.91, 101, **6**.92, 102, **9**.96, 102, **10**.98 n. 37, 102, **15**.101, 102, **16**.103, **17**.357

expiry of obligations **9**.96

See also prescription, effect *and* time-barred debt *below*

recovery of paid debt **9**.96, 97

unjust enrichment and **9**.96, **17**.357–8, 360–1, 371

natural obligation

debt declared void **2**.89, **3**.90; in case of minor **2**.89, **17**.357, 384–6

debt discharged in bankruptcy **2**.89, **8**.95, 102, **15**.102; new promise, need for **2**.88, 89, **8**.95, **17**.357; recovery of paid debt **8**.95

time-barred debt **2**.89, 90; as moral obligation **5**.92, 102, **6**.92, 102, **15**.102; new promise, need for **2**.89, **17**.357

partial payment, effect **7**.93–4

prescription, effect **7**.93–4

See also expiry of obligations *above and* time-barred debt *below*

on action to rescind **3**.90–1

obligation to pay **3**.90, 91, 101, **9**.97, **10**.97, **15**.101

partial payment, effect **7**.93–4

presumptive prescription **2**.88–9, 101, **3**.91, **15**.101; payment of debt **2**.88–9, **3**.91; promise to pay as evidence of non-payment **2**.89, 101, **15**.101; rebuttal **2**.89, **3**.91

promise made in knowledge that debt time-barred **7**.93, 102, **15**.102; novation **7**.94; promise in writing in ignorance that debt time-barred **10**.98, 102, **15**.102, **16**.103

promise to pay subsequent to **2**.89; as waiver of defence **8**.95, 102, **9**.97, 102, **10**.98, **15**.102, **16**.103; oral **10**.98

recovery of paid debt **3**.90, **7**.93, **10**.98

right of action accruing on date of written promise/acknowledgment **13**.100

promise as acknowledgment of indebtedness **9**.96, **16**.103

requirements **9**.96–7; protection of promisor and **9**.96–7, **17**.357–8, 371–2; signature of person making acknowledgment **13**.100; writing **9**.96, **11**.99, **13**.100, 104, **16**.103, 104, **17**.357

promise as gratuitous unilateral obligation, writing, need for **11**.99, 102, **15**.102

time-barred debt **17**.384–6
  in absence of consideration **12**.99, 102,
    13.100, **15**.102, **17**.356–7
voidable contract
  action to rescind: in absence of **2**.89–90;
    as response to action to enforce
    promise **2**.89; time limits **3**.90–1
  promise as confirmation of contract
    2.89–90, **3**.90–1, 101, **5**.92, **15**.101; in
    absence of consideration/cause **4**.91,
    12.100, 103, **13**.103, **15**.103; defect of
    age and **3**.90–1, 101, **5**.92, 102, **6**.93,
    102, **8**.95–6, 102, **13**.100–1, 103, 104,
    15.101, 102, 103, **16**.104, new
    contract, need for **8**.95, 96, **9**.97–8,
    102, **15**.102; promise made in
    knowledge that contract voidable,
    need for **7**.93, 94, 102, **15**.102; time-
    barred action **3**.91; writing, need for
    10.99, 102, **15**.102, **16**.103
  promise as gift **4**.91, 101, **15**.101
  recovery of paid debt **6**.93
debt, right to reclaim arrears in case of
  promise to reduce rent
condonación/pactum de non petendo
  distinguished **5**.270
estoppel and **12**.274–5, 277, 363, **13**.275–6,
  277, 363, **15**.277, **16**.278, **17**.363
extension of term (*clause de retour à*
  meilleur fortune) **2**.268
  effect **2**.268
  further period of grace **2**.268–9
promise as
  contract of 'renunciation' **4**.269, 277,
    15.277; formalities **4**.269 n. 5, 277,
    15.277; renunciation of part of claim
    4.269
  deferral of payment **2**.276, **6**.271, 277,
    8.272, 277, **9**.272, 277, **15**.277, **16**.278
  gift/donation **3**.269, **5**.270, 277, **8**.272,
    277, **9**.272, 277, **15**.277
  gratuitous renunciation **4**.269
  modification of contract **6**.271, 277,
    9.273, 277, **10**.273, 277, **12**.275,
    15.277, **17**.387–8
  variation of lease **11**.274, 277, **15**.277
  waiver of debt. *See* waiver of debt *below*

promise by debtor to pay as natural
  obligation **3**.269
promise made in order to secure future
  payment of part or all of rent **3**.269,
    4.269, **7**.271
remission of debt. *See* waiver of debt
  below
waiver of debt **5**.362, **17**.362
  consideration/cause, need for **5**.270–1
  contract of *remissão* **6**.271
  effect **2**.267–8, **3**.269
  formalities **8**.272; writing, need for
    5.270, **6**.271
  implied **2**.268, **5**.270, 277, **15**.277; tacit
    acceptance by debtor **2**.268, **3**.269
  remise de dette **2**.267, **3**.269
deed/promise under seal
  applicability **12**.55
  promise to: lend goods without charge
    13.187, 188; remunerate for services
    rendered without charge **12**.86,
    13.83, 86, **15**.86; store goods without
    charge **13**.142, 143
  as evidence of intention to create legal
    obligations **12**.55, 64, **15**.64
  delivery, relevance **13**.60
  origin **17**.340
  procedure **12**.55, **13**.59–60, 65, **15**.65, **17**.338
  requirements **12**.55, **13**.65, **15**.65
    immediate effectiveness **13**.60
    intention to create deed on face of
      instrument **12**.64, **13**.60, **15**.64
    signature, relevance **13**.60
    valid execution **13**.60
délai de grâce **2**.268
delivery of goods, relevance
  as evidence of special relationship **12**.141,
    148, **15**.148
  bailment **12**.137, 141, **13**.142–3, **16**.191–2
  contract of agency **7**.157–8, **8**.42
  contract of deposit/promise to store
    goods without charge **2**.119–21, 144,
    349, **3**.123, 145, **4**.124, 125, 145,
    5.126–7, 145, **6**.127–8, 146, **7**.129, 146,
    346, 349, **8**.131, 147, **10**.133–4, **15**.144,
    145, 146, 147, **16**.149, 150, **17**.346,
    349, 354

delivery of goods, relevance (*cont.*)
contract of donation **6**.39, **8**.41–2
contract/promise of loan of goods
    without charge **2**.171–2, 174, **3**.176,
    189, **5**.190, **6**.179, **8**.180, 190, **9**.182–3,
    190, **10**.183, 191, **15**.189, 190, 191,
    16.191–2
deed/promise under seal **13**.60
don manuel/donation manuelle **3**.33, **10**.45–6
gift/donation **3**.29, 31, 33, 63, **4**.34 n. 41,
    8.41–2, **15**.63
promise to do favour **5**.156, **7**.352, **12**.164,
    17.344–5, 352
deposit. *See* contract of deposit/promise to
    store goods without charge
depositum **1**.344, **12**.137, **17**.344
dette de reconnaissance **3**.71
devoir de conscience **2**.28
Dienstvertrag **8**.307 n. 27
doaçao remuneratória. *See* services rendered
    [without charge], remuneration for,
    remunatory donation
dol. *See* fault/*faute*/*dol*
donación remuneratoria. *See* services
    rendered [without charge],
    remuneration for, remunatory
    donation
donation. *See* gift/donation
dowry/gift propter nuptias
agreement to marry as consideration
    1.11, 13, **12**.11, 13, 54, **16**.66, **17**.340–1,
    376
reliance on promise, need for **12**.54, 65,
    15.65, **17**.341
applicable rules **6**.40
critical date **7**.41 n. 66
definition **2**.26
enforceability
    acte sous seing privé **3**.29
    heir/beneficiary, importance of
        distinction **2**.26
    where conditional on marriage
        (*condition subsequent mixte*) **2**.27
legal formalities/requirements
    acceptance, relevance **2**.26, **3**.29, **7**.41
    exceptional rules **9**.44, 64, **15**.64,
        17.340; reasons for **1**.8, **17**.342

notarization **2**.26, **6**.40
    writing **13**.59, **16**.66, **17**.340, 342
liability of estate **9**.44
obligation to give **8**.43
    maintenance obligations distinguished
        2.26
    natural obligation (*obligation naturelle*)
        2.26–7, **3**.29–30, 63, 66, **15**.63, **16**.66,
        17.340
promise of as settlement or
    acknowledgment of claim to **8**.43
proportionality and **8**.43, **9**.44 n. 84, 381,
    17.381
rescission
    on dissolution of marriage **6**.40, **7**.41 n.
        66
    marriage not performed **6**.40
    third party rights acquired before
        marriage **7**.41 n. 66
dringende reden **4**.178
duress. *See* economic duress

economic duress 17.362
See also abuse of circumstances
as defence to action in contract **2**.220
as tort **2**.220
distinguished from
    abuse of economic dependence **2**.220
        n. 3
    economic difficulties **2**.220
    unfair contract terms (*clauses abusives*)
        2.220 n. 3
French/English approach distinguished
    2.220
jurisdiction in relation to **2**.223
limited applicability **2**.221, 240, 251,
    15.251
remedies
    avoidance/rescission of contract **2**.220,
        281, **5**.227, **8**.229; annulment by
        court **10**.230
    damages **2**.220
    specific performance of original
        contract **3**.224–5, **16**.237–8
requirements
    determining influence **2**.220, 221–2,
        251, **3**.224, **4**.225, 226, **10**.230, **12**.234,

13.236; status of parties, relevance **2**.221, 223, **4**.226, **5**.227, **7**.228 n. 26, **10**.230. *See also* abuse of economic dependence

direct or indirect dependence on person making threat **10**.230, 363, **17**.363; third party as originator of 'threat', relevance **2**.220

fear of considerable and actual harm **3**.224, **5**.227, **7**.228 n. 26, **11**.232, 375, **17**.375

illegitimate or unjust threat **2**.220, 221, 251, **3**.224, **5**.227–8, **6**.227–8, 363, **8**.245, 252, **10**.230, **12**.233–4, **13**.250, 253, **15**.252, 253, **16**.254, **17**.363

imminent and serious harm **2**.221, **5**.227, 237, **8**.228–9, **10**.230, **15**.237, **17**.363

relevance of right to: damages for non-performance **4**.225, **11**.231–2, 237, 363, **15**.237, **17**.363; judicial authorization to substitute performance **2**.222–3; seek specific performance **2**.222, 223, **4**.225–6, **17**.363; take emergency action **2**.222; take legal proceedings **13**.236

'threat capable of overwhelming a reasonable person' **3**.224

vitiation of consent **12**.234. *See also* relevance of right to *above*

threat to terminate employment before term **11**.248, **12**.248–9, 253, **15**.253

employment contract

hiring of labour (*louage d'ouvrage*) distinguished **3**.302

validity in case of fixed 10-year term **7**.245, 252, 253, 362, **15**.252, 253, **17**.362

work contract distinguished **3**.302, **9**.308

employment contract, termination

at will **5**.243–4, 251–2, **15**.251–2

contract without fixed term, notice **3**.242

fixed-term contract before term

as abuse of circumstances **4**.243, **5**.251, **15**.251

damages/indemnity **3**.241–2, 251, 253, 362, **5**.243, 252, 253, 362, **15**.251, 252, 253, **17**.362

inducement to stay: as *causa credendi* **5**.243–4, 252, **15**.252; employer's right to offer **3**.242, 251, **7**.245, 252, **15**.251, 252; enforceability **5**.244, **10**.247, 252, **15**.252; right to terminate for non-payment **10**.247 obligations of: confidentiality **3**.242; non-competition **3**.242, 251, **15**.251

promise of reward **2**.300–1

terminal bonus

See also pension, promise to pay as natural obligation

gift, whether **2**.240, **4**.243, 364, **5**.244, 364, **8**.246, **9**.246, 252, **15**.252, **16**.254, **17**.364

obligation, whether **8**.246, **9**.246

employment restrictions imposed by employer

requirements **2**.239, 251, **15**.251

consideration/cause, relevance **2**.239–40

equitable criteria 10.216, 367, **15**.216, **17**.367, 373

estoppel 12.65, **13**.65, **15**.65

See also abuse of right; good faith; waiver of right

balance of interests and **13**.188

consideration and **1**.13, **12**.13, 274–5, 277, 363, **13**.275, 277, 363, **14**.13, **15**.277, **16**.278, **17**.342, 363

damages and **12**.263, 275

definition **12**.57

development of doctrine **17**.343

estoppel by representation distinguished **1**.13, **12**.13, **13**.62

failure to keep promise to

attend social engagement **13**.115

do favour **13**.166

lend without charge **12**.186–7, **13**.188, 189

pay more than agreed **12**.249, **13**.251

reduce rent **12**.274–5

store goods without charge **12**.139, 141, **13**.144

grace period compared **2**.268–9

liability in tort and **12**.141, 149, 275, **15**.149, **17**.343

estoppel (cont.)
requirements
detriment **12**.186, 187, 263, 363,
13.61–2, 189, 276, 363, **17**.342, 363
intention that promisee should act on
promise **13**.62, 214
intention to be bound **13**.62, 189, 214,
276
pre-existing legal rights **12**.57–8, 65, 66,
115, 117, 139, 149, 186–7, 249, 263,
274, 363, **13**.62, 66, 117, 144, 149, 166,
188, 214, 251, 264, 363, **14**.363, **15**.65,
117, 149, **16**.66, 117, 278, **17**.342, 363
reliance on promise **4**.257, **12**.66, 187,
262, 263, 274–5, 363, **13**.62, 66, 115,
213, 214, 363, **16**.65–6, 278, **17**.342, 363
right to withdraw from statement and
13.61
waiver distinguished **12**.262–3
evidence
promise as **17**.385–6
writing
as evidence of intention **11**.50
supplemented by witnesses **2**.69
evidence of
See also burden of proof
acceptance of offer **2**.256
assumption of responsibility, promise
12.163–4
breach of pre-contractual obligation **10**.47
contractual agreement
acceptance of offer **2**.256, 265, **15**.265
oral/parole **11**.112, 136
witnesses **5**.286
intention to create legal obligation
between family members **2**.69, **12**.54,
55, 113
between friends **10**.135, **11**.162, 168,
12.186, **13**.143, **15**.168, **16**.149,
17.353–4
professional status of promisor **9**.160,
13.165–6, **17**.353
promise to lend goods without charge
4.178, **12**.187, **13**.189
services rendered gratuitously **4**.126,
11.80–1; importance of services
9.159–60, 168, **10**.161–2, **15**.168

natural obligation/*obligation naturelle*
2.68–9, 84, **15**.84, **16**.86
non-payment of debt **2**.89
promise to do more than agreed **11**.261
promise to pay terminal bonus **11**.248
special relationship
delivery of goods **12**.141, 148, 168–9,
15.148, 168–9
professional status of promisor **12**.148,
164, 168, **15**.168, **16**.170
unilateral obligation **11**.48–9
waiver of debt **5**.270
ex aequo et bono, damages/compensation
3.302, **4**.303–4, 315, 317, 369, **15**.315,
16.317, **17**.369
exclusive dealing clause **2**.197, **3**.198, 199,
4.202, **6**.204, **9**.207
exécution en nature **2**.222
exigibilité **3**.90
extortion, unjustified demand for extra
payment **7**.228

faculté de remplacement **2**.222
fairness
See also just cause
abuse of right and **2**.195
performance of contract and **10**.207
voiding of contract and **2**.195
fault/*faute/dol* **2**.25, 121, 145, 152, **10**.47
See also liability for breach of contract/
pre-contractual obligation; liability
in tort
fiduciary relationship
brokerage contract **10**.326
contract of deposit/promise to store
goods without charge **10**.133
forbearance. *See* waiver of right
force majeure
contract of agency and **10**.161, 168, 352,
15.168, **16**.169, **17**.352
obligations of depositee and **2**.121–2, 144,
3.350, **15**.144, **16**.150, **17**.350
promise to lend goods without charge
3.176, 189, 192, 348, **15**.189, **16**.192,
17.348
requirements
absence of fault **3**.124

impossibility of performance **2**.122, 196, **3**.123–4, 145, **15**.145

independence of parties' will **2**.122

unforeseeability **2**.122

foundation (*fundación/fundação*). See charitable organization, foundation (*fundación/fundação*)

framework contract (*contrat cadre*). See *contrat cadre*

frustration 11.136, 148, **15**.148, **17**.373

See also just cause

right of inspection **6**.258, 259

Gefälligkeitshältnis **8**.131

general rules of law (*droit commun*), derogation from, real estate agency contract **2**.321

gentlemen's agreement

See also courtesy act/promise

damages for breach **2**.105, **6**.108, 116, 157, **15**.116

promise to do favour **2**.151, **6**.157, 167, **15**.167

promise to store goods without charge **2**.119

Geschäftsbesorgungsvertrag **17**.358–61

See also negotiorum gestio

good faith and **9**.309, 316, 317, 367, 369, **15**.316, **16**.317, **17**.369

termination, right of **9**.309

good faith and **9**.309, 317, **16**.317

work contract (*Werkvertrag*) distinguished **9**.308–9

Geschäftsführung ohne Auftrag. See *negotiorum gestio*

gestion d'affaires. See negotiorum gestio

gewichtige reden **4**.125

gift/donation

See also contract of donation; contract for services without charge (*mandatum*); contract re; dowry/gift *propter nuptias*; services rendered [without charge], promise to pay remuneration for

classification as

confirmation of voidable contract without consideration/cause **4**.91

honouring of moral obligation **8**.77–8, **10**.247

promise of dowry exceeding obligation **8**.43

reward for merits **8**.246

disguised donation (*donation déguisée*) **2**.241, **3**.33

distinguished from

option contract **8**.290, 297, **9**.291, **15**.297

promise of gift **3**.31

terminal bonus **7**.245, 252, 364–5, **8**.246, 364, **9**.246, 252, **10**.364, **15**.252, **16**.254, **17**.364–5

tip **9**.45

unilateral modification of contract **8**.260, 265, **9**.260, 265, **16**.265

don manuel **3**.33

conditional **3**.33–4

promise, enforceability **3**.33

evidence of **11**.48–9

indirect donation (*donation indirecte*) **2**.241

assignment of debt (*cession de créance*) **3**.33

reduction of rent **3**.269

renunciation of a right (*renonciation á un droit*) **3**.33

stipulation for benefit of third party (*stipulation pour autrui*) **3**.33

waiver of debt (*remise de dette*) **3**.33

'liberality of usage'

definition **7**.76

delivery, need for **7**.76

proportionality and **7**.76, 85, **15**.85

terminal bonus **7**.245

gift/donation, enforceability of promise of

charitable gift. See charitable gift

compliance with legal formalities, need for **2**.24, 25, 26, 27, 28, 240–1, 251, **3**.29, 32, 34, **15**.251, **17**.364

conditional promise

condition precedent **4**.35

condition subsequent mixte **2**.27

condition suspensive **3**.33–4; condition precedent distinguished **3**.34 n. 40

form of promise, relevance **3**.31, **16**.65

legal person as beneficiary **2**.27, **9**.44–5

See also charitable gift

gift/donation, enforceability of promise of (cont.)

liability of estate 2.24, 4.35, 5.38, 9.43, 44, 10.46, 12.51, 57, 15.61

intention expressed in will 12.57

recall and reduction 7.41

remunatory donation 6.75

rights of wife and children 6.39

liability of heir, in case of written promise 5.37

public policy and 2.28

recovery of expenses incurred in expectation of 2.25, 4.35, 6.38, 12.57-8

See also estoppel

in case of obligation created despite failure to comply with formalities, requirements: causation 11.50; knowledge and acquiescence of donor 1.9, 11.9, 50-1, 64, 247, 15.64; material effect ('not unimportant') 11.50-1, 64, 15.64; reasonableness 11.50-1; reliance on promise 11.50-1, 64, 247, 253, 254, 15.64, 253, 16.254

compliance with legal formalities and 11.50-1

consideration doctrine and 13.58

contractual liability 2.25

deception of victim 2.25, 62, 15.62

good faith, relevance 8.42

inequality of bargain 2.25

pre-contractual obligation to act in good faith 3.34, 35, 63, 4.35-6, 6.39, 10.46-8, 64, 15.63, 64; *culpa in contrahendo. See culpa in contrahendo*

reliance damages 4.34-5

tortious liability 2.25, 62, 7.41, 15.62

reliance doctrine and 17.342-4

gift/donation, legal formalities/requirements

acceptance of gift 2.24, 26, 3.29

contract of donation (*contrato de remissão*) 6.271

on delivery 10.45

express 3.29, 31, 33, 63, 15.63

formal 7.40-1, 63, 15.63

prior to delivery 10.45

in writing 5.37, 6.38; contract of donation (*contrato de doaçao*) 6.38; institution of proceedings as 5.37

acceptance of promise 8.42, 11.81

capacity of parties 2.28

causa donandi 5.37, 252, 270-1, 277, 15.252, 277

compliance with formal requirements, effect 2.28, 3.31, 5.37

consideration/cause. *See* consideration/cause

datio rei. See delivery to donee *below*

delivery to donee 2.241, 3.29, 31, 33, 63, 4.34 n. 41, 8.41-2, 15.63

donor's right to recover 10.46

or intermediary 34 n. 41

'liberality according to usage' 7.76, 245

enrichment 9.44-5

failure to comply, effect 3.34, 9.79, 11.49-51

on entitlement to withdraw 11.49-50

nullity 3.32, 9.43, 10.45; renunciation of right to invoke 3.32 n. 36; right to invoke 10.45

validity of contract and 11.49-50

immediate divestment of right to 3.31, 33

intention to create legal obligation 10.247, 11.80-1, 12.113

intention to give 3.269, 5.37, 6.271, 11.48, 12.54-5

presumption of/against 11.48, 12.54

Schenkungsabsicht 8.245, 246, 252, 15.252

seriousness, need for 12.55

irrevocability 2.27, 3.29, 31, 33-4, 63, 15.63

notarization. *See* notarization

promise under seal 12.55

purpose

distinguishment between enforceable and non-enforceable promises 7.40

evidentiary function 7.40

protection of donor 3.28, 34, 4.35-6, 9.43, 10.46, 17.337-40; in case of movable property 10.46; 'cautionary function' 7.40, 17.337-8; consent freely given 2.28

significance **16**.65

trust. *See* trust

writing **5**.37, 63, 156, **6**.38–9, 63, **11**.48–50, 64, 80–1, 86, 360, **15**.63, **16**.86, **17**.338, 360

  signature of donor and witness **13**.59, 65, **15**.65

gift/donation, revocability of promise on grounds of ingratitude 6.39, 75

gift/promise of gift as

  contract **4**.35, **8**.41–2

    See also contract of donation; contract for services without charge (*mandatum*)

  contractual debt **2**.24

  'customary present' (*cadeau d'usage*) **3**.29, 63, 342–3, **15**.63, **17**.342–3

  gratuitous contract of deposit distinguished **9**.132

  gratuitous unilateral obligation **11**.49

    between family members **11**.49–50, **12**.54–5

    charitable gift. *See* charitable gift

    consideration, relevance **11**.81, 99

    critical date **11**.81

    services rendered gratuitously **11**.80–1, 86, **15**.86

  natural obligation/*obligation naturelle* **2**.26–7, **3**.29–30

    See also natural obligation (*obligation naturelle*)

  onerous bilateral contract **2**.27, **5**.36–8

  unilateral contract **2**.25, **5**.36, **10**.45

    unilateral promise distinguished **6**.38

good faith 17.373

  See also abuse of right; bad faith (*contra bonos mores*); common decency; pre-contractual obligation

  as limitation of exercise of rights **4**.201, **9**.182 n. 32

  brokerage contract **7**.324, **10**.327, 333, **15**.333

  change of circumstances and **4**.201, 215, **6**.203, 215, 288–9, **9**.206–7, 216, **10**.209, **11**.209–10, 216, **15**.216, **16**.299, **17**.367

    circumstances 'unprovided for' **4**.201

unfairness and **12**.211

in common law jurisdictions **12**.376, **13**.376, **17**.376

Geschäftsbesorgungsvertrag and **9**.309, 316, 317, 367, 369, **15**.316, **16**.317, **17**.369

interpretation of contract and **9**.272, **10**.273, **11**.209–10, 367, 375, **17**.367, 375

objective fairness as test **4**.286

option contract (*contrat de promesse*) **17**.367

performance of contract and **7**.205, 216, **10**.207, 209

promise to do more than agreed and **10**.261

real estate agency contract **9**.325, 333, **12**.329

requirement to take other party's interests into account **7**.289

revocability of

  offer **4**.285, **16**.298

  promise of reward **9**.309, 316, 317, 369, **15**.316, **16**.317, **17**.369

'sole discretion' clause, relevance **4**.286, **7**.289–90, 297, **9**.292, 298, **12**.294, **15**.297, 298

timeliness of termination of contract of deposit **10**.135–6

Geschäftsbesorgungsvertrag **9**.309

loan of goods **9**.182, **10**.184, 191

gratuitous bailment

See also loan of goods without charge, promise

definition **12**.137, 148, **13**.142, **15**.148, **17**.349

estoppel and **12**.139, 141, 186–7, **13**.144, 187, 188, 189

legal classification

  contract **12**.137, **13**.142

  mixed **12**.137

  sui generis **12**.137

  tort **12**.137, 139, **13**.142, 149, **15**.149

  uncertainty **12**.137, 138, 148, **15**.148

liability

  after delivery **12**.138, 148, 187, **13**.188, **15**.148, **17**.346

gratuitous bailment (*cont.*)

liability (*cont.*)

before delivery **12**.137, 141, **16**.150;
consideration, need for **12**.137, 148,
150, 186–7, 191, 376, **13**.130, 142–3,
149, 189, 191, 376, **15**.148, 149, 191,
16.149, 150, **17**.346, 376

between friends **12**.142, **13**.143

cancellation of alternative contract,
relevance **13**.144

collateral contract **12**.138, 148, 187, 346,
347, 349, **13**.346, 347, 349, **15**.148,
16.149, **17**.346, 347, 349; storage as
consideration for purchase **13**.143

loss of alternative possibility, relevance
13.144

professional status of bailee, relevance
12.137, 139, 142, 148, **15**.148

seller of goods **12**.140, 142

in tort. *See* liability in tort, failure to
keep promise, storage of goods
without charge

loan of goods without charge as **12**.186–7,
191, 346, **13**.187–9, 191, 346, **15**.191,
17.346

obligations

care of goods **12**.138

limitation in absence of consideration
to those imposed by law **13**.142, 149,
15.149

restoration of goods **13**.188;
termination at will **12**.138, 346,
13.346, **17**.346

uncertainty **12**.148, 187, **15**.148

release from liability, grounds **12**.137,
142, 186, 349–50, **13**.143, 144, 149,
349–50, **15**.149, **16**.150, **17**.349–50

in case of fixed term **12**.138, 346,
13.236, 346, **17**.346

timeliness of termination of bailment,
relevance **12**.138

gratuitous contract

gift distinguished **8**.132, **9**.159

promise to do favour **9**.159–60, **17**.344

promise to store goods without charge as
2.119, 120–1, 122, 144, **7**.129, **8**.130,
9.132–3, 147, **15**.144, 147, **17**.344–5

relevance of classification as **2**.122

gratuitous option contract. *See* option
contract (*contrat de promesse*)

gratuitous promise

See also civil law of contract, historical
development; common law of
contract, historical development;
gift/donation, enforceability of
promise of

courtesy promise distinguished,
transportation promises **7**.109

donation rémunératoire **2**.241

enforceability **11**.191, **12**.138, 140, **13**.143,
17.342

'just' or reasonable consideration **7**.130

liability for breach **4**.125

gratuitous nature, relevance **4**.125,
154, 155

misfeasance **12**.139–40, 164

nonfeasance **12**.140–1, 148, 164, **13**.165,
15.148, **16**.170

professional status of promisor,
relevance **4**.125, 155

tort **7**.130

potential benefit to promisor, effect
11.311

gratuitous unilateral obligation

historical origin **1**.14, **11**.14

promise to

do favour **5**.156, 352, **9**.159, **11**.352,
17.352

do more than agreed **11**.261, 265,
15.265

loan goods **3**.175

make gift **11**.49–50, **12**.54–5

pay debt not legally due **11**.99, 102,
15.102

pay more than agreed **11**.232, 247–8,
252, **15**.252

pay remuneration for services
rendered **11**.80–1, 86, 360, **15**.86,
17.360

store goods without charge **3**.123,
10.133, **11**.136

writing, need for **5**.156, **11**.112, 136,
147–8, 149, 162, 232, 247, 252–3, 261,
352, 374, **15**.147–8, **16**.149, 254,
17.342, 352, 374

Gute Sitten **8**.110

hiring of labour (*louage d'ouvrage*) contract
See also brokerage contract
distinguished from
contract of agency **3**.321
employment contract **3**.302
unilateral termination, right of **3**.302, 321
homologation, statutory provisions on promises distinguished **1**.8–9, **11**.8–9, 50

immoral act, liability in tort **10**.231, 237, **15**.237
implied assumpsit. *See* consideration/cause, implied assumpsit
imprévision **2**.21, **10**.208 n. 46
See also changed circumstances
inequality of bargaining power 2.25, **3**.199, 215
insurance agency
lastgeving **4**.153
liability, remuneration, relevance **4**.153–4
interest on unpaid salary 10.247
Ireland, English law and **13**.59 n. 141
ius gentium **1**.3–4

just cause 6.179–80, **7**.305–7, 316, 317, 369, **15**.316, **16**.317, **17**.369
See also fairness; frustration

Konkursverfahren **8**.95

laesio enormis **1**.19
See also lésion
lastgeving **4**.153
lease, variation
See also debt, right to reclaim arrears in case of promise to reduce rent
writing, need for **11**.274, 277, 278, 362, **15**.277, **16**.278, **17**.362
legal persons, as beneficiaries of gifts **2**.27
legitimate expectations 3.198, 199, **6**.203
Leihvertrag **8**.181
lésion
attempt to change contract price and **2**.281
critical date **2**.281, 296, 367, **3**.284, 296,

367, **8**.291, 297, **15**.296, 297, **16**.298–9, **17**.367
economic duress and **2**.220, 281, **5**.227, **8**.229
invalidity of consent distinguished **2**.281
option contract (*contrat de promesse*) and **2**.282, **3**.284
protection of promisor and **2**.281, **17**.373
requirements **2**.96, 281, 367, **3**.367, **15**.296, **17**.367
time limits **2**.281
liability for breach of contract/pre-contractual obligation
gross negligence **10**.47, 161
misfeasance/nonfeasance **13**.165, 347, **17**.347
wilful conduct **10**.47
liability in tort
See also bad faith (*contra bonos mores*)
act contrary to morality **10**.231, 237, **15**.237
contract/tort, relevance of distinction **2**.122–3
contractual relationship, relevance **13**.143
courtesy transportation, suspension of performance **7**.109
damages. *See* damages for breach of
detrimental reliance and **12**.313
economic loss, sufficiency **4**.154, 167, **8**.110, **12**.139, 150, 163, 168, 350–1, **13**.165, 169, 347, 350–1, **16**.150, 170, **17**.347, 350–1
effect of changes on doctrine of consideration **12**.141–2
estoppel. *See* estoppel
failure to keep promise
as breach of duty arising out of voluntary relationship **12**.31, **13**.192, 347, 351, **16**.192, **17**.347, 351
free services/social engagement **2**.106, 115, **4**.107–8, **15**.115, **16**.117; bad faith, need for **8**.110, **9**.111, 116, **10**.112, **15**.116, **16**.117
gift/donation **2**.25, 62, **7**.41, 63, **15**.62, 63, **17**.343. *See also* gift/donation, enforceability of promise of gratuitous nature, relevance **4**.125, 154, 155

liability in tort (cont.)

failure to keep promise (*cont.*)

loan without charge **12**.346, **13**.189, 191, 192, 346, 347, **15**.191, **16**.192, **17**.346, 347

storage of goods without charge **2**.121, 122–3, **7**.130, **11**.351, **12**.139–42, **13**.142, **17**.351; delivery of goods, relevance **12**.141, 148, 150, **13**.143–4, **15**.148, **16**.150; fault, need for **2**.121, 145, **15**.145; status of promisee/ bailee, relevance **12**.142

to do favour **4**.154–5, **12**.163–5, 352, **17**.352; reliance on promise and **12**.164–5; standard of care, relevance **4**.155, 167, **15**.167, **17**.352–3

fairness as basis **2**.121

fault (*faute*)

breaking-off of commercial negotiations **2**.25

failure to complete formalities, whether **2**.25

need for **2**.25, 121, 145, **15**.145

harm (*dommage*) **2**.25

liability to rescuer acting voluntarily **2**.71

natural obligation liability as alternative **2**.68

negligent provision of services

special relationship, need for **12**.139–40, 148, 150, 163–4, 350–1, **13**.165, 350–1, **15**.148, **16**.150, **17**.350–1, 383–4; professional status of promisor **12**.148, 164, 168, **15**.168, **16**.170

nonfeasance **8**.168, **12**.140–1, 148, 164, 350–1, **13**.165, 169, 191, 250–1, 347, **15**.148, 168, 169, **16**.170, 192, **17**.347, 350–1

requirements

absence of public policy objection **13**.165

foreseeability **13**.165

proximity between wrong-doer and person suffering damage **13**.165

strict **2**.71

termination of real estate agency **2**.320, 332, 370, **15**.332, **17**.370

unjustified demand for extra payment **7**.228

violation of 'rule of unwritten law pertaining to proper social conduct' **4**.108, 115, 154, 167, **15**.115, 167

liberality

consideration/cause distinguished **5**.126, 156, 167, 179, **15**.167

gift/donation **7**.76, 245

historical development **1**.4–5, 6, 8

promise to do favour **5**.156, 167, **15**.167

proportionality and **7**.76, 85, **15**.85

terminal bonus **7**.245

loan of goods without charge, promise

See also civil law of contract, historical development; gratuitous bailment; Roman law

as

contract of loan for use. *See* contract of loan for use (*prêt à l'usage/ commodatum*)

courtesy promise **7**.180

pactum de contrahendo **8**.181

Prekarium (loan terminable at will) **8**.181, 190

preliminary consensual contract **4**.177, 190, **10**.183, 191, **15**.190, 191; enforceability **4**.177, 190, **15**.190; requirements **4**.177

rental agreement **8**.181 n. 28

binding nature **3**.176, 189, **15**.189

damages. *See* damages for breach of enforceability. *See* specific performance

estoppel **12**.186–7, 191, **13**.188, 189, 191, **15**.191

pre-contractual liability **7**.181, 190, **15**.190

promesse de prêt **2**.171

release from liability, grounds

absence of contract **7**.180

in case of *Prekarium* **8**.181, 190

force majeure **3**.176, 189, 192, 348, **15**.189, **16**.192, **17**.348

inconvenience to borrower, relevance **3**.176, **4**.178, **6**.180, **8**.181–2, **11**.185, **12**.187, **17**.345–6, 382–4

timeliness, relevance **11**.185

unforeseen circumstances **2**.174, **3**.176,

189, **10**.184, 191, **15**.189, **16**.192,
  17.345, 382–4
requirements
  consideration **12**.185
  delivery, relevance **4**.178, **12**.185, 186
  intention to create legal obligation
    4.177, 178, **16**.192, **17**.353–4; evidence
    of **4**.178; promisee's right to assume
    4.178
  reliance on promise **4**.177, **7**.181,
    11.185, 191, **12**.186, 187, **16**.192,
    17.346
  writing **11**.185, 191, **15**.191
locatio conductio operis. *See* obligation of
  result
louage d'ouvrage. *See* hiring of labour (*louage
  d'ouvrage*) contract

maintenance obligations 2.26–7
mandat à titre gratuit. *See* contract of agency
  (*mandatum*)
mandatum **8**.42, 63, 65, **12**.137, 148, **15**.63,
  148, **16**.65, **17**.352
  See also contract for services without
    charge (*mandatum*)
material damage, need for
  contract of deposit/promise to store
    without charge **11**.350, **17**.350
  enforceability of promise to lend goods
    without charge **11**.185, 191, 346–7,
    15.191, **17**.346–7
  recovery of expenses incurred in reliance
    on promise **11**.50–1, 64, 112, 113, 116,
    136–7, 148, **15**.64, 116, 148
mediação imobiliária. *See* real estate agency
  contract
modicité **3**.29
modificatio in peius **7**.158
moral equivalent 2.27
moral impossibility 2.69
moral obligation
  payment of debt **7**.93
  recovery of performance or value **6**.75
  social engagement, failure to keep and
    9.110–11, 116, **15**.115
  See also promise, moral/legal promise,
    distinction

**moral obligation, promise of remuneration
  for fulfilling 14**.82
  See also natural obligation/*obligation
    naturelle*; *negotiorum gestio*
  consideration, need for **12**.81–3
  enforceability **5**.76, **6**.75–6, 102, **8**.77–8,
    10.79–80, 86, 247, 252, 364, **15**.86,
    102, 252, **16**.254, **17**.364
  gift, whether **8**.77–8
  legal formalities/requirements **6**.102,
    7.102, **8**.77–8, **10**.86, **15**.86, 102
  harm to donor **8**.78
  importance to donee of services
    rendered **8**.78
  professional status of promisee,
    relevance **8**.78, **12**.82–3

natural law, enforceability of promises
  1.7–9
natural obligation/*obligation naturelle*
  3.29–30
  See also contract of donation; contract of
    rescue (*convention d'assistance*)
  applicability **3**.30 n. 21
  debt. *See also* debt not legally due,
    enforceability of promise to pay;
    debt, right to reclaim arrears in case
    of promise to reduce rent; declared
    void **2**.89, **17**.357; discharged in
    bankruptcy **2**.88, 101, **3**.90, 101, **4**.91,
    101, **8**.94–5, 102, **15**.101, 102, **17**.357;
    of gratitude (*dette de reconnaissance*)
    3.71; recovery of arrears of rent in
    case of debtor's promise to pay
    3.269; time-barred **2**.89, 101, **3**.90,
    101, **4**.91, 101, **5**.92, 102, **6**.92, **8**.95,
    15.101, 102, **16**.103, **17**.357
  promise to pay terminal bonus **10**.247,
    252, 364, **15**.252, **16**.254, **17**.364
  remuneration in absence of liability in
    tort **2**.68
  services rendered without charge. *See*
    services rendered [without charge],
    promise to pay remuneration for, as
    natural obligation
basis
  family relationships **5**.73, 358, **17**.358

natural obligation/*obligation naturelle*
(cont.)
basis (*cont.*)
  moral or social duty **7**.77, **10**.79
  statutory **2**.67–8, 89, **3**.29–30
conversion to civil obligation **2**.26, 68–9,
  3.30, **4**.91, **16**.66
  by contract **4**.72, **10**.79–80
  in case of prior moral obligation
    5.73–4, 92, **10**.79–80
  evidence of **2**.68–9
  promise to: pay discharged debt **3**.90,
    16.103; pay pension not due **3**.242,
    251, **15**.251; remunerate **3**.71–2
definition **3**.30
dowry **2**.26–7, 62, **15**.62, **17**.340
pension **3**.242, 364, **17**.364
promise
  as unilateral contract **2**.68
  enforceability **2**.67–9, **3**.71–2, 242, 251,
    364, **5**.73, **15**.251, **17**.364; difficulty/
    rarity of enforcement by courts **2**.69;
    professional status of person
    rendering service, relevance **2**.68,
    3.72, **4**.73; promior's status,
    relevance **2**.68, **5**.73–4
  gift distinguished **2**.68, **4**.358, **17**.358
  novation **2**.68
recovery of performance or value **2**.67 n.
  2, **3**.30, **7**.76–7, 85, **10**.79, **15**.85
requirements **4**.91
  evidence of **2**.68–9, 84, **15**.84, **16**.86,
    17.358
  interpretation **2**.68
  unequivocal recognition of obligation
    2.67
  validity **2**.68
  writing **2**.68–9, **16**.86, **17**.358;
    notarization **2**.68–9
negligence in case of
bailment **12**.139–40
brokerage contract **10**.327
contract of agency **7**.157–8, **10**.161
contract/pre-contractual obligation **10**.47,
  161
gross negligence **8**.159, **10**.47, 161
  definition **17**.384

promise to do favour **7**.157–8, **8**.159, 168,
  352, **10**.161, **12**.164, 168, **15**.168,
  17.352
provision of services **12**.139–40, 148, 150,
  163–4, 168, 350–1, **13**.165, 350–1,
  15.148, 168, **16**.150, 170, **17**.350–1,
  383–4
work contract (*contrat d'entreprise/*
  Werkvertrag) **8**.159, 168, **15**.168
negotiorum gestio
See also contract of agency (*mandatum*);
  Geschäftsbesorgungsvertrag
definition **6**.74–5
quasi-contract **2**.70
  equitable consequences deriving from
    agreement, applicability **2**.70–1
remuneration for damage/harm suffered
  4.72, **6**.75
  in case of necessary action **3**.303, **6**.87,
    8.78, 85, **15**.85, **16**.87, **17**.358, 359, 360
  legal duty, relevance **2**.70–1, **6**.74–5, 87,
    8.78, **9**.86, **15**.86, **16**.87
  professional status of person rendering
    service, relevance **2**.70–1, **4**.84, **6**.75,
    85, **8**.78, **9**.79, 86, **15**.84, 85, 86, **16**.87
  promise, as acknowledgment of claim
    6.85, **8**.78, 85, **9**.79, 86, **15**.85, **16**.86,
    87, **17**.359, 360
  promise of payment, relevance **6**.74–5,
    85, **8**.85, **15**.85
  status of person receiving service,
    relevance **6**.85, **8**.85, **15**.85; duty of
    that person to provide service, need
    for **6**.75, **8**.78; parent of adult/minor
    child distinguished **8**.78, 85, **9**.79,
    15.85, **16**.87
  useful and necessary expenses **2**.301,
    315, **15**.315
search for lost property in response to
  offer of reward **2**.301, **3**.303
unjust enrichment and **8**.359, **9**.359,
  17.359, 360–1
notarization
advantages/disadvantages **17**.339–40
agreement to pay sum above a certain
  level **2**.68, **10**.80
contract of donation **6**.39, **8**.41–2, **10**.80

court's right to examine requirement on
  own initiative **10**.45
dowry **2**.26, **6**.40
enforceability of promise
  of gift **3**.32, 33–4, 63, 242, **4**.34–5, 243,
    7.40, 63, **8**.41–2, 63, **9**.43, 64, 246,
    10.45–6, 64, **15**.63, 64, **17**.338, 357
  to pay for services rendered without
    charge **7**.76; status of person
    providing services, relevance **7**.76
  to sell **2**.280, **6**.287
exemption
  disguised gift (*donation déguisée*) **2**.241,
    3.33
  immediate delivery of movable (*don
    manuel/donation manuelle*) **2**.241, **3**.33,
    10.45–6
  indirect gift (*donation indirecte*) **2**.241,
    3.33
  limitation to small amounts/*modicité*
    2.24, **3**.29
  insinuatio/stipulatio as origin **1**.2, 338,
    339–40, **17**.338, 339–40
  real property transactions **6**.39, 287, 297,
    9.291, 297, **10**.292, 298, **15**.297, 298
novation
  contract voidable for defect of age **7**.94
  effect
    creation of new contractual
      obligations **5**.258
    extinction of previous obligations **5**.226
    increase in burden on one of parties,
      relevance **2**.265, **5**.258, **15**.265
    modification of contract and **2**.220, **5**.227
    as consideration/*causa* for new contract
      5.226–7, 237, **15**.237
  natural obligation/*obligation naturelle* and
    2.68
  parties' conduct, relevance **5**.258
  requirements **5**.226–7, 257–8, 265, **15**.265
    animus novandi **5**.257
    change of price, sufficiency **5**.227, 237,
      257, **15**.237
  time-barred debt **7**.94
    unequivocal intention to waive right of
      prescription, need for **7**.94
nullité absolue **3**.32

**obligation of best endeavours (*obligation de
    moyens*)** **2**.120, 300, 301, 320, **9**.308–9,
    316, **15**.316
obligation cum potuerit **6**.271
obligation de faire **2**.280, 282–3
obligation de moyens. *See* obligation of best
    endeavours (*obligation de moyens*)
obligation naturelle. *See* natural obligation/
    obligation naturelle
obligation of result **3**.302, **8**.307, **9**.308, 316,
    15.316
opdracht **4**.153, 352, **17**.352
  lastgeving **4**.153
option contract (*contrat de promesse*)
  See also contract, offer; unilateral
    promise, to sell
  changed circumstances, relevance **5**.287,
    9.291, **17**.367
  'basis of contract' theory and **5**.287,
    297, 367, **15**.297, **16**.299, **17**.367, 373
  consideration/cause, relevance **7**.288, 297,
    9.291, 297, **10**.298, **12**.366, **13**.366,
    15.297, 298, **17**.366
  enforceability **7**.288
  gift distinguished **8**.290, 297, **9**.291,
    15.297, **16**.298
  good faith and **17**.367
  notarization **10**.293
  pre-contractual agreement distinguished
    7.289, **8**.290
  registration **5**.286–7
  remedies for breach
    damages **2**.282, 296, **5**.286, **15**.296
    lésion. *See* lésion
    specific performance **2**.282, **5**.286
  third party rights **5**.286–7
  time limits for exercise of option **5**.287,
    8.290, **9**.291–2, **16**.298
  unjust enrichment and **17**.388–9

pacta sunt servanda **5**.202, 287, **6**.203, **10**.209
    n. 51
pactum de contrahendo **8**.130, 131, 181, 290
  See also pre-contractual obligation
pactum de non petendo **5**.270
pension, promise to pay as natural obligation
    3.242, 251, 364, **15**.251, **17**.364

pension, promise to pay as natural obligation (*cont.*)
    See also employment contract, termination, terminal bonus
***politicato* 1**.37
pre-contractual obligation
    See also pactum de contrahendo
    bad faith and **6**.244, 252, 362, 364, **7**.130, 146, 150, **15**.146, 252, **16**.150, **17**.362, 364
    basis of liability **10**.48, 134
        culpa in contrahendo **8**.42, **10**.48
        negotiations **10**.48
    breach of promise and **3**.34, 63, **4**.35, **6**.39, **10**.46–8, 64, **15**.63, 64
    negative interest damages **7**.130
    reliance damages. *See* damages for breach of, pre-contractual obligation
    changed circumstances and **8**.131, 147, 181, 290, **15**.147
    liability for breach, requirements
        burden of proof **10**.47
        conduct contrary to good faith and business practices **10**.46–7
        dependence on promise **6**.244, 252, **15**.252
        harm **10**.47; causally related to fault **10**.47
        violation in course of negotiations **10**.46
    promise to
        lend goods without charge **7**.181, 190, **8**.181, **15**.190
        pay more than agreed **6**.244, 252, 253, 362, **10**.247, **15**.252, 253, **17**.362
        sell goods **7**.289
        store goods without charge **7**.130, **8**.130, 131, **10**.134, 147
    remedies
        damages **6**.244
        specific performance **10**.134
    withdrawal from negotiations **10**.47
        fault **10**.47
pre-nuptial gift. *See* dowry/gift *propter nuptias*
***Prekarium* 8**.181, 190

prescription
    effect on debt. *See* debt not legally due, enforceability of promise to pay, prescription, effect
    novation. *See* novation
    presumptive **2**.88–9, 101, **3**.91, **15**.101
    reactivation of obligation **2**.89
***prêt à l'usage* 2**.171
professional status, relevance
    liability (*responsabilités professionnelles*) **3**.153
    commercial agency **3**.153
profiteering contract. *See* usurious contract
***promesse bilatérale* 3**.32 n. 33
***promesse de prêt* 2**.171, 174–5
***promesse unilatérale* 3**.32 n. 33
***promesse unilatérale de vente* 2**.193–4
promise
    as
        act of courtesy. *See* courtesy act/promise
        bilateral promise (*promesse bilatérale*) **3**.32 n. 33
        expression of future intention **11**.112
        offer **3**.32 n. 33, **13**.213, 217, **15**.217, **16**.217–18; standing offer **12**.210, 211
        relevance of classification **16**.169
        unilateral contract **1**.36, **2**.25, **3**.32 n. 33, **5**.36–7, **6**.38, 203, **10**.45; *promesse unilatérale* **3**.32 n. 33
    breach, damages for **2**.26
    conditional, liability for frustration of condition **1**.334, **11**.328, **15**.334
    in course of business **1**.9, **5**.156, **11**.9, 112, 116, 117, 162, 168, 209, 216, 246–7, 248, 253, 254, 261, 265, 266, 347, 375, **12**.294, **15**.116, 168, 216, 253, 265, **16**.117, 254, 266, **17**.347, 375
    gratuitous. *See* gratuitous promise
    intention to create legal relations, need for **4**.124, 145, **6**.127, 145–6, **8**.109, 131–2, **12**.142, **13**.143, **15**.145–6, **16**.149, **17**.353–4
        See also promise to do favour, requirements
        between friends **3**.123, 145, 152, **4**.153, **6**.156, **12**.113, **15**.145

business relations **11**.136, **12**.113, **13**.115, **16**.170

professional status, relevance **8**.131, 147-8, **11**.136, **15**.147-8

promisee's right to assume **4**.124, 125, 126, 178, **8**.109

moral/legal promise, distinction **2**.105-6, 151-2, **9**.110-11, 116, **15**.116

See also courtesy act/promise; gentlemen's agreement

court's discretion **2**.105, 115, 151, **15**.115

remedy in tort in absence of contract **2**.106, 115, **15**.115

non-gratuitous **11**.209, 216, 310-11, 316, 317, 328, 369, **15**.216, 316, **16**.317, **17**.369

writing, need for **11**.328

promise of reward

as

conditional contract **4**.303, **9**.308, **10**.309-10

contract **2**.301, **7**.307; reciprocal promises **13**.315

contract of agency **6**.304

employment contract **2**.300-1

gestion d'affaires **2**.301, 315, **3**.303, **15**.315

hiring of labour (*louage d'ouvrage*) contract **3**.302

non-gratuitous contract, benefit to promisor **11**.311

non-gratuitous promise **11**.310-11, 316, 317, 369, **15**.316, **16**.317, **17**.369

offer **4**.303-4, **11**.311; of unilateral contract **12**.311, 317, 368-9, **13**.368-9, **15**.317, **16**.317, **17**.368-9

unilateral contract **2**.301, **3**.303, 369, **12**.311-14, 368, **13**.314-15, 317, 368, **15**.317, **16**.317, **17**.368, 369

unilateral promise **6**.305

work contract (*contrat d'entreprise*/*Werkvertrag*) **2**.300-1, **3**.302, **8**.307-8, **9**.308-9

contract for services **9**.308-9

recovery of expenses and **2**.300-1, 315, 369, **3**.302, 315, 367, **4**.303-4, 369, **6**.304-5, 316, **7**.307, **8**.307-8, 316, 367, **9**.316, **15**.315, 316, **16**.317, **17**.367, 369

gestion d'affaires **2**.301, **3**.303

revocability of promise to general public **2**.301, 315, **4**.303-4, 315, **5**.304, **15**.315, **16**.317, **17**.368-70, 389-91

Auslobung **8**.308, 316, **9**.308, 316, **15**.316

in case of: just cause **7**.305-7, 316, 317, 369, **15**.316, **16**.317, **17**.369; serious reasons **4**.304

notice of revocation as for original promise **5**.304, 315, **6**.305, 315-16, **7**.305, 316, **9**.309, **10**.310, 316, **12**.311-12, 317, **15**.315-16, 317, **16**.317, **17**.369

relevance of: acceptance of offer **5**.304, **6**.305, **12**.312; date of publication **7**.305; expenditure on search **12**.312-13, **13**.314-15, 317, **15**.317; fixed term **6**.305, **7**.305; knowledge of offer **5**.304, **6**.305, **9**.309, **10**.310; knowledge of withdrawal of offer **8**.308, 316, **10**.310, **15**.316; passage of time **2**.301, 315, **11**.310-11, 316, **15**.316; performance in response to promise **7**.307, **9**.309, **12**.311-13, 317, 368, **13**.368, **15**.317, **16**.317, **17**.368; reservation of right to revoke **10**.310; specific action to secure **6**.305; undertaking not to revoke **3**.303-4, 315, **15**.315

revocability of promise to individual **2**.300-1, 315, **6**.305, **7**.306-7, **10**.309-10, **15**.315, **16**.317, **17**.368-70, 389-91

in case of just cause **7**.306, 316, 317, **15**.316, **16**.317

causa credendi and **5**.304, 315, **15**.315

good faith, need for **9**.316, 369, **15**.316, **17**.369

relevance of: acceptance **6**.305, **7**.306, **11**.310; expenditure on search **12**.312-13, **13**.314-15, 317, **15**.317; knowledge of offer **7**.306, 316, **15**.316; passage of time **10**.309-10, 316, **11**.310-11, 316, **15**.316; performance in response to promise **7**.306-7, 316, **8**.308, **15**.316, **16**.317

unjust enrichment and **2**.301

promise to do favour

as

acte de complaisance **2**.151

contract of agency **9**.159–60, **16**.169;
contrat de mandat **3**.152, 352, **17**.352;
mandat à titre gratuit **2**.152; *opdracht*
4.153, 352, **17**.352

contract of agency (*contrato de mandato*)
5.155–6, 352, **7**.157, 352, **17**.352

contract for services: professional
status, relevance **5**.156, 352, **9**.160,
17.352; remuneration, relevance
5.156, **6**.156–7, **9**.159

contract to perform a particular piece
of work (*Werkvertrag*) **8**.158;
professional status, relevance **8**.158

courtesy act/promise **3**.152, **10**.161

friendly service (*servicio amistoso*) **5**.156,
167, **15**.167

gentlemen's agreement **2**.151, **6**.157,
167, **15**.167

good faith obligation **4**.155

moral obligation **2**.151

part of contract of sale **4**.155, 167,
5.156, **12**.163, 168, **13**.166, 169, **15**.167,
16.170

contract, consideration, need for **12**.163,
168

liability

negligence **7**.157–8, **10**.161, **12**.164, 168,
15.168; gross **8**.159, **10**.161; implied
clause exempting from **8**.159, 168,
352, **15**.168, **17**.352

standard of care **4**.154–5, **15**.167,
17.352–3

in tort. *See* liability in tort

requirements

consideration/*causa*, liberality as **5**.156,
167, **15**.167

delivery **5**.156, **17**.344–5

intention to create legal relations
6.156, 157, **8**.158, 167–8, **9**.159–60,
11.162, **12**.166, **16**.169, **17**.353–4, 382

writing **5**.156, 352, **11**.162, 168, **15**.168,
16.169–70, **17**.352

promise to do more than agreed

as novation **5**.257–8

as offer to modify/modification of
contract **2**.255–6, 265, **4**.256, **5**.257,
6.258, **7**.259–60, **8**.260, **13**.264,
15.265, **17**.387–8

binding nature **3**.256, **6**.258, **7**.260, **10**.261

acceptance, relevance **7**.260, **15**.265

illegal promise **6**.258

consideration, need for **12**.261–2, 266,
376, **13**.264, 266, 376, **15**.266, **17**.376

formalities **8**.260, **11**.261

parties' conduct, relevance **10**.261,
13.264–5

promise to pay for benefits received or owed

motivation, relevance **17**.385–6

protection of promisor and **17**.363–4,
371–2, 384–6

unjust enrichment **17**.363–4, 372, 384–6

promise to pay more than agreed **17**.361–5

See also economic duress; extortion;
usurious contract

absence of modification/novation of
contract **5**.227, 362, **17**.362, 387–8

as unilateral obligation, writing, need for
11.232

consideration

need for **5**.243, **12**.232–3, 364, 376,
13.234–6, 250, 364, 376, **17**.364, 376

non-competition undertaking **13**.250

performance of contract as **11**.232,
12.232–3, **13**.234–6, 250, **16**.238

expenditure in expectation of, relevance
4.243, **9**.246, **12**.249, 253, **13**.251,
15.253

pre-contractual obligation. *See* pre-
contractual obligation

**promise to sell at fixed price, whether
binding in case of change of market
price** **2**.193–7, **3**.197–9, 213–15,
4.200–2, **5**.202–3, **6**.203–4, **7**.204–5,
8.205–6, **9**.206–7, **10**.207–8,
11.209–10, **12**.210–13, **13**.213–15

in absence of

agreement that sale for own
consumption **8**.205–6, 216, **15**.216

consideration **12**.210–11, 216, **13**.213,
215, 217, **15**.216, **16**.217–18;
acceptance of offer **12**.210, **16**.217–18

exclusive dealing clause **2**.197, **3**.198, 199, **4**.202, **6**.204, **9**.207

minimum/usual purchase requirement **8**.206, **9**.206; interpretation of contract and **11**.209–10, **12**.212, **16**.218

abuse of right and **2**.195–7, **3**.198, 199, **9**.206, **16**.217

as non-gratuitous promise **11**.209, 216, **15**.216

diversity of reasons against **16**.215

good faith and **4**.201, **6**.203–4, **7**.205, 216, **9**.206–7, **10**.207, 216, **11**.209–10, 216, **12**.211, **15**.216, **17**.367

interpretation of contract and **4**.201, **7**.205, **9**.206, 216, **12**.212, **16**.217–18, **17**.367

pacta sunt servanda and **5**.202, **6**.203, **10**.209 n. 51

rebus sic stantibus **5**.202

supervening hardship and **7**.204

unforeseen circumstances theory and **2**.196, **3**.199, **4**.200, 202, 215, **5**.202, **6**.203, **7**.204–5, **15**.215

unilateral offer to sell, uncertainty of obligation and **2**.193–4, 197

promise to take less than agreed. *See* waiver of debt

promise under seal. *See* deed/promise under seal

promissory estoppel. *See* estoppel

proportionality

abuse of right and **3**.198, 199

changed circumstances and **5**.202, **7**.204, **10**.208

charitable gift **17**.381

dowry/gift *propter nuptias* **8**.43, **9**.44 n. 84, 381, **17**.381

gift (*cadeau d'usage*) **3**.29

immoral act and **10**.231

liberality of usage **7**.76, 85, **15**.85

protection of promisor and **17**.38–81, 379, 381

services rendered, promise of remuneration **2**.241, **5**.74, **6**.85, **7**.77, 85, **10**.80, **15**.85

usurious contract **10**.231

voidable contract and **8**.291, 297, **15**.297, **16**.298

protection of promisee 11.375, **17**.375

protection of promisor/donor in case of

charitable gift **17**.381

coercion **2**.281

consideration and **1**.18

dowry/gift *propter nuptias* **8**.43, **9**.44 n. 84, 381, **17**.381

gratuitous transactions **11**.374–5, **17**.374–5

historical origin **1**.8

loan without charge **2**.348–9, **3**.348–9, **11**.347, **17**.347, 348–55, 371

promise of

gift/donation **3**.28, 34, **4**.35–6, **7**.40, **9**.43, **10**.46, **17**.337–40, 363, 379–82; proportionality **17**.379

money/property **1**.16, **17**.379–82

reward **17**.369–70

service **17**.371

promise to

contract **2**.240–1

pay for benefits received or owed **17**.363–4, 371–2, 384–6

pay debt not legally due **9**.96–7, **17**.357–8, 371–2

real estate agency contract **17**.370–1

reliance on promise, relevance **17**.381–2

storage of goods without charge **2**.349, **7**.349, **9**.132, **12**.349, **17**.349–51, 355, 371

unjust enrichment **17**.372

public benefit 2.27, **6**.40

public deed. *See* notarization

public policy, promise of gift/donation, enforceability **2**.28

quasi-contract, *negotiorum gestio* **2**.70

real estate agency contract

See also brokerage contract

agent's obligations

See also remuneration of agent *below*

absence **9**.326, 333, **15**.333

best endeavours **2**.320

in case of termination **12**.329

damages for breach **12**.329

real estate agency contract (cont.)
agent's right to recover expenses
2.319–20, **6**.333, 370, **9**.325, 326,
12.329, **13**.34, 330–2, 334, **15**.333,
334, **16**.334, **17**.370
seller's knowledge of, relevance
13.330–1, 334, **15**.334
as
contract **11**.327–8
contract for services **2**.318, **6**.323
non-gratuitous promise **11**.328
promise *sub conditione* **11**.328
unilateral contract **12**.334, **15**.334
general rules of law (*droit commun*),
derogation from **2**.321
good faith and **9**.325, 333, **12**.329, **15**.333
legal requirements
fixed term **6**.323
name of person to whom payment is to
be made **2**.319
remuneration **6**.323
writing **2**.319, 332, **6**.323, **15**.332
protection of promisor/donor in case of
17.370–1
remuneration of agent **2**.319
court's power to reduce **2**.321
dependence on: effectiveness of
agent's role **2**.319, **9**.325, **13**.331;
result **2**.319–21, 332, 370, **6**.323,
8.324–5, 333, **9**.325, 333, **12**.329, 334,
13.31, 330, **15**.332, 333, 334,
16.334–5, **17**.370; terms of valid
contract **2**.319, **4**.322, 332–3, **9**.326,
11.327–8, **13**.330–2, **15**.332–3,
16.334–5
sole agency. *See* sole agency *below*
termination of contract, effect
2.319–20; fixed term, relevance
6.323, **8**.325
seller
obligation to sell, whether **8**.325, 333,
9.325, **12**.312, 328–9, 334, **13**.331,
15.333, 334, **16**.334
protection of **2**.321, **9**.325–6, 333,
12.329, **15**.333
sole agency
damages for breach **12**.329

remuneration of agent **2**.320, **9**.325,
12.329; contract concluded other
than by agent **2**.320, **13**.331; penalty
clause **2**.320, 332, **15**.332, **16**.334;
seller's fault **6**.323, **8**.325, 333, 370,
15.333, **17**.370; termination after
conclusion of fixed term **6**.323,
16.335; termination and **2**.320, 370,
4.322, **6**.323, 333, 370, **12**.329, 334,
13.331, **15**.333, 334, **17**.370; third
party's help, relevance **2**.320
requirement **4**.322, 333, **7**.324, 333,
8.325, **15**.333
seller's right to terminate **11**.328, 334,
370, **12**.370, **13**.370, **15**.334, **17**.370
specific performance **12**.329, 334, **13**.331,
15.334
standard contract **4**.322, 333, 335, 370,
15.333, **16**.335, **17**.370
termination
fixed term, relevance **8**.325
liability in tort **2**.320, 332, 370, **15**.332,
17.370
remuneration and. *See* remuneration
of agent *above*
right of **17**.389–91
sole agency. *See* sole agency, seller's
right to terminate *above*
real property transactions, requirements
2.296, **15**.296, **16**.298
See also contract *re*; lease, variation
changed circumstances, relevance
10.292–3, **11**.293
contract to sell **8**.290, 297, **15**.297
gift **6**.39
motivation of parties, relevance **11**.293
notarization **2**.280, **6**.39, 287, 297, **9**.291,
297, **10**.291, **15**.297
protection of parties and **9**.291
registration **2**.280, **5**.286–7, **10**.292
writing **11**.274, 293, 298, 362, **15**.298,
17.362
rebus sic stantibus. See changed
circumstances
recall and reduction 7.41
redelijkjeid en billijkheid **4**.286
See also good faith

rei interventus **1**.8, **11**.9
    statutory provisions on promises
        distinguished **11**.9, 50
reliance on promise, relevance 4.34–6, 257,
        9.43, **12**.51, 58, **13**.62, **15**.64, **16**.65–6
    breach of contract of deposit/promise to
        store without charge **11**.136, 150,
        346–7, **16**.150, **17**.346–7
    charitable gift **17**.381
    consideration/*causa*, circumvention of
        rule **12**.51, 58, 114, 137–8, 148, 185–6,
        293–4, **15**.148, **17**.342
    dowry/gift *propter nuptias* **12**.54, 65, **15**.65,
        17.341
    estoppel **4**.257, **12**.66, 187, 262, 274–5,
        363, **13**.62, 66, 115, 213, 214, 363,
        16.42, 65–6, **17**.363
    failure to keep social engagement **11**.113,
        116, **12**.113–14, **15**.116
    modification of contract **2**.256, 265,
        6.258, **15**.265
    negligent provision of services **12**.139,
        17.384
    promise of
        gift **17**.342–4
        reward **12**.313
    promise to
        do favour **11**.113, 116, 148, 150, 162,
            168, 352, **12**.164–5, **15**.116, 148, 168,
            16.150, 170, **17**.352
        do more than agreed **11**.261, 265, 266,
            15.265, **16**.266
        lend goods without charge **4**.177, **7**.181,
            11.185, 191, **12**.186, 187, **16**.192
        sell **6**.288, **12**.295
        store goods without charge **11**.350, **17**.350
    protection of promisor/donor **17**.381–2
    real estate agency contract **17**.371
    recovery of expenses in expectation of
        enforcement of promise **11**.50–1, 64,
        15.64
    rei interventus **1**.8, **11**.9
    scholastics **1**.6
    waiver of right **12**.263
remedies
    See also damages for; *lésion*; restitution;
        specific performance

    limitation of right to normal use **3**.198
    termination of contract **2**.197
remise de dette **2**.267, 276, **3**.269, 276, **15**.276
remissão **6**.271
rental agreement 8.181 n. 28
requirements contract. *See* promise to sell at
        fixed price, whether binding in case
        of change of market price
rescission of contract. *See lésion*
rescue contract. *See* contract of rescue
        (*convention d'assistance*)
restitution, practical difficulties **2**.196
restrictive covenant. *See* employment
        restrictions imposed by employer
reward for merits, as gift **8**.246
Roman law
    See also civil law of contract, historical
        development; common law of
        contract, historical development
    actio doli **1**.48
    as basis of
        medieval law of contract **1**.3–8
        modern law of contract **1**.127–8;
            agency **1**.169
        modern law relating to gifts **1**.354–5,
            373, 373–4
    causae **1**.5
    contract *consensu* **1**.2
        binding effect of consent **1**.2
        lease **1**.2, 5
        mandatum **1**.2, 5, 169, **17**.344
        partnership **1**.2
        sale **1**.2, 5
    contract *re* **1**.127–8, 344–5, 351, **17**.351
        binding effect of delivery **1**.2
        commodatum **1**.2, 5, 7, 344–5, 351
        depositum **1**.2, 5, 7, 344–5, 351
        mutuum **1**.2, 5, 7
        pignus **1**.2, 7
    formalities other than delivery or consent
        insinuatio **1**.338, 339–40
        stipulatio **1**.2
    gratuitous promise to store or loan goods
        1.6–7, 344–5
    innominate contract, performance, need
        for **1**.2
    politicatio **1**.37

Roman law (cont.)
promise, enforceability, acceptance, need
for **1**.14, 37, 351, **17**.351
protection of promisor/donor **1**.346, 349,
355
unjust enrichment **1**.373–4
votum **1**.37

Schenkungsabsicht **8**.245, 246
services rendered [without charge], promise
to pay remuneration for
See also storage of goods without charge,
failure to keep promise
as contract
implied assumpsit/act at request of
promisor **12**.81, 87, 359, **13**.87, 359,
15.87, **17**.340, 359, 360
moral obligation, relevance **9**.79
professional status of person rendering
service, relevance **9**.79, **10**.80
as contract of donation **7**.76, **10**.79–80
as gift **4**.72, 84, 358, **7**.76, **9**.79, **15**.84, **17**.358
as gratuitous unilateral obligation
11.80–1, 86, 360, **15**.86, **17**.360
professional status of person rendering
service, relevance **11**.81
status of person receiving service,
relevance **11**.81
as moral obligation **8**.77–8, **12**.81–3
See also moral obligation
consideration/cause, whether **2**.241
as natural obligation **2**.67–71, 358,
3.30–1, 63, 71–2, 358–9, **4**.72–3,
5.73–4, 84–5, 358–9, **7**.76–7, **8**.358,
15.63, 84–5, **16**.86–7, **17**.358–9
See also natural obligation/*obligation*
naturelle
as onerous contract **2**.241, **5**.74
as remunatory donation **2**.241, 251, **5**.74,
359, **6**.75, 85, **7**.76, **15**.251, **17**.359, 360
causa donandi **5**.244, 252, **15**.252
definition **5**.87, **6**.75, 87, 244, **7**.76 n. 37,
16.87
exceptions **6**.75
historical origin **1**.8
'liberality according to usage'
distinguished **7**.76

requirements: delivery **6**.244, **7**.245;
rules applying to ordinary gifts/
donations **4**.243, 251, **6**.75, 87, 244,
359, 362, **7**.76, **15**.251, **16**.87, **17**.359,
362; writing **5**.74, **6**.87, 244, 252, 359,
11.248, **15**.252, **16**.87, **17**.359
status of parties, relevance **5**.74
sum above usual level **5**.74, **6**.85, **10**.80,
15.85
as rescue agreement (*convention*
d'assistance) **2**.69–71, 359–60,
17.359–60
rescue as offer **2**.359–60, **17**.359–60
as salary **9**.246, 364, **17**.364
increase in **8**.245, **10**.247, 252, **11**.248,
15.252
payment as part **6**.244, **7**.252, **15**.252
as terminal bonus **2**.241, **7**.245, 252,
8.246, 364, **9**.246, **15**.252, **16**.254,
17.364
enforceability **7**.77, 85, 86, **15**.85, **16**.86,
17.358–61
ad hoc nature of decision **7**.77
causa praeterita **7**.77, 245, 364–5, **17**.364–5
requirements: *cause suffisante* **7**.77;
consideration **12**.359, 376, **13**.359,
376, **17**.359, 376; monetary value for
service **2**.241, **7**.77, 85, **15**.85;
proportionality **2**.241, **5**.74, **6**.85, **7**.77,
85, **10**.80, **15**.85
unjust enrichment and, *Second*
Restatement of Contracts **14**.359,
16.359
legal formalities/requirements **5**.74
intention of promisor, *animus*
donandi/animus solvendi distinguished
7.77
notarization. *See* notarization
negotiorum gestio, relevance of doctrine
2.70–1, **4**.72–3, 84, **6**.74–5, 85, **8**.78,
9.86, **15**.84, 85, 86, **17**.3, 359
See also negotiorum gestio
servicio amistoso **5**.156
social engagement, agreement to keep
as
contract **2**.105–6, 115, **3**.106–7, **4**.107,
6.108, **9**.111, **10**.111–12, 116, **11**.112,

12.117, **13**.114–15, 117, **15**.115, 116–17, **16**.117; writing, need for **5**.108, 116, **15**.116

contract of donation **6**.108

courtesy promise **2**.106 n. 3, **3**.106–7, 123, **7**.108–9, **10**.111–12, **13**.115, 117

creation of legal relationship **12**.113

expression of future intention **11**.112

gratuitous unilateral promise: given in course of business **11**.112, 116, 117, **15**.116, **16**.117; writing, need for **11**.112, 116, 354 n. 15, **15**.116, **17**.354 n. 15

intention to keep legal obligations **11**.112

legally binding promise **8**.109–10; intention/cause, need for **8**.110, **15**.117

damages for breach. *See* damages for breach of

duty to notify of inability to fulfil **9**.111

liability in tort for breach. *See* liability in tort

sole discretion clause **4**.286, **7**.289–90, 297, **9**.292, 298, **10**.293, **12**.294, 298, **13**.296, 298, **15**.297, 298

See also condition potestative

special relationship

evidence of

delivery of goods **12**.141, 148, 168–9, **15**.148, 168–9

professional status of promisor **12**.148, 164, 168, **15**.168, **16**.170

relevance

contract of deposit/promise to store goods without charge **12**.139–40, 148, **15**.148

negligent provision of services **12**.139–40, 148, 150, 163–4, 350–1, **13**.165, 350–1, **15**.148, **16**.150, **17**.350–1

speciality principle **2**.27

specific enforcement. *See* specific performance

specific performance **2**.119

in case of economic duress. *See* economic duress

contract of agency **5**.156

contract of deposit/promise to store goods without charge **3**.123, 145, **5**.126, 145, **7**.129, **15**.145

in absence of contract **2**.120, 350, **3**.350, **5**.145, **6**.128, 146, **7**.350, **8**.131, 147, **15**.145, 146, **16**.149

between friends **2**.119, **13**.143; in case of gratuitous contract **2**.119, 120, **16**.150

breach of collateral contract **2**.120, **12**.138, 148, 349, **13**.349, **15**.148, **16**.149, **17**.349

contractual obligation **5**.127, **6**.128

liability in tort **13**.144

pre-contractual obligation **10**.134, 147, **15**.147

contract/promise of loan for use **2**.172, **5**.179, **11**.185, **12**.187, **13**.188

distinction **2**.174–5

requirements: detriment **11**.185, 191, **15**.191; knowledge and acquiescence of donor **11**.185, 191, 350, **15**.191, **17**.350

inconvenience of claimant, relevance **13**.188

infringement of rights of defendant and **2**.175

option contract (*contrat de promesse*) **2**.282, **5**.286

promise to do (*obligation de faire*) **2**.280, 282–3

promise to do favour **11**.162, **16**.170

real estate agency contract **12**.329, 334, **13**.331, **15**.334

standard of care

contract of agency **2**.166, **3**.152, 167, **7**.158, 167, **15**.167, **16**.169

contract of deposit/promise to store goods without charge **2**.119–20

promise to do favour **4**.154–5, 167, **15**.167, **17**.352–3

quantum of damages **2**.152, **4**.153, 167, **15**.166, 167, **16**.169

sums exceeding usual or obligatory level or financial means, treatment as gift or remunatory donation

customary gift **3**.29, 63, **15**.63

sums exceeding usual or obligatory level or financial means, treatment as gift or remunatory donation (*cont.*)
services rendered without charge 5.74, **6**.85, **10**.80
dowry/gift *pro nuptias* **8**.43, **9**.44 n. 84
supply contract
See also promise to sell at fixed price, whether binding in case of change of market price
escalation clause **3**.198
exclusive dealing clause **2**.197, **3**.198, 199, **4**.202, **6**.204, **9**.207
requirements, certainty of price/quantity **3**.197–8

***teoria de la base del negocio* 5**.202–3, 215, **15**.215
tort. *See* liability in tort
***transaction à titre onéreux* 3**.28 n. 11
trust
See also charitable organization
absence of concept in civil law **10**.46
advantages/disadvantages **17**.339
charitable trust **13**.61
definition **12**.56, **13**.60, **17**.338
gift distinguished **12**.56, **17**.338
requirements **13**.65, **15**.65
certainty of: intention **13**.60; object **13**.61; subject matter **12**.56–7, 64, **13**.61, **15**.64
evidentiary **13**.61
immediate divestment of ownership **12**.56, **17**.338
third party
as intermediary **12**.56, 64, **15**.64
right to enforce **13**.60

unforeseeable circumstances 2.144–5, **3**.124, 145, **10**.134–5
See also changed circumstances
unilateral contract 2.25 n. 3, **5**.36
See also contract *solo consensu*
contract of deposit. *See* contract of deposit/promise to store without charge
conversion to bilateral contract **2**.301

definition/requirements **3**.107, **5**.36, **10**.133
See also offer *and* performance as *below*
common/civil law distinguished **5**.36, **12**.311, 316–17, **13**.34, **15**.316–17, **16**.317
promise inviting performance **13**.314
exchange of contracts giving rise to **2**.120–1
natural obligation (*obligation naturelle*) and **2**.68
offer
acceptance: knowledge of offer, relevance **12**.311; need for **1**.15, **5**.36–7, **6**.38, **12**.15, Roman law **1**.36; performance as. *See* performance as, acceptance of offer *below*
withdrawal **12**.311–14, 317, **15**.317; abuse of right **16**.317; as anticipatory breach of contract **12**.313–14; effect **12**.313–14
performance as
acceptance of offer **1**.15, **12**.15, 311, 317, 334, 368–9, **13**.368–9, **15**.317, 334, **16**.317, **17**.368–9; 'starting to perform'/'preparations to perform' **4**.303, 315, **12**.312–13, 317, **13**.314–15, 317, **15**.315, 317
condition of benefit **12**.311, 317, **13**.317, **15**.317, **16**.317
consideration for promise **12**.311, **13**.314
promise to reward **2**.301, **3**.303, 369, **12**.311–14, 317, 368–9, **13**.368–9, **15**.317, **16**.317, **17**.368–9
revocability **1**.15, **3**.302, 315, **12**.15, 311–14, 317, **15**.315, 317
promise to sell
at fixed price **6**.203
revocability, motivation, relevance **5**.29, **6**.288, **8**.290–1, **9**.291, **13**.296, **15**.297
synallagmatic contract distinguished **2**.27, 197, 282
unilateral promise, as **6**.203, 204, 287
unilateral promise distinguished **2**.68, **6**.38

unilateral promise
in absence of contract **4**.256
acceptance, in case of options **2**.280–1
presumption of intention to incur
smaller obligation **8**.272
remedies for breach. *See* damages for
breach of; specific performance
to sell (*promesse unilatérale de vente*)
2.193–4
as contract **4**.284–6, **6**.287–8, **8**.290,
297, **15**.297
as option contract (*contrat de promesse*)
2.282, 296, **3**.6, 284, **5**.286–7, **7**.288–9,
10.293, **15**.296
as sale **2**.281
binding effect **7**.289, **13**.295
changed circumstances **3**.284, **4**.285–6,
5.287, **6**.287–8, **9**.291, **10**.292–3,
11.293, **12**.295, **13**.296
obligation limited to promisor **3**.283
offer distinguished **2**.283, **3**.283 n. 9,
7.288–9, **12**.293, **13**.295
pacta sunt servanda and **5**.287
pre-contractual agreement **7**.289
requirements: notarization **2**.280,
6.287, **10**.292–3; registration **2**.280,
10.292–3; writing **6**.287
validity/enforceability distinguished
2.280
unjust enrichment
absence of *causa* and **9**.96
as principle underlying rules on
enforcement of promises **17**.373, 382–4
breach of promise to reward and **2**.301
burden of proof **9**.97
negotiorum gestio **8**.359, **9**.359, **17**.359, 360
option contract and **17**.388–9
payment of debt not legally due **9**.96,
17.357–8, 360–1, 371
promise to pay for benefits received or
owed **17**.363–4, 372, 384–6
protection of promisor and **17**.372
Roman law **1**.373–4
services previously rendered without
charge **17**.360–1
Restatement of Contracts (Second) **14**.359
transfer of property without *causa* **9**.96

usurious contract
definition **6**.227, 237, **10**.231, **15**.237
disproportion **10**.231
improper advantage **10**.231
relative status of parties and **10**.231
remedies/effect
tort liability **10**.231
voidability of contract **6**.227, 363,
17.363
voidness **10**.231

venire contra factum proprium **4**.257, 285,
6.259 n. 11
See also abuse of right; estoppel
Verwahrung **9**.132
violence. *See* economic duress
votum **1**.37

waiver of right
binding nature **7**.259–60, 272, 277, **8**.260,
9.260, **10**.261–2, **13**.264, **15**.277
consideration, relevance **5**.270–1, 277,
12.262, 266, 362, 376, **13**.264, 266,
362, 376, **15**.266, 277, **16**.266, **17**.362,
376
debt. *See* debt, right to reclaim arrears in
case of promise to reduce rent
definition **12**.262
estoppel compared **12**.262–3
illegality **6**.258–9, 265, 266, 362, **15**.265,
16.266, **17**.362
parties' conduct, relevance **6**.259
implicit **13**.264
modification of contract distinguished
13.264
reliance on, relevance **12**.263, 362,
13.362, **16**.266, **17**.362
'renunciation' as contract **4**.257, 269, 277,
15.277
effect **4**.257, 269
formalities **4**.269 n. 5, 277, **15**.277
gratuitous **4**.257, 269
right to revoke **12**.262, **13**.264, 266,
15.266
waiver of warranty of hidden defects
3.256
Wegfall der Geschäftsgrundlage **8**.131, **10**.208

Werkvertrag 8.158
wilsverklarung 4.304
wilsvertrouwensleer 4.201
work contract (*contrat d'entreprise/***
Werkvertrag) 6.258, **10**.260-1
classification as
contract to undertake investigation
2.300-1
promise of reward to individual
2.300-1, **3**.302, **8**.307-8
promise to do favour **8**.158-9;
professional status of promisor,
relevance **8**.158
distinguished from
contract for services (*Dienstvertrag*)
8.307
employment contract **3**.302, **9**.308
Geschäftsbesorgungsvertrag **9**.308-9
liability

negligence: gross **8**.159; implied
exemption **8**.159, 168, **15**.168
modification **8**.258, **10**.261
obligation of
best endeavours **2**.300, **9**.308-9, 316,
15.316
result **3**.302, **8**.307, **9**.308-9
payment due on completion **10**.261
unilateral termination **3**.302, 315,
8.307-8, **15**.315
right to recover: agreed fee **9**.308, 316,
15.316; *ex aequo et bono*
determination **3**.302; expenses
2.300-1, **3**.302, 315, 369, **8**.307-8, 316,
369, **15**.315, 316, **17**.369; lost profit
3.302, 315, 317, 369, **8**.307, 316, 317,
369, **15**.316, **16**.317, **17**.369

zorgvuldigheidsnorm 4.154